# ZIONISM, PALESTINIAN NATIONALISM AND THE LAW

During the last decade of the British Mandate for Palestine (1939–1948), Arabs and Jews used the law as a resource to gain leverage against each other and to influence international opinion. The parties invoked "transformational legal framing" to portray the essentially political-religious conflict as a legal dispute involving claims of justice, injustice, and victimisation, and giving rise to legal/equitable remedies.

Employing this form of narrative and framing in multiple "trials" during the first 15 years of the Mandate, the parties continued the practice during the last and most crucial decade of the Mandate. The term "trial" provides an appropriate typology for understanding the adversarial proceedings during those years in which judges, lawyers, witnesses, cross-examination, and legal argumentation played a key role in the conflict. The four trials between 1939 and 1947 produced three different outcomes: the one-state solution in favour of the Palestinian Arabs, the no-state solution, and the two-state solution embodied in the United Nations November 1947 partition resolution, culminating in Israel's independence in May 1948.

This study analyses the role of the law during the last decade of the British Mandate for Palestine, making an essential contribution to the literature on lawfare, framing and narrative, and the Arab-Israeli conflict.

**Steven E. Zipperstein**, a former US federal prosecutor, is a Senior Fellow at the UCLA Center for Middle East Development and a Lecturer in the UCLA Luskin School of Public Affairs and the UCLA Global Studies program, and in the Department of History at UC Santa Barbara. Zipperstein is also a Visiting Professor of Law at Tel Aviv University, and is the author of *Law and the Arab-Israeli Conflict: The Trials of Palestine* (Routledge, 2020).

## UCLA CENTER FOR MIDDLE EAST DEVELOPMENT (CMED)

Series Editors: Steven Spiegel, *UCLA*

*Elizabeth Matthews, California State University, San Marcos*

The UCLA Center for Middle East Development (CMED) series on Middle East security and cooperation is designed to present a variety of perspectives on a specific topic, such as democracy in the Middle East, dynamics of Israeli-Palestinian relations, Gulf security, and the gender factor in the Middle East. The uniqueness of the series is that the authors write from the viewpoint of a variety of countries so that no matter what the issue, articles appear from many different states, both within and beyond the region. No existing series provides a comparable, multinational collection of authors. Thus, the series presents a combination of writers from countries who, for political reasons, do not always publish in the same volume. The series features a number of sub-themes under a single heading, covering security, social, political, and economic factors affecting the Middle East.

**19. The Foreign Policy of Smaller Gulf States**
Size, Power, and Regime Stability in the Middle East
*Máté Szalai*

**20. Zionism, Palestinian Nationalism and the Law**
1939–1948
*Steven E. Zipperstein*

**21. Elections and Public Opinion in Turkey**
Through the Prism of the 2018 Elections
*Edited by Ali Çarkoğlu and Ersin Kalaycıoğlu*

For more information about this series, please visit: https://www.routledge.com/UCLA-Center-for-Middle-East-Development-CMED-series/book-series/CMED

# ZIONISM, PALESTINIAN NATIONALISM AND THE LAW

## 1939–1948

*Steven E. Zipperstein*

Routledge
Taylor & Francis Group
LONDON AND NEW YORK

First published 2022
by Routledge
2 Park Square, Milton Park, Abingdon, Oxon OX14 4RN

and by Routledge
605 Third Avenue, New York, NY 10158

*Routledge is an imprint of the Taylor & Francis Group, an informa business*



*British Library Cataloguing-in-Publication Data*
A catalogue record for this book is available from the British Library

*Library of Congress Cataloging-in-Publication Data*
Names: Zipperstein, Steve E., author.
Title: Zionism, Palestinian nationalism and the law : 1939-1948 / Steven E. Zipperstein.
Description: Abingdon, Oxon ; New York, NY : Routledge, 2022. | Series: UCLA Center for Middle East Development (CMED); 20 | Includes bibliographical references and index.
Identifiers: LCCN 2021028410 (print) | LCCN 2021028411 (ebook) | ISBN 9781032125817 (Hardback) | ISBN 9781032125848 (Paperback) | ISBN 9781003225263 (eBook) | ISBN 9781000484335 (Adobe PDF) | ISBN 9781000484380 (ePub)
Subjects: LCSH: Constitutional history–Palestine–History–20th century. | Palestine–Politics and government–1917–1948. | Jewish-Arab relations. | Palestine–International status–History–20th century.
Classification: LCC KMQ1210 .Z57 2022 (print) | LCC KMQ1210 (ebook) | DDC 342.009/5694–dc23
LC record available at https://lccn.loc.gov/2021028410
LC ebook record available at https://lccn.loc.gov/2021028411

ISBN: 978-1-032-12581-7 (hbk)
ISBN: 978-1-032-12584-8 (pbk)
ISBN: 978-1-003-22526-3 (ebk)

DOI: 10.4324/9781003225263

Typeset in Bembo Std
by KnowledgeWorks Global Ltd.

To the Memory of my Father

# CONTENTS

# FIGURES

# TABLES

# MAPS

# CASES AND STATUTES

## Cases

*The Mavrommatis Palestine Concessions*, Permanent International Court of Justice, Series A, No. 2 (30 Aug. 1924).

*Lehrer v. Postmaster General*, High Court No. 88, Supreme Court of Palestine Sitting as the High Court of Justice (1928).

*District Governor, Jerusalem-Jaffa District v. Suleiman Murra*, [1926] A.C. 321.

*Ffrost v. Stevenson* (1937) 58 C.L.R. 528 (High Court of Australia).

International Court of Justice, *International Status of South-West Africa*, Advisory Opinion, 010-19500711-ADV-01-01, I.C.J. Reports 1950.

International Court of Justice, *Legal Consequences for States of the Continued Presence of South Africa in Namibia (South West Africa) Notwithstanding Security Council Resolution 276* (1970), I.C.J. Reports (21 June 1971).

*Public Committee Against Torture v. Government of Israel*, HCJ 5100/94 (1999).

*Legal Consequences of the Construction of a Wall in the Occupied Palestinian Territory*, Advisory Opinion, I.C.J. Reports 2004, International Court of Justice (2004).

*Ahmad et al. v. Prime Minister*, Israel Supreme Court (sitting as the High Court of Justice), HCJ 9132/07 (2008).

*Case of Certain Norwegian Loans*, Judgment of 6 July 1957, I.C.J. Reports 1957.

*Armed Activities on the Territory of the Congo (Democratic Republic of the Congo v. Uganda)*, Judgment, I.C.J. Reports 2005.

*In The Matter Of The Chagos Marine Protected Area Arbitration* (Mauritius v. U.K, Case No. 2011-03) Award, Permanent Court of International Arbitration (18 March 2015).

*Ungar v. Palestine Liberation Organization*, 402 F.3d 274 (1st Cir. 2005).
International Criminal Court, No. ICC-01/18, *Situation in The State of Palestine* (5 February 2021).

## Statutes

International Criminal Court (ICC) Statute, 17 July 1998, in force 1 July 2002, United Nations Treaty Series vol. 2187, No. 38544 ("Rome Statute")

# PREFACE AND EXPLANATORY NOTE

An often-overlooked aspect of the early years of the Arab-Jewish dynamic in Palestine involves the significant role the law played in the conflict. As I wrote in my earlier study, *Law and the Arab Israeli Conflict: The Trials of Palestine* (Routledge, 2020), during the British Mandate, the Jews and Arabs developed a custom and practice of using the law to seek relief from a succession of outside authorities, from the Ottomans to the British to the League of Nations.

The British also repeatedly relied on legal frameworks during the Mandate years, treating the *Status Quo* as a principle of substantive law, issuing various White Papers replete with legal language and principles, seeking a formal legal opinion from the Law Officers of the Crown regarding Jewish and Muslim rights at the Wailing Wall, and relying on various Commissions of Enquiry to investigate and adjudicate violent outbreaks and their underlying causes.

By the late 1920s and 1930s, therefore, the conflict had become as much a battle fought in the courtroom as in the streets, playing out in three separate trials and focusing primarily on two issues: the legality of the Balfour Declaration and the Mandate for Palestine, and the parties' rights and claims to the Wailing Wall. The term "trial" provides an appropriate typology for understanding the adversarial proceedings during those years in which judges, lawyers, witnesses, cross-examination, and legal argumentation played a key role in the conflict.

In two instances – the Shaw Commission in 1929 and the Lofgren Commission in 1930 – Arabs and Jews faced off in full-blown, dramatic trials before British and international judges, in which outside counsel made opening statements and closing arguments, introduced exhibits, and cross-examined each other's witnesses under oath. In a third instance, the 1936–1937 Peel Commission, the parties used witness testimony and extensive written submissions to continue their legal advocacy.

The present study focuses on the crucial decade between 1939 and 1948, when the parties continued weaponising the law as a tool in the conflict both before and after World War II. Seen through the lens of framing theory, the parties employed what I describe as *transformational legal framing* to characterise their essentially political conflict as a legal dispute involving claims of *justice, injustice, and victimisation*, giving rise to legal remedies such as damages and equitable remedies such as restitution, recission, and restoration. Both parties, especially the Palestinian Arabs, continue employing transformational legal framing to the present day.

This dynamic continued in four additional trials during the final decade of the British Mandate, beginning with the London Conferences in 1939 and the British White Paper of May 1939, and continuing after the War with the Anglo-American Committee of Inquiry in 1946 and the United Nations Special and Ad Hoc Committees for Palestine in 1947.

The London Conferences and May 1939 White Paper rendered a verdict against Zionism and in favour of Palestinian Arab nationalism, endorsing the *one-state solution* for the Palestinian Arabs and virtually halting European Jewish immigration to Palestine on the eve of the Holocaust. This represented by far the best offer the Palestinian Arabs would ever receive during the entire history of the conflict, yet the Palestinian Arab leadership rejected it.

The end of World War II ushered in a new era of American involvement in the conflict, with Whitehall rapidly losing its ability to control events in Palestine. The British and American Governments formed the "Anglo-American Committee of Inquiry" in late 1945 to take testimony from dozens of witnesses in the United States, Europe, and the Middle East. The Committee ultimately rendered a unanimous verdict against the May 1939 White Paper and in favour of the *no-state solution* for Palestine, with ongoing foreign trusteeship. The Committee also unanimously endorsed a large increase in Jewish immigration to Palestine. But Britain sabotaged the plan over concerns that additional Jewish immigration to Palestine would anger the Arab states and drive them into an alliance with the Soviet Union.

By early 1947, a depleted and frustrated British Government handed the entire Palestine matter to the United Nations. The UN convened two additional trials in the summer and fall of 1947, both of which delivered verdicts in favour of the *two-state solution.*

Just as they had done in response to the May 1939 British offer of the one-state solution, the Palestinian Arabs likewise rejected and renounced the United Nations November 1947 offer of the two-state solution. Palestinian Arab leaders responded to the latter offer by launching a violent and bloody civil war, joined by the surrounding Arab states following Israel's declaration of independence in May 1948.

By the end of the 1948–1949 Israeli War of Independence, the Palestinian Arabs in the West Bank and East Jerusalem had pledged their loyalty to Jordan's King Abdullah I, and remained under Jordanian occupation until June 1967. The Palestinian Arabs living in the Gaza strip remained under Egyptian occupation from late 1948 to June 1967, except for a brief period during 1956–1957. Throughout the entire two-decade period of Jordanian/Egyptian occupation, the Palestinian Arabs in both the West Bank and Gaza held firm to their renunciation of the two-state solution.

When Israel replaced Jordan as the occupying power in the West Bank and Egypt as the occupying power in Gaza after the June 1967 War, the Palestinian Arabs continued to reject the two-state solution for the next quarter century, until the 1993 Oslo Accords. Even after Oslo, however, the Palestinian Arabs refused offers of sovereignty from Israeli Prime Ministers Ehud Barak in 2000–2001 and Ehud Olmert in 2007–2008.

★★★★★

Modern-day analyses of the Israel-Palestinian conflict unfortunately tend to conflate Palestinian *political* claims with *legal* claims. The better approach would be to treat the two sets of claims separately.

Although the Palestinians may have a valid *political* argument for self-determination, their *legal* case is far weaker. As a matter of international law, the Palestinian rejection of the November 1947 United Nations offer of statehood constituted a *renunciation* and *waiver* of Palestinian Arab sovereignty over any portion of Mandate-era Palestine. The Palestinians expressly reaffirmed the waiver of sovereignty over the West Bank and Gaza in the original Palestine National Charter of 1964.

Nevertheless, the Palestinians today insist they are *legally* entitled to the *same* outcome they renounced for decades: statehood in a portion of Palestine. The Palestinians have brilliantly employed transformational legal framing to persuade the United Nations and most of the international community to back their legal claims. Indeed, in February 2021 the International Criminal Court issued a controversial, split decision finding the Palestinians have *already* achieved statehood for purposes of invoking the Court's jurisdiction.

The transformational framing of the inherently political conflict into a legal dispute represents the culmination of a process the parties began more than a century ago. The arguments made in the conflict today find their roots in the trials conducted during the British Mandate years, especially in the four trials examined in this study.

Few prior studies of the Arab-Israeli dispute have examined how the parties used the law as a weapon against each other from the very onset of the conflict. No prior study has examined the conflict from the perspective of transformational legal framing. Nor has any prior study focused on the legal implications of the Palestinian Arab rejection of the United Nations' offer of the two-state solution in November 1947. This study attempts to fill those gaps.

Most observers on both sides agree that the two-state solution offers the fairest *political* outcome for the Israeli-Palestinian conflict. This does not mean, however, that the Palestinian Arabs are *legally entitled* to that outcome. Chimerical legal claims based on "rights," "victimhood," and "injustice" should not obfuscate the reality that the conflict is inherently political and must be resolved by diplomats through negotiation, not by lawyers and judges through litigation and jurisprudential gymnastics.

# ACKNOWLEDGEMENTS

First and foremost, I offer my deepest gratitude to Professor Steven L. Spiegel of the University of California, Los Angeles for his tremendous support and guidance in this and many other endeavours. Dean and Professor Elizabeth G. Matthews of California State University, San Marcos provided great encouragement. Thanks also to Joe Whiting of Routledge for his kind support and excellent suggestions and to Ella Panczel of Routledge and Radhika Jolly of KnowledgeWorks Global Ltd. for their editorial assistance.

Professor Richard Hecht of the University of California, Santa Barbara helped me enormously with this project, generously sharing his insights, wisdom, and expertise. I am also profoundly grateful to Professor Michael F. Lofchie of the University of California, Los Angeles for nearly a lifetime of mentoring and inspiration.

My dear friends Ira Raphaelson and Senior United States District Judge Michael M. Baylson read significant portions of the manuscript and provided extremely helpful comments and suggestions.

I benefitted greatly from communications with Professor Elad Ben-Dror, Dr Fima Lifshitz, Dr Tobias Nobigrot, Sergio Garcia-Granados, and Carla Garcia-Granados. I am also very grateful to Rabbi Alan Podet for allowing me to access his files and papers regarding the Anglo-American Committee of Inquiry at the American Jewish Archives in Cincinnati and for briefing me on his long-ago interview of Loy Henderson.

I am indebted to the three anonymous referees for their very careful review of the manuscript and their excellent suggestions for improvement.

I received very kind and generous assistance from Evelina Stulgaityte of the Special Collections department at the Tarlton Law Library, University of Texas School of Law; Dana Herman of the American Jewish Archives in Cincinnati;

Jacques Oberson of the League of Nations Archives in Geneva; Debbie Usher of the Middle East Centre Archive at St. Antony's College, Oxford; Lior Hecht Yacoby of the Weizmann Archives in Rehovot; Maxwell Zupke of the UCLA Young Research Library Special Collections department; and the staffs of the Columbia University Rare Book and Manuscript Library in New York City, the British National Archives in London, the Modern Records Centre at the University of Warwick, the Bodleian Libraries in Oxford, the Central Zionist Archives in Jerusalem, the Israel Museum in Jerusalem, and the United Nations Archives in New York City.

I am also grateful to the UCLA Center for Middle East Development research team under the superb leadership of Warren Fahmy, and the excellent work of the following students: Donya Aframian, Hanna Al-Malssi, Suzan Bedikian, Francesca Bonaudo, Brandon Broukhim, Talia Cohen, R. William Dahlin, Yutong Dai, Jumico Evi, Seena Fakhimalizad, Haya Fakhoury, Kam Feiz, Justin Feldman, Talla Khelghati, Claudia Marza, Jack Payne, Maripau Paz, Sarah Peach, Allyson Ping, Wafeeq Ridhuan, Joshua Roizman, Michael Rosenkrantz, Matthew Rutzen, Jack Shea, Laura Slote, Bella Stenvall, Jenna Welsh, Dana Wilks, and Cayden Zayne.

Despite the enormous help from so many people, I alone am responsible for any errors, omissions or mistakes in this study.

Finally, I would not have been able to start, much less finish this project, without the constant support, love, and encouragement from my dear wife Diane Zipperstein and from our wonderful children and grandchildren.

My beloved father Herbert Zipperstein passed away in July 2021, while this book was in production. All who knew and loved my Dad admired his charismatic personality, his wonderful sense of humour, his keen intellect, and his profound devotion to family. I dedicate this book to him – may his memory be a blessing forever.

# INTRODUCTION

One of the most striking aspects of the Arab-Israeli conflict involves the role the law has played for the last century. During the British Mandate (1922–1948) the Arabs, Jews, and British all used the law, both procedurally and substantively, as a means of gaining leverage against each other and influencing international opinion. The Palestinian Arabs and Jews both invoked what will be described in Part I of this study as *transformational legal framing* to situate their inherently political conflict within a narrative of *justice, injustice, and victimisation*, especially during various British and international inquiry commissions and other quasi-legal proceedings from the 1920s to the 1940s.

These proceedings may appropriately be described as "trials," given the dominant role of judges, lawyers, witnesses, cross-examination, evidence, and legal argumentation. Some of the proceedings bore a closer relationship to courtroom trials than others, but in each instance, the parties sought to cast the political and religious disputes between them within an adversarial legal framework, thereby rendering the "trial" typology appropriate.

Indeed, each trial "corresponded to political efforts to define national belonging as well as the rule of law."[1] The trials featured extensive litigation regarding the meaning of the apparently conflicting British pledges to the Arabs in the McMahon-Hussein correspondence of 1915–1916 and the Jews in the Balfour Declaration of 1917, as well as the meaning of various provisions of the Covenant of the League of Nations and the Mandate for Palestine, always against the backdrop of competing Palestinian Arab and Jewish nationalist narratives.

The present study focuses on the last four trials of the Mandate period, between 1939 and 1947. The trials ended with vastly different verdicts: the *one-state* solution in 1939; the *no-state* solution in 1946; and the *two-state* solution in 1947. The Palestinian Arabs, much to their later regret, rejected each of these verdicts. The Jews likewise rejected the one-state and no-state solutions but actively lobbied for and embraced the two-state solution when the United Nations offered it in late 1947, culminating in Israeli statehood in May 1948.

Nevertheless, the Palestinian Arabs, by framing the conflict for the last 90 years in legal terms and proffering a narrative based on "justice," "injustice,"

DOI: 10.4324/9781003225263-1

and "victimhood," have succeeded in positioning their claims as based not only on politics but also on *legal* rights and remedies. The Palestinians have so successfully employed transformational legal framing and so completely out-manoeuvred the Jewish side that most of the world community today accepts the Palestinian narrative of the conflict, without regard to the factual history and legal ramifications of Palestinian Arab actions during the 1930s and 1940s.

The Palestinian Arabs continue employing transformational legal framing as a tool in the conflict today. For example, they persuaded the International Court of Justice to issue an Advisory Opinion in July 2004 declaring illegal the separation barrier dividing most of the West Bank from Israel. The Palestinian Arabs have also successfully situated their Boycott, Divestment and Sanctions campaign against Israel within the global "social justice" movement. In late 2016, the Palestinians won a huge legal victory in the UN Security Council, obtaining a resolution (with the United States abstaining in the waning days of the Obama Administration) declaring Israel's occupation of the West Bank and East Jerusalem a "flagrant violation of international law." And most recently, the Palestinians succeeded in persuading the International Criminal Court (ICC) to treat Palestine as a "state" for purposes of invoking the ICC's jurisdiction to preside over potential prosecutions of alleged Israeli "war crimes" in the West Bank, Gaza, and Jerusalem.

This study therefore continues the author's previous examination of how the Arabs, Jews, and British each used the law and the legal process during the period 1915–1937 to advance their positions and gain leverage against each other, especially in the Shaw Commission trial of 1929, the Lofgren Commission trial of 1930, and the Peel Commission trial of 1936–1937.[2]

The present study covers the crucial period between 1939 and 1948 to continue exploring the early legal encounters between the parties and the origins of many of the fundamental legal arguments in the Arab-Israeli conflict. By examining how the Arabs, Jews, and British transformationally framed the conflict through legal narrative, we can gain new insights into how the early legal clashes between Zionism and Palestinian Arab nationalism remain highly relevant to the conflict today.

## The four trials

The four trials between 1939 and 1947 each involved intensive participation by judges, lawyers, and witnesses. Table 0.1 shows the interplay between the four trials:

### *London Conferences, 1939*

Part II of this study analyses how the Jews, and especially the Arabs and British, used the law during the London Conferences of 1939. The failure of the Conferences cleared the way for Britain to issue the May 1939 White Paper endorsing the one-state solution for Palestine.

**TABLE 0.1** The Trials of Palestine, 1939–1947

| *Trial* | *Judge/Jury* | *Verdict* |
|---|---|---|
| London Conferences, 1939 | UK Government | **One-state solution**: Palestine to be independent after ten years; Jewish immigration capped at 75,000 total for first five years, thereafter subject to Arab consent |
| Anglo-American Committee of Inquiry, 1946 | US-UK (*British/American judges served as co-chairs*) | **No-state solution**: Palestine to continue under indefinite Mandate/Trusteeship; Jewish immigration to resume |
| United Nations Special Committee on Palestine (UNSCOP), 1947 | 11 countries (*Swedish Judge served as Chairperson*) | **Majority: two-state solution/partition:** Palestine to be divided into separate Jewish and Arab states |
| UN Ad Hoc Committee on Palestine, 1947 | General Assembly (*Australian Judge served as Chairperson*) | **Majority: two-state solution/partition:** Palestine to be divided into separate Jewish and Arab states |

## *Background*

In late November 1938, two months after Prime Minister Neville Chamberlain signed the Munich Agreement and appeased Adolph Hitler's belligerent expansionism, Chamberlain's Cabinet accepted a recommendation from Colonial Secretary Malcolm MacDonald for another form of appeasement, this time in favour of the Palestinian Arabs.

With the likelihood of war with Germany looming, Britain decided to adopt an unabashedly pro-Arab policy in Palestine, hoping to prevent Hitler and his ally the Grand Mufti of Jerusalem, Haj Amin al-Husseini, from using Zionism and Jewish immigration to Palestine as a wedge to drive the Palestinian Arabs and surrounding Arab states away from Britain and into an alliance with Nazi Germany.

The policy shift included abandoning the two-state solution (partitioning Palestine into separate Jewish and Arab states) the Palestine Royal Commission had recommended in its landmark July 1937 Report. In its place, Whitehall decided on a *one-state solution* under Palestinian Arab rule, preferring Palestinian Arab nationalism over Zionism.

But before announcing its new Palestine policy, the British Government convened a conference in London with the Palestinian Arabs and Jews to discuss Palestine's future. The conference, like the previous inquiry commissions Britain had established to investigate Palestine-related issues, was intended to allow the Jews and Arabs to make their legal and policy arguments to the

British Government while simultaneously providing legal and political cover for Britain's eventual policy change.

Britain, seeking to cloak with legal legitimacy its predetermined Palestine policy shift in favour of Palestinian Arab nationalism and against Zionism and Jewish immigration, embraced the façade of legal process and discussion during the London Conferences to lay the juridical foundation for the May 1939 White Paper.

The London Conferences, although not a courtroom proceeding in the traditional sense, effectively put Zionism and the Balfour Declaration on trial, as Whitehall sought to build a legal record justifying the radical change in Palestine policy it would eventually adopt in the White Paper of May 1939. The White Paper endorsed the "One-State" solution for Palestine, with Jewish immigration severely restricted and ultimately terminated after five years, Jewish land acquisition largely banned, and the Palestinian Arabs achieving statehood after ten years. The White Paper slammed shut the doors of Palestine to European Jews seeking escape from Nazism, condemning millions to death in Hitler's gas chambers.

## *The London Conferences*

The London Conferences convened in early February 1939 at St. James's Palace. Britain invited delegations representing the Palestinian Arabs, the surrounding Arab states, and the Jewish Agency. The Palestinian Arabs refused to sit together with the Jews, forcing the British Government to conduct parallel conferences with each side. Colonial Secretary Malcolm MacDonald served as the lead interlocutor for the British Government. For the next six weeks, MacDonald conducted parallel meetings and discussions with the Palestinian Arabs and their Arab neighbours, and separate discussions with the Jewish delegation.

## *McMahon-Hussein legal subcommittee*

Shortly after the London Conferences began, Britain agreed to create an Arab-British subcommittee to examine the Arab and British legal arguments involving the McMahon-Hussein correspondence of 1915–1916. The Palestine Royal Commission had previously found the correspondence, despite its ambiguous language, did not support the Arab claim that McMahon had promised Palestine to Sherif Hussein as one of the areas for future Arab independence. McMahon himself had written to the *Times* in late July 1937 making clear he never intended to include Palestine in the areas pledged to the Arabs, and that Hussein well understood Palestine had been excluded.

Nevertheless, the British Government invited and even encouraged the Palestinian Arabs during the London Conferences in 1939 to press their legal case regarding the McMahon-Hussein correspondence. The Palestinian Arabs hired the former Chief Justice of the Palestine Supreme Court to act as their lawyer for the McMahon-Hussein issue, while the British Government designated its highest legal officer, the Lord Chancellor, to take the lead for the British side during the subcommittee's discussions. The Arab legal team forcefully argued the ambiguous language in McMahon's letters to Hussein should be construed in favour of the Palestinian Arabs, to avoid an otherwise unjust outcome.

The Arab legal team also utilised the 1918 "Hogarth Message" to great effect, arguing it stood as compelling contemporaneous evidence of Britain's intent to construe the Balfour Declaration as narrowly as possible.

The McMahon-Hussein subcommittee produced an extraordinary joint Arab-British legal report, in which the British Government conceded half the Palestinian Arab claim, agreeing Hussein had intended to *claim* Palestine among the areas of Arab independence. But Britain still insisted McMahon himself never intended to *pledge* Palestine to the Arabs.

MacDonald was only too willing to consider the Arab arguments, as they helped bolster the British Government's desire to build a legal record justifying the eventual policy shift he had already recommended to the Cabinet even before the Conferences had convened. Thus, from MacDonald's perspective, allowing the London Conferences to serve as the functional equivalent of a "trial" of Zionism (with the verdict already decided) would serve British objectives perfectly.

The London Conferences collapsed in mid-March 1939 with no agreement between the parties. The Zionists knew they had lost all support from the British Government and therefore had no incentive to capitulate. The Palestinian Arabs, for their part, knew Britain was predisposed in their favour and therefore had every incentive to continue pushing for more concessions.

### *The May 1939 White Paper*

Ultimately, the British Government unilaterally announced its new Palestine policy in the form of a White Paper published 17 May 1939. The White Paper's key elements included a one-state solution, meaning a majority-ruled Palestinian Arab State would emerge within ten years. During the first five of those years, Jewish immigration would be permitted to continue, but slowed to a trickle, with only 75,000 total immigrants allowed during the entire five-year period, thereby locking in a two-to-one Arab majority. Any Jewish immigration after the five-year period would be subject to Arab veto power. The White Paper also proposed banning nearly all Jewish land acquisition in Palestine, a policy the Mandatory Government codified in early 1940 with a new Land Transfers Ordinance.

The White Paper represented a sweeping verdict in favour of Palestinian Arab nationalism and a crushing defeat for Zionism. But the Palestinian Arabs rejected the White Paper, upset that it fell short of their demands for *immediate* statehood and an *immediate* halt to Jewish immigration. The Palestinian Arab leadership insisted instead on framing the White Paper as an "injustice" due to the minor inconveniences of a ten-year waiting period until full statehood and a five-year continuation of minimal Jewish immigration. Blinded by their all-or-nothing approach, the Palestinian Arabs needlessly squandered the best chance they would ever receive in the entire history of the conflict for statehood throughout the entirety of Palestine.

### *Appeal before the Permanent Mandates Commission*

One month after Britain issued the White Paper, the Permanent Mandates Commission (PMC) of the League of Nations convened in Geneva to consider the legality of the new British policy.

The PMC served as the body overseeing the implementation of various post-World War I mandates around the world on behalf of the League of Nations. Since the establishment of the Palestine Mandate in 1922, the PMC (the members of which included several lawyers) had acted as a sort of appellate court, where both the Palestinian Arabs and Jews had frequently used the Petition process to challenge various British actions as violations of the Mandate's provisions.

The PMC treated the Palestine Mandate as a legal document embodying international legal rules approved by the League of Nations. It had frequently expressed sympathy toward Zionist aspirations in Palestine and scepticism regarding the legality of various British actions during the Mandate years and had occasionally subjected British officials to harsh cross-examination.

In June 1937, the PMC considered the legality of the new British White Paper policy and found it conflicted with various provisions of the Mandate. A majority of the PMC members voted to disapprove the White Paper, a stunning defeat for Britain. Ultimately, however, the PMC's decision had no impact on British policy, as Germany's invasion of Poland and the onset of World War II several weeks later rendered the PMC and the League itself nonentities on the world stage.

The Palestinian Arab leadership's refusal to accept the White Paper and Britain's offer of the one-state solution ended up costing their people dearly, and they continue paying the price today.

## *Anglo-American Committee of Inquiry, 1945–1946*

The second "trial," covered in Part III of the present study, involved the twelve-member Anglo-American Committee of Inquiry, which conducted a three-month series of courtroom-style hearings from January through March 1946 regarding the short-term plight of European Jewish Holocaust refugees and the long-term future governance of Palestine. Co-chaired by British and American judges, and containing four additional members with legal training, the Anglo-American Committee heard testimony from scores of witnesses, subjecting many of them to rigorous and occasionally hostile cross-examination. The Committee also received extensive written submissions from the parties. As the proceedings progressed, the Committee's hearings evolved into a "trial" of the White Paper and British Policy in Palestine since 1939.

Despite the underlying conflict between British and American political objectives, the Committee reached a unanimous verdict following three weeks of tense deliberations in Lausanne, Switzerland in April 1946. The Committee rejected the White Paper's policies restricting Jewish immigration and land acquisition as illegal under the terms of the Mandate. The Committee also renounced the White Paper's "one-state solution" in favour of the Palestinian Arabs, urging instead a "no-state solution," with the Mandate or a successor Trusteeship continuing for Palestine indefinitely.

## *Background and formation of the Committee*

Following World War II, Britain focused on developing a short-term solution to the plight of European Jewish refugees and the Jewish Agency's insistence that Britain allowed at least 100,000 refugees immediately into Palestine, as well as the longer term issue of Palestine's future governance. Britain, depleted and exhausted after years of war and still committed to the White Paper policy for Palestine, enlisted the Truman Administration's assistance to address both issues, hoping to force the Americans to share the political and financial responsibility for the outcome. The British Government hoped the strategy would not only buy time but would also convince the Truman Administration to support the White Paper policy.

President Truman, however, frustrated Britain's desire to lure the American Government into an orchestrated policy outcome for Palestine. In August 1945 and repeatedly thereafter, Truman publicly called on Britain to allow 100,000 Jewish Holocaust refugees to immigrate immediately to Palestine.

Britain reacted by resorting to its time-honoured custom for addressing Palestine controversies, proposing yet another commission of inquiry, this time a joint Anglo-American Committee to investigate the plight of the European Jews and the future of Palestine. The Truman Administration tentatively accepted the British offer to participate in the Joint Committee as a means of obtaining a seat at the table of Middle East policy, which Britain and, to a lesser extent, France had monopolised since the Sykes-Picot Agreement of 1916.

After considerable wrangling over the Joint Committee's Terms of Reference and the deadline to complete its work, the Americans finally agreed to participate. The British and American Governments appointed the Anglo-American Committee of Inquiry in late 1945 to investigate the immediate post-War plight of European Jewry, and the longer term governance of Palestine. The Committee contained 12 members, six British and six American, including several lawyers and judges. Justice Sir John Singleton of the King's Bench Division of the High Court in London and Judge Joseph C. Hutcheson, Jr. of the United States Court of Appeals for the Fifth Circuit in Houston, Texas, co-chaired the Committee.

## Committee hearings

The Anglo-American Committee convened in Washington, DC in January 1946 to commence four months of work, including three months of hearings and nearly one month of deliberations. The Committee conducted a "trial," not in the traditional meaning of the word, but in the sense that the twelve Committee members acted collectively as judges and jurors during three months of hearing testimony from scores of witnesses, subjecting many of them to searing cross-examination.

The Committee members conducted hearings in Washington and London, as well as Cairo and Jerusalem, taking testimony from and cross-examining a multitude of Arab and Jewish witnesses. In addition to courtroom-style hearings, various Committee members toured the rubble of the European war zones and saw at first hand the immeasurable suffering of Europe's surviving Jews. Committee members also visited Baghdad, Amman, Damascus, Jedda, and Beirut for discussions with Arab leaders.

The Palestinian Arab witnesses invoked their familiar legal narrative and framing, repeatedly characterising the conflict as a battle between "justice" and "injustice," and interweaving legal narrative throughout their testimony and written submissions. The Jewish witnesses did the same, most memorably the Zionist leader Chaim Weizmann, who, having learned well from the mistakes made in the 1929 Shaw Commission trial, cleverly appropriated the Arab "justice/injustice" narrative for the Jewish side during his testimony to the Committee, reframing the issue as involving a choice between "the least injustice."

By the time the Committee was ready to commence its deliberations, it was clear that the key issue on trial was not Jewish refugee immigration to Palestine, or even the future form of government for Palestine. Instead, the Committee realised the White Paper and British policy itself had been on trial from the beginning and now awaited a verdict.

## Deliberations and verdict

The Committee spent its final three weeks locked in tense, difficult, and fractious deliberations over their verdict. When they began deliberating, the Committee seemed hopelessly divided into at least two and perhaps three separate factions. But by the time they finished, the Committee rendered a unanimous verdict, issuing a stunning denunciation of the White Paper and British policy in Palestine.

The verdict proved enormously embarrassing for the British Government. Its Palestine policy had been adjudged guilty of betraying Britain's legal obligations under the Mandate. Not a single British member of the Committee dissented from the verdict.

Part of the Committee's rejection of the White Paper involved the Committee's explicit renunciation of the "one-state solution" for Palestine. The Committee decided the key to peace in Palestine depended instead on a "no-state solution," meaning neither the Jews nor the Arabs would dominate each other. Thus, the Committee recommended the Mandate or a successor Trusteeship arrangement should continue indefinitely.

### *Post-verdict manoeuvring*

The British Government tried to moot the Committee's verdict quickly, persuading the Truman Administration to engage in new discussions regarding yet another proposal (the "Morrison-Grady Plan") for Palestine, this time involving a form of cantonisation or "provincial autonomy."

Ultimately, Truman withdrew from the talks, leaving Britain scrambling to try to achieve a settlement between the Palestinian Arabs and the Zionists. When those efforts finally collapsed in early 1947, and with its Palestine policy in tatters, Britain had no choice but to turn the matter over to the United Nations.

The British Government's White Paper policy had unanimously been adjudged guilty of violating the Mandate and discriminating against Jewish immigration to Palestine and Jewish land acquisition in the country. At the same time, however, both the Anglo-American Committee and the Morrison-Grady plans rejected statehood in Palestine for Jews and Arabs alike, preferring a "no-state solution" under which Palestine would continue as a ward of the international community indefinitely.

## *United Nations Special Committee (UNSCOP) and Ad Hoc Committee, 1947*

Part IV of this study examines the third and fourth "trials" – the proceedings before the United Nations Special Committee on Palestine (UNSCOP) from June to August 1947 and the follow-on UN Ad Hoc Committee for Palestine from September to November 1947.

### *UNSCOP*

The third "trial" between 1939 and 1947 occurred under the aegis of the United Nations Special Committee on Palestine (UNSCOP). UNSCOP was formed in May 1947, following Britain's decision to hand the Palestine issue to the United Nations. The Special Committee followed the example of the long series of Palestine-related commissions that had preceded it, naming several lawyers among its 11 members and a Swedish high court judge as its Chairperson.

In July 1947, UNSCOP conducted public hearings and various *in camera* meetings in Jerusalem, hearing testimony from more than 30 witnesses and receiving thousands of pages of written submissions. Once again, a trial-type process, replete with legal framing and narrative, played a crucial role in determining Palestine's future. This time, Palestinian Arab Nationalism stood in the dock, rather than Zionism or British Policy. The UNSCOP trial thus focused on the legitimacy of the Palestinian Arab claim to *all* of Palestine.

The Palestinian Arabs, perhaps sensing the tide had turned in favour of Zionism, chose to boycott the Special Committee, seriously damaging their credibility with the United Nations and severely handicapping their ability to influence the outcome. However, representatives of various Arab states participated and made arguments on behalf of the Palestinian Arabs. The Special Committee also conducted two days of meetings in Beirut and paid a courtesy call on Transjordan's King Abdullah in Amman.

The Arab and Jewish witnesses invoked the long-standing legal framing and narrative the parties had developed during various "trials" occurring since the early 1920s.

After completing its deliberations, a majority of the Special Committee rejected both the "one-state" and "no-state" solutions, reverting instead to the Palestine Royal Commission's July 1937 recommendation for a "two-state" solution. The Special Committee majority recommended terminating the Mandate and dividing Palestine into separate Jewish and Arab sovereign states, with Jerusalem remaining a *corpus separatum* under international control. A minority of the Special Committee's members issued a separate recommendation for a "one-state" solution for Palestine, endorsing Palestinian Arab sovereignty over all of Palestine within a federal-state governance structure.

## *Ad Hoc Committee*

Shortly after UNSCOP issued its report, the United Nations appointed a follow-on committee, known as the "Ad Hoc Committee on the Palestine Question," to conduct yet another "trial," focusing in more detail on the UNSCOP majority's two-state solution (partition) and the minority's one-state solution.

A former Australian High Court judge chaired the Ad Hoc Committee. The Palestinian Arabs abandoned their boycott, opting to participate in the Ad Hoc Committee's hearings. The leading Palestinian Arab representative appeared three times before the Ad Hoc Committee during the fall of 1947.

The Ad Hoc Committee was divided into two subcommittees to prepare reports on the UNSCOP majority and minority recommendations. The second subcommittee endorsed the one-state solution, issuing a detailed report containing a lengthy discussion of the legal arguments in favour of Palestinian Arab sovereignty over all of Palestine and against Jewish statehood in even a tiny portion of the country.

The legal arguments mustered by the second subcommittee reprised and expanded on the long-standing Palestinian legal framing of the conflict and, in many respects, offer the best summary of the Palestinian Arab legal case as of November 1947. The second subcommittee also identified a variety of legal issues it wanted the General Assembly to refer to the International Court of Justice, including whether the General Assembly itself possessed any legal jurisdiction over Palestine.

At the conclusion of its proceedings, the Ad Hoc Committee by majority vote endorsed the two-state solution and rejected the second subcommittee's proposals to terminate the Palestine Mandate immediately and create a single, Arab-ruled state. The Ad Hoc Committee also rejected Arab requests to seek rulings on various issues from the International Court of Justice.

### *The General Assembly and the two-state solution*

The UN General Assembly approved the UNSCOP and Ad Hoc Committee partition proposal on 29 November 1947 in Resolution 181(II). This represented the first-ever formal international endorsement of a solution for the Palestine conflict, in which two states would be formed, one Arab and one Jewish. Both the United States and the Soviet Union endorsed the two-state solution, in a remarkable show of unity for two countries already locked in their post-War global rivalry.

The Jews accepted the General Assembly's verdict, but the Palestinian Arabs renounced the verdict and immediately launched a bloody civil war. The surrounding Arab countries ultimately joined the war when the Jews declared statehood in May 1948 in the portion of Palestine the General Assembly had allocated to them.

## Legal consequences of the Palestinian Arab rejection of the two-state solution

Part V of the present study examines the relevance of the trials during the decade between 1939 and 1947 to the conflict today. While many studies have examined the competing legal claims of the parties, none has focused on the legal significance and implications of the Palestinian Arab rejection of the United Nations' offer of the two-state solution in Resolution 181(II) of 29 November 1947.

Most existing scholarship, advocating on behalf of one side or the other, has focused on the legal status of the area that became known as the "West Bank" as of the 3 April 1949 Armistice Agreement between Israel and Jordan. Other scholars, also advocating on behalf of one side or the other, have debated the legal status of Palestine as of the Treaty of Versailles and the Covenant of the League of Nations. Still others focus on the moment the British Mandate officially began in 1923 following the Treaty of Lausanne, and the moment it officially terminated on 14 May 1948.

This study is the first to argue that under international law, the Palestinian Arabs' immediate rejection of the United Nations 29 November 1947 offer of statehood constituted a *waiver* and *renunciation*, at that precise moment, as a matter of law. Thus, from that moment forward, the Palestinians waived and renounced *all* claims to statehood in any portion of Palestine, and specifically the portion of Palestine the General Assembly had offered them. The Palestinians expressly reaffirmed the waiver in the original 1964 Palestine National Charter, often referred to as the PLO Charter. That waiver and renunciation, as a matter of law, *estopped* the Palestinians from thereafter changing their minds and asserting claims of sovereignty over any portion of Palestine, including the portion the General Assembly had offered for their state.

The Palestinian waiver/estoppel in late 1947 remains highly relevant to the current Israeli-Palestinian dispute. While the two-state solution might represent the most desirable outcome for the conflict as a matter of *politics* and *policy*, the Palestinians do not have a right to their own state as a matter of *law*, because they waived that right when they renounced the General Assembly's offer of statehood on 29 November 1947.

Therefore, because the Palestinians today have a weak *legal* claim to statehood, they lack standing to participate in international judicial bodies such as the ICC. The ICC, which only has jurisdiction over disputes between *states*, nevertheless recognised Palestine as a "state" in a bizarre and highly controversial split decision in February 2021, thereby permitting the Palestinian Authority to invoke the ICC's jurisdiction to investigate various "war crimes" complaints against the Israeli Government. But Palestine cannot legally be deemed a "state" in 2021, because the Palestinians *renounced* and *waived* statehood in response to the UN's offer of sovereignty over a portion of Mandate Palestine in November 1947 and maintained that position for many subsequent decades. Therefore, Palestine lacks standing to participate as an ICC member state, and the ICC lacks jurisdiction to pursue claims against Israel on behalf of the Palestinians.

Moreover, the Palestinian waiver of statehood in November 1947 undermines the modern claims of Palestinian lawyers and legal scholars, such as Victor Kattan, who incorrectly argue, "a Palestinian state has existed since 1919, and a Palestinian government was established – even if momentarily – in the territories occupied by the armed forces of Egypt and Jordan during the 1948 war following the termination of the mandate."[3]

Instead, the Palestinian rejection of the General Assembly's November 1947 offer of statehood irrevocably waived all Palestinian claims to statehood from that moment to the present day. Nor did the brief existence of a sham "All-Palestine" Government in October 1948 provide any legal basis for modern-day Palestinian claims of legally cognisable sovereignty over the West Bank and Gaza.

## Conclusion

The study concludes by assessing whether any lessons can be derived from the various "trials of Palestine" and the parties' early and ongoing experiences using transformational legal framing and narrative to define the conflict.

The Palestinians continue employing transformational legal framing to the present day to cast themselves as the "victims of injustice," entitling them to *legal* rights and remedies. But this construct ultimately fails to serve the long-term *political* interests of either the Palestinians or the Israelis. Indeed, it is highly unlikely that Palestinian efforts to impose judicial remedies on Israel will succeed.

The most appropriate process for resolving the inherently political conflict must be based on diplomacy and negotiation, not litigation.

## Notes

1 M. Arjomand, *Staged: Show Trials, Political Theater, and the Aesthetics of Judgment* (Columbia University Press, 2018) (emphasis added).
2 S. Zipperstein, *Law and the Arab-Israeli Conflict: The Trials of Palestine* (Routledge, 2020).
3 V. Kattan, "My two-part post criticising the Government of Israel's submission to the International Criminal Court" (30 January 2020), https://victorkattan.com/work/1077-2/ (last accessed 18 April 2021).

# PART I

# Theoretical framework

# 1

# FRAMING THE ISRAELI-PALESTINIAN CONFLICT

## Introduction

Studies of framing, narrative, and critical discourse theory have proliferated since Goffman (1974) published his seminal work on frame analysis nearly a half-century ago.[1] Few studies, however, have focused on the role of framing and narrative in the Israeli-Palestinian conflict. To the extent any such scholarship exists, it has focused mostly on the modern era and largely ignored the British Mandate period.

The present study and the author's prior study of the "Trials of Palestine" during the 1920s and 1930s demonstrate how framing and narrative – specifically, *transformational legal framing*, invoking tropes of "justice," "injustice," and "victimisation" – have played a key role in the conflict, not only in recent decades, but also ever since the inception of the conflict more than a century ago.[2]

Framing theory, therefore, provides a useful theoretical orientation for interrogating the role of *legal* discourse in the fundamentally *political* conflict between Palestinian Arab nationalism and Jewish nationalism during the British Mandate years – especially during the crucial decade between 1939 and 1948 – and in the conflict today.

As noted above and discussed further below, a new framing/reframing typology, *transformational legal framing,* is necessary to adapt framing theory to the Israeli-Palestinian conflict. "Transformational Legal Framing" describes how parties in the political and social arenas employ framing to convert inherently *non-legal* political movements and social causes into *legal* battles for and against *justice* and *injustice*. Movement and cause members are transformationally framed as *victims* of legal wrongdoing, entitling them to pursue legal remedies such as damages, reparations and criminal prosecution of alleged wrongdoers, and equitable remedies such as restitution, rescission, and restoration.

DOI: 10.4324/9781003225263-3

The discussion below begins with a review of the classically understood modalities and typologies of framing. It proceeds next to an examination of legal framing and master legal frames, including an examination of diagnostic legal framing, prognostic legal framing, and motivational legal framing. It then describes the justice/injustice subframes of diagnostic legal framing.

Finally, the new typology of *transformational legal framing* is proposed as the appropriate analytical framework for the Arab-Jewish conflict beginning during the British Mandate years and continuing to the modern Israeli-Palestinian conflict. The prevalence in the modern era of "lawfare," and the intervention of both the International Court of Justice and the International Criminal Court in the conflict exemplify the success of transformational legal framing entrepreneurs, especially on the Palestinian Arab side.

## Modalities and typologies of framing

Frame analysis and its intellectual companion, critical discourse theory, have produced a dynamic and robust outpouring of scholarship in the last 40 years. Nevertheless, the field has yet to coalesce into a single discipline. De Bruycker (2017), for example, described the fragmented nature of framing studies:

> Framing is studied in different research disciplines, including communication studies, political science, psychology and sociology. There is no clear consensus across these disciplines on how framing should be studied. The fractured and diffuse nature of framing studies brings about some demanding and complex challenges for interest group scholars who engage in this type of research. Most importantly, researchers draw on different types of frames, analytical frameworks and methodological approaches which impedes cooperation and convergence between the different studies.[3]

Leachman (2013) has defined framing as "an expressive act that has symbolic ramifications for both internal and external movement audiences, which movement actors take into consideration as they formulate movement strategy."[4] Muller and Slominski (2019) more recently defined framing as a means for policy advocates, sometimes described as *frame entrepreneurs*, to "shape the debate surrounding a policy issue with the aim of influencing policy outcomes."[5]

De Bruycker (2017) offers a more detailed typology of framing, including distinctions between "issue-specific" and "generic" frames, and "emphasis" versus "equivalence" frames:

> Issue-specific frames are tied to the specific nature of the issue or conflict under scrutiny and emerge by looking from the bottom–up. Generic frames are not tied to a specific policy debate or issue, but can be identified across issues ... Emphasis framing refers to emphasizing

> one aspect of an issue over others … [E]quivalence framing was developed in psychology research and involves presenting similar information in a different way.[6]

Gamson (1992) took a somewhat different approach, starting by describing what he called "interpretative frames." In the context of social movements, interpretive frames can be characterised as "collective action frames," with three components: an emotively defined injustice, an analysis of agency, and an identity component defining both the "we" of interested people and a "they" who hold opposing values.[7]

Carroll and Ratner (1996) have theorised how "whole cycles of protest might be organized in part around the construction of 'master frames' – schemata that integrate the specific agendas of diverse movements into central interpretive frameworks."[8] Gillan (2008) has stressed the importance of hermeneutic approaches to frame studies.[9]

Despite the multidisciplinary approach to frame studies, many (but not all) scholars have adopted Entman's (1993) oft-quoted definition of framing as selecting some aspects of a "perceived reality" and rendering them "more salient in a communicating text, in such a way as to promote a particular problem definition, causal interpretation, moral evaluation, and/or treatment recommendation for the item described."[10]

De Bruycker (2017), however, disagrees with Entman's definitional emphasis on communication, choosing instead to focus on the key role of framing in *defining* policy debates:

> [M]acro-level framing is seen as the collective definition process of what is at stake in a policy debate. Framing is then the process of how a policy debate is defined and understood. From this perspective frames are seen as the building blocks that construct a policy debate, rather than an emphasis in communication as in Entman's definition. A frame is then a perspective from which a policy problem can be made sense of and acted upon. Frames are identified by looking at the overall dominating aspects of a policy debate that are emphasized by institutions, advocacy coalitions and the news media. From this point of view framing is both a bottom–up process, where different sides of a policy debate promote their own frames, and a top–down process, which structures conflict and mobilization patterns … frames are seen as instruments of change or as strategic tools that interest groups rely on to obtain their political and policy goals.[11]

Junk and Rasmussen (2019) explain the importance of framing in social and political movements, particularly emphasising how framing can impact policy definition and policy outcomes, as "frames have the ability to affect how policy makers grasp and process complex policy choices and, hence, work in favor of certain interests over others."[12]

## *Legal framing*

Despite the enormous focus on framing and critical discourse theory, scholars have paid scant attention to *legal* framing and narrative. Jacques Derrida (1992) began the inquiry with his famous examination of Kafka's parable "Before the Law:"

> It seems that the law as such should never give rise to any story. To be invested with its categorical authority, the law must be without history, genesis or any possible derivation. That would be *the law of the law*. Pure morality has no history: as Kant seems first to remind us, no intrinsic history. And when one tells stories on this subject, they can concern only circumstances, events external to the law and, at best, the modes of its revelation.[13]

One year after Derrida's memorable exposition on Kafka, the critical legal theorist Robert Cover (1983) offered a framework for contextualising the role of legal *narrative*:

> Once understood in the context of the narratives that give it meaning, law becomes not merely a system of rules to be observed, but a world in which we live. In this normative world, law and narrative are inseparably related. Every prescription is insistent in its demand to be located in discourse – to be supplied with history and destiny, beginning and end, explanation and purpose ... The codes that relate our normative system to our social constructions of reality and to our visions of what the world might be are narrative. The very imposition of a normative force upon a state of affairs, real or imagined, is the act of creating narrative ... Narratives are models through which we experience and study transformations that result when a given simplified state of affairs is made to pass through the force field of a similarly simplified set of norms.[14]

Cover also noted how legal narrative frequently emerges against a backdrop of violence: "[T]he jurisgenerative principle by which legal meaning proliferates in all communities never exists in isolation from violence."[15]

Despite Cover's contribution, scholarly attention to law and framing has remained relatively sparse but has regained momentum in the recent past. Marshall (2003), for example, described the interplay between the everyday lives of "ordinary people" and the law as giving rise to "legal consciousness:"

> To ordinary people, law is not simply the official texts of judicial opinions and legislative acts that embody formal legal rules, nor is it just the formal legal institutions of courts, lawyers and police. Instead, the law of everyday life – what Ewick and Silbey call "legality" – embraces "the meanings, sources of authority, and cultural practices that are commonly recognized

> as legal, regardless of who employs them or for what ends. In this rendering, people may invoke and enact legality in ways neither approved nor acknowledged by law." Thus, individuals' lives are not simply constrained by legality. In fact, in their choices and social practices, people also create their own sets of legal meanings. This interactive process between meaning and practice is legal consciousness.[16]

Leachman (2013) built on Marshall's work, noting "[l]egal *concepts* are words, labels or categories associated with the law, which people use to interpret everyday life. Through legal framing, social movement actors strategically link together these legal concepts (and nonlegal ones) to convince others to support their cause."[17]

More recently, Muller and Slominski (2019) focused on law as a "master frame,"[18] urging more focus on "the particularities of the *legal* discourse itself" and how "norms entrepreneurs develop legal arguments to achieve political objectives."[19] Muller and Slominski, thus, posit three variations of legal framing: *diagnostic* legal framing, *prognostic* legal framing, and *motivational* legal framing.[20]

Diagnostic legal framing, according to Muller and Slominski, "communicates that a particular issue needs to be considered within the master frame of the law, as opposed to treating it primarily as a political, economic or moral issue." Prognostic legal framing involves "suggesting specific remedies to the diagnosed legal problems." Motivational legal framing "provides a 'call to arms' to generate mobilization" among policymakers.[21]

Muller and Slominksi applied their legal framing construct to public policy debates in the European Union, describing how "the interaction of legally savvy frame entrepreneurs with the law-thick world of EU politics has generated a distinct 'legal' discourse, which has gradually shaped political deliberations both within the EU and beyond."[22]

Muller and Slominski also cautioned that legal frame entrepreneurship requires certain attributes for success:

> At the same time, we identify two scope conditions for effective legal framing. First, legal framing benefits from the ability of applying law to facts. This requires frame entrepreneurs that have intimate knowledge about procedures, sequences of decision-making, and policy matters that revolve around crucial legal issues. Second, we argue that legal claims by frame entrepreneurs that are in accordance with established legal meanings are more persuasive and more difficult to ignore than those which operate in areas of legal contestation or produce new legal arguments.[23]

### *Justice/injustice frames*

Scholars including Gamson (1992) and others have been focused on the role of justice/injustice in framing analysis but without necessarily characterising such frames as attributes or subframes of legal master frames. Anheier (1998), for example, defined "injustice framing," as "allow[ing] the movement to dramatize problems, to highlight causes for characteristic negative developments, and to identify the parties responsible."[24]

Other scholars have also focused on "injustice" frames, although they disagree regarding the exact characterisation of such frames. Benford and Snow (2000), for example, take a somewhat narrower approach than Gamson (1992) to the prevalence of injustice frames in social movements:

> Regarding diagnostic framing, several case studies focus on the development and articulation of what Gamson and colleagues refer to as "injustice frames." A plethora of studies call attention to the ways in which movements identify the "victims" of a given injustice and amplify their victimization. Taken together, these studies support Gamson et al.'s initial conceptualization of injustice frames as a mode of interpretation – prefatory to collective noncompliance, protest, and/or rebellion – generated and adopted by those who come to define the actions of an authority as unjust. While the empirical evidence reported in the foregoing studies clearly demonstrates that injustice frames are commonplace across a variety of types of social movements, there is little theoretical or empirical support for Gamson's more sweeping assertion that all "collective action frames are injustice frames;" nor is there support for the less ambitious assertion that all collective action frames contain an injustice component.[25]

Capek (1993) examined justice framing in the context of environmental movements, noting:

> Defining a situation as unjust is more than an act of categorization; it implies a strategy for action. Residents in contaminated communities are generally pushed by their experiences toward a particular set of mobilizing strategies. A typical (although not inevitable) path is to opt for direct action tactics upheld by an "environmental justice" frame ... In constructing their claims and seeking redress, therefore, grass-roots antitoxics activists are far less likely than traditional established environmental groups (such as the Sierra Club) to appeal to the supposedly neutral arbitration of scientific studies conducted by private or public sector experts. Instead, environmental justice is premised on the notion that the rights of toxic contamination victims have been systematically usurped by more powerful social actors, and that "justice" resides in the return of these rights.[26]

Carroll and Ratner's (1996) research among social action groups in Canada revealed various subcategories of injustice frames, including the *political economy injustice frame*, *the identity politics injustice frame*, and the *liberal injustice frame*. The political economy injustice frame focuses on the dynamics of power and oppression. The identity politics injustice frame also focuses on power, especially how power "is often attached to identity markers such as gender and race," and "the possibility of power shifts as people reject old (e.g., patriarchal) models of human relations. In this frame, counterpower is conceived as empowerment, as sharing power."

Finally, the liberal injustice frame envisions "a plurality of groups vying for power, each with its own interests and resources ... injustice per se is grounded in the denial of rights; 'disfranchisement' is often invoked as a metaphor for oppression."[27]

More recently, Baumgart-Ochse (2017) described "injustice" framing as a modality of diagnostic legal framing:

> Referring to injustice is, in fact, a diagnostic frame which from the early writings in social movement theory to contemporary research has been regarded as a central – if not the central – leitmotif in framing processes whereby "injustice frames appear to be fairly ubiquitous across movements advocating some form of political and/or economic change."[28]

While the focus on justice/injustice framing is somewhat useful for the Israeli-Palestinian conflict, further theoretical refinement of legal framing is necessary.

## *A new typology: Transformational legal framing*

Legal frame entrepreneurs have achieved varying degrees of success in recent years, especially when seeking to transform otherwise non-legal disputes and conflicts by employing discursive and rhetorical "justice," "injustice," and "victimisation" frames and reframes.[29]

Nevertheless, the diagnostic, prognostic, and motivational typologies do not provide a sufficiently precise model for addressing situations in which frame entrepreneurs seek to frame/reframe inherently *political* disputes as *legal* disputes, characterising the movement's grievances, goals, and objectives as grounded in *legal rights* and *justice* rather than politics and policy, and vesting movement members with newfound legal rights and remedies. This suggests the need for an additional framing modality.

Pedriana (2006) notes that "because 'law may be the source of new expectations for existing relations,' aggrieved groups can also sustain successful challenges by reframing a movement's grievances and objectives around new or alternative legal symbols."[30] This modality of "reframing" may instead be regarded as an entirely new framing typology – *transformational legal framing*.

Transformational legal framing describes how social (or in the Israel-Palestine conflict, nationalist) movements employ framing to *redefine* the terms of their engagement and shift discourse from politics and policy to the law and legal rights.

Transformational legal framing aims to infuse social and political movements and causes with *legal* significance, converting inherently non-legal *causes* into *legal disputes* about *justice* and *injustice*. Transformational legal frame entrepreneurs recast their constituencies as *victims* of a legal wrong or injustice, entitling them to hold the wrongdoer(s) civilly and/or criminally liable, and receive damages, restitution, reparations, specific performance, restoration, rescission, and other legal and equitable remedies.

As Pedriana (2006) notes:

> [L]aw is a unique type of symbolic resource; it is not only a means by which a movement can, by appealing to deeply resonant legal symbols, garner legitimacy and support for the movement. Law in part also represents the ends of that process. In other words, translating a cultural frame into an officially recognized legal right is itself one of the central objectives of social movements.[31]

## *Transformational legal framing in the Israel-Palestine conflict*

Agne (2007) has noted that "[f]rames and conflict framing have been especially useful in the study of intractable conflicts."[32]

The Jewish-Arab conflict in Palestine is perhaps the most intractable of all the world's political conflicts, pitting competing Jewish and Arab political and nationalist movements against each other for the past century. Religion and religious nationalism have also fueled the conflict, especially during the 1920s and 1930s, when the Mufti successfully stirred Palestinian Arab nationalist sentiment based on false accusations that the Jews intended to wrest control of the *Haram al Sharif* in Jerusalem from the Muslims.

Burgis-Kasthala (2014) has explained how law, particularly international law, plays a role in creating frames and narrative in disputes such as the Israel-Palestine conflict:

> If we understand international law as a language and a practice of ordering the world around rights and responsibilities, then the study of international law must interrogate not only the normative implications of this language – the rules, but also the ways in which this language is generated within specific contexts by its principal interlocutors: judges, advocates, academics, law students, and practitioners in government and civil society. Understanding the import of a given rule or law also relies on particular interpretive methods that in turn are informed by wider disciplinary practices, social relations, and, especially, narratives … an evolving discourse and practice within Palestine does suggest that international legal ideals are being embraced, often in contrast with earlier, unsuccessful, politically-characterized ventures. Through their acts of stating and sometimes over-stating the centrality of international law in shaping and perhaps solving the conflict, Palestinian lawyers, activists, and intellectuals are contributing to a growing legalization of political debate within Palestine.[33]

Gamson (1992) also noted the tendency of Israelis and Palestinians to make "strong and competing claims about deep historical injustices."[34]

In his study of "legal fundamentalism" in the Israeli-Palestinian conflict, Strawson (2010) described how Israelis and Palestinians have used international law as a resource in the conflict for more than a century:

> This use of law has engendered a festering sense of justice amongst Palestinians and Israelis that has fostered conflict rather than offering a means for its resolution. Each side has become cocooned within a legal righteousness in which its own legitimacy is unimpeachable while that of the other is compromised. This has nourished the existential character of the conflict. As a consequence war, occupation, and defiance of the international community are justified as the exercise of legal rights. A cycle of law has sustained a cycle of violence.[35]

Throughout the early history of their disputes in Palestine, the Arabs and Jews each employed transformational legal framing to advocate their positions and influence international opinion.

### *Transformational legal framing during the British mandate*

From the inception of the Jewish-Arab conflict in Palestine, all three protagonists – Arab, Jewish, and British – utilised transformational legal framing to gain leverage against each other and to influence international opinion in the conflict.

Strawson (2010) has described how the Palestinian Arabs viewed their position relative to Zionism and British rule in Palestine through their own normative gloss on the principles of international law:

> No arguments were advanced as to why Zionism would be illegal; it was merely asserted and this became an approach that is to characterize much of the Palestinian legal narrative ..., the [Arab] delegation seemed to assume that a pure and just international law existed beyond the realm of the actual international society [the League of Nations] which was creating Palestine at that very moment. The implicit legal narrative imagined an international law based on values and doctrines that were in accord with a Palestinian perspective. It was early evidence of legal fundamentalism and confused the international legal doctrine that the Palestinians wished to see in place with the doctrines that were in place.[36]

Although Strawson did not employ framing analysis in his study, his characterisation of how the parties used the law aligns with the transformational legal framing typology proposed in this study.

Indeed, both the Jews and the Palestinian Arabs tried, from the very onset of the conflict 100 years ago, to characterise their competing historical narratives as competing legal claims.

The Palestinian Arabs repeatedly deployed transformational legal framing to create a narrative characterising the conflict as a battle between the "justice" of Palestinian Arab nationalism and the "injustice" of Zionism. Zionism was portrayed as a powerful, oppressive force of Western-style settler colonialism and the local Palestinian Arabs as the victims of a grievous injustice.[37] Strawson (2010) notes how as early as the back-and-forth exchange of correspondence between the Colonial Office and the Palestine Arab delegation preceding the Churchill White Paper of 1922, the Palestinians characterised Zionism as "illegal."[38]

The Palestinian Arabs largely succeeded during the Mandate years in employing transformational legal framing to create the long-running narrative of Palestinian victimisation, of Palestinian Arabs as the aggrieved party suffering a series of injustices from the Balfour Declaration to the Occupation, and of Palestinian Arabs as entitled to legal remedies including the abrogation of the Balfour Declaration and sovereignty over all of pre-Mandate Palestine.

Palestinian transformational legal framing has continued to the present day, and in recent years, the Palestinian Arabs have dramatically stepped up their demands for legal and equitable remedies, including the rescission of the Balfour Declaration, the restoration of Palestinian land, and the prosecution of Israelis they hold responsible for "crimes" in occupied areas.[39]

The Jews also employed transformational legal framing from the very beginning of the Zionist movement. At the first Zionist Congress in Basle, Switzerland, in late August 1897, the delegates agreed it was necessary to characterise the desire for a Jewish homeland in Palestine as a *legal* right. A drafting committee proposed language stating, "The aim of Zionism is to create for the Jewish people a home in EretzIsrael secured by law." Other delegates preferred the phrase "secured by international law." Ultimately the Basle Congress adopted Herzl's compromise formula: "Zionism seeks to establish a home for the Jewish people in Eretz Israel secured under public law."[40]

This meant, according to Strawson (2010), that the Zionist leadership from the inception of the movement intended to place "great emphasis on a legal campaign to secure their objectives."[41] The legal campaign, according to Strawson, included the following narrative:

> [The Jewish] argument rested on the assumption that historic rights have the capacity to be transformed into legal rights. It was precisely to oppose such a conclusion that the Palestinians had argued earlier that the Jews did not have such legitimate historical rights. This argument that connects historical claims to contemporary legal rights anticipate many battles that indigenous peoples were to fight in the Americas and Australasia in the latter part of the twentieth century. Moreover, historical claims including the right to return which [Zionist advocates] applied to Jews were to become central in Palestinian legal narratives after the establishment of Israel in 1948.[42]

The Jews likewise utilised transformational legal framing from the earliest days of the conflict with the Palestinian Arabs to create their own narrative regarding the "justice" of reconstituting their ancient homeland in Palestine. Stoyanovsky (1928), for example, argued the Mandate created an international legal obligation for Britain, as Mandatory, to administer Palestine as a trustee, charged with safeguarding and implementing the promise made to the "virtual" Palestinian people, namely, the *Jewish diaspora* scattered across the globe:

> There can hardly be any question now whether Jews constitute a distinct national entity in the eyes of international law ... If, therefore, the question of the national character of the [Jewish People] may remain open – as in fact it does – for purposes of ethnographical or sociological research, it seems to have been definitely settled from the point of view of international law. The status of Jews no longer constitutes a mere political issue within certain States, or a diplomatic issue between States ... Jews as such have now become subjects of rights and duties provided for by international law.[43]

Stoyanovsky also characterised the Jewish people's historical connection to Palestine as grounded in *legal* rights. Because the Jewish people never expressly or implicitly renounced their claims to Palestine, "no exclusive rights could either morally or legally have been acquired over that territory by any other people."[44]

The Zionist leader Chaim Weizmann repeatedly invoked transformational legal framing throughout the Mandate years, testifying at one key moment in 1946 that recognising Jewish national aspirations in Palestine would create a "lesser injustice" for the local Arabs than would the denial of those rights to the Jews.[45]

The British also used transformational legal framing, both substantively and procedurally, throughout the Mandate period. The British Government employed transformational legal framing substantively, characterising the League of Nations Mandate as a *legal* document imposing a variety of contradictory and conflicting *legal* obligations. By framing the Mandate that way, the British Government allowed itself room to justify its inconsistent yet politically expedient Palestine policy decisions throughout the Mandate years as consistent with its interpretation of particularised *legal* requirements of the Mandate.[46]

Britain also employed transformational legal framing as a procedural device, repeatedly using the mechanism of judicial and quasi-judicial "enquiry commissions" to address political and religious conflicts in the context of competing aspirations pitting Palestinian Arab nationalism against Zionism. Britain employed transformational legal framing in the procedural sense by sending judges to "adjudicate" disputes that more appropriately should have been the province of diplomacy and negotiation. By imposing judicial process and procedure on an inherently political dispute, Britain sought to persuade international opinion, including its overseers at the Permanent Mandates Commission (PMC) of the League of Nations, of the procedural fairness, objectivity, and normative credibility with which it addressed disputes between the Arabs and Jews of Palestine.

Arabs and Jews alike embraced Britain's transformational procedural legal framing throughout the Mandate years. Both sides sent small armies of lawyers to argue their cases in the various trials the British authorities convened in Palestine, beginning with the Palin and Haycraft Commissions of the early 1920s and continuing through the Shaw, Lofgren, and Peel Commissions of the late 1920s–1930s and culminating in the Anglo-American Committee of Inquiry in 1946 and the United Nations Special Committee on Palestine (UNSCOP) hearings in 1947. Both Arabs and Jews repeatedly invoked transformational legal framing, casting their claims as based on "justice" and "injustice." Both sides jockeyed for position as the true "victims," each seeking remedies for various "injustices" perpetrated against them.

Benford and Snow (2000) commented on the dynamics of competing frames, which played a crucial role in the Arab-Jewish conflict over Mandatory Palestine during the various "trials" before the British Government, the Anglo-American Committee of Inquiry, and the United Nations between 1939 and 1948, and continue to the present day:

> Those who oppose the changes advocated by a movement sometimes publicly challenge the movement's diagnostic and prognostic framings. Attempts "to rebut, undermine, or neutralize a person's or group's myths, versions of reality, or interpretive framework" have been referred to as counterframing. Opponents' counterframes, in turn, often spawn reframing activity by the movement: attempts "to ward off, contain, limit, or reverse potential damage to the movement's previous claims or attributes." Such square-offs between movements and their detractors have been referred to as "framing contests."[47]

Moreover, both Arabs and Jews repeatedly resorted to what Natasha Wheatley (2015) has described as "legal hermeneutics" in the hundreds of petitions they filed with the PMC during the Mandate years. Wheatley identifies several examples of Arab legal hermeneutics in petitions to the PMC:

> The Arab Executive tested different argumentative strategies. It repeatedly emphasized the Arabs' majority status, the contradiction between the Balfour Declaration and the prior McMahon–Hussein correspondence, and its conviction that the Zionist vision of a "Jewish Religio-Political state" was, "since the separation of church and state … incompatible with the standards of modern civilization." A favoured strategy involved recourse to the principles of the "new world order." It drew attention to the covenant's recognition of the "provisional independence" of the former

> Ottoman territories and its commitment to the wishes of the population. The Balfour Declaration, wrote the Palestine Arab Delegation, is "contrary to the spirit of the Mandate system contained in Article 22 of the Covenant which provides for the happiness and well-being of the people of the land and for the recognition of their independence"... Putting together' a world of rights and one of rightlessness, petitions capture the League as a forum for international, non-diplomatic politics in which the acquisition and recognition of rights across colonial distributions of power were routinely probed and challenged. In their litigious interpretations, petitioners combined those two worlds together in the fabric of the law, in the knot of syntax, grammar and sense.[48]

Wheatley also describes how Jewish petitioners used legal hermeneutics in their petitions to the PMC to animate their own legal narrative:

> The fragility and precariousness ascribed to the law indicated the fraught nature of its operation on the ground. While the text became less plausible as law to the disfranchised Palestinian Arabs, devoid of the characteristics that make law useful, Zionist petitioners clung insistently and creatively to this increasingly brittle enunciation of their national rights, even as they, too, hedged their bets in the invocation of alternative sources of right.[49]

After the August 1929 violence in Jerusalem, Hebron, and elsewhere in Palestine, the parties ramped up their use of legal framing and narrative in their petitions to the PMC. Wheatley notes how the Arabs employed legal rhetoric to support their claims of exclusive ownership and control of the Western (Wailing) Wall and the pavement in front of the Wall. The Arabs also increasingly used legal narrative to argue the international community lacked jurisdiction over those sites.[50] As Wheatley notes, the Palestinian Arabs were "'playing law,' playing mandate, pushing their claims through the funnel of the text to render them admissible to the international community: partaking, that is, in an international legalism whose legality they did not accept."[51]

It is, of course, one of the great historical ironies of the conflict that whereas the Palestinian Arabs repeatedly objected to international jurisdiction over key aspects the conflict during the 1920s and 1930s, today they *insist* that the International Court of Justice and the International Criminal Court are fully vested with such jurisdiction.[52]

The Jewish side, on the other hand, argued repeatedly during the Mandate years that the League of Nations and the international community indeed were vested with jurisdiction to establish and uphold Jewish rights in Palestine, even if, as Wheatley explains, the plain language of international law might not have addressed the issue directly:

> Where before it was only necessary to refer to the provisions of the mandate to establish the right of the Jews to a national home in Palestine, after 1929 the historical connection of the Jews with Palestine was often invoked as the foundation of that right – a right that had subsequently been recognized in the mandate. Rather than being the wellspring of entitlement, the mandate gave voice to a pre-existing right – a right thus capable of surviving whatever might befall the mandate's reign. Emblematically, in a memorandum submitted to the PMC in 1930, Vaad Leumi asserted that "the Mandate was intended to give practical effect to that historical connection"; through the mandate, the Jews' "historical and cultural associations with Palestine have been acknowledged by all principal nations." Here the mandate gave effect to, acknowledged or recognized rights, but it did not create them. Authorities coexisted in complex interactions. History provided certainty when the texts of international law failed to do so.[53]

Orzeck (2015) takes a different approach, focusing on critical discourse theory to analyse legal hermeneutics during the late Mandate period. In her study of the 1947 UNSCOP, Orzeck noted:

> My method, in analyzing these texts [Jewish presentations to UNSCOP], is informed by rhetoric studies as a field and Critical Discourse Analysis as a cross-disciplinary research method. In particular, I heed the calls made by scholars associated with this field and method that those analyzing texts be attuned to, among other things, the roles played by context and medium in shaping the discourses therein.[54]

## *Transformational legal framing in the Israel-Palestine conflict today*

The Palestinian Arabs and their supporters have continued using transformational legal framing to support their victimisation, justice, and injustice narratives since the birth of the State of Israel in 1948, and especially after June 1967, when Israel replaced Jordan as the occupying power in the West Bank. A large number of Palestinian and pro-Palestinian lawyers and legal scholars have all joined the fray, using transformational legal framing to convert the conflict from the realm of politics to one grounded in justice, injustice, and victimhood.[55]

The Egyptian diplomat and lawyer Nabil Elaraby, for example, wrote more than five decades ago that "[i]f peace is to be honestly strived for in the Middle East, the key measure undoubtedly lies in applying the rule of law and justice."[56]

The late Palestinian literary scholar Edward Said (1979a,b; 2006) gained worldwide fame as an early practitioner of transformational legal framing of the Israeli-Palestinian conflict. Said repeatedly employed transformational legal framing to describe the modern Israeli-Palestinian conflict as one involving justice, injustice, victimisation, and the suppression of Palestinian rights.[57] Said frequently invoked narratives of justice, injustice, and victimhood in his writings and speeches. "For Palestinians," he once wrote, "*a vast collective feeling of injustice* continues to hang over our lives with undiminished weight … I do not think that anyone can honestly disagree that *since 1948 the Palestinians have been the victims*, Israelis the victors."[58]

The Palestinians today have continued employing transformational legal framing in the conflict with the Israelis. Almost on a daily basis, the Palestinians demand "justice" and characterise themselves as "victims" of "injustice" at the hands of Israeli perpetrators and Israeli government policy.[59]

The Palestinians have also very effectively framed themselves as part of the same, decades-long global "justice" movement that once included the struggle against South African apartheid and more recently the Black Lives Matter movement. The Palestinians have taken the conflict to the very sympathetic International Court of Justice[60] and the International Criminal Court[61] during the past 20 years, and the results have proven strikingly successful thus far.

Atalia Omer (2009) explains the importance of the Palestinian effort to transformationally frame the local conflict with Israel as part of the larger, global conflict between justice and injustice:

> Sociologist Sidney Tarrow (2005), who worked extensively on the question of transnational activism, argues that "global framing" or linking local concerns such as Palestinian displacement with global topics of some vogue such as "indigenous rights" and "neoliberal imperialism" – as has been the tactic of Palestine solidarity groups – has constituted an effective and common "framing" strategy for generating a social solidarity and global protest movement in support of a local conflict … The rhetorical maneuvering or what Tarrow calls "global framing" that uses words/concepts such as "imperialism", "colonialism", and "indigenous people" contributes to analysing oppressive Israeli policies as symptomatic or endemic of broader systemic dominating structures. As highlighted, this idea that Israel and Zionism are intricately connected with broader systems of injustice is a common theme in the global Palestine solidarity movement.[62]

One manifestation of Palestinian transformational legal framing on a global level has involved the Boycott, Divestment and Sanctions (BDS) movement against Israel. The BDS website characterises its effort to isolate Israel economically, culturally, and politically through a massive boycott campaign as a "legal" response to Israeli "illegality" in the Occupied Territories.

Baumgart-Orsche (2017) notes how the BDS campaign has wrapped itself in the "global justice" movement:

> In 2005, Palestinian activists called on civil society organizations and "people of conscience" worldwide to impose boycotts, implement divestment initiatives and urge their respective states to impose embargoes and sanctions against Israel until it recognizes the Palestinian right to self-determination.

> This call for Boycott, Divestment, Sanctions (BDS) can be seen as a continuation of earlier attempts at pressuring Israel to change its policies toward the Palestinians. However, the BDS campaign at the same time represents a new approach. Instead of urging states to take action, it moves the Palestinian issue from the level of international politics to the transnational level of non-state actors. In order to mobilize civil society and business actors, the campaign has been deliberately framed by its Palestinian initiators as being a part of the Global Justice Movement (GJM). It employs the globally shared language of justice and human rights, thus appealing to allegedly universal, uncontested norms … By embedding itself within the GJM, the BDS campaign borrows these prognostic and motivational frames which are familiar to civil society activists across the world …[63]

McMahon (2014), a staunch BDS advocate, has nevertheless warned against the risks inherent in transformational legal framing. Such framing, according to McMahon, invokes the same legal structures and systems that gave rise to the very injustices the BDS campaign seeks to remedy. Thus, the BDS campaign's "juridical nature … makes recourse to the same international law that legitimised the existence of the state of Israel." McMahon, therefore, sounds a note of caution about over-reliance on legal framing:

> Understood critically, law is an instrument of the dominant. It does not change power relations. It perpetuates them. Moreover, law does not create equality. Its existence is evidence of ongoing inequality. In making recourse to juridical notions, the BDS campaign, in an attempt to realise Palestinian rights, invokes the very mechanisms those antagonistic to the realisation of Palestinian rights control. Trying to use the master's tools to change the master's order runs the real risk of perpetuating that order.[64]

Omer (2009), however, raises a different concern, focusing on whether the Palestinians stand to gain any long-term benefit from their use of transformational legal framing:

> [T]he Palestine solidarity movement that has emerged in Western cities and transformed into a global civil resistance to Israeli occupation exhibits a similar proclivity for abstraction and sweeping generalization … [T]his idea that Israel and Zionism are intricately connected with broader systems of injustice is a common theme in the global Palestine solidarity movement … The [Palestine Solidarity Movement's] exclusive focus on Palestinian history and narratives of injustice and its concomitant abstraction and caricaturing of Zionism ultimately works against the interest of conflict transformation and healing. Only recognition of the interrelatedness and interlocking of Palestinian and Israeli histories would enable a substantive transformation of the underlying paradigms.[65]

Noura Erakat (2019), the most recent exponent of transformational legal framing from the Palestinian Arab perspective, nevertheless has re-emphasised the conflict as a battle between legality and illegality. Erakat argues "[t]he very origins of the Palestinian-Israel conflict suggest that it is characterized by outright lawlessness."[66] Erakat, therefore, continues the century-long Palestinian narrative, transformationally framing the *political* conflict between Israelis and Palestinians as a *legal* conflict between lawless wrongdoers and innocent victims.

The United Nations Security Council provided significant support for this viewpoint when it adopted Resolution 2334 on 23 December 2016 (with the outgoing Obama Administration choosing to abstain rather than veto). The Resolution embraced the Palestinian transformational legal frame, condemning Israeli settlement activity in the West Bank and East Jerusalem as "a flagrant violation under international law."[67]

In recent years, the Palestinians have expanded their use of transformational legal framing, taking full advantage of both traditional and social media. For example, they and their supporters characterise the Gaza Strip, from which Israel withdrew *completely* in 2005, as "the world's largest open-air prison."[68] But Gaza hardly resembles a penal institution. The terrorist organisation Hamas seized power in a bloody 2007 armed coup against the Palestinian Authority and has ruled Gaza ever since. Hamas conducted joint military exercises with Gaza's other terrorist groups in December 2020, showing off massive amounts of weapons and military equipment.[69]

Hamas and other terrorist groups have launched rockets from Gaza toward Israel on multiple occasions since Israel's 2005 withdrawal, most recently launching more than four *thousand* rockets at Israel in May 2021. Hamas also fired Iranian-supplied anti-tank missiles and deployed Iranian-made aerial drones and underwater drones in the May 2021 conflict. If Gaza is a "prison," it is unique in the annals of criminal justice.

Palestinian frame entrepreneurs invoked transformational legal framing during and following the May 2021 Gaza conflict. For example, at a rally in Paris two days following the 21 May 2021 ceasefire, the president of the France Palestine Solidarity Association exclaimed, "this fight concerns all those who are attached to the values of justice, dignity and law."[70]

Palestinian frame entrepreneurs have also leveraged the Covid-19 pandemic to characterise alleged Israeli actions as "war crimes," including absurd and unsubstantiated accusations that Israel deliberately infected Palestinians with the virus and then denied the Palestinian Authority access to vaccines."[71]

The following chapters will examine Palestinian Arab, Jewish, and British transformational legal framing during the last four "trials" of the Mandate years: the London Conferences (1939), the Anglo-American Committee of Inquiry (1946), and the United Nations Special and Ad Hoc Committees on Palestine (1947). The final chapter will consider the irony that despite the concerted efforts of the Palestinian Arabs to employ transformational legal framing in the conflict, their *legal* claim to sovereignty over the West Bank, Jerusalem, and Gaza (in contrast to their political claim) rests on very thin ice.

## Notes

1 E. Goffman, *Frame Analysis: An Essay on the Organization of Experience* (Harper Colophon, 1974).
2 *See, e.g.*, I. Pappe, *The Framing of the Question of Palestine by the Early Palestinian Press: Zionist Settler-Colonialism and the Newspaper Filastin, 1912–1922*, Journal of Holy Land and Palestine Studies 14:1 at 59–81 (2015).
3 I. De Bruycker, *Framing and Advocacy: A Research Agenda for Interest Group Studies*, Journal of European Public Policy 24 at 776 (2017) (citations omitted). Benford and Snow have also noted how frame studies became popular in a variety of disciplines, including psychology, linguistics and discourse analysis, communication and media studies, political science and policy studies, and sociology. R. Benford and D. Snow, *Framing Processes and Social Movements: An Overview and Assessment,* Annual Review of Sociology at 611 (2000).
4 G. Leachman, *Legal Framing*, Studies in Law, Politics and Society 61 at 42 (2013).
5 P. Muller and P. Slominski, *Legal Framing and the EU's External Relations: How NGOs Shaped the Negotiations for an Israel-Europol Cooperation Agreement*, Journal of European Public Policy 26:6 at 908 (2019); *see also* E. McKee, *Environmental Framing and its Limits: Campaigns in Palestine and Israel*, International Journal of Middle East Studies 50 at 451 (2018) ("The work of framing gives meaning to advocacy and activism, and activists often strive to bend and stretch existing communicative frames to expand the reach of their messages. Sociopolitical context shapes and limits framing in all cases of activism").
6 I. De Bruycker, *op. cit.*, at 777–9.
7 W. Gamson, *Talking Politics* (Cambridge Univ. Press, 1992); *see also* K. Gillan, *Understanding Meaning in Movements: A Hermeneutic Approach to Frames and Ideologies*, Social Movement Studies 7:3 at 249 (2008).
8 W. Carroll and R. Ratner, *Master Frames and Counter-Hegemony: Political Sensibilities in Contemporary Social Movements*, Canadian Review of Sociology and Anthropology 33:4 at 411 (1996).
9 K. Gillan, *op. cit.*, *passim*.
10 R.M. Entman, *Framing: Toward Clarification of a Fractured Paradigm*, Journal of Communication 43:4 at 51–8 (1993).
11 De Bruycker, *op. cit.*, at 779–80 (citations omitted).
12 W.M. Junk and A. Rasmussen, *Framing by the Flock: Collective Issue Definition and Advocacy Success*, Comparative Political Studies 52:4 at 486 (2019).
13 J. Derrida, *Acts of Literature* at 191 (Routledge, 1992) (emphasis in original). Derrida later would refer to the interplay between law, religion, and politics in the Arab-Israeli conflict. J. Derrida, *Specters of Marx: The State of the Debt, The Work of Mourning and the New International* at 72–3 (Routledge, 1994).
14 R. Cover, *Nomos And Narrative*, Harvard Law Review 97:4 at 4, 5, 10 (1983).
15 *Id.* at 40.
16 A.M. Marshall, *Injustice Frames, Legality, and the Everyday Construction of Sexual Harassment*, Law & Social Inquiry 28:3 at 661–2 (2003) (citations omitted).
17 G. Leachman, *op. cit.*, at 29 (emphasis in original).
18 P. Muller and P. Slominski, *op. cit.*, at 910.
19 *Id.* at 909 (emphasis in original).
20 *Id.*
21 *Id.* at 911–3.
22 *Id.* at 907 (2019).
23 *Id.*

24 H. Anheier et al., *Movement Cycles and the Nazi Party: Activities of the Munich NSDAP, 1925*–1930, American Behavioral Scientist 41:9 at 1264 (1998).
25 R. Benford and D. Snow, *op. cit.*, at 615 (citations omitted).
26 S. Capek, *The "Environmental Justice" Frame: A Conceptual Discussion and an Application*, Social Problems 40:1 at 8 (1993) (citation omitted); *see also* D. Schlosberg, *Theorising Environmental Justice: The Expanding Sphere of a Discourse*, Environmental Politics 22:1 at 37–55 (2013); W. Carroll and R.S. Ratner, *op. cit., passim* (discussing injustice framing invoked by various social movements in Vancouver, Canada).
27 W. Carroll and R. Ratner, *op. cit.*, at 415–7 (1996).
28 C. Baumgart-Ochse, *Claiming Justice for Israel/Palestine: The Boycott, Divestment, Sanctions (BDS) Campaign and Christian Organizations*, Globalizations 14:7 at 1174 (2017) (citation omitted).
29 Transformational frame entrepreneurs have succeeded in more recent decades in recharacterising the anti-pollution movement of the 1970s as the "environmental justice" movement of the 2000s; or the civil rights movement of the 1960s as the "racial justice" movement of the 2000s, expanding further as the catch-all "social justice" and "global social justice" movements of the modern era. *See also* W. Gamson et al., *Encounters with Unjust Authority* at 123–24 (Dorsey Press, 1982).
30 N. Pedriana, *From Protective to Equal Treatment: Legal Framing Processes and Transformation of the Women's Movement in the 1960s*, The American Journal of Sociology 111:6 at 1724 (2006) (citation omitted).
31 *Id.* at 1729.
32 R. Agne, *Reframing Practices in Moral Conflict: Interaction Problems in the Negotiation Standoff at Waco*, Discourse and Society 18:5 at 552 (2007).
33 M.L. Burgis-Kasthala, *Overstating Palestine's UN Membership Bid? An Ethnographic Study on the Narratives of Statehood*, European Journal of International Law 25:3 at 690, 700 (2014); *see also* N. Khader, *Interview with Noura Erakat: Framing the Palestinian Narrative*, Journal of Palestine Studies 44:1 at 106–17 (2014).
34 W. Gamson, *op. cit.*, at 54.
35 J. Strawson, *Partitioning Palestine: Legal Fundamentalism in the Palestinian-Israeli Conflict* at 1 (Pluto Press, 2010).
36 J. Strawson, *op. cit.*, at 53–4. Strawson further describes how the Colonial Office itself framed the Palestinian Arabs' political objections to the Balfour Declaration as inferior to the Declaration's status as an internationally recognized, legally binding commitment on the British Government. *Id.* at 55.
37 Describing Zionism as a form of "settler colonialism" conveniently ignores crucial historical facts, including (i) the continuous presence of Jews in Palestine (especially Jerusalem, Tiberias, Tzfat, and Hebron) for centuries *before and after* the Muslim conquest of 638 A.D.; (ii) the Ottoman Empire's acceptance of Jewish immigration from Europe in the late 19th and early 20th centuries; and (iii) Jewish land acquisition in Ottoman and British Palestine occurred through lawful, arms-length purchases from willing *Arab* sellers at mostly above-market prices.
38 *See, e.g.*, W. Boustany, *The Palestine Mandate, Invalid and Impracticable: A Contribution of Arguments and Documents Towards the Solution of the Palestine Problem* (American Press, 1936).
39 *See, e.g.*, E. Alimi, *Israeli Politics and the First Palestinian Intifada: Political Opportunities, Framing Processes and Contentious Politics* (Routledge, 2007).
40 *See generally* L. Epstein, *The Dream of Zion: The Story of the First Zionist Congress* (Rowman & Littlefield, 2016); C. Klein, *Zionism Revisited*, Israel Affairs 11:1 at 240 (2005) ("It should be recalled that Herzl had obtained a law degree (from the University of Vienna). He actually signed the *Judensstaat* as Theodor Herzl, Doctor of Law. The distinction between public law and private law is one of the basics of all European legal systems. This concept was used instead of the proposed concept of (public) international law which might have antagonized the Sultan"); "Zionist Congress In Basel," *New York Times*,

31 August 1897 at 7 (quoting Theodore Herzl saying, "My plan is simple enough. *We must obtain sovereignty over the whole of Palestine – our never-to-be-forgotten, historical home*") (emphasis added). The *New York Times* seems to have forgotten Herzl's 1897 statement, as it recently published an op-ed making the blatantly false claim that Jewish statehood was *never* central to Zionist thought until after the Holocaust. *See* P. Bienert, "I No Longer Believe in a Jewish State," *New York Times*, 8 July 2020 ("[B]efore the Holocaust, many leading Zionists did not believe [in Jewish statehood]. 'The aspiration for a nation-state was not central in the Zionist movement before the 1940s' … A Jewish state has become the dominant form of Zionism. But it is not the essence of Zionism").

41 J. Strawson, *op. cit.*, at 15.

42 *Id.* at 67.

43 J. Stoyanovksy, *The Mandate For Palestine: A Contribution To The Theory And Practice Of International Mandates* at 55 (Longmans Green, 1928).

44 *Id.* at 66.

45 *See* Ch. 8, *infra*.

46 For an interesting discussion of British framing of the Palestine issue for the past century, *see* R. Hollis, *Palestine and the Palestinians in British Political Elite Discourse: From 'The Palestine Problem' to 'The Two-State Solution'*, International Relations 30:1 at 3–28 (2016).

47 R. Benford and D. Snow, *op. cit.*, at 626 (citations omitted).

48 N. Wheatley, *Mandatory Interpretation: Legal Hermeneutics and the New International Order in Arab and Jewish Petitions to the League of Nations*, Past and Present 227:1 at 219–20, 248 (2015). For a discussion of Sinn Fein's master framing strategy with the League of Nations, *see* W. J. Swart, *The League of Nations and the Irish Question: Master Frames, Cycles of Protest, and "Master Frame Alignment"*, The Sociological Quarterly 36:3 at 465–81 (1995).

49 N. Wheatley, *op. cit.*, at 247.

50 *Id.* at 228–9 ("These overarching historical narratives were brought into direct conversation with the text of the mandate, forming an intricate patchwork of claims. In 1930 the British appointed a special commission to disentangle Muslim and Jewish rights to the wall. A June 1931 response from the (Nashashibi-led) Palestine Arab Liberal Party involved the mandate in a complex of rival jurisdictions. Reminding the British that they derived all their authority in Palestine from the mandate, the party asserted that article 14, which provided for the investigation of rights to Palestine's holy places, could not sanction the commission, as this issue must fall under article 13, which prevented any interference with 'purely Moslem sacred shrines.' Turning the mandate back on the British, the Liberal Party declared the 'illegality of the appointment of the Commission.' But the mandate was not the only law invoked. The commission was also illegal because the whole Muslim world inherently possessed rights to this sacred site, and the commission had failed adequately to hear the case of the 'Defenders of the Islamic Faith' — the 'Moslem Kings and Princes.' Even referring to the site as a 'waqf property' flew in the face of a higher authority: 'The doctrines of the sacred Volume of the Kuran exclude such places from being subject to any positive law and indeed express provisions in the Kuran vest ownership of all Holy Places of Worship in the MOST HIGH'. The British had stepped on God's toes. It was 'impossible for any secular authority to repeal the doctrines of the Sacred Volume of the Kuran'. A legalistic rendering of the mandate thus intermingled with alternative claims that transcended temporal norms entirely").

51 *Id.* at 236.

52 *See* Ch. 16, *infra*.

53 N. Wheatley, *op. cit.*, at 229–30.

54 R. Orzeck, *The Jewish Agency's Case Before the UNSCOP: Image and Discourse*, Jerusalem Quarterly 63/64 at 8 (2015).

55 *See, e.g.*, S. Akram, "Myths and Realities of the Palestinian Refugee Problem: Reframing the Right of Return," in S. Akram et al., *International Law and the Israeli-Palestinian Conflict: A Rights-Based Approach to Middle East Peace* at 13–44 (Routledge, 2011).

56 N. Elaraby, *Some Legal Implications of the 1947 Partition Resolution and the 1949 Armistice Agreements*, Law and Contemporary Problems 33:1 at 109 (1968).

57 E. Said, *The Question of Palestine* (Random House, 1979). Said's position as a Columbia University professor, and his popularity in New York City intellectual and social circles made him a media darling, and he quickly became the leading frame entrepreneur for Palestinian nationalism (and apologist/defender of Palestinian terrorism) in the United States and Western Europe.

58 E. Said, "A Method for Thinking About Just Peace," in P. Allena and A. Keller, *What is a Just Peace?* at 182, 187 (Oxford Univ. Press, 2006) (emphasis added).

59 Even some Jewish organizations have employed transformational legal framing on behalf of the Palestinians. J Street, for example, has emerged as a leading pro-Palestinian frame entrepreneur. *See, e.g.*, J Street Press Release, "J Street Deeply Concerned by Ongoing Evictions of Palestinian Families in Occupied East Jerusalem" (discussing Sheikh Jarrah and Silwan residential housing disputes and proclaiming, "[i]t's therefore critical that the Biden administration urgently warn the Israeli government that these provocative and *unjust evictions are illegal under international law*") (emphasis added), https://jstreet.org/press-releases/j-street-deeply-concerned-by-ongoing-evictions-of-palestinian-families-in-occupied-east-jerusalem/#.YJrRyLVKhyw (last visited 11 May 2021).

60 International Court of Justice, *Legal Consequences of the Construction of a Wall in the Occupied Palestinian Territory* (Advisory Ruling), General List No. 131 (9 July 2004).

61 The Palestinians successfully persuaded the International Criminal Court to issue a highly controversial, split decision in early February 2021, ruling Palestine is a "state" for purposes of the Court's enabling instrument (the Rome Statute). The controversial and bizarre ruling has paved the way for the Court to hear cases brought against Israel for alleged war crimes in the West Bank, Gaza, and East Jerusalem. International Criminal Court, No. ICC-01/18, *Situation in The State of Palestine* (5 February 2021). The Court's website provides the relevant background: "On 1 January 2015, the Government of Palestine lodged a declaration under article 12(3) of the Rome Statute accepting the jurisdiction of the International Criminal Court (ICC) over alleged crimes committed 'in the occupied Palestinian territory, including East Jerusalem, since June 13, 2014.' On 2 January 2015, the Government of Palestine acceded to the Rome Statute by depositing its instrument of accession with the UN Secretary-General. The Rome Statute entered into force on 1 April 2015. Upon receipt of a referral or a valid declaration made pursuant to article 12(3) of the Rome Statute, the Prosecutor, in accordance with Regulation 25(1)(c) of the Regulations of the Office of the Prosecutor, and as a matter of policy and practice, opens a preliminary examination of the situation at hand. Accordingly, on 16 January 2015, the Prosecutor announced the opening of a preliminary examination into the situation in Palestine in order to establish whether the Rome Statute criteria for opening an investigation are met. Specifically, under article 53(1) of the Rome Statute, the Prosecutor shall consider issues of jurisdiction, admissibility and the interests of justice in making this determination. On 20 December 2019, the Prosecutor announced that following a thorough, independent and objective assessment of all reliable information available to her Office, the preliminary examination into the Situation in Palestine has concluded with the determination that all the statutory criteria under the Rome Statute for the opening of an investigation have been met. However, given the legal and factual issues attaching to this situation, pursuant to article 19.3 of the Rome Statute, the Prosecutor requested from Pre-Trial Chamber I a jurisdictional ruling on the scope of the territorial jurisdiction of the International Criminal Court under article 12(2)(a) of the Rome Statute in Palestine. On 28 January 2020, ICC Pre-Trial Chamber I issued an order setting the procedure and the schedule for the submission of observations on the Prosecutor's request under article 19(3) of the Rome Statute related to the scope of the Court's territorial jurisdiction in the Situation in the State of Palestine. Pre-Trial Chamber I is expected to make a decision on this matter in due course." International Criminal Court website, https://www.icc-cpi.int/palestine (last visited 30 December 2020).

62 A. Omer, *'It's Nothing Personal:' The Globalisation of Justice, the Transferability of Protest, and the Case of the Palestine Solidarity Movement*, Studies in Ethnicity and Nationalism, 9:3 at 499, 506 (2009).

63 C. Baumgart-Orsche, *op. cit.*, at 1173, 1174–5; *see generally* E. Rettig and E. Avraham, *The Role of Intergovernmental Organizations in the "Battle over Framing:" The Case of the Israeli–West Bank Separation Barrier*, International Journal of Press/Politics 21:1 at 111–33 (2016); N.A. Hatoum, *Framing Visual Politics: Photography of the Wall in Palestine*, Visual Anthropology Review, 33:1 at 18–27 (2017); *see also* A. Bakan, Y. Abu-Laban, *Palestinian Resistance and International Solidarity: The BDS Campaign*, Race & Class, 51:1 at 29–54 (2009). Blizzard (2017) has described how BDS frame entrepreneurs have counter-framed the Israeli response to the BDS movement: "Through framing Israel as the 'victim' of 'Muslim backwardness' and appealing to the nefarious modern drift toward Islamophobia, pro-Zionists attempt to undermine BDS and sponsor a moral assessment that BDS is illegitimate, unethical, and dangerous. By reinforcing artificial 'faux-conflict framing,' pro-Zionist media blur the 'occupier/apartheid/colonial/settler state versus nonviolent human rights movement' factual character." E. Blizzard, *Peace Journalism in Palestine's BDS Campaign*, Peace Review: A Journal of Social Justice, 29:4 at 469 (2017); *see also* O. Barghouti, *Opting for Justice: The Critical Role of Anti-Colonial Israelis in the Boycott, Divestment, And Sanctions Movement*, Settler Colonial Studies, 4:4 at 407–12 (2014); J. Peteet, *Language Matters: Talking About Palestine*, Journal of Palestine Studies 45:2 at 25 (2016) ("Discussion of Israel-Palestine is bounded by a set of terms, phrases, and lexicons as well as strategies for argument and debate, that is, talking points readily discerned by their consistent mantra-like repetition. While these repertoires and categories shape understandings, they simultaneously work to marginalize and render a Palestinian narrative 'unthinkable.' These bundled linguistic repertoires and categories are deeply entangled with power and until recently unquestionably accompanied the colonial endeavor in Palestine").

64 S. McMahon, *The Boycott, Divestment, Sanctions Campaign: Contradictions and Challenges*, Race & Class, 55:4 at 66, 72–3 (2014).

65 A. Omer, *op. cit.*, at 513–4 ("Indeed, this theme defines the distinctive discourse of a Palestine solidarity movement and clarifies its location in a so-called global civil society that recognises what critical theorist Nancy Fraser (2009) views as the heterogeneity of justice discourses, an inevitable upshot of the erosion of the Westphalian and bounded scale of justice. In her recent book Scales of Justice: Reimagining Political Space in a Globalizing World, Fraser writes to this effect: 'No wonder ... that activists contesting transnational inequities reject the view that justice can only be imagined territorially, as a domestic relation among fellow citizens. Positing post-Westphalian views of 'who counts,' they are subjecting the Westphalian frame to explicit critique.' Transnational social activism and its familiar strategy of global framing then point to the changing topographies of justice discourses and increased recognition on a post-Westphalian reframing. Fraser subsequently attempts to develop a post-Westphalian framework for debating questions of justice by underscoring the possibility and necessity of reimagining political space and thus re-conceiving the scope of justice as a three dimensional discourse, addressing political, cultural, and economic levels of injustice. Here she cites human rights activists and international feminists among other examples whose focus on trans-border questions of justice challenge the interpretation of justice as a domestic relation among fellow citizens within bounded territorial parameters"); *see also* B. Voltolini, *Non-State Actors and Framing Processes in EU Foreign Policy: The Case of EU–Israel Relations, Journal of European Public Policy*, 23:10 at 1502–19 (2016).

66 N. Erakat, *Justice For Some: Law and the Question of Palestine* at 3 (Stanford Univ. Press, 2019).

67 United Nations Security Council, Resolution 2334, S/Res/2334 (23 Dec. 2016).

68 *See, e.g.*, Norwegian Refugee Council, "Gaza: The World's Largest Open-Air Prison" (26 April 2018), https://www.nrc.no/news/2018/april/gaza-the-worlds-largest-open-air-prison/ (last visited 12 May 2021).

69 "Palestinian Groups Conduct First-Ever Joint Military Drill," *Al Monitor*, 29 December 2020, https://www.al-monitor.com/originals/2020/12/palestinian-factions-groups-joint-military-drill-gaza-israel.html (last visited 12 May 2021).

70 *Times of Israel*, 23 May 2021, https://www.timesofisrael.com/israeli-flag-dragged-through-london-street-as-thousands-rally-in-european-cities/?utm_source=The+Daily+Edition&utm_campaign=daily-edition-2021-05-23&utm_medium=email (last accessed 23 May 2021) (quoting Bertrand Helibron).

71 The Israeli NGO Palestinian Media Watch (PMW) has compiled a broad range of articles from official and unofficial Palestinian Arab media making wild and unsubstantiated claims of Israeli Covid-19 "war crimes" against Palestinians. *See* PMW website, https://palwatch.org/analysis/1666 (last accessed 28 February 2021).

PART II

# The London Conferences – Zionism on trial and the one-state solution

# 2

# PRELUDE TO THE LONDON CONFERENCES

## Background

By late 1938, the situation in Palestine had reached an inflection point for the three key players – Arab, Jewish, and British. All three parties, long-accustomed to availing themselves of the law in their constant struggle for leverage against each other and to influence international opinion, stood ready once again to bring the full weight of their legal framing and narrative to bear as 1939 dawned.

Throughout the 1920s and 1930s, the British Government used the law and the legal process, including Commissions of Inquiry and courtroom-style trials to adjudicate Arab-Jewish disputes, including the Palin, Haycraft, Shaw, Lofgren, and Peel Commissions. These Commissions, run largely by judges and lawyers, allowed outside lawyers to make opening statements and closing arguments, take direct testimony from and cross-examine witnesses under oath, and introduce thousands of pages of documentary evidence into the record. The Commissions each rendered verdicts, assigning blame after violent outbreaks and recommending changes in British policy toward Palestine, mostly to appease Arab sentiment.[1]

By late 1938, the British Government, growing impatient with the constant strife in Palestine after more than two decades as the country's caretaker, and wary of the possibility of losing Arab support to the Nazis, decided the time had come to reassess its policy regarding the Jewish National Home in Palestine. This time, however, the Government decided not to form a judicial-type body to conduct a "trial." Instead, the British Government itself would act as judge and jury, making factual assessments, inviting legal and policy arguments from the parties, and ultimately rendering a verdict on Zionism, Jewish

DOI: 10.4324/9781003225263-5

immigration, and a political solution for Palestine that would stand as a final expression of British hostility toward Zionism and sympathy with Palestinian Arab nationalism.

## *The Palestinian Arabs in late 1938*

The Arab position in Palestine had deteriorated significantly during the 1930s. British support for Jewish immigration and land acquisition, both of which had increased dramatically between 1922 and 1937, posed an intolerable threat to Arab nationalist aspirations in Palestine.

Making matters worse from the Palestinian Arab perspective, the Palestine Royal Commission (or Peel Commission) in July 1937 had recommended a two-state solution, partitioning Palestine into separate Jewish and Arab states.[2] Map 2.1 shows the Royal Commission's proposed boundaries for the separate Arab and Jewish states:

The Palestinian Arabs viewed the partition plan as a breach of Britain's legally binding promise in the McMahon-Hussein correspondence to guarantee future Arab independence in *all* former Turkish-ruled Arab lands, including Palestine, in exchange for the Arabs siding with Britain against Turkey during World War I. The Arabs also bitterly opposed the Peel Commission's recommendation that the portion of Palestine set aside for the Arabs be merged into Transjordan rather than receive independent statehood.

The Arabs, deeply angry and frustrated at Britain's seeming refusal to stem the influx of Jews into Palestine, commenced a bloody three-year revolt in 1936, costing hundreds of Arab, Jewish, and British lives.[3]

In early 1938, a pan-Arab and pan-Muslim Congress convened in Cairo to discuss the Palestine issue. Jamal Husseini, the Mufti's cousin, and the famed Palestinian Arab lawyer Auni Bey Abdul-Hadi represented the Palestinian Arabs. The Congress published a document and various resolutions broadly invoking the Palestinian Arab transformational legal framing.[4] For example, the document attacked the Balfour Declaration as "null and void *ab initio*," noting the Arabs "do not recognize the legality of the Balfour Declaration, even if it aimed only at the establishment of a Spiritual Home for the Jews."[5]

The document also criticised the Peel Commission's proposed two-state solution:

> Partition would create in Palestine two neighboring hostile states between which it is impossible to imagine the possibility of an exchange of inhabitants, property and holy places, such as mosques, churches and cemeteries. Furthermore, partition would deprive the Arabs of their land, which constitutes the bulk of their wealth in the territory proposed to be ceded to the Jewish State.[6]

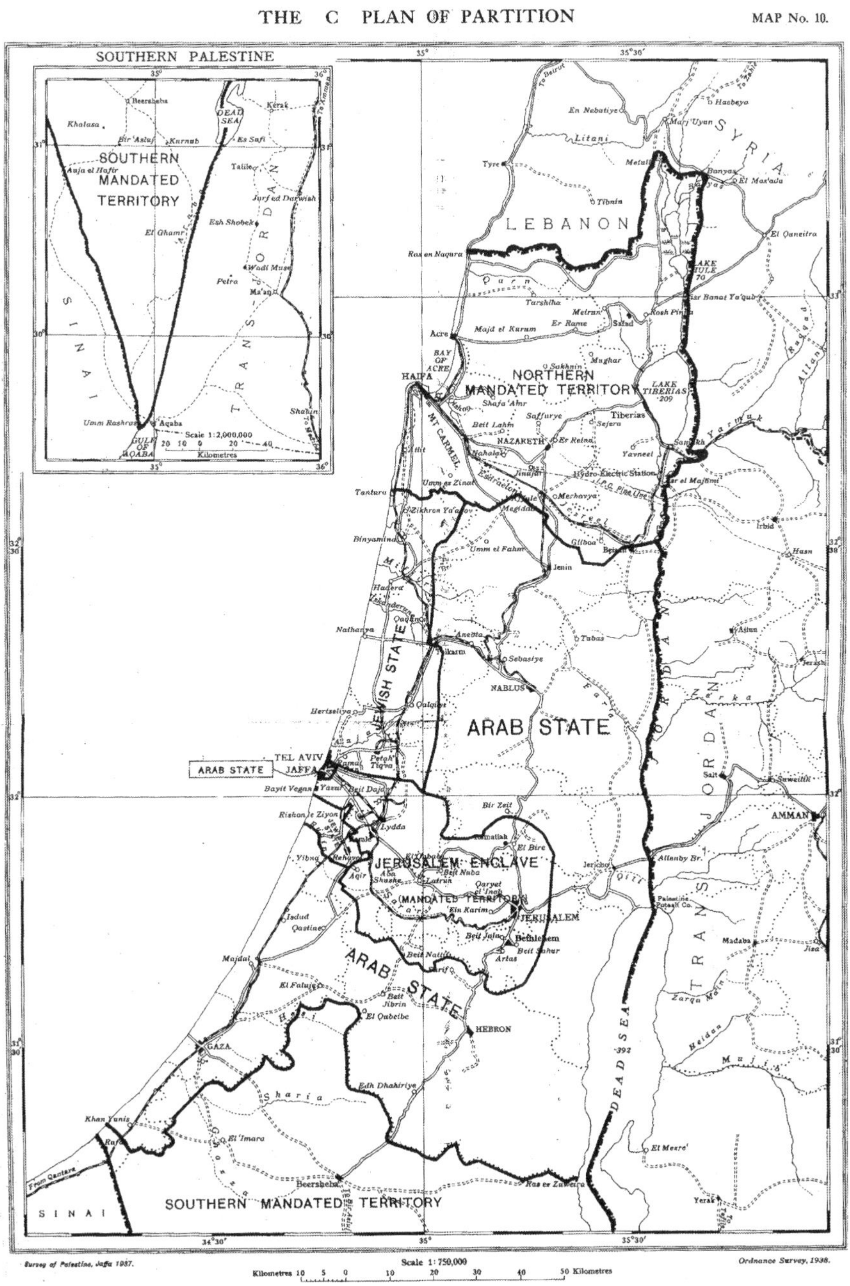


MAP 2.1 The Palestine Royal Commission Partition Plan, July 1937

### *The European Jews and Palestinian Jews in late 1938*

The Jewish position likewise had deteriorated significantly in both Palestine and Europe during 1938.

In Europe, the 30 September 1938 Munich Agreement between German Chancellor Adolph Hitler and British Prime Minister Neville Chamberlain paved the way for Hitler's conquest of Czechoslovakia six months later. Hitler dramatically ramped up the persecution of Germany's Jewish population with the *Kristallnacht* pogrom of 9–10 November 1938, less than six weeks after he and Chamberlain had signed the Munich Agreement.

As 1939 began, the outlook for European Jews had never been worse. The Jewish Agency desperately urged the British Government to allow more European Jews to immigrate to Palestine. The Arab Higher Committee, representing the one million Palestinian Arabs (who at that time outnumbered the Jews in Palestine by more than two to one), adamantly opposed any further Jewish immigration.

In Palestine, although the Jewish population had risen dramatically during the first two decades of British rule, Jews still comprised only one-third of Palestine's overall population. Moreover, with the Arab revolt still raging, the British Government in July 1937 amended the Palestine Immigration Ordinance, dispensing with the long-standing policy that Jewish immigration to Palestine be limited *solely* by the economic absorptive capacity of the country. Instead, the British Government imposed an unprecedented and extremely low numerical cap on Jewish immigration of 8,000 (only one thousand per month) for the period between August 1937 and March 1938.[7]

The project of establishing a National Home for the Jewish people in Palestine faced an uncertain future, as the British Government by late 1938 had abandoned the Royal Commission's partition plan. The Woodhead Commission, appointed to conduct a follow-on technical analysis of the Royal Commission's partition proposal, issued a report on 9 November 1938 (ironically, only hours before the *Kristallnacht* pogrom began, shown in Figure 2.1) deeming partition unworkable.[8]

### *Britain in late 1938*

The British, for their part, were growing increasingly weary of the intractable Arab-Jewish conflict in Palestine. British soldiers and police officers had lost their lives during the Arab revolt starting in 1936. Despite multiple commissions of inquiry and expert studies throughout the 1920s and 1930s, Britain struggled to find a formula for reconciling diametrically opposed Jewish and Arab nationalist aspirations with Britain's conflicting legal obligations under the League of Nations Mandate for Palestine.

By late 1938, however, Britain's top priority focused on avoiding or at least delaying the looming confrontation with Nazi Germany. Chamberlain, shown

FIGURE 2.1 *Kristallnacht*, 9–10 November 1938 (Public Domain)

together with Hitler in Figure 2.2, sacrificed the Sudeten Czechs in September 1938 to appease Hitler, and he now stood ready to sacrifice Zionism to appease the Arabs.[9]

Chamberlain and his Foreign Minister, Lord Halifax, wanted the Arab states to side with Britain in the event of war with Germany, much as Britain had lured Sherif Hussein into an alliance two decades earlier against Turkey during World War I. Britain's top priorities in the Middle East were to protect the strategically vital Suez Canal and keep the Arabs in the British fold, lest the Arabs join forces with Germany and jeopardise Britain's crucial land and sea bridges to India and beyond.[10]

Having capped Jewish immigration at only one thousand per month for the eight-month period between August 1937 and March 1938, the British Government began exploring its options once the eight-month period neared expiration. In early February 1938, H.F. Downie of the Colonial Office wrote a long minute laying out various possibilities for Britain's future immigration policy. Downie candidly admitted the Government had "crossed the Rubicon and threw over the principle that economic absorptive capacity should be the *sole* criterion" governing Jewish immigration to Palestine.[11] The Government now faced the decision of whether to continue imposing a numerical cap or restore

**FIGURE 2.2** Chamberlain and Hitler, Munich, 30 September 1938 (Public Domain)

the economic absorptive capacity principle as the sole limitation on Jewish immigration.

After summarising the input received from the High Commissioner in Palestine (Sir Harold MacMichael, who favoured continuing strict limits on Jewish immigration to placate Arab sentiment), Downie recommended the Government either adopt a new policy under which it would be permitted to consider factors in addition to economic absorptive capacity or continue imposing immigration caps in place for an additional 12 months. Downie recommended a cap of 8,500 for the first six of those months, April to October 1938.[12]

Ultimately, the Government extended the restrictions of the amended Palestine Immigration Ordinance for an additional one-year period, from 1 April 1938 through 1 April 1939.[13] The Government capped total additional immigration for the six-month period 1 April 1938–1 October 1938 at 8,300.[14]

In May 1938, Malcolm MacDonald, the son of former Prime Minister Ramsay MacDonald, replaced William Ormsby-Gore as Colonial Secretary. MacDonald undertook a review of British policy in Palestine, including visiting Palestine for two days in early August 1938.

On 31 August, MacDonald wrote to the Cabinet that while he still favoured partition, his view could change depending on the outcome of the Woodhead

Commission's investigation, and whether partition "proves practicable from the point of view of conditions inside Palestine and [Arab] opinion outside the country."[15]

On 13 September 1938, MacDonald met with the Zionist leader Chaim Weizmann. According to Weizmann's notes of the meeting, MacDonald said he did not know what the Woodhead Commission planned to say regarding partition, but in the same breath warned Weizmann the Commission "might propose something which the Jews would find unacceptable."[16] MacDonald (whom Weizmann referred to by the code name "B") added,

> "B" himself still thinks that partition would be the best solution, but recently he had been impressed by several facts, namely: (a) the danger of including a substantial Arab minority in the Jewish State, particularly when that State will be surrounded by powerful Arab neighbors in sympathy with the minority's national aspirations ... (b) the dangerous situation created in the Near East (and even as far East as India) by the support which the Arabs get – both moral and material – from their sympathizers, and from Italy and Germany; (c) lastly, he had been studying the McMahon correspondence, and thought that there might, in fact, be a conflict in policies.[17]

Weizmann and Ben-Gurion had a follow-up meeting with MacDonald on 20 September 1938. Ben-Gurion reported the next morning to the Zionist Executive that MacDonald said "he had been reading the McMahon correspondence again, and it seemed to him the that Arabs of Palestine had after all been treated abominably. The promise made to them had not been kept."[18]

## Invitation to London

Against this backdrop, and in the wake of the Woodhead Commission's November 1938 rejection of the Royal Commission's partition proposal and the Government's agreement that partition was no longer practicable,[19] the British Government decided to make one last attempt to reach a diplomatic solution to the conflict. "[F]aced with a stark choice between continuing to support the Jewish national home ... and somehow surrendering the obligation to Zionism contained in the Mandate,"[20] the Government announced in late 1938 it would invite representatives of the Jews, the Palestinian Arabs, and the neighbouring Arab states to London in early 1939 to discuss the future of Palestine.[21]

The British Government's announcement warned that if the London discussions failed to produce an agreement between the two sides "within a reasonable period of time," the British Government would act unilaterally and "take their own decision in light of their examination of the problem and of the discussions in London, and announce the policy which they would pursue."[22]

Indeed, even before the London meetings convened in early February 1939, the British Government, with the prospect of war looming, decided the time had come to adopt an unambiguously pro-Arab policy in Palestine. At a Cabinet meeting on 21 December 1938, two Ministers advocated their reasons for embracing a strongly pro-Arab approach:

> The Secretary Of State For Air said that it was the view of the Air Staff, if another crisis should find us with a hostile Arab world behind us in the Middle East, that our military position there would be quite untenable and that with the loss of our military position would go the loss of our vital land, air and sea communications with the Far East …
>
> The Secretary Of State For Foreign Affairs said … there was no disagreement on the extreme desirability of our not arousing antagonism with the Arabs, and that the forthcoming negotiations at the London Conference must be so conducted as to ensure the Arab States would be friendly toward us. But until the conference met, we could not say how far we should have to go to meet their needs.[23]

The British Government therefore invited representatives of the Jews, Palestinian Arabs, and surrounding Arab states to travel to London in February 1939. All three parties made extensive use of transformational legal framing and narrative during the conferences. The outcome proved disastrous for Zionist aspirations in Palestine and catastrophic for European Jewry.

One historian analysed Britain's Palestine predicament at the dawn of 1939:

> On the eve of World War II in 1939, the issues that were most important to British decision makers at the time centered on the diplomatic efforts abroad, bureaucratic infighting at home, and the dynamics of parliamentary politics. By analyzing how the government interpreted risk in the context of imminent war, it becomes clear that only one option was politically sound enough to be measured against the broader needs of national interest.[24]

That one option, as we will see, was to spell disaster for the Jews.

## Notes

1 S. Zipperstein, *Law and the Arab-Israeli Conflict: The Trials of Palestine* (Routledge, 2020).
2 Cmd. 5479, *Palestine Royal Commission Report* (July 1937).
3 *See generally* Y. Porath, *The Palestinian Arab National Movement: From Riots to Rebellion, 1929-1939* (Vol. II) at 228–1 (Routledge, 1977); M. Hughes, *From Law and Order to Pacification: Britain's Suppression of the Arab Revolt in Palestine, 1936–39*, Journal of Palestine Studies 39:2 at 6–22 (Winter 2010); M. Yazbak, *From Poverty to Revolt: Economic Factors in the Outbreak of the 1936 Rebellion in Palestine*, Middle Eastern Studies 36:3 at 93–113 (2000).
4 League of Nations Archive, R4078/6A/37120/668, *Resolution of the Inter-Parliamentary Congress, Cairo* at 6 (October 1938).

5 *Id.*
6 *Id.*
7 Cmd. 5513, *Palestine: Statement of Policy* para. 6 (July 1937). This was the first time in the history of the Mandate that the Government had abandoned the guiding principle behind its immigration policy since 1922; namely, that immigration would be permitted without numerical caps, subject only to the economic absorptive capacity of Palestine. *See, e.g.*, Cmd. 1700, *Palestine: Correspondence with the Palestine Arab Delegation and the Zionist Organization* at 19 (hereafter "Churchill White Paper") (July 1922); Weizmann Archives 10-1486, Letter from Prime Minister Ramsay MacDonald to Weizmann, para. 15 (13 February 1931). The Government's new policy, in which it capped immigration at a total of 8,000 over an eight-month period regardless of the country's economic absorptive capacity, represented a radical shift in policy. The Government issued this directive in connection with its receipt of the Report of the Palestine Royal Commission, otherwise known as the Peel Commission. Section 5A of Immigration (Amendment) Ordinance, 33 of 1937, in No. 33 in 75113/4/37; *see also* Hansard, HC Deb.Vol. 333 cols. 40-41W (14 March 1938). The Peel Commission had recommended Palestine be partitioned into separate Jewish and Arab states. The British Government decided to appoint a follow-on technical panel, known as the Woodhead Commission, to study the Peel Commission's partition proposal in detail and make recommendations. The Woodhead Commission issued its report in November 1938, in which it found partition unworkable.
8 Cmd. 5634, *Policy in Palestine: Despatch Dated 23rd December, 1937, from the Secretary of State for the Colonies to the High Commissioner of Palestine* (Jan. 1938) (announcing formation of Woodhead Commission and Terms of Reference); Cmd. 5854, *Palestine Partition Commission Report* (Nov. 1938) (Woodhead Commission Report); Cmd. 5893, *Palestine: Statement by His Majesty's Government in the United Kingdom* (Nov. 1938) at para. 3 ("His Majesty's Government, after careful study of the [Woodhead] Commission's report, have reached the conclusion that this further examination has shown that the political, administrative and financial difficulties involved in the proposal to create independent Arab and Jewish states inside Palestine are so great that this solution of the problem is impracticable"). In February 1938, Colonial Secretary William Ormsby-Gore submitted a memorandum to the Cabinet recommending the immigration restrictions be continued for an additional year beyond March 1938. CAB 24/275/10, C.P. 46 (38), Memorandum by the Secretary of State for the Colonies (Secret), Control of Immigration into Palestine paras. 17–20 (24 February 1938). The Cabinet approved the recommendations on 2 March 1938. CAB 23/92/10, Minutes (Secret) of Cabinet Meeting at 13 (2 March 1938).
9 L. Dinnerstein, *America, Britain, and Palestine: The Anglo-American Committee of Inquiry and the Displaced Persons, 1945–46*, Diplomatic History 4:3 at 283–301, 285 (1980).
10 For further background regarding the evolution of British policy toward Palestine during the summer and fall of 1938, *see* M.J. Cohen, *Appeasement in the Middle East: The British White Paper on Palestine*, The Historical Journal 16:3 at 571–80 (1973).
11 CO 733/364/1, Downie minute (7 February 1938); *see also* CO 733/364/1, Downie minute (4 March 1938) ("The truth is that we have already deserted the principle of economic absorptive capacity and are unlikely to return to it until boundaries of Jewish and Arab areas have been defined, and then only for a transition period pending the termination of the present Mandate. If the worst comes to the worst and partition falls through and we have to carry on under something like the existing Mandate, some modification of the principles governing Jewish immigration is surely inevitable"); M.J. Cohen (1973), *op. cit.* (strategic importance of Suez Canal to Britain as of 1938–39, and importance of Palestinian Arab cause to Britain's relations with surrounding Arab states).
12 *Id.* Weizmann met secretly with Colonial Secretary Malcolm MacDonald in July 1938, urging the British Government to move forward and implement the Peel Commission's partition plan to enable Jewish immigration to resume. MacDonald, foreshadowing the policy the British Government would adopt less than a year later in the White Paper, floated the idea of a five-to-ten year period during which Jewish immigration would

be slowed, resulting in a maximum of 40% Jews in Palestine, with a small number of Jews permitted to settle in Transjordan. Weizmann rejected the idea, arguing it would place the Jews at the mercy of the Arabs. Weizmann Archives 9-2077, Note of Interview (Secret) between "B" (code for MacDonald) and W (4 July 1938). Weizmann sent a follow-up letter several days later to MacDonald, laying out in great detail Weizmann's frustration that British immigration policy had undergone an abrupt change following the issuance of the Peel Commission report, with the British willing to restrict Jewish immigration to placate Arab opposition to the Peel Commission's inclusion of portions of the Galilee region in the area earmarked for the Jewish State. Weizmann also noted in the letter that Britain's Ambassador to Egypt, Sir Miles Lampson, had originally proposed a five-year halt to Jewish immigration (when Weizmann met with him in Cairo in February 1938) to calm both the Arabs in Palestine and Egypt. Weizmann Archives 4-2079, Letter from Weizmann to MacDonald (12 July 1938). Weizmann and MacDonald met again in mid-September 1938. According to Weizmann's notes of the meeting, MacDonald raised the possibility of abandoning partition and "revival of the Mandate and the principle of absorptive capacity – but, of course, applied cautiously? To this I replied that there was to my mind no question that the dropping of partition would be considered as a victory by the Arab terrorists." Weizmann Archives 13-2091, Summary Notes of Two Conversations with "B" (code for MacDonald) (13–14 September 1938).

13 Hansard, HC Deb. vol. 333 cols. 41-41W (14 March 1938) (Colonial Secretary Ormsby-Gore reading from a 10 March 1938 letter from the Colonial Office to the High Commissioner of Palestine regarding the extension of immigration restrictions for an initial period of six months to be followed by an additional six months with the possibility of quota changes); *see also* CO 733/364/1, H.F. Downie's minute explaining the basis for and details of continuation of immigration restrictions (19 January 1938).

14 CO 733/364/1, Downie minute (22 June 1938).

15 CAB 24/278/25, C.P. 190 (38) (Secret), Memorandum by the Secretary of State for the Colonies at 1–2 (21 August 1938).

16 Weizmann Archives 13-2091, Summary Notes (Most Secret) of Two Conversations with "B" (Malcolm MacDonald) (13–14 September 1938).

17 *Id.* at 1–2.

18 Weizmann Archives 15-2093, Summary Note (Secret) of Meeting of Executive, London (21 September 1938). For further background and discussion of the McMahon-Hussein correspondence, *see* S. Zipperstein, *op. cit.*, ch. 1.

19 CAB 24/280/5, C.P. 250 (38) (Secret), Final Draft of the Statement of Policy, Memorandum by the Secretary of State for the Colonies at para. 4 (5 November 1938); *see also* Cmd. 5893, *op. cit.*, at para. 4 ("His Majesty's Government, after careful study of the [Woodhead] Commission's Report, have reached the conclusion that this further examination has shown that the political, administrative and financial difficulties involved in the proposal to create independent Arab and Jewish states inside Palestine are so great that this solution of the problem is impracticable."); *see also* C. Beckerman, *Unexpected State, British Politics and the Creation of Israel* at 105 (Indiana University Press, 2020).

20 C. Beckerman, *op. cit.*, at 205.

21 Cmd. 5893, *op. cit.*, at para. 5 ("It is clear that the surest foundation for peace and progress in Palestine would be an understanding between the Arabs and the Jews, and His Majesty's Government are prepared in the first instance to make a determined effort to promote such an understanding. With this end in view, they propose to invite representatives of the Palestinian Arabs and of neighbouring States on the one hand and of the Jewish Agency on the other, to confer with them as soon as possible in London regarding future policy …").

22 Cmd. 5893, *op. cit.*, at para. 6.

23 CAB 23/96/12, Minutes (Secret) of a Meeting of the Cabinet at 24–5 (21 December 1938); *see also* C. Beckerman, *op. cit.*, at 110–1.

24 C. Beckerman, *op. cit.*, at 107.

# 3

# THE LONDON CONFERENCES

## Introduction

The London Conferences opened on 7 February 1939 at St. James's Palace. The Conferences are referred to in the plural, as they proceeded in parallel due to the Palestinian Arabs' refusal to sit in the same room with the Jewish delegates.[1] Prime Minister Chamberlain was forced to give his opening speech *twice* on 7 February 1939, once to the Arab delegates and later the same morning to the Jewish delegates.[2] Thereafter the British delegation conducted separate meetings with the Palestinian and Arab delegations and with the Jewish delegation.

Not surprisingly, the Conferences ended six weeks later in failure.

The Conferences represented yet another example of how the British, the Jews, and the Palestinian Arabs continued using the law and legal arguments to advance their positions and influence international opinion during the Mandate years.

Although the Conferences were convened to address the political future of Palestine, they ended up focusing largely on four legal issues:

First, the future governance of Palestine, which the parties described as "the constitutional issue";

Second, Arab claims that the British Government had in October 1915, through its High Commissioner in Egypt (Sir Henry McMahon), promised Palestine to the Arabs, thereby rendering the November 1917 Balfour Declaration and the December 1922 Mandate for Palestine legally invalid;

Third, the British Government's legal authority to restrict Jewish immigration to Palestine; and

Fourth, the British Government's legal authority to restrict Palestine land sales to Jewish buyers.

The composition of the delegations reflected the large role the law played in the discussions. The British delegation included Sir Grattan Bushe, the Legal

DOI: 10.4324/9781003225263-6

Advisor to the Colonial Secretary. The Jewish delegation included Leonard Stein, the Jewish Agency's Honorary Legal Counsel and Weizmann's long-time confidant. The Palestinian delegation included the famous lawyer Auni Bey Abdul Hadi, who had served as counsel to the Arab side during the Shaw and Lofgren Commission trials and had testified as a witness before the Peel Commission.[3] The Iraqi delegation included a British lawyer as its legal advisor.

The Conferences featured intense legal debates regarding the meaning and proper interpretation of the 1915–1916 McMahon-Hussein correspondence, as well as various provisions of the 1917 Balfour Declaration and the 1922 Mandate for Palestine.

The British Government realised, well before the Conferences convened, that the Palestinian Arabs were likely to renew their long-standing legal arguments regarding the McMahon-Hussein correspondence, as part of their effort to convince Britain to repudiate the Balfour Declaration and the Mandate and establish an Arab State in Palestine.

The Palestinians had argued since the early 1920s that the McMahon-Hussein correspondence formed a *legally binding* treaty between Britain and Sherif Hussein, under which the Arabs would receive their independence following World War I in all Ottoman-controlled lands of the Middle East, including Palestine. The Arabs argued, as a matter of law, that Article 22 of the Covenant of the League of Nations codified McMahon's written pledges to the Sherif.[4]

The Arabs further argued that Article 20 of the Covenant abrogated the Balfour Declaration, due to the Declaration's inconsistency with McMahon's prior promise of Palestine to the Arabs.[5] The Arabs also challenged the legal validity of those portions of the Mandate incorporating the Balfour Declaration or otherwise reflecting any commitments to the Jews.

The famous Christian Arab scholar George Antonius had recently published the text of the McMahon-Hussein correspondence as an Appendix to his October 1938 book, "The Arab Awakening."[6] Antonius succeeded in raising the public profile of the correspondence and increasing the pressure on the British Government to address whether in fact it had promised Palestine to the Arabs in October 1915, two years before the Balfour Declaration.

The British Government, therefore, began preparing several weeks before the Conferences began for extensive legal debates with both the Palestinian Arabs and the Jews.

## British legal preparations for the London Conferences

The British Government's preparations for the upcoming London Conferences focused as much on legal as on political and policy issues. The Government, perhaps recognising the need to shore up its legal position, even began studying the legal rules and procedures necessary for obtaining an amendment to the Mandate for Palestine, in the event the Conferences were not successful and the Government were to unilaterally implement policy changes which might require approval from the League of Nations.[7]

Ultimately, the Government determined it had the legal power under the existing terms of the Mandate to make the policy changes it had discussed in late 1938 and, therefore, would not need to seek permission or a change in the Mandate from the League of Nations.[8]

Two key British Government memoranda written before the Conferences began, one by the Colonial Secretary and the other by a Foreign Office lawyer, demonstrate the British Government's focus on the law as it prepared for the upcoming discussions with the Palestinian Arabs and the Jews.

The first memorandum (the MacDonald memorandum) addressed the overall Arab and Jewish legal arguments, Britain's responses to those arguments, and the Colonial Secretary's recommendations for drastic changes in British policy toward Palestine. The second memorandum (the MacKenzie Memorandum and the Lord Chancellor's response to the memorandum) focused exclusively on the Arab legal claims regarding the McMahon-Hussein correspondence.

## *The MacDonald memorandum*

On 18 January 1939, Colonial Secretary Malcolm MacDonald (Figure 3.1) submitted a lengthy memorandum to the Cabinet discussing the Arab and Jewish political and legal claims regarding the Jewish presence in Palestine and Jewish

**FIGURE 3.1** Malcolm MacDonald (National Portrait Gallery, London)

immigration to the country.[9] The memorandum offers the most comprehensive view of the official British mindset regarding Palestine and the complexity of the overall legal and geostrategic backdrop as of early 1939. The memorandum also served as a roadmap for the British approach to the upcoming London Conferences.

The MacDonald Memorandum first addressed the Jewish legal claims. The Jewish side had, according to MacDonald, based its legal case on two key points. The first Jewish argument held that *all* Jews, everywhere in the world, had a *legal right* to enter Palestine. That right derived from the preamble to the Mandate for Palestine, stating "recognition has thereby been given to the historical connection of the Jewish people with Palestine and the grounds for reconstituting their national home in that country." The Jewish side further relied on former Colonial Secretary Winston Churchill's declaration in his famous 1922 White Paper that "it is essential that [the Jewish people] should know that it is in Palestine as of right and not on sufferance."[10]

The MacDonald Memorandum quickly disposed of the first Jewish legal argument, flatly stating:

> We cannot accept the contention that all Jews as such have a right to enter Palestine. Such a principle is not a corollary of recognition of the historical connection of the Jews with Palestine, and the passage quoted from Mr. Churchill's Statement of Policy implies no more than that the Jews who have already entered, or might be allowed to enter, Palestine are or would be *in* that country as of right; that is to say, that they are equals in national status of the indigenous inhabitants. It would clearly be absurd to admit that all the millions of Jews in the world have a right, which they should be allowed to exert if they wished, to settle in Palestine.[11]

The second Jewish legal argument relied on Article 6 of the Mandate as *requiring* Britain to "facilitate Jewish immigration" to Palestine. The only limiting factor was whether Palestine had sufficient economic capacity to absorb additional immigrants at any given point in time. Churchill originally announced the "economic absorptive capacity" principle in his 1922 White Paper as the Government's official interpretation of Britain's obligation under Article 6 of the Mandate to "facilitate" Jewish immigration to Palestine "under suitable conditions."[12]

The Permanent Mandates Commission (PMC) of the League of Nations, responsible for overseeing Britain's performance of its duties as the mandatory power in Palestine and a frequent critic of British policy in Palestine (especially, as we will see, of the British Government's May 1939 White Paper), subsequently endorsed Churchill's interpretation, thereby enshrining the economic absorptive capacity principle as part of Britain's international legal obligations under the Mandate.[13] Prime Minister Ramsay MacDonald (Malcolm MacDonald's father) had reiterated in a 1931 letter to Chaim Weizmann that the principle of economic absorptive capacity represented the *only* limitation on Jewish immigration to Palestine.[14]

The Zionists argued that Palestine, as of early 1939, had sufficient economic capacity to absorb an additional one million Jews, which would have the effect of catapulting the Jews into the majority position in the country.[15] The Zionists further argued Britain would be violating the terms of the Mandate if it refused entry to those Jews, or if it took other steps to cement the current two-thirds Arab majority and deny eventual statehood to the Jews in Palestine.

The MacDonald Memorandum acknowledged Jewish immigration rates had never exceeded Palestine's economic absorptive capacity. But the memorandum also noted Britain's obligation under Article 6 of the Mandate was to facilitate Jewish immigration to Palestine only "under suitable conditions." While conditions may have been "suitable" during the 1920s and most of the 1930s to permit immigration subject only to Palestine's economic absorptive capacity, by 1939 the situation had changed considerably due both to the Arab revolt and the need for Britain to maintain good relations with the Arab and Muslim worlds in the event of war with Germany.[16]

Thus, the MacDonald Memorandum argued, Britain was fully within its legal authority under Article 6 to consider these changed circumstances in assessing the "suitability" of additional Jewish immigration to Palestine, *regardless* of the country's economic capacity to absorb additional Jewish immigrants. Therefore, the Memorandum noted, Britain possessed the legal authority to impose *further* limitations on Jewish immigration to Palestine, *beyond* the economic absorptive capacity principle.

The Memorandum then turned to a discussion of the Arab legal claims. First, the Arabs had consistently argued for nearly two decades that the McMahon-Hussein correspondence and Article 22 of the Covenant of the League of Nations established absolute Arab sovereignty over *all* of Palestine. The Balfour Declaration and the Preamble to the Mandate were, therefore, legally null and void. Accordingly, Britain expected the Arabs would assert legal demands for terminating the Mandate and granting immediate Arab statehood in Palestine.

Second, the Arabs argued the experiment of a Jewish National Home in Palestine, even if it were legally valid to begin with, should now be deemed completed. The Jewish population of Palestine had soared to 400,000 during the first two decades of the Mandate, comprising nearly one-third of Palestine's total population. The Jews already in Palestine could remain as a protected minority under Arab sovereignty, but no *additional* Jewish immigrants should be allowed to enter the country, to ensure the Jews would never become the majority and attempt to wrest control from the Arabs. The Arabs also demanded the prohibition of all further land sales to Jewish buyers.

The MacDonald Memorandum did not concede any of the Arab arguments but candidly acknowledged the British Government's responsibility for having made conflicting promises to both sides. "It is impossible to escape the conclusion," wrote MacDonald, "that the authors of the various declarations made to

Jews and Arabs during the war, which are really very difficult to reconcile, were rather confused about the whole business."[17] MacDonald urged the Cabinet to be prepared for the London Conferences to fail to produce an agreement between the parties, meaning Britain would need to be ready to impose its own solution unilaterally:

> [A]t the outset of the discussions we should have our own clear idea of what would be a just and workable solution to the present problem ... In determining this solution we must exercise a perfectly impartial understanding of the case for each side in the dispute, and be as fair as possible to each; we must keep in mind and endeavour to fulfill the British Government's and the League of Nations' promises to both parties; and we cannot forget our own British interests in the Near and Middle East ...[18]

The MacDonald Memorandum, therefore, made the following policy recommendations to the Cabinet:

First, the Memorandum recommended against Palestine becoming either a wholly Jewish or wholly Arab State. The time had come, according to the Memorandum, to make clear the "vague and dangerous" term "Jewish National Home" in the Balfour Declaration *precluded* the establishment of a Jewish state without Arab acquiescence. This interpretation represented a British "modification" of the Balfour Declaration, "to the extent that something [Jewish statehood in Palestine] which was not precluded in it before *was now being made dependent on Arab consent*."[19]

The Memorandum likewise rejected the Arab demand for statehood, agreeing with the Palestine Royal Commission's rejection of the Arab legal arguments regarding the impact of the McMahon-Hussein correspondence and Article 22 of the Covenant of the League of Nations.

Therefore, the memorandum recommended Britain not terminate the Mandate and not grant statehood either to the Jews or the Arabs but instead to continue the Mandate while trying to find a way to foster the development of self-governing institutions in Palestine, as required by Article 2 of the Mandate.

Second, regarding Jewish immigration, the Memorandum noted how Britain's permissiveness toward Jewish immigration to Palestine had caused an anti-British backlash throughout the Arab and broader Muslim world (including the very large Muslim population of India, where Britain still remained the Colonial ruler as of 1939). The Memorandum described the situation in stark, even hyperbolic language: "It would be hard to conceive of anything more damaging to our prestige than the loss of the sympathy and friendship of the Moslem world." Accordingly, the Memorandum urged the Cabinet to "*radically* alter our outlook on the Palestine problem."[20]

This meant, according to MacDonald, that Britain had paid "too little heed to the rights of the Arabs of Palestine ... it is necessary to respect the deep and genuine feelings of the Arabs, and to make concessions to them, perhaps considerable concessions."[21]

The MacDonald Memorandum, thus, proposed two new alternative policies regarding future Jewish immigration for the Cabinet's consideration:

First, that Jewish immigration to Palestine be permitted to continue based on the principal that it not exceed the economic absorptive capacity of the country, but that in no event and regardless of the country's economic absorptive capacity would the Jewish population of Palestine be permitted to exceed 40% of the total population of Palestine (compared to 29% as of January 1939) at the end of ten years. This would create an average yearly quota of 30,000 Jewish immigrants over the ten-year period. If the Arabs refused to agree to the 40% figure, the British Government should be prepared to agree to 35%, or a yearly quota of 15,300 Jewish immigrants. At the expiration of the ten-year period, the Arabs and Jews would discuss with the British Government new rules applicable to future immigration; or

Second, if the Arabs would be willing to agree to a 40% cap on the Jewish population, the Arabs would have the right to veto any future Jewish immigration to Palestine after the expiration of the ten-year period.[22]

MacDonald added, however, that additional concessions to the Arabs might be necessary to avoid further hostility toward Britain among the Arab and larger Muslim world.[23]

Third, the memorandum recommended legislation to limit further land sales in Palestine to Jews.[24] The Jews, of course, had acquired land from the beginning of the First Aliyah in 1882 and onwards through lawful *purchases*, usually at above-market prices, from willing Arab sellers, not expropriation or colonisation.[25] Nevertheless, MacDonald sought to appease *Arab* objections to *Arab* land sales by placing restrictions on *Jewish* buyers.

Fourth, the memorandum recommended steps be taken to continue the development of self-governing institutions in Palestine, both at the local and national level. The local level would be easier, given the *de facto* separation of Arabs and Jews among their own towns and villages. At the national level, however, the options were limited and very difficult. The two possibilities would be either a binational state (the "one state solution," in today's parlance) or a return to some version of partitioning Palestine into separate Jewish and Arab "areas," perhaps with the Arab area joining some form of federation with Lebanon, Syria, and Transjordan.[26]

MacDonald candidly summed up the frustrating nature of the Arab-Jewish problem in Palestine from the British perspective:

> I doubt whether, however much we may be able to improve relations between Jews and Arabs, they will ever be able to co-operate ... Though they do, in fact, belong to the same race, mixing them is like trying to mix oil and water. Their civilisations are different; their religions are different; their temperaments are different; their interests would clash at many points; they do not like each other; each of them wants to be the master.[27]

The Cabinet Committee on Palestine, chaired by Prime Minister Chamberlain, convened soon after receiving MacDonald's memorandum. Less than two weeks later, the Cabinet Committee sent a secret report to the entire Cabinet, taking a tough stance on future Jewish immigration to Palestine:

> Immigration ... is the most crucial of the questions to be examined at the London Conferences ... [T]he time has come to set definite limits to the expansion, without the consent of the Arabs, of the Jewish National Home ... [i]t must, we think, now be definitely accepted that, beyond a certain point, future Jewish immigration into Palestine must be dependent on the goodwill of the Arabs, and that we must endeavour to convince the Jews that this is the case.[28]

## *The MacKenzie memorandum and the Lord Chancellor's response*

On 23 January 1939, the British Foreign Office, anticipating the Palestinian Arabs would use the conference as a forum for maintaining and advancing their narrative regarding the legal force of the McMahon-Hussein correspondence, issued to the Cabinet a secret memorandum entitled "The Juridical Basis of the Arab Claim to Palestine."[29] The Foreign Secretary, Lord Halifax, circulated the memorandum to the Cabinet, along with a cover note entitled, "Palestine: Legal Arguments Likely to be advanced by Arab Representatives."[30]

J. Z. Mackenzie of the Foreign Office wrote the memorandum in December 1938. W.E. Beckett, the Legal Advisor to the Foreign Office, endorsed the memorandum's analysis and conclusions. The memorandum identified and analysed the expected Arab legal arguments regarding the McMahon-Hussein correspondence and the Balfour Declaration.

Although the MacKenzie Memorandum did not concede any legal arguments to the Arabs, it acknowledged certain "weak points" in the British legal case for defending its long-standing argument that McMahon had not promised Palestine to the Arabs in his 1915–1916 correspondence with the Sherif. The Memorandum admitted "there are points of serious weakness" in the Government's case. The correspondence lacks that self-evident and decisive clarity which ought to form the basis of international acts.[31] No prior British Government document had ever questioned so seriously the legal validity of Britain's position regarding the Arab claim to Palestine.

Lacy Baggallay of the Foreign Office sent the MacKenzie Memorandum to H.F. Downie at the Colonial Office for his review before the upcoming London Conferences. Baggallay commented in his cover letter, "I must say that, after going into the whole question of the McMahon-Hussein correspondence again, our position in regard to this correspondence seems to me even weaker than it did before!"[32]

Downie, however, felt no need to reconsider the Government's position, rejecting the notion that a strict legal analysis should trump the British Government's long-standing policy position:

> The idea that the fundamental issue whether or not Palestine is to be turned into an Arab state can be decided (or even seriously affected by) a legal interpretation of the McMahon correspondence is too ridiculous to need refutation ... Surely we need only concern ourselves with refuting the offensive insinuation (which constitutes the sting of the Arab case) that His Majesty's Government has been guilty of bad faith in the matter. On this point there is no reason why we should condescend to argument with the Arabs. We have always maintained that our intention was to exclude Palestine from the pledges given to the Sherif.[33]

After the MacKenzie Memorandum had been circulated to the Cabinet, Baggallay asked an Arabic language expert in the Foreign Office, A.C. Trott, to analyse the original Arabic versions of the correspondence to determine any weaknesses in the British arguments.[34] Trott sent a long memorandum to Baggallay several days later. The memorandum noted many ambiguities in the original Arabic that could be used to support either the British or the Arab arguments regarding the meaning of the correspondence, but none that undermined the British interpretation.[35]

Meanwhile, following the Cabinet's receipt of the MacKenzie memorandum, the Lord Chancellor (Lord Frederic Maugham) requested a meeting with the Foreign Office. Baggallay and Beckett met with the Lord Chancellor on 30 January 1939 to discuss the Memorandum. The Lord Chancellor, apparently worried that the Foreign Office seemed too eager to concede weakness in Britain's legal position, said the Memorandum "did not state the [legal] case for His Majesty's government as well as it could be stated."[36]

For example, the Lord Chancellor criticised the Memorandum for according insufficient weight to McMahon's intent at the time he engaged in the correspondence with Sherif Hussein. The Lord Chancellor noted that while McMahon's intent might not be "strictly relevant to any construction of the letter ... it was permissible to take into account the whole of the surrounding circumstances when attempting to get at the true meaning of the words used."[37] According to the Lord Chancellor, those circumstances included the enormous importance to Britain and France of the strategically crucial ports of Acre, Haifa, and Jaffa and the extreme unlikelihood that McMahon would have promised those ports to the Sherif. The Lord Chancellor also viewed as relevant the even more remote likelihood that McMahon would have ceded the Holy Sites throughout Palestine to solely Muslim control.[38]

The Lord Chancellor separately argued the general reservation in favour of French interests supported the Government's position that Palestine had been excluded from the pledge, and "if the Sherif of Mecca was unaware of the fact that the claims of France extended to Palestine at that time, the onus lay on him to make sure of the extent of those claims."[39]

The Lord Chancellor reported to the Cabinet two days later on his meeting with Baggallay and Beckett:

> The Lord Chancellor referred to the Memorandum by the Secretary of State for Foreign Affairs in regard to legal arguments likely to be advanced by Arab representatives. He was by no means satisfied that the British case was fairly stated in the Memorandum which had been circulated by the Foreign Secretary and he had taken the opportunity of discussing it with the Foreign Office official who prepared it. He did not altogether agree with the view taken in this Memorandum in regard to the McMahon correspondence and he would fully expect that if the matter was submitted to some such body as the Hague Tribunal they would take the view that the pledges in the McMahon correspondence did not apply to Palestine. If the discussions at the conference turned on legal points he would be happy to offer any assistance to the Colonial Secretary.[40]

As we shall see, the Lord Chancellor's views continued to evolve during February and March 1939 regarding the strength of Britain's legal position, especially after he had considered the legal impact of a message delivered in early 1918 by a British envoy (Commander David Hogarth) to Sherif Hussein regarding the meaning of the Balfour Declaration.[41]

## The London Conferences

"It very quickly became clear," according to one leading historian, that the London Conferences represented "another stage in the attempt to resolve the question of Palestine in an agreed arrangement that would be acceptable to the Arabs."[42] Britain sought to cloak the process in legitimacy by using the law and legal framing/narrative, justifying its preordained policy shift in favour of the Palestinian Arabs as legally required under the express terms of the Mandate.

Both the Arab and Jewish sides sent large delegations to the London Conferences. Chaim Weizmann, President of the Jewish Agency led the Jewish side (Figure 3.2), along with David Ben-Gurion, who by early 1939 held the title of Chairman of the Jewish Agency Executive and had begun to eclipse Weizmann as the leader of the Zionist movement.

The Arab delegations (Figure 3.3) included members of the Arab Higher Committee, following a lengthy and bitter intra-Palestinian dispute regarding the composition of their delegation.[43] The British banned the Grand Mufti of Jerusalem, Haj Amin al-Husseini (in self-exile in Beirut) from attending, but they allowed the Palestinian Delegation to be dominated by the Arab Higher Committee, most of whom were supporters of the Mufti and took direction from him.

FIGURE 3.2 Jewish and British Delegations at the Opening Session of the London Conferences, St. James's Palace, 7 February 1939 (Alamy photos)

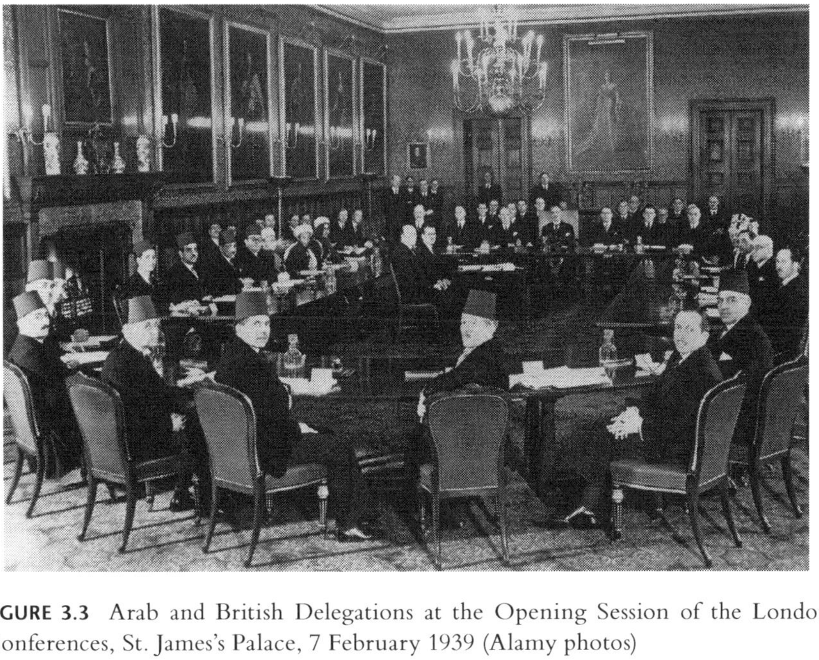

FIGURE 3.3 Arab and British Delegations at the Opening Session of the London Conferences, St. James's Palace, 7 February 1939 (Alamy photos)

The non-Palestinian Arab delegations consisted of representatives from various Arab states, including Egypt (Prince Mohamed Abdul Moneim and Ali Maher Pasha), Iraq (Nuri Said and Taufik Suwaidi), Saudi Arabia (Prince Faisal and Fuad Bey Hamza), Trans-Jordan (Tewfik Pasha Abdul Huda) and Yemen (Prince Saif al-Islam al-Husain). The All-India Muslim League also submitted a written document to the League of Nations at the beginning of the London Conferences in support of the Palestinian Arab cause.[44]

The Arabs had initially demanded verbatim transcripts be prepared of all Conference proceedings but relented when the British Government offered instead to prepare official secretarial minutes summarising each meeting.[45] H.F. Downie of the Colonial Office acted as the Secretary and prepared the minutes of all the official meetings of the Conferences. The minutes were never published.[46]

For the next six weeks, a team of seven British officials, led by Colonial Secretary Malcolm MacDonald and including the Undersecretary of State for Foreign Affairs (R.A. Butler) and the Colonial Office's Legal Advisor (Sir Grattan Bushe), met separately with the Arab and Jewish delegations. The meetings included enormous amounts of legal argumentation from both sides, in keeping with the parties' long-standing custom and practice of using the law to advance their respective positions and gain leverage against each other. Both sides set the tone in their opening statements, separately reprising many of the same legal arguments they had developed several years earlier during their presentations to the Shaw, Lofgren, and Peel Commissions.[47]

## *Opening remarks*

Weizmann made a brief statement on the first day of the conference, following Prime Minister Chamberlain's opening speech to the Jewish delegation.[48]

Jamal Husseini, in his opening statement for the Palestinian Arabs, immediately invoked the Palestinian Arab legal narrative, framing the Balfour Declaration and the Mandate as illegal and arguing the British Government had previously promised Palestine to the Arabs in the McMahon-Hussein correspondence of 1915–1916.

Husseini's legal arguments maintained the thematic continuity of the Palestinian Arab presentations to the Shaw and Peel Commissions in 1929 and 1937. By reiterating those arguments at the opening of the London Conferences in 1939, the Palestinian Arabs signalled the primacy of transformational legal framing and narrative as a key part of their effort (in tandem with the violence perpetrated in Palestine) to gain leverage with the British Government. The *Times* headline for its story the next morning regarding Husseini's opening statement captured the essence of the Palestinian Arab legal framing/narrative: "*The Arab Case: An Appeal for Justice.*"[49]

Three days later, on 10 February 1939, Colonial Secretary Malcolm MacDonald wrote to Sir Alexander Hardinge, Private Secretary to King

George VI. MacDonald reported he had met twice with the Jewish delegation and once with the Arab delegation. MacDonald presented the Arab case to the Jewish delegation, noting the British Government did "not necessarily associate" itself with the Arab side. Nevertheless, MacDonald confided to Hardinge that "a good many" of the Jewish delegates felt disappointed with the Government's statements. "So the conferences are both launched," MacDonald wrote, "but they have not really got into the rough weather yet. There is plenty of it ahead." MacDonald closed the letter by promising to keep Hardinge and the King informed of the progress of the London Conferences.[50]

For the next several weeks, the British delegation conducted multiple separate meetings with the Jewish and Arab delegations, until the talks collapsed on 15 March 1939.

## *British meetings with the Jewish delegation*

The first British meeting with the Jewish side convened on 1 February, 1939, six days prior to the formal opening of the Conferences. Colonial Secretary MacDonald announced during the meeting the British Government would be open to hearing from both sides "arguments in favour of the amendment" of the Balfour Declaration and/or the Mandate.

Weizmann seemed shocked at MacDonald's statement:

> [T]his attitude on the part of the Government might be interpreted as implying that the Mandate and the Balfour Declaration, which previous British Governments had always treated as beyond question, were now to be thrown into the melting pot and that the history of twenty-three years was to be torn up.[51]

Weizmann met again with MacDonald three days later, on 4 February 1939. According to MacDonald's typewritten notes of the meeting, Weizmann spoke very bluntly to MacDonald, telling him the Jewish side had secretly learned of British intentions to satisfy Arab demands and reach an agreement with the Arabs "at all costs."[52] Weizmann wanted to know if the British Government truly intended to "surrender to the Arabs."[53]

Weizmann also mentioned the American Government was poised to amend the Neutrality Act, meaning between 100,000 and 250,000 American Jews could soon be available to fight for Britain in the event of war with Germany. Weizmann asked MacDonald to weigh that prospect against Britain's desire to appease the Arabs to keep them on Britain's side.[54]

Weizmann, who had given a brief statement at the formal opening of the conference on 7 February, saved his full opening speech for the second official British-Jewish meeting on the evening of 8 February. Weizmann had notified MacDonald in advance of the importance of the speech he would give, and both MacDonald and Foreign Secretary Lord Halifax attended. A Foreign Office official later described Weizmann's speech as a "most eloquent, moving and adroit appeal."[55]

## *Weizmann's opening speech*

Weizmann's speech laid the entire Jewish case before the British delegation. He criticised the British Government for failing to implement the Peel Commission's partition plan, which gave the Jews far less than they had hoped for, but still provided at least the possibility of statehood in a small portion of Palestine. Weizmann claimed that Britain's Ambassador to Egypt, Sir Miles Lampson (later Lord Killearn) had surprised him in a February 1938 meeting by asking Weizmann to agree to a five-year halt of the Zionist project, for the sake of calming rising anti-British sentiment in Egypt and elsewhere in the Arab world.[56]

Weizmann argued the Balfour Declaration and the Mandate provided the legal basis for massive Jewish immigration from Europe to Palestine and imposed a legal obligation on Britain to facilitate such immigration. Weizmann blasted the British desire, for the sake of political expediency, to reinterpret the Balfour Declaration and the Mandate to the detriment of the promises earlier British Governments had made to the Jewish people:

> I cannot believe that it is possible to conceive that the Government after twenty years, is retreating from a moral and political position, and would seek an interpretation of the Mandate which might lead to a further curtailing of our fundamental rights. I for one consider it impossible, and impossible not only from a purely Jewish point of view but because there are *legally binding documents*; and, if I may say so with the utmost possible respect, speaking not as an Englishman, but as a Britisher, it is inconceivable from a British point of view.[57]

Weizmann noted the only legal limitation on Jewish immigration had been established in the 1922 Churchill White Paper, which laid down the principle that Jewish immigration to Palestine should not exceed the "economic absorptive capacity" of the country.

Weizmann also stressed the extreme danger Hitler posed to European Jewry, prophetically emphasising "the fate of 6,000,000 people was in the balance."[58]

Weizmann further rejected various suggestions of alternative places of refuge for European Jewry, such as British Guiana, East Africa, or perhaps elsewhere in South America, noting "If Moses had chosen to bring us to America our problem would have been easy, but he did not choose to do so and he is not here to discuss it."[59]

Weizmann concluded by invoking the Jewish "justice" narrative: "I pray you, who have carried justice, fairness, good government into the remotest corners of the globe – indeed, I claim, and I have the right to claim – that you should do justice to my people in this dark hour."[60]

### *British-Jewish meetings continue*

On Friday, 10 February, the British and Jewish delegations held their third formal meeting. MacDonald summarised the Palestinian Arab case and Britain's evolving view of its legal obligations under the Mandate to the Palestinian Arabs:

> Our obligations under the Mandate were to both Jews and Arabs. One of these obligations was that of safeguarding the rights of the Arab population ... and the term 'rights' must cover the national rights of the Arabs. The present troubled state of Palestine was an illustration of how the Arab population enjoying these rights resented our policy. If we pushed our Jewish policy through against such strongly expressed opposition, we were ignoring Arab rights and infringing the Mandate.[61]

MacDonald's contention that the Mandate imposed a *legal* obligation on Britain to protect Palestinian Arab national aspirations flowed directly from the argument in his 18 January 1939 Memorandum to the Cabinet. MacDonald had urged the British Government to acknowledge the language regarding Arab rights in both the Balfour Declaration and the Mandate precluded the establishment of a Jewish state *without* Arab acquiescence.

David Ben-Gurion, who had studied law in Istanbul, responded on behalf of the Jewish side to MacDonald's presentation. Ben-Gurion objected to MacDonald's view that the Mandate precluded a Jewish state in Palestine without Arab consent. First, Ben-Gurion noted the concept of Arab "consent" was not mentioned in either the Balfour Declaration or the Mandate, "in which Great Britain undertook obligations to the whole world by recognising the prior rights of the Jews in Palestine. As against these rights, those of the Arab population of Palestine were secondary."[62]

Second, to the extent Britain based its argument for Arab consent on the numerical majority status of the Arabs in Palestine, Ben-Gurion objected because the Jewish status as the minority population had been the result of British restrictions on Jewish immigration during the Mandate.

Third, Ben-Gurion emphasised the Mandate's requirement in Article 2 for the development of "self-governing institutions" did not authorise Britain to create a majority-ruled Arab State. Instead, as Ben-Gurion argued in legalistic fashion:

> [I]f 'the self-government of Palestine' had been meant, the Mandate would have said so. The reference to the development of self-governing institutions came after, and was therefore subordinate to, the clause referring to the establishment of the Jewish National Home; if the former were to be interpreted as applying to the State of Palestine as a whole, it would vitiate the whole intention of the Mandate.[63]

At the next meeting of the Jewish and British delegations (10 February 1939), Weizmann said the Jewish side disagreed with MacDonald's interpretation of Britain's legal obligations under the Mandate and added that the Jewish Agency would submit a legal memorandum responding more fully to MacDonald.

On 18 February, Ben-Gurion met privately with MacDonald and "Mr. D" (likely H.F. Downie of the Colonial Office, who had been serving as Secretary of the London Conferences). According to Ben-Gurion's notes of the meeting, Ben-Gurion told MacDonald the Jewish side could never accept a complete stoppage of Jewish immigration:

> We cannot agree to any arrangement, either temporary or permanent, which involves or implies a denial of our fundamental rights, such as that we are in Palestine 'as of right,' or that we are re-constituting there our National Home. We can in no way countenance the idea that our return to Palestine is dependent on the consent of the Arabs. Any suggestion involving such an idea, explicitly or implicitly, we are bound to reject.[64]

MacDonald then asked Ben-Gurion if he saw any possible arrangement or solution. Ben-Gurion said his preferred outcome would be "a Jewish State in a Semitic Federation with the neighboring Arab States." Ben-Gurion said he had discussed the idea with some of the Arab leaders. Surprisingly, Ben-Gurion indicated one of the most prominent members of the Palestinian Arab delegation – the famed lawyer Auni Bey Abdul Hadi – "was prepared in principle to accept it."[65]

Ben-Gurion also suggested partition along the lines of the Peel Commission recommendation. Interestingly and very surprisingly, Ben-Gurion also floated the possibility of a five-year fixed rate of Jewish immigration but with no Arab veto on Jewish immigration beyond the five-year period.[66]

## *Jewish agency legal memorandum*

The Jewish Agency submitted the legal memorandum it had promised several days earlier to the Colonial Secretary on 20 February. The legal memorandum made a variety of arguments reiterating the long-standing Zionist legal narrative.

First, the memorandum argued the Mandate conferred no legal right upon the Arabs either to authorise or veto Jewish immigration to Palestine or to veto the establishment of the Jewish National Home in Palestine. No such right can be inferred from or read into the language of the Balfour Declaration's language regarding the "civil and religious rights of existing non-Jewish communities" in Palestine; nor from the language in Article 2 of the Mandate requiring Britain to safeguard the "civil and religious rights of all the inhabitants of Palestine"; nor from the language in Article 6 of the Mandate requiring Britain to ensure "the rights and position of other sections of the population are not prejudiced."

None of these provisions, according to the legal memorandum, could reasonably be read to confer any sort of veto power on the Palestinian Arabs, as doing so would render meaningless Britain's obligations under the Mandate to "secure the establishment of the Jewish national home," (Article Two), "facilitate Jewish immigration," and "encourage ... close settlement by Jews on the land." (Article Six).

Second, regarding MacDonald's argument that Britain would be infringing the Mandate if it did not recognise an Arab veto over further Jewish immigration, the Jewish Agency memorandum argued not only the plain language of the Mandate contradicted MacDonald's view, but also so did the Balfour Declaration and the 1922 Churchill White Paper, which as of 1939 still represented the British Government's official and internationally recognised interpretation of the Balfour Declaration, including the principle of economic absorptive capacity as the *sole* limitation on Jewish immigration.

Third, the Jewish Agency argued the phrase "shall facilitate Jewish immigration *under suitable conditions*" in Article 6 of the Mandate was not intended as an escape clause which Britain could trigger any time it wanted to end or limit Jewish immigration. The "under suitable conditions" language could not logically be read as undercutting Britain's primary obligation under Article 2 "to secure the establishment of the Jewish national home."

## *Colonial Office internal response*

The Colonial Office prepared an internal file note analysing and responding to the legal arguments in the Jewish Agency's legal memorandum.[67] The file note reflected the British Government's own emerging legal narrative, representing a change from the Government's prior legal framing of the conflict.

First, the Colonial Office dismissed the Jewish arguments against an express or implied Arab veto right as irrelevant. The main issue involved the influx of 300,000 Jews into Palestine during the Mandate years and the intense Arab opposition to any further immigration lest the Jewish population at some future point become the majority in the country. These changed circumstances (as compared to the circumstances prevailing 17 years earlier, at the onset of the Mandate) gave Britain the *legal* right under the terms of the Mandate to update and alter its immigration policy.

Second, the Colonial Office rejected the notion that Britain was required to permit continued Jewish immigration as part of its obligation to secure the creation of a Jewish National Home. The two obligations stood separately under the language of Articles 2 and 6 of the Mandate. Thus, Britain was under *no* legal obligation to permit Jewish immigration *indefinitely* as part of its *separate* obligation to secure the creation of the Jewish National Home.

Third, Article 6 of the Mandate also required Britain to "ensure the rights and position of other sections of the population are not prejudiced" and to permit

Jewish immigration only "under suitable conditions." Thus, Britain stood on firm legal ground in deciding to limit Jewish immigration to Palestine for reasons other than the country's economic absorptive capacity. Changed circumstances in the country rendered the conditions no longer "suitable" for ongoing, relatively unlimited Jewish immigration without prejudicing the rights and position of the Palestinian Arabs.

Finally, the Colonial Office rebuffed the Zionist legal argument regarding the overall purpose and intent of the Mandate. The Colonial Office chided the Jewish Agency memorandum for failing to mention Article 22 of the Covenant of the League of Nations, noting, "[i]t may well be argued that it would be contrary to the whole spirit of the Mandate system enshrined in the Covenant to impose further Jewish immigration on the Arabs against their will in present circumstances."[68]

## *British "suggestions" to the Jewish delegation*

MacDonald floated various "suggestions" to the Jewish delegation at the next formal British-Jewish meeting, on 24 February. These suggestions constituted the first formal British offer to both sides. MacDonald presented the same suggestions to the Arab Delegations three days later. The suggestions included the following key concepts:

- First, the Mandate "in due course" would end, and an independent Palestine State would take its place;
- Second, a conference of Jews, Arabs, and British experts would be convened later in 1939 in London to work out the constitutional details of the new Palestine state. The conference would also be tasked with setting the length of the transition period from Mandate to independence, as well as agreeing on steps to safeguard the Jewish National Home and protect British interests; and
- Third, during the transition period, local Arabs and Jews would be added as non-voting members of the Palestine Government advisory council and executive council, serving alongside British officials.[69]

Ben-Gurion later described the Government's 24 February "suggestions" as a complete shock to the Jewish Delegation, especially the proposal for an independent Palestine State.[70]

The next day, 25 February 1939, Weizmann, Ben-Gurion, and Shertok met with MacDonald and a small subset of the British delegation to discuss the British suggestions. Weizmann opened by saying he was very unhappy with the Government's 24 February "suggestions," as "they must in fact mean the ultimate creation of an independent Arab State in which the Jews would have the status of a permanent minority and the growth of the Jewish National Home would be stopped."[71]

On the following day, former United States Supreme Court Justice Louis Brandeis cabled Prime Minister Chamberlain:

> Having discussed in detail the problem of the Jewish National Home in Palestine with the late Lord Balfour prior to the publication of the Balfour Declaration and the acceptance of the Mandate I cannot believe that your Government has fully considered how gravely shattered would be the faith of the people of this troubled world in the solemn undertaking of even democratic governments if Great Britain so drastically departed from her declared policy in reference to the Jewish National Home. I urge you to consider the cruel plight of the Jews in the world today and not to crush their most cherished and sanctified hopes ...[72]

Weizmann formally responded to the 24 February "suggestions" in his opening remarks when the two sides reconvened on 27 February:

> [The British Government's] suggestions ... pass over in expressive silence the Balfour Declaration and the Mandate. They ignore the historical connection of the Jewish people with Palestine and its internationally established right to re-constitute its National Home in that country. They ignore the internationally recognized principle that 'Jewish immigration should be authorised to the extent allowed by the country's capacity of economic absorption.' ... The suggestions thus constitute a repudiation by His Majesty's Government of the solemn pledges given to the Jewish people in the Balfour Declaration, reaffirmed by successive British Governments, and endorsed in the Mandate by the League of Nations and the United States of America.[73]

Weizmann announced the Jewish side saw no basis to continue further discussions.

### *Weizmann letter to McDonald*

But discussions did continue. Weizmann, Ben-Gurion, and Rabbi Stephen S. Wise met with Prime Minister Chamberlain on 2 March. Weizmann and Ben-Gurion said the Jewish side would never agree to the Government's "suggestion" that an independent state be established in Palestine without Jewish consent. The Prime Minister tried to reassure them by framing the suggestions as conditional on safeguarding Jewish and British interests in Palestine, but Weizmann and Ben-Gurion were not persuaded. The meeting concluded with Weizmann asking whether the Government would be willing to entertain alternative proposals, and the Prime Minister agreed to do so.[74]

Several days later, Weizmann sent a letter to MacDonald, complaining that despite the Prime Minister's willingness to consider alternative proposals, the

British representatives had adhered to their 24 February suggestions for creating an independent Palestine State without Jewish consent while severely restricting Jewish immigration for a number of years and stopping it completely thereafter. "These provisions," Weizmann wrote, "are clearly calculated to crystallise the Jewish National Home both numerically and territorially."[75]

The letter next invoked the Jewish legal framing and narrative regarding the proper interpretation of the Mandate. First, the letter noted that unlike the Mandates for Syria and Lebanon, the Palestine Mandate contained *no* language requiring the creation of a "Palestinian" State. Instead, the Palestine Mandate spoke only of creating "self-governing institutions," which must be read in light of the immediately preceding language in the Mandate requiring Britain to place the country "under such political, administrative and economic conditions as will secure the establishment of the *Jewish* National Home."[76]

Second, the letter argued Britain lacked the authority to impose *any* discriminatory or restrictive measures interfering with its "positive" obligation to create the Jewish National Home. This meant Britain legally was barred from hindering Jewish immigration, barred from impeding Jewish land purchases, and barred from taking other measures to reduce Palestine's economic capacity to absorb further Jewish immigrants.[77]

The letter concluded by setting forth the Jewish Agency's response to the British Government's suggestions. Weizmann proposed three alternative solutions for Palestine: (i) continuing the Mandate, in tandem with the development of self-governing institutions on the basis of parity between Jews and Arabs, to ensure the non-domination of either race by the other; (ii) terminating the Mandate and establishing a Jewish State in some portion of Palestine adequate to allow for further immigration and land settlement on a substantial scale; or (iii) terminating the Mandate and creating a single, federal state with Jewish and Arab autonomous provinces, with full Jewish control of immigration to the province(s) under Jewish control, and a single federal government based on Arab-Jewish parity.[78]

The Jewish and British sides reconvened in an unusual Saturday afternoon meeting on 11 March to discuss Weizmann's letter. MacDonald noted his Government disagreed with Weizmann's interpretation of Britain's obligation under the Mandate to facilitate Jewish immigration to Palestine. MacDonald emphasised the "under suitable conditions" clause of Article 6, noting the Government's view that "conditions that were suitable at one time might not be suitable at another."[79]

MacDonald continued:

> British Governments had never supposed that one rule regarding immigration should prevail for all times and in all circumstances. They had felt for many years that conditions in Palestine were such that their obligations could be interpreted as meaning that immigration should be allowed up to the limit of economic absorptive capacity. But the situation had changed, and the British Government definitely did not hold that opinion now. At present the British Government thought it necessary to take not only

economic, but political and psychological considerations into account. They did not think it right or obligatory under the Mandate to continue to follow the principle of economic absorptive capacity in the face of the deep rooted and genuine opposition of the national Arab movement.[80]

## *Ben-Gurion argues the Jewish legal case*

A discussion then ensued between Ben-Gurion and MacDonald regarding whether the British Government would be willing to condition Palestinian statehood on the consent of both Arabs and Jews. Ben-Gurion, who had studied law in Istanbul before World War I, argued that as a matter of law the Jews had the right to consent:

> The Jewish Delegation held that the Mandate could not be replaced by an independent State in which the Jews would be in the minority. The legal, political and moral position in Palestine was such that no independent State could be set up under conditions which precluded *a priori* Jewish consent. Such conditions would be the threat of deprivation of Jewish rights under the Balfour Declaration and the Mandate.[81]

The discussions between the British and Jewish sides continued the next day, Sunday 12 March. MacDonald addressed the three alternative forms of statehood Weizmann had proposed in his 10 March letter. MacDonald quickly ruled out partition, based on the findings of the 1938 Woodhead Commission that partition would be unworkable. As for the unitary or federal state options, MacDonald suggested the British Government would be willing to consider both but noted the Arabs would need much more time to accept anything other than a single state under their control.[82]

Ben-Gurion retorted that the Jews would never consent to a single, unitary state. Ben-Gurion noted that while the Palestinian Arabs might constitute the majority population of the country as against the Palestinian Jews, the Balfour Declaration and the Mandate also conferred rights on the entire *worldwide* Jewish diaspora to join their brethren in Palestine to help reconstitute the Jewish National Home. Given the Jewish Delegation represented the interests of *both* Palestinian and non-Palestinian Jews, the delegation could never consent to an arrangement cementing the current minority status of the Jewish population of Palestine under permanent Arab domination.

Ben-Gurion once again invoked the Zionist legal framing and narrative when addressing this issue:

> Palestine was to be the Jews' National Home, and this had been the primary object of the Mandate ... if the maintenance of the principle that Palestine was their home embittered the Arabs, then they were sorry, but they could not help it. That was the one thing they could never renounce ... Since the

> Jews had already acquiesced in the loss of Palestine east of the Jordan, they could not be accused of being unwilling to compromise. But any constitution in the remaining part of Palestine which was based on an Arab majority would place the Jews in a position of no longer being 'at home.' They had believed their status in Palestine to be already *res judicata*.[83]

As the Conference neared collapse, Weizmann met alone with MacDonald on 14 March. Weizmann continued invoking legal arguments, even at this late stage. For example, Weizmann complained bitterly at MacDonald's reliance on the January 1918 "Hogarth Message" to Sherif Hussein as somehow relevant or persuasive evidence of a material modification of the Balfour Declaration. Weizmann sarcastically noted the Hogarth Message "had been secret and had lain hidden in the archives of the Foreign Office for the last twenty years."[84]

Weizmann further argued, again in legal terms, that if the British Government

> [H]ad made contradictory declarations of policy, it was scarcely for the British Government to decide which of the two policies was binding. *It was a matter which ought to go to the Hague Court or to some impartial tribunal.* It was utterly wrong that the British Government should be both the party in dispute and the judge.[85]

## *British-Jewish talks collapse*

The British and Jewish delegations met for the last time the following evening, 15 March 1939. German troops had invaded Czechoslovakia and occupied Prague earlier that day, casting a pall over both the Jewish and British delegations.

MacDonald presented the revised and final British proposals for Palestine to the Jewish delegation, including (i) the establishment, after a transition period of unspecified length, of an independent Palestine State; (ii) the new Palestine State would be neither a Jewish nor an Arab State, but the interests of both sides would be safeguarded; (iii) an aggregate cap on Jewish immigration of 75,000 over the next five years, subject to the country's economic absorptive capacity, resulting in the Jewish population reaching a maximum of one-third of the overall population of Palestine by the end of the five-year period; (iv) any additional Jewish immigration after the expiration of the five-year period would be subject to Arab consent; and (v) vesting the High Commissioner in Palestine with the authority to prohibit and regulate transfers of land.[86]

MacDonald cabled High Commissioner Harold MacMichael in Palestine the following day to report on the status of the discussions with the Arab and Jewish delegations. MacDonald predicted the Jews "will most certainly reject our proposals." MacDonald said the Palestinian Arabs also opposed the British proposals, but the neighbouring Arab states were trying to bring the Palestinian Arabs on board by pressuring the British to agree to a fixed date of ten years for the Palestinian state to be established. MacDonald asked MacMichael for his views.[87]

MacMichael cabled back the next day, noting the Palestinian Arabs would not be satisfied even with a Jewish immigration cap of 75,000. The Palestinian Arabs, according to MacMichael, wanted all Jewish immigration halted immediately. The Palestinian Arabs also demanded a fixed date for the end of the transition period and their gaining control of Palestine as a majority Arab State. MacMichael, however, recommended against agreeing to a fixed date "in the absence of guarantees of cooperation" from the Palestinian Arabs with the remainder of MacDonald's proposals.[88]

## *British meetings with the Arab delegations*

The British delegation met jointly with the Palestinian Arabs and the representatives of the Arab states in plenary sessions from early February through mid-March. The British and Palestinian Arab delegations also formed a smaller, joint committee to meet separately to discuss their differing interpretations of the McMahon-Hussein correspondence.

### *Arab-British plenary meetings*

The British and Arab delegations commenced their separate meetings on 9 February 1939. Jamal Husseini, the lead delegate for the Palestinian Arabs, read an opening statement.[89] The statement had been typewritten on the letterhead of the Egyptian Embassy in London and signed by both Husseini and George Antonius.[90]

Husseini's opening statement was laced with the long-standing Palestinian Arab legal framing and legal narrative. He began by arguing the Palestinian Arab case was based on "self-evident justice." He then took aim at the Balfour Declaration and the Mandate, again basing his argument on legal concepts, in what the *Times* would characterise as "an appeal for justice:"[91]

> The Arabs have never recognised and never will recognise the Balfour Declaration or the Mandate. The first contained a promise which Great Britain was not entitled to make without Arab consent and which was, in any case, invalid, since it conflicted with a previous and binding British pledge. The second is an illegal document. The terms of the Mandate which could only have derived their sanction from the Covenant of the League of Nations are demonstrably in conflict with the letter and spirit of the relevant article (namely Article XXII) of the Covenant. The Palestine Arab delegation are prepared to present an argument to prove conclusively the invalidity of the Balfour Declaration and the basic illegality of the Mandate. They consider that the measures taken in virtue of the provisions of the Mandate, such as facilities given Jews to enter Palestine, acquire land, and enjoy other exceptional privileges … must be regarded as null and void and deserving, on legal as well as on moral and political grounds, to be abrogated.[92]

Husseini summarised the four key Palestinian Arab demands as (i) establishing an independent Arab State in Palestine; (ii) abandoning the attempt to establish a Jewish National Home in Palestine; (iii) abrogating the Mandate and "the illegalities resulting from it"; and (iv) halting Jewish immigration and land sales to Jews immediately.[93]

At the next meeting, on 11 February, Husseini again addressed the McMahon-Hussein correspondence in legal terms, noting "a question of contract was at issue, and ... such a question could not be discussed on the basis of the intention of the parties, but the text of the documents."[94]

The representatives of the Arab states also invoked the Palestinian legal framing and legal narrative in their remarks. For example, on 13 February, Iraqi Prime Minister Nuri al-Said opened the discussion by expressing sympathy with the plight of European Jewry, while simultaneously making clear the Arab view that "the unfortunate position of the Jews in Europe would not be used as an argument for *denying justice* to the Arabs of Palestine."[95]

Nuri next turned to the McMahon-Hussein correspondence, invoking many of the legal arguments the Arabs had been making for the past nearly 20 years. For example, Nuri argued, in decidedly legal terms, that McMahon had been communicating on behalf of the British Government, and therefore, his explanation years later regarding his personal intent was irrelevant:

> Sir Henry McMahon was therefore only an instrument in the matter and his personal opinion at a later date was not relevant to the argument. When a dispute between parties over the interpretation of documents arose in an English court, it was the custom to take the grammatical and literal sense of the words as binding, and intentions were not taken into account unless it was evident that at the time both parties had been using certain words in a special sense.[96]

Nuri further argued that the Balfour Declaration had caught the Arabs by surprise, coming as it did while the war against Turkey was still underway. The Arabs sought reassurances from the British Government, which they received from Commander Hogarth in his January 1918 message to Sherif Hussein. The Hogarth Message, according to Nuri, had clarified the "National Home" Britain promised the Jews in the Balfour Declaration would amount to nothing more than a Jewish "spiritual or cultural center" in Palestine, without prejudice to Palestinian Arab political and economic rights in Palestine.[97] Thus, Nuri argued, Britain undertook legal obligations regarding future sovereignty in Palestine solely to the Arabs and not the Jews.

On 14 February, Prince (and future King) Faisal of Saudi Arabia made a lengthy legal argument on behalf of the Palestinian Arab cause. Faisal began by asserting the familiar Arab legal argument that the McMahon-Hussein correspondence had promised independence to the Arabs of Palestine. Faisal argued that the international community had supported that view when it enacted

Article 22 of the Covenant of the League of Nations, promising independence for *all* former Ottoman-ruled Arab lands.[98]

Faisal then attacked the legality of the Balfour Declaration:

> The Balfour Declaration was illegal on four grounds; first, because it was subsequent to the undertaking given to the Arabs which, therefore, had the prior right in the event of conflict; secondly, because it was made without consultation with the Arabs; thirdly, because it was inconsistent with Article 22 of the Covenant; … and fourthly, because it was inconsistent with international law and morality.[99]

On 16 February, MacDonald opened the British-Arab meeting by acknowledging the Palestinian Arab view that the Balfour Declaration and the Mandate were illegal. However, MacDonald reiterated the British Government and the League of Nations were committed to upholding *both* documents and were committed to protecting Jewish rights in Palestine. But MacDonald then made a huge concession to the Arab side:

> The meaning of the National Home promise in the Balfour Declaration had never been properly defined. Certain of its authors (for example Mr. Lloyd George and President Wilson) had, however, expressed the view that it was intended to lead up to a Jewish commonwealth; so far this had been a possibility, and a possibility most threatening to the Arabs of Palestine. *His Majesty's Government did not think it right that this uncertainty should continue any longer, and would propose to make a public announcement to the effect that they did not contemplate that Palestine should become a Jewish state* – unless of course the Arabs should themselves wish it.[100]

In response to a question from George Antonius (Figure 3.4) MacDonald clarified the British Government "would not contemplate a sovereign Jewish State in *any part* of Palestine" and expressed the hope that "this definite interpretation of the Balfour Declaration would … bring some measure of reassurance to the Arabs of Palestine."[101]

Both Jamal Husseini and Antonius argued forcefully in favour of the immediate establishment of a democratic, majority-ruled state in Palestine, promising the minority Jewish population would be treated well:

> Jamal Husaini said that the Arabs did not wish to get rid of the Jews, but that if the Jews wished to leave Palestine, so much the better. If they wished to remain, the Jews would be given the same status as others and there would be no question of domination.[102]

MacDonald countered that while Britain did not favour the establishment of a Jewish State, it likewise did not favour the establishment of an independent *Arab*

**FIGURE 3.4** George Antonius (Public Domain)

State but instead preferred the establishment of an independent *Palestine* state in which neither Jew dominated Arab nor Arab dominated Jew.[103]

The British and Arab delegations convened again on 27 February 1939. MacDonald opened the meeting by presenting the same list of "suggestions" for the Arabs to consider that MacDonald had already presented to the Jewish side three days earlier.

In response to questions from Jamal Husseini regarding ongoing Jewish immigration, MacDonald said the British Government envisioned immigration would be allowed to continue at a reduced rate for the next five years, but "not to exceed a figure which would leave the total Jewish population, at the end of the period, in a very considerable minority."[104] MacDonald added the caveat that any additional Jewish immigration would also be subject to the economic absorptive capacity of the country.

Husseini also asked about further land sales to Jews. MacDonald said the Government was contemplating vesting the British High Commissioner in Palestine with full powers to prohibit or restrict land sales to Jews, as "the time had arrived to restrict land sales to Jews in the interest of Arab cultivators."[105]

The day after the 27 February meeting between the British and Arab delegations, and three days after MacDonald had presented the same suggestion to the

Jewish side, the *Times* reported "[t]he Arabs were jubilant about the proposals, the Jews cast down and bitter."[106]

On 1 March, the British and Arab delegations met to discuss the suggestions the British delegation had shared at the 27 February meeting. Jamal Husseini criticised the proposals as vague and not satisfying Palestinian Arab demands for an independent, majority-ruled state under their control. MacDonald seemed taken aback by Husseini's rejectionist approach, while reiterating the British Government's different conception of the precise contours of Palestinian statehood:

> The British Delegation's suggestions ... represented an immense concession to the point of view of the Palestinian Delegation ... the Palestinian Delegation had demanded the creation of an independent Arab State, whereas the British Delegation's suggestion involved an independent Palestinian State, in which the whole people of Palestine, Arabs and Jews alike, would equally enjoy self-government. Mr. MacDonald suggested that he thought the British Delegation's suggestions represented a very great concession, since they gave to the people of Palestine the gift of freedom, the most prized possession of all peoples.[107]

On 15 March, the British and Arab delegations met again. MacDonald presented the Arabs with the same proposals he would read to the Jewish side during their meeting that same day.[108] The Arab delegates viewed the proposals as vague and unsatisfactory. They pressed MacDonald to explain *exactly* what Britain meant by proposing an independent "Palestine" state, in which neither Arabs nor Jews would "dominate" the other. How would this differ, they demanded to know, from any other democratic country governed by a majority yet containing a substantial minority population? Did the British intend to confer a form of super-minority status on the Jews, perhaps vesting them with veto power over the majority Arab population who presumably would end up in control of the government?[109]

MacDonald answered all the Arab questions patiently but grew frustrated at the seeming Arab reluctance to appreciate how far the British had gone to accede to Arab demands, especially regarding Jewish immigration:

> Under the new proposals, the last word on immigration, after five years, would be with the Arabs. This was a *revolutionary* change in British policy, a reversal of policy on the most important question. Hitherto the Arabs of Palestine had feared the indefinite continuance of immigration which might lead eventually to a Jewish majority. It would now rest with them to decide whether the Jewish population of Palestine should go beyond approximately one-third of the total.[110]

Ultimately, as MacDonald advised the Cabinet at its meeting on 22 March, the Palestinian Arabs rejected the British proposals due to "our refusal to put a definite time limit to the transition period. The Palestinian Arabs had thought that the failure to put a time limit on the transition period would have the effect of encouraging the Jews in an attitude of non-co-operation."[111]

Even after the London Conferences ended in failure, Prime Minister Chamberlain remained determined to try to win over the Arabs with even further concessions. On 18 March 1939, Chamberlain asked Sir Miles Lampson, the British Ambassador to Egypt, what further concessions might be made to the Palestinian Arabs to persuade them to cease their violence. Chamberlain told Lampson he was prepared to delay publication of the new Government White Paper pending further outreach to the Palestinian Arabs.[112]

For the next several weeks, and prior to the 17 May publication of the White Paper, the British Government continued discussions with the Arab states, who sent additional proposals in April 1939. The proposals called for a ten-year transition period, more restrictions on Jewish immigration during the first five years, and the drafting of a new constitution at the end of the first three years.[113]

### *Arab-British Joint Committee regarding the McMahon-Hussein correspondence*

On 15 February 1939, the British and Arab delegations convened for their sixth formal meeting. The meeting was dominated by discussion of the McMahon-Hussein correspondence, including the Arab view that the dispute regarding the proper interpretation of the correspondence required "a careful legal examination."[114] The Prince of Yemen, for example, emphasised the legal nature of the dispute regarding the correspondence:

> His Royal Highness said there should be no difference of opinion among those who wanted to take a fair view, and certainly among scholars, that the only method of interpreting legal documents was to bring out the clarity of the meaning of the words in their ordinary and every day sense.[115]

The Prince suggested the matter of the McMahon-Hussein correspondence be referred to a subcommittee that comprised British and Palestinian Arab representatives and legal experts, as well as representatives from the surrounding Arab states. The subcommittee, later renamed the Joint Committee, would submit its report to the entire British-Arab conference for approval. MacDonald agreed with the suggestion, and the formation of the Joint Committee was approved.[116]

The Joint Committee met four times in London between 23 February and 16 March 1939. The Joint Committee considered the long-standing Arab legal arguments regarding the McMahon-Hussein correspondence and the British responses to those arguments.[117]

The Arab members of the Joint Committee included the historian George Antonius and the famed Palestinian lawyer Auni Bey Abdul Hadi, who had represented the Arab side before the Shaw, Lofgren, and Peel Commissions.

Sir Michael McDonnell, the former Chief Justice of Palestine, served as legal adviser to the Arab members of the Joint Committee and participated actively as their advocate during the Committee's discussions.

The British members included the Lord Chancellor (who acted as overall Chair of the Joint Committee), Sir Grattan Bushe, the Legal Adviser to the Colonial Office, and Lacy Baggallay of the Foreign Office. The Lord Chancellor announced at the Joint Committee's first meeting that

> [H]e was not present in any judicial capacity and that he made no claim to decide, as a judge, whether the views of His Majesty's Government in the United Kingdom upon the questions at issue, or the views of the Arabs, were right: he was present as the representative of His Majesty's Government only, with the sole function of expounding and advocating their views upon these questions.[118]

The Joint Committee considered various new legal arguments the Arab side had not previously offered during the various legal proceedings and commissions of inquiry that had convened during the Mandate years. The most important of those arguments involved the meaning of the so-called Hogarth Message of 4 January 1918, delivered to Sherif Hussein two months after the Balfour Declaration. George Antonius, one of the Arab members of the Joint Committee, disclosed the existence of the Hogarth Message in his book *The Arab Awakening*, published only a few months prior to the start of the London Conferences.[119]

According to Antonius, the Sherif was "greatly disturbed" by the 2 November 1917 Balfour Declaration and requested an explanation, lest he change his mind about continuing to support the British against Turkey during World War I. The British Government dispatched Commander David George Hogarth to Jeddah to meet with Hussein during the first week of January, 1918. Hogarth did not deliver anything in writing to Hussein. But according to Antonius, Hussein's contemporaneous notes reveal Hogarth, acting on instructions from London, gave Hussein an "explicit assurance that 'Jewish settlement in Palestine would only be allowed in so far as would be consistent with the *political* and economic freedom of the Arab population.'"[120]

Antonius argued the wording of the Hogarth Message, especially the phrase "*political* and economic freedom," should be viewed as a "fundamental departure from the text of the Balfour Declaration."[121] According the Antonius, the Hogarth Message *expanded* the Balfour Declaration's promise to the Arabs to protect the *civil* and religious rights of existing non-Jewish communities in Palestine and simultaneously *narrowed* the scope of the Declaration's promise to the Jewish people of a National Home in Palestine. Hogarth's use of the broader term "political," according to Antonius, meant Britain *never* intended the Balfour Declaration to permit the Jews to become the majority population in Palestine or to achieve Jewish statehood in *any* portion of Palestine.[122]

In the eyes of the Arab advocates, the Hogarth Message represented the smoking gun the Palestinian Arabs had long sought. For them, it meant game, set, and match.

Subsequent commentators, however, have vigorously disputed Antonius' reliance on the Hogarth Message as reliable evidence of British intent regarding the Balfour Declaration. One historian has assailed Antonius' account as having "no basis in fact" and "worthless," noting the drafters of the Hogarth Message intended it to serve as "nothing more than a reiteration of the Balfour Declaration."[123]

Another commentator, relying on Hogarth's own contemporaneous notes and correspondence, argued the phrase "in so far as is compatible with the political and economic freedom of the Arab population" was *not* intended to concede *any* claims of Arab sovereignty over Palestine and at most should be understood as referring *only* to local self-government.[124] Even more significantly, Hogarth reported to London that Hussein raised *no* objections to the Balfour Declaration.[125]

But one passage from Hogarth's subsequent notes of his meeting with the Sherif tends to support the Palestinian Arab interpretation of the Hogarth message:

> The King would not accept an independent Jew State in Palestine, *nor was I instructed to warn him that such a state was contemplated by Great Britain.* He probably knows little or nothing of the actual or possible economy of Palestine and his ready assent to Jewish settlement there is not worth very much. But I think he appreciates the financial advantage of Arab co-operation with the Jews.[126]

The British Government was aware of the significance of this phrase in Hogarth's note and decided not to publish it when it released the text of the Hogarth message as an Appendix to the Joint Committee's report. Baggallay minuted the phrase would be "rather damaging" if made public.[127] Both Baxter and Butler of the Foreign Office agreed with Baggallay, and the decision was made to keep Hogarth's notes concealed from public view.[128]

The Hogarth Message made a big impact on Lord Maugham, who told the Cabinet in early March:

> [H]aving made a careful study of the pledges and undertakings given at various dates, in particular the statement made by Commander Hogarth to the Sherif of Mecca as to the meaning of the Balfour Declaration, he [the Lord Chancellor] felt satisfied that the honour of this country demanded some such limitation of Jewish immigration as the Colonial Secretary now proposed.[129]

The Hogarth Message was not the only piece of evidence brought before the Joint Committee. Other evidence tended to support the British claim that the Sherif understood that McMahon had not included Palestine in his pledge.

For example, another first-hand recollection, made public only four days before the Joint Committee's first meeting, came from Colonel C.E. Vickery, who served as the British Agent at Jeddah to Hussein (by this time King of the Hedjaz) from 1919 to 1920. Vickery described a meeting with King Hussein in 1920, during which they discussed McMahon's 24 October 24 1915 letter. According to Vickery:

> I read the letter through very slowly; it was not written in very scholarly Arabic and had no English translation in the margin, and it was quite evident that Palestine was not included in the proposals to the King. I can say most definitely that the whole of the King's demands were centered round Syria, and only round Syria. Time after time he referred to that vineyard, to the exclusion of any other claim of interest. He stated most emphatically that he did not concern himself at all with Palestine, and had no desire to have suzerainty over it for himself or for his successors.[130]

The most important piece of first-hand evidence came from McMahon himself, who went public with his version of the events in a July 1937 letter to the *Times*, published several days after the release of the Palestine Royal Commission (Peel Commission) Report. As noted earlier, Iraqi Prime Minister Nuri al-Said had already argued prior to the formation of the Joint Committee that McMahon's intent carried no legal weight in construing the meaning of his letters to the Sherif.[131] But McMahon's letter to the *Times* addressed not just his own intent but also the Sherif's understanding of McMahon's intent:

> Sir,
>
> Many references have been made in the Palestine Royal Commission [Peel Commission] Report and in the course of the recent debates in both Houses of Parliament to the 'McMahon Pledge,' especially to that portion of the pledge which concerns Palestine and of which one interpretation has been claimed by the Jews and another by the Arabs.
>
> It has been suggested to me that continued silence on the part of the giver of the pledge may itself be misunderstood.
>
> I feel, therefore, called upon to make some statement on the subject, but I will confine myself in doing so to the point now at issue – i.e., whether that portion of Syria now known as Palestine was or was not intended to be included in the territories in which the independence of the Arabs was guaranteed by my pledge.
>
> I feel it is my duty to state, and I do so definitely and emphatically, that it was not intended by me in giving this pledge to King Hussein to include Palestine in the area in which Arab independence was promised.
>
> I also had every reason to believe at the time that the fact that Palestine was not included in my pledge was well understood by King Hussein.
>
> Yours faithfully,
>
> A. Henry McMahon[132]

Faced with conflicting evidence, the British side decided to agree with the Arab members of the Joint Committee that the Sherif intended to *include* Palestine in his original letter to McMahon. However, the British side stood behind McMahon and his July 1937 explanation of his intent to *exclude* Palestine from the areas earmarked for Arab independence:

> The United Kingdom representatives ... maintain that on a proper construction of the Correspondence Palestine was in fact excluded. But they agree that the language in which its exclusion was expressed was not so specific and unmistakable as it was thought to be at the time.[133]

Despite the British-Arab disagreement regarding the meaning of McMahon's 24 October 1915 letter to the Sherif, the British side agreed to the following language in the Joint Committee's final report, joining with the Arab side in declaring:

> In the opinion of the Committee it is, however, evident ... that His Majesty's Government were not free to dispose of Palestine without regard to the wishes and interests of the inhabitants of Palestine, and that these statements must all be taken into account in any attempt to estimate the responsibilities which – upon any interpretation of the Correspondence – His Majesty's Government have incurred towards those inhabitants as a result of the Correspondence.[134]

The Palestinian Arabs, thanks to Antonius' work in unearthing the Hogarth Message, had achieved a huge victory. The British, who for the past two decades had rejected *all* Arab claims regarding the McMahon-Hussein correspondence, now agreed the Arab claims had "greater force than has appeared hitherto,"[135] requiring Britain to take those claims into consideration as it formulated a new policy for Palestine. Given the British had already decided to take a new direction in Palestine even before the London Conferences convened, the Joint Committee's work provided additional cover for Britain's dramatic policy change and abandonment of its support for Zionism.

The Jewish Agency, excluded from the Joint Committee and suspicious of its activity, wrote to MacDonald on 28 March, offering its own interpretation of the McMahon-Hussein correspondence. The Jewish Agency argued the correspondence did not promise Palestine to the Arabs and complained the Jews had not been included on the Joint Committee. The letter concluded with a largely legal point, namely, that the Jewish people held an "inalienable right" to reconstitute its home in Palestine, based on the terms of the Balfour Declaration and the Mandate.[136]

The Colonial Office rejected the Jewish Agency's letter in an internal memorandum explaining the Jewish side lacked standing to intervene in the debate regarding the McMahon-Hussein controversy, which involved purely British and Arab interests.[137]

The British Government reiterated the Joint Committee's findings in the White Paper, published two months later:

> In the recent discussions the Arab delegations have repeated the contention that Palestine was included within the area in which Sir Henry McMahon, on behalf of the British Government, in October, 1915, undertook to recognise and support Arab independence. The validity of this claim, based on the terms of the correspondence which passed between Sir Henry McMahon and the Sharif of Mecca, was thoroughly and carefully investigated by the British and Arab representatives during the recent conferences in London. Their report, which has been published, states that both the Arab and the British representatives endeavoured to understand the point of view of the other party but that they were unable to reach agreement upon an interpretation of the correspondence ... His Majesty's Government regret the misunderstandings which have arisen as regards some of the phrases used. For their part they can only adhere, for the reasons given by their representatives in the Report, to the view that the whole of Palestine west of Jordan was excluded from Sir Henry McMahon's pledge, and they therefore cannot agree that the McMahon correspondence forms a just basis for the claim that Palestine should be converted into an Arab State.[138]

## *Tripartite British-Arab-Jewish informal meetings*

Twice during the London Conferences, the British convened tripartite meetings with the Arab states (Egypt, Iraq, and Saudi Arabia, but not the Palestinian Arabs) and the Jews sitting together. The first such meeting occurred on 23 February 1939.[139] The Iraqi delegation's legal advisor also attended the meeting. The official British minutes of the meeting left out the substance of the discussion. One of the Jewish delegates, Professor Selig Brodetsky, took extensive notes.[140] According to Brodetsky, the parties exchanged pleasantries and reiterated their positions but accomplished little else.

Near the end of the meeting, Ben-Gurion emphasised the right of European Jews to immigrate to Palestine:

> [We] ought to be ready to make concessions to the Arabs on the basis of give and take provided the Arabs were willing to recognize the special status of the Jews in Palestine; if they refused, then there could be no discussion ... if there was anything to discuss with the Arab states at all, it was not the fate of the Yishuv but that of the Jews who were yet in Palestine.[141]

The second Arab-Jewish meeting took place on 7 March 1939.[142] The Egyptian delegate, Ali Maher Pasha, implored the Jewish side to "[m]ake a proclamation yourselves that for the sake of peace you are willing to stop immigration, or at least to limit it."[143] Weizmann responded with an olive branch, saying although 50,000–60,000 Jews could enter Palestine each year, it might be possible to "slow-down" that rate on the basis of give-and-take negotiations with the Arabs. MacDonald said there seemed to be "common ground" regarding reduced immigration, but Ben-Gurion immediately clarified the Jewish side was not offering a "slow-down."[144]

Several days later Ben-Gurion described the 23 February and 7 March meetings with the Arab states in a letter to his wife:

> We had two meetings with the representatives of the Arab countries (Iraq, Egypt and Saudi Arabia), one on February 23 and the other on March 7. The Chief spokesman on the Arab side at both meetings was the Egyptian delegate, Ali Maher Pasha. The first time he spoke about the Jews in Palestine as if they were Jews living in Egypt and Iraq, and promised us equal rights ... The second time he did not think of talking that way. By then he understood that the Jews in Palestine are not like the Jews in Egypt and Iraq. And although we have not yet persuaded the Arab countries to support Zionism, they now understand Zionism better than they did before, and they respect it more.[145]

## Termination of the London Conferences

On 15 March, just prior to MacDonald's final meetings with the Jewish and Arab sides, the British Cabinet convened to discuss the Conferences.[146] MacDonald claimed with unjustified optimism that the Jews (to whom MacDonald had presented the Government's final proposals on 13 March) were "fairly satisfied" with the British Government's proposal for an independent Palestine State (rather than a Palestinian *Arab* State). However, MacDonald more accurately reported that the Jewish side strongly opposed the proposed arrangements for the transition period, fearing proportional representation on the Advisory and Executive Councils would favour the Arabs and position them for eventual majority rule over the entire country. Most importantly, however, the Jews bitterly opposed the proposed restrictions on immigration and land sales.

MacDonald also previewed the anticipated Arab reactions to the proposals. MacDonald accurately predicted the Arabs would demand a fixed end to the transition period and a demand for Arab statehood in Palestine immediately upon the termination of the transition period. The Arabs would also oppose the five-year aggregate limit of 75,000 Jewish immigrants, preferring a complete ban on immigration, or at most the admission of no more than a total of 20,000 Jews over the next five years.

On 17 March 1939, the London Conferences were terminated following the Arab and Jewish formal rejections of the British proposals.[147] The Palestinian Arabs provided a written statement to the British Government, explaining their decision to reject the British proposals was based on (i) the failure of the British Government to agree to a fixed time period for the transition period from the Mandate to Palestinian statehood; (ii) the failure of the British Government to agree to an immediate halt to Jewish immigration, noting the "present population is larger than the country can support"; and (iii) the failure of the British Government to agree to an immediate ban on land sales to Jews.

MacDonald lamented, during his comments at this final meeting, the failure of the Palestinian Arabs to appreciate how far the British Government had gone to satisfy their demands:

> The British Government were trying to help the Palestinian Arabs to obtain their rights in practice by reducing the power of the Jews in this matter to a minimum. Progress throughout the transition period up to and including responsible government was to be independent of Jewish co-operation. Moreover, the Arabs were being given a veto on Jewish immigration, and the Jews would know that they could no longer rely on British support in that direction. The British Government were facing a practical problem and trying to face it in such a way as to remove any obstacles which could be removed to the attainment of Arab political rights. If the Palestine delegation was not satisfied it was free to say so, but what they could not do was to charge the British Delegation with throwing obstacles in the way.[148]

Britain had made far-reaching concessions to the Palestinian Arabs, including agreeing to cap Jewish immigration at an aggregate total of 75,000 for the next five years and giving the Arabs an outright veto on any Jewish immigration thereafter, thus locking in a permanent two-to-one Arab majority. Interestingly, it was the Saudi delegate, Fuad Bey Hamza, who originally had suggested the 75,000 figure to the British. Both Ali Maher of Egypt and Taufiq Suwaidi of Iraq agreed with the 75,000 figure and conveyed the offer to the Palestinian Arab delegation.[149] But the Palestinians rejected the offer, demanding instead that all Jewish immigration cease immediately.

In addition, the Palestinian Arabs were to be the beneficiaries of the original *one-state solution*, receiving independence and sovereignty over *all* of Palestine following a transition period. But the Palestinians insisted on a fixed date for attaining their independence.[150] The Palestinians also rejected the British insistence that the Jews would be permitted to maintain a "national home" in Palestine, which the British described as something more than mere minority rights but far less than autonomy in any portion of the country.

Despite the Arab misgivings regarding the lack of a fixed termination date for the transition period, this was the greatest offer ever made to the Palestinian Arabs in the entire history of the conflict, the true "deal of the century." They stood to gain eventual statehood and sovereignty over *all* of Palestine, with a British guarantee that the Jewish population would *never* exceed one-third of the country's total population prior to Arab statehood.

From the British and Jewish perspectives, this reflected a radical shift in Palestine policy. The Balfour Declaration was all but abandoned in favour of near total appeasement of every Arab demand. Britain chose to breach its binding legal obligations to the Jewish people under the Balfour Declaration and the Mandate, opting instead to use the law as a fig leaf for bowing to Arab demands based on the legally shaky McMahon-Hussein correspondence and Hogarth Message.

After the Conferences concluded, the British Government delayed the issuance of the White Paper for two months while it continued negotiating with representatives of the Arab states (but not the Palestinian Arabs) in Cairo.[151] Britain made three additional concessions during those talks, most importantly setting a ten-year aspirational termination date for the transition period. The Foreign Secretary noted at a 1 May 1939 Cabinet meeting that "it had been remarkable that the Arabs had not insisted on automatic self-government after ten years."[152]

But even these additional British concessions were not enough to satisfy the Palestinian Arabs, who rejected the British offer, insisting on obtaining *all* their demands to vindicate their sense of "justice." The Palestinian Arabs may have hoped the Arab states could obtain better terms for them, which they did during the post-conference negotiations with the British. Or perhaps, the Palestinian Arabs were counting on their position growing even stronger in the event war were to break out between Britain and Germany.

Regardless of the reason, the Palestinians squandered their best opportunity during the entire history of the conflict to acquire sovereignty and statehood in *all* of Palestine.[153]

## Notes

1 CO 733/415/17, Conferences on Palestine, 1939: Notes on General Arrangements at 2; FO 371/23223, Conferences on Palestine, United Kingdom Delegation, Programme for Opening Meetings (4 February 1939). Although the Egyptian, Saudi, and Iraqi delegates agreed to participate in two "informal" meetings under British auspices with the Jewish side, those meetings produced no agreement. Esco Foundation for Palestine, *Palestine: A Study of Jewish, Arab, and British Policies*, Vol. II at 891 (Yale Univ. Press, 1947).

2 CO 733/415/17, "Conferences on Palestine, 1939: Notes on General Arrangements" at 6.

3 Auni Bey was one of the principal architects of the Palestinian Arab strategy during the 1920s and 1930s to frame the political conflict between Zionists and Palestinian Arab nationalists as a *legal* dispute. Auni Bey developed the legal framing and narrative that dominated Palestinian rhetoric during those early years and into the modern era. In addition to his participation both as lawyer and witness in the various trials pitting the Jews, Arabs and British against each other in the 1920s and 1930s, Auni Bey also wrote extensively on the subject, framing the Palestine conflict in legal narrative. *See, e.g.*, A. Abdul Hadi, *The Balfour Declaration*, The Annals of the American Academy of Political and Social Science, 164:1 at 12–21 (1932); League of Nations Archives, R2286, 6A/23373/224, "On the Palestine White Paper of 1930," Memorandum by Ouni Bey Abdul Hadi on behalf of the Arab Executive Committee (December 1930).

4 Article 22 of the Covenant of the League of Nations provided, in part, that, "Certain communities formerly belonging to the Turkish Empire have reached a stage of development where their existence as independent nations can be provisionally recognized subject to the rendering of administrative advice and assistance by a Mandatory until such time as they are able to stand alone." League of Nations, The Covenant of the League of Nations (1919). Arab lawyers and legal scholars have argued ever since that Article 22 was intended to codify McMahon's pledge to Hussein, guaranteeing self-determination in Palestine only to the majority local Arab population who had lived under Turkish rule and not to Jewish/Zionist immigrants from overseas.

5 Article 20 of the Covenant of the League of Nations provides, "The Members of the League severally agree that this Covenant is accepted as abrogating all obligations or understandings inter se which are inconsistent with the terms thereof, and solemnly undertake that they will not hereafter enter into any engagements inconsistent with the terms thereof. In case any Member of the League shall, before becoming a Member of the League, have undertaken any obligations inconsistent with the terms of this Covenant, it shall be the duty of such Member to take immediate steps to procure its release from such obligations." League of Nations, The Covenant of the League of Nations (1919). Arab lawyers and legal scholars have argued ever since that this language nullified the Balfour Declaration as inconsistent with McMahon's pledge to Hussein, as codified in Article 22.

6 G. Antonius, *The Arab Awakening: The Story of the Arab National Movement* (Hamish Hamilton, 1938).

7 The Foreign Office began discussions with the League of Nations Secretariat in January 1939 regarding the procedure it would need to follow to work with the PMC and the Council of the League of Nations to obtain amendments to the Mandate. *See, e.g.*, FO 371/23248, *Question de la convocation, en 1939, d'une session extraordinaire de la Commission permanente des Mandats consacree a la Palestine, Note preliminaire* (9 January 1939); FO 371/23248, various minutes discussing procedure for obtaining amendment of the Mandate (10, 12, 13, and 17 January 1939).

8 CO 733/410/9, Note from Sir Grattan Bushe, Colonial Office Legal Advisor (19 January 1939) (concluding the only contemplated action requiring an amendment of the Mandate would have been the dissolution of the Jewish Agency, a step the British Government never ended up taking); League of Nations, Permanent Mandates Commission, Minutes of the Thirty-Sixth Session, Held at Geneva from 8 June to 29 June 1939, Official No. C.170.M.100.1939.VI, Minutes of 14th meeting at 110 (16 June 1939) (Colonial Secretary Malcolm MacDonald argues "the White Paper did not require any alteration of the Mandate; and, in coming to that conclusion, [the British Government] had naturally consulted with its own legal advisors on the matter").

9 CAB 24/282/4, C.P. 4 (39), Memorandum by the Secretary of State for the Colonies (Secret) (hereafter "MacDonald Memorandum") at paras. 54, 74 (18 January 1939).

10 Cmd. 1700, *Palestine: Correspondence with the Palestine Arab Delegation and the Zionist Organisation* (hereafter "Churchill White Paper") at 19 (1922).

11 MacDonald Memorandum, para. 14 (emphasis in original).

12 Churchill White Paper, *op. cit.*, at 19.

13 *See, e.g.*, League of Nations, Permanent Mandates Commission, C.355,M.147.1930.VI, Seventeenth Session, *Report to the Council of the League of Nations on the Work of the Session* at 142 (4 August 1930) ("The Commission views with approval the Mandatory Power's intention of keeping Jewish immigration proportionate to the country's capacity of economic absorption, as clearly intimated in the [Churchill] White Paper of 1922"); League of Nations, Permanent Mandates Commission, Minutes of the Thirty-Second (Extraordinary) Session, 23d Meeting (13 August 1937) ("M. Rappard pointed out that the mandate spoke of facilitating immigration. It had been found – and M. Rappard thought that everybody felt it to be reasonable – that that provision should be limited by the absorptive capacity. He admitted that 'absorptive capacity' was an extraordinarily

facile phrase which it was very difficult to interpret, especially in the present case, where immigration might very often increase the absorptive capacity, as it was immigration of capital as well as of labour. Admittedly, the phrase was elastic, but it described the policy that was inherent in the mandate"). The PMC frequently criticized British policy during the 1920s and 1930s as inconsistent with Britain's obligations to facilitate Jewish immigration and land acquisition. *See, e.g.,* S. Zipperstein, *op. cit.*, at 193–194.

14 Weizmann Archives 10-1486, Letter from Prime Minister Ramsay MacDonald to Chaim Weizmann (13 Feb. 1931).

15 *See generally* I. Troen, *Calculating the "Economic Absorptive Capacity" of Palestine: A Study of the Political Uses of Scientific Research*, Contemporary Jewry 10:2 at 31–32 (1989); S. Reichman, Y. Katz and Y. Paz, *The Absorptive Capacity of Palestine, 1882–1948*, Middle Eastern Studies 33:2 at 351–53 (1997).

16 MacDonald Memorandum, paras. 36, 55; *see also* C.P. 60 (38), Conclusions (Secret) of a Meeting of the Cabinet (21 December 1938) ("if another crisis should find us with a hostile Arab world behind us in the Middle East... our military position there would be quite untenable").

17 MacDonald Memorandum, para. 18.

18 *Id.*, para. 21.

19 *Id.*, paras. 25–31.

20 *Id.*, para. 38 (emphasis added).

21 *Id.*, para. 40.

22 *Id.*, para. 52.

23 *Id.*, para. 54.

24 *Id.*, para. 57.

25 *See* S. Zipperstein, op. cit.

26 *Id.*, paras. 23–31, 60, 65.

27 *Id.*, para. 62.

28 CAB 24/283/2, C.P. 29 (39), Cabinet Committee on Palestine Report (Secret) at paras. 7, 8, and 12 (30 January 1939).

29 FO 371/23219, MacKenzie memorandum (original draft dated 19 December 1938).

30 CAB 24/282/19, Memorandum (Secret) by Lord Halifax, Secretary of State for Foreign Affairs, *Palestine: Legal Arguments Likely to be Advanced by Arab Representatives* (23 January 1939, hereafter "Halifax Memorandum").

31 *Id.* at paras. 29, 46.

32 FO 371/23219, Letter from Baggallay to Downie (19 January 1939); *see also* CO 733/409/13 (same).

33 CO 733/409/13, Letter from Downie to Baggallay (1 February 1939).

34 FO 371/23222, McMahon-Hussein Correspondence: Notes for Mr. Trott (23 January 1939).

35 FO 371/23222, A.C. Trott, McMahon-Hussein Correspondence: Results of the examination of the Arabic texts of certain obscure passages (31 January 1939). Baggallay minuted his satisfaction with Trott's memorandum, noting it would "be of great use to future investigators and historians." Trott's conclusions also led Baggallay to say "I do not think it is necessary now to re-examine the legal case of His Majesty's Government ..." (Baggallay minute, 6 February 1939).

36 FO 371/23222, Baggallay minute (30 January 1939) and memorandum by Baggallay, *The Juridical Basis of the Arab Claim to Palestine: Views of the Lord Chancellor* (30 January 1939); *see also* CO 733/409/13 (same).

37 *Id.*

38 *Id.*

39 *Id.* The Lord Chancellor reiterated these and other arguments in support of the British position at a 24 February 1939 meeting of the Joint British-Arab Committee set up to consider the McMahon-Hussein correspondence. Cmd. 5974, *Report of a Committee set up to consider Certain Correspondence between Sir Henry McMahon and the Sharif of Mecca in*

*1915 and 1916*, Annex B at 20–29 (1939). The Colonial Office Legal Advisor, Sir Grattan Bushe (who would serve on the Joint Committee alongside the Lord Chancellor) reacted to the Lord Chancellor's arguments with a candid and ironic minute, writing "I doubt the arguments are very sound, *but we should never get anywhere on purely legal arguments*." CO 733/409/13, Bushe minute (6 February 1939) (emphasis added). The Lord Chancellor failed to mention one important legal argument that had been the subject of a letter to the *Times* several months earlier from the international legal scholar Ernst Frankenstein, who argued Britain had lacked the legal authority to promise Palestine *either* to the Arabs in October 1915 *or* the Jews in November 1917. However, following the end of World War I, the Principal Allied Powers chose to incorporate the Balfour Declaration into the Mandate, thereby vesting the Balfour Declaration with the status of international law, whereas the Principal Allied Powers did *not* do the same regarding McMahon's correspondence with the Sherif regarding Palestine. Thus, according to Frankenstein, even if McMahon *had* promised Palestine to the Sherif in 1915, the Principal Allied Powers *never* elevated that promise to the status of international law, as they had done with the Balfour Declaration. *The Times*, 23 August 1938 at 6.

40 CAB 23/97/3, Minutes (Secret) of Cabinet Meeting at 22 (1 February 1939).

41 *See* n.130 *infra* and accompanying text.

42 Y. Ben-Arieh, *The Making of Eretz Israel in the Modern Era: A Historical-Geographical Study (1799–1949)* at 573 (De Gruyter/Magnes, 2020).

43 *See* CO 733/408/15, Unsigned and undated report detailing tension between Palestinian Arab factions occurring at various meetings in Beirut in early January 1939 regarding representation at the London Conferences and policy positions to be advocated by the Palestinian Arabs. The Palestinian Arabs were divided into two camps. The Grand Mufti, Haj Amin al Husseini, controlled the Arab Higher Committee. The Nashashibi family, equally anti-Zionist but opposed to the Mufti's terror campaign, controlled the rival National Defense Party. *See* "The Palestine Conference," *The London Times* at 13 (23 January 1939) (discussing rivalry and tension between the Mufti and the Nashashibis). The British refused to allow the Mufti to attend the conference due to his role in agitating the Arab revolt. During December 1938 and January 1939, Colonial Secretary MacDonald kept the British Cabinet apprised of the status of the evolving Palestinian Arab delegation, as well as the anticipated attendance of the Arab States and the Jewish representatives. *See, e.g.*, CAB 23/96/12, Minutes (Secret) of a Meeting of the Cabinet at 23–24 (21 December 1938) (describing efforts to include moderate Palestinians to counterbalance the Mufti's supporters). The British Ambassador to Egypt, Sir Miles Lampson (later Lord Killearn), noted in his diary entry for 21 January 1939 that the Prime Minister and the various Arab states were making a "prize muddle of the whole business" by suggesting the Mufti travel to Cairo for negotiations regarding which of his political opponents would be asked to join the Palestinian delegation. Killearn Papers, GB 165-0176, Box 3, Middle East Centre Archive, St. Antony's College, Oxford. On 30 January, MacDonald and several other British officials met with Jamal Husseini, George Antonius, and other members of the Palestine Arab Higher Committee to try to persuade them, for the sake of showing a unified front to the world, to include Ragheb Nashashibi and at least one other member of the National Defense Party in their delegation. Husseini flatly refused, and Antonius accused the Jews of actively working behind the scenes to sow discord among the various Palestinian Arab factions. FO 371/23222, Conferences on Palestine, 1939, United Kingdom Delegation, Note of Informal Discussion with Palestinian Arab Delegation, paras. 4, 5 (31 January 1939). On 8 February, the day after the opening sessions, MacDonald reported to the Cabinet that the Mufti's supporters had accepted Ragheb Nashashibi but were still refusing to agree to the second proposed National Defense Party delegate. CO 733/406/11, Cabinet 6(39), Conclusions (Secret) of a Meeting of the Cabinet (8 February 1939). The dispute was resolved several days later, thereby permitting the British to negotiate with a single, albeit not completely unified Palestinian Arab delegation. CO 733/406/11, Cabinet 7(39), Extract (Secret) from Conclusions

of a Meeting of the Cabinet (15 February 1939) (MacDonald reported "since the last meeting of the Cabinet it had been possible to being the two separate Delegations of Palestinian Arabs into a single Delegation. The Conference had now settled down to separate discussions between British representatives and the representatives of the Arabs and of the Jews respectively"). *See also* Esco Foundation for Palestine, *Palestine: A Study of Jewish, Arab and British Policies* Vol. II at 888–89 (1947) (discussing Husseini-Nashashibi rivalry, including the Mufti's "systematic and ruthless plan of extermination of his opponents"). To induce the Palestinian Arabs to attend the London Conference, the British Government agreed to fund their travel expenses. CO 733/415/17, Conferences on Palestine, 1939: Notes on General Arrangements at 2. Intra-Arab rivalries were not confined to the Palestinians. The day before the formal opening session of the Conferences, the Yemeni Prince complained when he heard the Saudi Prince was to enter the ceremonial room at St. James's Palace before him. FO 371/23223, Formal Opening of Palestine Conferences at St. James's Palace (Baggallay minute, 6 February 1939).

44 League of Nations Archive, R4078/6A/668/37120, Letter from Abdur Rahman Siddiqi, All-India Muslim League, to Secretary General, League of Nations, enclosing "Statement of Indian Muslim Views on Palestine" (9 February 1939). Siddiqi's cover letter states the document had also been submitted to the British Government for its consideration during the London Conferences.

45 CO 733/415/17, "Conferences on Palestine, 1939: Notes on General Arrangements" at 10.

46 *Id.* at 17.

47 *See generally* S. Zipperstein, *op. cit.*

48 FO 371/23223, Conferences on Palestine, United Kingdom-Jewish Agency Delegation, Notes of the First Meeting held at St. James's Palace, London, at 4–6 (7 February 1939).

49 The *Times*, 11 February 1939 at 11.

50 CO 733/406/11, Letter from Malcolm MacDonald to Sir Alexander Hardinge (10 February 1939). MacDonald's letter to Hardinge raises the obvious question why the Colonial Secretary would have briefed Buckingham Palace about the ongoing discussions with the Arab and Jewish delegations. The file does not reflect whether Prime Minister Chamberlain knew of or authorized MacDonald's direct communications with the Palace.

51 FO 371/23223, Conferences on Palestine, United Kingdom Delegation, (Secret) Note of Informal Discussion with Members of the Jewish Agency Executive (1 February 1939).

52 FO 371/23223, Note of Mr. MacDonald's Discussion with Dr. Weizmann (4 February 1939).

53 *Id.*

54 *Id.*

55 FO 371/23223, Conferences on Palestine, United Kingdom-Jewish Agency Delegation, Draft Notes of the Second Meeting held at St. James's Palace, London, (unsigned minute, 12 February 1939).

56 *Id.* at D1–D2 (8 February 1939); *see also* Weizmann Archives 24-2047, Short Note of Meeting of Jewish Agency Executive, at 3 (19 February 1938) (Weizmann identifies Britain's Ambassador to Egypt Sir Miles Lampson as the architect of Britain's newly anti-Zionist policy, noting Lampson's top aide, Walter Smart, was Antonius' brother-in-law).

57 *Id.* at C1 (emphasis added).

58 *Id.* at F1. Five weeks later the Jewish Community of Poland sent a desperate telegram to Prime Minister Chamberlain: "In the darkest and most tragic hours of history and life of Jewry three and a half million Jews in Poland appeal to His Majesty's Government the authority which has undertaken responsibility to create a seat in Palestine for the Jewish people to consider both the confidence which the Jewish people have placed in England and the most sacred hopes of Jewry and not to apply a policy in Palestine which throws the Jewish masses into an abyss of despair." CO 733/407/6, Telegram from United Zion-

ist Organization of Poland and Agudas Israel of Poland to Prime Minister (17 March 1939). The British Government never responded to the telegram, and by 1944 only 75,000 Polish Jews had survived the Holocaust. *See* S. Zipperstein, "Uncovered, Polish Jews' pre-Holocaust plea to Chamberlain: Let us into Palestine," *Times of Israel*, 21 January 2020.

59 FO 371/23223, Conferences on Palestine, United Kingdom-Jewish Agency Delegation, Draft Notes of the Second Meeting held at St. James's Palace, London, at H1 (8 February 1939).

60 *Id.*

61 FO 371/23223, Conferences on Palestine, United Kingdom-Jewish Agency Delegation, Draft of Secretary's Notes of the Third Meeting held at St. James's Palace, London, at 7 (10 February 1939).

62 *Id.* at 10.

63 *Id.* at 12.

64 Weizmann Archives 12-2129, Note of Interview (Secret) with M.M., at 6 (18 February 1939).

65 *Id.* at 6–7.

66 *Id.*

67 FO 371/23226, Conferences on Palestine, Colonial Office Note (Confidential) on Jewish Agency's Memorandum of 20th February (28 February 1939).

68 *Id.* at 7.

69 George Antonius Papers, Middle East Centre Archive, St. Antony's College, Oxford, GB 165-0011, Box 2/5/2, Conferences on Palestine, United Kingdom-Arab Delegation, Draft Notes of the Eleventh Meeting held at St. James's Palace, London, at A1-B3 (27 February 1939). MacDonald obtained approval from the Cabinet Committee on Palestine at a meeting the day earlier (23 February) to propose the suggestions. CAB 24/284/3, Minutes (Secret) of meeting of Cabinet Committee on Palestine at 4–7 (23 February 1939).

70 Weizmann Archives 24-2135, Minutes of the 27th Meeting of the [Jewish Agency] Executive at 4 (7 March 1939).

71 FO 371/23226, Conferences on Palestine, (Secret) Note of Informal Conversation with Representatives of the Jewish Agency Delegation, at 1–2 (25 February 1939; note dated 27 February 1939, prepared by H.F. Downie of the Colonial Office). MacDonald told the British Cabinet at a briefing several days later that the Jewish ranks were divided, with Weizmann more willing to accept an independent and federal Palestine State with some limitation on Jewish immigration during the transition period (a cap of 20,000 per year but with no Arab veto on immigration beyond five years), but Ben-Gurion, Shertok and "other extreme Zionists" opposed Weizmann's willingness to make concessions. MacDonald said the representatives of the Arab States had privately expressed their willingness to agree to 10,000 Jewish immigrants per year for the next five years, subject to an Arab veto thereafter. MacDonald asked the Cabinet to allow him to negotiate further on the immigration and other issues for the next few days, knowing the British Government had already made up its mind to impose a cap on Jewish immigration for the next five years with an Arab veto thereafter. Nevertheless, MacDonald wanted to keep the discussions going for a few more days so the Jews would not "feel that they were being hustled." CO 733/406/11, C.P. 10 (39), Extract (Secret) from Conclusions of a Meeting of the Cabinet (8 March 1939); *see also* CO 733/406/11, C.P. 9 (39), Extract (Secret) from Conclusions of a Meeting of the Cabinet (2 March 1939) (MacDonald reports tension between Weizmann and Ben-Gurion to the Cabinet).

72 FO 371/23226, Cablegram from Louis D. Brandeis to Prime Minister Neville Chamberlain (26 February 1939). Brandeis had retired from the Supreme Court two weeks earlier, on 13 February 1939.

73 FO 371/23226, Conferences on Palestine, United Kingdom-Jewish Agency Delegation, Draft of Secretary's Notes of the Ninth Meeting held at St. James's Palace, London, at A1–A2 (27 February 1939).

74 FO 371/23229, Conferences on Palestine, Note (Secret) of Prime Minister's conversation with Dr. Weizmann, Mr. Ben-Gurion and Rabbi Wise (2 March 1939).

75 Weizmann Archives 22-2136, Weizmann Letters to MacDonald at para. 2 (9 and 10 March 1939). An earlier draft of the letter had also noted how the British Government had initially offered a much higher rate of immigration, between 15,000 and 30,000 per year, and for a longer period of time (ten vs. five years). Weizmann Archives 12-2136, Draft Letter to MacDonald (8 March 1939).

76 *Id.* at para. 3.

77 *Id.* at para. 4.

78 *Id.* at para. 6.

79 FO 371/23229, Conferences on Palestine, Informal Discussions with Jewish Delegates, Secretary's Notes of the Third Meeting held at St. James's Palace, London, at 2 (11 March 1939).

80 *Id. at 3.* The British Government had convinced itself by this point that it had only two options regarding Jewish immigration: either allow immigration to continue, subject only to the country's economic absorptive capacity, and against the will of the Arab majority (who feared the Jews would sooner or later overtake them unless immigration were halted), or restrict immigration for a period of time and then ban it altogether unless the Arabs would consent. The British rejected the former approach, as it would mean ruling the Arabs by force in perpetuity, in violation of the core purposes of Article 22 of the Mandate. *See, e.g.*, CO 733/410/5, Code Telegram No. 129 from Foreign Office to Sir Ronald Lindsay, British Ambassador to the United States (20 March 1939).

81 FO 371/23229, Conferences on Palestine, Informal Discussions with Jewish Delegates, Secretary's Notes of the Third Meeting held at St. James's Palace, London, at 9 (11 March 1939).

82 MacDonald reiterated to Weizmann three days later that a unitary, federal state represented the British Government's preferred outcome. Weizmann Archives 17-2137, Letter from MacDonald to Weizmann (15 March 1939).

83 FO 371/23229, Conferences on Palestine, Informal Discussions with Jewish Delegates, Secretary's Notes of the Fourth Meeting held at the Colonial Office, at 11–12 (12 March 1939).

84 FO 371/23230, Conferences on Palestine, Note of Conversation between Mr. MacDonald and Dr. Weizmann (14 March 1939) at 3.

85 *Id.* at 4 (emphasis added).

86 FO 371/23230, Conferences on Palestine, United Kingdom-Jewish Agency Delegation, Draft of Secretary's Notes of the Tenth Meeting held at St. James's Palace, London, at A3–A7 (15 March 1939).

87 FO 371/23230, Cypher Telegram No. 169 (Secret) from the Secretary of State for the Colonies to the High Commissioner for Palestine (16 March 1939). The Foreign Office sent similar cables, describing the British Government's final proposals, to the British Ambassadors in Cairo, Baghdad, Jedda, and Washington, DC. CO 733/406/11, Cypher Telegram Nos. 184/85, 55/56, 34/35 and 119/120 (14 March 1939). In a separate telegram to the British Ambassador in Washington, DC, the Foreign Office asked the Ambassador to explain to the State Department that Britain had rejected the Arab demand for an Arab State in Palestine, as Britain was not prepared to define the precise nature of the future Palestine State until the end of the transition period, depending on the level of cooperation from both Arabs and Jews. CO 733/406/11, Cypher Telegram No. 121 from Foreign Office to R.C. Lindsey (15 March 1939).

88 FO 371/23230, Cypher Telegram from the High Commissioner for Palestine to the Secretary of State for the Colonies (17 March 1939).

89 George Antonius Papers, Middle East Centre Archive, St. Antony's College, Oxford, GB 165-0011, Box 2/5/1, Conferences on Palestine, United Kingdom-Arab Delegation, Draft Notes of the Second Meeting held at St. James's Palace, London, at 1 (9 February 1939).

90 George Antonius Papers, Middle East Centre Archive, St. Antony's College, Oxford, GB 165-0011, Box 2/5/1, Statement by the Palestine Arab Delegation (9 February 1939).
91 *The Times*, "The Arab Case: An Appeal for Justice" (11 February 1939).
92 George Antonius Papers, Middle East Centre Archive, St. Antony's College, Oxford, GB 165-0011, Box 2/5/1, Statement by the Palestine Arab Delegation (9 February 1939) at 4.
93 *Id.* at 7–8.
94 George Antonius Papers, Middle East Centre Archive, St. Antony's College, Oxford, GB 165-0011, Box 2/5/1, Conferences on Palestine, United Kingdom-Arab Delegation, Draft Notes of the Third Meeting held at St. James's Palace, London, at C1 (11 February 1939).
95 George Antonius Papers, Middle East Centre Archive, St. Antony's College, Oxford, GB 165-0011, Box 2/5/1, Conferences on Palestine, United Kingdom-Arab Delegation, Draft Notes of the Fourth Meeting held at St. James's Palace, London, at A1 (13 February 1939) (emphasis added).
96 *Id.* at B2.
97 *Id.* at B3–B4.
98 George Antonius Papers, Middle East Centre Archive, St. Antony's College, Oxford, GB 165-0011, Box 2/5/1, Conferences on Palestine, United Kingdom-Arab Delegation, Draft Notes of the Fifth Meeting held at St. James's Palace, London, at A1–A3 (14 February 1939).
99 *Id.* at B1.
100 George Antonius Papers, Middle East Centre Archive, St. Antony's College, Oxford, GB 165-0011, Box 2/5/1, Conferences on Palestine, United Kingdom-Arab Delegation, Draft Notes of the Seventh Meeting held at St. James's Palace, London, at B1 (16 February 1939) (emphasis added). Antonius corrected the original typewritten version of MacDonald's statement by interlineating in pencil, rendering the new version as "His Majesty's Government … did not contemplate that a Jewish State should be established in Palestine." The difference between the original version and Antonius' version was that MacDonald said Palestine would not become a Jewish State, whereas Antonius corrected the statement to say a Jewish State would not be established in *any portion* of Palestine.
101 *Id.* (emphasis added.)
102 *Id.* at C4.
103 *Id.* at F1–F2.
104 *Id.* at C3.
105 *Id.* at D1.
106 *Id.*, 28 Feb. 1939 at 14.
107 George Antonius Papers, Middle East Centre Archive, St. Antony's College, Oxford, GB 165-0011, Box 2/5/2, Conferences on Palestine, United Kingdom-Arab Delegation, Draft Notes of the Twelfth Meeting held at St. James's Palace, London, at C1–C2 (1 March 1939).
108 George Antonius Papers, Middle East Centre Archive, St. Antony's College, Oxford, GB 165-0011, Box 2/5/2, Conferences on Palestine, United Kingdom-Arab Delegation, Draft Notes of the Thirteenth Meeting held at St. James's Palace, London, at A3–A7 (15 March 1939). The British Cabinet Committee on Palestine (which included Prime Minister Chamberlain) approved the proposals at a meeting two days earlier. FO 371/23229, Cabinet Committee on Palestine, Draft Conclusions (Secret) of the Eighth Meeting of the Committee (13 March 1939).
109 *Id.* at B1–E4.
110 *Id.* at C4 (emphasis added).
111 CO 733/406/11, Cabinet 14(39), Extract (Secret) from Conclusions of a Meeting of the Cabinet, para. 5 (22 March 1939). MacDonald told the Cabinet the representatives of the Arab States, although also publicly opposed to the British proposals,

privately said they regarded the British proposals as "wise and reasonable." *See also* CO 733/406/11, Cypher Telegram (Nos. 198, 65 and 39) from Foreign Office to British Ambassadors to Egypt, Iraq and Saudi Arabia (20 March 1939) ("The main reason given by the Arabs for rejecting British proposals was the absence of a time limit for the transition period").

112 CO 733/406/11, Telegram No. 199 from Lampson to Foreign Office (18 March 1939).

113 Esco Foundation for Palestine, *op. cit.*, Vol. II at 900-01.

114 George Antonius Papers, Middle East Centre Archive, St. Antony's College, Oxford, GB 165-0011, Box 2/5/1, Conferences on Palestine, United Kingdom-Arab Delegation, Draft Notes of the Sixth Meeting held at St. James's Palace, London, at C3 (15 February 1939) (statement of Prince Said ul-Islam of Yemen).

115 *Id.* at D1.

116 *Id.* at E5, F2; *see also* CO 733/415/17, Conferences on Palestine, 1939: Notes on General Arrangements at 8–9.

117 For further background regarding those legal arguments, *see* S. Zipperstein, *op. cit.*, ch. 1.

118 Cmd. 5974, *Report of a Committee Set Up to Consider Certain Correspondence Between Sir Henry McMahon [His Majesty's High Commissioner in Egypt] and the Sharif of Mecca in 1915 and 1916* at 4 (16 March 1939).

119 G. Antonius, *op. cit.*, at 267-68. Jamal Husseini years later described Antonius as one of the two "main Arab strategists" during the 1939 London Conferences. W. Khalidi, *On Albert Hourani, the Arab Office, and the Anglo-American Committee of 1946*, Journal of Palestine Studies, 35:1, 60–79 at 64 (2005).

120 Cmd. 5964, *Statements Made on Behalf of His Majesty's Government during the Year 1918 in regard to the Future Status of Certain Part of the Ottoman Empire (1939) (including the Hogarth Message)*; G. Antonius, *op. cit.*, at 269. Antonius' book is widely regarded as a classic text of the history of Arab nationalism in the early 20th century. Unfortunately, however, Antonius dedicated his book to the notorious anti-Semite Charles R. Crane, who had served as co-Chair of the King-Crane Commission. President Woodrow Wilson sent the Commission to Palestine and Syria in 1919 to study the proposed post-War mandates and the Arab desire for self-determination. Crane told William E. Dodd, the incoming United States Ambassador to Germany in 1934, that Hitler should be allowed to "have his way" with the Jews. W. E. Dodd and M. Dodd, *Ambassador Dodd's Diary* at 24–25 (diary entry, 4 July 1933) (Victor Gollancz, 1945). Crane also complained to Sir John Chancellor, the former British High Commissioner in Palestine, that "I do not like the idea of attributing everything that goes wrong in the Jewish world to Hitler. The minute they are caught in one of their tricks they immediately cry Hitler! Hitler!!" Chancellor Papers, MSS. Brit. Emp. S.284, Bodleian Libraries, Oxford, Box 20/MF16 (Letter from Crane to Chancellor, 11 February 1934).

121 G. Antonius, *op. cit.*, at 268.

122 *Id.* at 267–69.

123 E. Kedourie, *In the Anglo-Arab Labyrinth: The McMahon-Husayn Correspondence and Its Interpretations 1914–1939* at 282-84 (Frank Cass, 1976). According to Kedourie, Sir Mark Sykes, who drafted the Hogarth Message, "could not have had in mind any substantive, let alone fundamental, change in the Balfour declaration; for this reason if no other: such a change would have required ministerial authority." *Id.* at 283.

124 Esco Foundation for Palestine, *op. cit.*, Vol. I at 191–93.

125 C. Sykes, *Crossroads to Israel: 1917–1948* at 30 (Indiana University Press, 1965).

126 FO 371/23229, Hogarth note to High Commissioner, Cairo (extract) (15 January 1918) (emphasis added).

127 FO 371/23229, Baggallay Minute (10 March 1939); *see also* FO 371/23229, Letter from Baggallay to MacDonald (9 March 1939)("we should give the Arabs enough to show that the message was in fact delivered in the form intended, but need not go into the matter of King Hussein having given the impression that he would refuse to have a Jewish State").

128 FO 371/23229, Baxter and Butler Minutes (both 11 March 1939).

129 CAB 23/97/10, Minutes (Secret) of Cabinet Meeting at 16 (8 March 1939); CO 733/406/11, C.P. 10 (39), Extract (Secret) from Conclusions of a Meeting of the Cabinet (8 March 1939) (same). The Lord Chancellor, who in January felt the legal arguments in support of Britain's position had not been articulated strongly enough in the MacKenzie memorandum, by early March came to harbour serious doubts about the strength of the British argument, telling the Cabinet "the correspondence in question was extremely unsatisfactory … it was very difficult to contend that the letter of the 24[th] October, 1915, contained any specific exclusion of Palestine." CAB 23/97/9, Minutes (Secret) of Cabinet Meeting at 5 (2 March 1939); CO 733/406/11, C.P. 9 (39), Extract (Secret) from Conclusions of a Meeting of the Cabinet (2 March 1939) (same).

130 The *Times*, 21 February 1939 at 10.

131 *See supra* n. 99 and accompanying text.

132 H. McMahon, Letter to the Editor, "Independence of the Arabs, The 'McMahon Pledge,' A Definite Statement," The *Times*, 23 July 1937.

133 Cmd. 5974, *Report of a Committee Set up to Consider Certain Correspondence Between Sir Henry McMahon and the Sharif of Mecca in 1915 and 1916*, para. 18 (16 March 1939); *see also* CO 733/406/11, Code telegram from Foreign Office to British Ambassadors to Egypt, Iraq and Saudi Arabia (19 March 1939) (summarizing the Joint Committee's report and Britain's position that the McMahon pledge had excluded Palestine).

134 Cmd. 5974, *op. cit.*, para. 22. The British and Arab delegations unanimously adopted the Committee's report at their last formal session on 17 March 1939. George Antonius Papers, Middle East Centre Archive, St. Antony's College, Oxford, GB 165-0011, Box 2/5/2, Conferences on Palestine, United Kingdom-Arab Delegation, Draft Notes of the Fourteenth Meeting held at St. James's Palace, London at A6 (17 March 1939).

135 CO 733/406/11, Code telegram from Foreign Office to British Ambassadors to Egypt, Iraq and Saudi Arabia (19 March 1939).

136 CO 733/411/16, Letter from Selig Brodetsky on behalf of the Jewish Agency to MacDonald (28 March 1939).

137 CO 733/411/16, J.S. Bennett, Colonial Office, Note on Jewish Criticisms of the Report of the "McMahon-Hussein Committee" (3 April 1939).

138 Cmd. 6019, *Palestine: Statement of Policy* (hereafter "MacDonald White Paper") para. 7 (May 1939).

139 FO 371/23225, Conferences on Palestine, 1939, Informal Discussions with Arab and Jewish Delegates (23 February 1939); *see also* Weizmann Archives, 14-2131 (same).

140 Weizmann Archives, 15-2131, Minutes of the Fifth Meeting of the Palestine Conferences Discussion Committee (24 February 1939).

141 *Id.* at 5.

142 FO 371/23228, Conferences on Palestine, 1939, Informal Discussions with Arab and Jewish Delegates (7 March 1939).

143 *Id.*

144 *See* M.J. Cohen, *op. cit.*, at 587–88; *see also* M.J. Cohen, *Palestine: Retreat from the Mandate, the Making of British Policy, 1936–45* at 80 (Paul Elek Ltd. 1978).

145 D. Ben-Gurion, *Letters to* Paula, 16 March 1939 at 239 (Univ. of Pittsburgh Press, 1971).

146 CO 733/406/11, C.P. 11 (39), Extract (Secret) from Conclusions of a Meeting of the Cabinet (15 March 1939). That same day (15 March 1939) the German Army invaded Czechoslovakia and occupied Prague.

147 CO 733/406/11, C.P. 14 (39), Extract (Secret) from Conclusions of a Meeting of the Cabinet (22 March 1939); *see also* CO 733/406/11, Telegram No. 176 from Secretary of State for the Colonies to High Commissioner for Palestine (17 March 1939) ("Formal letter has been received from Jewish Delegation rejecting British Delegation's proposals on ground that they do not afford basis of agreement. Final meeting held with Arab Delegations this afternoon at which British proposals were rejected by Palestine Arab Delegation … [d]elegations of neighbouring states supported attitude of Palestine Arabs").

148 George Antonius Papers, Middle East Centre Archive, St. Antony's College, Oxford, GB 165-0011, Box 2/5/2, Conferences on Palestine, United Kingdom-Arab Delegation, Draft Notes of the Fourteenth Meeting held at St. James's Palace, London, at B5 (17 March 1939).

149 FO 371/23229, Conferences on Palestine, Note (Secret) of Informal Discussion with Delegates of Egypt, Iraq and Saudi Arabia (10 March 1939) (Saudi Delegate Fuad Hamza suggested a total of 75,000 Jewish immigrants be allowed into Palestine during the next five years, comprising 12,000 ordinary immigrants per year, plus 25,000 Jewish refugees); CO 733/406/11, Code Telegram from Foreign Office to British Ambassadors in Egypt, Iraq and Saudi Arabia (20 March 1939); *see also* FO 371/23232, C.W. Baxter (Counsellor, Foreign Office) Minute (5 April 1939) ("Fuad Hamza, Ali Maher and Taufiq Suwaidi agreed to put the [75,000] figure to the Palestine Arabs").

150 *Id.*

151 CAB 23/99/3, Minutes (Secret) of Cabinet Meeting at 13 (26 April 1939) (Colonial Secretary MacDonald informs the Cabinet that the Government was "no longer negotiating with the representatives of the Palestinian Arabs," hoping instead the neighbouring Arab States "would issu[e] a statement to the effect that, while the White Paper did not give the Arabs all that they had asked for, they advised the Palestinian Arabs to cease their violent courses and to return to constitutional methods of procedure"). The Arab States ultimately declined to make any such statement following the publication of the White Paper.

152 CAB 23/99/4, Minutes (Secret) of Cabinet Meeting at 7 (1 May 1939).

153 Less than two months after the White Paper was published, Auni Bey privately admitted during a meeting in Cairo to A.J. Kingsley Heath (Deputy Inspector General of the Palestine Police) his private belief that "since the White Paper proposals had, to a great extent, conceded Arab demands, there was no point in fighting for points of detail." CO 733/408/15, Letter from Kingsley Heath to Sir Harold MacMichael, High Commissioner for Palestine at 2 (14 July 1939); *see also* CO 733/401/15, Letter from MacMichael to Sir Cosmo Parkinson, Permanent Undersecretary of State for Colonial Affairs (14 July 1939) (explaining MacMichael had send Kingsley Heath to Cairo on the pretext of a "Holiday" to make contact with Auni Bey "in view of the tentative approaches from Palestinians in Egypt").

# 4

# THE WHITE PAPER

## Key elements of the White Paper

The failure of the London Conferences led the British to act unilaterally, issuing the MacDonald White Paper (Figure 4.1) on 17 May 1939.[1] The most important elements of the White Paper included:

First, the British Government dealt a catastrophic blow to Zionism, declaring "unequivocally that it is not part of their policy that Palestine should become a Jewish State."[2]

Second, instead of a wholly Jewish or Arab State, the British Government declared its support for the establishment within ten years (unless circumstances at the time would warrant postponement) of an "independent Palestine State" with treaty relations with Britain, "in which the two peoples in Palestine, Arabs and Jews, share authority in government in such a way that the essential interests of each are secured."[3]

Third, during the ten-year transitional period, local Arabs and Jews would have "an opportunity to participate in the machinery of government."[4] Palestinian Arabs and Jews would eventually assume control of certain government departments (assisted by British advisers), and Arabs and Jews would be offered seats on the Executive Council, the body advising the High Commissioner.

Fourth, Jewish immigration would be capped at a *maximum* of 75,000 (10,000 per year plus 25,000 refugees) over the next five years (May 1939 through May 1944), subject to the country's economic absorptive capacity.[5]

Fifth, at the end of the five-year period, "no further Jewish immigration will be permitted unless the Arabs of Palestine are prepared to acquiesce in it."[6]

Sixth, the High Commissioner of Palestine would be vested with authority to prohibit or restrict land sales to Jews.[7]

DOI: 10.4324/9781003225263-7

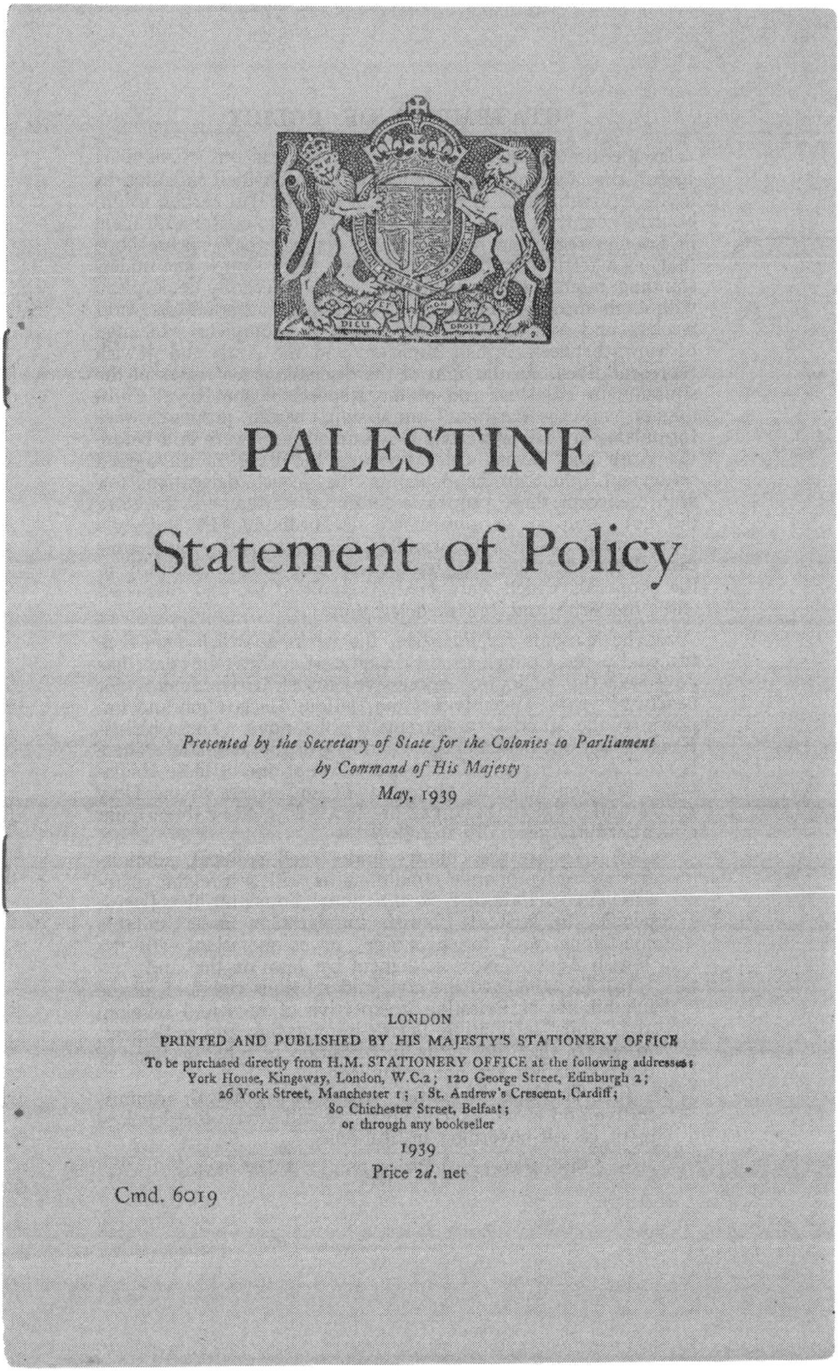

# PALESTINE

## Statement of Policy

*Presented by the Secretary of State for the Colonies to Parliament*
*by Command of His Majesty*
*May, 1939*

LONDON
PRINTED AND PUBLISHED BY HIS MAJESTY'S STATIONERY OFFICE
To be purchased directly from H.M. STATIONERY OFFICE at the following addresses:
York House, Kingsway, London, W.C.2; 120 George Street, Edinburgh 2;
26 York Street, Manchester 1; 1 St. Andrew's Crescent, Cardiff;
80 Chichester Street, Belfast;
or through any bookseller
1939
Price 2*d*. net

Cmd. 6019

**FIGURE 4.1** The Palestine White Paper, 17 May 1939 (Public Domain)

The White Paper adopted nearly all the Arab demands for Palestine, laying the groundwork for a future one-state solution by dramatically restricting Jewish immigration and land purchases. The Arabs received an absolute veto over future Jewish immigration after the initial five-year period, thereby locking in a two-to-one Arab majority throughout Palestine. Significantly, the White Paper did not give the Jews *any* ability to veto or postpone the creation of the independent Palestine State after ten years, abandoning MacDonald's initial concept of a reciprocal veto structure, in which the Arab veto of future Jewish immigration would be offset by a Jewish veto over Palestine statehood. The White Paper instead left the decision regarding the timing of statehood solely to the British Government.[8]

The Palestinian Arab strategy, combining violence on the ground in Palestine with transformational legal framing and a keen sense of Britain's desire to appease and neutralise the Arabs as potential Nazi allies, had succeeded in achieving an enormous change in British policy, a *volte face* beyond all expectations. Ironically, despite Britain's overarching effort to placate Arab demands, the Mufti nevertheless chose to spend most of the coming War in Berlin collaborating with the Nazi regime and urging Hitler to bomb Tel Aviv rather than trying to build a state for his people in Palestine.

The earliest drafts of the White Paper were circulated within the British Government in mid-March, even as the London Conferences were still underway. The Lord Chancellor requested a draft and made only minor changes.[9]

The Cabinet Committee on Palestine met on 6 April 1939 to consider drafts of the White Paper. At the 14 April meeting, MacDonald walked the Committee through the draft White Paper's language regarding the future, post-Mandate Government of Palestine, which he noted had been "the crucial subject of discussion with the Arab States" during the London Conferences. MacDonald noted the Foreign Office had "attached great importance to the wishes of the Representatives of the Arab States being met to the maximum practicable extent."[10]

Foreign Office officials privately said the White Paper did not *preclude* the possibility of an independent *Arab* State in Palestine at the end of the transition period, regardless whether the White Paper in fact promised such a result up front.[11] MacDonald sent the draft White Paper to the entire Cabinet on 13 April for their review.[12]

The Arabs had placed great emphasis on their demand that the transition period be set for a fixed period and in no event greater than ten years. MacDonald said the British delegation had pushed back against a finite transition period during the London Conferences, because "in our opinion it would be a great mistake to attempt now to prescribe a definite date in the future for the coming into being of the independent Palestine State when it was impossible to forecast what the circumstances might be when that date arrived."[13]

Nevertheless, MacDonald explained, "in view of the importance which the representatives of the Arab states had attached to their proposal it had been thought desirable to go some way to meet them."[14] Therefore, the draft White Paper proposed a ten-year transition period to Palestinian statehood, during which the British Government would do everything within its power to create conditions for achieving that objective, unless circumstances at the end of the ten-year period, in the sole discretion of the British Government, would require postponement.[15]

The full Cabinet convened several times during April and May 1939 to consider various drafts of the White Paper.[16] At its meeting on 17 May 1939, the Cabinet authorised MacDonald to release the White Paper later that same day.[17] The Lord Chancellor said the White Paper was "consistent" with the Balfour Declaration.[18] MacDonald said the Government should be prepared for the possibility that the League of Nations Council might ask the Permanent Court of International Justice in the Hague to determine whether the White Paper unlawfully breached the Mandate. Lord Halifax, the Foreign Secretary, expressed "anxiety" about the prospect of the Council of the League, which was "much under the influence of Zionist opinion," referring the matter to the Permanent Court for judicial review of the legality of the White Paper.[19]

Within one month of issuing the White Paper, the British Government vested the High Commissioner in Palestine with authority to promulgate regulations governing land transfers, retroactive to the 17 May publication date of the White Paper. The new regulations, flagrantly discriminating against Jews in violation of the Mandate, were published in early 1940.[20]

## Legal reactions to the White Paper

The White Paper provoked a firestorm in the Jewish world. The Jewish Agency denounced it as a betrayal of the Jewish People, especially those facing Nazi persecution. The Jewish Agency also accused Britain of capitulating to Arab terror.

The Palestinian Arabs, dissatisfied at not receiving everything they had demanded, publicly denounced the White Paper for failing to halt Jewish immigration immediately and for failing to confer immediate statehood on Palestine and its existing Arab majority.

The British Government also faced vocal opposition in Parliament to the new policy. The White Paper survived a 23 May 1939 vote in the House of Commons by an uncomfortably thin majority for Prime Minister Chamberlain's Conservative Government.

Official reaction in the United States was also critical, but several influential voices in American society, including the editorial page of the Jewish-owned *New York Times*, stepped forward to support the White Paper and provide much-needed political cover for the British Government in the United States.[21]

The White Paper also provoked strong legal responses from all three parties – Jewish, Arab, and British, consistent with their use of the law throughout the Mandate years as a means of gaining leverage against each other and influencing international opinion. The Jewish side challenged the legal validity of the White

Paper, alleging it conflicted with Britain's legal obligations under the Mandate. The Arab Higher Committee likewise attacked the White Paper for denying the Palestinian Arabs "justice" and their "natural rights." The British Government reacted by constructing an elaborate legal artifice in defence of the White Paper.

The Permanent Mandates Commission (PMC) of the League of Nations convened in Geneva one month after the White Paper's issuance to consider various legal and policy arguments, in what amounted to yet another trial of British policy in Palestine.

## *Jewish legal reaction to the White Paper*

The Zionist leader Chaim Weizmann (Figure 4.2) already knew the key provisions of the White Paper several weeks before it was published. He urged key members of the British Government and British society to speak out against the proposed change of policy.

Weizmann also launched a *legal* attack on the anticipated White Paper, even before it was officially released. On 17 April, for example, Leonard Stein, the long-time Honorary Counsel to the Jewish Agency, prepared what he described as "rough notes in response to a request for an immediate preliminary survey" addressing whether the proposed restrictions on land sales to Jews would violate

**FIGURE 4.2** Chaim Weizmann (library of Congress)

the non-discrimination language of Article 2 ("irrespective of race and religion") and Article 15 ("no discrimination of any kind") of the Mandate. Stein concluded that the Jews would have a strong claim that any restrictions on land sales to Jews would violate the Article 15 ban on "discrimination of *any* kind."[22]

On 15 May, Weizmann wrote to Sir John Simon, the former British Attorney General and Solicitor General (and future Lord Chancellor). Simon and Lord Hailsham had co-authored a 1930 letter to the *Times of London* criticizing the 1930 White Paper and suggesting an advisory opinion be sought from the Permanent Court of International Justice in the Hague. Weizmann wondered if Simon would be willing to make the same recommendation regarding the anticipated 1939 White Paper:

> This is why I would now like to ask you – do you still adhere to this view? Great Britain has always stood by the principle that law and justice should govern relations between nations great and small, and that there should be no attempts at riding rough-shod over the rights of the weaker. Great Britain, moreover, holds Palestine under a legal deed. Why should not the case which is now about to arise over it be openly examined by the highest international Tribunal?[23]

Weizmann, in his memoirs, characterised the London Conferences as dominated by an atmosphere of "utter futility."[24] That sense of futility exploded into anger on 16 May 1939, the day before the White Paper was issued, when Weizmann accepted an invitation to tea with MacDonald at Hyde Hall, MacDonald's country home approximately 50 miles northeast of London. The meeting was extremely acrimonious, with both men later describing it as one of the worst encounters of their lives. After several ugly exchanges, Weizmann accused MacDonald of "covering up his betrayal of the Jews under a semblance of legality."[25]

Weizmann's comment captured precisely Britain's cynical use of transformational legal framing to create a fig leaf of legitimacy for a political decision that would end up dooming millions of European Jews to Hitler's gas chambers.

Following the 17 May 1939 publication of the White Paper, the Jewish Agency issued three formal documents. The first document, the Jewish Agency's Official Statement reacting to the White Paper, was published as a letter to the *Times* on 18 May 1939. The statement condemned the White Paper, among other reasons, as "devoid of any moral basis and contrary to international law."[26]

The second document, a letter dated 31 May from Weizmann to Sir Harold MacMichael, the British High Commissioner in Palestine, set forth the Jewish Agency's detailed response to the White Paper.[27]

The third document, a formal memorandum challenging the legal validity of the White Paper, was attached to a subsequent letter from Weizmann to MacMichael, dated 4 June 1939.[28] Weizmann asked MacMichael to transmit both the 31 May letter and the 4 June legal memorandum to the PMC of the League of Nations for consideration at its upcoming June 1939 meeting.

Both the 18 May official statement and the 31 May letter made legal arguments against the White Paper. For example, the 18 May official statement attacked the White Paper as "contrary to international law."[29] The 31 May letter noted the White Paper conflicted with the Mandate, which had conferred "internationally recognised rights" on the Jewish people to reconstitute their National Home in Palestine. Nothing in the Mandate, the letter argued, gave the British Government *any* lawful authority to guarantee a permanent Arab majority in Palestine. Nor did the Mandate grant Britain the legal authority to limit Jewish immigration, other than based on the "economic absorptive capacity" principle originally expounded in the 1922 Churchill White Paper and endorsed by the Council of the League of Nations in 1930.

Moreover, the 31 May letter argued that on "purely legal grounds" Britain lacked authority to disregard or suspend its obligations under the Mandate to facilitate Jewish immigration and secure the establishment of the Jewish National Home. Nothing in the Mandate, Weizmann argued, allowed Britain to give the Palestinian Arabs a veto over further Jewish immigration into Palestine. Finally, the 31 May letter argued the contemplated restrictions on land sales to Jews violated the nondiscrimination language of Article 15 of the Mandate.[30]

These arguments set the stage for the Jewish Agency's legal memorandum several days later, analysing and attacking the legal validity of the White Paper.[31] As noted, Weizmann sent the legal memorandum to MacMichael as an attachment to his letter of 4 June 1939.[32] The legal memorandum was intended to serve as a sort of appellate brief to the PMC from the Jewish Agency, consistent with the Jewish Agency's practice over the past two decades.

The legal memorandum, running more than 30 pages, began by noting that the Mandate constituted the controlling international legal authority regarding Britain's governance of Palestine. The Balfour Declaration, which the Mandate's preamble had expressly incorporated, "must also be taken into account" as part of Britain's core legal obligations in Palestine. Britain, therefore, was "authorized to take such measures, and such measures *only*, as can be shown to be consistent with the Mandate according to its true intent and purpose." Moreover, the legal memorandum argued both the Balfour Declaration and the Mandate "must be fairly construed, without resort to sophistical glosses or verbal jugglery, in conformity with the principle that international agreements must be interpreted and carried out in good faith."[33]

The legal memorandum next argued the January 1918 Hogarth Message bore no legal relevance to interpreting Britain's obligations under the Mandate, because the League of Nations did not know about the Hogarth Message when it drafted and approved the terms of the Mandate. The Sherif had never mentioned it at the Versailles Conference. Nor did any Palestinian Arabs ever mention it during the 1922 discussions with Churchill preceding the issuance of the Mandate, or at any other time, until the London Conferences. The Arabs obviously had never viewed the Hogarth Message as significant because they never mentioned it, even though their leader the Sherif was the *recipient* of the message. Britain had only recently disclosed the Hogarth Message to prop up the 1939 White Paper. Therefore, the legal memorandum argued, the Hogarth Message was entitled to no weight in determining Britain's legal obligations under the Mandate.[34]

The legal memorandum next argued the primary and fundamental purpose of the Mandate was to require Britain to establish a National Home for the Jewish People in Palestine, including the possibility of Jewish statehood in Palestine. The White Paper, however, contradicted those aims: it guaranteed a permanent two-to-one Arab majority in Palestine; it aimed to create a single Palestinian State under majority Arab control; and it relegated the Palestinian Jews to second-class status.

The White Paper sought to achieve those objectives through the immediate and drastic reduction of Jewish immigration. The immigration restrictions, argued the legal memorandum, violated Britain's legal obligations under the Mandate in at least three ways. First, by restricting Jewish immigration, but not restricting Christian or Muslim immigration, the White Paper violated the anti-discrimination language of Article 15 of the Mandate, providing that "no person shall be excluded from Palestine on the sole ground of his religious belief." Second, the arbitrary restrictions on immigration during the first five years after the issuance of the White Paper violated Britain's obligation under Article 6 of the Mandate to "facilitate Jewish immigration." Third, granting the Arabs the right to veto further Jewish immigration after the expiration of the initial five-year period also violated the express terms of Article 6 as well as the entire purpose of the Mandate, namely, to reconstitute the Jewish National Home in Palestine.

This meant, according to the legal memorandum, that "Jewish immigration is singled out in Article 6 as the immigration to be facilitated. It is now proposed to be singled out as the immigration to be subjected to special restrictions, and eventually to an Arab veto, from which immigration of other types is apparently exempt." The memorandum elaborated further on this point, noting Article 6 imposed an active, *positive* obligation on Britain to facilitate Jewish immigration under suitable conditions, whereas the White Paper implied "there is no real difference between facilitating immigration and putting a stop to it." The memorandum disputed the British Government's position that the qualifying phrase in Article 6 – "under suitable conditions" – could somehow be "torture[d] … into a justification for subjecting Jewish immigration to an Arab veto."[35]

The memorandum next argued that the traditional British view that the Mandate had imposed a double (and equal) undertaking on the British – to facilitate Jewish immigration while simultaneously protecting the rights and position of the non-Jewish population of Palestine – would be turned on its head by the White Paper's position that after five years "the undertaking to the Jews need be given *no* weight at all."[36]

Echoing the letter Weizmann had sent a few days earlier to Sir John Simon, the legal memorandum next noted how Sir Simon and Lord Hailsham had publicly questioned the legality of the less drastic immigration restrictions the British

Government had proposed in the 1930 White Paper. "If this is their view of the White Paper of 1930," the legal memorandum claimed, "it is not difficult to infer what their comments would have been if the proposals before them had been those now announced."[37]

The legal memorandum also spent considerable energy demonstrating how the White Paper conflicted with the British Government's own prior interpretations of the Mandate, especially as articulated in the 1922 White Paper and the 1931 MacDonald letter, both of which were binding on the British Government. The legal memorandum noted the British Government, the Jewish Agency, and the Council of the League all understood Jewish immigration to Palestine could be limited *only* by the economic absorptive capacity of the country, and nothing else. Under Article 6 of the Mandate, as all parties had interpreted it for nearly two decades, Britain was *not* legally authorised to impose arbitrary numerical caps on Jewish immigration, regardless of the country's economic capacity to absorb a far higher number, as the White Paper had done.

The legal memorandum concluded by arguing the White Paper's intention to establish a majority, Arab-ruled Palestine conflicted with Britain's legal obligation under the Mandate to secure the establishment of a National Home for the Jewish people in Palestine.

> It is difficult to understand how his Majesty's Government can have persuaded themselves that it would be contrary to their obligations to the Jews under the Mandate, and to the assurances given to the Jewish people in the past, that the Jewish population of Palestine should be made the subjects of an Arab State against their will … The status of a minority in the nominal enjoyment of minority rights is not the status which was contemplated for the Jews when His Majesty's Government promised them to facilitate the establishment in Palestine of a National Home for the Jewish People, or when that promise was subsequently incorporated in the Mandate.[38]

Finally, the legal memorandum complained that the White Paper's exclusion of the Jewish Agency from involvement in future discussions regarding the political status of Palestine contravened the provisions of Article 4 of the Mandate.

Taken as a whole, the legal memorandum was surprisingly weak. It was not well organised. The sentences were long and verbose. The arguments were more focused on politics and policy than principles of law. In many respects, the weakness of the legal memorandum echoed the weakness of the Jewish legal performance throughout the Mandate years, especially before the Shaw Commission in 1929. Despite these weaknesses, however, the memorandum (along with Weizmann's 31 May letter) seemed to make a favourable impression on several members of the PMC, as will be discussed in Chapter 5.

Following the PMC's meetings in June 1939, Stein continued exploring legal options for challenging the White Paper, including the possibility of asking the Permanent Court of International Justice in the Hague to rule on the legality of the White Paper. However, in a secret letter to Joseph Ivor Linton of the Jewish Agency Executive in August 1939, Stein candidly admitted the weaknesses in the Jewish legal case against the White Paper, advising that the chances of success at the Hague Court were not promising.[39]

For example, Stein did not feel at all confident about the Jewish Agency's chances of legal success against the immigration and constitutional provisions of the White Paper. Regarding immigration, Stein said "I am inclined to doubt whether, if we relied on the Mandate alone, we could be sure of its being held, on the construction of the actual words of the Mandate, that the fixed quota was a breach of the Mandate."[40]

Regarding the constitutional provisions and the concern that the White Paper had telegraphed the formation of a majority Arab State in Palestine, Stein again conceded weakness in the Jewish case:

> [M]uch would depend on the view taken by the Court as to the extent to which this particular Mandate must have certain parts of Article 22 of the Covenant read into it, and as to the true construction of these parts of Article 22. As to whether the constitutional proposals are inconsistent with the Jewish National Home obligations, the difficulty is that the expression "Jewish National Home" can hardly be said as a matter of law, to have a clear and definite meaning, and the Mandate makes no attempt to define it.[41]

Stein, thus, counselled caution before bringing the case before the Hague Court, for two reasons. First, the Court for political reasons might be reluctant to rule against Britain. Second, the Jews would face an uphill battle convincing the court that the White Paper had clearly violated the Mandate, given the ambiguity in the Mandate's language and the Court's ability to construe that language in a variety of ways:

> The truth is, I think, that the Mandate is a political rather than a legal document, and a Court of Law would have considerable difficulty in construing it, or in forming an opinion as to whether, as a matter of law, some particular course of action is inconsistent with it. The result would, I think, depend largely on whether the Court took a broad or narrow view – whether it looked strictly at the actual text of the Mandate, or whether it was prepared to consider what the Mandate was *meant* to mean … I cannot help feeling, however, that although, in a clear case, the Court would decide judicially on the merits of the case, political considerations might have some weight in a case in which (as here) it is a question of construing a document which is so vaguely worded that different minds may well take different views as to what it means. In other words, the ambiguity of the Mandate might, perhaps, furnish a loophole for anyone who would, for political reasons prefer – if reasonably possible – not to decide against the British Government.[42]

Stein's only expression of confidence involved the non-discrimination language of Article 15 of the Mandate, which provided a basis for challenging the White Paper's willingness to give the High Commissioner authority to limit or ban land transfers to Jews.

## *Arab legal reaction to the White Paper*

The White Paper, according to one British historian writing with classic understatement, "was not received with acclaim by the Arabs."[43] Any Arabs willing to say anything even remotely favourable about the White Paper were threatened. The Mufti's followers assassinated one member of the Arab National Defense Party who dared to signal the White Paper might be acceptable.

Thus, the Arab Higher Committee for Palestine issued a formal response to the White Paper on 30 May, 1939.[44] Incredibly, despite the enormously favourable outcome of the London Conferences from the Arab perspective and the heavily pro-Arab policies embodied in the White Paper, the Palestinian Arabs rejected what for them truly would have been the "Deal of the Century" – at least the 20th century.

Teeming with repeated references to Palestinian "natural rights" and "justice," the Arab Higher Committee's response nit-picked its way through various provisions of the White Paper, finding fault with each. The constitutional provisions were not good enough, because the Jews were allowed to "participate" in the independent Palestine State. The immigration provisions were not satisfactory, because the British Government failed to impose an *immediate* ban on all further Jewish immigration. And the land transfer restrictions were not acceptable either, because the Jews should have been banned immediately from buying even a single additional dunam of land, arable or not, anywhere in the country.

The Palestinians, who had used the law so effectively during the first two decades of the Mandate, achieved enormous success in London by persuading the British to make the drastic policy changes embodied in the White Paper. But the Palestinians, in a cruel twist of irony, refused to embrace the stunning victory they achieved in London, in which they won almost everything they had demanded. Instead, they insisted on litigating every last point in their lengthy bill of particulars.

By maintaining their absolutist, uncompromising demands for "justice" and insisting the British give them *everything* they wanted – with no appreciation of the larger political context, in which Britain was trying to keep the Arabs close, but without risking the loss of American support – the Palestinians blew their best chance *ever* for statehood.[45] The Mufti's irredentism and extremism proved catastrophic to Palestinian Arab nationalism, dooming his people to a state of statelessness lasting well into the 21st century.

## *British legal reaction to the White Paper*

The British Government anticipated the Jewish side would attempt to stir opposition to the White Paper in Parliament and at the PMC (the body entrusted with overseeing the performance of various Mandatories), scheduled to meet in June 1939. Just as it had focused on legal issues in defending Britain's position in the run up to the London Conferences, the British Government likewise focused on legal issues in preparing its defence of the White Paper.

As a first step in preparing to rebut those anticipated attacks, H.F. Downie of the Colonial Office sought legal advice from Sir Grattan Bushe, the Colonial Office's Legal Advisor, regarding the potential remedies the League of Nations might be able to invoke against Britain if the PMC were to find the White Paper in violation of the Mandate.

Bushe advised the PMC and the League had little or no chance of forcing any remedies on Britain. Bushe noted three key factors in Britain's favour. First, Britain held the Palestine Mandate not as a bestowal from the League, but instead in its capacity as one of the Principal Allied Powers of World War I, who received the territories Turkey had surrendered in the Treaty of Lausanne. Second, Bushe explained "the question of the seat of sovereignty in the case of mandated territories" had never been resolved as a matter of international law.[46] Third, Britain held a seat on the Council of the League, giving it a likely veto over any adverse action or remedy the League might contemplate imposing on Britain.[47]

Thus, according to Bushe, the League very likely would be powerless to force Britain to amend the White Paper, or to replace Britain as the Mandatory power in Palestine. Nor was it likely the League would be able to succeed in an action against Britain in the Permanent International Court of Justice.

MacDonald was slated to defend the White Paper before the House of Commons on 22 May, 1939. MacDonald wrote to the Attorney General, D.B. Somervell, on 15 May seeking legal guidance to help with his defence of the White Paper and to stave off a Jewish effort to persuade the House to ask the Government to refer the matter to the Permanent International Court of Justice in the Hague:

> In connection with the temporary restrictions on immigration the Jewish Agency have already proposed that we should invite the League of Nations Council to obtain an advisory opinion from the Hague Court before any action is taken, and we have declined to accept this proposal. The suggestion will no doubt be renewed in Parliament after the White Paper is published. I understand that the only way in which we could be brought before the Court is pursuant to Act [sic] 26 of the Mandate or by reason of a decision by the Council to refer the matter for an advisory opinion. The idea that we should make our policy dependent upon a decision of the Hague Court hardly calls for serious consideration, but there is no doubt that the legal aspect of the question will be vigorously pressed in the forthcoming [House of Commons] debate, and I should like to be fortified with your valuable advice.[48]

The next day, the Colonial Office sent the Attorney General a summary of the legal issues they expected the Jewish side would raise with Parliament in the coming days, and in Geneva with the PMC at is meeting scheduled to commence 8 June 1939.[49]

Somervell responded to MacDonald's request for legal advice and delivered a five-page memorandum to the Colonial and Foreign Offices on 18 May 1939.[50]

The Attorney General argued that Britain's paramount legal obligations under the Mandate were to secure the creation of the Jewish National Home and to develop self-governing institutions. The Attorney General argued Britain had already fulfilled the first obligation, given the enormous increase in the Jewish population of Palestine during the first two decades of the Mandate. The Attorney General argued Britain had no obligation under the Mandate to permit Jewish immigration to continue indefinitely, especially if doing so would impair Britain's ability to fulfil its second paramount obligation and develop self-governing institutions, or otherwise jeopardise peace in the country.[51]

The Attorney General said this meant the British Government was not legally obligated to regulate immigration solely on the basis of the economic absorptive capacity of Palestine but was free under the language of the Mandate to consider other factors. Thus, Britain was under no legal obligation to "continue immigration to the maximum forever regardless of all other obligations and considerations,"[52] especially if doing so would conflict with Britain's more important obligations under the Mandate. This argument constituted the "centre of gravity" of the Government's legal position, according to the Attorney General.

Charles W. Baxter, Head of the Eastern Department at the Foreign Office minuted, after reading the Attorney General's memorandum, that "we are on quite strong ground from the legal point of view."[53]

Downie also prepared two internal memoranda responding to the arguments contained in Weizmann's 31 May letter and the Jewish Agency's 5 June legal memorandum.

Regarding Weizmann's 31 May letter, the Colonial Office memorandum rejected Weizmann's contention that, as a matter of law, Jewish immigration could be limited *only* by the economic absorptive capacity principle. The Colonial Office memorandum found no support in either the preamble or the operative provisions of the Mandate for Weizmann's position. In fact, the memorandum argued, Britain had a very strong basis to argue that as of mid-1939, it had *already* met its obligations to facilitate Jewish immigration and secure the creation of the Jewish National Home. Because those obligations had been fulfilled, there was nothing in the Mandate requiring Britain to continue facilitating Jewish immigration indefinitely.[54]

The Colonial Office memorandum criticised Weizmann's 31 May letter in many other respects, sometimes in very dismissive language. For example, the memorandum criticised Weizmann's claim that the Mandate gave every Jew in the world the right to immigrate to Palestine as "so fantastic that it hardly calls for refutation."[55]

The memorandum next addressed what it characterised as the "most effective part" of Weizmann's letter, namely, Weizmann's argument that by locking in a two-to-one Arab majority, the British Government was all but guaranteeing the "Palestine State" it contemplated would in fact become a majority-ruled Palestinian *Arab* State. The memorandum said, in response:

> We are not limiting Jewish immigration with the object of preventing the establishment of a Jewish State (i.e., a Jewish majority). We are limiting Jewish immigration because the point has now been reached when, if we continue to facilitate such immigration against the will of the Arabs, a "fatal enmity between the two peoples will be perpetuated" and the complete fulfillment of our obligations under the Mandate will be impossible.[56]

The second Colonial Office memorandum responded directly to the 5 June 1939 Jewish Agency legal memorandum regarding the White Paper. The memorandum began with a sharp attack on the general tenor of the Jewish Agency memorandum, erroneously predicting the PMC would support the White Paper:

> In spite of its reprobation of "sophistical glosses or verbal jugglery," this memorandum makes full use of every forensic device (even the cheapest), and generally treats the important political issues at stake in the spirit of the sharp attorney. The Secretary of State will no doubt take his stand at Geneva on the broad issues and will not be drawn into controversy over these legalistic irrelevancies. I feel sure that, if he adopts this attitude, he will be supported by the majority of the Permanent Mandates Commission.[57]

The second memorandum turned next to the substance of the Jewish Agency's legal arguments. The memorandum rejected the Jewish Agency's view that Britain's primary obligation under the Mandate was to secure the creation of the Jewish National Home and to support Jewish immigration and land purchases as part of that process. Instead, the memorandum argued, the Mandate imposed two separate obligations on the British Government – one to the Jews and the other to the Arabs of Palestine – and those obligations were of "equal weight."[58]

In that regard, the second memorandum rejected the Jewish Agency's argument that the word "position" in Article 6 of the Mandate meant only the *economic* position of the Palestinian Arabs, rather than their *political* position. The second memorandum further rejected the Jewish Agency's contention that Britain was locking in a permanent two-to-one Arab majority as "nonsense … [t]here is no guarantee in either direction as regards these proportions."[59]

The second memorandum then addressed an interesting argument the Jewish Agency had made regarding the phrase "under suitable conditions" in Article 6 of the Mandate. The Jewish Agency had argued the phrase was not intended to act as a check on Jewish immigration but instead to ensure Jewish immigration be facilitated in a "suitable" manner. The second memorandum conceded the strength of the Jewish argument on this point but discounted the point as "minor."[60] This reasoning seemed in conflict with MacDonald's position during the London Conferences, when he argued repeatedly that the "under suitable conditions" language formed the *entire* legal basis for Britain's decision to jettison the economic absorptive capacity principle and impose a new and unprecedentedly harsh quota on Jewish immigration.

The Colonial Office remained focused on defending the legality of the White Paper for the next several months. In a 3 March 1940 note, for example, Sir William Malkin addressed the Jewish claim that the recently promulgated land transfer restrictions violated the non-discrimination language of Article 15 of the Mandate. Malkin doubted the validity of the argument, noting sarcastically that a Jewish buyer would not have been able to invoke a legal right under Article "to buy e.g. the Church of the Holy Sepulchre and that if the Administration prevented him from doing so, this would involve a breach of the Mandate."[61]

Moreover, the Colonial Office argued, somewhat disingenuously, that if the land sale restrictions were discriminatory against Jewish *buyers*, they were also discriminatory against Arab *sellers*, thereby cancelling out *any* discriminatory impact against a single group.[62]

## British parliamentary debates regarding the White Paper

The White Paper provoked significant political controversy in Britain. Parliament debated the merits of the White Paper during several sessions in late May and early June 1939.

Even before the publication of the White Paper, Weizmann urged various prominent Britons to send letters to the *Times* opposing the Government's new Palestine policy. Weizmann also lobbied various MPs to take a strong stance against the White Paper.[63]

One of those MPs whom Weizmann briefed was Sir Winston Churchill, the former Colonial Secretary and author of the 1922 White Paper.[64] In a 23 May 1939 House of Commons speech, widely regarded as one of the most brilliant of his career, Churchill spoke forcefully against the White Paper. He began by saying "I should feel personally embarrassed in the most acute manner if I lent myself, by silence or inaction, to what I must regard as an act of repudiation" of the commitments Britain made to the Jews in the Balfour Declaration.[65]

Churchill noted that his 1922 White Paper had made clear that the Mandate's requirement of creating self-governing institutions in Palestine, presumably to be dominated by the Arabs who comprised more than two-thirds of the population, "was to be *subordinated* to the *paramount* pledge and obligation of establishing a Jewish National Home in Palestine."[66]

Churchill aimed his strongest criticism at the White Paper's restrictions on Jewish immigration to Palestine:

> Now I come to the gravamen of the case. I regret very much that the pledge of the Balfour Declaration, endorsed as it has been by successive Governments, and the conditions under which we obtained the Mandate, have both been violated by the Government's proposals. There is much in this White Paper which is alien to the spirit of the Balfour Declaration, but I will not trouble about that. I select the one point upon which there is plainly a breach and repudiation of the Balfour Declaration—the provision that Jewish immigration can be stopped in five years' time by the decision of an Arab majority. That is a plain breach of a solemn obligation … what sort of National Home is offered to the Jews of the world when we are asked to declare that in five years' time the door of that home is to be shut and barred in their faces?[67]

Other members of Parliament framed the issue in legal terms. House Member Archibald Sinclair, for example, echoed demands from others that the Government first seek an opinion regarding the White Paper's legality from the Permanent International Court of Justice in the Hague:

> [W]e ought in these grave matters of the true interpretation of the Mandate to obtain … an opinion from the Hague Court … My contention is that such an opinion from the Hague Court should be obtained forthwith, and, having been obtained, that His Majesty's Government should either consult Parliament afresh or go straight to the Mandates Commission. But Parliament ought not to commit itself to proposals which there is at least a strong case for regarding as conflicting with the fundamental principles of the Mandate until they have been approved by the Mandates Commission.[68]

The House ultimately approved the White Paper by an unimpressive margin, with only 268 votes (of a total strength of 413 seats) in favour, 179 against, and 110 abstentions.[69]

The House again addressed the legality of the White Paper two weeks later, when the following exchange occurred between Prime Minister Chamberlain and MP Lipson:

MR. LIPSON: May I ask whether it is within the competence of the [Permanent] Mandates Commission to decide whether the [White Paper] proposals are legal or not?

THE PRIME MINISTER: The only provision on such a matter is in Article 26 of the Palestine Mandate, where it is laid down that if any dispute should arise between the Mandatory Power and another member of the League of Nations as to the interpretation of the application of the provisions of the mandate, such dispute, if it cannot be settled by negotiation, shall be submitted to the Permanent International Court of Justice.[70]

The House of Lords also debated whether the White Paper could be reconciled with Britain's legal obligations under the Mandate. Lord Snell, who had served as a member of the 1929–1930 Shaw Commission, framed Britain's obligations under the Mandate in decidedly legal terms:

> The Mandate, as I understand it, was the most important international obligation ever entrusted to a single nation … We accepted this Mandate knowing perfectly well what it involved. The Mandate is but an elaborated interpretation of the Balfour Declaration and in the Balfour Declaration the purpose of it was made perfectly clear, a declaration of sympathy with Zionists aspirations … The question for us, my Lords, is: Is the Mandate a legal document, or is it not? If it is not, then those of us who are laymen have been grievously misled. Various Governments have sheltered themselves behind its provisions on the ground that they were bound, their hands were tied and they could not move at their own will … Now, it seems to me that that conferred upon our country an almost sacred obligation. Whatever the letter of the Mandate may be interpreted to mean, the spirit of it, beyond all doubt, was the establishment of a National Home for the Jewish people … If we do not know what the Mandate means there are statesmen still living who know what it meant to them at the time the Mandate was formulated. Mr. Lloyd George, giving evidence before the Royal Commission, said: The idea was that the Jewish State was not to be set up immediately by the Peace Treaty without reference to the wishes of the majority of the inhabitants. On the other hand it was contemplated that when the time arrived for according representative institutions to Palestine, if the Jews had meanwhile responded to the opportunity afforded to them and had become a definite majority all the inhabitants, then Palestine would thus become a Jewish Commonwealth.[71]

Despite the opposition in Parliament, the Chamberlain Government was determined to push ahead with the new White Paper policy. The Zionists, shattered and embittered, asked the PMC of the League of Nations to declare the new British policy unlawful.

## Notes

1 MacDonald White Paper; *see also* CO 733/406/11, Code telegram from Foreign Office to British Ambassadors in Egypt, Iraq, Saudi Arabia, and the United States (19 March 1939) (describing the key principles to be included in the White Paper).

2 MacDonald White Paper, para. 4. MacDonald prepared an undated handwritten draft of the White Paper on the stationery of his country home, Hyde Hall in Essex. MacDonald's original handwritten draft stated this somewhat differently: "They therefore declare that, after twenty years' experience, the Balfour Declaration should no longer be read as envisaging the possibility of Palestine becoming a Jewish State, and that is no part of their policy to promote such a change." CO 733/410/9, MacDonald draft at 2–3.

3 MacDonald White Paper, paras. 8, 10(1) and 10(7). MacDonald's original handwritten draft made no mention of a fixed period for the transition, indicating instead the Mandate would continue until the Jews and Arabs had demonstrated the ability to cooperate and work together (effectively giving the Jews a veto over the future creation of an independent Palestine State). CO 733/410/9, MacDonald draft at 4–8.

4 MacDonald White Paper, para. 10(3).

5 *Id.* para. 14(1). MacDonald's original handwritten draft set the limit at 100,000 immigrants over the next five years, which would have brought the Jewish population of Palestine to 35% of the total. CO 733/410/9, MacDonald draft at 12.

6 MacDonald White Paper, para. 14(3).

7 *Id.*, para. 17. MacDonald's original handwritten draft said the land transfer prohibitions and restrictions "will not necessarily be permanent." CO 733/410/9, MacDonald draft at 14. That language was not included in the published version of the White Paper. In February 1940, the High Commissioner for Palestine issued the Land Transfer Regulations contemplated by the White Paper. The regulations divided the country into three zones. Land sales to Jews were prohibited in Zone A (6,615 sq. miles), largely corresponding to the modern-day West Bank, Galilee, upper Negev, and Gaza. Land sales to Jews were permissible but highly restricted in Zone B (3,295 sq. miles), consisting mostly of the lower Negev desert, portions of the Huleh Valley and the area around Ashkelon. Land sales were not restricted in Zone C (only 519 sq. miles), corresponding roughly to the modern-day Tel Aviv metropolitan area, from Bat Yam to Netanya as well as other municipal areas, plus a small industrial area south of Haifa. Cmd. 6180, *Palestine Land Transfers Regulations* (28 February 1940).

8 MacDonald White Paper, para. 10(7). Several days later, Viscount (and former Palestine High Commissioner) Herbert Samuel said during a speech in the House of Lords that the White Paper had given the Jews at least an implicit veto over the creation of the Palestine State, in exchange for giving the Arabs a veto over future Jewish immigration after the expiration of the initial five-year period. The Marquess of Dufferin and Ava, who had been a member of the British Delegation during the London Conferences, disagreed with Samuel's reading of the White Paper, noting "I must make it clear that if my noble friend cares to read into these words a Jewish veto on the establishment of the independent Palestinian State, he must do it on his own authority. I myself do not accept that interpretation, nor does His Majesty's Government." Hansard, HL Deb. vol. 113 c105 (23 May 1939).

9 CO 733/410/9, Letters to Colonial Office on behalf of the Lord Chancellor with suggested edits to the draft White Paper and requesting opportunity to review a revised draft (21 March and 31 March 1939).

10 FO 371/23232, Cabinet Committee on Palestine, Draft Conclusions of the Ninth Meeting of the Committee (Secret) at 2 (6 April 1939).

11 *See, e.g.*, FO 371/23235, E3488 (Baxter minutes, 27 and 28 April 1939). Baxter and other Foreign Office staffers were concerned about draft language in the White Paper stating the McMahon-Hussein correspondence could not be the basis for acknowledging the Arab right to statehood in Palestine. The Foreign Office suggested softer language to the Colonial Office, noting "[t]he present wording might be held to rule out the formation of a Palestine government with an Arab majority; *but this is not the intention.*" *Id.* (Baxter minute, 6 May 1939). Baxter had served as a member of the British Delegation in all the meetings with the Jewish side during the conference, during which MacDonald had repeatedly tried to reassure the Jewish delegates that Britain did *not* intend to create a majority-ruled Arab state in Palestine.

12 CAB 24/285/1, Memorandum by the Secretary of State for the Colonies (13 April 1939).

13 *Id.* at 4.

14 *Id.*

15 *Id.* at 5.

16 CO 733/410/9, Cabinet 21(39), Extract (Secret) from Conclusions of a Meeting (19 April 1939); Cabinet 24(39), Extract (Secret) from Conclusions of a Meeting (26 April 1939); Cabinet 25(39), Extract (Secret) from Conclusions of a Meeting (1 May 1939); Cabinet 26(39), Extract (Secret) from Conclusions of a Meeting (3 May 1939).
17 CAB 23/99/7, Minutes (Secret) of a Meeting of the Cabinet at 16 (17 May 1939).
18 *Id.* at 12.
19 *Id.* at 12–13; *see also* FO 371/23235, CP 28(39), Extract from Cabinet Conclusions at 2,3 (17 May 1939); *see also* CO 733/410/9 (same).
20 *See* CO 733/418/13, Palestine Land Transfer Regulations: Notes on League of Nations Aspect (4 March 1940).
21 The *New York Times* editorial, written only six months after *Kristallnacht* and less than four months before Germany's invasion of Poland, declared "[t]he pressure on Palestine is now so great that immigration has to be strictly regulated to save the homeland itself from overpopulation ..." *New York Times*, 18 May 1939 at 24. Weizmann was so furious that he refused to meet with *Times* publisher Arthur Hays Sulzberger during Sulzberger's visit to London a few days later, dismissing Sulzberger as a "cowardly Jew." Clairvoyantly anticipating the *Times'* efforts decades later to drive a wedge between American Jews and Israel, Weizmann said, "what I would like to understand however is whether the general attitude and feeling of the [American] Jews is very different from Sulzberger's and his paper." B. Litvinoff and N. Rose (eds.), *The Letters and Papers of Chaim Weizmann*, Series A, Letters (hereafter "Weizmann Letters"), Vol. XIX (Transaction/Israel University Press, 1980), Letter No. 84 at 93, Weizmann to Solomon Goldman (30 May 1939).
22 Weizmann Archives 6-2144, L. Stein, "Note on Proposed Land Legislation in Relation to Non-Discrimination Provisions of the Mandate" (17 April 1939) (emphasis added).
23 Weizmann Letters, Letter No. 65 at 70, Weizmann to Sir John Simon (15 May 1939).
24 C. Weizmann, *Trial and Error* at 494 (Harper and Bros. 1949).
25 C. Sanger, *Malcolm MacDonald: Bringing an End to Empire* at 171 (McGill-Queen's University Press, 1995); *see also* N. Rose, *Chaim Weizmann* at 348 (Viking, 1986); *see also* C. Sykes, *op. cit.*, at 195 ("when Weizmann came out of the house [after his meeting with MacDonald] he was pale and trembling with anger").
26 Jewish Agency Statement, "A Beach of Faith," the *Times*, 18 May 1939 at 9.
27 CO 733/410/18, Weizmann Archives 16-2153, Weizmann to Sir Harold MacMichael (31 May 1939).
28 CO 733/410/18, Weizmann Archives 20-2154, Weizmann to Sir Harold MacMichael (4 June 1939).
29 Jewish Agency Statement, "A Beach of Faith," the *Times*, 18 May 1939 at 9.
30 CO 733/410/18, Weizmann Archives 16-2153, Weizmann to Sir Harold MacMichael (31 May 1939).
31 CO 733/410/18, Jewish Agency for Palestine, *Memorandum on the Legal Aspects of the Statement of British Policy in Palestine (Cmd. 6019)* (hereafter "Legal Memorandum"), 5 June 1939; *see also* Weizmann Archives 20-2154. The British lawyer Leonard Stein, who had served for many years as the Jewish Agency's Honorary Counsel, wrote the memorandum. CO 733/410/18, Notes on Jewish Agency Memorandum of the Legal Aspects of the White Paper at 1 (9 June 1939).
32 CO 733/410/18, Letter from Weizmann to Sir Harold MacMichael, High Commissioner, Jerusalem attaching Jewish Agency Legal Memorandum (4 June 1939).
33 *Id.*, para. 1 (emphasis added).
34 *Id.*, paras. 2–3.
35 *Id.* para. 10.
36 *Id.* (emphasis added).
37 *Id.* para 11.
38 *Id.* para. 25.
39 Weizmann Archives 16-2164, Letter (Secret) from Stein to Linton (11 August 1939).
40 *Id.* at 2.

41 *Id.*
42 *Id.* at 3–4.
43 C. Sykes, *op. cit.*, at 198.
44 League of Nations Archives, Geneva, R4076/6A/30296/668, *Reply of the Arab Higher Committee for Palestine to the White Paper Issued by the British Government on May 17, 1939* (30 May 1939).
45 The Arab Higher Committee's reply to the White Paper ended by proclaiming, in all capital letters, "PALESTINE SHALL BE INDEPENDENT WITHIN AN ARAB FEDERATION AND SHALL REMAIN FOREVER ARAB." *Id.* at 14. Nevertheless, several Arab and Palestinian leaders expressed support for the White Paper privately but were afraid to oppose the Mufti publicly. Y. Porath, *op. cit.*, at 290–291. Only Auni Bey Abdul Hadi seemed to understand the Palestinian Arabs had blown a tremendous opportunity, confiding to Kingsley Heath his wish the Palestinian Arabs would stop fighting over "details" since the White Paper "had, to a great extent, conceded Arab demands." CO 733/408/15, Letter from Kingsley Heath to High Commissioner MacMichael (14 July 1939).
46 CO 733/418/13, Note from Downie to Bushe and MacDonald confirming legal advice received from Bushe at 3 (18 May 1939); *see also* N. Wheatley, *op. cit.*, at 211 (issue of sovereignty over mandated territories "rankled in the context of widespread academic debate as to who was sovereign in the territories under sacred trust: the mandatory power, the inhabitants of the territory, the League itself or some new combination. While the League abstained from taking a definitive position, it reluctantly affirmed that the mandatory powers possessed administrative and legislative authority over the territory, but not full sovereignty").
47 CO 733/418/13, Note from Downie to Bushe and MacDonald confirming legal advice received from Bushe at 3–4 (18 May 1939).
48 CO 733/410/17, Letter from MacDonald to Attorney General Donald Somervell (15 May 1939).
49 CO 733/410/17, Letter from Sir Grattan Bushe to Attorney General Donald Somervell, enclosing memorandum entitled "Palestine Statement of Policy: The Legal Aspect" (16 May 1939).
50 CO 733/410/17, Letter from Attorney General D.B. Somervell to MacDonald enclosing Memorandum entitled "Palestine" (18 May 1939); FO 371/23235 (same).
51 For a contrary legal view, *see* E. Frankenstein, *The Meaning of the Term 'National Home for the Jewish People'*, Jewish Yearbook of International Law at 41 (1948) ("The concept of the Jewish National Home, as expressed in the Mandate, is adapted to a unique situation, that of a people *moving back* to its home. This *movement* is the very essence of the concept; if it is arrested, the National Home may transform itself into a State or crystallize into a minority, but it ceases to be a National Home")(emphasis added).
52 *Id.* at 4.
53 FO 371/23235, Baxter minute (19 May 1939).
54 CO 733/410/18, Colonial Office Memorandum at 1–3, 11 (6 June 1939). The memorandum was written on Colonial office stationery but was not signed, although Downie was in fact the author.
55 *Id.* at 5.
56 *Id.* at 8.
57 CO 733/410/18, Notes on Jewish Agency Memorandum on the Legal Aspects of the White Paper (9 June 1939). The memorandum was written on Colonial Office stationery and initialed by Downie. Downie noted he had also written the first memorandum dated 6 June 1939 responding to Weizmann's 31 May letter.
58 *Id.* at 1.
59 *Id.* at 4.
60 *Id.* at 5.
61 CO 733/418/13, Sir W. Malkin's Memo on Legal Aspects at 1 (4 March 1940).

62 CO 733/418/13, R. Makins, "Palestine Land Transfers Regulations: Notes on Legal Aspects" at 2–3 (3 March 1940). Makins admitted the weakness of this argument, noting it could be "regarded as a debating point;" *see also* CO 733/392/8, Letter from D.G. Harris to H.F. Downie (15 March 1939) (discussing need for immediate legislation implementing land transfer restrictions, "otherwise we may be embarrassed by a flood of sales in anticipation of it," and acknowledging the potential conflict between such legislation and the language of Article 15 of the Mandate prohibiting discrimination "of any kind").

63 *See, e.g.*, Weizmann Letters and Papers, *op cit.*, Letter No. 70 at 72, Weizmann to Reginald Coupland (member of Palestine Royal Commission, 1936–1937) (17 May 1939); Letter No. 71 at 73–74, Weizmann to Admiral George King-Hall (17 May 1939).

64 *Id.*, Letter No. 80, Weizmann to Churchill (23 May 1939), editor's n.1 at 88; *see also id.*, Telegram No. 59 at 65–66, Weizmann to Churchill and Amery (4 May 1939) (arguing Palestine Jews could be valuable wartime asset for Britain, and urging Churchill and Amery to share the telegram with other "friends" in Parliament).

65 Hansard, HC Deb. vol. 347, col. 2168 (23 May 1939).

66 *Id.*, col. 2170 (emphasis added).

67 *Id.*, cols. 2711–2772, 78.

68 *Id.*, col. 2157.

69 *Id.* cols. 2194–2197.

70 *Id.*, HC Deb. vol. 348, cols. 413–414 (7 June 1939).

71 HL Deb. Vol. 113, cols. 92–94 (23 May 1939).

# 5

# APPEAL TO THE PERMANENT MANDATES COMMISSION

## Introduction

The Permanent Mandates Commission (PMC) of the League of Nations took up the White Paper at its regularly scheduled meetings in Geneva in June 1939.[1]

The PMC had, almost since its inception, functioned as a sort of appellate court where aggrieved Jewish and Arab parties, continuing a custom and practice they had pursued since the onset of the Mandate, would seek relief via highly legalistic petitions challenging various British actions and policies in Palestine as impermissible under the Covenant and the Mandate.[2] The PMC thus represented yet another forum in which Jews, Arabs, and the British Government would invoke legal narrative and transformational legal framing to gain leverage against each other and influence international opinion.

The PMC and the League of Nations were far more sympathetic to Zionism than today's United Nations, and the PMC had frequently expressed disagreement with British policies in Palestine for they perceived to be less than faithful to the letter of the Mandate and the Balfour Declaration. Weizmann frequently lobbied various members of the PMC behind the scenes, and he did on this occasion as well.[3]

Thus, the proceedings before the PMC in June 1939 should be regarded as the substantive equivalent of an appellate court hearing a Jewish appeal of the legality of the White Paper.

## Debate regarding the White Paper's legality

The PMC's consideration of the White Paper, as the British Government later complained in an internal document, was "confined to the juridical aspect, namely, whether the policy set out in the [White Paper] is in strict conformity with the terms of the Mandate for Palestine."[4]

DOI: 10.4324/9781003225263-8

Colonial Secretary Malcolm MacDonald personally appeared on behalf of the British Government, accompanied by his Legal Advisor, Sir Grattan Bushe. MacDonald made a lengthy, detailed, and highly legalistic opening statement to the PMC at its 15 June 1939 session. Among other arguments, MacDonald relied heavily on the Hogarth Message to support the British Government's position that the phrase "without prejudice to the civil and religious rights" in the Balfour Declaration was also intended to include the *political* rights of the indigenous Palestinian Arab population.

MacDonald characterised the Hogarth Message as "important evidence" of the intent of the drafters of the Balfour Declaration. Therefore, the British Government believed it had the authority to issue the White Paper, and that doing so "did not require any alteration of the Mandate; and, in coming to that conclusion, it had naturally consulted its own legal advisors on the matter."[5]

### Commissioners Van Asbeck and Rappard challenge the White Paper's legality

Several members of the PMC were highly sceptical of the White Paper's legality, believing it conflicted with Britain's obligations under the Mandate. For example, Commissioner Frederick Mari Asbeck (the Baron van Asbeck) said the Mandate imposed *one* overriding international legal obligation on Britain – to establish the Jewish National Home in Palestine. Van Asbeck slammed MacDonald and the British Government for shirking that obligation.

Britain's obligation to protect the civil and religious rights of the existing non-Jewish population of Palestine was *subordinate* to that obligation, according to van Asbeck. The phrase "civil and religious rights" meant exactly what it said and could not be stretched to include "political" rights for the Palestinian Arabs. If the League had intended to include political rights for the Arabs, it would have added that language to the Mandate. And if Britain had intended for the Mandate to include such rights, it should have so requested when the wording of the Mandate was negotiated.[6]

Commissioner van Asbeck also discounted MacDonald's new-found reliance on the Hogarth Message, especially because the British Government had *never* previously relied on it or brought it to the PMC's attention:

> The basis for that change of emphasis was the Hogarth message ... But it could not have been known to the British and Allied statesmen, otherwise they would have been much more careful when referring to a Jewish State or Commonwealth; and it was unknown in 1922, or it would naturally have been referred to in the Churchill White Paper. It was unknown in 1930 when, at the seventeenth (extraordinary) session [of the PMC], the whole question of Palestine came up before the Mandates Commission. It was unknown to the Royal Commission which did not mention that important message in its report, although it was accustomed

> to examine thoroughly the material available; and it was not mentioned by the accredited representative of the mandatory Power in his explanations to the Commission at its thirty-second (extraordinary) session [of the PMC] in 1937, although there had then been ample occasion and necessity for bringing the message fully to light ... If, under the terms of the Hogarth message, the Arabs had the right to oppose immigration, and, in that respect, retained their previous freedom, that was the very antithesis of the Balfour Declaration and of the mandate which contained a very important obligation to facilitate immigration ... the Balfour Declaration had in view a Jewish, and the Hogarth message an Arab, majority.[7]

Commissioner William Rappard (Figure 5.1), a Swiss lawyer and law professor who had been a frequent critic of British policy in Palestine, also asked why no British official had ever previously mentioned the Hogarth Message to the PMC or the League of Nations during the negotiations leading to the Mandate in 1922 or anytime thereafter. Rappard expressed great scepticism regarding the evidentiary value of the Hogarth Message, noting "a great deal was now being made after some seventeen years of silence."[8]

**FIGURE 5.1** Commissioner William Rappard, Permanent Mandates Commission of the League of Nations (Public Domain)

Commissioner van Asbeck also attacked the White Paper's abandonment of the economic absorptive capacity principle in favour of an Arab veto on future Jewish immigration after the initial five-year period had expired. Van Asbeck challenged this "new interpretation [of the Mandate], and one based on data unknown to the Mandates Commission and the Council of the League."[9]

### *MacDonald on the defensive*

MacDonald tried to defend the White Paper in response to these arguments. MacDonald again emphasised the legal significance of the Hogarth Message, regardless of Britain's prior failure to rely on it:

> The Hogarth Message had some importance even in relation to the Mandate itself, because, according to the continental system of law at any rate, if there were any doubt about the meaning of phrases in a document, the Court might admit other relevant documents as evidence to be used in solving any problems of interpretation which arose ... [The Hogarth Message] was quite an important and genuine piece of evidence, which it was quite proper, under the continental system of law, to regard as relevant to the consideration of what certain phrases meant in the Balfour Declaration and in the Mandate.[10]

MacDonald also relied on Article 22 of the Covenant of the League of Nations as a legal basis for justifying the new restrictions on Jewish immigration.

But the majority of the PMC members remained unconvinced. PMC Chairman Pierre Orts of France summarised his view:

> The Mandate, in which the Balfour Declaration had been enshrined, placed Palestine under an international lien. It was only natural that the lien should seem a heavy one to the Arab inhabitants of the country. The Balfour Declaration was, however, an historic fact ... was not consent to the establishment of a Jewish National Home in Palestine the price – and a relatively small one – which the Arabs had paid for the liberation of lands from the Red Sea to the border of Cilicia on the one hand, Iran and the Mediterranean on the other, for the independence they were now winning or had already won, none of which they would ever have gained by their own efforts, and for all of which they had to thank the Allied Powers and particularly the British force in the Near East?[11]

## The PMC's deliberations and report to the League Council

Following several days of debate with MacDonald, the PMC members met privately to discuss the legality of the White Paper. The PMC unanimously agreed, and so reported to the Council of the League, that "the policy set out in the

White Paper was not in accordance with the interpretation which, in agreement with the mandatory Power and the Council [of the League of Nations], the Commission had always placed upon the Mandate."[12]

Four of the seven members of the PMC went further, saying they "did not feel able to state that the policy of the White Paper was in conformity with the Mandate, any contrary conclusion appearing to them to be ruled out by the very terms of the Mandate and by the fundamental intentions of its authors."[13]

The remaining three members believed "existing circumstances would justify the policy of the White Paper, provided the Council did not oppose it."[14]

Britain's representative on the PMC, Lord Hankey, expressed his views about Chairman Orts and his fellow PMC members in a private letter to MacDonald shortly after the PMC had concluded its deliberations:

> [Orts] is the most bigoted and intransigent of the whole narrow-minded, legalistic crew and there was never any doubt that he would come down against the White Paper ... As I kept telling my colleagues until they must have been sick of me, we should not do anyone any good with our divided views and we must do as little harm as possible. Human lives are more important than the *amour propre* of the old gang of the P.M.C. In the end I got it home to all except the old "school marm" [Commissioner Valentine Dannevig of Norway]. She didn't seem to care how many people were killed! The most charitable view is that she never took it in – for when I expressed surprise personally and in private conversation that she, a woman, should be so impervious to the humanitarian aspect, she appeared not to have realized it at all![15]

## The British Government's response to the PMC

The Cabinet met on 19 July 1939 to discuss the PMC's conclusions and how the Council of the League of Nations might react to those conclusions. The Cabinet requested the Foreign Office's legal advisor be consulted to advise the Government "as to what the position would be in the various situations which might arise when the matter came before the Council of the League."[16]

Three days later the Government prepared a draft response to the PMC majority's conclusion that the White Paper violated the Mandate. The Government expressed frustration that the PMC had treated the issue as solely a legal matter while ignoring the larger political context:

> As the power responsible for the administration of the Mandate, His Majesty's Government are obviously not in a position to neglect political considerations in their interpretation of the obligations which the Mandate imposes upon them. In light of their responsibilities, it is inconceivable to them that a document such as the Mandate for Palestine should be treated as if it were a purely legal instrument of the nature of a deed of sale or even of a legislative enactment ...[17]

This statement is remarkable and highly ironic, given the British Government and its officials in charge of administering Palestine had, for nearly the last 20 years, consistently treated the Mandate as a *legal* document, imposing *legal* obligations on the British Government. Now, faced with an adverse finding from a majority of the PMC that the White Paper had violated that same document, the British chose to downplay the legal significance of the Mandate, arguing the document was written so ambiguously that the British Government could interpret it in any way it wanted:

> [T]he Palestine Mandate is susceptible of wide interpretation, and ... the interpretations which have hitherto been placed upon it have not been complete. Attention had been drawn above to the impossibility of ignoring political considerations in the implementation of such a document as the Palestine Mandate, and His Majesty's Government have no doubt that those who framed the Balfour Declaration and the Mandate deliberately avoided the use of precise terms in order to allow a generous latitude of interpretation in light of unforeseen developments.[18]

The sudden British retreat from treating the Mandate as a binding legal document underscored how Britain manipulated the law and legal procedure during the Mandate to suit its political objectives. The Palestinians likewise mastered the same sort of manipulation of the law through transformational legal framing during the Mandate and continuing to the modern era of the conflict, as will be seen in later chapters of this study.

On 2 August, the Foreign Secretary circulated a memorandum to the Cabinet discussing the Government's legal and diplomatic options for defending the White Paper at the upcoming 8 September 1939 meeting in Geneva of the Council of the League of Nations, during which the Council would consider the PMC's majority view that the White Paper did not conform to the Mandate. Once again, despite the Government's heavy reliance on the law and legal reasoning in justifying the White Paper during its formulation in the winter and spring of 1939, the Foreign Secretary, mindful of the legally shaky basis for the White Paper, advised against risking an adverse ruling from the Permanent Court of International Justice:

> The British delegation should strongly discourage any suggestion that a legal ruling should be obtained, either from a special committee of jurists, or from the Hague Court, before the White Paper policy is put into effect ... It is desirable, in this connexion, that the greatest care should be taken by His majesty's Government not to over-emphasize the legal aspect of the problem; for example, it should be unwise for His Majesty's Government to challenge the Permanent Mandate Commission's "observations" in such a way as to become involved in a legal controversy with the Commission. The line to be taken is that there have been many changes in Palestine since 1922, that the Council has to consider the situation as it now is, and so forth.[19]

**FIGURE 5.2** Council of the League of Nations, Geneva (Alamy Photos)

On 5 August 1939, the Foreign Office sent to the Secretary General the Government's official response to the PMC's decision.[20] Interestingly, the Government's final response deleted the language from the earlier draft denying the legal nature and legal force of the Mandate.

Ultimately, there was no need for Britain to worry about defending the legality of the White Paper before the Council of the League of Nations (Figure 5.2). The Nazi invasion of Poland only a few weeks later, on 1 September 1939, not only spelled the beginning of World War II and the demise of the League of Nations but also left the White Paper intact during the entirety of the Holocaust.

Prime Minister Chamberlain had, *in less than eight months*, appeased Hitler, the Mufti, and the surrounding Arab states and left millions of helpless European Jews with no escape from Hitler's Final Solution.

## Notes

1 League of Nations, Permanent Mandates Commission, Minutes of the Thirty-Sixth Session, Held at Geneva from June 8 to June 29, 1939, Official No. C.170.M.100.1939.VI (June 1939).

2 *See* N. Wheatley, *op. cit.*, at 206–207 ("Jews and Arabs in the former Ottoman territory turned this new legal architecture into a mode of politics. They wrote hundreds of petitions to the League and its Permanent Mandates Commission (PMC) that engaged closely with the structure of the system and its laws … Both Jews and Arabs devoted extraordinary attention to composing their petitions [to the Permanent Mandates Commission] in an emphatically legal style. They combed the League's Covenant and the Mandate for Palestine with interpretative zeal, dissecting sentence structures, comparing

and counting articles, and arguing for the priority of one subsection over another. No comma or clause was left unexamined as both communities looked to unearth guarantees of their rights in the League's laws.").

3 CO 733/390/5, Letter from Lord Hankey (British member of the PMC) to MacDonald at 1 (30 June 1939) ("the Jews ... have carried out an active propaganda [campaign] with the members of the P.M.C.").

4 FO 371/23248, Cabinet Committee on Palestine, Memorandum (Secret) by the Secretary of State for the Colonies, Draft Commentary on the Observations of the Permanent Mandates Commission at para. 2 (July 1939).

5 League of Nations, Permanent Mandates Commission, Minutes of the Thirty-Sixth Session, Held at Geneva from June 8 to June 29, 1939, Official No. C.170.M.100.1939. VI at 95–102, 110 (June 1939). Downie also prepared a lengthy set of questions and answers for MacDonald to use in preparation for his appearance before the PMC. CO 733/410/9, H.F. Downie, Palestine: Points for Geneva (10 June 1939).

6 League of Nations, Permanent Mandates Commission, Minutes of the Thirty-Sixth Session, Held at Geneva from June 8 to June 29, 1939, Official No. C.170.M.100.1939.VI at 115 (June 1939). The original PMC verdict is located in the League of Nations Archives, R4079/6A/38140/668, Folios 85–96 ("Observations of the Permanent Mandates Commission on the policy laid down in the document entitled 'Palestine: Statement of Policy of May 1939'").

7 *Id.* at 116.

8 *Id.* at 105.

9 *Id.* at 116.

10 *Id.* at 119.

11 *Id.* at 183–184.

12 *Id.*, Annex 14, *Report to the Council on the Work of the Commission* at 275, para. 9.

13 *Id.*, para. 14.

14 *Id.*, para. 15. Lord Hankey, the British member of the PMC, attempted unsuccessfully to obtain even stronger language from the minority members of the PMC expressing support for the White Paper based on the British Government's *legal* argument that the White Paper did not violate the Mandate. League of Nations Archive, R4079/6A/38689/668, Folio 78, *Variante su dernier paragraphs de la conclusion* (with handwritten note indicating "*Prepare por Lord Hankey*") (28 June 1939) ("Finally, other members of the Commission ... believe also that present circumstances justify the policy of the White Paper, and they see not sufficient reasons for adding to the difficulties of the responsible Mandatory Power by dissenting from the view expressed by the Accredited [British Government] Representative [Malcolm MacDonald] *on the highest legal advice available to it that its policy is consistent with the Mandate*") (emphasis added).

15 CO 733/390/5, Letter from Lord Hankey to MacDonald at 2, 7–8 (30 June 1939).

16 CAB 23/100/6, Minutes (Secret) of Cabinet Meeting at 11 (19 July 1939).

17 FO 371/23248, C.P. 38(20), Minutes (Secret) of Meeting of the Cabinet Committee on Palestine, Draft Commentary on the Observations of the Permanent Mandates Commission at para. 3 (22 July 1939). This language was removed from a subsequent draft.

18 *Id.*, para. 12.

19 CAB 24/288/24, C.P. 174 (39), Memorandum (Secret) by the Secretary of State for Foreign Affairs, Forthcoming Discussions at Geneva regarding the Palestine White Paper at 4 (2 August 1939).

20 League of Nations Archives, R4079/6A/38140/668, Letter from Lacy Baggallay, Foreign Office, to Secretary General, League of Nations, enclosing document entitled "Comments of His Majesty's Government in the United Kingdom" (5 August 1939).

# 6
# ASSESSMENT

The London Conferences, although not a "trial" in any sense of the word, provided a forum for all three parties – Arab, Jewish, and British – to frame the issues through the respective legal narratives they had developed over the last 15 years.

The London Conferences represented a continuation of Britain's use of legal arguments to justify its political approach to the Arab-Jewish conflict in Palestine during the Mandate years. The Palestinian Arabs and their supporters from the surrounding Arab states made very effective use of the law during the Conferences, forcing Whitehall to admit Sherif Hussein had not intended to cede Arab claims to Palestine in his 1915–1916 correspondence with Sir Henry McMahon.

The Arabs also succeeded in their effort to cast the Hogarth Message as a clarification of the Balfour Declaration, providing the British Government with a convenient legal basis for backtracking on its previous commitments to the Zionists. The Jews, for their part, valiantly but unsuccessfully argued the Mandate imposed legal obligations on Britain to continue permitting Jewish immigration and land acquisition in Palestine.

With the Nazi threat looming, Britain decided on a dramatic reversal of its Palestine policy. Britain's overriding political goal at the London Conferences was to appease the Arabs and stave off a potential Nazi-Arab alliance. The best way to achieve that goal was to use the London Conferences as a vehicle for announcing a major policy shift in Palestine, severely limiting Jewish immigration and providing a glide path to the one-state solution and Palestinian Arab sovereignty over all of Palestine.

Britain, therefore, structured the London Conferences as a forum for putting Zionism and the Balfour Declaration "on trial." Britain, seeking to cloak its predetermined policy decisions with legal legitimacy, embraced the façade of legal

DOI: 10.4324/9781003225263-9

process and discussion throughout the Conferences to lay the juridical foundation for the White Paper policy.

The Palestinian Arabs and the Arab states held the strongest hand of all the parties at the London Conferences. The Arabs realised the political momentum was swinging in their favour following Britain's appeasement of Hitler on 30 September 1938 and Britain's 9 November 1938 abandonment of the Peel Commission's two-state proposal. The Arabs also gained leverage through the violence they had perpetrated during their ongoing revolt in Palestine. Thus, the Arabs found themselves well-positioned in London to frame the Palestine conflict as grounded in the alleged illegality of the Balfour Declaration and the Mandate, and especially the alleged illegality of ongoing Jewish immigration and land acquisition.

The Arab and British transformational legal framing during the London Conferences found the perfect foil in the creation of the Arab-British subcommittee to examine the legal arguments involving the McMahon-Hussein correspondence. The Palestine Royal Commission had previously found the correspondence somewhat ambiguous, but not supporting the Arab claim that Palestine had been promised to them in 1915. The British author of the correspondence, Sir Henry McMahon, wrote to the *Times* in July 1937 to state publicly that he never intended to pledge Palestine to the Arabs, and that Hussein well understood Palestine had been excluded.

The Arab side used their legal justice/injustice narrative with great skill in London, especially in the McMahon-Hussein Committee. Antonius and his legal team argued the ambiguous language in McMahon's letters to Hussein should be construed in favour of the Palestinian Arabs, to avoid an otherwise unjust outcome. Antonius and his lawyers also utilised the Hogarth Message to great effect, arguing it stood as compelling contemporaneous evidence of Britain's intent to interpret McMahon's pledge to Hussein as broadly as possible, and the Balfour Declaration as narrowly as possible.

Nevertheless, the British Government found it expedient to allow the Palestinian Arabs once again to make their legal case regarding the McMahon-Hussein correspondence. The Palestinian Arabs obliged, presenting their legal arguments very forcefully. The Palestinians also made effective use of "newly discovered evidence," the so-called Hogarth Message to Sherif Hussein in January 1918, supposedly clarifying the Balfour Declaration was not intended to degrade Arab political rights in Palestine.

The Palestinian Arabs hired the former British Chief Justice of the Palestine Supreme Court to act as their lawyer for the McMahon-Hussein issue, while the British Government had its highest legal officer, the Lord Chancellor, take the lead for the British side during the subcommittee's discussions. The result was an extraordinary joint report, in which the British Government conceded half the Palestinian Arab claim, acknowledging Hussein had intended to include Palestine in the areas of Arab independence, but insisting McMahon had not intended to pledge Palestine to the Arabs.

MacDonald was only too willing to accept the Arab legal framing, as it helped bolster the British Government's desire to build a legal record that would justify the eventual "radical" policy shift he had already recommended to the Cabinet even before the Conferences had convened. Thus, from MacDonald's perspective, allowing the London Conferences to serve as the functional equivalent of a "trial" of Zionism (with the verdict already decided) would serve British objectives perfectly.

Yet the Palestinian Arab penchant for framing the justice/injustice narrative as all-or-nothing ended up costing them dearly. During the London Conferences, they truly were offered the "deal of the century" – the one-state solution, a state which would be theirs alone. The Arabs, blinded to the enormous opportunity the White Paper offered them by their objection to a mere 75,000 additional Jews entering the country over the next five years, and by their unhappiness at having to wait ten years for their independence, made the *mistake* of the century by saying no to the White Paper.

The Jews held the weakest hand at the London Conferences, with no leverage and nothing to offer the British Government. Yet the Jewish side clung to their own legal narrative in attempting to convince the British Government not to backtrack on its commitments under the Balfour Declaration and the Mandate. The Jewish legal arguments, however, fell on deaf British ears.

The London Conferences and the White Paper represented, therefore, yet another instance during the Mandate years in which all three parties – British, Arab, and Jewish – relied heavily on the law to gain leverage against each other and influence international opinion. Weizmann had it exactly right during his tense 16 May meeting at Hyde Hall with MacDonald, when he accused MacDonald of cloaking British policy in the guise of the law. But both the Jewish and Arab delegations had also wrapped their political arguments in the cloak of legal reasoning, just as the parties had done since even before the onset of the Mandate.

The parties' long-established custom and practice of relying on the law and legal argumentation in many ways came to dominate the London Conferences even more than their previous legal battles before the Shaw, Lofgren, and Peel Commissions between 1929 and 1937. And that is not surprising, given the stakes as of February 1939 when the London Conferences began.

For the Jews, whose hopes had diminished dramatically during 1938 – with the nearly parallel rise of Nazism and evaporation of British support for partition – the London Conferences offered a desperate, last-ditch chance to save the Zionist project, and hopefully rescue as many trapped European Jews as possible. For the Jews, the stakes truly amounted to life or death.

For the Palestinian Arabs, increasingly angry at Britain's failure to end Jewish immigration and the National Home experiment once and for all, the London Conferences represented their best chance to seize the mantle of nationalism from the Zionists and claim Palestine as their own, as a truly *Arab* country deserving the same political status as their brethren in Iraq, Saudi Arabia, and Egypt.

For the British, the stakes could not have been greater. Chamberlain's failure in Munich to stem the Nazi juggernaut had put Britain in a terrible bind. The Government badly needed to prevent the Arab states from joining with Hitler while simultaneously making sure not to alienate the United States and its 4.5 million strong Jewish community.[1]

Britain's decision to adopt the White Paper must, however, be remembered for the terrible outcome it caused for the Jews of Europe. Trapped under the increasing reach of Nazi occupation, the White Paper meant certain death for millions of Jews with no place to escape. The British historian Christopher Sykes, whose father Sir Mark Sykes negotiated the famous agreement with his French counterpart Francois Georges-Picot in 1916 to carve up the Ottoman Empire, wrote the following about the White Paper:

> [N]o English person can possibly be proud of the White Paper … Nothing can disguise the fact that there was odious moral cruelty in inflicting so heavy a disappointment on millions of people to whom Palestine was the only hope left on earth … This moral harshness was all the more atrocious because it meant that British rule became consciously involved in enormous physical cruelty as well.[2]

Britain, therefore, used the London Conferences (including the Joint Committee regarding the McMahon-Hussein correspondence) and the legal arguments it made during and after the Conferences, to justify the radical change in policy embodied in the White Paper. The British, in a supreme twist of irony, convinced themselves and tried to convince the PMC that if they were going to sacrifice Zionism and European Jewry, it was only because the Mandate *required* them to do so.

Britain, therefore, succeeded in appeasing both the Germans and the Arabs within less than a year but ended up with little or nothing to show for their efforts.[3] By June 1940, the Nazis were bombing the civilian population of London. The Mufti relocated to Berlin, where he broadcast messages during the war urging the Arabs and the Bosnian Muslims to fight with the Nazis, and imploring the *Luftwaffe* to bomb Tel Aviv.

But British officialdom clung to the illusion they in fact had served their national interests, as evidenced by a handwritten minute by Downie in March 1940. Commenting on German propaganda aimed at the Arab states, Downie wrote, in reference to the White Paper, "What would the Germans have said if we had let down the Arabs!"[4]

In the end, however, it was the Palestinian Arab leaders who let down their own people. Rather than embrace the White Paper as the final nail in the Zionist coffin and the key to Palestinian Arab statehood, the Mufti and his allies rejected it as not good enough. Those Palestinian leaders who knew better were afraid to stand up to the Mufti, who had proven extremely ruthless at murdering his enemies and crushing any dissent. If those Palestinian leaders had shown more courage, history might well have been different. Instead, the Palestinians wasted their best-ever chance for statehood when they formally rejected the White Paper in late May 1939.

The London Conferences did not represent the last legal battleground involving the parties during the Mandate years. The legal battles continued after World War II before the Anglo-American Committee of Inquiry and the United Nations Special Committee on Palestine. But the legal conflicts surrounding the London Conferences and the White Paper were the last *purely* British-Arab-Jewish legal battles of the Mandate, representing the culmination of Britain's long-brewing split with Zionism and its embrace of Palestinian Arab nationalism.

## Notes

1 *See* Y. Porath, *op. cit.* at 290.
2 C. Sykes, *op. cit.* at 199.
3 For a contrary view of the Munich-White Paper appeasement analogy, *see* C. Beckerman, *op. cit.* at 134 ("Far from an analogy with the Munich Agreement of 1938 – which was a foreign policy anomaly pursued to avoid war with another European power – MacDonald's White Paper was merely the routine exercise of diplomacy within Britain's own empire. While labelled 'appeasement' by some of those MPS who opposed Munich, the comparison was an emotional reaction to an otherwise normal act of concession and compromise … The decision was made in the context of a crisis, but it also reflected a rational weighing of costs versus benefits").
4 CO 733/418/13, Palestine Land Transfers Regulations: Notes on League of Nations Aspect, Downie's handwritten comment in margin at para. 8 (4 March 1940).

# PART III

# The Anglo-American Committee of Inquiry – British policy on trial and the no-state solution

# 7

# ENTER AMERICA

## Formation of the Anglo-American Committee

### Background

The 1939 London Conferences resulted in the British Government unilaterally rendering a resounding verdict in favour of Palestinian nationalism and against Zionism. The Government, anxious to keep the Arabs on its side during the anticipated War with Nazi Germany, cast aside the Balfour Declaration and the Mandate, opting instead for the one-state solution, with Palestine gaining independence in ten years as an Arab-dominated state. No further Jewish immigration would be permitted without Arab consent after the first five of those years, and nearly all further Jewish land acquisition was banned immediately.

But for the Palestinian Arabs, nothing short of complete capitulation to *all* their demands, including the *immediate* stoppage of Jewish immigration, would suffice. In rejecting the White Paper of 1939, the Palestinians lost their greatest opportunity since the end of the Ottoman Empire for independence and sovereignty over all of Palestine.

World War II, of course, changed everything for Palestine, as it had for the rest of the world. The murder of six million European Jews in the Holocaust – more than *one-third* of the *entire* global Jewish population – left the victorious yet depleted British Government with two immediate and interrelated challenges: first, the need to formulate a *short-term* policy response to demands from both the Zionist leadership and President Truman that Britain immediately grant one hundred thousand Palestine immigration certificates to European Jewish refugees; and second, the need to construct a *long-term* policy for the future governance of Palestine.

The British Government, consistent with its longstanding custom and practice during the Mandate, addressed both issues by once again resorting to legal process and procedure. But this time Britain, exhausted after years of war and wary

DOI: 10.4324/9781003225263-11

of Jewish influence in the United States, insisted the American Government participate in the process and share the financial, diplomatic and potential military responsibility for the outcome. Britain proposed, and the United States accepted, the idea of forming a Joint Committee of Inquiry in late 1945 to investigate the plight of European Jewry and the political future of Palestine, and to make recommendations to both governments.

Britain hoped it would be able to educate its American counterparts about the dizzying complexities of the Palestine problem and the reasonableness of the White Paper policy paradigm. Britain aimed to make the Americans realise that transferring tens of thousands of European Jews to Palestine carried the enormous risk of angering the Palestinian Arabs and driving the surrounding Arab states into the waiting arms of the Soviet Union.

Whitehall identified three key objectives for involving the Americans: (i) persuading the Americans to take Britain's lead on Palestine policy; (ii) coaxing the Americans into contributing their fair share of the political, financial, and military burdens of Britain's presence in Palestine; and (iii) maintaining Britain's strategic foothold in the Middle East as a bridge to India and as a bulwark against posy-war Soviet expansionism.

Britain's notion was that the Committee, co-chaired by British and American judges, and including four additional members with legal training, would investigate the plight of European Jewry and the situation in Palestine, taking testimony and receiving written evidence from witnesses in Washington, London, Europe, Jerusalem, and the surrounding Arab states, and render a legally compelling verdict affirming the White Paper policies regarding Jewish immigration and Palestine's long-term future.

The Anglo-American Committee spent four months conducting what turned out to be a "trial" of British policy regarding Jewish immigration and Palestine's long-term political future. But the verdict ended up shocking the British Government, as the Committee unanimously and overwhelmingly rejected the White Paper.

The Committee also unanimously endorsed the granting of the 100,000 immigration certificates and the resumption of the pre-White Paper policy permitting free Jewish immigration, subject only to Palestine's economic absorptive capacity. It also recommended rescission of another key vestige of the White Paper – the 1940 Land Transfer Ordinance. Even more significantly, the verdict rejected the White Paper's "one-state" solution in favour of the Palestinian Arabs, opting instead for a "no-state solution" and the indefinite continuation of the Mandate or a successor Trusteeship for Palestine.

The Committee was deeply moved by the plight of Europe's surviving Jews and their overwhelming desire to leave Europe and immigrate to Palestine. The Committee was also impressed with Palestinian Jewish economic achievements and with the community's sheer will-power to absorb tens of thousands of additional Jewish immigrants. Golda Meir, for example, testified that every Jewish family in Palestine would willingly take as many refugees as possible into their own homes.

The Committee was also convinced that creating either a single, binational state, or partitioning Palestine into two separate states would lead to war between Arabs and Jews. It opted instead for no statehood for either party.

The Committee's verdict represented a compromise after three months of testimony and fact-finding, and three subsequent weeks of bitterly fought deliberations, especially pitting the two judges – and their desire to uphold the political aims of their respective governments – against each other.

The Committee's verdict also left both the Jewish and Arab sides unhappy. The Jews reacted favourably to the recommendation regarding the 100,000 immigration certificates, but Prime Minister Attlee quickly dashed their hopes by announcing in the House of Commons that none of the immigration certificates would be issued until the *Haganah* and other armed Jewish groups in Palestine had surrendered all their weapons.

The British Government, bitterly disappointed with the verdict, tried to manoeuvre the Americans into setting the verdict aside in favour of a new "provincial autonomy" plan for Palestine. The effort almost succeeded, until one of the American members of the Anglo-American Committee made a dramatic, last-ditch plea to President Truman in late July 1946 to reject the British proposal. That crucial moment in the Oval Office marked the beginning of the end of British influence in Palestine and paved the way for Israeli statehood less than two years later.

## The White Paper and Jewish immigration during the War

World War II began with Germany's invasion of Poland on 1 September 1939, less than four months following the British Government's publication of the MacDonald White Paper, and less than one month after the Permanent Mandate's Commission verdict that the White Paper had violated the terms of the Mandate. The outbreak of the War ended any possibility for the Council of the League to issue a final ruling regarding the White Paper's legality.

Britain adhered to the White Paper policy throughout the War. By May 1945, the White Paper's cap of 75,000 total Jewish immigrants still had not been reached. Britain continued enforcing the monthly Jewish immigration limit during the War, even after it learned of the Holocaust. In fact, fewer than the maximum cap of 1,500 immigrants per month entered Palestine during the War years. As of the end of the War in May 1945, the overall limit of 75,000 would not have been reached until approximately December 1945 – six years and seven months after the White Paper had been issued.[1]

Throughout the War years, the Zionists continued advocating for the White Paper's repeal to alleviate the desperate situation confronting European Jewry. In May 1942, at the Biltmore Conference in New York City, the Zionists adopted resolutions rejecting the legality of the White Paper and, for the first time, rejecting partition and demanding the one-state solution in the form of a Jewish commonwealth in the whole of Palestine.[2] Despite the "Biltmore Program," however, Zionist leaders repeatedly expressed the willingness to accept a two-state solution in the form of partition during discussions with the British and American Governments in 1946.

## *Emerging American interests in the Middle East*

The United States emerged from World War II with new interests in the Middle East. The State Department began focusing in the waning months of the War on building strong ties with the Arab states, to ensure US access to oil and commercial air routes through the region.

On 14 February 1945, three days following the conclusion of the Yalta Conference, President Roosevelt met Saudi King Abdul Aziz Ibn Saud aboard the *USS Quincy*, which had sailed through the Suez Canal to the Great Bitter Lake in Egypt.[3] US Ambassador to Saudi Arabia Colonel William A. Eddy, a known anti-Zionist, served as Roosevelt's interpreter for the meeting (Figure 7.1).[4] Among other topics, the two leaders discussed Palestine and US policy.

Eddy later reported his pleasure with the outcome of the Roosevelt-Ibn Saud meeting in a secret memorandum to Secretary of State Edward Stettinius. Eddy wrote, "[t]he President had planned to modify the King's attitude regarding Palestine, but was instead convinced by the King of the Arab point of view. The President stated ... he would not support the Zionist movement for a Jewish National Home in Palestine."[5]

**FIGURE 7.1** President Franklin Roosevelt and Col. William Eddy with King Ibn Saud aboard the *USS Quincy*, 14 February 1945 (Public Domain)

Roosevelt confirmed the substance of the 14 February discussion in a letter to Ibn Saud in early April 1945, written exactly one week prior to Roosevelt's death. The President's letter said the United States would not take action in Palestine without full consultation with Arabs and Jews:

> I communicated to you the attitude of the American Government toward Palestine and made clear our desire that no decision be taken with respect to that country without full consultation with both Arabs and Jews. Your Majesty will also doubtless recall that during our recent conversation I assured you that I would take no action ... which might prove hostile to the Arab people.[6]

## *Formation of the Arab League*

In March 1945, as the War drew to a close, the Arab states formed the Arab League. The Charter of the Arab League contained a special Annex regarding Palestine, reprising some of the same legal arguments the Mufti and Auni Bey Abdul Hadi had been advocating since the 1920s.

The Annex asserted Palestine enjoyed independent *legal* status as a sovereign entity, based on the Covenant of the League of Nations:

> ANNEX ON PALESTINE. At the end of the last Great War, Palestine, together with the other Arab States, was separated from the Ottoman Empire. She became independent, not belonging to any other State.
>
> The Treaty of Lausanne proclaimed that her fate should be decided by the parties concerned in Palestine.
>
> Even though Palestine was not able to control her own destiny, it was on the basis of the recognition of her independence that the Covenant of the League of Nations determined a system of government for her.
>
> Her existence and her independence among the nations can, therefore, no more be questioned *de jure* than the independence of any of the other Arab States.
>
> Even though the outward signs of this independence have remained veiled as a result of *force majeure*, it is not fitting that this should be an obstacle to the participation of Palestine in the work of the League.
>
> Therefore, the States signatory to the Pact of the Arab League consider that in view of Palestine's special circumstances, the Council of the League should designate an Arab delegate from Palestine to participate in its work until this country enjoys actual independence.[7]

Azzam Pasha became Secretary General of the Arab League. Less than one year later he would appear as a witness before the Anglo-American Committee during its hearings at the Mena Palace Hotel near Cairo.

## *Jewish post-war demands to allow Holocaust survivors into Palestine*

When the War in Europe ended in May 1945, Weizmann wrote to Churchill requesting rescission of the White Paper and restating the demands of the Biltmore Program.[8] Weizmann enclosed a memorandum from the Jewish Agency requesting the British Government announce immediate support for a Jewish commonwealth in Palestine.[9]

On 18 June 1945, the Jewish Agency formally requested the British Government rescind the White Paper and issue 100,000 immigration certificates for Jewish survivors of the Holocaust, including 25,000 orphaned children.[10]

Britain rejected both requests, for fear of angering the Arab states and rousing Muslim sentiment in India. Britain, loath to alienate the Arabs and Indian Muslims in 1939 for fear of driving them into Hitler's arms, now harboured the same fears in 1945 regarding the Soviet Union.[11] The most Britain would consider for the short-term was a continuation of the White Paper policy beyond the end of 1945 (after the White Paper's original quota of 75,000 had been filled) and permitting ongoing Jewish immigration to continue at the same rate of 1,500 per month – but subject to Arab consent.[12]

That consent, however, was unlikely to be forthcoming. The Palestinian Arabs by 1945 had achieved the two-to-one majority in Palestine the White Paper had promised, and they adamantly refused to consider any further Jewish immigration. The Palestinian Arabs emphasised they were not responsible for the Holocaust, and argued it would be unfair and even *illegal* to foist *any* of Europe's remaining Jews on Palestine. The Arabs insisted Palestine lacked the physical space and resources to accommodate any Holocaust survivors or other Jewish immigrants.

## The Harrison report and "the 100,000"

Not long after Roosevelt's death, President Truman expressed sympathy with Jewish demands for Britain to issue 100,000 immigration certificates to European Jewish refugees. Truman sent Earl G. Harrison, Dean of the University of Pennsylvania Law School and the US representative to the Intergovernmental Committee on Refugees, to Europe in June 1945 to investigate and report back on the Jewish Holocaust survivors in Germany and Austria.

Harrison sent his short but powerful ten-page typewritten report to Truman in July 1945. The Report addressed both the desire of the surviving Jews to emigrate to Palestine, as well as their horrendous living conditions as displaced persons:

> [T]he issue of Palestine must be faced. Now that such large numbers are no longer involved and if there is any genuine sympathy for what these survivors have endured, some reasonable extension or modification of the White Paper of 1939 ought to be possible ... The Jewish Agency has submitted to the British Government a petition that one hundred thousand immigration

> certificates be made available. A memorandum accompanying the petition makes a persuasive showing with respect to the immediate absorptive capacity of Palestine … *As matters now stand, we appear to be treating the Jews as the Nazis treated them except that we do not exterminate them.* They are in concentration camps in large numbers under our military guard instead of S.S. troops. One is led to wonder whether the German people, seeing this, are not supposing that we are following or at least condoning Nazi policy.[13]

Harrison's report "moved" and impressed Truman with the urgency of the European Jewish plight, and the linkage of that plight with the Palestine issue.[14] Truman wrote to Prime Minister Clement Attlee on 24 July 1945 urging the British Government to "find it possible without delay to take steps to lift the restrictions of the White Paper on Jewish immigration to Palestine."[15]

## British and American reactions to the Harrison report

The British Government, however, rejected the Harrison report as "not … based on a proper investigation."[16] Britain wanted to separate the refugee issue from the Palestine issue, fearing a mass transfer of European Jewish Holocaust survivors to Palestine would be extremely expensive both financially and politically for Britain. Britain feared such a move would enrage the local Arabs and the surrounding Arab states, jeopardising Britain's standing in the Arab world, and requiring Britain to commit more military and financial resources to Palestine.

Britain, still the Mandatory power in Palestine, therefore continued to pursue a pro-Arab, anti-Zionist line, urging the surviving European Jews to try to rebuild their lives in Europe or elsewhere rather than emigrate to Palestine. The British Government realised, however, that American pressure regarding the 100,000 Jewish immigration certificates had weakened Britain's position. Britain no longer operated with the freedom of action in Palestine it had enjoyed between the two World Wars. It had been one thing to risk the occasional slap on the wrist from the Permanent Mandates Commission of the League of Nations. But risking the wrath of President Truman and the US Congress over European Jewish immigration carried far more serious potential economic and political consequences for Britain.

British officialdom privately expressed deep frustration with the Americans for criticising British policy from the sidelines. British officials lambasted their American counterparts for failing to appreciate the many nuances, conflicting interests and political cross-currents at play in both the short- and long-term policy considerations for Jewish immigration and Palestine's overall future. Britain wanted the Americans to appreciate the political difficulties inherent in linking the Jewish refugee issue to the Palestine issue.

Moreover, Britain refused to accept the notion that Palestine offered the *only* place of refuge for European Jewry. Instead, Britain argued, most European Jews would likely prefer to rebuild their lives in Europe. Those who wanted to leave should be given a choice of various locations, such as the Dominican Republic, rather than automatically sent to Palestine, which would cause huge problems for Britain with the local Arabs, the surrounding Arab states, and the restive Muslims of India.

Britain, growing tired of Americans carping from the sidelines, devised a policy of drawing the Americans into the short-term immigration and long-term Palestine issues and saddling the United States with a large portion of the political, financial, and military burdens for Palestine.

Thus, in early July 1945 Lord Halifax (former Foreign Secretary and now Britain's Ambassador to the United States) sent a lengthy cable to the Foreign Office urging the British Government to involve the United States "in any attempt to solve the Palestinian and other connected problems."[17]

Soon afterward the Foreign Office prepared a list of options for Jewish immigration to Palestine. The Foreign Office noted the least unfavourable course for Britain would be to seek Arab consent to continue Jewish immigration at the existing rate of 1,500 per month once the White Paper quota ran out in late 1945, at least on a temporary basis.[18]

The State Department was also identifying various future options for Palestine during the summer of 1945. Professor William Yale of the University of New Hampshire, serving on temporary assignment at the State Department, sent a memorandum to the Near East Division identifying four potential plans for Palestine: (i) a Jewish State; (ii) an Arab State; (iii) Partition, and (iv) Trusteeship.[19]

On 22 August Prime Minister Attlee appointed a Cabinet Committee on Palestine, chaired by Lord Morrison, to formulate a proposed British policy for Palestine. The Committee issued an *ad interim* report to the Cabinet less than three weeks later, on 8 September 1945.[20]

On 31 August President Truman sent a copy of the Harrison Report to Attlee and urged the Prime Minister once again to grant the 100,000 immigration certificates. In so doing, Truman explicitly linked the Jewish refugee issue to the Palestine issue:

> I should like to call your attention to the conclusions and recommendations [of the Harrison Report] ... especially the references to Palestine. It appears that the available certificates for immigration to Palestine will be exhausted in the near future. It is suggested that the granting of an additional one hundred thousand of such certificates would contribute greatly to a sound solution for the future of Jews still in Germany and Austria, and for other Jewish refugees who do not wish to remain where they are or who for understandable reasons do not desire to return to their countries of origin.
>
> On the basis of this and other information which has come to me I concur in the belief that no other single matter is so important for those who have known the horrors of concentration camps for over a decade as is the future of immigration possibilities into Palestine ... As I said to you

> in Potsdam, the American people, as a whole, firmly believe that immigration into Palestine should not be closed and that a reasonable number of Europe's persecuted Jews should, in accordance with their wishes, be permitted to resettle there …
>
> The main solution appears to lie in the quick evacuation of as many as possible of the non-repatriable Jews, who wish it, to Palestine. If it is effective, such action should not be long delayed.[21]

## British-American tensions regarding Jewish immigration to Palestine

On 6 September 1945, British Foreign Secretary Ernest Bevin convened a meeting in London with Britain's ambassadors to the Arab states and the Palestine High Commissioner to consider Britain's short- and long-term future options for Palestine. The minutes of the meeting reflect discussion of various options for Palestine, including outright partition or a federal state including Transjordan. The federal state would be ruled by an Arab King (presumably but not necessarily Abdullah) and would contain three quasi-autonomous provinces – Jewish, Palestinian Arab, and Transjordanian – each "with a measure of home-rule, similar to that enjoyed in Scotland."

Bevin and the Ambassadors agreed to refer the matter to the Colonial Office for further study, knowing Britain would need to come up with a proposal acceptable to the United Nations and the United States. Bevin and the Ambassadors also agreed to recommend Jewish immigration to Palestine be allowed to continue at the existing rate of 1,500 per month after the White Paper's overall cap of 75,000 had been reached in the next two months.[22]

On 8 September, two days after Bevin's meeting, the Cabinet Palestine Committee issued its *ad interim* report. The Committee recommended the British Government should: (i) continue the 1939 White Paper policy, including the 1,500 per month Jewish immigration quota on a short-term basis, subject to Arab consent; (ii) inform the United States and the surrounding Arab states of its intention to refer the long-term policy questions regarding Palestine to the newly established United Nations; and (iii) reinforce its military garrison in Palestine to guard against Jewish violence in response to Britain's decision to maintain the White Paper's immigration restrictions.[23]

British-American tensions flared repeatedly over the Jewish immigration issue in the fall of 1945. On 14 September Prime Minister Attlee sent a "personal and top secret" cable to Truman. Attlee said he had learned Truman planned to issue a statement that same evening urging Britain to grant the 100,000 immigration certificates. Attlee could hardly suppress his anger, telling Truman that doing so "could not fail to do grievous harm to relations between our two countries."[24]

On 16 September Attlee responded formally to Truman's 31 August letter enclosing the Harrison Report. Attlee emphasised President Roosevelt's pledge to consult with both the Jews and Arabs before any decisions were made regarding Palestine. Implementing Harrison's recommendation and granting the 100,000 immigration certificates would, according to Attlee, anger the Arabs and inflame Muslim sentiment in India. Attlee concluded:

> We have got the matter under urgent examination, with a view to the formulation of a long-term policy which we propose to refer to the World Organization [United Nations] as soon as practicable. Meanwhile we are considering how to deal with the immigration problem in [the] interval and I shall be very happy to let you know as soon as I can what our intentions are in this matter.[25]

## *British internal review of short-term immigration and long-term Palestine issues*

On 28 September 1945, the Colonial Secretary, George Henry Hall, submitted a memorandum to the Cabinet containing the joint recommendations of the Colonial Office and the Foreign Office for short- and long-term policy for Palestine. Given Britain's desire to retain its strategic foothold in the eastern Mediterranean, the memorandum recommended the Government apply to the newly formed United Nations Organization for approval to convert Palestine from a Mandate to a Trusteeship, presumably with Britain appointed as Trustee.[26]

The memorandum identified six possible outcomes for Britain's long-term policy in Palestine:

a. The present system of governing, without either the consent or the co-operation of the governed.
b. The White Paper proposals, envisioning a unitary Palestinian State with constitutional bodies on which Arabs and Jews would sit in predetermined proportions.
c. The plan recommended by the Ministerial Committee of 1943–44 which involves the partition of Palestine and the setting up of independent Jewish and Arab states.
d. Lord Altrincham's scheme for an International Trust, with international control of immigration.
e. The scheme which I [Hall] have circulated … which envisages the division of Palestine into Jewish and Arab provinces, each with a considerable degree of autonomy, with a unitary government at the Centre.
f. The scheme suggested by the Foreign Secretary for a federation embracing Arab and Jewish areas of Palestine and Transjordan.[27]

The memorandum described the above six possibilities as representing "all practicable systems of government that might be introduced."[28]

By early October 1945, Lord Halifax, Britain's Ambassador to the United States, was urging his Government to continue the rate of Jewish immigration at 1,500 per month while simultaneously referring the Palestine situation to the United Nations to take the pressure off British shoulders. Interestingly, and consistent with Britain's prior approach to dealing with the Permanent Mandates Commission, Lord Halifax described Britain's political challenge in decidedly legalistic language in a 3 October 1945 cable:

> In any case we should avoid a situation in which in the event of trouble in Palestine His Majesty's Government would become a *defendant before the United Nations Organisation at the instance of any power that might wish to put us in the dock*.[29]

## Joint Anglo-American Committee of Inquiry

### *Bevin's proposal*

The Cabinet convened on 4 October to consider Lord Halifax's 3 October telegram and Hall's 28 September memorandum. The Prime Minister focused on the increasing pressure from Washington regarding the 100,000 immigration certificates, which he said would "lead to an explosion in the Middle East, [but] would not solve the situation of the Jews in Europe."[30]

Foreign Minister Bevin suggested a "fresh approach," in which Britain and the United States would form a Joint Committee to examine both the short-term immigration issue and the longer term future of Palestine, with the aim of submitting proposals to the United Nations.[31]

Bevin envisioned the Committee's work would focus on three issues: (i) what immediate steps could be taken to ameliorate the situation of the European Jews; (ii) how many Jews could reasonably be allowed to immigrate to Palestine in the immediate future; and (iii) whether the Jewish refugees could be resettled in places other than Palestine.

Bevin's objective was for the Joint Committee to produce a report treating the Jewish refugee issue as completely separate from the Palestine issue. The Zionists were focused on linking the two issues together, arguing the gates of Palestine must be opened to the refugees, as there was no future for them in Europe and no suitable alternative home anywhere else in the world. Bevin, on the other hand, fearing further Jewish immigration to Palestine would jeopardise Britain's relationship with the Arab world and cause an uprising among India's Muslim population, wanted to solve the refugee problem without Palestine, and he needed American support to do so.[32]

The Cabinet endorsed the idea in principle and instructed Bevin (Figure 7.2) to work together with the Colonial Secretary to submit a proposal to the Cabinet Committee on Palestine at its meeting the following week.[33] The Cabinet wanted a "careful enquiry in which the United States would be associated with us."[34]

On 9 October Bevin and Hall submitted a joint memorandum to the Cabinet Committee on Palestine, formally proposing the creation of an Anglo-American

**FIGURE 7.2** Ernest Bevin (Public Domain)

Committee of Enquiry under a rotating chairmanship. The proposed Terms of Reference specified: (i) examining the current position of the Jews in Europe; (ii) estimating how many Jews could not be returned to their countries of origin; (iii) considering whether European Jews could immigrate to "other countries, including the United States"; and (iv) identifying other available means of meeting the immediate needs of the situation.[35] Palestine was not mentioned at all, but subsumed within the "other countries" language of the third proposed Term of Reference.

While Palestine was not included as a specific item in the proposed Terms of Reference, the joint memorandum noted the Committee would also need to investigate the situation in Palestine and hear from both Jews and Arabs. Given the British Government's desire to apply for United Nations approval for a Trusteeship in Palestine, the Committee would serve as a vehicle for helping devise a long-term policy, as well as forcing the United States "to bear a share of the responsibility for it. She will no longer be able to play the part of the irresponsible critic."[36]

Consistent with Britain's longstanding approach to the Palestine issue, it wanted the Committee to operate as a legal body, using legal procedure to produce recommendations flowing from legal fact find-finding and based on legal reasoning. Britain, therefore, suggested the Committee be co-chaired by highly respected British and American judges, with power to take testimony from witnesses, examine documents, and render a verdict in the form of a written report. Ultimately the 12-member Committee contained not just the two judges as co-chairs, but four additional members with legal training.

The Cabinet met on 11 October 1945 and approved the Bevin/Hall joint recommendations to establish a Committee of Inquiry and to persuade the United States to participate.[37]

## *British-American negotiations regarding committee formation*

On 13 October, the Foreign Office cabled instructions to Lord Halifax in Washington DC for discussing with the American Government the formation of a joint Anglo-American Committee of Inquiry. The instructions contained the draft Terms of Reference that made no mention of "Palestine," saying instead the proposed Joint Committee would "examine the possibility of relieving the position in Europe by immigration into other countries outside Europe."[38]

On 14 October Lord Halifax cabled back to London to report his view that the Americans would most likely to agree to form a Joint Committee of Inquiry with Britain, as there appeared to be a growing feeling in Congress that the US Government "ought not (repeat not) to shirk all responsibility."[39]

On 22 October, the US Government accepted the British proposal to form a Joint Committee of Enquiry, but the wording of the Terms of Reference had not yet been agreed. The State Department asked the British Government to delay the public announcement until after the New York mayoral election scheduled for 6 November.[40] The White House did not want to risk criticism from the Jewish Republican candidate that by agreeing to establish the Joint Committee of Inquiry with the British Government, the Administration had backed away from its repeated insistence that the 100,000 immigration certificates be issued as soon as possible.[41]

Bevin informed the Cabinet on 13 November the Americans had accepted the invitation to form the Joint Committee of Inquiry "to examine the question of European Jewry and, in light of that examination, to make a further review of the Palestine problem." Bevin told the Cabinet President Truman "still adhered to the views expressed [regarding the 100,000 immigration certificates] in the letter which he had addressed to the Prime Minister on 31st August."[42]

Bevin made the formal public announcement to the House of Commons that same afternoon, 13 November 1945:

> Having regard to the whole situation and the fact that it has caused this worldwide interest which affects both Arabs and Jews, His Majesty's Government decided to invite the Government of the United States to co-operate with them in setting up a joint Anglo-American Committee of Inquiry, under a rotating chairmanship, to examine the question of

> European Jewry and to make a further review of the Palestine problem in the light of that examination. I am happy to be able to inform the House that the Government of the United States have accepted this invitation.[43]

Bevin also told the House that Jewish immigration would continue at the present rate of 1,500 per month while the Joint Committee conducted its work.[44]

### *Zionist legal reaction to formation of the Anglo-American Committee*

That same afternoon (13 November 1945) Weizmann, ever ready to use the law in advancing Zionist objectives, asked New York lawyer Abraham Tulin for a *legal opinion* regarding Bevin's announcement of the proposed work of the Anglo-American Committee of Inquiry, including the proposed Terms of Reference. Tulin sent Weizmann a letter with his preliminary legal analysis the following day, 14 November.[45]

Tulin noted the rights of the Jewish people both derive from, and are circumscribed by, the Palestine Mandate, the Palestine Treaty of 1924 between the United States and the United Kingdom, and Article 80(1) of the Charter of the United Nations, preserving pre-existing rights regarding potential future Trusteeships.[46]

Tulin next argued for interpreting the first Term of Reference, requiring the Committee to examine the political, economic and social conditions in Palestine as they bear upon the problem of Jewish immigration, to include "the constitutional legal rights which the Jewish people has in and to Palestine and the constitutional legal obligations which the British Government has assumed under the [Palestine Mandate and the 1924 Anglo-American Palestine Treaty]."[47]

Tulin then argued in favour of according full legal rights to the Jewish people regarding the various elements of the Mandate, including "the internationally covenanted and legal right to establish the Jewish National Home in Palestine"; the Jewish Agency's "legal and official status before the Anglo-American Committee"; Britain's "internationally covenanted duty to facilitate Jewish immigration into Palestine under suitable conditions" and not to discriminate against the Jewish inhabitants of Palestine. Therefore, Tulin argued, the Anglo-American Committee would "have the full right and power to inquire and report as to the legality of the MacDonald White Paper of 1939 and the restrictive land purchase regulations enacted pursuant thereto, which are so discriminatory against Jews."[48]

After briefly discussing the remaining Terms of Reference, Tulin concluded his legal analysis as follows:

> [T]he Terms of Reference to the Anglo-American Committee spell grave danger to the cause of a Jewish Palestine unless they are clarified so as to make the existing constitutional status the basis and foundation of the Committee's inquiry and give the Jewish Agency for Palestine official

> status before the Committee in practically all phases of its inquiry. The danger is particularly grave, since the Committee is expected to make the recommendations which may be embodied in the proposed new Trusteeship Agreement for Palestine. I think that the Jewish Agency has definite rights in the premises that have not yet been abrogated and which should be forcefully asserted.[49]

### *Negotiations over Terms of Reference*

The British and American Governments embarked on the process of forming the Committee with differing objectives. The British Government wanted the inquiry to focus on European Jewry without reference to Palestine. Whitehall was loath to concede any linkage between the European Jewry and Palestine issues, or that Palestine represented the only possible home for the surviving European Jews. The British Government was "reluctan[t] to admit, after a war in which we have fought against the principle of racial discrimination, that the Jews have no future in Europe."[50]

Truman, on the other hand, insisted on that very linkage, repeatedly stressing throughout the summer and fall of 1945 that he wanted Britain to allow 100,000 Holocaust survivors to immigrate to Palestine:

> It was apparent that London opposed opening Palestine to massive immigration, and equally apparent that Washington, or at least Truman, remained committed to Palestine as a refuge for a large portion of the Jewish DPs. Bevin announced the Anglo-American Committee of Inquiry on November 13 in the House of Commons. Repeating his position that the Jews should remain in Europe and live in their native lands without fear of discrimination, he reminded listeners that the mandate for Palestine required Britain to encourage Jewish settlement only if the rights of the Arabs were not prejudiced, and underlined that Britain had never been able to reconcile the Arabs to the Jewish presence in Palestine. Truman ... made no mention of rebuilding Jewish communities in Europe, and emphasized that the committee would examine conditions in Palestine as they related to Jewish immigration.[51]

The British and American Governments, therefore, squabbled over the Terms of Reference for the Joint Committee. Lord Halifax and Secretary of State Byrnes negotiated over the language for several weeks, specifically the extent to which the Terms of Reference should contain any reference to Palestine and to the possibility of Jewish refugees remaining in Europe or finding new homes in countries other than Palestine. Lord Halifax and US Secretary of State James Byrnes had an especially tense meeting on 29 October 1945, with Byrnes insisting the US Government would not permit the British Government to downgrade Palestine's importance to the Committee's work.[52]

The two governments fought over other procedural issues as well, including whether to impose a deadline of 120 days for the Committee to issue its report, whether the governments should indicate up front whether they would consider extending the deadline, and whether an interim report from the Committee would be acceptable.[53]

The Americans pressed for a hard deadline for the Committee to conclude its work, eager to protect the Administration from any criticism that the Committee had been formed simply to delay indefinitely any relief for the Jewish refugees. Ultimately Britain agreed to a 120-deadline for the Committee to complete its work.

On 10 December 1945, nearly a full month after announcing the formation of the Joint Committee of Inquiry, the two governments finally reached agreement on the following Terms of Reference, which they made public on 14 December 1945[54]:

1. To examine political, economic, and social conditions of Palestine as they bear upon the problem of Jewish immigration and settlement therein, and the well-being of the peoples now living therein.
2. To examine the position of the Jews in those countries in Europe where they have been the victims of Nazi and Fascist persecution and the practical measures taken or contemplated to be taken in those countries, to enable them to live free from discrimination and oppression and to make estimates of those who wish, or will be impelled by their conditions to migrate to Palestine, or other countries outside Europe.
3. To hear the views of competent witnesses and to consult representative Arabs and Jews on the problems of Palestine as such problems are affected by conditions subject to examination under paragraph 1 and paragraph 2 above, and by other relevant facts and circumstances, and to make recommendations to His Majesty's Government and to the Government of the United States for *ad interim* handling of those problems, as well as for their permanent solution.
4. To make such other recommendations to His Majesty's Government, and the Government of the United States, as may be necessary to meet the immediate needs arising from conditions subject to examination under paragraph 2 above, by remedial action in the European countries in question, or by the provision of facilities for emigration to, and settlement in, countries outside Europe.

Commenting on the difficult and at times acrimonious British-American negotiations leading to the agreed Terms of Reference and the 120-day deadline for the Committee to complete its work, one leading historian noted:

> The tortuous tradition of Middle East diplomacy continued. The American administration placated its Jewish electorate by creating the public impression that the committee was a business venture, bound by time-limit to procure a speedy solution to the plight of the displaced persons of Europe. The Foreign Office, having proved a very uneven match in the negotiating process, could at least console itself at the attainment of its tactical goals

– that of buying time, and of associating the United States with its mandatory responsibilities. However, it was appreciated that the dubious tactical goals had been achieved at the cost of severe damage to Britain's strategic goals in the Arab world.[55]

## Formation of the Committee

Once the US and British Governments had agreed on forming the Joint Committee and settled the Terms of Reference, the next step was to appoint the Committee members and staff. The British and American Governments agreed the Joint Committee would comprise 12 members, six from each country.

Interestingly, both the British and American Governments, consistent with Britain's longstanding practice during the Mandate of using lawyers, judges and the legal process to address the Jewish-Arab conflict, decided to select two judges, one from each country, to serve as Co-Chairs of the Joint Committee. The British Government strongly urged the Americans to appoint people of "weight and impartiality."[56]

### *The cast of characters: judges, lawyers, and others*

The Committee contained 12 members, half of whom were lawyers and/or judges.

#### *British members*

The British members were led by Justice Sir John Singleton, who served as the British Chairman and Co-Chair of the Committee.[57] Justice Singleton served on the Kings Bench Division of the High Court of Justice. Singleton was not Whitehall's first choice, as they had initially approached Sir James Frederick Rees, Vice Chancellor of the University of Wales.[58] Rees, however, declined the offer.[59]

Bevin then wrote to Singleton and offered him the position. Bevin's letter emphasised the need to find people to serve on the Committee "of impartial judgment and of sufficiently high standing for their report to be accepted as authoritative by all reasonable people."[60] Bevin, consistent with the British Government's practice regarding its previous Palestine-related commissions, noted the importance of Singleton's legal and judicial experience to the Committee's work:

> I am writing to ask whether you will help us in this most important task by agreeing to serve as British Chairman of the Committee … I very much hope that you will see your way to accepting the Chairmanship in which your legal training and experience will be of greatest value.[61]

Singleton accepted Bevin's offer and became the British Co-Chair of the Committee.

Richard Crossman, a brilliant young MP who also served on the Committee, described Singleton in his unpublished diary in somewhat unflattering terms:

> [A]lmost a caricature of a judge. The smooth aged skin with plum flesh underneath: the waistcoat beautifully out over the slight paunch, the Pickwickian boyishness and simplicity, combined with a judicial precision of wording and cautiousness. He is judicial in the strictly *legal* sense i.e. he has very strong and simple political prejudices (quite apart from his two years as a Conservative M.P.) which he does not accept as prejudices, and tries to be patient and fair-minded ... He is most keen to avoid making up our minds before we hear the evidence, but he is unaware that, in so doing, we may easily unconsciously side-track the inquiry as to various noncontroversial issues ...[62]

William Phillips, one of the American members of the Committee, described Justice Singleton as the "John Bull in our midst. Like our judge [Hutcheson], he was also an expert draftsman, but reflecting his judicial attitude, there was about him a touch of pomposity which was not altogether appreciated even by his own colleagues."[63]

Leslie Rood, a state department official who served as one of the two American secretaries to the Committee, described Singleton many years later as a "hanging judge" for the tough and strict manner he would display during the hearings.[64]

The other British members were Lord Morrison (Baron of Tottenham and Lord President of the Cabinet Council); Richard Crossman (former Oxford Don and Labour MP, shown in Figure 7.3); Reginald Manningham-Buller (MP, a barrister who had served as a clerk to Justice Singleton years earlier); Sir Frederick Leggett (former Deputy Secretary of the Ministry of Labour and National Services, with a reputation as an expert conciliator); and Wilfred Crick (economist and advisor to Midland Bank).[65] The British secretaries to the Committee were H.G. Vincent and Harold Beeley of the Foreign Office.

Crossman commented about the other British members of the Committee in his unpublished diary. Crick was "close to the judge politically, but more thoughtful ... but without any imagination." Lord Morrison was a "puzzle ... with an air of imperturbability, good humour and shrewdness." Leggett had "kind eyes" and a "springy, youthful gait with a constant stream of stories about conciliation in labour disputes, or about Ernie Bevin, whom he worships, or best of all, about both ... his stories all intimate his own power to settle disputes, by permitting the two sides to argue themselves into exhaustion (that will hardly work this time!)."[66]

The American member William Phillips, in turn, described Crossman as the "brilliant member of the British delegation, if perhaps a bit unstable."[67]

**FIGURE 7.3** Richard Crossman (Public Domain)

## *American members*

The State Department encountered difficulty finding "suitable persons to accept the task, they are to [Secretary Byrnes'] extreme displeasure shilly-shallying about giving definite answers."[68]

Ultimately the Americans formed their side of the Committee, led by Judge Joseph C. Hutcheson, Jr. of the US Court of Appeals for the Fifth Circuit in Houston, Texas. Judge Hutcheson served as Co-Chair of the Committee alongside Justice Singleton.

Hutcheson had long been interested in Zionism, but he staunchly opposed Jewish statehood in Palestine. In a 1944 letter to Will Rogers Jr., he slammed the idea of a Jewish State in Palestine, bluntly proclaiming it would be a "sham nation and a sham army to secure a sham place at the peace table."[69]

Crossman adopted the nickname "Texas Joe" for Judge Hutcheson, after hearing Chief Justice Harlan Fiske Stone use the moniker during the Committee's courtesy visit to the Supreme Court building in January 1946 in Washington, DC.[70] Crossman described Hutcheson in his diary, comparing him favourably to Justice Singleton:

> [Hutcheson is in] almost every way, the antithesis of Sir John Singleton. Small and wiry, informal and undiplomatic, "Texas Joe" was a character – and he knew it. He was nearly 70, an appeal judge of a circuit court, who

> must certainly have been in the running for a Supreme Court appointment. He called himself a Jeffersonian Democrat, but was in fact a conservative Texan who regarded Roosevelt and the New Deal as the ruin of the Democratic Party ... "Texas Joe" had a hearty contempt for politicians, and he had no innate respect for officials. A democrat in the real sense of the word, he only respected people for their merits, and detested hypocrisy and prevarication.[71]

James McDonald, another American member of the Committee, described Hutcheson (Figure 7.4) as:

**FIGURE 7.4** Judge Joseph C. Hutcheson (Hutcheson Papers, University of Texas, Tarlton Law Library Rare Books and Special Collections)

[Shrewd], very honest, determined to find, if possible, a "just solution." He is handicapped by what seems to me [an] unjustifiable feeling that our problem is analogous to litigation, whereas it is in fact primarily one of political adjustment. He also has very strong feelings against any form of Jewish state and is quite unsympathetic to anything which smacks of Jewish nationalism. He is, however, a tremendous worker, with an extremely keen mind, and will probably end up with a surprising comprehension of the whole problem.[72]

The other American members were Frank Aydelotte (former President of Swarthmore College and current Director of the Institute for Advanced Study in Princeton, New Jersey); Frank Buxton (editor of the Boston Herald); Bartley Crum (a San Francisco-based lawyer who would later gain fame as counsel to the "Hollywood Ten" and to the actress Rita Hayworth in her divorce from Prince Aly Khan); James McDonald (former High Commissioner for Refugees); and William Phillips (former US Undersecretary of State, former Ambassador to Italy, and former Presidential envoy to British India with the rank of Ambassador). The American secretaries to the Committee were Leslie Rood and Evan Wilson of the State Department.

Table 7.1 shows the members of the Anglo-American Committee of Inquiry.

The Foreign Office seemed impressed with the American members of the Committee. A file minute described Judge Hutcheson as having "an excellent

**TABLE 7.1** Members of the Anglo-American Committee of inquiry

| *Commissioner* | *Country* | *Profession* |
|---|---|---|
| Justice Sir John Singleton (Co-Chair) | United Kingdom | High Court of Justice, King's Bench Division |
| Judge Joseph Hutcheson (Co-Chair) | United States | Judge, US Court of Appeals for the Fifth Circuit |
| Frank Aydelotte | United States | Director, Institute for Advanced Study, Princeton |
| Frank Buxton | United States | Editor, Boston Herald |
| Wilfred Crick | United Kingdom | Economist and Advisor, Midland Bank |
| Richard Crossman | United Kingdom | MP, Labour |
| Bartley Crum | United States | Lawyer, San Francisco |
| Sir Frederick Leggett | United Kingdom | Former Deputy Secretary of the Ministry of Labour and National Services |
| James McDonald | United States | Former High Commissioner for Refugees |
| Reginald Manningham-Buller | United Kingdom | Barrister and future Lord Chancellor |
| Lord Herbert Morrison | United Kingdom | Lord President of the Cabinet Council |
| Ambassador William Phillips | United States | Former Undersecretary of State, former US Ambassador to Italy and envoy to India |

legal mind. He is Presbyterian." Aydelotte was described as "very friendly to Britain." Buxton was an "upper class New Englander." His newspaper, the Boston Herald, seemed to "have a record of fairly enlightened conservatism. It seems *not* to be Jewish owned. The Jewish influence is of course less strong in Boston than in other large cities." McDonald was "likely to be the most troublesome" but "he has the reputation of being entirely worthy." Phillips was known to the British Government from his service in India, where he had criticised British rule, but viewed as "still friendly to us."[73]

Crossman described Phillips in his published diary as "the best-mannered member of the Committee." Aydelotte "was the only academic of the Committee, but his abilities were more administrative than professorial ... [h]e showed a remarkable resemblance to Happy of *Snow White and the Seven Dwarfs*, not only in his appearance but in his sunny temperament." Buxton "displayed throughout a truly American suspicion of British imperialism." McDonald "remained throughout the most enigmatic of our American colleagues ... who had publicly committed himself to supporting Zionism, and this made him suspect that we suspected him." Crum, shown in Figure 7.5 with his celebrity client Rita Hayworth, was "an extremely successful Californian lawyer."[74]

**FIGURE 7.5** Bartley Crum with his client, the actress Rita Hayworth, 1951 (Public Domain)

Interestingly, none of the British or American officials who vetted Judge Hutcheson seemed aware of a highly important law review article the judge had published nearly two decades earlier describing his judicial philosophy. Hutcheson revealed in the article how much he relied on intuition and pure hunch in deciding difficult cases, a philosophy that would play a huge role in how he ended up reconciling the competing claims of Arabs and Jews:

> I decide the case more or less offhand and by rule of thumb. When the case is difficult or involved, and turns upon a hairsbreadth of law or of fact, that is to say, "when there are many bags on the one side and on the other" and Judge Bridlegoose would have used his "little small dice," I, after canvassing all the available material at my command, and duly cogitating upon it, give my imagination play, and brooding over the cause, wait for the feeling, the hunch – that intuitive flash of understanding which makes the jump-spark connection between question and decision, and at the point where the path is darkest for the judicial feet, sheds its light along the way.[75]

The State Department advised the British that the Arabs might object to McDonald, "who is on record as favouring Palestine as the major solution for the problem of the Jews in Europe, and that the Jews may not like Mr. Phillips, who is supposed to have considerable sympathy with the Arabs. But these two cancel each other out."[76]

"We were selected," Crossman would say six months later, "six British and six American, because we had one common characteristic – a total ignorance of the subject."[77]

The selection of two judges to serve as co-chairs of the Committee guaranteed the Committee would function more as a legal/judicial body than a diplomatic one. This represented Britain's effort once again to use the law and legal process to adjudicate the conflicting claims of Zionism and Palestinian nationalism. Britain expected the addition of the Americans to the Committee, with a judge as their co-chair, would maintain this model, which had worked relatively well for the British during the Mandate years.

One historian has described the judicial-type nature of the Committee's work:

> The Committee operated along the model of a courtroom, modified to allow for 12 interrogators. They were prepared to deal with people who came before them as hostile witnesses in a trial if they suspected a lack of frankness. In fact, more than half the 12 men had formal legal training.[78]

We were "more like a jury than a Commission," Crossman wrote later.[79] But the last thing Britain expected was that Judge Hutcheson would end up commandeering the Committee and steer it toward a unanimous verdict overwhelmingly renouncing the White Paper and British policy in Palestine.

## Diaries and other contemporaneous records of the Committee

At least five members of the Committee – Crossman, Aydelotte, Phillips, Crum, and McDonald – kept diaries or contemporaneous notes of their experiences serving on the Committee. Crossman, Crum, and Phillips published their recollections after completing their service on the Committee. McDonald (Figure 7.6) passed away in 1964, but his diary was not published until 2015.

Evan Wilson of the State Department, who served as one of the two American Secretaries to the Committee, published his own recollections of the Committee's work several decades later as one chapter in a broader book about the Truman Administration's decision to recognise Israel.

These diaries and recollections, along with the transcripts of the witness testimony and the written submissions from the witnesses and other interested parties, provide valuable evidence regarding the role of the law, legal procedure, and transformational legal framing during the Committee's work.

Crossman also wrote several letters to his then-wife Zita Crossman during his service on the Committee, at least two of which he wrote while witnesses were in the middle of testifying. Crossman's letters to Zita and his diaries (especially the unpublished, raw version), reflect his candid and often witty, sarcastic and always self-congratulatory observations on the Committee's work, the personalities of the Committee members, and the clashes among them, especially between Justice Singleton and Judge Hutcheson.

**FIGURE 7.6** James McDonald (Public Domain)

With this eclectic collection of legal and judicial personalities in place, the Committee convened in early January 1946 in Washington, DC to commence work.

We turn now to examining the role of the Committee, focusing on how the Committee availed itself of the law and the legal process in rendering judgment on the short-term fate of the surviving European Jews and the long-term future of Palestine.

## Notes

1 As of late September 1945, 72,000 of the 75,000 immigration certificates permitted under the White Paper had been issued. The British Government estimated that at a rate of 1,500 new certificates issued per month, the quota would be reached before the end of December 1945. CAB 129/2/6, C.P. (45) 156, Cabinet Palestine Committee, Report (Top Secret) by the Lord President of the Council, paras. 3, 5 (8 September 1945); CAB 129/2/46, C.P. (45) 196, Palestine: Memorandum (Top Secret) by the Secretary of State for the Colonies, para. 8 (28 September 1945) (3,000 immigration certificates under the White Paper quota remained unallotted as of late September 1945).

2 Declaration adopted by the Extraordinary Zionist Conference at the Biltmore Hotel of New York City, paras. 6, 8 (11 May 1942). Thereafter the "Biltmore Program" represented the fundamental Zionist demand for statehood in Palestine, although the Zionist leadership privately continued to tell both the British and American governments that it remained open to partitioning the country into separate Jewish and Arab states.

3 *See generally* B. Riedel, *Kings and Presidents: Saudi Arabia and the United States since FDR* at 1–26 (Brookings, 2019).

4 *See* W.A. Eddy, *FDR Meets Ibn Saud* (American Friends of the Middle East, Inc., 1954); W.A. Eddy, *King Ibn Sa'ūd: Our Faith and Your Iron*, Middle East Journal 17:3 at 257, 261 (1963) (Eddy served as "sole interpreter" at the 14 February 1945 Roosevelt-Ibn Saud meeting).

5 Rabbi Alan Podet Papers, Jacob Rader Marcus Center of the American Jewish Archives, Cincinnati, Ohio, MS 163, Box 1/2, Memorandum (Secret) No. 101 from William A. Eddy to Secretary of State (11 April 1945). Eddy's source was an individual named Garry Owen, who reported on a conversation with the Lebanese businessman Najib Salha at Salha's home in Cairo.

6 Foreign Relations of the United States (hereafter "FRUS") 867N.01/4-545, Letter from President Franklin Roosevelt to King Abdul Aziz Faisal (5 April 1945); E. Wilson, *The Palestine Papers, 1943-1947*, Journal of Palestine Studies, 2:4 at 38, 43–44 (1973). The exchange of correspondence between Roosevelt and Ibn Saud was made public in the United States on 19 October 1945, six months after Roosevelt's death. R. Radosh and R. Radosh, *A Safe Haven, Harry S. Truman and the Founding of Israel* at 107–108 (Harper Collins, 2009).

7 Charter of the Arab League (22 March 1945), http://arableague-us.org/wp/wp-content/uploads/2012/06/Charter%20of%20the%20Arab%20League.pdf (last accessed 12 April 2020).

8 Weizmann Archives 15.1-2585, Letter from Weizmann to Churchill (22 May 1945).

9 Weizmann Archives 15-2585, Jewish Agency Memorandum (17 May 1945). The Jewish Agency in October 1944 formally requested the British Government "inaugurate a new era for Palestine and the Jewish people by drawing the logical conclusion from the Balfour Declaration as originally conceived. At this juncture, they [the Jewish Agency] regard as imperative a decision designating Palestine as a Jewish Commonwealth." Weizmann Archives, 9-2525, para. 7 (16 October 1944).

10 Letter from Moshe Shertok to Palestine High Commissioner Lord Gort, reprinted in Jewish Agency for Palestine, Documents relating to the Palestine Problem 90–93 (1945), *cited in* J. Heller (ed.), *The Letters and Papers of Chaim Weizmann*, Series A (Letters), Vol. XXII, editor's introduction at x, n. 3 (Israel Universities Press, 1979).

11 R. Crossman, *Palestine Mission* at 122 (Hamish Hamilton, 1946) ("The White Paper had become the keystone of British Middle Eastern policy. In 1939 the Middle Eastern experts had argued that it was essential for achieving Arab neutrality in the event of war with Germany and Italy. Now in 1946 they argued it could not be rescinded without throwing the Arabs into the arms of Russia").
12 CAB 129/2/6, C.P. (45) 156, Cabinet Palestine Committee, Report (Top Secret) by the Lord President of the Council, paras. 6, 30–33 (8 September 1945).
13 Harrison report to President Truman at 5–7 (July 1945) (emphasis added), *reprinted in* Department of State Bulletin at 456 (30 September 1945).
14 H. Truman, *Memoirs, Volume Two: Years of Trial and Hope* at 138 (Doubleday, 1956); M.J. Haron, *Palestine and the Anglo-American Connection*, Modern Judaism, 2:2 at 199–211, 200 (1982); M. Ottolenghi, *Harry Truman's Recognition of Israel*, The Historical Journal, 47:4 at 968 (2004); A. Radosh and R. Radosh, *op. cit.*, at 94 ("Truman's first reaction upon reading the Harrison report... was shock").
15 PREM 8/627, Memorandum to the Prime Minister from the President (24 July 1945).
16 E. Wilson, *op. cit.*, at 47 ("The British were unhappy with the Harrison Report").
17 CAB 95/14, P.(M) (45) 13, Palestine Cabinet Committee, Note by the Secretaries (3 September 1945), enclosing E4849/15/G, Cable (Top Secret) from Lord Halifax to Foreign Office (1 July 1945).
18 FO 371/45378, Palestine Policy: Foreign Office Appreciation of International Repercussions, paras. 12–13, 23 (July 1945), *reprinted in* M. Cohen (ed.), *The Rise of Israel (Vol. 35): The Anglo-American Committee on Palestine 1945-1946* at 5–10 (1987).
19 Rabbi Alan Podet Papers, Jacob Rader Marcus Center of the American Jewish Archives, Cincinnati, Ohio, MS 163, Box 3/4 (August 1945); *see generally* M.N. Penkower, *The Earl Harrison Report: Its Genesis and Its Significance*, The American Jewish Archives Journal 68:1 at 1–75 (2016).
20 CAB 129/2/6, C.P. (45) 156 (Top Secret), Cabinet Palestine Committee, Report by the Lord President of the Council (8 September 1945).
21 FRUS, 867N.01/8-3145, President Truman to Prime Minister Attlee (31 August 1945).
22 FO 371/45379, Minutes of Meeting held at the Foreign Office (6 September 1945), *reprinted in* M.J. Cohen (ed.), *The Rise of Israel (Vol. 35): The Anglo-American Committee on Palestine 1945-1946* at 26–31 (1987).
23 CAB 129/2/6, C.P. (45) 156 (Top Secret), Cabinet Palestine Committee, Report by the Lord President of the Council, para. 33 (8 September 1945).
24 FRUS, N.A. 867N.01/9-1445, Cable (Top Secret and Personal) from Prime Minister Attlee to President Truman, para. 2 (14 September 1945).
25 FRUS, N.A. 867N.01/9-1745, Memorandum (Top Secret) from Prime Minister Attlee to President Truman (16 September 1945). Truman's own State Department agreed with the British Government's view that no steps should be taken in Palestine absent prior consultation with both the Arabs and Jews, as American interests and prestige needed to be protected. *See, e.g.*, FRUS, N.A. 867N.01-145, Memorandum from Loy Henderson, Director, Division of Near Eastern Affairs to Dean Acheson, Acting Secretary of State (1 October 1945). Acheson sent a memorandum the following day to President Truman reflecting Henderson's position and emphasizing that American failure to consult the Arabs regarding future Jewish immigration policy for Palestine would "constitute the severest kind of blow to American prestige not only in the Near East but elsewhere." FRUS, N.A. 867N.01/10-245, Memorandum (Top Secret) from Dean Acheson, Acting Secretary of State, to President Truman (2 October 1945).
26 CAB 129/2/46, C.P. (45) 196 (Secret), Palestine: Memorandum by the Secretary of State for the Colonies, para. 16 (28 September 1945).
27 *Id.*, para. 19.
28 *Id.*
29 FO 371/45400, Telegram No. 6593 (Secret) from Lord Halifax to Prime Minister Attlee and Foreign Secretary Bevin (3 October 1945), *reprinted in* M.J. Cohen (ed.), *The Rise of Israel (Vol. 35): The Anglo-American Committee on Palestine 1945-1946* at 58–59 (1987).

30 CAB 128/1/21, C.M. (45) 38, Conclusions (Secret) of a Meeting of the Cabinet (4 October 1945).
31 *Id.* Bevin's proposal "was very much Bevin's own brainchild to involve the US in this way, and it is clear from his comments and the attitude of the Prime Minister and the Colonial Secretary that the US Government's pressure was felt and keenly resented as being irresponsible." M. Jones, *Failure in Palestine: British and United States Policy after the Second World War* at 59 (Bloomsbury, 1986).
32 *Id.* at 63.
33 CAB 128/1/21, C.M. (45) 38, Conclusions (Secret) of a Meeting of the Cabinet at 140–142 (4 October 1945).
34 CAB 128/1/23, C.M. (45) 40, Conclusions of Cabinet Meeting (11 October 1945).
35 CAB 95/14, Cabinet Palestine Committee, Proposed Anglo-American Commission of Enquiry, Note (Top Secret) by the Secretary of State for Foreign Affairs and the Secretary of State for the Colonies (9 October 1945). The Palestine Committee submitted its proposal the following day to the full Cabinet. CAB 129/3/16, C.P. (45) 216, Palestine: Report (Top Secret) by the Lord President of the Council (10 October 1945). Colonial Secretary Hall had initially opposed the idea of an Anglo-American Committee of Enquiry, fearing it would subordinate British interests to American desires, risking a "complete loss of face in the Middle East and all hope of Arab cooperation for any purpose will be at an end." Memorandum by the Secretary of State for the Colonies, para. 2 (October 1945), *reprinted in* M.J. Cohen (ed.), *The Rise of Israel (Vol. 35): The Anglo-American Committee on Palestine 1945-1946* at 89 (1987).
36 *Id.*; *see also* L. Dinnerstein, *op. cit.*, at 286–287.
37 CAB 128/1/23, C.M. (45) 40, Conclusions (Secret) of a Meeting of the Cabinet (11 October 1945).
38 PREM 8/627, Telegram No. 10268 (Cypher) from Foreign Office to British Embassy, Washington, DC (13 October 1945).
39 PREM 8/627, Telegram (Top Secret) from British Embassy, Washington, DC to Foreign Office (14 October 1945).
40 M.J. Cohen, *Truman and Israel* at 124 (University of California Press, 1990).
41 PREM 8/627, Telegram No. 7013 (Top Secret) from British Embassy, Washington, DC to Foreign Office (22 October 1945) and Telegram No. 6964 (Top Secret) from Lord Halifax to Bevin, para. 2 (19 October 1945); PREM 8/627, Telegram No. 7157 (Top Secret) from Halifax to Bevin (27 October 1945) (reporting Truman Administration wanted British government to wait until after the upcoming New York election to announce the formation of the Anglo-American Committee, for fear of inflaming the "million or so Jewish voters ... and altogether destroy the prospects of the Democratic candidate whose Republican rival for Mayor was ... a Jew"); PREM 8/627, Telegram No. 7159 (Top Secret) from Halifax to Bevin (27 October 1945) (reporting Byrnes' "shame-faced embarrassment" at Truman Administration's need to wait until after the New York mayoral election to announce the formation of the Anglo-American Committee of Inquiry); *see also* A. Kochavi, *The Struggle Against Jewish Immigration to Palestine*, Middle Eastern Studies, 34:3 at 149 (1998).
42 CAB 128/2/5, C.M. 52 (45), Conclusions of a Meeting of the Cabinet, para. 7 (13 November 1945).
43 Hansard, HC Deb. Vol. 415, col. 1929 (13 November 1945); *see also* Cabinet (45) 52, Conclusions of the Cabinet Meeting (13 November 1945) (Bevin told the Cabinet he intended to address the House of Commons that same afternoon to announce the formation of the Anglo-American Committee of Inquiry).
44 *Id.*, col. 1931; *see also* A. Kochavi, *op. cit.*, at 149.
45 Weizmann Archives 45-2611, Letter from Abraham Tulin to Chaim Weizmann (14 November 1945). For further discussion of the Jewish and Arab reactions to Bevin's 13 November 1945 announcement, *see* M.N. Penkower, *Palestine to Israel, Mandate to State, 1945-1948, Volume I: Rebellion Launched* at 116–118 (Touro University Press, 2019).

46 Weizmann Archives 45-2611, Letter from Abraham Tulin to Chaim Weizmann, 2–3 (14 November 1945).
47 *Id.*, 3–4.
48 *Id.*, 4–6.
49 *Id.*, 14–15.
50 PREM 8/627, Telegram No. 7013 (Top Secret) from British Embassy, Washington, DC to Foreign Office (22 October 1945) (reporting Secretary of State Byrnes "is unhappy about comparatively slight emphasis on Palestine [in draft Terms of Reference]... he is going to have a shot at redraft of Terms of Reference and said he would try to find something that would meet both your difficulties and his own [referring to potential backlash from Jewish voters in the New York election scheduled for 6 November 1945]"); PREM 8/627, Telegram No. 7026 (Top Secret) from Halifax to Bevin (23 October 1945) (noting Halifax expected to have a "stiff tussle" over the proposed Terms of Reference); PREM 8/627, Telegram No. 7036 (Top Secret) from Halifax to Bevin (24 October 1945) (Americans pushing for Terms of Reference to "place greater emphasis on Palestine"); PREM 8/627, Telegram No. 7037 (Top Secret) from British Embassy, Washington, DC to Foreign Office (24 October 1945); (quoting draft Terms of Reference proposed by US Government); PREM 8/627, Telegram No. 10750 (Top Secret) from Foreign Office to British Embassy, Washington, DC (25 October 1945) (instructing Halifax to reject American draft Terms of Reference as placing too much emphasis on Palestine, creating risk of alienating Palestinian Arabs and surrounding Arab States and further instructing Halifax to deliver revised proposed Terms of Reference); PREM 8/627, Telegram No. 7113 (Top Secret) from British Embassy, Washington, DC to Foreign Office (25 October 1945) (reporting discussion with Secretary of State Byrnes regarding British revised proposed Terms of Reference and Byrnes' negative reaction); PREM 8/627, Telegram No. 10754 (Top Secret) from Bevin to Halifax (26 October 1945) (instructing Halifax to persuade Byrnes to agree to keep phrase "or other countries outside Europe" in the Terms of Reference, noting "he will see that we are not minimizing Palestine in any way, but Palestine cannot deal with the whole emigration problem"); PREM 8/627, Telegram No. 7192 (Top Secret) British Embassy, Washington, DC to Foreign Office (28 October 1945) (reporting State Department has withdrawn its offer of revised Terms of Reference, declaring "it is not possible for the two Governments at this time to agree upon the Terms of Reference"); PREM 8/627, Telegram No. 7206 (top Secret) from Halifax to Bevin (29 October 1945) (reporting Halifax and Byrnes had met that morning, the meeting "was frank, sometimes rough, and ended amicably," with Byrnes assuring Halifax they would be able to reach agreement on the Terms of Reference very quickly once the New York mayoral election scheduled for 6 November had occurred); PREM 8/627, Telegram No. 11317 (Top Secret) from Foreign Office to British Embassy, Washington, DC, para. 2 (9 November 1945); *see also* PREM 8/627, Telegram No. 7422 (Top Secret) from British Embassy, Washington, DC to Foreign Office (6 November 1945) (Lord Halifax reports Secretary of State Byrne "would not budge" in negotiations over including Palestine in Terms of Reference; Byrnes also noted President Truman personally involved in approving final Terms of Reference); *but see* PREM 8/627, Telegram No. 7264 (Top Secret) from British Embassy, Washington, DC to Foreign Office (31 October 1945) (reporting effort by Assistant Secretary of State Loy Henderson to suggest changes to proposed Terms of Reference to enable Britain to achieve its objectives without provoking White House rejection; Henderson (an Arabist who found common cause with the British against Zionist aspirations) said he was acting without authority in this regard). For a more detailed discussion of the negotiations and squabbles over the Terms of Reference, *see* A.H. Podet, *The Success and Failure of the Anglo-American Committee of Inquiry, 1945-1946: Last Chance in Palestine* at 57–74 (Edwin Mellen Press, 1986).
51 M.J. Haron, *op. cit.*, at 201.
52 *See, e.g.*, PREM 8/627, Telegram No. 11227 (Top Secret) from Foreign Office to British Embassy, Washington DC (7 November 1945); *id.* Telegram No. 7445 (Top Secret) from Lord Halifax, British Ambassador to the United States to Foreign Office (7 November

1945) ("This is very annoying but I got a hint late last night that rats were at work. This is the President himself. . . I told [Secretary of State James] Byrnes this morning that their political difficulties, whatever they were, could really not be held comparable with the hard possibilities of outbreaks and dead bodies in Palestine"); *id.*, Telegram Nos. 11263 and 11264 (both Top Secret) from Foreign Office to British Embassy, Washington, DC (8 November 1945); FRUS, 867N.01/11-2545, Telegram from Byrnes to Halifax (27 November 1945); FO 371/45387, Telegram No. 12555 (Secret and Personal) from Bevin to Halifax (7 December 1945).

53 FO 371/45386, Letter from US Ambassador John G. Winant to Bevin (19 November 1945); FRUS, 867N.01/11-1945, Memorandum of Conversation between Byrnes and Halifax (19 November 1945); FO 371/45386, Telegram Nos. 7822 and 7823 (Secret) from British Embassy, Washington, DC to Foreign Office (both 22 November 1945); FRUS, 867N.01/11-2045, Letter from Halifax to Byrnes (20 November 1945); FRUS, 867N.01/11-2445, Letter from Halifax to Byrnes (24 November 1945); FRUS, 867N.01/11-2545, Letter from Byrnes to Halifax (25 November 1945); FO 371/45386, Telegram No. 7896 from British Embassy, Washington, DC to Foreign Office (26 November 1945) (relaying text of 25 November 1945 letter from Byrnes insisting on maintaining 120-day deadline for Committee to complete its report).

54 FO 371/52503, US Department of State Confidential Future Release No. 936 (13 December 1945); *see also* PREM 8/627, Telegram No. 11264 (Top Secret), from Foreign Office to British Embassy, Washington, DC (8 November 1945); FRUS, 867N.01/12-1045, Telegram from Byrnes to Halifax (10 December 1945); FO 371/45388, Telegram No. 8287 from British Embassy, Washington, DC to Foreign Office (11 December 1945) (quoting text of diplomatic notes to be exchanged between British and US governments setting forth their agreement to form the Joint Committee of Inquiry).

55 M.J. Cohen, *The Genesis of the Anglo-American Committee on Palestine, November 1945: A Case Study in the Assertion of American Hegemony*, The Historical Journal, 22:1 at 206 (1979).

56 PREM 8/627, Telegram No. 7509 (Top Secret), from British Embassy, Washington DC to Foreign Office, para. 3 (9 November 1945).

57 FO 371/45386, Letter from Sir A. Napier to Sir A. Cadogan (23 November 1945) ("Mr. Justice Singleton is willing to be appointed British member of the Palestine Anglo-American Committee of Enquiry").

58 FO 371/45385, Letter from Bevin to Rees (16 November 1945).

59 FO 371/45386, Letter from Sir George Henry Gater, Colonial Office to Sir Alexander Cadogan, Foreign Office (22 November 1945) ("But, with Rees' refusal of the Chairmanship, the key post is still unfilled, and it is a matter of the highest importance that we should get the right man for this position"). Singleton was the third choice among three judges originally under consideration. FO 371/45384, R. Howe minute (22 November 1945).

60 FO 371/45387, Letter from Foreign Secretary Bevin to Justice Singleton, 1 (25 November 1945).

61 *Id.*, 2. The Foreign Office Advised the British Embassy in Washington, DC several days later that Justice Singleton had agreed to serve as British Chairman of the Committee. FO 371/45387, Telegram No. 12019 (Cypher) from Foreign Office to British Embassy, Washington, DC (30 November 1945).

62 Crossman Papers, GB 165-0068, Middle East Centre Archive, St. Antony's College, Oxford, Anglo-American Committee Papers, File 2, handwritten diary (30 December 1945).

63 W. Phillips, *Ventures in Diplomacy* at 448–449 (Beacon Press, 1953).

64 Rabbi Alan Podet Papers, Jacob Rader Marcus Center of the American Jewish Archives, Cincinnati, Ohio, MS 163, Box 2/4, Podet's typewritten notes of interview of Leslie Rood (26 August 1975).

65 FO 371/45386, Telegram No. 11802 (Secret) from Foreign Office to British Embassy, Washington, DC (24 November 1945) (identifying other British members of the Committee). Crick accepted Bevin's invitation to serve on the Committee, writing to the

Foreign Secretary that he would do so "with all my mind and strength." FO 371/45385, Letter from Crick to Bevin (10 November 1945); *see also* FO 371/45385, Letter from Leggett to Bevin (19 November 1945) (accepting Bevin's invitation to serve on the Committee); FO 371/45385, Letter from Bevin to Leggett (22 November 1945) (thanking Leggett for accepting invitation to serve on the Committee); FO 371/45385, Letter from Bevin to Crossman (22 November 1945) (thanking Crossman for accepting invitation to serve on the Committee).

66 Crossman Papers, GB 165-0068, Middle East Centre Archive, St. Antony's College, Oxford, Anglo-American Committee Papers, File 2, handwritten diary (30 December 1945).

67 W. Phillips, *op. cit.*, at 449.

68 FO 371/45387, Telegram No. 8032 (Secret) from British Embassy, Washington, DC to Foreign Office (30 November 1945); *see also* M.N. Penkower (2019), *op. cit.*, at 149–150 (discussing Hutcheson's predisposition against a Jewish State in Palestine).

69 Hutcheson Papers, Box L13, Folder 2, Letter from Hutcheson to Will Rogers, Jr., American League for a Free Palestine (25 April 1944).

70 B. Crum, *Behind the Silken Curtain: A Personal Account of Anglo-American Diplomacy in Palestine and the Middle East* at 11 (Simon & Schuster, 1947) ("Suddenly, from an open door, boomed a great voice shouting, 'Where the hell are you, Texas Joe?' It was the then Chief Justice of the United States, the late Harlan Fiske Stone, looking for his old friend, the Circuit Judge from the West").

71 R. Crossman, *Palestine Mission, op. cit.*, at 29–30.

72 N. Goda, *op. cit.*, at 50, McDonald Diary Entry (18 January 1946).

73 FO 371/45387, J.G. Donnelly Minute (7 December 1945) (emphasis in original).

74 R. Crossman, *Palestine Mission, op. cit.*, at 30–31.

75 J.C. Hutcheson, *The Judgment Intuitive: The Function of the Hunch in Judicial Decision*, Cornell Law Review 14:3 at 278 (1929).

76 FO 371/45387, Telegram No. 8168 (Secret) from British Embassy, Washington, DC to Foreign Office (6 December 1945).

77 Crossman Papers, GB 165-0068, Middle East Centre Archive, St. Antony's College, Oxford, Anglo-American Committee Papers, File 1, Speech to the Royal Institute of International Affairs, Chatham House, "The Palestine Report" (13 June 1946).

78 A.H. Podet, *op. cit.*, at 147–148.

79 R. Crossman, *op. cit.*, at 7. For more in-depth biographical information about the committee members and staff, *see* A.H. Podet, *op. cit.*, at 82–124.

# 8

# COMMITTEE HEARINGS

## Process and procedure

The British High Commissioner in Jerusalem, Sir Alan Cunningham, cabled the Colonial Secretary in December 1945, suggesting the Anglo-American Committee of Inquiry begin by asking Jewish and Arab organisations in Palestine to identify the witnesses wishing to testify in Jerusalem, and to submit written summaries of their testimony in advance. The High Commissioner also requested he be informed whether the Committee's hearings in Jerusalem would be open to the press and/or public, or conducted in secret.[1]

The Committee adopted the suggestion and followed this practice, notifying the public it would prefer to receive written submissions from interested parties, and that, time permitting, it would invite certain of them to offer oral testimony.[2]

The Committee also requested it be provided with written submissions from witnesses the day before their testimony, and that transcripts of witness testimony be provided to the Committee members at the end of each day.[3]

As the first round of hearings were about to begin in Washington, Justice Singleton advised the British Embassy in Washington that he did not want to take any testimony in secret, preferring instead the hearings be public.[4] By the end of the hearings, however, the Committee had heard secret testimony from British military officials in Cairo and Jerusalem, as well as from a small number of civilians.

The transcripts of the hearings reveal a remarkable amount of philosophical discussion between Committee members and witnesses about topics as wide-ranging as the meaning of Zionism; the definition of a Jewish National Home and a Jewish State; whether Jews constitute a race, a nationality, or a religious group; whether Palestine, which the Arabs had always considered as "southern Syria," ought to be treated as a separate country unto itself; and whether it

DOI: 10.4324/9781003225263-12

would be possible for Europe's surviving Jews to resume life as Europeans, or whether Palestine offered the only realistic place where they could live.

Those discussions frequently became fertile ground for transformational legal framing. Jewish witnesses invoked Jewish legal rights under the Balfour Declaration and the Mandate to immigrate to Palestine. Jewish witnesses also insisted upon Jewish legal rights to buy land in Palestine and Jewish legal rights to reconstitute the ancient Jewish homeland in Palestine.

Arab witnesses, on the other hand, invoked the familiar "justice/injustice" narrative, arguing the Jews had no historical connection to Palestine. The Arab witnesses framed the Zionists as illegal colonisers who arrived after the Balfour Declaration had illegally promised them a National Home in Palestine, in breach of the McMahon pledge of Palestine to the Arabs. The Arab witnesses also argued that it was unjust to foist the European Jewish refugee problem on a Palestinian Arab population who had nothing to do with the Holocaust.

Several of the Committee members, especially Crossman, McDonald and Crum, continued musing on these issues outside the hearing room in their discussions with Holocaust survivors in Europe and their private discussions with Arabs and Jews in Palestine.

## Washington

The Committee began its hearings in Washington, DC in early January 1946. The Committee, shown in Figure 8.1, conducted seven full days of hearings and

**FIGURE 8.1** Anglo-American Committee of Inquiry, Washington, DC, 5 January 1946 (Getty Images)

received testimony from 37 witnesses in a conference room on the second floor of the State Department in Washington, DC.

## *Judicial nature of the hearings*

Judge Hutcheson opened the Committee's inaugural session on Monday, 7 January 1946. He asked that the Terms of Reference be read aloud for the record. He then made a brief statement on his own behalf, emphasising from the outset the judicial nature of the Committee's work:

> As a United States Judge, engaged for more than a quarter of a century in the business of judging, I have long known that while knowledge must precede understanding and understanding must precede judging, this is not always enough. Sometimes if we must judge aright we must let our minds be bold ... let me say to my colleagues, to you who, furnishing us with material and information and appearing before us, are our co-adjutors, as well as to you everywhere who watch and pray without ceasing that justice may be done ...[5]

Once the hearings began, it became clear the Committee would function more as a court than a mere fact-finding body. This procedural dynamic positioned each of the Committee members not only as judges/jurors but also as cross-examiners. Witnesses were, in several instances, subjected to sometimes hostile, courtroom-style questioning from various Committee members, a dynamic that only encouraged the witnesses to continue using legal framing and narrative to advocate for their side of the case.

Ironically, the emphasis on courtroom-style practice and procedure hampered the Committee's ability to recommend practical, politically feasible solutions rather than rendering a judicial verdict:

> [W]ith the two judges presiding, the Committee was more a court of inquiry than a latter day Crusade. And a severe court it was. Judge Hutcheson disqualified evidence which was not submitted in the procedural way that had been decided upon; witnesses had to commit themselves to their testimony by attaching their signatures to their typescript evidence; time and again various subjects, mainly of a political character, were ruled out as not in accord with the Terms of Reference; private conversations of commissioners with witnesses were considered as being of secondary importance to the inquiry ... With the Terms of Reference interpreted to the effect that the Commission was expected to give a judicial verdict rather than provide a political solution, the contribution of the [Committee] to an essentially political problem could not be great.[6]

Justice Singleton in particular proved an intimidating figure to many of the witnesses, and so did Judge Hutcheson:

> One correspondent who accompanied the Committee described Singleton as a "real hangman. Singleton looks like death warmed over. When he points his pencil at the person giving testimony he scares him half to death." The judges cornered and pressed witnesses with questions of "Yes" or "No," and often challenged their signed statements, drawing protests from other commissioners that they were acting like prosecutors. Nevertheless, the courtroom style cross-examination of the testimonies turned out to be the most revealing part of the hearings.[7]

Like Singleton, Hutcheson believed his experience as a federal judge was all he needed to analyse the problem and reach the correct verdict. Hutcheson particularly scoffed at any suggestion that the American Committee members could benefit from the help of a Middle East expert to counter the expertise of the British staffer Harold Beeley (who had never visited the region, but was still regarded as one of Britain's leading experts on Palestine). As McDonald recalled:

> Crum, Buxton and I, sometimes with the mild help of Phillips, tried to persuade the Judge to act to strengthen our research group. We specifically urged the addition of [Paul] Hanna, the author of the excellent book, *British Policy on Palestine*. The Judge, however was unwilling to admit either that we needed additional help or that Hanna was necessarily our man. Part of the Judge's reasoning was based on his conviction that he as a judge, with 27 years on the bench, will be able to find the truth and that he does not need, as some of the rest of us feel we need, more technical assistance.[8]

In nearly every respect, therefore, the hearings amounted to a trial, in which the issues of Zionism, Arab nationalism, and especially the White Paper and British policy in Palestine all stood in the dock.

## *Harrison testimony*

The first witness (Judge Hutcheson initially used the term "appearer" instead of witness, but eventually adopted the term "witness") to testify before the Committee was Earl G. Harrison, Dean of the University of Pennsylvania Law School and author of the July 1945 report to President Truman regarding the harsh situation of the surviving European Jews. Harrison focused on the plight of the German and Austrian Jewish refugees. He noted most of them wanted to leave the displaced persons camps where they were held under military guard and relocate to Palestine. Harrison estimated 100,000 German and Austrian Jews would leave for Palestine if they were allowed to do so.[9]

When Harrison completed his opening remarks, Judge Hutcheson mentioned he had asked the Committee before the hearing not to question any of the "appearers."[10] Now, however, he decided to "breach" that suggestion by putting questions to Harrison.[11] Other members of the Committee continued with their own questions to Harrison, and thereafter, every witness who testified before the Committee was subject to questioning, and sometimes aggressive and hostile cross-examination.

## Schwartz testimony

The next witness was Joseph J. Schwartz of the American Joint Distribution Committee, who also emphasised the desire of the 100,000 Jews interned in Germany and Austria to leave as soon as possible for Palestine.[12]

Schwartz described the situation of the surviving Jews of Poland – whose Jewish population numbered some 3 million immediately prior to the War, and had been decimated to less than 75,000 – in utterly heartbreaking terms:

> Poland, which was the cradle of Jewish culture and Jewish religious life, now has altogether eight Rabbis in the entire country. Poland, which was the center of Jewish cultural and artistic achievement, now has only a handful of people, a handful of writers and actors and artists who have survived the rubble. There are only 5,000 Jewish children left in all of Poland … In all of Poland you will find not more than 100 intact Jewish families; that is, where father, mother and children are alive. Most of the people in Poland are individual survivors of family groups. They have no more families and no family ties; they have nothing …[13]

Schwartz testified that Polish anti-Semitism continued raging even after the War. He was in Poland when a Jewish orphanage in the town of Rofit "was attacked three times, and on two occasions hand grenades were thrown" into the orphanage.[14]

Schwartz noted only ten per cent of the pre-War population of Jewish children had survived the War, meaning *ninety per cent* of all European Jewish children had been murdered in the Holocaust.[15]

Schwartz estimated (a "conservative" estimate, he testified), that based on the Joint Distribution Committee's interviews of Holocaust Survivors, at least 600,000 European Jews wanted to leave Europe for Palestine.[16]

## Hershfield testimony

Isidore Hershfield, counsel to the Hebrew Immigrant and Aid Society, testified next. Hershfield argued the surviving European Jews had a legal right to immigrate to Palestine, which had "as a matter of law, international law, been established as the Jewish homeland."[17]

## Nathan testimony

The next witness to testify was Robert Nathan, an independent economist whom the American Palestine Institute hired to conduct a study of Palestine's economic capacity to absorb additional immigrants. Nathan and his associate, Oscar Gass, spent three months in Palestine between December 1944 and February 1945. Nathan and Gass both testified during the hearing.

Nathan described the development of Palestine since 1920 as "rather phenomenal" and "unparalleled," during which the proportion of Arabs to Jews had dropped from nine-to-one down to two-to one.[18] Although Jews comprised one-third of the population, they owned only 6% of the land.[19]

Nathan and Gass reported their conclusion that Palestine had the economic capacity to absorb between 615,000 and 1,125,000 new immigrants over the next ten years.[20] Justice Singleton used this as his first opportunity to begin laying out the British case – including defending the 1939 White Paper – against further Jewish immigration and land acquisition. McDonald wrote in his diary that Singleton had "clearly lost his patience, or as some put it, his temper"[21] during his cross-examination of Gass:

JUSTICE SINGLETON: But what I would like to know is, and is it your view, that the acquisition of more land by the Jews would increase the friendship between the Arabs and the Jews, or would have no effect, or would make the relations more difficult – which? That is all I ask.

GASS: [I]f the acquisition of agricultural land by Jews were an isolated process, accompanied by no further economic changes in the Palestinian economy, it could do nothing but create hardship and as such, ill feeling. Since it is accompanied by other processes it doesn't create the same kind of hardship and ill feeling."[22]

Singleton pressed the point further with Nathan. Referring to the much-criticised policy of the Jewish National Fund to bar the employment of Arab workers on Jewish-owned land, Singleton asked:

JUSTICE SINGLETON: If that policy is pursued, and if more land is acquired by Jews, it must mean, in that regard, less employment for Arab laborers?

NATHAN: I think that is true in that regard if one doesn't assume all the other implications.[23]

## Impatience with witnesses

During the first day of hearings in the State Department's second floor conference room (Figure 8.2), both Judge Hutcheson and Justice Singleton began flexing their judicial muscles, showing impatience with witnesses they believed were taking too long to answer their questions.[24] Singleton harshly scolded Gass for giving "the longest answer I have ever heard."[25]

FIGURE 8.2 Anglo-American Committee Hearing, State Department Conference Room, Washington, DC (Getty Images)

Hutcheson, not to be outdone, later warned Gass "that a witness who goes around the back door to get to the front door does us very little good. If you could ... shoot to the point, you would get us somewhere,"[26] and "you must take some training in witnessing."

## *Tulin and Neumann legal testimony*

The next day, 8 January 1946, featured a series of witnesses from the American Zionist Emergency Council and the American Jewish Committee, all of whom were accompanied by Abraham Tulin, the New York lawyer who wrote the 14 November 1945 memorandum for Weizmann regarding the legality of the Committee's Terms of Reference.

The most important of the Washington, DC witnesses from the Jewish legal perspective was Emanuel Neumann, a New York lawyer who testified in support of the legal case for Zionism:

> The Balfour Declaration, the Mandate, and international treaties were all designed to bring about a fundamental change in the Jewish position in the world. They were all designed, among other things, to provide all Jews

> who found themselves in any way in conflict with their environment with a home to which they might freely go, with a national home in which to re-establish their national existence. Such a home was provided and is available to them as of right … particularly [under] the Mandate, it is clear that several specific rights have been recognized and granted, such as the right to enter Palestine, the right to state lands and waste lands, the right to colonize, to develop the natural resources, the recognition of the Jewish Agency for Palestine, the recognition of Hebrew as an official language, etc. But all of these and other specific rights stem from one basic right accorded to the Jewish people: the right to national restoration in Palestine.[27]

Neumann then offered his view of the proper legal construction of the Balfour Declaration:

> There have been repeated attempts to represent the Balfour Declaration as being vague, ambiguous and subject to conflicting interpretations. Subtle minds and skillful hands have long been at work in a persistent effort to generate about it a pea-soup fog and to sow doubt and confusion regarding its substance … There is hardly a legal instrument or political document which does not in the course of time give rise to commentary and exegesis. But I venture to assert that when all is said and done, the underlying purpose of that declaration and what it intended to signify is exceedingly clear, leaving little room for doubt. If any doubt is entertained, it can, in almost every instance, be resolved by the usual methods, by applying ordinary rules of construction: (a) by the internal evidence; (b) by the attendant circumstances; (c) by the explanatory statements of its authors; and (d) by its antecedents.[28]

Neumann then zeroed in on the meaning of the term "National Home" as used in the Balfour Declaration. He first noted the Zionist movement had begun using the word "home" as a euphemism for Jewish self-determination in Palestine as early as 1895. He argued that future US Supreme Court Justice Louis Brandeis equated the term "home" with Jewish "home rule" in Palestine, much as Irish nationalists at the same time were demanding "home rule" for themselves.

Neumann next noted the language in the Balfour Declaration about safeguarding the civil and religious rights of the non-Jewish population in Palestine. Neumann argued that if Balfour had intended the Jews to remain a minority in Palestine under majority Arab rule, logically the civil rights clause in the Declaration would have applied *to the Jews* rather than the non-Jewish population.[29] But the civil rights clause had in fact been directed toward the non-Jewish population. The logical inference, therefore, was that Balfour intended Palestine would someday become a Jewish majority state, subject to protecting the civil and religious rights of the non-Jewish minority.

Neumann next addressed the word "in" as used in the Balfour Declaration's phrase, "National Home for the Jewish People *in* Palestine." Neumann argued the word "in" was not meant to limit the term "National Home" geographically. "If, for instance, we speak of the hope for a democratic regime 'in' Spain, do we mean in a corner of Spain, in Barcelona? Not at all."[30]

Neumann's testimony gave the Committee an early dose of the Zionist legal framing and narrative that they were to hear throughout the hearings, especially when they arrived in Jerusalem.

## Gold testimony

Dr. Henry Raphael Gold, a Rabbi and physician, testified the following day, 9 January 1946, on behalf of the Mizrachi religious Zionist movement and its affiliates.

Dr. Gold mentioned in his opening statement how the Jews had received vague offers to live outside Europe in places other than Palestine. However, according to Dr. Gold, nothing could replace Palestine as an adequate home for the Jewish people:

> There were other offers ... but they were like the offerings of a marriage of convenience to one who was determined to find his beloved. Outside of his native land for which the Jew as a citizen was always willing to work and fight, Palestine was the only other land for which the Jew was willing to make continuous and heroic sacrifices[31]

Dr. Gold emphasised the point further in response to questioning from McDonald, noting "no other country as a mere territory could take the place of Palestine because of the fact that Palestine is so deeply rooted in the religious consciousness of the Jewish people."[32]

Other members of the Committee asked Dr. Gold what form of political solution he envisioned for Palestine, including whether all or part of Palestine should be designated as a Jewish State. Crum continued the line of questioning:

MR. CRUM: Rabbi, as I understand your position, you envisage a commonwealth ultimately in which a majority of the persons residing there are Jewish?

DR. GOLD: That is right.

MR. CRUM: It is also your position, as I understand it, that no Arab is to be displaced either in the course of time or through the creation of such a commonwealth. Indeed, as I understood your testimony, the rights of all minority groups must be thoroughly protected ... [W]hat you ultimately seek is a commonwealth in which merely the majority of persons who reside in such state or commonwealth are Jewish, either by faith or by race. Is that correct?

DR. GOLD: Correct.

MR. CRUM: Would the guarantees of which you speak mean that minorities would have the rights that they have in other democratic states, including the right to vote, the right to aspire to office, and all the other rights which go along with any democratic community? Is that right?

DR. GOLD: That is right.[33]

## Miller testimony

Dr. Irving Miller, Chairman of the Executive Committee of the American Jewish Congress, perhaps anticipating the Arab testimony to come the following day, invoked the Jewish "justice" narrative during his testimony. For example, in response to a question from Judge Hutcheson, Miller noted:

> We say that if the nations of the world are firmly convinced that the establishment of a Jewish commonwealth is a matter of simple elementary justice, then the nations of the world will also consider it to be a matter of justice to see that such a commonwealth shall be as protected as every other small people on the face of the earth.[34]

## Proskauer testimony

One of the most important Jewish legal witnesses appearing in Washington, DC was former Judge Joseph M. Proskauer (Figure 8.3), testifying in his capacity as President of the American Jewish Committee. Proskauer began his testimony with a legalistic appeal to the British members of the Committee on behalf of the surviving remnants of European Jewry. Proskauer argued Britain had a *legal obligation* under the Mandate to issue the 100,000 immigration certificates.

Proskauer further argued, again employing highly legalistic framing, that the Permanent Mandates Commission's disapproval of the 1939 White Paper meant Britain was legally compelled to rescind the White Paper:

> I believe I have made a case for the abolition of the White Paper for good and all but whether I have or not, speaking in Judge Hutcheson's language, I want a dissolution of the preliminary injunction.[35]

Proskauer, however, also made clear the American Jewish Committee stood apart from the Zionist movement and was not advocating Jewish statehood. He quoted various Zionist statements from the 1920s and 1930s to argue the Zionist movement had from time to time seemed to advocate a single Palestinian state in which both Arabs and Jews would live together harmoniously.[36]

Judge Hutcheson commended Prosakauer at the conclusion of his opening statement: "I would like to say that your approach is familiar and pleasant to me because it is the approach and the attitude of what I call judicial. It is practical."[37]

**FIGURE 8.3** Judge Joseph Proskauer (library of Congress)

Later in his testimony, in response to a question from Aydelotte, Proskauer suggested if at some future date the Jews were to become the majority population in Palestine, the country could become a secular, democratic Jewish state with equal rights for the minority Arabs. Proskauer, however, in response to a question from Judge Hutcheson, said he opposed the creation of a Jewish *theocratic* state in Palestine.[38] On the other hand, if the Arabs retained their majority status in the future, Proskauer envisioned something more like Switzerland, with ethnic cantons under a common federal government.

Proskauer also testified, in response to questions from Justice Singleton, that the American Jewish Committee opposed partition as a solution to the Palestine problem: "It is like dividing a sandwich into a great many microscopic portions, nobody gets enough to eat."[39]

Singleton asked Proskauer whether he believed Palestine should become a Jewish state, and if so, when:

JUSTICE SINGLETON: Now, sir, in answer to the Chairman [Hutcheson], you said there was no point, it seemed to you, in announcing a Jewish state today. I gather that your view is that, in any event, there must be a considerable period, there must be a considerable period of years looking for conciliation before a state is created?

PROSKAUER: That is my view and ... I think it is the view of very substantial people in the Zionist movement itself. I do not think, in that respect, I am in antagonism at all with important Zionist leaders.[40]

The Committee also questioned Proskauer regarding Jewish immigration. Proskauer reiterated his position that Britain should issue the 100,000 immigration certificates immediately. He noted Jews had the legal right to immigrate to Palestine, subject only to the economic absorptive capacity of the country. Proskauer, again invoking the Zionist legal framing and narrative, insisted "Jewish immigration into Palestine stands on a different legal and historical basis from general immigration into Palestine."[41]

## *Crossman's reaction to the Jewish case*

Crossman commented in his published diary that he felt as if Britain had been "indicted" by the Jewish witnesses in Washington, DC:

> Subjected to this deluge of oratory, we Englishmen were driven on the defensive and found ourselves asking questions not to obtain information but to counter hostile argument ... We were there to take punishment – and we took it. Sometimes, glancing along the table to my right, I was anxious lest Sir John Singleton would explode. He was used to being dictator in his own court, dispenser of the King's justice. Now he had to sit quiet while, in defiance of the proprieties of British legal procedure, his country was held up to scorn, and each British member of the Committee was made to feel that he was held personally responsible for the death of 6,000,000 Jews.[42]

Nevertheless, Crossman admitted to himself that he began "swinging over to the Jewish side" during the Washington hearings. He also warned, however, that the Zionists had "overstated their case" and "really worried our Texan judge and fair-minded men like Crum and Aydelotte and Phillips, who support Jewish immigration into Palestine, but are beginning to react against the totalitarian claims of the Zionists. As Americans they are shocked."[43]

## *Hitti testimony*

The Committee began hearing the Arab case during its last session of the first week of hearings, on Friday, 11 January 1946. Dr. Philip Hitti and Dr. John Hazam of the Arab American Affairs on Palestine testified separately.

Dr. Hitti, a highly respected Professor of Semitic Literature at Princeton University, began as the first witness for the Arab side. Dr. Hitti first challenged the Jews' historical claim to Palestine. He claimed Jewish sovereignty over the entirety of ancient Palestine lasted for a relatively brief time, from 1020 to

930 B.C. under Kings Saul and Solomon. That brief period, according to Dr. Hitti, did not provide a basis for the modern Zionist claim of a Jewish right to "reconstitute" their ancient homeland in Palestine.[44]

Dr. Hitti then attacked Zionism as "the rankest kind of imperialism." He threw cold water on the Zionist idea of establishing a Jewish state in Palestine, making a variety of predictions that turned out to be less than accurate:

> It is unpracticable and indefensible as a Jewish state. It is an anachronism. Even if it is established, it cannot be maintained. It is unpracticable; it is indefensible, not only on historical and scholarly grounds, but also from the military point of view. It is unpracticable from the economic point of view.[45]

Dr. Hitti went further, and in his zeal to debunk any Jewish connection to Palestine made an argument that would be unthinkable for any advocate of Palestinian Arab nationalism today, asserting, "there is no such thing as Palestine in history, absolutely not."

Dr. Hitti supported his argument by quoting from a 1938 book published by British archaeology professor John Garstang:

> Since Palestine on three sides has no definite boundaries, it is not well adapted to become the cradle of one particular race, nor can it claim for its population a continuous national history. Indeed, only at long intervals and for relatively short periods has it ever been ruled from within ... It is essentially apart of Syria, with which it shares a common seaboard and the parallel range of mountains.[46]

Dr. Hitti said the Arabs would be willing to accord the Jewish population of Palestine protected minority status as residents of a single, Arab-majority state. He described the competing claims of Palestinian and Zionist nationalism as irreconcilable. This led to a testy exchange with Crossman:

CROSSMAN: Your view is that anything like a Zionist solution could only be imposed by force on the Arabs?

DR. HITTI: Yes, sir.

CROSSMAN: Your view is even if the Zionist solution were not adopted, any amount of immigration which gave the Jews a majority in Palestine could only be imposed by force on the Arabs?

DR. HITTI: Yes, sir.

...

CROSSMAN: Therefore, the view you are putting to the Committee is a mandatory power has only the choice of imposing by force one view on another part of the community.

DR. HITTI: That is the way it looks to me now.

CROSSMAN: So you are actually putting it up to the mandatory power that it will be right to suppress one part for the sake of the other because there is no other solution?

...

DR. HITTI: Sure, it's the Mandate which brought us into the impasse.

CROSSMAN: I am not asking who brought it in.

DR. HITTI: Yes, but you are trying to put the responsibility on me.

CROSSMAN: I think everyone who expresses a view on a subject of this sort has a moral responsibility for the view he expresses.[47]

## *Hazam testimony*

Dr. John Hazam, Professor of History at the College of the City of New York, testified as the next witness for the Arab side. He began by invoking the Palestinian "injustice" narrative, criticising the Balfour Declaration as a "distinct injustice to the native population of the country."[48]

Dr. Hazam described the "injustice" as stemming from the loss of various rights the Palestinian Arabs enjoyed under Turkish rule, the inability to regain those rights "so long as the interests of the national home were allowed priority," and the unfairness of addressing European anti-Semitism by allowing Jews to immigrate to Palestine, a country that had nothing to do with Jewish persecution in Europe:

> Why the Arabs should be imposed upon and suffer for the consequences of Europe's religious intolerance is a baffling but legitimate question. The Arabs, it should be repeated, were not the creators of any of these problems. The Jewish problem existed for countless centuries before there was ever a modern Palestine question. Nor did the Arabs create the Palestine question. That question is a recent special, deliberate, artificial and secret concoction of the Zionists and their fair-weather friends in the British Cabinet, each with his own special axe to grind ... *The Zionists cannot with sober conscience demand justice for themselves in Europe and at the same time inflict a flagrant injustice on another people in Palestine.*[49]

Dr. Hazam then rejected the Zionist argument that Jewish immigration had helped improve the standard of living in Palestine, especially by beginning to industrialise the economy:

> The Arabs who concentrate on agriculture are not averse to a certain measure of industrialization, but they prefer to bring that about gradually in their own way and through their own efforts. They are opposed to Zionist aims of defacing the Holy Land, the well-preserved sanctuary of world religions, by factory smokestacks and turning the shoreline into amusement centers. The Arabs do not want the Holy Land to be converted into a cross between Pittsburgh and Coney Island.[50]

Dr. Hazam further defined the "injustice" inflicted on the Palestinian Arabs stemming from the British breach of the McMahon pledge of Arab independence to Hussein during World War I.[51]

## Totoh testimony

The next witness for the Arab side was Dr. Khali Totoh, Executive Director of the Institute for Arab American Affairs. Dr. Totoh also invoked the "injustice" narrative, saying early in his testimony "we cannot get justice out of the acts of the Zionists or at the hands of the British Government which has sponsored Zionism."[52]

Crossman also had a testy exchange with Totoh. Crossman was upset with Totoh for his veiled threat that the Arabs would seek an alliance with the Soviet Union if the British and American Governments did not meet their demands regarding Palestine:

CROSSMAN: I should like to develop one line of thought which you dropped into the discussion but did not develop. You said if the Arabs did not get their way they might resort to a use of powers. You said that you did not want to expand on that. During 1939 and 1940, if I understood you rightly, we had some experience of what I think you meant, which was that if we did not capitulate the Arabs would support [Nazi Germany]. I should like to know what you meant.

DR. TOTOH: I meant that there is a power [the Soviet Union] which is maneuvering quite openly in the Middle East. It is currying favor, and I would hate to have the Arabs bamboozled in any way.

CROSSMAN: I should like to know whether you think it is better to persuade Britain and America to work out a policy which would virtually result in blackmail?

DR. TOTOH: I would not call it blackmail. That is not my intention.[53]

## Einstein testimony

The last witness to testify before the Committee at the end of the first week of hearings in Washington, DC was Albert Einstein (Figure 8.4). Einstein's testimony came as a disappointment to both the British and the Zionists.

Einstein criticised British rule in Palestine as intended to "dominate, with the help of a few officials, the people of Palestine," in the same way Britain had dominated the people of India. He blamed the British authorities for failing to achieve peace between Arabs and Jews in Palestine. Einstein advocated for allowing the "great majority of Jewish refugees in Europe to settle in Palestine," but he flatly opposed Jewish statehood.[54]

Crum and McDonald both wrote about Einstein's testimony in their diaries of the Committee's work. Crum, for example, recalled how Einstein's entrance

**FIGURE 8.4** Albert Einstein testifying before the Anglo-American Committee, Washington, DC, 11 January 1946 (Getty Images)

into the hearing room on the second floor of the State Department building caused a stir:

> Although another witness was testifying, the moment the door opened and the audience caught sight of the figure so familiar to them in newsreels, they burst into applause. With his great mane of flowing white hair racing almost to his shoulders, with his slow step, he looked almost like a patriarch stepping out of a Biblical tale. Judge Hutcheson rapped sharply for order. Later, when Dr. Einstein's turn came, Judge Hutcheson said, "Now all who feel I have restrained them from giving an appropriate welcome to Dr. Einstein may say so." The room echoed with applause. Dr. Einstein murmured to a friend beside him, "I think they ought to wait first and see what I say."[55]

McDonald described Einstein's appearance as "sensational ... but not very significant."[56]

Monday, 14 January 1946 was the last day the Committee conducted hearings in Washington DC. At the conclusion of the day's proceedings, Judge Hutcheson made a statement, reflecting once again his view that the Committee was conducting a trial-type proceeding:

> I will say as a judge for many years who tried cases trying to catch the points of difference which are immaterial and eliminating them so as to finally come down to solid bedrock in the case ... it may be that we find the core question is so tough and so uncompromisable that we can't find any solution by conciliation but must only find it by judgment, that is, by determining the principles which shall control, and render judgment accordingly ...[57]

## London

While the Committee was still in Washington, it issued a public announcement indicating it would hear evidence in London from 25 to 31 January 1946 at the Royal Empire Society, in what Crossman described as "an excellent room but the heating had broken down and there was a cold draught on Sir John's bald head."[58]

### *Transatlantic sea voyage*

Before leaving London to take testimony in Europe and the Middle East, Justice Singleton wrote to Foreign Secretary Bevin, asking the British Government to purchase personal accident insurance for the British members and staff of the Committee.[59] The Committee also advised the British and American Governments that it intended to deliberate and write its report in Switzerland, after hearing testimony in Europe and the Middle East.

After enduring a difficult Atlantic crossing in cramped, uncomfortable quarters below decks aboard the *Queen Elizabeth*, the Committee specifically requested their governments to book rooms for 28 people at the Beau Rivage hotel in Lausanne, along with a conference room seating 16 and 5 additional rooms for use as offices.[60]

During the Atlantic crossing, the Committee members met to decide upon an agreed statement of the issues they would need to address in their final report. Crossman later wrote that on the last day of the sea trip, he persuaded the Committee members to discuss the "Arab question."

### *State Department secret file*

Crossman also recalled the moment when the American Committee members, during the trip across the Atlantic, were shown for the first time a secret State Department file containing communications from President Roosevelt and his administration to various Arab leaders, pledging to consult with them before any decisions were made regarding Palestine:

> It was very dramatic. Phillips produced the relevant American documents, in particular the Roosevelt Ibn-Saud conversation in which Roosevelt gave an assurance he would not assist the Jews. After this he went back to Washington and assured the Zionists of his full support. Texas Joe used the phrase "a duplicitous son-of-a-bitch."[61]

Crum was deeply shocked and angered when he saw the State Department secret file containing proof of Roosevelt's duplicity. Crum, a Republican who had campaigned for Roosevelt, felt betrayed. From that moment Crum had made up his mind: "To a lawyer, studying the documents alone, legal justice lay unquestionably on the side of the Jewish case …"[62]

## *Brodetsky and Montefiore testimony*

The hearings resumed in London on Friday, 25 January 1946. Professor Selig Brodetsky, the President of the Board of Deputies of British Jews (and future President of the Hebrew University of Jerusalem), invoked the Zionist legal narrative, arguing the Balfour Declaration acquired the force of international law when the League of Nations incorporated it into the Mandate for Palestine.[63]

The next witness was Leonard G. Montefiore of the Jewish Colonization Association. Judge Hutcheson, displaying his hostility toward political Zionism, questioned Montefiore regarding whether the idea of Jewish statehood in Palestine was intended simply to provide a refuge for persecuted European Jews, or whether it represented a larger, political aspiration for Jews everywhere:

JUDGE HUTCHESON: "Yes, take me. I do not want a State. I have got a mixed mongrel pedigree, but mainly Scotch and English, but I do not want a State. I am satisfied to be an American. Why is not the Jew satisfied? I think the American Jew is, is he not?

MONTEFIORE: I think there is no doubt of that.

JUDGE HUTCHESON: Is not the British Jew satisfied to be a Britisher?

MONTEFIORE: Yes.

JUDGE HUTCHESON: So, as you put it, the Palestine problem is one of Europe and Palestine more than of Jewry and religion, is it not?

MONTEFIORE: I think that may be true.[64]

Crossman commented on this exchange in his diary:

> Texas Joe, after one or two attempts at humour, became more and more irritated at the Jewish state. One Jewish witness, anxious to show that the Jews were a nation, infuriated him by suggesting that they possess citizenship of their present countries but nationhood as Jews. Texas Joe said this was high treason in America. To which the witness naively replied that America wasn't yet a nation but might become so in time.[65]

## Jackson testimony

The hearings resumed in London on Monday, 28 January 1946 with the testimony of Nathan Jackson, representing the *Poale Zion*, the Jewish Socialist Workers' Party, who argued for Jewish statehood in Palestine.[66] Judge Hutcheson once again displayed his dislike of political Zionism:

JUDGE HUTCHESON: I would like to ask you a question. You drew a parallel which I didn't exactly understand. You said that just as Britain is a British state and France is a French state – in the first place I don't exactly know what you mean by Britain bring a British state. You mean England and Scotland? Is that what you are talking about?

JACKSON: I mean there are in this country all kinds of national groups, English, Scottish, Welsh. The state is British. There isn't such a person as British …

JUDGE HUTCHESON: This isn't a British, Scotch or Welsh state. Why then in Palestine should we have a Jewish state? Why don't you have a Palestinian state?

JACKSON: Because the position of Jews in the world is such that … it is necessary that they have control of their own destiny as a people.

…

JUDGE HUTCHESON: The trouble with me is how people calling themselves Jews or Scotch or Germans or whatnot can expect to come into a land which they do not populate in anything like the majority, in fact, it was begun in a very small minority, and demand that their characteristics, their colonies and their point of view shall be enforced upon others.[67]

Justice Singleton also grew testy and "icy" with several Jewish witnesses in London. Crum wrote later that "it was apparent that [Singleton] had the constant problem of remembering that the witnesses before him were not prisoners in the dock …"[68]

## Unterman testimony

The next witness to testify was Rabbi Isser Unterman, representing the Mizrachi Federation.

Judge Hutcheson again expressed his scepticism toward Zionism, barely concealing his sarcasm:

JUDGE HUTCHESON: You say you should have that place [Palestine] because it is the only place where you can gratify your nationalist ambitions?

UNTERMAN: More than that. It is not merely gratifying nationalist ambitions; it is something more. In our case it is a question of leading a complete Jewish life. The Arabs have ample territory in which to lead a full Arab life if they desire to do so. We Jews have no place in the world except Eretz Israel, that is, the Land of Israel.

JUDGE HUTCHESON: If that happy condition exists in Palestine, if it is to be a place where everybody will love everybody else and nobody will feel unkindness toward another, it is a beautiful condition, will there be a general exodus of the Jews from Britain and America to Palestine or will they just have to be miserable living in the state in which they are in those countries?[69]

## *Marks testimony*

Sir Simon Marks (of Marks and Spencer fame) testified next on behalf of the Zionist Federation of Great Britain and Ireland, arguing Palestine should become a Jewish State.[70] Crossman ridiculed Marks in his diary as "behaving like a small greengrocer in his Sunday clothes."[71]

## *Reid testimony*

The next day (29 January) began with testimony in London from the virulently anti-Zionist M.P. Thomas Reid, who had served on the Woodhead Commission, sent to Palestine in 1938 to study the technical feasibility of the Royal Commission's partition recommendation. The Woodhead Commission ultimately found partition unworkable and Britain dropped the idea in favour of the May 1939 White Paper. Reid took credit in his testimony before the Anglo-American Committee for helping "overthrow" the Peel Commission's partition recommendation through his work on the Woodhead Commission.[72]

Reid opposed Jewish statehood in Palestine, preferring instead the one-state solution in favour of the Palestinian Arabs. Reid argued Zionism had harmed the Jewish people by provoking an anti-Semitic backlash in Palestine and elsewhere:

> I think the greatest foes of Jewry are the political Zionist leaders who are creating anti-Jewish feeling all over the world by this Palestinian policy of theirs. It is bound to create enormous anti-Jewish feeling everywhere, especially in the East.[73]

Reid went further, saying, "I simply cannot understand the attitude that because the Jews are suffering in Europe then Palestine must bear the burden."[74]

Reid also argued Britain had complied with its obligation to establish a Jewish National Home in Palestine. He defended the 1939 White Paper as "just." The White Paper, according to Reid, served as a fair and proper means of giving the Jewish people five years' notice that Jewish immigration to Palestine and the process of establishing the Jewish National Home would cease.[75]

## *Spears testimony*

General Sir Edward Spears, another rabid anti-Zionist, testified next. General Spears headed the British military mission at Versailles and served as Britain's

Ambassador to Syria and Lebanon in the early 1940s. Spears repeatedly invoked the Palestinian Arab legal framing as he discussed the issues in his testimony.

For example, early in his testimony General Spears mentioned the McMahon-Hussein correspondence. He agreed with former Palestine Chief Justice Michael McDonnell (who had served as counsel to the Arab side during the 1939 London Conferences) that Palestine had been included in the areas promised to the Arabs.[76] General Spears summarised his position regarding conflicting Zionist and Palestinian nationalist claims:

> Now, in other words, sir, my contention is that we promised a home for the Jews, that we have in fact provided a home for the Jews in Palestine, that we never promised a state, a Jewish state, that in fact our promise to the Arabs made it impossible that we should promise or attempt to form a Jewish state in Palestine.[77]

General Spears also raised the Hogarth message in his testimony, noting its importance so close in time to the Balfour Declaration as evidence Britain never intended the term "National Home" to mean Jewish statehood in Palestine.[78]

General Spears went even further, comparing Zionism to Nazism in shocking language less than one year after the Holocaust. Unfortunately, such language is still used today in certain Palestinian Arab circles and elsewhere:

> [T]he Zionist policy in Palestine has many similar features to the Nazi policy. The policy of the *Herrenvolk*, who claim because they have got a claim to superior intelligence, industry and worth, to have the right to have the will over the weaker people … The idea of *Lebensraum*, the Nazi idea of Lebensraum, is also very evident in the Zionist philosophy … The training of the youth is very similar under both organizations that have designed this one and the Nazi one … The intimidation of their own people, the masses of perfectly peaceful Jews in Palestine who only want to follow their own avocations, but there is most terrific intimidation taking place all the time.[79]

## *Royden testimony*

With General Spears' testimony still top of mind, that same afternoon the Committee engaged in a discussion of anti-Semitism during the testimony of Maude Royden. The following exchange ensued between Royden and Judge Hutcheson, in which Hutcheson displayed his own anti-Semitism:

ROYDEN: I have asked my Jewish friends if they can explain it. They are apt to say of course it may be due to the fact that Jews have better brains and we are jealous. I think quite possibly there is something in that. They have certainly got good brains, but what the fundamental cause is I am sorry I cannot give it.

JUDGE HUTCHESON: I should like to follow up and make this suggestion, do you not think that running through it all and at all times, perhaps aggravated and added to from time to time by other rivulets, the great stream which has been responsible for that tendency is the fact that the Jews have called themselves and been called a peculiar people, that is, a separate people.[80]

McDonald took issue with Hutcheson's comment, noting German Jews had been almost completely assimilated, yet Germany had been ground zero for the worst manifestation of anti-Semitism in world history. Hutcheson, unmoved, said "I deny that."[81]

Crum then questioned Royden regarding the McMahon-Hussein correspondence, which she had earlier cited as evidence of British promises of Palestine to the Arabs. Royden was prepared for the questions, and riposted by again invoking legal framing:

CRUM: You know, do you not, McMahon has denied in a letter to the Times that Palestine was included?

ROYDEN: Yes, I know he did, but as I say *we cannot really go by interpretations people put on their speeches, words, afterwards; what we have to go by is what they actually said and wrote at the time.*

CRUM: Have you read the correspondence between Prince Feisal and Dr. Weizmann?

ROYDEN: Yes.

CRUM: Have you read the agreement concluded between Prince Feisal and Dr. Weizmann?

ROYDEN: *It was subject to conditions; as those conditions were not fulfilled, the contract went by default.*[82]

## *Samuel testimony*

The next witness was Viscount Herbert Samuel (Figure 8.5), who had served as Britain's first High Commissioner to Palestine from 1920 to 1925. Samuel, who Crossman described as "very statesmanlike,"[83] urged the Committee to recommend the immigration restrictions of the 1939 White Paper be lifted and that 50,000 Jews be allowed to immigrate into Palestine each year.[84]

The following day featured an appearance from former Colonial Secretary Leo Amery, who advocated for partition as "the only possible solution of the Palestine problem."[85]

## *Feisal testimony*

The Emir (future King) Feisal of Saudi Arabia testified on Friday, 1 February 1946, the last day of the London hearings, together with representatives of Iraq, Syria, Lebanon and Egypt, whom General Spears had arranged to appear before

**FIGURE 8.5** Viscount Herbert Samuel (Public Domain)

the Committee. The witnesses expressed sympathy with the humanitarian plight of European Jewry, but insisted the issue be treated separately from Zionist aspirations in Palestine.

## *Al Khawi testimony*

Faris Bey al Khawi, the Syrian representative, invoked the Arab legal narrative, framing the legal issue by reference to the first paragraph of Article 22 of the Covenant of the League of Nations:

> To those colonies and territories which as a consequence of the late war have ceased to be under the sovereignty of the States which formerly governed them and which are inhabited by peoples not yet able to stand by themselves under the strenuous conditions of the modern world, there should be applied the principle that the well-being and development of such peoples form a sacred trust of civilisation and that securities for the performance of this trust should be embodied in this Covenant.

Crum challenged al Khawi's legal arguments against Jewish immigration:

CRUM: May I ask the Syrian delegate, did I understand you to say that it was your view that the Mandatory was without legal power to permit further immigration?

...

AL KHAWI: Yes, we say that distinctly everywhere – that the Mandatory Power is not authorized; they have no right to introduce strangers into a country which is in their hands as a sacred trust for the amelioration and good being of the inhabitants themselves.

CRUM: Upon what do you base that statement from a legal point of view?

AL KHAWI: Yes, from a legal point of view, I am saying the legal point of view does not give way for the Mandatory Power to deport people and introduce others in their place.

CRUM: Have you read the terms of the Mandate?

AL KHAWI: Do you think I agree to the terms of the Mandate?

CRUM: Whether you object.

AL KHAWI: No, we don't agree. All the Arabs have always been protesting against the terms of the Mandate.

CRUM: Of course, you are familiar, are you not, with the fact that the [Permanent] Mandates Commission of the League rejected the White Paper of 1939?

AL KHAWI: They may do whatever they like, but we don't accept anything.[86]

## *Impressions of London testimony*

McDonald (shown in Figure 8.6 alongside the Zionist leader Chaim Weizmann) wrote in his diary that the Arab witnesses in London "made an impression of such unyieldingness that it would be impossible to win them by any sort of compromise."[87]

Crossman summed up in his unpublished diary where matters stood as of the end of the London hearings:

> Judging from London, the personal position of the twelve of us is something like this. McDonald and Buxton are much nearer to the Zionists but they are very different people. Buxton is an independent-minded New Englander, honest, straight, anti-British Empire and very much disturbed by the Jews' talk of the necessity of a majority [in Palestine]. But he is also vastly suspicious of the Colonial Office and the Arabs. McDonald is so close to the Zionists that some people suspect he is in actual connection with them ... I refused to accept Sir John and Buller's view that we should have no private contacts "outside the courtroom."
>
> Next to McDonald and Buxton come Crum and I; the two most politically-minded members with no anti-Semitic prejudices ... We both think we are open-minded but in the end we shall find ourselves pleading for more Jewish immigration than the majority want.

FIGURE 8.6 James McDonald with Chaim Weizmann (Public Domain)

Then comes the professional conciliators; Leggett, from the Ministry of Labour and Phillips from the State Department. They will be looking for some let-out which can be sold to both sides and avoid trouble. They are middle-of-the-road men, unlike Singleton and Morrison, and for that matter, Texas Joe, whose middle-of-the-road will tend to be violently pro-Arab ...

Crick is the real unknown quantity. Buller is emotionally and traditionally pro-Arab and against those vulgar thrusting Jews pushing their way into the British Empire in that neighbourhood. Aydelotte is pro-Arab because it is somehow *recherche* academic."[88]

## *Bevin's curious statements*

During the London hearings Crossman went to the House of Commons to vote on a pending coal mining bill. While there he spoke to both Prime Minister Clement Attlee and Foreign Ernest Secretary Bevin:

> Attlee listened attentively but only permitted himself to say that the Zionist pressure was very irritating. Ernest Bevin in a three minute conversation asked me whether I had been circumcised.[89]

Bevin made another statement to the entire Committee during a luncheon on 28 January 1946 given in their honour at the Dorchester Hotel. Bevin said, apparently off the cuff, that if the Committee reached a unanimous verdict he would accept it and implement it. Bevin's statement made a big impression on the Committee members and played a key role in Hutcheson's later efforts during the Committee's deliberations in Lausanne to push for unanimity.

Crossman recorded Bevin's luncheon comments in his published diary:

> It was a pleasant, informal affair, and we did not expect any serious speeches. Then unexpectedly, Mr. Bevin, in proposing the health of the Committee, launched into a personal statement of policy. He jokingly thanked us for removing the responsibility from his shoulders for at least 120 days, and then stated slowly but emphatically that if we achieved a unanimous report he would personally do everything in his power to put it into effect ... Mr. Bevin's speech, though obviously impromptu, made an enormous impression on all of us, especially my American colleagues.[90]

Phillips, however, thought Bevin's comment "seemed injudicious to me, as there was no foreseeing what the conclusions of twelve independent men might be."[91]

## Europe

The Committee did not conduct formal, *en banc* hearings on the European continent, as it had done in Washington, DC and London and would later do in Cairo and Jerusalem. Instead, the Committee divided into subcommittees and spent nearly the entire month of February 1946 visiting the American, French, and British zones of Germany and Austria, as well as Poland, Czechoslovakia, Italy, and Greece. The subcommittees took witness testimony and interviewed Jewish Holocaust survivors in each location, primarily to ascertain whether they desired to try to rebuild their lives in Europe, or whether they would be willing to consider places other than Palestine, or whether they preferred Palestine or nothing.

### *The plight of the Holocaust refugees*

The terrible plight of the Holocaust survivors, homeless and stateless, with no possessions and no families, and still held in "displaced persons" camps – the post-War term for concentration camps – made a deep impression on all the Committee members. McDonald, for example, recorded an utterly heart-breaking observation in his diary: "one of the most tragic sides of the refugee problem is that there are almost no Jewish babies among the refugees, for these and most of the older people could not survive the horrors of the concentration camps."[92]

Phillips commented on a memorable demonstration of young Jewish refugees near his hotel in Santa Maria dei Bagni, Italy:

> It was only too clear that Zionist propaganda was at work … Yet when I realized what these young people had been through, that they were all that remained of their respective families, and that each had witnessed scenes of indescribable horror, I could understand and sympathize deeply with their longing for a home and country of their own.[93]

McDonald also stopped in Nuremburg to observe the Nazi War crimes trials:

> The view from the visitor's gallery was unforgettable. The prisoner's box was, of course, the center of interest. There, in the front row in the following order, sat Goering, Hess, Ribbentrop, Keitel, Rosenberg, Frank, Frick, Streicher, Funk, and Schacht. In the back row sat: Doenitz, Raeder, von Neurath, and Fritzsche … The expressions on the faces of the prisoners, their attitudes towards one another, the signs that showed of wear and tear – all these made the occasion for me memorable. Goering, the obvious leader of the group, is still the showman and carried himself like a Hollywood star. Ribbentrop seemed a broken man. Hess's face was a death mask, and during the prosecutor's presentation, he seemed to be suffering from acute pain.[94]

From 17 to 25 February 1946, the full Committee was based in Vienna, although it continued dividing into subgroups and traveling through the American and British occupied zones of Austria.

On 28 February, Crossman wrote to his then-wife Zita, describing the simmering tensions among the Committee members, especially between the two judges. Those tensions would continue brewing for the next two months, ultimately reaching a boil during the Committee's deliberations in Lausanne in April:

> Texas Joe [Judge Hutcheson] … is now bristling with anti-Zionist fervour and holds the view that the whole matter can be settled on the Texan model by closing the frontier and deporting any Jews who try to get out of Poland … We held a meeting on Sunday evening [23 February] in the Bristol [Hotel in Vienna]. When the British went over there, Hutcheson and Buxton were just concluding a press conference with the American newspapermen, which caused us some annoyance. The meeting was bad-tempered and desultory, with the two judges sparring with each other.[95]

### *Controversy regarding proposed interim report*

Near the end of the Committee's stay in Vienna, a controversy erupted over whether the Committee should issue an *ad interim* report addressing the plight of the Jewish refugees and their desire to immigrate to Palestine. On 23 February, the full Committee met for the first time since their stay in London. Justice Singleton wanted to issue an interim report describing the differing policies in the British and American zones of Austria for handling Jewish refugees who were attempting to transit through as a first step toward an onward journey to Palestine.

Crum, on the other hand, wanted to file an interim report recommending the *immediate* issuance of the 100,000 immigration certificates. Crum threatened to resign unless his request was met. According to Crum, Hutcheson talked him out of it. "I learned later," Crum subsequently wrote, "that word had come from the White House, asking that no Interim Report be made."[96]

Crossman recorded the scene in his unpublished diary:

> [T]he sparks began to fly. Texas Joe [Judge Hutcheson] said he wanted no interim report at all ... Then Crum and Crick complicated the issue by stating that they did want a full Interim Report on the Jews in Europe to be prepared immediately. Leggett, Philips and McDonald urged that we could not decide the issue in principle ... The whole affair was puzzling because two or three days ago Texas Joe and Buxton had informally agreed to this sort of communication. But on Saturday Texas Joe was adamant that he would not sign any interim report or communication whatsoever ... M[anningham] Buller, however, is pertinacious, and stated that he wanted his dissent recorded in the minutes ... A long and unpleasant discussion ended in the extraordinary decision that, on this occasion alone, which should not be a precedent, Buller's dissent should be recorded ... Buller lost the reputation for straightness and impartiality which he had won with the Americans, who began to see that politics are also played in England. This has done not harm to Morrison and myself, and the Committee was really 10 to 1 against Buller, with Sir John embarrassed and neutral.[97]

Crossman significantly downplayed this episode in his published diary, writing only, "after lengthy and at times heated discussion, we followed the lead of Judge Hutcheson and decided to issue no interim report. The Committee had weathered its first crisis."[98]

## Cairo

The full Committee reconvened near Cairo at the beginning of March, where they heard testimony from eight witnesses from the Arab League and various other Arab witnesses in public, plus one witness and the military officials *in camera*. The Committee spent three days in Egypt, residing and conducting their hearings at the famed Mena House Hotel (near the pyramids in Giza).[99]

## Azzam Pasha testimony

Azzam Pasha, the Secretary General of the Arab League, testified on 1 March 1946. Azzam said the Jews would be welcome in Palestine if they renounced Zionism and agreed to live as a protected minority, to the same extent as Jews in other Arab countries.[100]

Azzam framed Zionism as a manifestation of European settler colonialism. He drew a distinction between the Arabic-speaking Jews who had lived for centuries as docile minorities enjoying *Dhimmi* status under Muslim rule in the Middle East and North Africa, in contrast to their European-Zionist brethren:

> [O]ur Brother has gone to Europe and to the West and has come back something else. He has come back a Russified Jew, a Polish Jew, a German Jew, an English Jew. He has come back with a totally different conception of things, Western and not an Eastern. If he had the intention to be an Eastern, to be one of us, we have no quarrel with him … the Jew, our old cousin, coming back with imperialistic ideas, with materialistic ideas, with reactionary or revolutionary ideas … the Zionist, the new Jew, wants to dominate and he pretends that he has got a particular civilizing mission with which he returns to a backward, degenerate race in order to put the elements of progress into an area which has no progress. Well, that has been the pretension of every power that wanted to colonize and aimed at domination. The excuse has always been that the people are backward and that he has got a human mission to put them forward … the Arabs simply stand and say "No." We are not reactionary and we are not backward. Even if we are ignorant, the difference between ignorance and knowledge is ten years in school. We are a living, vitally strong nation, we are in our renaissance; we are producing as many children as any nation in the world. We still have our brains. We have a heritage of civilization and of spiritual life. We are not going to allow ourselves to be controlled either by great nations or small nations or dispersed nations.[101]

Crossman wrote later in his diary how Azzam's appearance before the Committee quickly descended into chaos: "Every time Azzam tried to answer there was a babel of protest behind from him in Arabic, and, in front of him, in English from the two judges who had never seen such judicial procedure."[102]

## Ali Pacha testimony

On 5 March, the Egyptian lawyer and former judge Mohamed Zaki Ali Pacha testified. Zaki had served as one of the lawyers for the Muslim side in the Lofgren Commission trial of 1930 regarding the respective rights and claims of Jews and Muslims to the Western Wall in Jerusalem.[103] Zaki invoked the familiar Arab legal framing and narrative during his testimony.

Zaki first argued that Britain, not the Jews, had conquered Palestine at the end of World War I, meaning the Jews had no legal right to reclaim Palestine for themselves. Zaki then rejected the legal validity of the Balfour Declaration, arguing it had been issued without Arab consent. Zaki further argued the Mandate *required* Britain to govern Palestine in the best interests of the local Arabs, *not* the Jews.[104]

Justice Singleton then interjected, but Zaki insisted he was properly "judging" the case:

JUSTICE SINGLETON: It sounds to me though rather as though you are giving judgment, Sir.

ZAKI: I am not giving judgment, Mr. President. I am only giving my opinion as a jurist. I am giving judgment as if this case was submitted to me to judge, and I think it is interesting for you to know the opinion of a jurist on this question, if you are looking at it from a legal point of view …

JUSTICE SINGLETON: You are rather mixing up, perhaps deliberately, law and equity.

ZAKI: No, I am coming to equity, if you please … I have been speaking about law, and now I am going to speak about the rules of equity, the humanitarian question. Would it be possible that the Palestine Arabs would pay the indemnity of the persecution of the Jews of Europe? I do not think it is right to say so … if you look to this question from a humanitarian point of view, or from an equity point of view, I think the Arabs are more concerned in this question because this land is theirs; they have been living here for centuries and centuries, and the Jews are only coming now; so, Mr. President, I should like it to be known in all the Arab world that equity and justice – I am now speaking of justice – must be the aim of this Committee.[105]

JUSTICE SINGLETON: May I ask you, just out of curiosity, when did you cease to be a judge?

ZAKI: Only about four or five months ago.

Another witness, Ahmed Morad el Bekri, Grand Chief of the Sufi Sect, made the absurd argument during his testimony that Zionism aimed at conquering the entire Arab world, from "the Euphrates to the Sudan and on to the Atlantic."[106]

## *Bourgeiba testimony*

Habib Bourgeiba, the future President of post-independence Tunisia, testified very briefly, but took the opportunity to blame the Jews for the Holocaust:

> The solution of this problem of refugees is not to be found in carrying bodies of people from one place to another, but it is for the Jews themselves to change themselves, to change certain contentions which they hold which make them offensive sometimes to the locality where they live …[107]

## Jerusalem

By far the most important phase of the evidentiary hearings took place in Jerusalem, where the Committee spent three weeks, from 6 to 28 March 1946. The Committee heard public testimony from 54 witnesses and *in camera* testimony from an additional 8 witnesses, plus military officials.

The Committee arrived at the Jerusalem railway station on 6 March 1946 (Figure 8.7) after an overnight journey from Cairo. Crossman recorded their

**FIGURE 8.7** Anglo-American Committee Members arriving in Jerusalem, 6 March 1946 (Public Domain)

arrival in Jerusalem in his diary: "We steamed into Jerusalem, where the dignitaries were all on the platform, and photographs were taken."[108]

The Committee members stayed at the King David Hotel, across the street from the YMCA building where they would hold their hearings. Crossman was enamoured with the scene at the King David: "The atmosphere of the hotel is terrific, with private detectives, Zionist agents, Arab sheikhs, special correspondents, and the rest all sitting about discreetly overhearing each other."[109]

## *Weizmann testimony*

The Jerusalem hearings began two days later, on 8 March 1946 at the YMCA building with the dramatic testimony of Chaim Weizmann, at that time the President of the Jewish Agency.

Leonard Stein, a British lawyer who for years had served as Honorary Counsel to the Jewish Agency, drafted a lengthy outline of points for Weizmann to use during his testimony.[110] Stein suggested a brilliant formulation for taking the Palestinian Arab "justice/injustice" narrative and reframing it to Weizmann's advantage:

> But there can be no ideally just solution giving full satisfaction to everyone. *It is a question of the line of least injustice,* and, weighing on one scale the position and needs of the Jews, the expectations held out to them, the contribution already made by them on the faith of those expectations, and the interest of the world generally in the settlement of the Jewish problem, and on the other, the needs of the Arabs and the position of the Arab people as a whole, justice is on our side.[111]

Weizmann embraced Stein's suggestion. In his opening statement, with Jamal Husseini of the Arab Higher Committee seated directly behind him, Weizmann made one of the most memorable public comments of his career:

> I know there may be Arabs present, opponents or friends or whoever they are; I think probably opponents, but there is no counsel of perfection in this world, and *there is no absolute justice in this world.* What you are trying to perform, and what we are all trying in our small way to do is just *rough human justice,* and *I think the decision which I would like this Committee to take, if I dare to say this, would be to move on the line of the least injustice, and injustice there is going to be* … I say there may be some slight injustice politically if Palestine is made a Jewish State, but individually the Arabs will not suffer.[112]

Weizmann's reframing of the "justice/injustice" narrative, before a single Arab witness had testified in Jerusalem, turned the Arab "justice/injustice" narrative on its head. The Palestinian Arab legal narrative had always framed the competing goals of Palestinian Arab nationalism and Zionism in absolutist, all-or-nothing terms, with no compromise possible. In stark contrast, Weizmann's "least injustice" formulation reframed the narrative in relativist, comparative terms.

Weizmann's formulation also helped stake out a more practical position for the Zionist cause, signalling a willingness to accept the two-state solution (partition) rather than the Biltmore Program's demand for a single state, with Jewish sovereignty over all of Palestine. In so doing, Weizmann made clear that statehood in Palestine had *always* been the final goal of Zionism, since the inception of the movement. The key difference between Weizmann and other mainstream Zionists involved the *timing* of statehood, but not the ultimate *goal* of statehood. For Weizmann, the issue of statehood always came down to the question of not *if*, but *when*.[113]

As Weizmann was speaking (Figure 8.8), Crum reflected to himself on Weizmann's last appearance as a witness in the YMCA Building before the Peel Commission nine years earlier, in 1937:

> I wondered what must be going through Dr. Weizmann's mind as he sat before us. Seven [sic] years before he had sat before this very same table, pleading the same cause. Only the faces before him are changed. These are twelve new men he sees before him, twelve strangers who have come only lately upon this problem with which his entire life has been concerned.[114]

**FIGURE 8.8** Chaim Weizmann testifying before the Anglo-American Committee, 8 March 1946 (Public Domain)

When it was his turn to question Weizmann, Crum asked about the fairness of declaring Palestine a Jewish state while the Arabs enjoyed a two-to-one majority. To bolster his point, Crum quoted from a 1931 *Foreign Affairs* article by Zionist supporter and future US Supreme Court Justice Felix Frankfurter:

CRUM: What is in my mind is this. You have at present an Arab majority in Palestine … The word "Jewish State" presently implies, does it not, the imposition of a new majority upon an existing majority of people, does it not?

WEIZMANN: That is so, yes.

CRUM: What I would like to know is how is that justified in democratic practice?

WEIZMANN: The word "imposition" always means the use of force. Well, if you bring in Jews into the country and allow them to settle and allow the country to develop to its maximum and absorb as many people as can be absorbed, a majority would be created. I don't believe it is undemocratic if it is done without hurting others.

CRUM: May I read to you from a statement in *Foreign Affairs* in 1931. This is what is in my mind. It is a statement by Justice Frankfurter: "*Into the whole texture of Palestine life there comes the unflagging realization that Arab cannot dominate Jew nor Jew Arab*, and that only in a fellowship of reciprocal rights and reciprocal duties can be realized the distinctive values to the civilization of Jew and Arab." Do you concur in that statement?

WEIZMANN: I concur in that statement as far as the moral relationship between Arabs and Jews goes if there is a future Jewish State … I would say however sir if you remember my chief statement I would say I admit it implies a certain amount of injustice, but the question is the line of least injustice.[115]

The italicized portion of the Frankfurter quote would prove very influential with the Committee and would reappear in the Committee's final report several weeks later.

Buxton questioned Weizmann about President Truman's request that the 100,000 immigration certificates be issued, noting the request had been based on the Harrison report. Weizmann said the figure was reasonable, especially because approximately 25,000 of the proposed immigrants would be children, for whom it was not necessary to find employment in Palestine. But Weizmann also acknowledged that all 100,000 could not be absorbed immediately, or even during 1946.[116]

On 9 March 1946, Crossman and Crum visited Weizmann at his home in Rehovot. Crossman wrote a glowing letter to his wife after the visit, describing Weizmann's home as "wonderful" and "gleaming." Crossman subsequently also described Weizmann as "one of the few very great men I have ever met."[117]

In the same letter, Crossman told his wife tensions were mounting among the Committee members, now halfway through their third month together, especially between Justice Singleton and Judge Hutcheson:

> The committee is in a fairly bad, bickery mood and the old judges snarl at each other and Phillips, McDonald and I try to pacify them, and Crick

> and Leggett, who are sensible, stay away. The rest are fairly silly people and fairly petty. But I expect they consider me silly and socialist too. So what can one do? I find myself very much on my own here, and very much approached by both sides.[118]

Crossman wrote a short memorandum to Justice Singleton and Judge Hutcheson regarding his discussion with Weizmann, noting Weizmann believed partition was the "only practical solution." Shertok was present for a portion of the discussion, and he too supported partition. Weizmann said he knew Ben-Gurion would also support partition. Crossman said it was clear Weizmann wanted him to report the substance of his proposal to the co-Chairmen of the Committee, and Crossman suggested they designate himself, Phillips and Aydelotte "to study the physical, economic and political conditions of partition."[119]

Crossman viewed Weizmann's openness to partition as extremely significant. He asked Judge Hutchinson and Justice Singleton to invite Weizmann to testify *in camera*, but the judges never pursued Crossman's suggestion.[120]

## Ben-Gurion testimony

David Ben-Gurion, Chairman of the Executive of the Jewish Agency, was the next key Jewish witness to testify in Jerusalem, on 11 March 1946. Ben Gurion, who had studied law in Istanbul, also invoked transformational legal framing and narrative during his testimony (Figure 8.9).

**FIGURE 8.9** David Ben-Gurion testifying before the Anglo-American Committee, 11 March 1946 (Alamy Photos)

Ben-Gurion began by describing the Jewish "case" as "simple and compelling," resting on two principles:

> One, that we Jews are just like other human beings, entitled to the same rights as every human being in the world and we Jewish people are just like any other people entitled to the same equality of treatment as any free and independent people of the world. The second principle is, this is and will remain our country. We are here as of right. We are not here on the strength of the Balfour Declaration or the Palestine Mandate.[121]

Ben Gurion next defined Jewish statehood:

> When we say "Jewish independence" and a "Jewish state" we mean a Jewish country, and I will say what it is. We mean Jewish soil, we mean Jewish labour, we mean Jewish colony, Jewish agriculture, Jewish industry, Jewish seed. We mean Jewish language, schools, culture. We mean Jewish safety, security, independence, complete independence as for any free people.[122]

Ben-Gurion next addressed the 100,000 immigration certificates, saying without hesitation that if he were asked to choose between the certificates or Jewish statehood in Palestine, he would opt for statehood.[123]

Ben-Gurion next addressed the legality of the White Paper of 1939:

> It is illegal not because of setting aside absorptive capacity. It has nothing to do with that. There is no absorptive capacity principle at all. The White Paper is illegal for other reasons, because it is illegal to deny that we are here as of right. The [Preamble to the] Mandate said that recognition was given to the historical connection of the Jewish people with Palestine, to be created for reconstituting their national home here. The White Paper is a denial of that.[124]

Ben-Gurion, who according to Crossman had made a "bad impression"[125] on the Committee during his first appearance, returned for further testimony two weeks later, on 26 March 1946. Justice Singleton immediately launched into hostile, prosecutorial cross-examination. Singleton wanted Ben-Gurion to admit the Jewish Agency under Ben-Gurion's leadership exercised control over the *Haganah*, the Jewish defence organisation in Palestine which the British Government had accused of terrorism:

JUSTICE SINGLETON: The organization which you spoke of, I think, on the last occasion, or someone else spoke of – *Haganah* – is that under the Jewish Agency?

BEN-GURION: I haven't spoken of it. *Haganah* is a Hebrew word which means defense.

...

JUSTICE SINGLETON: Then the *Haganah* is not under some form of control by the Jewish Agency, is it?

BEN-GURION: No, the Agency is not engaged in any illegal or any secret activity.

JUSTICE SINGLETON: I did not ask you that. I asked you just this question: Is or is not the *Haganah* under some form of control by the Jewish Agency?

BEN-GURION: I can tell you about the Agency but not about the *Haganah*. I represent the Jewish Agency here and not the *Haganah*, and I can answer about the Agency. The Agency has nothing to do with any illegal or any secret activity of Jews in this country, and therefore it can have nothing to do with any secret organization.

JUSTICE SINGLETON: Mr. Ben-Gurion, you must know that that is not an answer to my question.[126]

Singleton continued pressing Ben-Gurion regarding the *Haganah*, asking about the organisation's funding, recruitment, leadership, and the location of its headquarters. Singleton also expressed anger at the Jewish Agency's refusal to issue a broad appeal to all Palestinian Jews to refrain from attacking British police and other targets.

Ben-Gurion's second appearance ended with further rancor:

JUSTICE SINGLETON: Mr. Ben-Gurion, I appreciate, believe me, that the Jewish Agency, and you representing the Jewish Agency, in time gone by did try to stop these things, but I am coming nearer to the present day, and I venture to point out that you, as leader, appear to have said it is difficult for you to raise your hand in the interests of peace.

BEN-GURION: No, I do not accept that paraphrase, Sir.

JUSTICE SINGLETON: I will read the words again if you prefer, but what I desire, while you are still here, is to allow me to beg of you to think again, and in the interests of Palestine and of the world to raise your voice and to raise your hand in the interests of peace.

BEN-GURION: I appreciate deeply what you have said, Sir.

JUSTICE SINGLETON: That is all I want to ask.

BEN-GURION: And I hope you will reciprocate and raise your voice, you have a mightier voice than I, for many outrages which have been done or are being done to us.[127]

Crossman commented in his diary on Justice Singleton's cross-examination of Ben-Gurion:

> We started with a strange passage between Sir John and Ben-Gurion, who is really the Lenin of the Jewish Agency – i.e. the dictator who runs the Jews in Palestine, including the illegal army. Sir John tried to make

him admit this in public through a series of rather artless direct questions about the extremist bombings, which merely gave Ben-Gurion the chance of saying that the White Paper had killed more Jews than the extremist bombs had killed Englishmen.[128]

## *Husseini testimony*

The day after Ben-Gurion's initial appearance, 12 March 1946, was devoted entirely to the testimony of the two most important Palestinian Arab witnesses – Jamal Husseini and Auni Bey Abdul Hadi.

While the Committee was still in Europe, the Arab Higher Committee sent a telegram to Foreign Secretary Bevin objecting to the creation of the Committee and threatening that "any resolution emanating [from] joint enquiry commission contrary [to] Arab demands will not bind Arabs ... should enquiry be insisted upon Arabs demand participation." The telegram also demanded that Britain allow the exiled Grand Mufti of Jerusalem, Haj Amin al Husseini, to return to Palestine and appear before the Committee.[129]

Jamal Husseini (Figure 8.10), cousin of the Mufti, testified "on behalf of the Arabs of Palestine." Jamal had been in exile until February 1946 when the Mandatory Government allowed him to return to Palestine. His cousin the Mufti remained in exile.[130]

**FIGURE 8.10** Jamal Husseini testifying before the Anglo-American Committee, 12 March 1946 (courtesy Israel Museum, Jerusalem)

Husseini began by noting he had been present for Weizmann's and Ben-Gurion's testimony and the "wild" statements both had made.[131] Husseini then laid out the Arab case, using the same "justice/injustice" narrative that he, the Mufti, and Auni Bey had been invoking since the 1920s.

First, Husseini argued "[t]he Arabs are convinced that their case is one of clear and self-evident justice. It is based on the natural right of a people to remain in undisturbed possession of their country ..."[132]

Second, Husseini reprised the familiar Palestinian Arab legal arguments that the Balfour Declaration was invalid because it conflicted with the McMahon-Hussein correspondence and Article 22 of the Covenant of the League of Nations:

> The Arabs have been denied the independence which had been promised to them in the British Government's pledges of the twenty-fourth of October, 1915 and confirmed in several subsequent pledges [the Hogarth Message] in 1918, in return for their share in the Allied victory. A Mandate was imposed upon them of which the terms were a flagrant violation, not only of the promises made to them and of their natural rights, but also of the right to political independence which was specifically recognized to them in the Covenant of the League of Nations.[133]

Husseini continued the legal narrative a short time later:

> The Arabs have never recognized and never will recognize the Balfour Declaration or the Mandate. The first contained a promise which Great Britain was not entitled to make without Arab consent and which was, in any case, invalid, since it conflicted with a previous and binding British pledge. The second is an illegal document. The terms of the Mandate, which could only have derived their sanction from the Covenant of the League of Nations, are demonstrably in conflict with the letter and spirit of the relevant article; namely, Article XXII of the Covenant. The Arabs can prove the invalidity of the Balfour Declaration and the basic illegality of the Mandate, and can show cause why the measures taken in virtue of the provisions of the Mandate ... must be regarded as null and void and deserving, on legal as well as on moral and political grounds, to be abrogated.[134]

Husseini then repeatedly framed the Balfour Declaration and the Mandate as a "grave injustice:"

> These are by no means the only Arab grievances, but enough has been said to show that the policy hitherto pursed in exercise of the Mandate in Palestine constitutes a grave injustice and one that is indefensible whether from the point of view of ordinary justice and morality or from that of political expediency. The Arab case is that, in the interests of everyone concerned, injustice must be redressed without further loss of time.[135]

Later, addressing Weizmann's "least injustice" framing, Husseini said, "[i]t is not a matter of 'the lesser injustice.' We cannot see how it is less unjust to give a country to people who have not lived in it and have only sentimental claims on it, than to take that country away from people whose very life it is."[136]

Justice Singleton began the cross-examination of Husseini, asking if Husseini wanted British troops to leave Palestine, and what he thought would ensue after a British withdrawal.

JUSTICE SINGLETON: Then are we to understand that it is your wish, the wish of the Arabs of Palestine, that that the British forces and police should be withdrawn from Palestine forthwith?

HUSSEINI: Surely, Sir.

...

JUSTICE SINGLETON: Have you considered what would happen the day following?

HUSSEINI: Yes, Sir.

JUSTICE SINGLETON: Quite clearly, bloodshed.

HUSSEINI: I do not think so. If these pampered children, if these spoilt children of the British Government, the Zionists, know for once that they are no more to be pampered and spoilt, then the whole condition will be turned to what it was before the war. We will become their friends probably. What I think is that many of their hotheads will be leaving the country ...

...

JUSTICE SINGLETON: You know it is possible at least that you may be wrong as to what would happen if the British troops withdrew, that there might be war.

HUSSEINI: Well, let it be, I say let it be ... if your Commission, for instance, say to the two parties this problem will not be solved unless we got out of Palestine, it may happen, it has happened all over the world, that people have come into clashes and they have solved their difficulties by their fists. Is that not the case of history?[137]

Judge Hutcheson followed Singleton, pressing Husseini on the "injustice" issue during his questioning. Husseini used the questions to continue invoking transformational legal framing:

JUDGE HUTCHESON: [The] Committee ... is seeking, not as you say, to force anybody to do anything, but to determine where the injustice and the right of the matter lies ...

HUSSEINI: Well, Sir, it can rely on one thing, justice.

JUDGE HUTCHESON: And in the pursuit of justice will it find it in following what you say or what the Zionists say or what neither of you say?

HUSSEINI: No, justice is found in what I say because I am here, I am occupying the land, so he is the invader, I am the invaded. Never in the world has the invader been in justice.

...

JUDGE HUTCHESON: So your point is your claim to justice is based mainly on the proposition that you were in possession of the land and the Zionists ... have been invading and are continuing to invade your land. That is your case?
HUSSEINI: Quite, Sir.[138]

Husseini also attacked Ben-Gurion's testimony. Husseini equated Zionism with Nazism, in another early example of the ugly and offensive narrative that has become so ingrained in anti-Zionist framing ever since: "I thought as if I were hearing Hitler from his grave; he had the same tone, the same spirit."[139]

Crossman caused a stir when he asked Husseini about the wartime activities of his cousin, the Mufti Haj Amin al Husseini, on behalf of the Nazis. Crossman displayed a photograph of the Mufti reviewing Bosnian Muslim troops who had volunteered at the Mufti's urging to fight with the Nazis. Husseini vigorously defended his cousin, arguing the Mufti had worked with the Nazis solely to protect the Palestinian Arabs from the Zionists, and *not* to help the Germans in the war against the British.[140]

Crossman boasted to his wife in a letter he wrote that afternoon, during Auni Bey Abdul Hadi's testimony, that he had "successfully grilled him [Husseini] for 20 minutes as to the Mufti's activities in Germany during the war ... he was quite open in saying that no Arab minded which side won, and that the real battle for Arabs was against the British mandate, which doesn't really help the Arab position."[141]

Crossman wrote another letter to his wife the next morning in which he related how his questions to Husseini regarding the Mufti had caused a "sensation" in the local press, resulting in pushback from his British colleagues:

> My British colleagues were somewhat frigid and talked darkly about people who like press publicity. Crick formally protested that these questions had made conciliation more difficult, to which I replied that I wasn't particularly sorry if the truth about the Higher Arab Committee [sic] made it more difficult to get into cahoots with them. At which point of course all the Americans rallied to my side.[142]

Crossman also commented in his published diary regarding Husseini's testimony, adding an interesting and deeply perceptive observation about Britain's relations with the Arabs and Jews:

> He added nothing to what we knew of the Arab case, but he spoke with a fatalistic acceptance of conflict which sounded to English ears more sincere than protestations of friendship. *Somehow we [Britain] like the Arabs even though they fight us and we dislike the Jews even if our interests run together.*[143]

After Husseini had testified, Gershon Agronsky, the publisher of the Palestine Post, met McDonald for lunch. According to Agronsky's typewritten notes of their discussion, McDonald described Husseini's testimony as a "great shock" to the British members of the Committee, who had "been taught to regard the Jewish Agency as a menace, and now [they have heard] this anti-British evidence [from Husseini]."[144] McDonald wrote in his diary that although Husseini's testimony was "sensational," Husseini's "open defense of the Mufti was a major strategic mistake."[145]

Agronsky asked McDonald about the possibility the Committee would recommend partition. McDonald said, "he was quite prepared, but he doubted whether any such thing was likely." McDonald also described how Judge Hutcheson had grown impatient and homesick. Hutcheson, McDonald said, was "an unknown quantity, but pressing to get through in time, and anxious that the writing of the report shouldn't take longer than two to three weeks."[146]

## *Abdul Hadi testimony*

Auni Bey Abdul Hadi (Figure 8.11) testified on behalf of the Arab Higher Committee during the afternoon following Husseini's testimony. Auni Bey was the most famed Palestinian lawyer of the 1920s–1940s. He had served as Prince Feisal's legal advisor at the Versailles Peace Conference in 1919, and as the Arabs' lawyer during the Shaw Commission trial of 1929 and the Lofgren Commission trial of 1930. Auni Bey testified as a witness before the Palestine

**FIGURE 8.11** Auni Bey Abdul Hadi, London, February 1939 (Getty Images)

Royal Commission in early 1937, and he co-led the Palestine Arab delegation to the London Conferences in 1939. He was also a co-founder of the *Istiqlal* Party.

Auni Bey began by echoing Jamal Husseini's framing of Zionism as a form of fascism: "When I heard Mr. Ben Gurion … it occurred to me that what I was hearing, I will not say the voice of Hitler, as my friend Jamal Bey Husseini said, but the voice of Mussolini, with his warlike emphasis."[147]

Auni Bey then launched into the same legal narrative and legal argumentation he had made many times in the past regarding the interplay between the McMahon-Hussein correspondence, the Balfour Declaration, the Mandate, and the Covenant of the League of Nations. He framed the Balfour Declaration and the portions of the Mandate implementing it as legally null and void.

Auni Bey also took aim at the Weizmann-Feisal agreement of January 1919, accusing Colonel T.E. Lawrence, who had acted as Feisal's translator, of tricking him into signing the agreement, even though Feisal had added a reservation of rights in Arabic, in his own handwriting, before signing the agreement.[148]

Crossman described Auni Bey's testimony as "not very impressive."[149] Crossman grew so bored during Auni Bey's testimony that he wrote a multi-page letter to his wife while Auni Bey was still in the witness chair. The letter painted a less than flattering portrait of the witness and Crossman's fellow Committee members:

> During the Hearings.
>
> My own sweet, an Arab [Auni Bey] has now been talking for 2 hours about the history of the Mandate. Texas Joe [Judge Hutcheson] sleeps, Sir John is keeping his eyes open. Only Phillips is even pretending to attend, as we have heard it all 20 times before. So I will finish off the letter to you which I started this morning.[150]

A short time later Crossman, growing increasingly weary from listening to Auni Bey, wrote to his wife, "this Arab has now spoken for 2-1/4 hours and the gentle hum of boredom hovers over the afternoon sleep."[151]

Crossman then noted the American committee members had become "disconcerted" by some of the testimony they had heard, "and have become positively pro-British in their indignation."[152]

Crossman, still writing to his wife as Auni Bey was testifying, described the intellectual life in Palestine:

> One of the troubles here is that there is such a *vast amount* of Jewish talent, and such a tiny group of Arab intelligentsia. I think I have met all the Arabs who are worth talking to already; but the list of Jewish leaders who are worth meeting is gigantic. I dined with Horowitz, a first rate economic planner last night; I dine with Ben Gurion who leads the anti-Weizmann Labour Wing of the Zionists tonight … There is really terrific *intellectual* activity among the Jews, not to mention business, farming, and general

> communal thrust and against them are pitted the poor, inefficient, idle, corrupt political leaders who are wasting our time today. They haven't sent us written material or prepared their case but just talk and talk and talk.[153]

Crossman would later describe a dinner meeting that same evening with Ben-Gurion, "in the Manager's suite at the Eden Hotel, by a beautiful log fire," as "one of the best dinners, both food and drink, I have ever had, and a vastly stimulating conversation."[154] Following so closely after his overnight stay at the Weizmann's' home in Rehovot only four days earlier, Crossman had been won over to the Zionist cause.

Meanwhile, while Crossman was writing the letter to his wife, Auni Bey pounded away at the Jewish case. He took a defiant, strident stand against Zionist aspirations in Palestine: "You may be sure," he testified, "that you can never establish a Jewish state in Palestine so long as there is one Arab living."[155]

Auni Bey concluded his testimony by invoking yet again the familiar Palestinian Arab legal narrative. He argued the Balfour Declaration was "invalid, *ultra vires*, and should be abolished because members of the League of Nations took it upon themselves not to enforce anything which is contrary to the terms of [Article 20] the Covenant of the League of Nations."[156]

But Auni Bey, so effective in the 1920s and 1930s, seemed by 1946 to have lost some of his persuasive force as a legal advocate for Palestinian Arab nationalism. McDonald, writing separately in his diary, found Auni Bey "dull, labored and nervous."[157]

## *Breuer testimony*

After the Committee once again made the short trek from the King David Hotel to the YMCA Building (Figure 8.12), the Jewish case resumed the following day, 13 March 1946, with a variety of witnesses representing the Agudath Israel, the Sephardic Communities of Palestine, and the Vaad Leumi.

Dr. Isaac Breuer, a highly regarded Jewish lawyer and Rabbi in Palestine who had testified before the Palestine Royal Commission in 1937, testified on behalf of *Agudath Israel*. Dr. Breuer, like so many of the prior Jewish and Arab witnesses, invoked transformational legal framing during his testimony:

> It [Jewish statehood in Palestine] is not only a demand of the entire Jewish People, but a demand of objective law, of objective justice, according to our deep conviction … In loyalty to the tradition of our People, we do not see in the Arab-Jewish problem a problem of world politics and not a power problem, but a problem of law. In loyalty to the tradition of our People, we are convinced that law alone is capable of bringing peace into the relations of nations. The Jewish People claims naught but its lawful rights. May you bring about a decision according to objective law, and let then, if necessary, power protect the law. Power must never pronounce on what is to be right, but objectively found law may claim to be protected by power.[158]

**FIGURE 8.12** Anglo-American Committee crossing street from King David Hotel to YMCA Building, March 1946 (Public Domain)

## *Eliash testimony*

Later that day, Dr. Mordechai Eliash (Figure 8.13), the most eminent Jewish lawyer in Palestine, who had served as lead counsel to the Jews during the Lofgren Commission trial of 1930 and as a witness before the Palestine Royal Commission in 1937, testified on behalf of the *Vaad Leumi.*

McDonald described Dr. Eliash as "in some respects almost the most brilliant spokesman to date. His basic argumentation and his answers to questions revealed a singularly acute and constructive mind."[159]

Phillips asked Dr. Eliash, who had been living in Palestine for the past 34 years, whether any attempts had been made to bring peace between the Jewish and Arab communities by educating their children together in the same schools. Dr. Eliash's answer would ring as equally true if it were given today:

> Certain attempts have been made along these lines, but they have always been futile. Any attempt or any invitation to Jews and Arabs to go into a melting pot to produce something which would call itself a Palestinian, would not succeed in Palestine. The desire for national aspiration and national existence is strong. I would say, in both communities, and the desire to develop one's language and one's culture is so strong that one wouldn't meet with great success by suggesting to Jews that if they rub off a bit of their Jewishness they might be less noxious.[160]

FIGURE 8.13 Dr. Mordechai Eliash (courtesy Central Zionist Archives, Jerusalem)

Crick asked Dr. Eliash about the term "in" Palestine as used in the Balfour Declaration and the Mandate. Phillips wanted to know whether that meant "the boundaries of your suggested Jewish State be identical with the boundaries of Palestine as defined today?" Dr. Eliash responded carefully: "My answer would be yes, *if* there is no partition."[161]

## *Magnes testimony*

The following day, 14 March 1946, featured testimony from three famous Palestinian Jews who supported Jewish immigration, including the immediate issuance of the 100,000 immigration certificates, but opposed Jewish statehood. The witnesses were Dr. Judah Magnes (Figure 8.14), Professor Martin Buber, and Moshe Smilansky.

Magnes handled the majority of the testimony and fielded nearly all the questions from the Committee. His testimony played a key role in influencing the Committee's verdict and final report.

**FIGURE 8.14** Judah Magnes testifying before the Anglo-American Committee, 14 March 1946. Martin Buber is seated to his right (Alamy Photos)

Magnes was born in San Francisco and ordained as a Reform Jewish Rabbi. He moved to Palestine after World War I and eventually co-founded the Hebrew University of Jerusalem and became its first Chancellor. Magnes had long championed the bi-national solution for Palestine, representing a small minority view in the Zionist movement.

During his testimony, Magnes invoked the "justice" narrative that both the Arab and Jewish witnesses had used. Magnes, however, framed the justice/injustice narrative differently from nearly all the other Jewish witnesses. Magnes idealistically argued "true justice" would require both sides to compromise their nationalist goals and give up their desire to dominate the other. Palestine, Magnes urged, should become *neither* a Jewish nor an Arab state, but a truly binational state in which both communities would cooperate for the benefit of all:

> Independence of one's own must not be gained at the expense of another's independence. Jewish settlement must oust no Arab peasant, Jewish immigration must not cause the political status of the present inhabitants to deteriorate and must continue to ameliorate their economic condition. The tradition of justice is directed toward the future of this country as a whole, as well as towards the future of the Jewish people ... A regenerated Jewish people in Palestine has not only to aim at living peacefully together with the Arab people but also at a comprehensive cooperation with it in opening and developing the country.[162]

Magnes continued by stressing Jewish-Arab equality as the governing principle upon which to build the binational, unitary state in Palestine:

> We regard the Arab natural rights and the Jewish historical rights as, under all the circumstances, of equal validity. We look upon Palestine as a bi-national Jewish-Arab land, a common motherland for these two Semitic peoples who have the privilege of acting as trustees for millions of their co-religionists all over the world. In such a land it is not fitting that one people should dominate the other. A Jewish State means domination of the Arabs by the Jews; an Arab State means domination of the Jews by the Arabs. The fear of this domination is deep and genuine in both peoples. This fear is the double-edged sword of the problem. It becomes the task of statesmanship to find the way of dissipating the fear and supplanting it with cooperation, development, peace.[163]

Proclaiming "no one can have all he wants in this country" and "a feasible and honorable compromise must be sought," Magnes argued two overriding principles should govern the Committee's consideration of the issues – political parity and numerical parity.

The first key principle, political parity, according to Magnes, meant a system of unitary government in which each community would enjoy limited autonomy over their own affairs, but under the umbrella of a single national government:

> We contend that sovereign independence in this tiny land, whether it be Jewish sovereignty or Arab sovereignty, is not possible ... the bi-national Palestine would deprive the Jews of their one opportunity of a Jewish State. Nevertheless, this bi-national Palestine would be the one country in the world where the Jews would be a constituent nation, that is, an equal nationality within the body politic and not just a minority as everywhere else.[164]

Magnes offered a vision for Palestine that many would characterise as utterly naïve and utopian. The binational state, Magnes argued, "would make this Holy Land into a delightful, peaceful Switzerland in the heart of this ancient highway between East and West ... a bi-national Palestine would become a beacon of peace in the world."[165] Magnes, therefore, opposed partition or a two-state solution as "a moral defeat."[166]

The second key principle, numerical parity, meant Jewish immigration should be hastened to grow the size of the Jewish community until it reached parity with the Arab population. "And the immediate thing to be done in this direction," Magnes argued "is to admit without further delay President Truman's 100,000 displaced persons."[167] Magnes argued that issuing the 100,000 immigration certificates would diminish the fervour among those in the Jewish community who were clamouring for statehood:

> There are others however who want the State for the sake of immigration. That is another reason why I say if immigration were given without the State there would be many people who would not be satisfied a hundred percent but who would acquiesce, would forgo the State.[168]

Magnes' testimony made an enormous impression on the Committee. Leggett commended Magnes in glowing terms: "May I just say how wonderful it has been to hear this afternoon a council of conciliation put forward." Hutcheson went even further, praising Magnes for his "courage and character" and for having the "moral courage to stand against a stream of vigorous tendency and propound the theory he thinks is just."[169] McDonald too was impressed, although he thought Magnes, despite his brilliance, somewhat unrealistic:

> Then came Dr. Magnes, who held his audience almost breathless for more than two hours. His statement was eloquent at times, deeply moving, and showed a moral courage of the very highest kind. His political thesis about a bi-partisan state did great credit to his breadth of understanding, but little, I fear, to his sense of statesmanship, for I don't think it is at all practicable.[170]

★★★★★

Two days after Magnes' testimony, Crossman confided in a letter to his wife that he was not getting along well with the other members of the Committee. "I am a bit lonely on the Committee now and isolated," he wrote, "partly it is jealousy and partly it is because I do happen to be an arrogant Socialist who despises them so why not dislike me?"[171] Crossman's isolation, especially from the other British members of the Committee, would prove to play a key role in their deliberations the following month in Lausanne.

Leslie Rood, one of the American secretaries to the Committee, received a telegram from his superiors in the State Department on 21 March 1946 identifying a range of places other than Palestine where the surviving European Jews could be relocated, including Alaska, Eritrea, Tripolitania, Madagascar, the Dominican Republic, British Guiana, Venezuela, and the Philippines.[172]

★★★★★

## *Cattan testimony*

The next significant witness was the Jerusalem-based Arab lawyer Henry Cattan, who testified on 23 March 1946 on behalf of the Arab Higher Committee. Cattan continued the Palestinian Arab transformational legal framing, arguing "the Arabs have a right, a natural and legal right, to Palestine as their country."[173]

Cattan then ran through the litany of familiar legal arguments the Mufti and Auni Bey Abdul Hadi had been making since the 1920s. He argued Britain had no legal standing to promise anything regarding Palestine to the Jews in

FIGURE 8.15 Anglo-American Committee members visiting the Dome of the Rock, March 1946 (Public Domain)

the Balfour Declaration. Even if Britain had such standing, Article 20 of the Covenant of the League of Nations rendered the Balfour Declaration void as against the British pledge of Palestine to the Arabs in the McMahon-Hussein correspondence.

Cattan also emphasized the importance of the Muslim Holy sites and Muslim ownership of the Haram Al-Sharif (Figure 8.15). He rejected any Jewish claim of legal rights or legal title to Palestine based on the Jews' historical connection to the land:

> Many states, many peoples, have historical connections, and in no case could that establish the basis to enforceable claim to territory. I do not think I need further go into that aspect of the question. I would ask you to consider that if such a claim were to be put before an International Court of Justice, any such claim of historical connection, whether by the Jews to Palestine or the Arabs to Spain, or the British to certain parts of the United States, or any other such claim, it would not be considered for a minute.[174]

Cattan further argued the Jews had no rights under the Balfour Declaration or otherwise to immigrate to Palestine, and that the White Paper of 1939 had

FIGURE 8.16 Henry Cattan (Public Domain)

rejected the concept of "economic absorptive capacity" as conferring any legal rights on prospective Jewish immigrants.[175]

McDonald described Cattan (Figure 8.16) as a "brilliant Arab lawyer," who had made "a carefully prepared appeal to a jury rather than to a judge."[176]

Crum, however, seemed impatient with Cattan's legal arguments:

CRUM: You are a barrister, are you not, and you know that litigants always think they are right, both sides always think that?
CATTAN: They do, but justice is there to tell them who is right.
CRUM: But in the ordinary course one of the litigants usually loses, doesn't he?
CATTAN: Yes.
CRUM: And he accepts the verdict of the court?
CATTAN: Right.
CRUM: That is all.[177]

One of the most interesting aspects of the Palestinian legal argument from the early 1920s to the mid-1940s was the claim that Palestine had never been a separate country, but instead had always been considered part of Syria. The argument seems counter-intuitive, as it completely undermines the Palestinians' own claim since the early 1960s that Palestine has always been a separate, discreet country belonging to them.

**FIGURE 8.17** Anglo-American Committee members visiting the Wailing Wall, March 1946 (Public Domain)

But the emphasis of the Palestinian legal framing and narrative between the 1920s and 1940s was to negate Jewish claims to Palestine by denying there was such a place as "Palestine." Instead, a long succession of Arabs argued during those years that "Palestine" did not exist as a separate political entity; it was merely a figment of the Zionist imagination. Palestinian nationalism was viewed during those years as part of the larger tableau of pan-Arab nationalism, and did not depend on the existence of a separate Palestinian country.

Crossman explored this point briefly with Cattan:

CROSSMAN: Would you say that Arab nationalism, I mean talking about Palestine Arabs, was Palestinian in its feeling or more general? Is it a nationalism which is Palestinian or Tran-Jordanian or Syrian, or do the Arabs feel a single nationalism?

CATTAN: They do feel a single nationalism. We are all related. We, the Arabs of the Middle East, are all related to one another. We feel in the same way, we live in the same way, we think in the same way.

Cattan also rejected Jewish feelings regarding the Wailing Wall (Figure 8.17) as justifying Zionist national aspirations in Palestine.

## *Crossman's views take shape*

Crossman wrote again to his wife after Cattan's testimony, describing the increasingly difficult dynamic within the Committee during their stay in Jerusalem. Crossman said the hearings were becoming "a bit trying and the Committee is getting testy and bored. Their only interest is to get the hell out of Palestine and to start finishing the job in Lausanne."[178]

Crossman had additional harsh words for his fellow Committee members. He expressed doubt whether the Committee would be able to reach agreement on a verdict once they began their deliberations in Lausanne:

> They are not very good most of them at *seeing* things so they don't much want to look at Palestine or to meet people or really to *understand* what it is all about. In fact, I am feeling rather outside the committee, though Leggett, Crick and Crum are still fine. The two old chairmen are really too crotchety and uninterested for words, though Texas Joe [Judge Hutcheson] is still a very nice man in private. I hesitate to think what will happen when we get to Lausanne and start trying to agree on a report, with two such chairmen in charge ... what *is* annoying is that my last few days in this lovely and fascinating country must be wasted mostly on hearings.[179]

Crossman said he would have preferred for the Committee to spend more time touring the country and gaining a better understanding the facts on the ground:

> [I]n my view, it is quite ridiculous leaving before we have really more than skimmed the problem here. But the fact, I think, is the committee would disintegrate if it tried to go on much longer ... God knows how on earth we are capable in our present state of knowledge of putting anything on paper at all.[180]

Crossman by this time had also formed a dismal opinion of the British Mandatory Government officials in Palestine:

> I find the administration here utterly nauseating. They are snobbish, cliquy, second-rate and reactionary. They like the Arabs because they are illiterate, inefficient, and easy to govern. They dislike the Jews because the Jewish leaders are ten times as able as they are.[181]

In the same diary entry, Crossman also wrote he had made up his mind on a solution to the conflict in Palestine: "Suddenly my mind got made up on the solution [partition] and only two people agree with me so far. So now thank heavens its [sic] good hard politics, and argument and in-fighting and out-fighting and all the things I enjoy."[182]

The hearings resumed two days later, on 25 March 1946, with a broad array of Arab and Jewish witnesses.

## *Ghory testimony*

Emile Ghory, a member of the Arab Higher Committee and General Secretary of the Palestine Arab party, expressed adamant opposition to any further Jewish immigration, much to the consternation of at least two Committee members:

CROSSMAN: Supposing that the Jewish State were abandoned and the Jewish majority, what would be the Arab attitude to further immigration?

GHORY: The Arabs are not prepared to accept any more immigration.

...

CROSSMAN: Supposing there was an independent Arab State, that would be the end of political Zionism.

GHORY: Yes.

CROSSMAN: In that situation, would the ban on immigration be complete?

GHORY: Yes, there would be a ban on immigration.

...

MANNINGHAM-BULLER: You regard, as I understand, every Jewish immigrant as a danger and a threat to the Arabs in Palestine.

GHORY: Yes, Sir.

MANNINGHAM-BULLER: Is that right?

GHORY: Yes, Sir.

MANNINGHAM-BULLER: Do you seriously take that view in fact, to an elderly, sick and infirm Jew who is now seeking a home and shelter for himself for the last few years of his life?

GHORY: Palestine is not an asylum.

...

MANNINGHAM-BULLER: Are the Arabs prepared to stop any old, infirm, sick Jew from coming to Palestine to spend his ... last few years in a Jewish home in Palestine?

GHORY: Yes, Sir. We are against any Jewish immigration irrespective of class, type or number of immigrants.[183]

## *Meyerson testimony*

Later that day, Goldie Myerson (later Golda Meir, Figure 8.18) testified on behalf of the *Histadrut* (Zionist Labor Federation). She urged the 100,000 immigration certificates be issued immediately. Meyerson said "there is no doubt in my mind" that all 100,000 immigrants could be housed and employed in Palestine before the end of 1946, even if that meant every Jewish family in the country taking in refugees.[184]

## *Shukeiri testimony*

Ahmed Shukeiri, a "very ambitious rising lawyer who had been appointed director of the Arab Office,"[185] and the future founder of the Palestine Liberation Organization, and the British-Syrian historian Albert Hourani, testified together on behalf of the Arab office immediately after Myerson.

Shukeiri went first, reiterating the Palestinian Arab legal narrative regarding the interplay between Articles 20 and 22 of the Covenant of the League of Nations and the Balfour Declaration. Shukeiri argued the Balfour Declaration

FIGURE 8.18 Golda Meir (Public Domain)

and the Mandate were "invalid and void *ab initio*, for neither Great Britain nor any other power in the world is entitled to promise a nation's territory to another."[186]

Shukeiri also threatened violence if Palestinian Arab demands were not met, in menacing language that presaged the following decades of war and terrorism:

> We hope that your decisions will not be swayed in any way by temporary convenience, and that you will not be influenced by such questions as who can make the most trouble. *But if it is a question of degree of violence, the Arabs are prepared to break the record – and not only in Palestine.*[187]

## Hourani testimony

Albert Hourani (Figure 8.19), an Oxford-educated intellectual with a reputation for brilliance, invoked the familiar Arab "justice/injustice" narrative in his opening statement:

> I think it is right to emphasize, without elaborating what needs no further elaboration, the unalterable opposition of the Arab nation to the attempt to impose a Jewish state upon it. This opposition is based upon the

**FIGURE 8.19** Albert Hourani (Public Domain)

> unwavering conviction of unshakeable rights and a conviction of the injustice of forcing a long settled population to accept immigrants without its consent being asked and against its known and expressed will – the injustice of turning a majority into a minority in its own country – the injustice of withholding self-government until the Zionists are the majority and able to profit by it.[188]

Hourani further described the Zionist proposal for a Jewish State in Palestine as a "terrible injustice."[189] Accordingly, Hourani explained, the Arabs rejected partition – if they rejected Jewish statehood in *all* of Palestine, they certainly also rejected it in *part* of Palestine.[190]

Hourani also scoffed at Magnes' proposal for a binational state:

> A bi-national state of the kind that Dr. Magnes suggests can only work if a certain spirit of trust and cooperation exists and if there is an underlying sense of unity to neutralize communal differences. But that spirit does not exist in Palestine. If it existed, the whole problem would not have arisen in this form and Dr. Magnes' solution would not be necessary. Since it doesn't exist, Dr. Magnes' solution is, under present circumstances, impossible.

> And if it were possible – if a bi-national state could be established – it would lead to one of two things: either to a complete deadlock involving perhaps the intervention of foreign powers, or else to the domination of the whole life of the state by communal considerations.[191]

McDonald asked both Hourani and Shukeiri a question which laid bare Palestinian Arab intransigence against the Zionist movement. McDonald asked whether Hourani would compromise and accept a two-state solution, or whether he would rather hold out for the one-state solution – meaning a Palestinian Arab state – no matter how long it would take:

MCDONALD: You have stated what you would like to have [an Arab State in all of Palestine] very clearly and very forcibly. Assuming that it couldn't be had immediately, would you prefer to wait a longer time to get the whole case … Or would you rather take less in a shorter time?

HOURANI: No, I would prefer to have the whole.

…

MCDONALD: How about you?

SHUKEIRI: I stand by the answer.[192]

Manningham-Buller pressed Hourani regarding immigration, specifically whether elderly and infirm European Jewish refugees should be permitted to relocate to Palestine. Hourani tried to evade the question before admitting he opposed allowing elderly and infirm Jews to immigrate to Palestine:

MANNINGHAM-BULLER: There are people in Europe now, old people … who can scarcely spend a year waiting … With regard to these old, sick people does the Arab office – in your capacity would you object to these individual Jews who have relatives here who are prepared to look after them, would you object to their coming to this country?

HOURANI: If I may say so, I feel the question is not adequately posed. It implies there is no other possible arrangement for these people.

MANNINGHAM-BULLER: With great respect, I don't think so. You said in your address to us that you wouldn't agree to immigration until you were satisfied that Great Britain and the United States had done all that was possible. Well, we have lost thousands of homes and houses during this war, but we have at the same time opened our doors to Jews who have relatives in Great Britain. I was only asking whether the Arabs would be prepared to open their doors to elderly Jews who had relatives now in Palestine as a humanitarian gesture.

HOURANI: May I make two replies to that? The first is that it would not be true to assume that the only choice before those refugees in Europe is either to come to Palestine or to die. There are other possible assignments. In the second place, with regret, as one says, it is impossible to divorce the question of immigration on whatever grounds you justify it from a peaceful settlement.

MANNINGHAM-BULLER: Let me assume at the moment that the only relations these elderly Jews in the world [have] are in Palestine. Would you be in favour of keeping them in their last few years away from the one relation who perhaps possibly can give them help?

HOURANI: In view of all that has happened and in view of the political aim of the Jewish Agency, I am afraid there in no alternative, but I insist that the Arabs are not responsible. These people ... are the victims of political Zionism.[193]

One modern pro-Palestinian commentator has speculated that as a result of this exchange with Manningham-Buller, "the force of [Hourani's] testimony was weakened, his credibility tarnished, and his morality called into question because he fell short on expressing a crucial emotion: sympathy."[194]

### *E. Samuel testimony*

Edwin Samuel, the son of former High Commissioner Herbert Samuel, also testified *in camera* on 25 March 1946. Samuel told the Committee "it is absolutely essential that there should be some form of control of immigration."[195] Samuel also called for ruling out either an Arab or a Jewish State, advocating instead a continuation of the Mandate in the form of a Trusteeship.

*****

The next day, reflecting on the hearings in Jerusalem and their stay in Palestine, Crossman lamented the Committee could not stay longer to conduct a more in-depth study, but tempers were too frayed inside the Committee by then:

> So now we shall just wind up our hearings in public and pack up and go. It is probably wise since if we tried to study this any more, tempers would get so bad and [Judge Hutcheson's] longing for Houston would grow so great that the committee would disintegrate altogether.[196]

*****

## Other Arab states

While the hearings were ongoing in Jerusalem, the Committee broke into small subcommittees between 15 and 24 March 1946 for side-trips to Transjordan, Iraq, Syria, Saudi Arabia, and Lebanon. The Committee conducted no formal hearings in those countries, but took testimony informally and met with a variety of officials and others to gather information.

One of the more interesting encounters took place in Lebanon between McDonald and the Maronite Archbishop, Ignacy Mubarak, who told McDonald he was a staunch Zionist, and that Palestinian Arab leaders who opposed Zionism were acting only for their "personal and political ends."[197]

In early February 1946, the British Embassy in Jedda, Saudi Arabia cabled London to advise that King Ibn Saud wanted to appear personally before the Committee. The Embassy noted the importance of not offending Ibn Saud, especially if the Committee were to hear testimony from the King's "enemies in Egypt or hear Amir Abdullah in person."[198] The decision was made to honour the King's request.

Justice Singleton, along with Buxton and Manningham-Buller, travelled to Iraq and Saudi Arabia in mid-March. In Baghdad they met with 24 people, conducting informal interviews rather than taking formal testimony.[199]

In Saudi Arabia, Justice Singleton and his colleagues met with King Ibn Saud in Riyadh on 19 March 1946. In response to a question from Buxton regarding further Jewish immigration to Palestine, the King replied, "to us death is preferable to acquiescence in the emigration, and all our efforts are directed toward the prevention of Jews immigrating into Palestine and purchasing land there."[200]

Harold Beeley, one of the two British secretaries to the Committee, accompanied the delegation and reported later to London that the King was "in excellent form" during the meeting, and that the Committee members "were deeply impressed."[201] Beeley enclosed with his report an English translation of the King's remarks, in which the King expressed the desire that Britain "act justly towards the Arabs and Palestine."[202]

Meanwhile, in Damascus, Judge Hutcheson, together with Morrison and McDonald, interviewed Dr. David Pinto, a representative of the Syrian Jewish community, who appeared robotic and scripted:

DR. DAVID PINTO: In the name of the Jewish congregations of Syria and the Lebanon we declare that we are loyal citizens of our countries and enjoy all the rights and have nothing to complain of. Therefore, we totally object to Zionist aspirations.

JUDGE HUTCHESON: Do you have something more to add?

PINTO: No.[203]

The brief interview under the watchful eye of Syrian officials made an enormous impression on Judge Hutcheson, although not the one the Syrian Government had hoped to convey. During the Lausanne deliberations, Judge Hutcheson mentioned what he had seen in Syria, citing it as evidence that the Jews would not survive under Arab domination in Palestine.

## Written submissions to the committee

The Anglo-American Committee of Inquiry received voluminous written submissions – *200 pounds of paper* per committee member by the time they had arrived in Lausanne – from nearly all the witnesses it heard and from a variety of Jewish, Arab, and other groups.[204] Many of the submissions reprised the Arab and Jewish legal narratives.

## *Senator Gillette legal memorandum*

For example, former United States Senator Guy Gillette of Iowa, now President of the American League for a Free Palestine, submitted a memorandum dated 3 January 1946. A significant portion of Gillette's memorandum addressed the "legal basis for the Hebrew State in Palestine."[205]

Gillette began his analysis by arguing the Jewish people originally were the legal owners of Palestine. Despite their expulsion from the country two millennia ago, they never ceded or waived their claim of legal title to Palestine. Gillette supported this argument by citing an 1891 article written by the "famed legal authority" Dr. William E. Blackstone, in which Blackstone argued:

> [S]ince Hebrews never gave up their title to Palestine, the general "law of dereliction" could not hold in their case, "for they never abandoned the land, they made no treaty, they did not even surrender … [s]ince then, having no sovereign head through whom they could speak they have disputed the possession of the land by continued protest."[206]

Gillette then discussed the Balfour Declaration and the Weizmann-Feisal January 1919 "treaty" in which Feisal pledged support for the Zionist program in Palestine. Gillette further argued, in much the same vein as the leading Arab legal scholars had been arguing for the prior two decades, that Palestinian independence had been legally authorised by Article 22 of the Covenant of the League of Nations.

But Gillette turned the Arab legal argument regarding Article 22 on its head. He insisted that because the Jews had never renounced their claim to Palestine, Article 22 must be construed as having made a legally binding pledge of self-determination and independence to the *Jews*, not the Arabs of Palestine.

Gillette further argued that Britain's acceptance of the Mandate bound it by force of international law to ensure the creation of the Jewish homeland in Palestine, consistent with his view that Article 22 embodied a pledge of independence to the Jews.[207]

## *Other Jewish memoranda*

The Committee also received three other legal submissions from the Jewish side. One came from Isaac Breuer, who had previously testified before the Committee;[208] the second came from the American Zionist Emergency Council;[209] and the third came from Judge Simon Rifkind.[210]

The Jewish Agency for Palestine submitted a variety of papers. One argued Jewish settlement in Palestine had made a positive impact on the local Arab population.[211] Another traced the historical connection of the Jewish people with Palestine.[212]

The American Jewish Committee submitted a lengthy memorandum, on the cover of which Judge Hutcheson wrote "a very fine document."[213]

The Jewish Resistance Movement submitted a memorandum from the "Head of Command," declaring "[w]e are prepared to give our lives for the renaissance of our people and state."[214]

On the other end of the Jewish spectrum, Jewish peace activist Haim Margolis-Kalvaryski, a peace activist in the *Brit Shalom* movement, submitted an *aide memoir* advocating for a binational, unitary state.[215] Martin Buber submitted a short memorandum advocating Arab-Jewish cooperation and binationalism.[216]

### Arab written submissions

The Arab submissions largely invoked the longstanding legal narrative the Arab side had been developing for the past 25 years against the Balfour Declaration and the Mandate, framing Arab grievances through the lens of the familiar "justice/injustice" narrative. Jamal Husseini's written submission, for example, argued:

> The Arab case is based on the fact that the policy hitherto pursued in Palestine constitutes a *grave injustice to the Arab people of a kind for which there is no parallel in modern times*; and that, until that injustice is adequately redressed in accordance with the accepted principles of morality and equity there can be no peace in the Holy Land.[217]

The Secretariat General of the Arab League submitted a memorandum to the Committee advocating the Palestinian Arab case in decidedly legal terms, arguing as Gillette had done on behalf of the Jewish side that the Arabs obtained legal title over Palestine hundreds of years ago:

> As to the legal argument, it is also a known fact that the Arabs who took over Palestine from the Byzantines and not from the Jews base their *legal right of possessing Palestine* on a treaty concluded in 636 A.D. between the Calif Omar and the Byzantines. They maintained full sovereignty in Palestine with the Jews living as citizens under the rule of an Arab majority; a recognized and accepted fact until the present time.[218]

The Arab League memorandum also invoked the Arab legal narrative regarding the interplay between the Balfour Declaration, the McMahon-Hussein correspondence and the Hogarth Message:

> [The Balfour Declaration] has *no legal validity* since Great Britain at the time was not in possession of Palestine and consequently had no right to dispose of the future status of the country. Furthermore, this Declaration is *devoid of all the essential legal functions* indispensable to the validity of such international documents. It was addressed to an individual who represented

> neither a state nor a government ... It was merely a unilateral, personal message, implying no reciprocal obligations between Great Britain and the Jews. In addition, the term "National Home" is a vague expression that *bears no definite meaning in international law* ... It is paramount to note also, that the Balfour Declaration contradicts all pacts, pledges, and declarations that Great Britain and her Allies made to the Arabs during the First World War, preceding, and following the Balfour Declaration.[219]

The Government of Transjordan, on behalf of King Abdullah (Figure 8.20), submitted a lengthy memorandum that also employed the Arab legal narrative. The memorandum disputed the Jews' historical connection to Palestine and contested the legality of the Balfour Declaration as against the McMahon pledge.[220]

The Mandatory Government in Palestine prepared a two-volume, nearly 1100-page "Survey of Palestine" for the Committee.[221] The Committee also received a top secret memorandum from the High Commissioner, Sir Alan Cunningham, arguing "partition in some form or other would be the only solution."[222]

With this mountain of evidence in its possession, the Committee retired to the luxurious Beau Rivage Hotel in Lausanne, Switzerland to deliberate its verdict.

**FIGURE 8.20** King Abdullah I (library of Congress)

## Notes

1 FO 371/52504, Telegram No. 1818 from High Commissioner, Jerusalem to Secretary of State for the Colonies (22 December 1945).
2 FO 371/52503, Cypher Telegram No. 125 from British Embassy, Washington to Foreign Office (6 January 1946); *see also* FO 371/52507, Telegram No. 201 (Secret) from Secretary of State for the Colonies to High Commissioner of Palestine (2 February 1946); FO 371/52504, Cypher Telegram No. 247 from British Embassy, Washington to Colonial Office in response to Palestine High Commissioner's Telegram No. 1818, para. 1 (10 January 1946).
3 FO 371/52505, Letter to C.W. Baxter, Foreign Office from H.G. Vincent (British secretary to the Anglo-American Committee of Inquiry), attachment A (9 January 1946).
4 FO 371/52504, Cypher Telegram No. 279 from British Embassy, Washington to Foreign Office (11 January 1946).
5 Hutcheson Papers, University of Texas, Tarlton Law Library, Rare Books and Special Collections (hereafter "Hutcheson Papers") Box L11, Folder 1, Transcript of Hearing before the Anglo-American Committee of Inquiry, Washington, DC, opening remarks of Judge Hutcheson at 4–5 (7 January 1946).
6 A. Nachmani, *Great Power Discord in Palestine: The Anglo-American Committee of Inquiry into the Problems of European Jewry and Palestine, 1945-1946* at 102 (Routledge 1987).
7 *Id.* at 102–103.
8 N. Goda et al., *To the Gates of Jerusalem: The Diaries and Papers of James G. McDonald, 1945-1947* at 47, McDonald diary entry, 18–23 February 1946 (Indiana University Press, 2015).
9 Hutcheson Papers, Box L11, Folder 1, Transcript of Hearing before the Anglo-American Committee of Inquiry, Washington, D.C. at 6–24 (testimony of Earl G. Harrison).
10 *Id.* at 5.
11 *Id.* at 16.
12 *Id.* at 29 (testimony of Joseph J. Schwartz).
13 *Id.* at 31–32.
14 *Id.* at 33.
15 *Id.* at 58.
16 *Id.* at 39.
17 *Id.* at 78.
18 *Id.* at 84–85 (testimony of Robert Nathan).
19 *Id.* at 86.
20 *Id.* at 94.
21 N. Goda, *op. cit.*, at 31, McDonald diary entry, 7 January 1946.
22 Hutcheson Papers, Box L11, Folder 1, Transcript of Hearing before the Anglo-American Committee of Inquiry, Washington, DC, testimony of Robert Nathan at 112.
23 *Id.* at 118–119.
24 *Id.* at 146.
25 Id. at 112 (testimony of Oscar Gass).
26 *Id.* at 136.
27 Hutcheson Papers, Box L11 Folder 2, Transcript of Hearing before the Anglo-American Committee of Inquiry, Washington, D.C., testimony of Emanuel Neumann at 52–53 (8 January 1946).
28 *Id.* at 54–55.
29 *Id.* at 57–58.
30 *Id.* at 73.
31 Hutcheson Papers, Box L11, Folder 3, Transcript of Hearing before the Anglo-American Committee of Inquiry, Washington, DC, testimony of Dr. Henry Gold at 33 (9 January 1946).
32 *Id.* at 41.
33 *Id.* at 45–46.
34 *Id.* at 67 (testimony of Dr. Irving Miller).

35 *Id.* at 74–76 (testimony of Judge Joseph Proskauer).
36 *Id.* at 89–92.
37 *Id.* at 94.
38 *Id.* at 100.
39 *Id.* at 116.
40 *Id.* at 118.
41 *Id.* at 126–128.
42 R. Crossman, *Palestine Mission, op. cit.* at 44–45.
43 *Id.* at 47.
44 Hutcheson Papers, Box L11, Folder 5, Transcript of Hearing before the Anglo-American Committee of Inquiry, Washington, DC, testimony of Dr. Phillip K. Hitti at 3–9 (11 January 1946).
45 *Id.* at 10. Dr. Hitti was not the only witness who wrongly predicted that the Jews could not defend Palestine. A British military expert later told the Committee "if British troops were withdrawn, the Jews would be strong enough to occupy the country *and might hold it for three years before being driven into the sea.*" FO 371/52526, H. Beeley minute (27 May 1946) (emphasis added).
46 Hutcheson Papers, Box L11, Folder 5, Transcript of Hearing before the Anglo-American Committee of Inquiry, Washington, DC, testimony of Dr. Phillip K. Hitti at 12–13 (11 January 1946) (quoting J. Garstang, *The Heritage of Solomon* [Williams and Norgate, 1938] at 115).
47 *Id.* at 31–32.
48 *Id.* at 44 (testimony of Dr. John Hazam).
49 *Id.* at 45–47, 52 (emphasis added).
50 *Id.* at 49.
51 *Id.* at 60, 72. Less than one year later, Hazam published a review of the books Crossman and Crum had each written regarding their experiences as members of the Committee. J. Hazam, *Palestine*, Middle East Journal 1:340 (January 1947). Hazam reiterated his position at the end of his review that "the Balfour Declaration and the Mandate … are regarded by the Arabs as null and void since they were made without their knowledge or consent."
52 *Id.* at 78–79 (testimony of Dr. Khali Totoh).
53 Id. at 93–94.
54 "Einstein Condemns Rule in Palestine," *New York Times*, 12 January 1946 at 7; *see also* B. Crum, *op. cit.*, at 24–28 (Einstein criticized British rule in Palestine, saying the Committee was merely a "smokescreen" to enable Britain and the United States to delay addressing the plight of European Jewry).
55 B. Crum, *op. cit.*, at 24–25.
56 N. Goda, *op. cit.*, at 37–38, McDonald diary entry, 11 January 1946.
57 Hutcheson Papers, Box L11, Folder 7, Transcript of Hearing before the Anglo-American Committee of Inquiry, Washington, DC, at 162 (14 January 1946).
58 Crossman Papers, GB 165-0068, Middle East Centre Archive, St. Antony's College, Oxford, Box 5, File 2, Diary Entry (undated).
59 FO 371/52508, Letter from Justice Singleton to Foreign Secretary Bevin (1 February 1946). Bevin responded several days later that the Government would indemnify the British members of the Committee up to £10,000 each against death or permanent disability. FO 371/52508, Letter from Foreign Secretary Bevin to Justice Singleton (6 February 1946).
60 FO 371/52508, Telegram No. 145 from Foreign Office to British Embassy, Bern requesting provisional booking be made at Beau Rivage hotel (7 February 1946). The Committee's request for a month's fully-paid stay at the five-star Beau Rivage may have been in reprisal for their unhappiness at their accommodations on the *Queen Elizabeth* during the crossing from New York to London following the hearings in Washington. Manningham-Buller wrote a bitter letter about the journey to Foreign Secretary Bevin,

complaining the Committee members were booked on the "Main Deck, in double bunks, three of us in each cabin," rather than receiving better rooms on the Promenade or Sun Decks. Manningham-Buller also complained that the British Committee members only received an expense allowance of USD $8 per day while they were in Washington, sarcastically describing the allowance as "a princely sum less than that received by an American stenographer attached to us." FO 371/52507, Letter to Foreign Secretary Bevin from Manningham-Buller (22 January 1946). Manningham-Buller's letter was forwarded to the British Embassy in Washington, DC, which had been responsible for arranging the sea voyage for the Committee. An official at the embassy expressed little sympathy for Manningham-Buller, responding to the Foreign Office that each member of the Committee signed a form before embarkation acknowledging the *Queen Elizabeth* was still serving as troop carrier. "The committee members were, we understand, accommodated on the Main Deck in large but sparsely furnished cabins, and we feel sure that everything possible was done to meet their needs." FO 371/52507, Letter from British Embassy, Washington, DC to Foreign Office (22 January 1946); *see also* Crossman Papers, GB 165-0068, Middle East Centre Archive, St. Antony's College, Oxford, Box 5, File 2, Diary Entry (January 1946) ("the whole Commission had been distributed in 12-bunk cabins on the main deck. I found myself sharing 12 bunks with two judges").

61 Crossman Papers, GB 165-0068, Middle East Centre Archive, St. Antony's College, Oxford, Box 5, File 2, Diary Entry (undated). Hutcheson may have had other reasons for referring to Roosevelt in that manner, including that Roosevelt had passed him over for an appointment to the United States Supreme Court. Buxton reminded Hutcheson about this many years later: "I may have told you that, when there was a vacancy in the Court and President Roosevelt asked [Justice Frankfurter] to suggest a nominee, Felix named one Joseph J. Hutcheson, Jr. Roosevelt shook his head negatively. A few minutes later, Felix repeated his suggestion and the President shook his vetoing head again. Felix surmised that someone had prejudiced the President strongly against you but never knew who it was." Hutcheson Papers, Box L8, Folder 12, Letter from Buxton to Hutcheson (12 July 1968); *see also* C. Zelden, *The Judge Intuitive: The Life and Judicial Philosophy of Joseph C. Hutcheson*, 39 South Texas Law Review 904, 909–910 (1998) ("One of the highlights of the Judge's years on the circuit bench came in 1937, when he was considered for a seat on the Supreme Court. Long viewed as one of the most preeminent and respected Southern legal scholars and judges of his day, Hutcheson was felt a logical candidate for the seat that opened up on the Supreme Court in 1937 following the retirement of Justice Willis Van Devanter. Hutcheson, however, did not get the nod. Though a life-long Democrat, Hutcheson was not a supporter of the New Deal. In fact, he was strongly opposed to 'that bastard Roosevelt,' a feeling only strengthened following the appointment of Hugo Black of Alabama to the High Court in 1937. The White House did pull Hutcheson's personnel file, but Roosevelt distrusted Hutcheson's anti-New Deal tendencies. The story goes that the President, after looking at Hutcheson's file noted, 'I know [he] is thoroughly qualified. I know his reputation and standing as a judge and legal scholar; but we can't afford to appoint him. Notwithstanding his progressive and liberal tendencies, we can't count on him. He may decide our way, and then again he may not'").

62 B. Crum, *op. cit.*, at 36–43.

63 Hutcheson Papers, Box L12, Folder 1, Transcript of Hearing before the Anglo-American Committee of Inquiry, London, testimony of Selig Brodetsky at 14 (25 January 1946).

64 *Id.* at 66–67 (testimony of L.G. Montefiore).

65 Crossman Papers, GB 165-0068, Middle East Centre Archive, St. Antony's College, Oxford, Box 5, File 2, Diary Entry (undated).

66 Hutcheson Papers, Box L12, Folder 2, Transcript of Hearing before the Anglo-American Committee of Inquiry, London, testimony of Nathan Jackson at 6, 10, 21 (28 January 1946).

67 *Id.* at 24–25.

68 B. Crum, *op. cit.*, at 58
69 Hutcheson Papers, Box L12, Folder 2, Transcript of Hearing before the Anglo-American Committee of Inquiry, London, testimony of Rabbi Isser Unterman at 52 (28 January 1946).
70 *Id.*, testimony of Sir Simon Marks at 92 (28 January 1946).
71 Crossman Papers, GB 165-0068, Middle East Centre Archive, St. Antony's College, Oxford, Box 5, File 2, Diary Entry (undated).
72 Hutcheson Papers, Box L12, Folder 2, Transcript of Hearing before the Anglo-American Committee of Inquiry, London, testimony of T.R. Reid at 26 (29 January 1946).
73 *Id.* at 16.
74 *Id.* at 26.
75 *Id.* at 23–26.
76 Hutcheson Papers, Box L12, Folder 3, Transcript of Hearing before the Anglo-American Committee of Inquiry, London, testimony of General Sir Edward Spears at 33 (29 January 1946). General Spears added "no responsible authority, no British government has ever promised that Palestine would be a Jewish state." *Id.* at 34.
77 *Id.* at 34.
78 *Id.* at 39–40.
79 *Id.* at 41–42.
80 *Id.* at 64 (testimony of Maude Royden).
81 *Id.* at 65–66. Hutcheson's comment, seemingly casting blame on the Jews themselves for anti-Semitism, reflected the Judge's racist tendencies. The Judge's private correspondence contains far more blatant evidence of his racism. *See, e.g.*, Hutcheson Papers, Box L8, Folder 12, Letter from Judge Hutcheson to Frank Buxton at 2 (12 August 1965) (containing crude racist joke).
82 Hutcheson Papers, Box L12, Folder 3, Transcript of Hearing before the Anglo-American Committee of Inquiry, London, testimony of Maude Royden at 68 (29 January 1946) (emphasis added). For further discussion of the January 1919 Weizmann-Feisal agreement, *see* S. Zipperstein, *op. cit.*, at 30–31.
83 Crossman Papers, GB 165-0068, Middle East Centre Archive, St. Antony's College, Oxford, Box 5, File 2, Diary Entry (undated).
84 *Id.* at 77 (testimony of Viscount Herbert Samuel).
85 Hutcheson Papers, Box L12, Folder 4, Transcript of Hearing before the Anglo-American Committee of Inquiry, London, testimony of Leo Amery at 97 (30 January 1946).
86 Hutcheson Papers, Box L12, Folder 5, Transcript of Hearing before the Anglo-American Committee of Inquiry, London, testimony of representatives of Arab States at 22-23 (1 February 1946).
87 N. Goda, *op. cit.*, at 68, McDonald diary entry, 31 January 1946.
88 Crossman Papers, GB 165-0068, Middle East Centre Archive, St. Antony's College, Oxford, Box 5, File 2, Diary Entry (undated).
89 *Id.*
90 R. Crossman, *op. cit.*, at 65–66.
91 W. Phillips, *op. cit.*, at 426; *see also* E. Wilson, *Decision on Palestine: How the U.S. Came to Recognize the State of Israel* at 73 (Hoover Institution Press, 1979) ("The highlight of our stay in London was a luncheon given by Foreign Secretary Bevin, which we all attended. Bevin gave a short speech, in the course of which he assured the members of the committee that if they came back with a unanimous report, he would do all in his power to carry it out, a remark that made a profound impression on the members and was very much on their minds when they were writing their report").
92 N. Goda, *op. cit.*, at 87, McDonald diary entry, 10 February 1946.
93 W. Phillips, *op. cit.*, at 428.
94 N. Goda, *op. cit.*, at 104–105 (McDonald diary entry, 20 February 1946). Phillips also attended a session of the Nuremberg trials. W. Phillips, *op. cit.*, at 426–427.
95 Crossman Papers, GB 165-0068, Middle East Centre Archive, St. Antony's College, Oxford, Box 5, File 2, Letter from Crossman to his wife Zita (28 February 1946).

96 B. Crum, *op. cit.*, at 129.
97 Crossman Papers, GB 165-0068, Middle East Centre Archive, St. Antony's College, Oxford, Box 5, File 2, Letter from Crossman to his wife Zita (24 March 1946). McDonald described the full Committee meeting on Saturday 23 February as "rather unpleasant and distressing," and the meeting the next day as "long and acrimonious." N. Goda, *op. cit.*, at 109 (McDonald diary entries, 23–24 February 1946).
98 R. Crossman, *Palestine Mission*, *op. cit.*, at 105.
99 FO 371/52508, Telegram No. 175 (Cypher) from Foreign Office to British Embassy, Cairo (2 February 1946); FO 317/52508, Telegram Nos. 173, 103, 50 and 99 from Foreign Office to British Embassies in Cairo, Baghdad, Jedda, and Beirut (2 February 1946), Telegram Nos. 26, 21, and 20 from British Embassy, Cairo to British Embassies in Baghdad, Jedda, and Beirut (25 February 1946).
100 Hutcheson Papers, Box L6, Folder 12, Transcript of Hearing before the Anglo-American Committee of Inquiry, Cairo, testimony of Azzam Pasha at 19–20 (1 March 1946).
101 *Id.* at 3–5.
102 Crossman Papers, GB 165-0068, Middle East Centre Archive, St. Antony's College, Oxford, Box 5, File 2, Letter from Crossman to his wife Zita (undated).
103 S. Zipperstein, *op. cit.*, ch. 4.
104 Hutcheson Papers, Box L6, Folder 12, Transcript of Hearing before the Anglo-American Committee of Inquiry, Cairo, testimony of Mohamed Zaki Ali Pacha at 31–32 (5 March 1946).
105 *Id.* at 33–34.
106 *Id.* at 29 (testimony of Ahmed Morad el Bekri).
107 *Id.* at 38 (testimony of Maitre Habib Bourkeiba).
108 Crossman Papers, GB 165-0068, Middle East Centre Archive, St. Antony's College, Oxford, Box 5, File 2, Diary Entry undated).
109 *Id.* The King David Hotel would be the site of a Jewish terrorist bombing attack just over four months later.
110 Weizmann Archives, 20-2626, L. Stein memorandum (31 January 1946).
111 *Id.* para. 14 (emphasis in original).
112 Anglo-American Committee of Inquiry, Transcript of Hearings in Jerusalem (Chaim Weizmann testimony) at 19–20 (8 March 1946) (emphasis added).
113 *Id.* at 17, 24.
114 B. Crum, *op. cit.*, at 168–169.
115 Anglo-American Committee of Inquiry, Transcript of Hearings in Jerusalem (Chaim Weizmann testimony) at 37–38 (8 March 1946). The article Crum quoted was F. Frankfurter, *The Palestine Situation Restated*, Foreign Affairs 9:3 at 434 (April 1931) (emphasis added). Frankfurter at the time was a Professor at Harvard Law School.
116 Anglo-American Committee of Inquiry, Transcript of Hearings in Jerusalem (Chaim Weizmann testimony) at 43–44 (8 March 1946). Weizmann later wrote to the Committee to correct his testimony on this point.
117 Crossman Papers, GB 165-0068, Middle East Centre Archive, St. Antony's College, Oxford, Box 5, File 2, Diary Entry (26 March 1946).
118 *Id.*, letter from Crossman to his wife Zita (undated, sometime between 11 and 15 March 1946).
119 *Id.*, File 1, "Note of a Conversation with Dr. Weizman [sic], During Evening of March 9th, 1946." Although Crossman's typewritten note records the date of the conversation as 9 March 1946, in his published diary he recorded the date as 10 March. Crossman also wrote in his published diary that he submitted his memorandum to Justice Singleton and Judge Hutcheson, with the suggestion that Weizmann be invited to testify *in camera* regarding his partition proposal. R. Crossman, *op. cit.*, at 134, 137. McDonald recorded in his diary that he "had a most interesting talk with Crossman, Crum, and Sir Simon Marks [who had traveled to Palestine from London]. Crossman developed a program [partition], which for the first time gave me a glimpse of a possible solution.

The details of it are, however, too confidential to confide to this diary." N. Goda, *op. cit.*, at 154 (McDonald diary entry, 13 March 1946). McDonald also spoke to Judge Hutcheson about Crossman's proposal, "who seemed at least willing to consider it." *Id.*

120 R. Crossman, *op. cit.*, at 137.

121 Anglo-American Committee of Inquiry, Transcript of Hearings in Jerusalem (David Ben-Gurion testimony) at 2 (11 March 1946).

122 *Id.* at 13.

123 *Id.* at 20–21.

124 *Id.* at 31.

125 R. Crossman, *op. cit.*, at 138.

126 Anglo-American Committee of Inquiry, Transcript of Hearings in Jerusalem (Ben-Gurion testimony) at 9–10 (26 March 1946). McDonald noted how Singleton had "quickly adopted and maintained throughout the role of prosecutor … [i]t was an unseemly demonstration." N. Goda, *op. cit.*, at 186 (McDonald diary entry, 26 March 1946). Justice Singleton's clumsy cross-examination of Ben-Gurion ran afoul of the advice Singleton himself had given years earlier in a speech to a group of barristers: "It is well to make sure of your ground before making an attack upon a witness, for an attack which fails has a repercussive effect … Do not go on cross-examining a witness … when you may get an answer you do not like." J. Singleton, *Conduct at the Bar and Some Problems of Advocacy* at 31–32 (Sweet & Maxwell, 1933).

127 Anglo-American Committee of Inquiry, Transcript of Hearings in Jerusalem (Ben-Gurion testimony) at 17 (26 March 1946).

128 Crossman Papers, GB 165-0068, Middle East Centre Archive, St. Antony's College, Oxford, File 2, Diary Entry (26 March 1946).

129 FO 371/52509, Telegram to Foreign Secretary, London from Arab Higher Committee, Jerusalem (14 February 1946).

130 W. Khalidi, *op. cit.,* at 72–73.

131 Anglo-American Committee of Inquiry, Transcript of Hearings in Jerusalem (Jamal Effendi Husseini testimony) at 1 (12 March 1946).

132 *Id.* at 2.

133 *Id.* at 3.

134 *Id.* at 3–4.

135 *Id.* at 5.

136 *Id.* at 6–7.

137 *Id.* at 14–15.

138 *Id.* at 16–17.

139 *Id.* at 12.

140 *Id.* at 22–27. The Mufti's wartime activity on behalf of the Nazis included making radio broadcasts from Berlin exhorting his fellow Arabs to "kill the Jews wherever you find them." B. Crum, *op. cit.*, at 39. This of course contradicted the common Arab refrain that the Arabs had nothing against the Jews and would be happy to live together with them in Palestine, so long as Palestine were recognized as an Arab State. Captured German documents also reveal the Mufti had urged Hitler in 1943 and 1944 to bomb Tel Aviv. Kings College, London, Foley Special Collections, Maughan Library, FCO4, Pamph. Box D754 E3, The Nation Associates, Memorandum Submitted to the United Nations entitled "The Record of Collaboration of King Farouk of Egypt with the Nazis and their Ally, the Mufti" (June 1948) (containing copies of Nazi military reports dated 29 October 1943 and 30 March 1944 discussing the Mufti's request for the Luftwaffe to bomb Tel Aviv, "*die Zidadelle des palestinensichen Judentums und der Emigration*"). The Palestinian movement to this day has never disavowed the Mufti's collusion with Hitler and his fervent desire that the Nazis murder not just the entire Jewish population of Europe, but the entire Jewish population of the planet. Although the Mufti himself explicitly linked *Palestinian Nationalism* to the success of Nazism, the Palestinians to this day continue invoking their long-running narrative falsely equating *Zionism* with Nazism.

141 Crossman Papers, GB 165-0068, Middle East Centre Archive, St. Antony's College, Oxford, File 2, Letter from Crossman to his wife Zita (12 March 1946).
142 *Id.*, Letter from Crossman to his wife Zita (undated).
143 R. Crossman, *Palestine Mission, op. cit.*, at 139.
144 Weizmann Archives, 8-2641A, G. Agronsky (Strictly Confidential), Lunch with James McDonald after Jamal's Evidence (12 March 1946). McDonald mentioned the lunch meeting with Agronsky in his diary entry for 12 March. N. Goda, *op. cit.* at 150. Agronsky sent his notes of the meeting to Weizmann, who wrote back to express his thanks for the "extremely interesting" information. Weizmann Letters and Papers, Series A, Letters, Vol. XXII, Letter No. 130, from Weizmann to Agronsky at 105 (15 March 1946).
145 N. Goda, *op. cit.* at 147, McDonald diary entry, 12 March 1946.
146 Weizmann Archives, 8-2641A, G. Agronsky (Strictly Confidential), Lunch with James McDonald after Jamal's Evidence (12 March 1946).
147 *Id.* at 35 (Auni Bey Abdul Hadi testimony).
148 *Id.* at 34–47.
149 R. Crossman, *Palestine Mission, op. cit.*, at 140.
150 Crossman Papers, GB 165-0068, Middle East Centre Archive, St. Antony's College, Oxford, File 2, Letter from Crossman to his wife Zita (12 March 1946).
151 *Id.*
152 *Id.*
153 *Id.* (emphasis in original).
154 Crossman Papers, GB 165-0068, Middle East Centre Archive, St. Antony's College, Oxford, Anglo-American Committee Papers, File 1, typewritten notes of meetings with Shertok, Horowitz and Ben Gurion (13 March 1946).
155 Anglo-American Committee of Inquiry, Transcript of Hearings in Jerusalem (Auni Bey Abdul Hadi testimony) at 36 (12 March 1946).
156 *Id.* at 42.
157 N. Goda, *op. cit.*, at 150 (McDonald diary entry, 12 March 1946).
158 Anglo-American Committee of Inquiry, Transcript of Hearings in Jerusalem (Isaac Breuer testimony) at 1–2 (13 March 1946).
159 N. Goda, *op. cit.*, at 153 (McDonald diary entry, 13 March 1946).
160 *Id.* at 45 (Dr. Mordechai Eliash testimony).
161 *Id.* at 49 (emphasis added). Two years later Dr. Eliash would become Israel's first Ambassador to the United Kingdom.
162 Anglo-American Committee of Inquiry, Transcript of Hearings in Jerusalem (Dr. Judah Magnes testimony) at 4 (14 March 1946).
163 *Id.* at 6.
164 *Id.* at 9.
165 *Id.* at 11–12.
166 *Id.* at 22.
167 *Id.* at 7.
168 *Id.* at 31.
169 *Id.* at 38.
170 N. Goda, *op. cit.*, at 157 (McDonald diary entry, 14 March 1946).
171 Crossman Papers, GB 165-0068, Middle East Centre Archive, St. Antony's College, Oxford, File 2, Letter from Crossman to his wife Zita (16 March 1946).
172 Rabbi Alan Podet Papers, Jacob Rader Marcus Center of the American Jewish Archives, Cincinnati, Ohio, MS 163, Box 3/6, Telegram No. 792 from State Department to Rood (21 March 1946).
173 Anglo-American Committee of Inquiry, Transcript of Hearings in Jerusalem (Henry Cattan testimony) at 13 (23 March 1946).
174 *Id.* at 13–14.
175 *Id.* at 25.

176 N. Goda, *op. cit.*, at 179 (McDonald diary entry, 23 March 1946).
177 *Id.* at 35.
178 Crossman Papers, GB 165-0068, Middle East Centre Archive, St. Antony's College, Oxford, Box 5, File 2, Letter from Crossman to his wife Zita (23 March 1946).
179 *Id.* (emphases in original).
180 *Id.*
181 Crossman Papers, GB 165-0068, Middle East Centre Archive, St. Antony's College, Oxford, Box 5, File 2, Diary Entry (undated).
182 *Id.*
183 Anglo-American Committee of Inquiry, Transcript of Hearings in Jerusalem (Emile Ghory testimony) at 13–15 (25 March 1946).
184 *Id.* at 86 (Goldie Myerson testimony) ("every Jew[ish home and tent] would be filled to capacity in order to bring more Jews into the country").
185 W. Khalidi, *op. cit.*, at 72–73.
186 Anglo-American Committee of Inquiry, Transcript of Hearings in Jerusalem (Ahmed Shukeiri testimony) at 100 (25 March 1946).
187 *Id.* at 99 (emphasis added).
188 *Id.* at 102 (Albert Hourani testimony).
189 *Id.* at 103.
190 A Zionist official grudgingly praised Hourani's testimony as "ably and brilliantly presented. He analyzed the problem with merciless logic and consistency." D. Horowitz, *State in the Making* at 67 (Alfred A. Knopf, 1953).
191 *Id.* at 105–106.
192 *Id.* at 126.
193 *Id.* at 124–125.
194 L.A. Allen, *Determining Emotions and the Burden of Proof in Investigative Commissions in Palestine*, Comparative Studies in Society and History 59:2 at 406–407 (2017). Allen cites the memoirs of Evan Wilson, one of the American secretaries to the Committee, to support her argument that Hourani's failure to express sympathy hurt the Palestinian case. But neither Wilson's memoirs nor the memoirs of any of the Committee members provide any support for claiming Hourani's testimony caused the Committee to adopt its eventual recommendation in favor of admitting 100,000 Jewish holocaust survivors into Palestine.
195 Hutcheson Papers, Box L6, Folder 14, Transcript of *In Camera* Hearing before the Anglo-American Committee of Inquiry, Jerusalem, testimony of Edwin Samuel at 1 (25 March 1946).
196 Crossman Papers, GB 165-0068, Middle East Centre Archive, St. Antony's College, Oxford, Box 5, File 2, Diary Entry (26 March 1946).
197 N. Goda, *op. cit.*, at 175 (McDonald diary entry, 21 March 1946).
198 FO 371/52508, Telegram No. 40 (Cypher) from British Embassy, Jedda to Foreign Office, para. 3 (2 February 1946).
199 FO 371/52513, Despatch No. 100 (Secret) from British Embassy, Baghdad to Foreign Secretary Bevin (19 March 1946).
200 *Id.*, notes of meeting with King Abdul Aziz (attached to Baxter letter) at 9.
201 FO 371/52514, Letter from H. Beeley to C.W. Baxter, Foreign Office (25 March 1946).
202 *Id.*, notes of meeting with King Abdul Aziz attached to Baxter letter at 6.
203 A. Nachmani, *op. cit.*, at 162.
204 R. Crossman, *op. cit.*, at 32.
205 Jabotinsky Institute Archives, HT 12-6/7, Memorandum Submitted by Honorable Guy M. Gillette, President, American League for a Free Palestine, to Anglo-American Committee of Inquiry, Washington, DC (3 January 1946).
206 *Id.* para. 1.
207 *Id.*, paras. 2–6.

208 Hutcheson Papers, University of Texas, Tarlton Law Library Rare Books and Special Collections, Box L6, Folder 4, "Judaism and the National Home: A Historical and Juristic Examination of the Position of the Jewish Religion in the National Home" (undated).
209 *Id.*, Box L24, Folder 4, "The American Zionist Case: Statement Submitted to the Anglo-American Committee of Inquiry, Washington, D.C. by the American Zionist Emergency Council" (January 1946).
210 *Id.*, Box L8, Folder 6, S. Rifkind, "The Basic Equities of the Palestine Problem" (January 1946).
211 *Id.*, Box L7, Folder 1, Document No. 2, "The Influence of Jewish Colonization on Arab Development in Palestine" (March 1946).
212 *Id.*, Box L7, Folder 2, "The Historical Connection of the Jewish People with Palestine" (March 1946).
213 *Id.*, Box L7, Folder 4, Document No. 4, "Statement of the American Jewish Committee to the Anglo-American Committee of Inquiry" (January 1946).
214 *Id.*, Box L7, Folder 5, Document No. 6, "The Jewish Resistance Movement" (25 March 1946).
215 *Id.*, Box L7, Folder 5, Document No. 9, H.M. Kalvaryski, "Aide Memoir" (undated).
216 *Id.*, Box L6, Folder 5, M. Buber, "The Meaning of Zionism" (March 1946).
217 *Id.*, Box L6, Folder 2, Document No. 4, "The Arab Case Submitted to the Anglo American Commission by Jamaal Husseini on Behalf of the Arabs of Palestine" (12 March 1946) (emphasis added); *see also* J. Nevo, *The Arabs of Palestine, 1947–1948: Military and Political Activity*, Middle Eastern Studies 23:1 at 7 (1987) ("The AHC's memorandum, submitted to the Committee, reiterated the claims that the Arabs were the lawful masters of the country, that the question of Palestine was exclusively an Arab question, and that the Balfour Declaration was considered null and void").
218 Hutcheson Papers, University of Texas, Tarlton Law Library Rare Books and Special Collections, Box L6, Folder 2, Document No. 1, "Memorandum by the Secretariat-General of the Arab League to the Anglo-American Committee of Inquiry on Palestine" at 2 (1 March 1946) (emphasis added).
219 *Id.* (emphasis added).
220 *Id.*, Box L7, Folder 9, Document No. 4, "Memorandum by the Trans-Jordan Government on the Palestine Problem" (19 March 1946) (copy on file at FO 816/83).
221 Government of Palestine, "A Survey of Palestine, Prepared in December 1945 and January 1946 for the Information of the Anglo-American Committee of Inquiry" (December 1945–January 1946), https://www.bjpa.org/content/upload/bjpa/a_su/A%20SURVEY%20OF%20PALESTINE%20DEC%201945-JAN%201946%20VOL%20I.pdf (last accessed 5 January 2021).
222 Crossman Papers, GB 165-0068, Middle East Centre Archive, St. Antony's College, Oxford, Box 5 File 2, Memorandum (Top Secret, "No Distribution Whatsoever") by His Excellency for Anglo-American Committee (22 March 1946).

# 9

# DELIBERATIONS AND VERDICT

## Prelude to deliberations

After completing the evidence-gathering phase of its mission, the Committee arrived in Lausanne, Switzerland on 29 March 1946, where they remained for three weeks at the Beau Rivage Hotel to deliberate and reach a verdict in the form of a written report and recommendations.

### *Lord Morrison's premature prediction*

As the Committee was preparing to leave Palestine on 28 March, Lord Morrison (who was in London) briefed Bevin on the Committee's tentative conclusions. Morrison reported – incorrectly as it turned out – that the Committee had agreed on three principles: (i) there should not be a Jewish state; (ii) the *Haganah* should be dissolved; and (iii) the Jewish Agency should be abolished or reconstituted.[1] Only the first of these recommendations would end up as part of the Committee's final verdict.

Lord Morrison had underappreciated the impact of the Committee's first-hand observations of the terrible suffering of the European Jews. Lord Morrison also discounted the impact of the Palestine visit on the Committee. Hutcheson, Buxton, Crossman, Phillips and Aydelotte all left Palestine with a far different view of the case than they had formed after the initial hearings in Washington, DC and London.

Thus, by the time they had left Palestine, the Committee members "embarked on a line of thought clearly opposed to the concepts of [the British Government] and its Foreign Secretary, Ernest Bevin."[2]

DOI: 10.4324/9781003225263-13

### *Judge Hutcheson's "Tentative Ruling"*

Judge Hutcheson prepared a lengthy memorandum after arriving in Lausanne entitled "Purely Tentative Thoughts on Our Terms of Reference." [3] Hutcheson wrote the memorandum in the style of what American judges usually refer to as a "tentative ruling," or a precursor to a formal judicial opinion, like those he was accustomed to writing as a sitting judge of the United States Court of Appeals for the Fifth Circuit. Judge Hutcheson's memorandum ended up bearing a striking similarity to the Committee's final verdict and report.

Judge Hutcheson began his memorandum in classic judicial fashion: "The matters for determination come up on a record presenting few disputed issues of fact."[4]

Hutcheson identified two key undisputed facts regarding the European Jewish refugees. First, almost all surviving German and Austrian Jews, and large sections of the remaining Jews elsewhere in Eastern Europe, wanted to leave the continent for Palestine. Second, other than the Dominican Republic, which had offered to receive some Jewish refugees after the War, "no opportunity seems to be offered for Jews to migrate out of Europe to other countries than Palestine."[5]

Judge Hutcheson then noted, "the political question of Palestine as a Jewish state or not must be met, faced and decided."[6]

Judge Hutcheson, clearly influenced both by Judah Magnes' testimony and Hutcheson's pre-existing opposition to Jewish statehood in Palestine, expressed hostility to Zionist political aspirations in Palestine. He accused the Zionists of exploiting the European Jewish crisis, claiming they "see in it an unparalleled opportunity to obtain their political majority" in Palestine "and capture[] control of the state."[7]

Judge Hutcheson launched into a blistering attack on the Zionist demand to create a Jewish state in Palestine:

> The bare statement of this proposition is so contrary to the fundamental principles of self-determination and does so much violence to the normal American feelings that there is something vicious in stacked elections and controlled plebiscites, that it is quite plain that those who propose it are either deceiving or self-deceived, and those who accept it are either not just men or they are uninformed. It is, however, on just this proposition that the whole future of political Zionism hangs, and it is quite clear that so understood it must be rejected. No amount of construction of the Balfour Declaration or of the Mandate, no amount of sophistry as to Arabs having large territories, the Jews none, no amount of special pleading as to the miseries of the Jews in Europe can justify it, and it must once and for all be definitely abandoned. The Jewish state thus definitely will be put aside, it remains only to consider the question of a reasonable Zionism as to Palestine and its relation to the refugee problem in Europe.[8]

Judge Hutcheson rejected Zionist demands for statehood in Palestine by noting that, in his view, statehood was never central to Zionism. Indeed, "while there was a hope that development might some day bring about a Jewish majority and Jewish dominance in Palestine, it was never of the essence of the homeland that this should come about."

Thus, Judge Hutcheson argued, again echoing Judah Magnes' testimony, the fairest outcome would be to place Palestine under Trusteeship, with arrangements guaranteeing equal political rights to Jews and Arabs "without reference to their majorities," thereby enabling Jews and Arabs to "live together as Palestinian citizens peacefully and prosperously."[9]

Judge Hutcheson concluded his analysis by emphasising what he viewed as the core principle: that any policy outcome should be based on the best interests of Palestine and its inhabitants. Judge Hutcheson thus rejected both the Zionist and Arab arguments regarding Jewish immigration, preferring instead that future immigration be controlled by the government of Palestine, and the Jewish Agency be abolished.

Nevertheless, Judge Hutcheson expressed great sympathy with the plight of European Jewry. To ease the emergency facing the surviving European Jews, he argued, "Palestine should receive within the next year as many Jews from Europe who are desirous of going and need to go there as its present economy can sustain."[10]

## *Justice Singleton's memorandum*

Justice Singleton also wrote a long memorandum when he arrived in Lausanne cataloguing all the acts of Jewish terrorism occurring in Palestine since the end of World War II.

Justice Singleton referred to his cross-examination of Ben-Gurion regarding the Jewish Agency's relationship with and knowledge of the *Haganah's* activity, noting "we cannot think his answers were frank … private armies ought not to exist: they constitute a threat to the peace of the world."

Singleton also noted that if British forces were withdrawn from Palestine, "there would be immediate and prolonged bloodshed the end of which it is impossible to predict."[11]

## *Other tentative views*

By the time he arrived in Lausanne, Crum had made up his mind regarding the core issue, which he described as decidedly legal in nature: "*The basic law of the Mandate has been violated by the agent entrusted with carrying it out.*"[12]

McDonald recorded in his diary how Judge Hutcheson, after dinner their first night in Lausanne, invited McDonald for a private chat:

> He said he wanted to find out where I stood. In the course of our talk he told me of his own position, which I found almost amazingly encouraging, so much did it differ from the impression which one got from his questions at the hearings and his private conversations. As he talked I, for the first

> time, became hopeful that we could work out a report which would be worthwhile.[13]

Meanwhile, Crossman had already concluded before arriving in Lausanne that partition represented the only practical solution to the conflict in Palestine. Crossman later wrote, in his published diary:

> My solution, therefore, of the problem we had been instructed to solve was that we should as an interim policy recommend rescinding the White Paper and the admission of 100,000 immigrants, and that our long-term recommendation should be partition ... I accepted Dr Weizmann's analysis. The choice was between two injustices, and we had to decide which injustice was the lesser ... I was convinced that all this was a lesser injustice which must be accepted for the sake of the building of a Jewish Commonwealth ... So I was driven to the conclusion that, since the Jews of Palestine were capable of fending for themselves, the only sane policy for Britain was to carry through the partition plan, which I had discussed with Weizmann ...[14]

Crossman wrote a lengthy analysis of his arguments in favour of partition shortly after he arrived in Lausanne. Crossman favoured partitioning the country into a Jewish state comprising the coastal plane, the Negev and the upper Galilee. The Jewish state would contain a large number of Arabs, who would be granted full civil and religious rights. Crossman preferred to describe the area set aside for the Jews not as a "Jewish State," but as a binational state under Jewish control.

Crossman further envisioned the hill country comprising the modern-day West Bank would become an Arab state, to be merged into Transjordan, just as the Peel Commission had recommended nearly a decade earlier. Crossman felt the Arabs would accept this outcome based on their testimony denying Palestine existed as a stand-alone country:

> The scheme gives not only to the Jews, but to the Arabs of the central mountain area, the immediate independence they demand. *Since the Arabs of Palestine have no Palestinian patriotism but an Arab nationalism*, there is no political injustice in giving them independence as citizens of Transjordan ... it provides a solution based on rough justice. The purely Arab area receives Arab independence. The Jews are given an area big enough for the development of a national home, but concede in return constitutional parity to their fellow Arab citizens.[15]

Crossman also favoured granting the 100,000 immigration certificates "without conditions and see the job through ourselves."[16] Crossman wrote in his unpublished diary:

> [I]f England had the same sort of timidity as my five colleagues, then she would not support the national home and push it through against solid Arab opposition. That was the problem. In what way could we in the Report indicate the appalling unfairness of Britain's single responsibility, and the need for world support for Britain. Obviously I concluded that we could only do that if we recommended unconditional support for the national home, and won world opinion including American opinion in support of Great Britain.[17]

## Deliberations begin

The Committee's first round of deliberations began on Monday, 1 April 1946. Crossman recalled the scene in his unpublished diary:

> Texas Joe began with a carefully drafted statement in favour of the bi-national state, and then we went round the table, each of us giving his views. It became clear that Sir John and Buller were more or less in favour of a modified White Paper policy, that Crick and Leggett saw the necessity for increased Jewish immigration ... and that all the Americans had decided to line up in favour of some form of binational state, and large-scale immigration ... only Crum spoke in favour of partition, and Hutcheson was careful not to rule it out. I supported large-scale immigration, expressed my doubt whether bi-nationalism would work, but stated that I would not raise partition unless any and every unitary solution proved unworkable.[18]

McDonald thought Judge Hutcheson's statement "masterly ... [it] amazed me because it was so out of keeping with many of his private comments and his questions during the public hearings. In his analysis, he showed no influence of prejudice or dislikes."[19]

Crossman described how the two judges clashed over procedure:

> Hutcheson said that you had to reach your conclusions first and then choose the facts which supported them: this was judicial procedure. Sir John argued that it wasn't ... I [Crossman] am sick to death of being told how Texas judges prepare their judgments ...[20]

Crossman had developed an intense dislike of Singleton by that point, noting "if he never opened his mouth at a meeting, was removed from the chairmanship, and was confined solely to drafting, he would be a most useful member of the British delegation."[21]

Singleton followed Hutcheson and advocated essentially a continuation of the White Paper policy. After the remaining members of the Committee offered their preliminary views, they could not "hide from ourselves the depth of difference."[22]

After further discussion, the Committee was divided into two subcommittees for purposes of writing the report: one focusing on European Jewry and the other on Palestine.

By Wednesday, 3 April, the Committee reached its first point of important agreement, reflecting how deeply Magnes' testimony had influenced their thinking. The Committee agreed that "both a Jewish State in the whole of Palestine and an Arab State in the whole of Palestine were injustices which must be unequivocally ruled out."[23]

Crossman recalled that Manningham-Buller argued for disbanding the Jewish armies as a precondition for any further Jewish immigration. Crossman objected, noting the only reason the Jewish armies had been formed was because the White Paper had nearly banned immigration. Removing the White Paper's immigration policy would likewise remove the underlying reason for the existence of the armed Jewish groups.

Singleton reacted angrily at Crossman after the meeting, accusing him of supporting terrorism. Crossman responding that Singleton's proposal would lead to all-out war between Arabs and Jews. "We parted unamicably," Crossman wrote with a tinge of sarcasm in his unpublished diary.[24]

## Tensions during deliberations; unanimity in doubt

At one point during the deliberations, according to Crossman, the British had not reached a unified position amongst themselves, and the American and British sides stood so far apart that "it looked as though the Americans would issue one report, Sir John and four Englishmen another, and I should be left alone in the middle."[25] The stress and tension within and among the American and British sides became palpable in Lausanne and threatened to scuttle the effort to reach consensus.[26]

Crossman outlined where the Committee members stood in the midst of their deliberations. Judge Hutcheson and three other Americans (Aydelotte, Buxton and Phillips) advocated issuing the 100,000 immigration certificates immediately and unconditionally, but they insisted Palestine should be neither an Arab nor Jewish state, and the Mandate should remain in force.

Justice Singleton and two other British members agreed with Judge Hutcheson regarding no statehood (Arab or Jewish) for Palestine, but they disagreed regarding the immigration certificates, insisting any additional immigration to occur slowly, and only if the *Haganah* and all other armed Jewish organisations were first disarmed and disbanded.

A third group (Crossman, Crum and McDonald) favoured partition, with unlimited Jewish immigration permitted into the new Jewish state.[27]

Crossman credited himself with beginning to break the logjam, even as the two judges refused to budge:

> But then things began to improve. I talked to Phillips, Phillips talked to Aydelotte, Aydelotte talked to Morrison, and finally Aydelotte and Leggett played golf on Sunday. Result – a nucleus of a middle group which will try to mediate between the obstinate intransigence of the two judges.[28]

Crossman then blamed the tense relationship between Judge Hutcheson and Justice Singleton for the failure of the deliberations to make any meaningful progress:

> The real trouble here is that these two judges aren't chairmen at all, but representatives of American and British isolationism at their worst. At the meetings, instead of taking the chair, and, in a relatively neutral way trying to guide the discussion, they put forward at great length and very stubbornly their own point of view. Anything which Texas Joe suggests is automatically opposed by Sir John and Manningham-Buller, and anything Sir John suggests is automatically opposed by all six Americans. The result is that we don't get very much further, since the extremes are always pulling away from each other, and dragging the moderates with them.[29]

Crossman humorously described how the Americans themselves began to realise they needed to move Judge Hutcheson to a more reasonable position:

> However, there now seems some chance that the common sense of the committee which really does exist, will prevail over the obstinancy of the two old chairmen … [V]ery fortunately Aydelotte, who started violently pro-Arab, not only changed his view in Palestine, but defeated Texas Joe at golf in Cairo. This produced a serious break in relations which was confirmed yesterday, when he not only defeated him twice, but won 25 francs off him as well. Yesterday evening Aydelotte said to me: "I don't know about other people, but I'm not going to let that old judge write our report for us. He's just one of six Americans." This is a wholesome sign. Buxton still backs Texas Joe solid, mainly out of an intense dislike of Manningham-Buller … As for Crum, he has been a great disappointment. He reads nothing, drinks too much and changes his mind according to the last newspaper he receives from the States. McDonald remains the great enigma …[30]

Crossman was no more charitable in his description of his British colleagues:

> On our side, there is a tight little social and political triangle of Sir John, M.B. [Manningham-Buller] and Vincent [one of the two British secretaries to the Committee] who work, eat and drink and for all I know sleep in the same bed. Morrison was away in London for a few days and Sir John thought he had nobbled him when he got back, but Morrison, despite

> all appearances, has a mind of his own, and we prised him out last night. Leggett and Crick wallow rather sweetly in an unstable middle position, veering to Sir John.[31]

Crossman later described the "most ticklish" issue involved Justice Singleton's insistence that the issuance of the immigration certificates be conditioned on disarming and disbanding the *Haganah*. Crossman felt this position, if adopted by the Committee, would provoke a Jewish backlash in both the United States (thereby weakening Britain's influence in Washington) and Palestine (thereby weakening Weizmann's influence with the Jewish Agency).[32]

## Judge Hutcheson takes command

Despite Crossman's statements in his diary giving himself sole credit for breaking the logjam and steering the Committee toward unanimity, Crum, McDonald and Phillips lauded Judge Hutcheson for playing the key role in keeping the Committee on track to deliver a unanimous verdict. Crum, for example, praised Judge Hutcheson lavishly:

> In the end, it was the leadership of Judge Hutcheson which kept us all together. He would not permit our initial differences to result in a breakup of the Committee into British and American groups. *It is not an overstatement to say that had it not been for him, the final report would not have been unanimous.* He labored from twelve to sixteen hours a day, drafting proposals and trying to reconcile points of view without yielding on basic principle.[33]

Arthur Lourie, the Political Secretary of the Jewish Agency, stationed himself in Geneva during the Committee's deliberations in Lausanne. Both McDonald and Crum (and possibly Buxton) were leaking secret details of the Committee's ongoing deliberations to Lourie.[34] Lourie sent two reports to the Zionist leadership about the deliberations, the first on 3 April 1946, after the Committee had been deliberating for several days, and the second on 21 April 1946.

Lourie's first memorandum, dated 3 April 1946, reported what Hutcheson had privately informed the other American committee members:

> [Hutcheson] now saw the matter in perspective … he favored the immigration of 100,000 this year and then free Jewish immigration under the [Jewish] Agency … As to the political solution, he believed binationalism was the best …

Lourie also reported Hutcheson had realised during his side trip to Syria, where he saw a local Jewish witness testifying under obvious duress, "that it was impossible to put Jews in an Arab State."[35]

Lourie noted his own view that "it has been clear for a long time that Hutcheson would be a key figure in the final decision – likely to take with him Phillips and Aydelotte." This news about Judge Hutcheson, Lourie reported, was "tremendously encouraging – not to say exciting."[36]

Lourie further reported the Committee had held its first full meeting on Monday, 1 April. The entire Committee except Lord Morrison were present. Hutcheson, according to Lourie's sources (McDonald and Crum), opened the discussion:

> Hutcheson then delivered his little bouquet. The White Paper *was a great injustice and could not stand.* He favored the immigration this year of 150,000 but was prepared to accept a figure of 100,000. Then there should be free immigration under the Agency. The land laws could not stand. The final solution should be bi-nationalism … he saw no reason why the Committee should not finish its work within 3 or 4 days.[37]

Crum's description of Judge Hutcheson's comments is remarkably similar to Lourie's secret memorandum:

> He [Judge Hutcheson] now saw our problem in perspective, he said. The White Paper *was a great injustice; it could not stand.* There should be substantial continuing immigration under the Jewish Agency. After what he had seen in Syria and the Lebanon – the precarious position of Jews under Arab rule – he realized that it was impossible to put Jews into an Arab state. Palestine could, therefore, be neither an Arab nor a Jewish state.[38]

According to Lourie, Singleton "had no inkling" of Hutcheson's position and "was, to put it mildly, shocked." Singleton's first reaction was to stall for more time. Manningham-Buller and Crossman took different positions on immigration, and on binationalism versus partition. The other Americans largely supported Hutcheson's position.

According to Lourie's sources, there was "a state of combined consternation in the British camp." Lourie's sources also described the broken relationship between the two judges:

> Relations between the two chairmen are very bad and they are not on speaking terms. Singleton feels he was tricked; after all his co-chairman had accepted their hospitality, visited their homes and country houses, playing the part of a friend, and now to turn around and do this caddish thing![39]

On 5 April, McDonald, at Justice Singleton's request, prepared draft language regarding the short-term immigration issue. McDonald discussed the draft with

Buxton, Crum and Hutcheson, and they settled on recommending 100,000 immigration certificates be issued during 1946.[40]

The Committee discussed the immigration issue the next day, 6 April 1946. Lord Morrison said increased Jewish immigration would require Britain to commit more troops and money to Palestine, and he challenged the Americans to do more than just offer advice. Crum sarcastically said Britain should legalise the *Haganah* if it needed more troops, drawing a sharp rebuke from Justice Singleton.[41] The tensions between the two sides ran so high that Judge Hutcheson cancelled a picnic planned for the next day, Sunday 7 April.[42]

On 8 April, Crossman floated his partition proposal, but only Crum supported it.[43]

On 9 April, Hutcheson received a telegram from President Truman. The President said he had been keeping track of the Committee's deliberations. He encouraged Judge Hutcheson to "[k]eep up the good work. Looking forward eagerly to receipt of report. Hope it will represent unanimous opinion of Commission [sic] members."[44]

On 12 April, Hutcheson presented a draft set of recommendations to the Committee. Discussion focused on the White Paper's restrictions on land sales to Jews, later codified in the 1940 Land Transfers Ordinance. Crossman supported the Americans in recommending repeal of the ordinance, with the proviso that the Jewish Agency should also repeal its ban on Arab workers on Jewish-owned lands.[45]

Saturday, 13 April 1946, turned out to be the key day in the deliberations. According to Arthur Lourie's sources:

> Hutcheson decided the time had come for a show-down. After seeing all his own group and establishing a united front – which involved above all straightening out the two "weak sisters" [Aydelotte and Phillips] he arranged to see the Britishers separately and told them "either – or." The Americans hadn't invited themselves into this but now they were in, they would make their report in accordance with the situation as they saw it – 100,000, mandatory obligations to be maintained, etc. – if the British were ready to go along – fine; if not there was no good messing around. The Americans would make their report without further delay and go home![46]

The British side met that same evening (13 April), arguing with each other until very late at night. Lourie reported it had been tough going for Justice Singleton with the other British members:

> But Singer [Singleton] had lost all influence over his own people following what must have been a terrific session of the British group on Saturday … which lasted until nearly 2 A.M. – an hour appropriate to Zionist tradition but totally unsuitable for respectable Englishmen to be seen fussing around.[47]

On 16 April, Truman cabled Hutcheson again:

> The world expectantly awaits a report from the entire Commission [sic] which will be the basis of an affirmative program to relieve untold suffering and misery … it is my deep and sincere wish that the American delegation shall stand firm for a program that is in accord with the highest American tradition of generosity and justice.[48]

Justice Singleton complicated matters by insisting the Americans agree to include language in the report committing US military assistance to Britain in the event the report were to provoke an outbreak of violence in Palestine against British troops. The Americans refused and ultimately reached a compromise with Singleton by including commentary to the fourth recommendation (that the Mandate or a successor Trusteeship remain in force) indicating Britain should receive help from other UN member states to keep the peace in Palestine.[49]

## Unanimous verdict

Ultimately, on 18 April 1946, the Committee reached agreement on a unanimous, compromise verdict: it recommended the 100,000 immigration certificates be "authorized" before the end of 1946 but left an ambiguous deadline for issuing or permitting the use of the certificates. In return, the British side dropped their demand for making the immigration recommendation conditional on Jewish disarmament.

The Americans agreed to include a lengthy description in the report of illegal Jewish armed activity in Palestine; a strong statement against the maintenance of illegal armies in Palestine; and an exhortation to the Jewish Agency to cooperate with the Mandatory Government against terrorism and illegal immigration.[50]

Phillips, writing several years later, credited Judge Hutcheson for driving the Committee to unanimity, even as the two judges remained at loggerheads:

> As I look back, Judge Hutcheson stands out as the one who contributed the most to the final report. He demonstrated a remarkable ability to draft a concise statement. Unfortunately he and Sir John never got on well together, and while both were excellent men in their way, the rest of us suffered somewhat from this undercurrent of friction between the two chiefs. Hutcheson was a bluff, shrewd, direct, stubborn and impatient man … But his strong personality and his fundamental honesty of purpose made us all, with the possible exception of Sir John, really fond of him.[51]

To celebrate their agreement and the completion of their work, Judge Hutcheson hosted a dinner at the Beau Rivage Hotel for the Committee and the secretaries on Thursday, 18 April 1946. Hutcheson worked with the Hotel chef to create a whimsical menu (Figure 9.1), featuring dishes such as "Balfour Soup," and

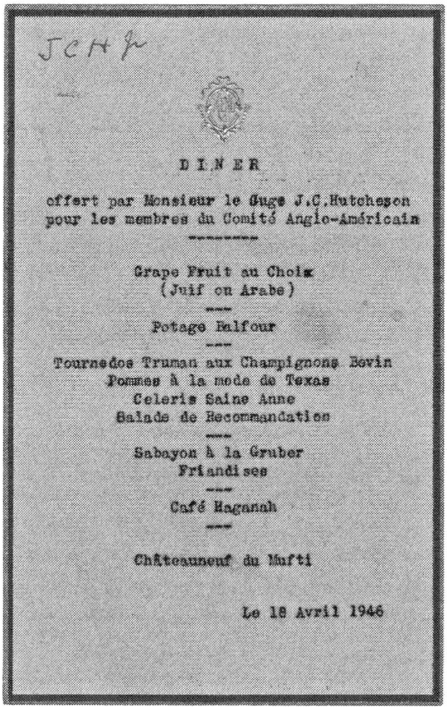

JCH Jr

DINER

offert par Monsieur le Juge J.C.Hutcheson
pour les membres du Comité Anglo-Américain

Grape Fruit au Choix
(Juif ou Arabe)

Potage Balfour

Tournedos Truman aux Champignons Bevin
Pommes à la mode de Texas
Celeris Saine Anne
Salade de Recommandation

Sabayon à la Gruber
Friandises

Café Haganah

Châteauneuf du Mufti

Le 18 Avril 1946

**FIGURE 9.1** Judge Hutcheson's copy of dinner menu (front side), Beau Rivage Hotel, Lausanne, 18 April 1946 (Hutcheson Papers, University of Texas, Tarlton Law Library Rare Books and Special Collections)

"Tournedoes Truman aux Champignons Bevin," along with beverages such as "Chateauneuf du Mufti" and "Café Haganah."

The Committee members and staff autographed the reverse side of Judge Hutcheson's menu (Figure 9.2).

## *Singleton's last-minute surprise*

The next day, 19 April 1946, Justice Singleton engaged in a "gross and amazing effort" to sneak language into the final report that no one else had seen, on items that had never been agreed. McDonald noted in his diary that evening how Singleton's last-minute insertion would have torpedoed the immigration portion of the Committee's verdict. The change would have required the Arab states be consulted *prior* to the issuance of the 100,000 immigration certificates and would have given the United Nations control over subsequent immigration. Singleton was caught red-handed, embarrassing the other British members. McDonald commended the other British members for not supporting the Judge's unethical tactics.[52]

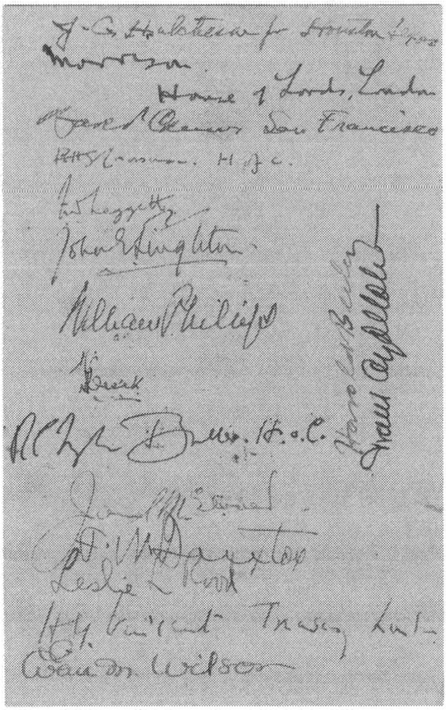

**FIGURE 9.2** Judge Hutcheson's copy of dinner menu (reverse side), Beau Rivage Hotel, Lausanne, 18 April 1946 (Hutcheson Papers, University of Texas, Tarlton Law Library Rare Books and Special Collections)

The incident was leaked to Lourie, who reported it to the Zionist leadership. He condemned Singleton as "virtually as a crook … no wonder Singer [Singleton] ended in a state of complete disgruntlement."[53]

## *Hutcheson's emotion*

The Committee members signed the report on Saturday, 20 April 1946. After everyone had signed, Hutcheson took his leave from the British Committee members to meet privately with the Americans, and "[t]here in saying goodbye to us he broke down, much to his disgust and to our embarrassment."[54]

Lourie, still monitoring the deliberations from Geneva, sent another report to the Zionist leadership on Sunday, 21 April, after the deliberations had concluded. Lourie had already been told how Hutcheson "quite broke down – tears and all – he was so overcome with emotion after the tension and strain of the past weeks."[55]

Lourie said his source (likely McDonald or Crum) reported how he was "in despair" when he left Palestine, believing the Committee would issue a majority report reaffirming the White Paper, slamming the Jewish Agency and calling for disarming the *Haganah*. The source told Lourie he was proud the final report came out so differently, saying it would make a "great contribution to the future of the National Home."[56]

Lourie credited Judge Hutcheson as "the key man in all this business." Lourie had far less regard for Justice Singleton:

> [Justice Singleton was] unregenerate, and having had a good deal too much to drink [at a cocktail party Singleton hosted for the Committee] on Friday night (incidentally the report was not signed till Saturday morning because he didn't want to sign on Good Friday), let himself go with great profanity about Dolly [Hutcheson] whom he regarded as having betrayed him and Harvey [McDonald] whom he regarded as Dolly's "evil genius."[57]

### *A "Compromise Document"*

On 22 April, Crossman wrote a memorandum to Hector McNeil, the Undersecretary of State for Foreign Affairs in the British Government. The memorandum described the Committee's deliberations and the bases for the reports' conclusions. Crossman began by explaining "The report was, of course, a compromise document. A week before it was finished it seemed certain that there would be two and probable that there would be three reports. It seemed almost impossible to achieve unanimity."[58]

Crossman wrote a separate, less formal note to McNeil the same day, offering the following summary and taking credit for steering the Committee to unanimous verdict:

> I think on the whole the results of this Committee are fairly satisfactory and I know that they are a great deal better than we had any right to hope a fortnight ago. At least we have achieved unanimity and I remember that almost the last thing you said to me was that my assignment was to get on with the Americans and to get them to agree to something. If that meant, as it did, sometimes not getting on quite so well with some of my British colleagues, that was, I fear, unavoidable. It has been a fascinating experience. I have learnt a lot and am really grateful to you and E.B. [Ernest Bevin] for giving me this chance.[59]

## The Committee's report and recommendations

The Committee issued its unanimous report to both Governments on 20 April 1946. The report was made public ten days later, on 30 April 1946.[60]

"No report," Phillips wrote later, "agreed to by six Americans and six Englishmen, each acting individually and independently, could be everything that one might have wished."[61]

The report represented the unanimous compromise verdict the members had reached during their deliberations in Lausanne. The compromise nature of the result echoed certain precedents during Palestine's legal history. For example, the Lofgren Commission had also delivered a unanimous, yet compromise verdict 16 years earlier regarding the respective rights and claims of the Muslims and Jews to the Wailing Wall and the narrow strip of pavement facing the Wall.

But on the most important issue of all – the White Paper of 1939 and British policy based on the White Paper – the Anglo-American Committee's verdict delivered a death blow. Even though the White Paper was not mentioned in the Committee's Terms of Reference, the Committee nevertheless unanimously rejected three key aspects of the British policy embodied in the White Paper.

First, the Committee rejected "the view that there shall be no further Jewish immigration into Palestine without Arab acquiescence."[62]

Second, the Committee called for the repeal of the 1940 Land Transfers Ordinance which had mostly banned Jewish land acquisition in Palestine.[63]

Third, the Committee rejected the White Paper's "one-state solution" in favour of the Palestinian Arabs:

> It is therefore neither just nor practicable that Palestine should become an Arab State, in which an Arab majority would control the destiny of a Jewish minority, or a Jewish State, in which a Jewish majority would control an Arab minority. In neither case would minority guarantees afford adequate protection for the subordinated group.[64]

The Committee's unanimous verdict meant "[t]he White Paper was trashed."[65] The White Paper had survived the Permanent Mandates Commission's harsh criticism in August 1939, but it could not survive a rigorous trial seven years later, resulting in a unanimous verdict rendered by six Britons joined by six Americans. The Committee upheld the legal validity of the Balfour Declaration and the Mandate and struck down the White Paper as contrary to both.

The Committee therefore unanimously recommended the issuance of the 100,000 immigration certificates.

However, the Committee rejected both the Jewish and Arab claims to Palestine, recommending instead that the Mandate or a successor Trusteeship continue indefinitely. Echoing both Magnes' testimony and Frankfurter's 1923 *Foreign Affairs* article, the Committee proclaimed "neither Jew shall dominate Arab nor Arab dominate Jew in Palestine."

This outcome disappointed the Zionists, who feared they had lost both British *and* American support for the dream of Jewish statehood in Palestine, or even a portion of Palestine.[66] At the very least, however, the Jews succeeded in obtaining a verdict that not only destroyed the legal basis for the White Paper but also paved the way for future Jewish immigration to Palestine.

Overall, the Committee made ten recommendations:

*Recommendation One*: The British and American Governments "together, and in association with other countries, should endeavor immediately to find homes for all … 'displaced persons,' irrespective of creed or nationality."

*Recommendation Two*: The 100,000 immigration certificates should be authorised "immediately" and issued "as far as possible" during the remainder of 1946, and "that actual immigration be pushed forward as rapidly as conditions will permit."

*Recommendation Three*: "In order to dispose, once and for all, of the exclusive claims of Arabs and Jews to Palestine, we regard it as essential" that "Jew shall not dominate Arab and Arab shall not dominate Jew in Palestine;" that "Palestine shall be neither a Jewish state nor an Arab state;" and the ultimate form of government to be established will "fully protect and preserve the interests in the Holy Land of Christendom and of the Moslem and Jewish faiths."

*Recommendation Four*: Palestine will continue under the Mandate pending the execution of a Trusteeship agreement with the United Nations.

*Recommendation Five*: The mandatory or trustee should "at once prepare measures designed to bridge the gap which now exists and raise the Arab standard of living to that of the Jews."

*Recommendation Six*: Over and above the 100,000 immigration certificates, the mandatory should return to the pre-White Paper policy required by Article 6 of the Mandate and facilitate Jewish immigration under suitable conditions, while ensuring that the rights and position of other sections of the population are not prejudiced.

Commenting on the recommendation regarding future Jewish immigration, the report reflected the formulation in Judge Hutcheson's tentative ruling:

> The well-being of all the people of Palestine, be they Jews, Arabs or neither, must be the governing consideration. We reject the view that there shall be no further Jewish immigration into Palestine without Arab acquiescence, a view which would result in the Arab dominating the Jew. We also reject the insistent Jewish demand that forced Jewish immigration must proceed apace in order to produce as quickly as possible a Jewish majority and a Jewish State. The well-being of Jews must not be subordinated to the Arabs; nor that of the Arabs to the Jews. The well-being of both, the economic situation of Palestine as a whole, the degree of execution of plans for further development, all have to be carefully considered in deciding the number of immigrants for any particular period.[67]

*Recommendation Seven*: The Land Transfers Ordinance of 1940, which had restricted land sales to Jews throughout nearly all of Palestine, should be rescinded. The Jewish Agency policy of employing only Jewish workers on Jewish-owned land should also be repealed.

*Recommendation Eight*: Plans for large-scale agricultural and industrial development of Palestine should be examined, discussed and executed with the full cooperation of the Jewish Agency and the surrounding Arab states.

*Recommendation Nine*: The Jewish and Arab educational systems should be reformed, and compulsory education should be adopted for both communities.

*Recommendation Ten*: Violence and terrorism committed by Jews and Arabs will not be tolerated, and the Jewish Agency must cooperate with the Mandatory to suppress both terrorism and illegal immigration.

The recommendations represented a mixed bag, with neither the Jews, the Arabs nor the British Government receiving what they wanted. The Jews were happy about the immigration certificates, but unhappy that the report did not recommend Jewish statehood or partition. The Arabs were angry about the immigration certificates and the lack of any recognition of their claims to statehood in *all* of Palestine, both of which represented huge reversals of the White Paper policy of 1939. The British Government was disappointed with Singleton's failure to link the issuance of the immigration certificates to the disarming of the *Haganah* and the dismantling (or severe weakening) of the Jewish Agency.

The verdict, albeit unanimous, pleased no one except Judge Hutcheson, who months later proclaimed the report an "excellent document."[68] More than two decades later, commenting on the Six-Day war in a letter to Buxton, Judge Hutcheson still viewed the Committee's recommendations as having offered a better outcome than partition.[69]

## Reactions to the report

### *Arab reaction*

The Anglo-American Committee report deeply angered the Palestinian Arabs and the Arab states. The Arab heads of state gathered in Inshas, Egypt, for their first-ever summit meeting on 28–29 May 1946. They demanded the immediate stoppage of Jewish immigration and land acquisition, and immediate Arab independence and sovereignty over Palestine. The heads of state also made clear they viewed the "attack" on the Palestinian Arabs as a hostile act against all Arab states.[70]

On 8 June 1946, the Arab states convened another summit at Bloudan, Syria. The delegates decided to provide arms and cash to the Palestinians. They also approved a series of secret retaliatory resolutions against Britain and the United States as punishment for the Anglo-American Committee report but decided to hold off on implementing the resolutions pending the potential implementation of the report. The delegates (including Jamal Husseini) also approved the reconstitution of the Palestinian Arab Higher Committee, under the leadership of Haj Amin al-Husseini, the ex-Mufti of Jerusalem and wanted war criminal for his collaboration with the Nazi regime.[71]

### British Government reaction

On 24 April 1946, Bevin advised the Cabinet that the government had received the Anglo-American Committee's report.[72] The British Government reacted with great consternation to the Committee's report.

For example, a 26 April 1946 Finance Ministry memorandum criticised the recommendation regarding the 100,000 immigration certificates as potentially imposing an enormous financial burden on Great Britain, nearly equalling Britain's projected ten-year expense for the *entire* colonial empire. Faced with the impossibility of bearing that burden alone, the memorandum offered a striking level of self-awareness of Britain's depleted economic and political power in the aftermath of World War II:

> The Foreign Secretary may feel that in the interests of Anglo-American solidarity we are bound to stand by the Report, which in America will probably get a good reception. The Chiefs of Staff will maintain that Palestine is our last hold in the Eastern Mediterranean and that at whatever cost, political or financial, we must continue as the power in possession. To this the answer is plain. *We cannot afford it* and in any event the United States will not allow us to remain indefinitely. Even if the issue is not brought to the Security Council at once either by the Arab States or by Russia, it is bound to come before the United Nations when Trusteeship terms come to be discussed. At that point no country, apart from America, will agree to a single power administration. We should resign ourselves to this fact and get what credit we can by advocating collective administration rather than having this policy forced on us.[73]

On 27 April 1946, a Committee of Officials issued a report to the Cabinet assessing the conclusions and recommendations of the Anglo-American Committee report.[74] The Committee said the report, if adopted, "would have disastrous effects on our position in the Middle East and might have unfortunate repercussions in India."[75] The Committee recommended that if the Government were to consider implementing the report's recommendations, it should insist on Jewish disarmament in Palestine as a condition precedent to issuing the 100,000 immigration certificates.[76]

Phillips lamented later that the White House and media focus on the recommendations to issue the 100,000 immigration certificates, without reference to the remaining recommendations, doomed the report to fatal opposition from the Arabs and the British Government:

> The British Government, which was making another attempt to effect an agreement between the Jews and Arabs was embarrassed … [t]hereupon the report of the Anglo-American Committee vanished from the scene and has never been revived. Four months of intensive labor went for nothing. The enormous expense of transportation and accommodations for the committee members and their large staff of experts, assistance and clerks was wasted. All that remains is an interesting little volume published by the Government Printing Office.[77]

At a 1 May 1946 Cabinet meeting, Prime Minister Attlee insisted the report's recommendations must be read together as a unified package and not individually. That meant, according to the Prime Minister, the *Haganah* must first be disbanded and disarmed *before* Britain would allow a large influx of Jewish immigrants to Palestine.[78]

The Prime Minister also wanted to "raise directly the question to what extent [Britain] could rely on the active collaboration of the United States in giving effect to [this] policy."[79] Attlee addressed the House of Commons later that same day to reiterate the Government's concerns with the report.[80] The Prime Minister drew a line in the sand, saying his Government would implement the recommendations of the Anglo-American Committee only *after* the Jews in Palestine had disarmed:

> It is clear from the facts presented in the report regarding the illegal armies maintained in Palestine and their recent activities that it would not be possible for the Government of Palestine to admit so large a body of immigrants unless and until these formations have been disbanded and their arms surrendered.[81]

Attlee's speech, as discussed below, stunned and angered the Zionist leadership.

Meanwhile, on 6 May 1946, Crossman met with Attlee. The Prime Minister said the British members of the Committee had let him down by producing a report that was "grossly unfair to Great Britain."[82]

Crossman wrote a long letter to Attlee the next day defending the report, especially the Committee's decision to recommend the 100,000 immigration certificates, noting "morally we are bound to rescue those Jews in Europe, and let them go to the only place which will welcome them, the National Home." Crossman said the Committee had heard ample testimony in Jerusalem regarding the country's economic capacity to absorb that number of immigrants. He also took issue with Attlee's criticism that the Committee had not conditioned its recommendation to issue the 100,000 immigration certificates on the Jews first disarming the *Haganah*.[83]

Attlee sent a handwritten response two days later, apologising for any unintended criticism of the British members of the Committee. Attlee said he was annoyed with the Americans, "who forever lay heavy burdens on us without lifting a finger to help."[84]

Several days later, on 8 May 1946, President Truman cabled Attlee and advised the White House was prepared to begin within two weeks the process of consulting with the Jews and Arabs regarding implementing the recommendations of the Anglo-American Committee report.[85] After consulting Bevin and the Cabinet, Attlee asked Truman to defer those discussions until after British and American experts could assess the financial and military implications of implementing the Committee's recommendations.

Attlee (shown with Churchill in Figure 9.3), stalling for time and seeking to delay any influx of Jewish refugees into Palestine, envisioned the formal consultations with Jews and Arabs would take place during a conference later that year to discuss the issues raised by the report. Attlee also told the Cabinet he intended to meet with the British members of the Anglo-American Committee to question them about their report.[86]

On 14 May 1946, Attlee and Colonial Secretary George Henry Hall met with Justice Singleton and the other British members of the Anglo-American Committee.

Justice Singleton began by portraying the Committee's report as having achieved Britain's short-term and long-term policy objectives for Palestine. He characterised the Committee' report as embodying three key conclusions. First, he said, "in no circumstances would Palestine become a Jewish State." Second, he emphasised how the report described the "private armies" (a clear reference to the *Haganah*) in Palestine as illegal. Third, Justice Singleton downplayed the

**FIGURE 9.3** Attlee and Churchill (Public Domain)

Committee's recommendation regarding the immigration certificates as a short-term blip, saying "after the admission of the first 100,000 immigrants, immigration would be conducted on a new basis, the well-being of Palestine as a whole being the sole criterion."[87]

As the meeting continued, Singleton's colleagues on the Committee offered their own comments, reflecting deep divisions among the British members. For example, Manningham-Buller said he opposed partition. Crossman said he supported partition.[88] Manningham-Buller supported the Government's position that the *Haganah* be disarmed before the 100,000 immigration certificates would be granted. But Leggett and Crossman disagreed, saying they opposed conditioning the immigration certificates on disbanding the *Haganah*.[89]

Lord Morrison also spoke during the meeting. He began by relaying intelligence he had received from Judah Magnes, who said the Committee's report had been received more favourably by Palestinian Jews than was generally believed. Lord Morrison then launched into a diatribe against the Zionists, making the shocking statement in front of the Prime Minister that "Jewish education was, in fact, being conducted on the lines of the Hitler Youth Movement."[90]

On 20 May 1946, the Prime Minister advised the Cabinet that President Truman had accepted the British Government's proposal to appoint a joint committee of experts to study the implications of the Anglo-American Committee report.[91] Truman and Attlee also agreed to invite the Arabs and Jews to submit written comments regarding the report within 30 days.[92]

On 26 May 1946, Attlee sent Truman a list of topics he suggested the experts from both countries needed to discuss regarding each of the Committee's ten recommendations.[93] Regarding the Committee's recommendation to issue the 100,000 immigration certificates, Attlee's list included items such as the cost of transporting, temporarily accommodating, and permanently housing the immigrants; the logistics for transporting the immigrants to Palestine; the supply of material for housing; and the capital investment necessary to create productive employment for the immigrants.

On 8 July 1946, Colonial Secretary George Hall sent a memorandum to the Cabinet, summarising the Anglo-American Committee's recommendations and noting "some of their implications and … the difficulties foreseen in giving effect to them."[94] The Hall memorandum briefly recounted the Government's position as to each of the ten recommendations. Interestingly, regarding the recommendation to issue 100,000 immigration certificates, Hall focused almost exclusively on the economic cost of absorbing that number of immigrants into Palestine, rather than the political cost.[95]

But Hall reacted very negatively to the Committee's recommendation that additional Jewish immigration be permitted without Arab consent beyond 100,000. Hall disputed the Zionist principle that any Jew, from anywhere in the world, could immigrate to Palestine as of right. He also argued against basing future Jewish immigration on the ambiguous principle of the "well-being of the entire population of Palestine." Instead, future Jewish immigration should depend on *Arab* willingness to accept more Jews beyond the initial 100,000 refugees:

> The Committee's recommendation thus leaves unsolved the most crucial question affecting the Administration of Palestine, *viz.*, the character and measure of future immigration. Of all their recommendations [this] will meet with the most obdurate and sustained opposition on the part of the Palestine Arabs. Nor is it to be expected the Jews will acquiesce in a formula which is in direct opposition to their claims regarding the free admission of Jews to Palestine which they regard, however erroneously, as deriving direct from the Balfour Declaration … An immigration policy based on the broad lines sketched by the Committee would appear to imply reversion to the old problem of economic absorptive capacity with all its vexatious uncertainties. On the other hand, it may well be argued that to exclude political considerations when assessing the phrase "the well-being of all the people of Palestine" is to make nonsense of the phrase. In short, the Committee's recommendation gives no definite lead for future policy; it leaves the situation as indefinite and unsatisfactory as it is to-day.[96]

Hall next addressed the Committee's recommendation that the Land Transfers Ordinance of 1940, which had largely banned land sales to Jews, be rescinded in favour of a policy promoting freedom of sale, lease or use of land. While admitting the 1940 Ordinance "has proved to be a thoroughly unsuccessful measure since its enactment," Hall expressed fear that the Committee's recommendation would provoke "intense indignation" among the Palestinian Arabs.[97]

Finally, Hall attacked the Committee's recommendations as harmful to Britain's strategic interests:

> [I]t is the unanimous view of His Majesty's Representatives that the adoption of the policy recommended by the Anglo-American Committee would have disastrous effects on Great Britain's position in the Middle East and might have unfortunate repercussions in India. Both the immediate and long-term reactions of the Arab States would be extremely unfavourable: acceptance of the report would undermine belief in the good faith of Great Britain and in the benefits to be obtained from friendship with this country and thus make the Arab peoples more easily accessible to Russian propaganda and influence.[98]

Hall therefore offered an alternative Colonial Office "provincial autonomy" proposal for the Cabinet to consider. The proposal, originally authored by Sir Douglas Harris of the Colonial Office in August 1945, advocated the creation of semi-autonomous Jewish and Arab provinces in Palestine, under the overall control of a central government. The Mandate itself would remain in force, and Jerusalem, Haifa harbour and the Negev would remain under British control.

The Jewish area "would be confined to a definite and fairly small compartment of Palestine," thereby freeing "three-quarters of the Palestinian Arabs, once and for all, from any fear of Jewish domination."[99] The Colonial Office had submitted the proposal anonymously to the Anglo-American Committee earlier in 1946, but the Committee made no mention of it in its final report.

The Cabinet met on 11 July 1946 to discuss Hall's provincial autonomy proposal. Bevin, who was in Paris, authorised Cabinet Secretary Sir Norman Brook to say Bevin favoured the provincial autonomy plan and recommended it to be discussed with the Americans. However, Bevin doubted provincial autonomy "would provide a lasting solution of the Palestine problem." Bevin therefore floated the possibility of a major shift in British policy, suggesting the Cabinet consider adopting partition as its long-term objective for Palestine. The provincial autonomy plan should be viewed as an intermediate step, with the ultimate objective that "the major part of the Arab province would be assimilated in the adjacent Arab states of Transjordan and the Lebanon, and the Jewish province established as an independent Jewish state, with perhaps a somewhat larger territory than that suggested for the Jewish province" in Hall's plan.[100]

The Cabinet expressed "general agreement that the recommendations in the report of the Anglo-American Committee offered no practical prospect of progress towards a solution of the constitutional problem in Palestine." The Cabinet therefore embraced "in principle" the provincial autonomy proposal but rejected an outright policy change in favour of partition:

> The Cabinet's general conclusion was that it would be inexpedient to put forward at this stage proposals for the partition of Palestine into two sovereign States. The [provincial autonomy plan] was, however, a constructive and imaginative plan which ... should be commended to the favourable consideration of the Jews and the Arabs if United States support for it could be secured.[101]

The Cabinet authorised Brook and his team to find "the appropriate moment for bringing forward this alternative plan [to the Americans]; and this would probably come after they had exposed the weaknesses in the recommendations ... of the Anglo-American Committee regarding the future constitution of Palestine and future immigration policy."[102]

## *American Government reaction*

Judge Hutcheson met with President Truman on 25 April 1946 and handed him the Committee's report. Hutcheson wrote to other American members of the Committee later that day, reporting the President "was greatly pleased that we had produced a unanimous report and with what I told him was the substance of it. He expressed himself in the warmest terms of gratitude to us all ..."[103]

Truman wrote in his memoirs that the Anglo-American Committee's report was "careful and complete" and "Judge Hutcheson and his colleagues had done a notably conscientious job."[104] The White House issued a statement on 30 April 1946, immediately following the publication of the Anglo-American Committee report, quoting a clearly pleased President Truman:

> I am very happy that the request which I made for the immediate admission of 100,000 Jews into Palestine has been unanimously endorsed by the Anglo-American Committee of Inquiry. The transference of these unfortunate people should now be accomplished with the greatest despatch. The protection and safeguarding of the Holy Places in Palestine sacred to Moslem, Christian and Jew is adequately provided in the report. One of the significant features of the report is that it aims to insure complete protection to the Arab population of Palestine by guaranteeing their civil and religious rights, and by recommending measures for the constant improvement in their cultural, educational, and economic position. I am also pleased that the committee recommends in effect the abrogation of the White Paper of 1939 including existing restrictions on immigration and land acquisition to permit the further development of the Jewish National Home … In addition to these immediate objectives, the report deals with many other questions of long-range political policies and questions of International Law which require careful study and which I will take under advisement.[105]

The President (shown in Figure 9.4 with Secretary of State James Byrnes) continued urging Britain to grant the 100,000 immigration certificates for the next several weeks.[106]

**FIGURE 9.4** President Harry Truman and Secretary of State James Byrnes (Public Domain)

The British and American Governments invited the Arabs and Jews on 20 May 1946 to submit their comments regarding the Anglo-American Committee report within 30 days. The American Government would later take the position that this invitation to submit comments had discharged Roosevelt's pledge to Ibn Saud to consult both sides before taking further action regarding Palestine.[107]

## *Jewish reaction*

Weizmann initially was pleased with the report due to the positive recommendation regarding the 100,000 immigration certificates. But Attlee's 1 May 1946 statement to the House of Commons, conditioning the 100,000 immigration certificates on Jewish disarmament, came as a shock to Weizmann.

"Attlee's statement came as a shattering blow," wrote Weizmann in a 4 May 1946 letter to Felix Frankfurter, noting it "may have grave consequences."[108] In a letter to Judah Magnes a few days later, Weizmann (apparently unaware that Magnes had been feeding information to Lord Morrison) wrote,

> I cannot help feeling uncomfortable about Attlee's behaviour and see in it not just a desire of obtaining some concessions from us – that would be legitimate – but I fear that they are still bent on the destruction of the National Home, which would mean plunging Palestine into a great disaster.[109]

On 11 May 1946, Crossman published an article in the *New Statesman*, in which he also criticised Attlee's linkage of the immigration certificates to Jewish disarmament:

> There is only one way of reversing the process [of Jewish] terrorism in Palestine: in conformity with the unanimous findings of the Committee, to annul the illegalities and injustices of the White Paper and simultaneously to call on the Jewish Agency to assist in liquidating the extremist groups ...[110]

On 13 May, Weizmann wrote directly to Attlee regarding "the grave situation which has arisen since the publication of the report of the Anglo-American Committee of Inquiry." Weizmann said the Jews would not agree to disarm. He argued forcefully that the best way to prevent further acts of Jewish violence would be for the British Government to move ahead immediately to allow the 100,000 immigrants to come to Palestine.[111]

On 23 May, Weizmann complained about Attlee's 1 May statement again, this time in a letter to the former Colonial Secretary, Oliver Stanley:

> The Prime Minister's statement came, therefore, as a bitter disappointment – a severe blow to us all. All this talk about consultation with Jews and Arabs – and the peculiar form in which it is conceived: is not real consultation: we are merely asked for another memorandum, with talks perhaps to follow – is really no more than a delaying device.[112]

Attlee replied to Weizmann on 28 May 1946, indicating he and President Truman intended to confer with both the Jewish and Arab communities in determining how to implement the Committee's report.[113]

## *Arab reaction*

The Arab Higher Committee, led by Jamal Husseini, wrote to Prime Minister Attlee on 2 May 1946, rejecting the Anglo-American Committee's report and invoking the Palestinian Arab legal narrative. Husseini argued the proposals amounted to "the suppression of our natural rights to determine our destiny, the breach of the promise made by Britain to the Arabs and the contradiction of the principles of the Atlantic Charter for which the Arabs have fought."[114]

Ibn Saud cabled Husseini to assure him of Arab support in the face of the "unsurpassable injustice" of the Anglo-American Committee's recommendations.[115] The Iraqi Government also objected to the report. In a 19 June 1946 *Note Verbale* from the Iraqi Ministry of Foreign Affairs to the British Ambassador in Baghdad, the Iraqi Government framed its criticism of the report through the prism of the Palestinian Arab legal narrative:

> *Justice* requires that the fate of Palestine should be determined by its *legitimate inhabitants* and not by others. The Iraqi Government *does not admit the legal character* of the Commission of Inquiry … The Iraqi Government considers also that there is *no legal justification* whatsoever for the interference of the Government of the United States … The Iraqi Government is certain that the Mandate over Palestine is fundamentally unsound, for the Balfour Declaration contained in the text of the Mandate and the resultant deprivation of the Arabs in Palestine of the enjoyment of their political and civil rights is *contrary to Article 22(4) of the Covenant of the League of Nations* … The Iraqi Government consider any retreat from the White Paper, by which Britain is bound in honour, to be a fresh challenge to the natural *and legal rights* of the Arabs in their own countries.[116]

The Iraqi Government lodged a similar protest with the US Embassy in Baghdad. "There is no *legal* justification," wrote the Iraqis, "for the interference of the United States Government in the situation in Palestine."[117]

The Emir (and future King) Abdullah of Transjordan also objected to the report, using the following bizarre analogy:

> I have no better comparison to this Committee's decision than the case of a man who, on seeing a piece of cake in the hand of a poor little orphan, inherited from his forefathers, slapped him on the face and tried to take from him the piece of cake in order to give it to another boy who has numerous wealthy and influential relatives and cousins all over the world. The above is the best comparison to the recommendations of the Joint Committee on the Palestine deadlock.[118]

The Egyptian Embassy in London sent a note to the Foreign Office on 10 May 1946, slamming the report as "thoroughly harmful to the rights of the Arabs, based on *no legal* or historic foundation and menacing the peace and security of a vital region."[119]

The Arab League raised similar legal objections in a telegram to the Foreign Office:

> League is glad United States Government recognized recommendations as advisory only, considers Committee possessed neither legality nor permanency … Arab rights being based on over thousand years settlement whereas Jews rely on weak historical association severed 2,000 years ago. This is contrary to practice and law of nations, discriminating against Palestine Arabs and depriving them of rights enjoyed in other Arab lands.[120]

The Anglo-American Committee's verdict failed to resolve the Jewish-Arab conflict in Palestine. It also marked the beginning of the end of Britain's monopoly over Palestine policy. The resounding and unanimous rejection of the White Paper completely undercut Britain's earlier justification of the White Paper as lawful under both the Balfour Declaration and the Mandate.

The Committee upheld both the Balfour Declaration and the Mandate as the binding legal instruments governing Palestine's future, but the Committee's verdict was not self-executing or enforceable. Indeed, the British Government immediately worked to persuade the Truman Administration to disregard the verdict entirely and adopt a completely different approach based on the Colonial Office's provincial autonomy scheme.

The British effort almost succeeded.

## Notes

1 FO 371/52513, H.T. Morgan minute (Top Secret) regarding Lord Morrison's report to Bevin.
2 A. Nachmani, *op. cit.*, at 179; *see also* L. Dinnerstein, *op. cit.*, at 293 ("Their experiences [in Europe] moved all of the members of the committee. Sir Frederick Leggett, previously hostile to the Jews, became 'emotionally exhausted' by this trip and wanted to do something to help the surviving remnant. Not only did he start greeting everyone with the term, 'Shalom,' but he told his colleagues: 'Unless we can do something and do it soon, we shall be guilty of having finished the job Hitler started.'").
3 Hutcheson Papers, University of Texas, Tarlton Law Library Rare Books and Special Collections, Box L7, Folder 4, Document No. 2 (Undated).
4 *Id.* at 1.
5 *Id.* at 1–2.
6 *Id.*
7 *Id.* at 4–5.
8 *Id. at 5.*
9 *Id.* at 7.
10 *Id.* at 8–9. According to McDonald, on 3 April 1946, Judge Hutcheson gave the other members of the Committee a "very reasonable memorandum as a basis for discussion." N. Goda, *op. cit.*, at 200 (McDonald Diary Entry, 3 April 1946). It is not known whether

the memorandum Judge Hutcheson provided the Committee is the same memorandum he wrote discussing his tentative view of how the case should be decided.

11 Crossman Papers, GB 165-0068, Middle East Centre Archive, St. Antony's College, Oxford, Anglo-American Committee Papers, File 1, "Public Security" at 15–6 (9 April 1946).

12 B. Crum, *op. cit.*, at 264 (emphasis in original).

13 N. Goda, *op. cit.*, at 193 (McDonald diary entry, 30 March 1946).

14 R. Crossman, *Palestine Mission* at 176, 180–1 (Hamish Hamilton, 1947).

15 Crossman Papers, GB 165-0068, Middle East Centre Archive, St. Antony's College, Oxford, Anglo-American Committee Papers, File 1, "Partition" at 3–4 (7 April 1946) (emphasis added).

16 *Id.*, Box 5, File 2, Diary Entry (Undated).

17 *Id.*

18 Id., Box 5, File 2, Diary Entry (4 April 1946).

19 N. Goda, *op. cit.*, at 195 (McDonald Diary Entry, 1 April 1946).

20 *Id.*

21 Crossman Papers, GB 165-0068, Middle East Centre Archive, St. Antony's College, Oxford, Box 5, File 2, Diary Entry (8 April 1946).

22 N. Goda, *op. cit.*, at 196–7 (McDonald Diary Entry, 1 April 1946).

23 Crossman Papers, GB 165-0068, Middle East Centre Archive, St. Antony's College, Oxford, Box 5, File 2, Diary Entry (4 April 1946); *see also* M.N. Penkower (2019), *op. cit.*, at 179–84.

24 Crossman Papers, GB 165-0068, Middle East Centre Archive, St. Antony's College, Oxford, Box 5, File 2, Diary Entry (4 April 1946).

25 *Id.*

26 *See* A. Nachmani, *op. cit.*, at 194–5; L. Dinnerstein, *op. cit.*, at 295–6 ("Resentment, bitterness, and acrimony handicapped working relationships among committee members and aggravated the taxing nature of their responsibilities").

27 Crossman Papers, GB 165-0068, Middle East Centre Archive, St. Antony's College, Oxford, Anglo-American Committee Papers, File 1, "Notes on Palestine Report of Anglo-American Committee," copy of memorandum sent to Hector McNeil at 1 (22 April 1946) (copy on file at FO 371/52524).

28 *Id.*

29 *Id.* Nearly two decades later, Buxton wrote to Hutcheson that he still thought, "and not pleasantly" about Justice Singleton, who he described as "not a nice baby." Hutcheson Papers, University of Texas, Tarlton Law Library Rare Books and Special Collections, Box L8, Folder 12, Letter from Buxton to Hutcheson (9 July 1965). In another letter, Buxton said he still felt "antipathy" toward Singleton. *Id.*, Letter from Buxton to Hutcheson (17 August 1965). Crossman also wrote to Judge Hutcheson in 1965, saying he had happy memories of the time when he was "devoted to an American Judge and acquired a detestation for an English one!" *Id.*, Letter from Crossman to Hutcheson (11 October 1965).

30 Crossman Papers, GB 165-0068, Middle East Centre Archive, St. Antony's College, Oxford, Anglo-American Committee Papers, File 1, "Notes on Palestine Report of Anglo-American Committee," copy of memorandum sent to Hector McNeil at 1 (22 April 1946) (copy on file at FO 371/52524).

31 *Id.*

32 *Id.*

33 B. Crum, *op. cit.*, at 265 (emphasis added).

34 N. Nachmani, *op. cit.*, at 196; N. Goda, *op. cit.*, at 201–2, citing Memorandum by M. Weisgal (5 April 1946), TL, Papers of David Niles, Box 29, Folder January–June 1946.

35 Central Zionist Archives, 26/287, Excerpt of Letter from A.L. [Arthur Lourie] – Geneva (3 April 1946), reprinted in M.J. Cohen (ed.), *The Rise of Israel (Vol. 35): The Anglo-American Committee on Palestine 1945-1946* at 222–4 (1987).

36 *Id.*
37 *Id.*
38 B. Crum, *op. cit.*, at 268.
39 Central Zionist Archives, 26/287, Excerpt of Letter from A.L. [Arthur Lourie] – Geneva (3 April 1946), reprinted in M.J. Cohen (ed.), *The Rise of Israel (Vol. 35): The Anglo-American Committee on Palestine 1945-1946* at 222–4 (1987); *see also* L. Dinnerstein, *op. cit.*, at 295–6.
40 N. Goda, *op. cit.*, at 203–4 (editor's note).
41 *Id.* at 205–6 (McDonald Diary Entry, 6 April 1946).
42 *Id.* at 207 (McDonald Diary Entry, 7 April 1946).
43 *Id.* at 207–8 (McDonald Diary Entry, 8 April 1946).
44 *Id.* at 202, quoting Telegram from Truman to Hutcheson, 9 April 1946.
45 *Id.* at 210–1 (McDonald Diary Entry, 12 April 1946).
46 Central Zionist Archives, 26/287, Excerpt from a Letter from A.L. [Arthur Lourie] – Geneva (21 April 1946), reprinted in M.J. Cohen (ed.), *The Rise of Israel (Vol. 35): The Anglo-American Committee on Palestine 1945-1946* at 220 (1987).
47 *Id.*
48 N. Goda, *op. cit.*, at 219–20, quoting telegram from Truman to Hutcheson, 16 April 1946, TL, Papers of David K. Niles, Box 29, Folder January–June 1946.
49 Crossman Papers, GB 165-0068, Middle East Centre Archive, St. Antony's College, Oxford, Anglo-American Committee Papers, File 1, "Notes on Palestine Report of Anglo-American Committee," copy of memorandum sent to Hector McNeil at 2 (22 April 1946) (copy on file at FO 371/52524). Crossman wrote in his memo to McNeil that he still favoured partition but did not want to sacrifice unanimity in the report. He said the report's recommendation to continue the Mandate or a similar Trusteeship could last "for at least a generation – possibly for fifty years," a prospect that would face "overwhelming objection" from both Jews and Arabs in Palestine, both of whom were already "perfectly fit and ready to govern themselves." *Id.* at 4. Phillips recalled that Crum and McDonald also consistently advocated for partition alongside Crossman. W. Phillips, *op. cit.*, at 446. McDonald described himself as "noncommittal but favorable" regarding partition. N. Goda, *op. cit.*, at 217 (McDonald Diary Entry, 8 April 1946).
50 N. Goda, *op. cit.*, at 220 (McDonald Diary Entry, 18 April 1946); *see also* M. Jones, *op. cit.*, at 80.
51 W. Phillips, *op. cit.*, at 447–8.
52 N. Goda, *op. cit.*, at 221 (McDonald Diary Entry, 19 April 1946).
53 Central Zionist Archives, 26/287, Excerpt from a Letter from A.L. [Arthur Lourie] – Geneva (21 April 1946), reprinted in M.J. Cohen (ed.), *The Rise of Israel (Vol. 35): The Anglo-American Committee on Palestine 1945-1946* at 220 (1987).
54 N. Goda, *op. cit.*, at 222 (McDonald Diary Entry, 20 April 1946).
55 *Id.*
56 Central Zionist Archives, 26/287, Excerpt from a Letter from A.L. [Arthur Lourie] – Geneva (21 April 1946), reprinted in M.J. Cohen (ed.), *The Rise of Israel (Vol. 35): The Anglo-American Committee on Palestine 1945-1946* at 220 (1987).
57 *Id.*
58 *Id.*
59 FO 371/52524, Letter from Crossman to McNeil (22 April 1946).
60 Cmd. 6308, *Report of the Anglo-American Committee of Enquiry Regarding the Problems of European Jewry and Palestine* (20 April 1946); published simultaneously by the US Department of States as *Anglo-American Committee of Inquiry: Report to the United States Government and His Majesty's Government in the United Kingdom* (20 April 1946).
61 W. Phillips, *op. cit.*, at 449.
62 Cmd. 6308, *op. cit.*, at 8.
63 *Id.*
64 *Id.* at 4.

65 W. Khalidi, *op. cit.*, at 74.
66 M. Golani, *Palestine Between Politics and Terror, 1945-1947* at 48 (Brandeis University Press, 2013).
67 Cmd. 6308, *op. cit.*, at 8.
68 Crossman Papers, GB 165-0068, Middle East Centre Archive, St. Antony's College, Oxford, Anglo-American Committee Papers, File 1, Letter from Hutcheson to Crossman (16 August 1946).
69 Hutcheson Papers, Box L8, Folder 12, Letter from Hutcheson to Buxton (2 August 1967).
70 W. Khalidi, "The Arab Perspective," in W. Louis and R. Stookey, *The End of the Palestine Mandate* at 110 (Univ. of Texas Press, 1986); *see also* Z. Elipeleg, *Why Was "Independent Palestine" Never Created?*, Jerusalem Quarterly 50, 3–22 (1989) ("In response to the publication of the findings of the Anglo-American Commission of Inquiry in April 1946, the Arab rulers gathered in Inshas near Cairo to discuss options. Among other things, it was decided that 'Palestine is Arab and cannot be separated from the rest of the Arab states, for it is the center of the great Arab nation and its destiny rests with that of the Arab states. Therefore we view the Palestinian problem as an inseparable part of the their basic national problems'").
71 W. Khalidi, *op. cit.*, at 110–2; *see also* Z. Elipeleg, *op. cit.*
72 CAB 128/5/37, C.M. 37 (46), Conclusions (Secret) of a Meeting of the Cabinet (24 April 1946).
73 T 220/20, Minute, "Anglo-American Committee on Palestine" (26 April 1946) (emphasis added).
74 CAB 129/9/23, C.P (46) 173, "Palestine: Report of Committee of Officials" (27 April 1946).
75 *Id.*, para 9.
76 *Id.*, para. 45.
77 W. Phillips, *op. cit.*, at 453–4.
78 CAB 128/5/39, C.M. 39 (46), Conclusions (Secret) of a Meeting of the Cabinet (1 May 1946).
79 *Id.*
80 FO 371/52520, Prime Minister's Statement in the House of Commons on the Report of the Anglo-American Committee of Enquiry (1 May 1946).
81 "Government Studying the Palestine Report," *The Times*, 2 May 1946 at 4.
82 Crossman Papers, GB 165-0068, Middle East Centre Archive, St. Antony's College, Oxford, Anglo-American Committee Papers, File 1, Letter from Crossman to Prime Minister Attlee (7 May 1946). The meeting was extremely awkward for both Crossman and Attlee. Attlee's personal assistant, Douglas Jay, recalled that Attlee sat silently while Crossman spoke for nearly 30 minutes, at the end of which, "[a]fter nearly half a minute's pause, Attlee commented, 'I saw your mother last week.'" D. Jay, *Change and Fortune: A Political Record* at 133 (Hutchinson, 1980).
83 *Id.* Crossman also sent a short set of notes to Hector McNeil, the Undersecretary of State for Foreign Affairs, defending the Committee's report, especially the recommendation to issue the 100,000 immigration certificates, noting the recommendation had been "worked out carefully" and "the rate of intake has been carefully left ambiguous in our recommendation." *Id.*, Notes for Hector McNeil (8 May 1946).
84 Crossman Papers, GB 165-0068, Middle East Centre Archive, St. Antony's College, Oxford, Anglo-American Committee Papers, File 1, Letter from Attlee to Crossman (9 May 1946).
85 FRUS, N.A. 867.01/5-646, Telegram from President Truman to Prime Minister Attlee (8 May 1946).
86 CAB 128/5/45, C.M. (46) 45, Conclusions (Secret) of a Meeting of the Cabinet (13 May 1946).
87 FO 371/52524, Note of a Meeting held at No. 10 Downing Street, on 14 May 1946, at which the Prime Minister and the Secretary of State for the Colonies met the British members of the Anglo-American Committee at 1 (17 May 1946).

88 *Id.* at 7, 9.
89 *Id.* at 6–8.
90 *Id.* at 4.
91 Truman had so advised Attlee in a 16 May telegram. FRUS, 867N.01/5–1646, Telegram (Top Secret) from Truman to Attlee (16 May 1946); *see also* FO 371/52526, Telegram No. 4799 from Foreign Office to British Embassy, Washington, DC (17 May 1946) (reporting content of Truman telegram).
92 CAB 128/5/50, C.M. (46) 50, Conclusions (Secret) of a Meeting of the Cabinet (20 May 1946).
93 FO 371/52526, Telegram No. 5151 (Top Secret) from Foreign Office to British Embassy, Washington, DC (26 May 1946) (containing message from Attlee to Truman with five-page list of topics for Anglo-American experts to discuss); FRUS, 867N.01/5–2746, Telegram from Attlee to Truman (same).
94 CAB 129/111/8, C.P. (46) 258 (Secret), Report of the Anglo-American Committee of Enquiry Regarding the Problems of European Jewry and Palestine, Memorandum by the Secretary of State for the Colonies (8 July 1946).
95 *Id.* paras. 5–8 (noting the direct and indirect costs of absorbing 100,000 immigrants into Palestine would amount to at least £110 million).
96 *Id.* para. 17.
97 *Id.* paras. 19–20.
98 *Id.* para. 25.
99 CAB 129/11/19, C.P. 46 (259) (Top Secret), Long-Term Policy in Palestine: Memorandum by the Secretary of State for the Colonies, paras. 9–15 (8 July 1946). The Colonial Office had been drafting the provincial autonomy plan since the summer of 1945. *See, e.g.*, CO 537/1754, John M. Martin minute (2 January 1946) (discussing drafting of provincial autonomy plan in Colonial Office and involving the Foreign Office).
100 CAB 128/6/5, C.M. 67 (46), Conclusions (Secret) of a Meeting of the Cabinet (11 July 1946).
101 *Id.*
102 *Id.*
103 Hutcheson Papers, University of Texas, Tarlton Law Library Rare Books and Special Collections, Box L8, Folder 12 (25 April 1946).
104 H. Truman, *op. cit.*, at 146.
105 FO 371/52521, Letter from British Embassy, Washington, DC to Foreign Office (1 May 1946) (containing text of President Truman's statement). Assistant Secretary of State Loy Henderson, a notorious anti-Zionist, told British officials in Washington, DC he had "made every effort to head off the unilateral statement by the President on Palestine … Henderson deeply regretted the occurrence, as he knew that it had added to the difficulties of the Palestine question." CO 537/1759, Telegram No. 2918 (Secret) from British Embassy, Washington, DC to Foreign Office (7 May 1946), reprinted in M.J. Cohen (ed.), *The Rise of Israel (Vol. 35): The Anglo-American Committee on Palestine 1945-1946* at 247 (1987). It is not known whether the White House authorised Henderson to provide this information to a foreign government.
106 FO 371/52539, President Truman's Statements on the Admission of 100,000 Jewish Immigrants to Palestine (15 July 1948). Truman's endorsement of the Committee's recommendation regarding the 100,000 immigration certificates threw Bevin into "one of the blackest rages I have ever seen him in," according to a close associate who later included the episode in a biography of Bevin. F. Williams, *Ernest Bevin: Portrait of a Great Englishman* at 260 (Hutchinson, 1952).
107 FRUS, 867N.01/7–2246, Telegram No. 5572 (Top Secret) from Secretary of State to US Embassy, London (23 July 1946).
108 Weizmann Archives 22-2656, Rehovot, Letter from Weizmann to Frankfurter (4 May 1946).

109 Weizmann Archives 26-2657, Rehovot, Letter from Weizmann to Magnes (8 May 1946).
110 R. Crossman, "War in Palestine?" *The New Statesman and Nation*, 11 May 1946.
111 Weizmann Archives 17-2658, Rehovot, Letter from Weizmann to Attlee (13 May 1946).
112 Weizmann Archives 4-2660A, Rehovot, Letter from Weizmann to Stanley (23 May 1946).
113 Weizmann Archives 27-2661A, Rehovot, Letter from Attlee to Weizmann (28 May 1946).
114 CAB 129/10/20, C.P. (46) 220 (Secret), Arab reactions in Palestine to the Report of the Anglo-American Committee of Inquiry (6 June 1946), reporting on and reprinting letter from Jamal Husseini to Prime Minister (2 May 1946).
115 M.N. Penkower (2019), *op. cit.*, at 214.
116 FO 371/52532, Correspondence (Confidential) with the States' Members of the Arab League, with the Jewish Agency for Palestine, and with the Palestine Arab Higher Committee, concerning the Report of the Anglo-American Committee of Enquiry regarding the Problems of European Jewry and Palestine (19 June 1946), reprinting *Note Verbale* from Iraqi Ministry of Foreign Affairs to His majesty's Ambassador, Baghdad (19 June 1946), reprinted in P. Toye and A. Seay (eds.), *Israel: Boundary Disputes with Arab Neighbours 1946-1964*, Vol. I at 143–4 (1995) (emphasis added).
117 Rabbi Alan Podet Papers, Jacob Rader Marcus Center of the American Jewish Archives, Cincinnati, Ohio, MS 163, Box 3/4, Telegram No. 356 from US *Charge D'Affaires* James S. Moose, Jr., US Embassy, Baghdad to Secretary of State (21 June 1946) (original document from files of Loy Henderson, US Department of State, Box 1100, given by Henderson to Rabbi Podet in August 1975) (emphasis in original).
118 FO 816/83, Letter to Palestine High Commissioner Sir Alan Cunningham from Abdullah (3 May 1946).
119 FO 371/52522, Royal Egyptian Embassy, London. *Aide Memoir* (6 May 1946) (emphasis added).
120 FRUS, 867N.01/6–1946, Telegram (Secret) from the Minister to Syria and Lebanon to the Secretary of State (19 June 1946); *see also* FO 371/52529, Telegram (Cypher) No. 543 from British Embassy, Beirut to Foreign Office (16 June 1946) (reporting the Arab League considered the Anglo-American Committee "without legal basis," and the Palestine Mandate legally invalid because "it deprived the Arabs of Palestine of their rights under paragraph 4 of Article 22 of Charter [sic] of League of Nations"); FO 371/52532, Correspondence (Confidential) with the States' Members of the Arab League, with the Jewish Agency for Palestine, and with the Palestine Arab Higher Committee, concerning the Report of the Anglo-American Committee of Enquiry Regarding the Problems of European Jewry and Palestine (19 June 1946).

# 10

# BRITAIN UNDERMINES THE VERDICT

## The Morrison-Grady provincial autonomy plan

### Introduction

Colonial Secretary Hall's provincial autonomy plan became the key focus of British discussions with the Americans in the wake of the Anglo-American Committee Report. Britain, hoping to convince the Americans to set aside the Anglo-American Committee's recommendations, persuaded the Americans as a first step to appoint a group of experts to meet with their British counterparts to consider the feasibility and cost of the Anglo-American Committee's recommendations.[1] Following the expert consultations, each government would appoint a high-level delegation to engage in further discussions.

President Truman therefore appointed a Cabinet-level Committee consisting of the Secretaries of State, War and Treasury, each of whom would be represented by alternates in the upcoming talks with the British Government after the expert teams had completed their preliminary technical discussions.

The State Department instructed US Ambassador W. Averell Harriman in London to commence discussions "of a purely exploratory nature" with the British Government regarding the logistics of transferring 100,000 European Jewish Holocaust survivors to Palestine. The US Government sent a team of experts to assist Harriman in the preliminary discussions with the British Government, preparatory to the arrival in London of the Cabinet Committee alternates.[2] The British Government appointed Cabinet Secretary Sir Norman Brook to engage with Harriman.[3]

### Provincial autonomy, not statehood

Britain's objective, as decided at the 11 July Cabinet meeting, was for its negotiators to convince the Americans to (i) endorse the Colonial Office's provincial

DOI: 10.4324/9781003225263-14

autonomy plan as an alternative to the Anglo-American Committee's recommendations; and (ii) defer action on the transfer of the 100,000 European Jewish refugees to Palestine until Britain could reach agreement with both the Arab and Jewish sides on the provincial autonomy plan at a planned conference in London during the fall of 1946.

The British Government feared that allowing mass Jewish immigration before Arab-Jewish agreement on a political settlement would spark large-scale violence in Palestine, requiring an enormous new commitment of British troops and treasure to keep the peace. Britain insisted therefore on deferring any increase in immigration until a political settlement could be negotiated.

The provincial autonomy plan called for Palestine to be divided into semi-autonomous Arab and Jewish provinces or cantons, under the control of a central government. The Jewish province would be confined to a small salient of land (comprising approximately 15% of Palestine) from Tel Aviv northwards, eastwards through a portion of the Galilee, and then northwards again through the Hula Valley. Neither the Arab nor Jewish sides would receive statehood under the provincial autonomy plan, but each would be granted limited autonomy in their respective provinces. The Mandatory Power (or successor Trustee) would function as the central or federal government and retain permanent control of Jerusalem and the Negev.

In mid-July, Henry Grady, an economist and diplomat (later the first United States Ambassador to India), representing Secretary of State Byrnes as his alternate, led a high-level American delegation to London to continue the discussions with British Cabinet Secretary Norman Brook regarding the immigration issues and the remaining nine recommendations of the Anglo-American Committee Report.[4]

Once Grady arrived, Brook presented the provincial autonomy plan as a preferable alternative to the Anglo-American Committee's Report. Brook simultaneously expressed the British Government's willingness to accept a 12-month target for completing the transfer of the 100,000 Jewish refugees to Palestine, but only *after* the Arabs and Jews had agreed to accept the provincial autonomy plan or some variation of it.

## *Grady hastily agrees to British proposal, including delaying immigration*

It did not take long for Brook to persuade the "inexperienced" and "outgunned"[5] Grady to accept Britain's proposals. Grady (and Morrison, shown in Figure 10.1 in separate photographs) thought it reasonable for the British Government to issue the 100,000 immigration certificates after the Jews and Arabs agreed to the provincial autonomy plan.[6] Indeed, only a few days after arriving in London, Grady reported progress in a 19 July 1946 cable to Secretary of State Byrnes:

**FIGURE 10.1** Lord Morrison (left) and Henry Grady (Public Domain)

> Since our arrival in London we have been in constant meetings with representatives of the British Cabinet and have explored numerous possible solutions to the Palestine problem. Our thinking is now along the lines of provincial autonomy under which plan Palestine would be divided into two partially self-governing Arab and Jewish provinces with an overall Central Govt. Jerusalem and the Hegeb [sic] would remain under the direct jurisdiction of the mandatory. This plan seems to offer the only means now apparent of moving the 100,000 into Palestine in the near future. It is strongly backed by the British Govt … The plan as presented by the British is almost a verbatim copy of the plan for provincial autonomy submitted anonymously to the Anglo-American Committee in January by Sir Douglas Harris of the Colonial Office.[7]

Byrnes was flabbergasted. In a return cable to Grady on 22 July 1946, Byrnes asked for clarification. If, Byrnes wrote, Grady had apparently agreed the 100,000 Jewish refugees would not be transferred until *after* the Arabs and Jews had reached agreement with the British Government regarding the provincial autonomy plan, such a process could take many months:

> Are we to understand from [your telegram] Brit do not contemplate transferring 100,000 displaced Jews from Europe to Palestine until agreement covering whole future of Palestine along lines Harris plan has been approved by both Jews and Arabs or, in case Jews and Arabs do not agree, by UN? If such is Brit attitude we are concerned lest transfer these Jews will be almost indefinitely delayed. It has been our hope that some kind of agreement might be reached between Brit and ourselves which would make it possible for transfer Jews begin near future.[8]

**FIGURE 10.2** King David Hotel bombing, 22 July 1946 (Public Domain)

But events in Palestine temporarily interceded. The bombing of the King David Hotel (Figure 10.2) in Jerusalem occurred the same day as Byrnes' return cable to Grady, 22 July 1946. The Cabinet was briefed the next day and decided to continue discussions with the United States regarding the provincial autonomy plan.[9]

On 23 July, details of the British-American discussions were leaked to the *Times of London*, including the contours of the provincial autonomy plan.[10] On 24 July, Brook notified the Cabinet that the British and American teams had completed their examination of the recommendations of the Anglo-American Committee of Inquiry, "and arrived at a common viewpoint on the broad principles of a policy for carrying out these recommendations."[11]

The joint Brook-Grady recommendation (soon renamed the "Morrison-Grady Plan") was to adopt the provincial autonomy plan for Palestine. The plan, a "complicated cantonal arrangement,"[12] would divide Palestine into four provinces with limited autonomy: an Arab province, consisting of about 40% of the area; a Jewish province, with 17%; and two British provinces, the Jerusalem district and the Negev, covering 43% of the area. The Arab province would be free to permit or refuse any Jewish settlements within its area. Land sales and Jewish immigration would be permitted in the Jewish provincial area.

The Jewish and Arab provinces would remain subordinate to an overarching British-controlled central government. President Truman viewed the arrangement as conferring very little control on the Jewish and Arab provinces, "except wholly local matters."[13]

Britain would issue the 100,000 immigration certificates for entry to the Jewish province, but only *after* both the Jews and Arabs agreed to the provincial autonomy plan, and only *after* the plan had been implemented.

Grady cabled Washington the same day to advise the State Department of the agreement he had reached with his British counterparts:[14]

> Joint committee unanimous in conviction plan agreed to is only realistic solution at this time particularly if any extensive Jewish immigration is to be realized. It leaves ample room for progress toward federation if Arabs and Jews find they can live together in harmony but in present state of tension provides for their segregation which British officials with long experience in Palestine Govt believe essential. Proposed provincial boundaries give Jews best land in Palestine, practically all citrus and industry, most of the coast line and Haifa port. Jewish legitimate demands including large measure of control of immigration and opportunity to develop national home, have been met with exception of Jerusalem and Negev. Christian interests must be taken into full account in Jerusalem and Bethlehem, and disposition of Negev is remaining undetermined until its potentialities can be ascertained.[15]

On the same day, 24 July, further details of the provincial autonomy plan (Map 10.1), including the delay in issuing the 100,000 immigration certificates, were leaked to the New York newspaper *PM*.[16] The *New York Times* carried the story on its front page two days later, complete with details of the plan and a map showing the boundaries of the proposed Jewish and Arab provinces.[17]

The Cabinet endorsed the plan on 25 July 1946. The Cabinet expressed its thanks to Brook for the "skill" he had shown "in conducting to so successful a conclusion the negotiations with the United States."[18] Following the Cabinet meeting, Attlee cabled Truman and asked him to "give urgent attention to the agreed recommendations of the two delegations and to let us have your views in the next few days."[19]

Zionist officials immediately expressed great concern. On 25 July, Dr Nahum Goldmann told Grady "if the reports accurately reflect the character of this proposal, it appears to me wholly unacceptable from our point of view."[20]

On 26 July, Grady cabled Byrnes regarding the timing of the 100,000 immigration certificates:

> I have again consulted Brook and there is not the slightest doubt that the British Government will give the green light on the 100,000 at the earliest possible moment. They do not expect formal approval of the plan from either side but are counting on "a measure of acquiescence from Arabs and Jews" and feel that it has been understood by both our Governments from the beginning that consultation and a measure of acquiescence from both is an essential preliminary to their expressing determination to go ahead with the whole plan including the 100,000. As soon as they have decided to go ahead with the plan they will at once implement the movement of the 100,000.[21]

The Morrison–Grady Plan, Based on Harris' Plan

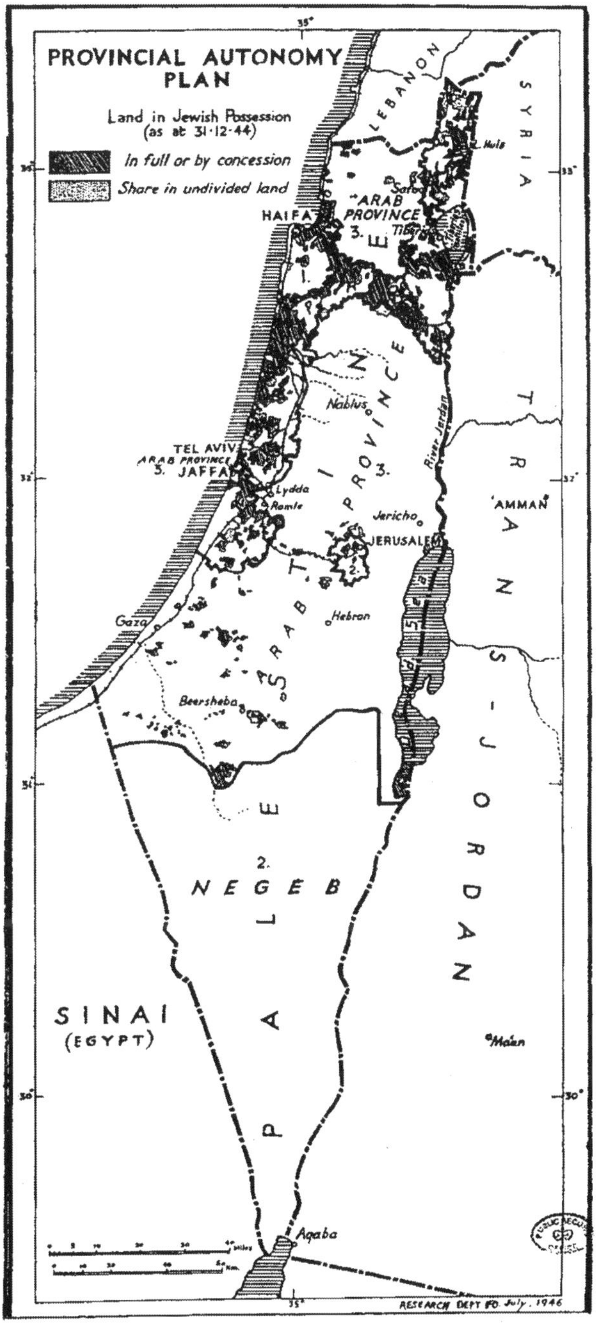


**MAP 10.1** The Morrison–Grady Provincial Autonomy Plan, July 1946 (Public Domain)

The same day, 26 July, Byrnes and Grady conferred by teletype. Grady insisted he "had not the slightest doubt as to the good faith to [sic] the British." Byrnes, however, reiterated the President's position that he wanted the Jewish immigration to begin *immediately*, and not conditioned on Arab-Jewish-British agreement regarding the provincial autonomy plan:

> We can appreciate British position. Nevertheless after the stand that the President has taken we do not see how we can enter into any arrangement which would prevent us from continuing to take the position that the 100,000 should move without awaiting for agreement on part of Arabs and Jews. That agreement might be delayed for months or years, and we would have to be silent … Any arrangement that might be made between us and the British should leave us free to insist on the transfer of the 100,000 beginning at once. We feel that we should be able to announce that we have not abandoned the position taken by the President in this regard. I understand British position but I feel that President cannot well recede from his position. All parts of program should proceed simultaneously but President's position has been that 100,000 immigration was to start immediately and he has so stated publicly time and again. Trouble with British plan is immigration never starts unless they get acquiescence of Jews and Arabs.[22]

On 27 July 1946, Grady cabled Byrnes, once again advocating for the Morrison-Grady Plan as the best way to secure the issuance of the 100,000 immigration certificates:

> I am convinced President can rely on the good faith of British Government to move with the greatest speed in the consultations … British can see the solution of the problem of Jewish immigration only through their provincial plan … I know British are as anxious for speed as we are.[23]

## The turning point: McDonald meets Truman

James McDonald, who had served on the Anglo-American Committee, met with President Truman, also on 27 July 1946. Senators Robert Wagner and James Mead, both Democrats from New York, also attended the Oval Office meeting.

McDonald brought a one-page memorandum he had prepared for the President. The memorandum argued against the provincial autonomy plan because it conditioned the issuance of the 100,000 immigration certificates on Arab approval, "an acceptance which I am almost certain will not be given." The plan likewise put the Jews to the Hobson's choice of either accepting the 100,000 immigration certificates and surrendering "all Jewish rights under the Balfour Declaration and the Mandate and of all their historic hopes" or rejecting the plan and losing the 100,000 immigrants.[24]

McDonald further argued in the 27 July memorandum that the provincial autonomy plan would create a "Jewish Ghetto" in an area comprising "but one-thirtieth of the original Palestine envisioned under the Balfour Declaration" and would leave the country "indefinitely under an even more rigid and absolute control by the British."[25]

With his memorandum in hand, McDonald entered the Oval Office with the two senators for what quickly turned into a highly contentious meeting with President Truman. The meeting, however, would prove to be one of the most pivotal in the entire history of Zionism, even though no Jews were present.

According to McDonald's typewritten summary of the meeting (a copy of which ended up in Weizmann's hands),[26] McDonald argued vociferously against the provincial autonomy plan. The provincial autonomy plan, McDonald insisted to the President, embodied all the disadvantages of partition, with none of the advantages. "You have been badly served. You sent bad men" to work with the British Government, McDonald told the President. "You must refuse to be a party to it."

McDonald said the provincial autonomy plan was so bad, "the Jews would rather not have the 100,000 [immigration certificates] than have the plan. I told him [Truman] that if we get the 100,000 at the price of this then he will go down in history as anathema. [Truman] exploded at this point."[27] The two Senators later told McDonald "they had never seen as frank a statement by a non-politician to the President."[28]

McDonald told the President he "had no object in coming in except to tell the truth." The President said "I want to hear it. I hear it too seldom." McDonald described the President as "definitely combative and at times even angry. But I have gotten too old to be troubled by the anger of a President."[29]

McDonald's candour made an impression on Truman. Two years later, Truman would appoint McDonald to serve as the first-ever United States Ambassador to Israel.[30]

## *Truman's volte-face*

The President and his Cabinet, mindful of the intense domestic political implications, decided on 30 July 1946 not to endorse the provincial autonomy plan but instead to recall Grady's team from London for consultations with the US members of the Anglo-American Committee.[31]

Rabbi Abba Hillel Silver of the American Zionist Emergency Council described Truman's decision to recall Grady as a "sudden, almost miraculous last minute shift."[32] The news shocked and angered British Ambassador Lord Inverchapel, who cabled London just after midnight on 31 July, advising Truman had decided to reject the Morrison-Grady Plan:

> It is acutely embarrassing for us that, on the eve of debate in Parliament, the President should have rejected the proposed statement approved both

> by Grady and Byrnes. The entirely anodyne announcement which Mr. Truman is preparing to make in its stead and his decision to recall the United States delegates for further consultation can hardly be otherwise interpreted than as denoting that at present, the administration intend drastically to recast the recommendations jointly agreed upon in London if not to reject them *in toto*. This deplorable display if weakness is, I fear, solely attributable to domestic politics which, it will be recalled, caused the administration last year to use every artifice to delay the announcement about the establishment of the Anglo-American Committee until after the New York elections. The director of the Near Eastern Division [Loy Henderson], the official in the State Department responsible for handing the Palestine question, frankly admitted as much in a talk with me this evening. But for the attitude of the Zionists, he declared, there was nothing in the joint [Morrison-Grady] recommendations which would not have been acceptable to the United States Government. Unfortunately, the Zionists had seen fit to condemn the recommendations root and branch.[33]

Later that same morning, 31 July 1946, US Ambassador Averell Harriman called on Prime Minister Attlee and delivered a letter announcing the President's decision to abandon the Morrison-Grady proposal and recall Grady to Washington for consultations. Harriman reported the meeting to Washington, noting:

> [Attlee] was confused, however, as to what the British Govt's position regarding the plan should now be. He said that the British Govt's confidence in the success of the plan had been based on the US giving it moral as well as financial support. He has doubts whether the British Govt could force it alone. He emphasized his fear of increased chaos in Palestine. He showed keen disappointment that this plan could not have the support of the US as it was the only one yet devised which in the opinion of the British Govt would make it possible to bring into Palestine promptly the hundred thousand Jews. I explained to him the public reaction to the plan in the US with which the President was confronted. He expressed the hope that the President would give sympathetic consideration to the serious difficulties which confronted the British Govt in Palestine and in the Middle East from Arabs as well as Jews.[34]

## Britain presses ahead with provincial autonomy

That same afternoon, 31 July 1946, Lord Morrison unveiled the provincial autonomy plan in a speech to the House of Commons, despite the American decision to recall Grady for consultations:

> The only chance of peace, and of immediate advance towards self-governing institutions, appears to lie in so framing the constitution of the country

> as to give to each the greatest practicable measure of power to manage its own affairs. The experts believe that, in present circumstances, this can best be secured by the establishment of Arab and Jewish Provinces, which will enjoy a large measure of autonomy under a central Government. It is their proposal that, for this purpose, Palestine shall be divided into four areas, an Arab Province, a Jewish Province, a District of Jerusalem and a District of Negeb. The Jewish Province would include the great bulk of the land on which Jews have already settled and a considerable area between and around the settlements. The Jerusalem District would include Jerusalem, Bethlehem and their immediate environs. The Negeb District would consist of the uninhabited triangle of waste land in the South of Palestine beyond the present limits of cultivation. The Arab Province would include the remainder of Palestine; it would be almost wholly Arab in respect both of land and of population.[35]

Byrnes, who was in Paris attending a peace conference, cabled Truman on 31 July after Lord Morrison's speech to the House. Byrnes noted that because the United States had walked away from the provincial autonomy plan, Washington had lost all leverage to demand Britain issue the 100,000 immigration certificates:

> The British are disappointed and do not like our action but the purpose of my message … was to let you know that if you declined to agree to the proposals it would not embarrass me. Yesterday I advised Wise and Goldmann that my opinion was, in the absence of agreement the British will not agree to the immigration of 100,000 or any part of it, and that they could not look to you to bring about such immigration because there was no way you could force Britain to act. I think it would be wise for the present not to make public any further demand about the 100,000 in order to avoid newspaper conflict with Attlee. Grady's committee returning immediately.[36]

## American recrimination

Truman's decision to recall Grady emboldened at least two members of Grady's staff to leak to the press their complaints that Grady had ignored his instructions from Washington to insist on rapid issuance of the 100,000 immigration certificates. The unnamed staffers accused Grady of caving early in the discussions to Britain's desire to condition issuance of the certificates on Arab-Jewish agreement with the provincial autonomy plan. Grady, they charged, "put up no fight for the previously agreed United States position that the admission of 100,000 refugees should be kept separate from the long-term proposals."[37]

The White House, apparently still trying to find a way to reconcile its objective regarding the 100,000 immigration certificates with the provincial autonomy plan, requested the State Department to summon the six American members of the Anglo-American Committee to attend a meeting at the State Department with Grady, to see if they could square their recommendations with Grady's. Hutcheson and his colleagues stood firm, criticising the provincial autonomy plan as a "bill of goods" that had been sold to Grady. McDonald wrote shortly afterwards that the meeting "gave the *coup d'grace* to the Grady proposal."[38]

In an August 1946 letter to Crossman, Judge Hutcheson wrote,

> My whole attitude has been that I feel that our report was an excellent document, that we deliberately avoided trying to set up the form the government should take because we were dealing with principles, and we didn't want someone to seize hold of the form we might suggest as though it were an essential part of our principles.[39]

Grady, still believing he had been right to make the deal with Brook, later disclosed in his draft, unpublished memoir that Truman told him privately he viewed the provincial autonomy plan as "the best of all the solutions proposed for Palestine."[40]

But Truman, unable to obtain the support of the American members of the Anglo-American Committee, and unable to overcome American Zionist opposition, officially notified Attlee on 12 August 1946 that he had "reluctantly come to the conclusion that I cannot give formal support to [the Morrison-Grady] plan in its present form as a joint Anglo-American plan."[41]

In early September 1946, Grady had lunch with his old friend Cyril Cane, the British Consul General in San Francisco. Grady, apparently without authorisation, shared in detail with Cane his grievances about Truman's rejection of the Morrison-Grady agreement. Cane promptly reported to the British Embassy in Washington, DC what Grady had told him:

> Grady … gave me a detailed account of his committee's work and the reasons for the non-acceptance of their recommendations … Grady was very anxious not to criticize the President and said that he (Truman) was in favor of the plan, but that he wanted backing and so called in the Hutchinson [sic] Committee in the hope that they would come out in favour of it. Unfortunately, Judge Hutchinson [sic] came to look upon his Committee's report as his brainchild and could not bear to have any changes made. The other members, of whom Crum is the most sinister and unprincipled, backed Hutchinson to the limit …[42]

## Jewish agency partition proposal

Meanwhile, on 7 August 1946, Nahum Goldmann of the Jewish Agency launched a new diplomatic initiative, advising Acting Secretary of State Dean

Acheson of a new proposal the Jewish Agency had approved two days earlier. The key elements of the plan included the following:

- The immediate partitioning of Palestine into three areas: Jewish, Arab and the Holy Places; the Jewish area roughly to include the territory assigned to the Jews by the Peel Commission partition plan, plus the Negev; the Arab area would include the remainder except for the Holy Places;
- Statehood for the Jewish area within three years;
- Permitting the Jews to set up their own administration and enjoy considerable home rule in economic matters pending the establishment of the independent Jewish state; and
- Permitting the Jews, immediately upon adoption of the Plan, to have full control of immigration into their area.[43]

On 9 August 1946, Truman's advisor David Niles told Goldman the President had accepted the Jewish partition proposal "without reservation."[44]

On 15 August 1946, Bevin and Hall briefed US Ambassador Harriman on a discussion with the Zionist leaders. The Zionists wanted assurances from Britain that if an Arab-Jewish conference were to be convened, then the Zionist partition proposal would form the basis for discussions between the parties.

Bevin and Hall said the British Government intended to propose the Morrison-Grady Plan instead, despite President Truman's decision not to support it. Bevin and Hall also told Harriman they would consider the Jewish Agency's partition proposal and proposals from the Arabs as well.[45] Indeed, the British Government knew as early as August 1946 that King Abdullah of Jordan and his Prime Minister both favoured "partition followed by an exchange of populations as the only practical solution to the Palestine problem."[46]

## Another failed London Conference

Attlee reiterated the Government's position in a cable to Truman on 19 August 1946, noting the Government would propose the Morrison-Grady Plan at the upcoming London Conference, and the Jews would be free to offer their own proposals.[47] But by then, the Jewish side had already advised Bevin they would not attend the conference unless the Jewish Agency proposals were made the basis of discussions.[48]

On 9 September 1946, the British Government convened the conference on Palestine at Lancaster House in London. Representatives of various Arab states were present, but no Jewish or Palestinian Arab representatives attended.[49] Attlee and the Syrian delegate spoke at the opening session. Over the next few days, Bevin offered certain principles as the basis for negotiations, including that "some institutions must be set up which will enable both peoples in Palestine to govern themselves more and more."[50]

The Arabs countered several days later, insisting among other things the Mandate be terminated and Palestine be declared an independent, "unitary state." The Arabs also demanded an immediate halt to Jewish immigration.[51] The British Government took the Arab counter-proposals under advisement, adjourning the conference on 2 October and announcing the conference would resume on 16 December 1946.[52]

President Truman reacted to the adjournment of the conference with a lengthy statement, once again urging Britain to issue the 100,000 immigration certificates immediately.[53] Truman's statement drew a sharp rebuke from Saudi King Ibn Saud, who again invoked the Arab and Palestinian injustice narrative:

> I am confident that the American people who spent their blood and their money freely to resist aggression, could not possibly support Zionist aggression against a friendly Arab country which has committed no crime except to believe firmly in those principles of *justice* and equality, for which the United Nations, including the United States, fought, and for which both your predecessor and you exerted great efforts. My desire to preserve the friendship of the Arabs and the East towards the United States of America has obliged me to expound to Your Excellency the *injustice* which would be visited upon the Arabs by any assistance to Zionist aggression.[54]

Ultimately, the London Conference reconvened in January 1947, with British officials conducting separate talks with the Jews and Arabs.[55] A month later, Britain, unable to reconcile conflicting Arab and Zionist demands, without American support for the provincial autonomy plan, and exhausted after nearly three decades of frustrating, difficult rule in Palestine, finally threw in the towel and handed the problem to the United Nations.

## Notes

1 President Truman appointed the Secretaries of State, Treasury, and War on 11 June 1946 as a Special Cabinet Committee on Palestine and related issues. The President asked the Committee to appoint alternate members to participate in discussions with the British Government regarding the Anglo-American Committee Report. Secretary of State Byrnes designated Grady as his alternate to lead the American side. Executive Order 9735 (11 June 1946); *Department of State Bulletin* at 1089-90 (23 June 1946); *see also* FO 371/52525, Telegram No. 4799 (Top Secret and Personal) from Foreign Office to Lord Halifax, British Embassy, Washington, DC (17 May 1946). Cabinet Secretary Sir Norman Brook took the lead for the British side in discussions with Brady and the American team. For further background, see M.N. Penkower (2019), *op. cit.*, at 230 *et seq.*; M.J. Haron, *op. cit.*, at 203–4.

2 FRUS, 867N.01/6–1046, Telegram (Secret) from Secretary of State to US Ambassador W. Averell Harriman, London (10 June 1946); FRUS, 867N.01/6–1446, Telegram (Secret) from Truman to Attlee (14 June 1946) ("I consider that our two Governments should without delay endeavor to make detailed plans for the transfer of the 100,000 Jews to Palestine. These plans would thus be ready for use when definite decisions are made. I feel moreover that considerable time would be saved, when the two Governments discuss all

of the various matters relating to the report, if such plans had already been devised. It is for this reason that we are instructing our Ambassador in London, Mr. Harriman, to initiate preliminary conversations at once with representatives of your Government relative to these technical and physical problems. He will be assisted by a group of representatives of the State and War Departments who are proceeding to London this week").

3 FRUS, 867N.01/6–1446, Telegram (Top Secret) from Attlee to Truman (14 June 1946).

4 The American team arrived in London on 12 July 1946. FRUS, 867N.01/7–1546, Telegram from US Embassy, London to State Department (12 July 1946).

5 M. Jones, *op. cit.*, at 134; E. Wilson, *op. cit.*, at 95 (State Department officials were "surprised" Grady had agreed "so readily" to the provincial autonomy plan).

6 L. Dinnerstein, *op. cit.*, at 298–9.

7 FRUS, 867N.01/7–1946, Telegram No. 6851 (Top Secret) from US Embassy, London (Grady) to Secretary of State (19 July 1946).

8 FRUS, 867N.01/7–1946, Telegram No. 5541 (Top Secret) from Byrnes to Grady (22 July 1946).

9 CAB 128/6/10, C.M. (46) 72, Conclusions (Secret) of a Meeting of the Cabinet (23 July 1946).

10 "Anglo-U.S. Talks on Palestine," *The Times*, 23 July 1946 at 4.

11 CAB 129/11/45, C.P. (46) 295 (Top Secret), Palestine: Statement of Policy (24 July 1946); *see also* CAB 129/12/8, C.P. (46) 308 (30 July 1946) (Top Secret) (same, slightly amended).

12 K. Roosevelt, *The Partition of Palestine: A Lesson in Pressure Politics*, The Middle East Journal 2:1 at 12 (1948).

13 H. Truman, *op. cit.*, at 151–2.

14 FRUS, 867N.01/72446, Telegram (Top Secret) No. 6970 from US Embassy, London (Grady) to State Department (24 July 1946). The text of Grady's telegram was nearly identical to the version Sir Norman Brook presented to the Cabinet in his 24 July 1946 Memorandum (C.P. (46) 295).

15 FRUS, 867N.01/7–2446, Telegram No. 6952 (Secret) from Grady to Byrnes (24 July 1946).

16 N. Goda, *op. cit.*, at 246, citing F. Kuh, "British Plan for Palestine," PM Daily 8, no. 32 at 1 (24 July 1946).

17 "Divided Palestine is Urged by Anglo-U.S. Cabinet Body, Delaying Entry of 100,000," *New York Times*, 26 July 1946 at 1.

18 CAB 128/6/11, C.M. 73 (46), Conclusions (Secret) of a Meeting of the Cabinet (25 July 1946); *see also* A. Kochavi, *op. cit.*, at 154.

19 Truman Archives, Telegram No. 3027 (Top Secret) from Attlee to Truman (25 July 1946).

20 FRUS, 867N.01/7–2546, Telegram No. 6975 (Confidential) from Grady to Byrnes (25 July 1946) (quoting letter received from Dr Goldmann earlier that day); *see also* FRUS, 867N.01/8–1246, Telegram No. 5973 (Top Secret) from Acting Secretary of State to US Ambassador Harriman (12 August 1946) ("Premature leaks from London re contents recommendations incorporated in Morrison Plan gave groups in this country opposed to plan opportunity mobilize so much public sentiment against it that Cabinet Committee and President felt they could not agree accept recommendations at least until they had studied and discussed them in detail. Alternates of Cabinet Committee, American members of Anglo-American Committee, the Cabinet Committee, other members of Cabinet and various interested persons and groups have participated in the discussions. During discussions, it has become clear that it would be unwise for President to give his formal support to Plan in its present form. President feels that in view opposition to Plan, he would not be able to prevail on Congress to agree to financial contributions for its implementation nor to rally sufficient public support to warrant undertaking by this Govt to give plan in its present form moral backing").

21 FRUS, 867N.01/7–2646, Telegram No. 7030 (Top Secret) from Grady to Byrnes (26 July 1946).

22 FRUS, 867N.01/7–2646, Record of Teletype Conference between Washington and London (Secret) (26 July 1946).

23 FRUS, 867N.01/7–2746, Telegram No. 7082 from Grady to Byrnes (27 July 1946).
24 James Grover McDonald Collection, Rare Book & Manuscript Library, Columbia University in the City of New York, Box 5, File 1, Memorandum from McDonald to President Truman (27 July 1946); *see also* R. Ovendale, *Britain, the United States and the end of the Palestine Mandate* at 147 (Royal Historical Society, 1989) (describing Zionist reaction to Morrison-Grady Plan: "Not only would it delay admission of the refugees but it would destroy practically all the rights of the Jewish people which had been internationally guaranteed").
25 James Grover McDonald Collection, Rare Book & Manuscript Library, Columbia University in the City of New York, Box 5, File 1, Memorandum from McDonald to President Truman (27 July 1946).
26 Weizmann Archives 19-2678 (Secret), J. McDonald, J.M.D.'s Report on his and Wagner's and Mead's Conversation with the President on 27 July 1946.
27 *Id.*
28 *Id.* Two days after the Oval Office meeting, McDonald wrote a conciliatory note to Truman and offered his help with the Jewish refugee problem. Truman responded quickly, saying he hoped he had not been "too hard" on McDonald during the Oval Office meeting. James Grover McDonald Collection, Rare Book & Manuscript Library, Columbia University in the City of New York, Box 5, File 1, Letter from McDonald to Truman (29 July 1946), Letter from Truman to McDonald (31 July 1946).
29 Weizmann Archives 19-2678 (Secret), J. McDonald, J.M.D.'s Report on his and Wagner's and Mead's Conversation with the President on 27 July 1946.
30 "Truman Appoints Mission to Israel," *New York Times*, 23 June 1948 at 24; *see also* James Grover McDonald Collection, Rare Book & Manuscript Library, Columbia University in the City of New York, Box 5, File 1, Letter from Truman to McDonald (21 July 1948) (congratulating McDonald on his appointment and asking McDonald to keep Truman "personally informed" regarding a variety of sensitive issues).
31 M.J. Cohen (1990), *op. cit.,* at 131–6.
32 Central Zionist Archives, Z5/1172, American Zionist Emergency Council (Confidential), Minutes of Executive Committee Meeting, 1 August 1946, *reprinted in* M.J. Cohen (ed.), *The Rise of Israel (Vol. 35): The Anglo-American Committee on Palestine 1945–1946* at 325 (Garland, 1987).
33 FO 371/52546, Telegram No. 4862 (Cypher) from Lord Inverchapel to Foreign Office (31 July 1946); *see also* FRUS, 867N.01/7–3046, D. Acheson, Memorandum of Conversation, by the Acting Secretary of State (30 July 1946) ("The Ambassador expressed regret as well as the thought that this development would cause an embarrassing situation for the Prime Minister. He said that he understood fully the considerations which had moved the President to this conclusion since he was thoroughly informed of the discussion of this matter in the American press").
34 FRUS, 867N.01/7–3146, Telegram No. 3744 (Top Secret) from Harriman to State Department (31 July 1946).
35 Hansard, HC Deb., vol. 426, col. 965 (31 July 1946). Lord Morrison finessed the bad news received earlier that morning regarding Truman's reversal, telling the House, "We had hoped before the Debate to receive from President Truman his acceptance, but we understand that he has decided, in view of the complexity of the matter, to discuss it in detail with the United States expert delegation who are returning to Washington for the purpose. The President is thus giving further consideration to the matter, and we hope to hear again from him in due course." *Id.*, col. 969.
36 FRUS, 740.00119 Council/7–3146, Telegram No. 3743 (Top Secret) from Byrnes to Truman (31 July 1946).
37 "Staff Raps Grady on Palestine Plan," *New York Times*, 3 August 1946 at 1.
38 N. Goda, *op. cit.*, at 252–3, quoting McDonald letter to Eddie Cantor (27 August 1946); *see also* R. Ovendale, *op. cit.*, at 150–1; E. Wilson (1973), *op. cit.,* at 51 (Wilson had served as one of the two American Secretaries to the Committee).

39 Crossman Papers, GB 165-0068, Middle East Centre Archive, St. Antony's College, Oxford, Anglo-American Committee Papers, Anglo-American Committee Papers, File 1, Letter from Judge Hutcheson to Crossman (16 August 1946).

40 H.F. Grady, *Adventures in Diplomacy* (draft, unpublished) at 163–4, Truman Library, accessible at https://www.trumanlibrary.gov/library/research-files/chapter-9-unpublished-manuscript-henry-grady-adventures-diplomacy?documentid=NA&pagenumber=14 (last accessed 4 August 2020).

41 FRUS, 867N.01/8–1246, Telegram (Top Secret) from Truman to Attlee (12 August 1946).

42 FO 371/52558, Letter from C. Cane to J. Balfour (Very Confidential) (7 September 1946).

43 FRUS, 867N.01/8–1246, Telegram No. 5973 (Top Secret) from Acting Secretary of State to Ambassador Harriman (12 August 1946).

44 N. Goldmann, *The Autobiography of Nahum Goldmann* at 235 (Holt, Rinehart, 1969). The Radoshes describe the August meeting between Niles and Goldmann as "a major turning point in the evolution of Truman's view of the Palestine Crisis." A. Radosh and S. Radosh, *op. cit.*, at 182.

45 FRUS, 867N.01/8–1546, Telegram No. 7552 (Top Secret) from US Embassy, London to State Department (15 August 1946).

46 FO 371/52556, Telegram No. 59 (Secret) from British Embassy, Amman to Foreign Office (27 August 1946).

47 FRUS, 867N.01/8–1946, Telegram (Top Secret) from Attlee to Truman, para. 4 (19 August 1946). The Chief Secretary of the Palestine Government, Sir John Shaw, sent formal notifications to the relevant Palestinian Arab and Jewish representatives that the London Conference would convene on 9 September, and that the British Government intended to include the Morrison-Grady Plan "as the first item on the agenda." Sir Alan Cunningham Papers, GB 165-0072, Box 5, File 2, Middle East Centre Archive, St. Antony's College, Oxford, Letters from Shaw dated 27 August 1946 to the Arab side and 5 September 1946 to the Jewish side.

48 FRUS, 740.00119 Council/8–2146, Telegram (Top Secret) from Harriman to Acting Secretary of States (21 August 1946) ("On Sunday [18 August] he [Bevin] had word from the Jews that they declined to participate except on their terms"); *see also* 867N.01/9–546, Memorandum of Conversation by the Assistant Chief of the Division of Near Eastern Affairs (Wilson) ("Mr. Epstein called at the request of Dr. Goldmann, of the Agency Executive, to inform the Department that the Executive had reluctantly decided that it could not accept the invitation of the British Government to the proposed conference on Palestine under the conditions proposed … He said that the decision had only been reached after the most serious consideration, but that the terms imposed by the British for the Agency's attendance were not acceptable. The most serious obstacle in this connection was the insistance [sic] of the British on putting forward the Morrison–Grady Plan as the basis for discussion").

49 FO 371/52565, Cover note to Bevin enclosing Memorandum (Secret) entitled "Palestine," prepared by Foreign Office for US Secretary of State Byrnes at para. 36 (23 November 1946).

50 FRUS, 867N.01/9–1746, Telegram No. 8214 (Secret) from US Embassy, London to State Department (17 September 1946).

51 FRUS, 867N.01/9–2346, Telegram No. 8349 (Secret) from US Embassy, London to State Department (23 September 1946).

52 FRUS, 867N.01/10–246, Telegram No. 8572 (Urgent) from US Embassy, London to State Department (2 October 1946); *see also* A. Kochavi, *op. cit.*, at 157.

53 FRUS, 867N.01/10–346, Telegram from Truman to Attlee (3 October 1946). The telegram contained the entire text of the President's statement, which was made public the following day, 4 October 1946.

54 FRUS, 867N.01/10–1546, Letter from Abdul Aziz Ibn Saud to President Truman (15 October 1946) (emphasis added).

55 C. Sykes, *op. cit.*, at 309–10.

# 11

# ASSESSMENT

The Anglo-American Committee, under the leadership of Justice Singleton and Judge Hutcheson, conducted a "trial," not in the traditional meaning of the word, but in the sense that the twelve Committee members acting as judges and jurors spent three months investigating the plight of European Jewry and the future governance of Palestine. The Committee took testimony from scores of witnesses, subjecting many of them to searing cross-examination.

The witnesses all invoked the transformational legal framing they had developed during the last 25 years before the previous inquiry commissions and the Permanent Mandates Commission. The Arab witnesses repeatedly framed the conflict as a clash between justice and injustice, interweaving legal narrative throughout their testimony and written submissions. Weizmann cleverly appropriated the Arab justice/injustice narrative for the Jewish side, reframing it as a matter of the "least injustice," appealing directly to the Anglo-American Committee's familiarity with the British common law notion of "balancing the equities."

The Committee toured the rubble of the European war zones and saw at first hand the immeasurable suffering of Europe's surviving Jews. The Committee members visited the key Arab capitals of Cairo, Baghdad, Amman, Damascus, Jedda, and Beirut and spent nearly three weeks in Jerusalem and Palestine.

The British Government pressed the Truman Administration to agree to form the Committee in an effort to alleviate the enormous pressure from the White House to permit the immediate immigration of 100,000 European Jewish refugees to Palestine. Whitehall hoped the strategy would not only buy time but would also convince the Truman Administration to support the White Paper policy and share the political, financial, and military burdens for keeping the peace in Palestine.

DOI: 10.4324/9781003225263-15

The Truman Administration, for its part, accepted the British offer to participate in the Joint Committee as a means of obtaining a seat at the table of Middle East policy, which Britain and, to a lesser extent, France had monopolised since the Sykes-Picot Agreement of 1916.

Bevin wanted Lord Halifax to keep Palestine out of the Terms of Reference, to avoid signalling the Committee and the public that the European Jewish refugee and the Palestine issues were linked. But the Harrison Report's impact on President Truman made that objective impossible for Halifax in his negotiations with Byrnes. Once the Terms of Reference were set, formally including both the Jewish refugees and the Palestine issues, the linkage had been cemented.

Ironically, once the Committee had delivered its verdict, Britain reversed course and insisted the immigration issue *must* be linked to the Palestine issue, arguing the verdict needed to be read as a unified whole and thus the immigration recommendations could not be implemented unless the *Haganah* was disarmed first.

Commenting on the conflicting British and American objectives, one historian noted,

> The fact remains that the British government did not accept the recommendations and the American government had neither the authority nor the will to execute them on her own. Moreover, the goals of the British and American governments differed widely. Officials in London and Washington did not perceive this dichotomy as acutely as did the members of the Anglo-American Committee of Inquiry. The British government really wanted support for a pro-Arab, anti-Russian policy in Palestine. Truman, more sympathetic than the British to aspirations of the Zionists and the plight of DPs in Europe, hoped to alleviate the sufferings of the European Jews while not alienating Palestinian Arabs. This, ultimately, could not be done. American politicians had to listen carefully to the representatives of the articulate, well-financed, and well-organized Zionists. The British did not. But the British government had to grapple with the problems of a disintegrating Empire, of which Palestine was only a part. And as a result of the conflicting national demands the Anglo-American Committee of Inquiry's report could not be accepted as written.[1]

But that assessment misses the key point. What the Committee did not appreciate at first, but by the time it had arrived in Lausanne appreciated fully, was that all along the key issue on trial was not the 100,000 immigration certificates, or even the future form of government for Palestine. Instead, by the time the Committee arrived in Lausanne, Hutcheson had grasped the larger picture, and so had most of the rest of the Committee. They realised the White Paper and British policy itself had been on trial from the beginning and now awaited the Committee's verdict.

The Committee spent its final three weeks locked in tense and often acrimonious deliberations over their verdict. When they arrived in Lausanne, the Committee seemed hopelessly divided into at least two and perhaps three separate factions. But by the time they left, the Committee had rendered a unanimous verdict, issuing a stunning denunciation of the White Paper and British policy in Palestine.

To that extent, therefore, Crossman's description of the Committee's Report as "a compromise document" missed the mark. The Committee's verdict overwhelmingly rebuked the White Paper, depriving it of all legal and moral validity, and forcing the British Government to abandon it once and for all.

In many respects, the Committee's verdict affirmed the Permanent Mandates Commission's position in August 1939 that the White Paper had violated the Mandate. But the Council of the League never had the chance to formally urge Britain to rescind the White Paper and/or take Britain to the Permanent Court of International Justice over the White Paper's violation of the Mandate. The twelve American and British members of the Committee finished the job by unanimously pronouncing the White Paper dead once and for all.

British policy had finally been adjudged guilty, by unanimous verdict of a tribunal containing six Americans and six eminent British citizens, of betraying Britain's legal obligations under the Mandate.

The remainder of the Committee's verdict, however, represented a carefully crafted compromise, upholding the legality of the Mandate and granting a form of equitable relief both to the Jews (the 100,000 immigration certificates) and the Arabs (no Jewish statehood). The Committee's willingness to compromise may have been driven by Bevin's commitment at the February luncheon that he would support and implement a unanimous verdict.

But the compromise left no one happy. The Arabs were upset that Britain had backtracked on the White Paper. The Jews, initially pleased with the recommendation to issue the 100,000 immigration certificates, quickly felt betrayed by Attlee's insistence on disarming the *Haganah* as a condition precedent for issuing the 100,000 immigration certificates. The British Government was infuriated with its own hand-picked Committee members, and by what it viewed as the Truman Administration's bowing to Zionist pressure.

Moreover, the Committee's compromise verdict failed to create a realistic road map for resolving the conflict. Britain's initial insistence on disarming the *Haganah* as a condition for allowing the 100,000 immigration certificates, and its subsequent effort to persuade Grady to set aside the Report in favour of the provincial autonomy plan, doomed the Report "to the oblivion of departmental archives, along with those of its many worthy predecessors."[2]

One historian has argued the Anglo-American Committee "discounted" the Arab witnesses "for their lack of sympathy" with the plight of European Jewry,[3] but there is little evidence to support that claim. The transcripts of the hearings reveal nearly every Arab witness expressed humanitarian *sympathy* with the plight of the European Jews, even while denying the Arabs bore any *responsibility* for the Holocaust or the refugee issue. The Arab witnesses emphasised the problem of European Jewry was a *European* problem requiring a *European* solution, *not* a Palestinian solution. Yet that did not mean the Arab witnesses had demonstrated a lack of sympathy for the Jewish refugees.

A more accurate assessment of the Arab witnesses would instead focus on their lack of *empathy* with the Zionist dream of building a Jewish state in even a small corner of Palestine. The Palestinian and other Arab witnesses uniformly rejected *any* form of Jewish statehood in *any* portion of Palestine, no matter how tiny.

Ironically, however, by framing the issue as an absolute battle between justice and injustice, the Palestinian Arabs likely lost their chance for statehood in all of Palestine. The Committee realised the 600,000 existing Jews in Palestine would face great peril if placed under Arab rule. Nor would it be acceptable to place the Arab majority under Jewish rule. The one-state solution in favor of the Palestinian Arabs embraced by the White Paper was, in the Committee's view, doomed to fail.

The Committee felt the same way about the two-state solution, rejecting it as not viable either, despite Crossman's efforts to promote it. No wonder Judge Hutcheson, who had always opposed partition, reacted so strongly against the Morrison-Grady provincial autonomy plan at the August 1946 State Department meeting with Grady.

The leading historian of the Anglo-American Committee, Amikam Nachmani, summed up the outcome of the Committee's work as a failure of British diplomacy, a failure of the legal process as a means of addressing the conflict, and a turning point in the history of the Middle East:

> [U]nder Hutcheson's guidance, the Committee torpedoed almost all the hopes invested in it … [i]f there were expectations that the [Committee] would acknowledge Britain's difficulties in Palestine, thus recognizing the White Paper as the equitable solution, the Committee's recommendation to abolish the White Paper put an end to them. The same was true of the hopes that some political solution would come out of the Inquiry; they were laid to rest by the legalistic approach to the problem and by the fact that the Bench ruled out whatever was not strictly judicial; and not within the terms of reference. It was only a year and a half later, in retrospect, that Hutcheson remarked: "In international relations many solutions must be accepted which fall short of doing justice." His insistence during the inquiry on admitting courtroom evidence only resulted in the non-consideration of the partition solution.[4]

Evan Wilson, who had served as one of the two American secretaries to the Committee, offered his own assessment decades later:

> To return to the Report of the Anglo-American Committee, it can be said that the Report, for all its generalities, represented a determined effort by men of good will to find a reasonable and moderate solution. By that

> time however, it was too late for the sort of compromise which the members of the Committee evidently had in mind. As for the Morrison-Grady proposals, they were not seriously considered by our policy-makers once they had been rejected by the President. In any case, as events were soon to show, the only way to bring about a settlement at this stage would have been for the British and American governments to agree on a fixed course of action and implement it jointly with the use of such force as might prove necessary.[5]

★★★★★

The Anglo-American Committee of Inquiry delivered a resounding verdict against the British Government's White Paper policy. The Committee rejected both the one-state solution in favour of the Palestinian Arabs and the White Paper's draconian limitations on Jewish immigration and land acquisition. Britain's failed Morrison-Grady gambit embarrassed Whitehall further, laying bare Britain's severely diminished post-War authority and prestige in Palestine.

Indeed, the Anglo-American Committee marked the beginning of the American ascent as the pre-eminent power in the Middle East. Nevertheless, the Anglo-American Committee's verdict failed to advance the prospects for a settlement of the Palestine problem. The Committee's endorsement of a "no-state" solution left both the Jews and Arabs equally dissatisfied, ultimately forcing Britain to ponder the harsh reality that it could no longer afford to continue serving as the Mandatory power in Palestine.

Judge Hutcheson, more than anyone else, brought about the demise of the White Paper by successfully manoeuvring and cajoling the Committee to deliver a unanimous verdict. And James McDonald, more than anyone else, doomed the Morrison-Grady plan by telling President Truman he would go down in history as "anathema" if he abandoned his repeated demands that Britain immediately issue the 100,000 immigration certificates. Thus, two Christian Americans, a federal appellate judge from Texas and a diplomat from Ohio, hastened the end of decades of British rule in Palestine and paved the way for the United Nations to decide the country's future.

## Notes

1 L. Dinnerstein, *op. cit.*, at 300.
2 M.J. Cohen (1979), *op. cit.,* at 206.
3 L. Allen, *op. cit.*, at 408.
4 A. Nachmani, *op. cit.*, at 271.
5 E. Wilson, *op. cit.*, at 53.

# PART IV

# UNSCOP and the UN Ad Hoc Committee – Palestinian nationalism on trial and the two-state solution

# 12

# UNSCOP HEARINGS AND VERDICT

## The United Nations and Palestine

By January 1947, the British Government realised it was running out of options in Palestine. The Morrison-Grady provincial autonomy plan had failed to win support from the Palestinian Arabs, the Zionists, and the Truman Administration. Britain's effort to revive the plan at the London Conference in September 1946 likewise failed, after the Zionists declined to participate in further negotiations about the proposal.

The Zionist leadership, however, indicated a willingness to discuss partitioning the country into two states, as the Peel Commission had recommended in July 1937. The Palestinian Arabs, meanwhile, continued to insist on immediate Arab sovereignty over *all* of Palestine, and a complete halt to further Jewish immigration.

### *Britain explores its legal options*

Against this backdrop, the British Government, as it had done since the beginning of the Mandate, sought legal advice regarding its options for Palestine. The legal advisers to the Foreign and Colonial Offices prepared a joint memorandum in January 1947 analysing whether Britain would need to obtain prior legal approval from the United Nations either for partitioning the country into separate Jewish and Arab states or imposing the provincial autonomy plan.[1]

The legal memorandum first noted, "the United Nations has no automatic jurisdiction over Palestine merely by virtue of its being a mandated territory." Article 77 of the UN Charter left "for subsequent agreement" any decision regarding which mandated territories would be "brought under the trusteeship system and upon what terms." Moreover, Article 80 of the Charter required

DOI: 10.4324/9781003225263-17

all pre-existing international agreements (such as the Palestine Mandate) to continue in force "except as may be agreed upon in individual trusteeship agreements."[2]

The legal memorandum next discussed whether Britain would need United Nations' approval to partition Palestine into separate Jewish and Arab states. The legal memorandum concluded such approval would be required:

> [I]nasmuch as Partition involves the creation of two independent states, i.e., the cessation of administration by the Mandatory Power in the areas made independent, Partition could not be said to be a continuance of administration in accordance with the obligations contained in the Mandate. Partition would therefore conflict with [Britain's] undertaking given at the League of Nations Assembly ...[3]

The legal memorandum, however, viewed Britain's authority to impose the provincial autonomy plan differently from its lack of authority to impose partition. The legal memorandum argued Britain had sufficient lawful authority under the terms of the Mandate to impose the provincial autonomy plan unilaterally, and therefore prior approval from the United Nations would not be required:

> The essential difference between "provincial autonomy" and "Partition" is that provincial autonomy does not involve the cessation of administration of any part of Palestine (excluding Transjordan) by the existing Mandatory Power. It does not therefore give rise to the same difficulties of conflict with Article 80 of the Charter ... The United Kingdom could continue to implement the obligations of the Mandate under the "Provincial autonomy" scheme because it will retain sufficient legal powers to do so. There would appear, therefore, to be probably no legal necessity to consult the United Nations before putting into effect the scheme of "provincial autonomy."[4]

Nevertheless, the memorandum cautioned the Government that any attempt to impose the provincial autonomy plan unilaterally, albeit permissible "as a matter of strict law," would likely be met with stiff political resistance at the United Nations, likely resulting in pressure to place Palestine under a United Nations-supervised Trusteeship.[5]

The Cabinet discussed the legal memorandum on 15 January 1947. Bevin summarised the recent history of Britain's efforts to find a solution in Palestine, blaming President Truman's insistence on the 100,000 immigration certificates for derailing Britain's plans. Bevin rejected the option of Britain unilaterally imposing the provincial autonomy plan, but he defended provincial autonomy as likely to garner more support at the United Nations than partition.[6]

## *Britain's last attempt: January–February 1947*

The London Conference reconvened on 27 January 1947 between the British Government and Palestinian Arab representatives. The British Government also conducted informal parallel discussions with Zionist officials.[7] By early February 1947, the talks had collapsed. Foreign Secretary Ernest Bevin and Colonial Secretary Arthur Creech Jones jointly submitted a memorandum to the Cabinet advising there was "no prospect" of settling the Palestine problem.[8] The Palestinian Arabs continued to insist on a one-state solution, with a Palestinian Arab Government ruling the entire country. The Palestinian Arabs also demanded a complete and immediate halt to any further Jewish immigration.[9]

The Zionists, on the other hand, demanded the creation of a Jewish State in "all" of Palestine. Unofficially, however, the Zionist leadership expressed support for partition and a two-state solution, so long as the Jewish State would contain "an adequate area of Palestine."[10]

Bevin and Creech Jones described in their joint February 1947 memorandum to the Cabinet the intractability of the parties' positions:

> The essential point of principle for the Jews is the creation of a sovereign Jewish State. And the essential point of principle for the Arabs is to resist to the last the establishment of Jewish sovereignty in *any* part of Palestine. These, for both sides, are matters of principle for which there is no room for compromise. There is, therefore, no hope of negotiating an agreed settlement.[11]

The memorandum sought authority from the Cabinet to propose a modified form of the same provincial autonomy plan the Jews and Arabs had already rejected.[12] The memorandum recognised there was little or no chance the parties would accept the revised scheme at this juncture, or that the revised scheme would "meet with any substantial measure of acquiescence from even one of the two communities in Palestine."[13]

Therefore, the memorandum recommended, "[i]f we are unable to report any such prospect of acquiescence, we believe that the only course then open to His Majesty's Government will be to submit the problem to the United Nations."[14]

The Cabinet approved the recommendations the next day, asking the Foreign Secretary and Colonial Secretary to report back within one week.[15]

## *Britain concedes defeat*

British officials discussed the modified provincial autonomy plan with the Zionist leadership on 10 February 1947 and the Palestinian Arab leadership on 12 February 1947.

On 13 February 1947, Bevin and Creech Jones notified the Cabinet the discussions with the Jewish and Arab representatives had failed. Not surprisingly, both the Jews and Arabs had "declined to accept these proposals as a basis for further negotiation."[16] Given the implacable opposition from both sides, as well as the lack of public support in Palestine for the provincial autonomy plan, Bevin and Creech Jones advised the Cabinet against any effort to impose the plan unilaterally.[17]

Bevin and Creech Jones therefore recommended the Cabinet authorise the Government to notify the UN Secretary General of Britain's intent to submit the Palestine problem to the judgement of the UN General Assembly. In the interim, Britain would continue administering Palestine pursuant to the League of Nations Mandate.[18]

The Cabinet considered the recommendation of the Foreign and Colonial Secretaries at a meeting the next morning, 14 February 1947. After discussing the recommendation, the Cabinet agreed to refer the Palestine issue to the United Nations:

> [I]t was the general view of the Cabinet that the right course was now to submit the whole problem to the United Nations ... This submission would not involve an immediate surrender of the Mandate; but His Majesty's Government would not be under an obligation themselves to enforce whatever solution the United Nations might approve. If the settlement suggested by the United Nations were not acceptable to us, we should be at liberty then to surrender the Mandate and leave the United Nations to make other arrangements for the future administration of Palestine.[19]

Foreign Secretary Bevin publicly announced, in a speech to the House of Commons on 18 February 1947, the Government's decision to refer the Palestine issue to the United Nations, and to withdraw from Palestine no later than 1 August 1948. Bevin, still bitter over the Anglo-American Committee report nine months earlier, took a final swipe at the Committee's verdict:

> His Majesty's Government have of themselves no power, under the terms of the Mandate, to award the country either to the Arabs or to the Jews, or even to partition it between them. It is in these circumstances that we have decided that we are unable to accept the scheme put forward either by the Arabs or by the Jews, or to impose ourselves a solution of our own. We have, therefore, reached the conclusion that the only course now open to us is to submit the problem to the judgment of the United Nations ... We shall explain that the Mandate has proved to be unworkable in practice, and that the obligations undertaken to the two communities in Palestine have been shown to be irreconcilable. We shall describe the various proposals which have been put forward for dealing with the situation, namely, the Arab Plan, the Zionists' aspirations, *so far as we have been able to ascertain them*, the proposals of the Anglo-American Committee, and the various proposals which we ourselves have put forward. We shall then ask the

> United Nations to consider our report, and to recommend a settlement of the problem. We do not intend ourselves to recommend any particular solution.[20]

The Jewish side lost no time commenting on Bevin's announcement. Hebrew University law professor Nathan Feinberg, for example, sent a letter only five days later to UN Secretary General Trygve Lie. The letter invoked Zionist transformational legal framing:

> It is hardly an exaggeration to say that the fate of the Jewish people, more than any other people, is bound up with law and justice ... The Jewish people has not renounced its claims [to Palestine]. More than any other people it is aware that justice, no less than peace, is indivisible. No new world order of law and justice can arise while the Jewish people is deprived of its rights and while the responsibilities which the nations of the world assumed towards it as an international obligation after the first world war have not been fulfilled.[21]

On 25 February 1947, Bevin addressed the House again, explaining further the Government's rationale for referring the Palestine matter to the United Nations and seeking the world community's recommendations for Palestine's future:

> The issue which the United Nations must consider and decide is, first, shall the claims of the Jews that Palestine is to be a Jewish State be admitted; second, shall the claim of the Arabs that it is to be an Arab State, with safeguards for the Jews under the decision [sic] for a National Home be admitted; or, third, shall it be a Palestinian State, in which the interests of both communities are as carefully balanced and protected as possible? ... That, therefore, raises the issue which has got to be decided and we, as Mandatory Power, cannot solve that problem until the United Nations have recommended which of these three alternatives is to form the basis of the future organisation of Palestine. We, as Mandatory Power, have no power to make that decision. Nothing that I can find in any of the documents, either at the League of Nations, or in the discussions between the great Powers at Versailles and after, indicates that we have that power. The Mandate certainly does not give it.[22]

Bevin's remarks to the House seem especially ironic. Although he asserted the British Government was powerless to alter Palestine's political future, the British Government sought to do exactly that when it unilaterally issued the May 1939 White Paper. Indeed, as discussed in Chapter Three, the Foreign Office's legal advisors concluded Britain possessed lawful authority as the mandatory to decide Palestine's political future unilaterally, without involving the League of Nations. Now, however, less than eight years later, the Foreign Secretary took the opposite position.

## *Referral to the United Nations*

Accordingly, on 2 April 1947, the British Government submitted a formal written notice to the United Nations, requesting the Secretary General place the question of Palestine on the Agenda of the General Assembly at its next regular Annual Session. The notice requested the appointment of a Special Committee under the auspices of the United Nations to undertake a study of the Palestine problem. The notice further indicated Britain would submit to the General Assembly an account of its administration of the League of Nations Mandate.

The notice also indicated Britain would ask the General Assembly to make recommendations, under Article 10 of the Charter of the United Nations, concerning the future government of Palestine. Finally, the notice requested a special session of the General Assembly be summoned as soon as possible for the purpose of constituting and instructing a Special Committee to prepare for the consideration of the question by the General Assembly at its next regular session.[23]

The British Government's notice set in motion a chain of events leading to two separate trials, conducted by two separate committees of the United Nations. Both trials occurred in the remarkably short span of six months, between June and November 1947. The verdicts delivered by those two committees – the United Nations Special Committee on Palestine (UNSCOP), and the General Assembly Ad Hoc Committee on Palestine – brought to an end three decades of British rule.

While both Committees resoundingly endorsed partition and the two-state solution, only the Jewish side accepted the verdicts, leading to the birth of the State of Israel on 15 May 1948. The Palestinian Arabs, however, just as they had done in rejecting the Peel Commission's two-state solution and the 1939 White Paper's one-state solution, rejected and renounced the United Nations' November 1947 offer of statehood in a portion of Palestine, choosing to launch war instead.

The Palestinian Arabs, unable to frame the conflict other than through their long-standing justice/injustice/victimisation narrative, made yet another self-destructive decision. The consequences and reverberations continue to this day.

## *UNSCOP formation and Terms of Reference*

On 29 April 1947, the UN General Committee (acting as the Agenda Committee for the General Assembly) voted to recommend the British Government's request that Palestine be placed on the agenda of the General Assembly. The General Committee also endorsed Britain's request to appoint a Special Committee, whose work would assist the General's Assembly's consideration of the question of Palestine at the second regular session of the General Assembly later that year.[24] The General Committee also voted to refer the matter to the UN First Committee for further study.[25]

The British Ambassador to the United Nations, Sir Alexander Cadogan, explained the British Government's position to the First Committee. Cadogan said Britain would welcome proposals from the United Nations, but he emphasised

Britain would not bear the lone responsibility for enforcing any solution, unless both the Arabs and Jews agreed:

> We have tried for years to solve the problem of Palestine. Having failed so far, we now bring it to the United Nations, in the hope that it can succeed where we have not. If the United Nations can find a just solution which will be accepted by both parties, it could hardly be expected that we should not welcome such a solution. All we say – and I made this reservation the other day – is that we should not have the sole responsibility for enforcing a solution which is not accepted by both parties and which we cannot reconcile with our conscience.[26]

On 13 May 1947, the First Committee recommended the appointment of a Special Committee on Palestine, comprising representatives from Australia, Canada, Czechoslovakia, Guatemala, India, Iran, the Netherlands, Peru, Sweden, Uruguay, and Yugoslavia.[27]

The First Committee also recommended the General Assembly should approve Terms of Reference delegating to the Special Committee "the widest powers to ascertain and record facts, and to investigate all questions and issues relevant to the problem of Palestine." The Terms of Reference would give the Special Committee the power to "conduct investigations in Palestine and wherever it may deem useful, receive and examine written or oral testimony, whichever it may consider appropriate in each case, from the mandatory Power, from representatives of the population of Palestine, from Governments and from such organizations and individuals as it may deem necessary."

The Special Committee would be given a deadline of 1 September 1947 to issue a report to the Secretary General of the United Nations.

The General Assembly debated the First Committee's recommendations and its proposed Terms of Reference for the Special Committee on 14 May 1947. The 14 May debate featured many interesting statements. The Syrian delegate, for example, referred to Palestine as part of Syria, not as a separate political entity:

> Palestine used to be a Syrian province. Geographical, historical, racial and religious links exist there. There is no distinction whatever between the Palestinians and the Syrians and, had it not been for the Balfour Declaration and the terms of the mandate, Palestine would now be a Syrian province, as it used to be.[28]

The Soviet delegate, Andrei Gromyko, in a surprise move, spoke in support of Jewish aspirations in Palestine, blaming the West for its failure to protect its Jewish population:

> The fact that no western European State has been able to ensure the defense of the elementary rights of the Jewish people, and to safeguard it against the violence of the fascist executioners, explains the aspirations of

> the Jews to establish their own State. It would be unjust not to take this into consideration and to deny the right of the Jewish people to realize this aspiration. It would be unjustifiable to deny this right to the Jewish people, particularly in view of all it has undergone during the Second World War. Consequently, the study of this aspect of the problem and the preparation of relevant proposals must constitute an important task of the special committee.[29]

Gromyko said the Soviet Union preferred for Palestine to become a single Jewish-Arab state with equal rights for both groups. If, however, "this plan proved impossible to implement, in view of the deterioration in the relations between the Jews and the Arabs ... then it would be necessary to consider the second plan which ... provides for the partition of Palestine into two independent autonomous States, one Jewish and one Arab."[30]

The next day, 15 May 1947, the General Assembly adopted Resolution 106, approving the formation of the Special Committee, otherwise known as "UNSCOP" and adopting the First Committee's recommended Terms of Reference.[31]

UNSCOP held its first meeting at the interim headquarters of the United Nations at Lake Success, New York, on 26 May 1947.[32] From that date until 31 August 1947 (the day the Special Committee members signed their Report), the Special Committee held 16 public meetings and 36 private meetings in Lake Success, Jerusalem, Beirut, and Geneva.

On 2 June 1947, the Special Committee met for the purpose, among other things, of selecting a Chairperson. The Uruguayan delegate nominated the Guatemalan lawyer and Ambassador Jorge Garcia Granados to chair the Special Committee. The Canadian delegate, Supreme Court Justice Ivan Rand, preferred a candidate who, like himself, had "long judicial experience and a long judicial career in his own country."[33] Rand therefore nominated Emil Sandstrom, the Chief Justice of Sweden.

The members took a vote by secret ballot and elected Justice Sandstrom as Chair of the Special Committee. They selected another lawyer, the Peruvian delegate Dr Alberto Ulloa, as Vice-Chair. Garcia Granados explained in his memoirs that Sandstrom's selection as Chair had been a foregone conclusion, agreed in advance by the United States and Britain, who used their influence to persuade the majority of the Special Committee members to select him, not so much for his legal/judicial expertise, but because he "came from a country in the northern European bloc; he had been a judge in Egypt under the benevolent British eye, and could not be altogether indifferent to the British point of view."[34]

Other members of the Committee also had substantial legal and judicial experience, including Sir Abdur Rahman of India, a Justice of the High Court of Lahore.

UNSCOP, comprised of several lawyers and judges and chaired by a judge, followed in the legal footsteps of many British-appointed commissions of inquiry regarding Palestine that had preceded it since the early 1920s. The heavy reliance

**FIGURE 12.1** UNSCOP Chair Emil Sandstrom (right) and member Enrique Fabregat (centre) (Public Domain)

on commissioners with legal and judicial expertise once again underscored the looming presence of transformational legal framing and legal narrative in the conflict.[35]

A Jewish Agency official would later describe Justice Sandstrom (Figure 12.1) as "reticent and reserved, usually stern and of few words, of judicious and intelligent appearance, and very courteous."[36] Justice Rand was an "obstinate, fiery and explosive liberal, of broad outlook and deep intellectual and moral caliber [who] sought truth, justice and morality in the tangled skein of the problem."[37] Judge Rahman was "openly and virulently pro-Arab. His manner was forthright and tactless, and he had a narrowly juridical approach to problems."[38]

Garcia Granados also described the Special Committee's purpose in decidedly legal terms, likening the Committee to a court of law:

> I took the opportunity to study, time and again, the historical and legal aspects of the task before us. The documentation seemed enormous. More than a dozen committees had examined this question, and we … were like a Supreme Court, which must revise all earlier rulings, read all arguments, then take up the matter where it had been left by the last adjudication and produce a just, irrevocable solution.[39]

Garcia Granados further noted the unique nature of the Special Committee in the history of Palestine since World War I:

> As a committee we were in a unique position. We were the highest tribunal and the first truly international body to investigate the Palestine problem. The inquiry committees which had preceded us had either been British or Anglo-American. They had been responsible only to their own governments. We were responsible to the nations of the world. This, I felt, was eminently right; for it had been the nations of the world, the League of Nations, which had given Great Britain the Mandate for Palestine, and made her their trustee to rule the Holy Land. Now that the task was too great for her, it was fitting that she return her trust to the community of nations for judgment – and solution.[40]

The Special Committee's secretariat consisted of three international staffers, Victor Hoo, Alfonso Garcia Robles, and Ralph Bunche. Bunche quickly took the labouring oar for the staff, earning the respect and admiration of nearly everyone who observed him. One leading Zionist official described Bunche in glowing terms:

> Dr. Ralph Bunche … at once penetrated into the ramifications of the complex issue with practiced skill and amazed everyone with his depth of understanding, his wide knowledge, and his dedication. He created a profound impression by his remarkable intelligence, the celerity with which he grasped a problem, his brilliance, and above all, his energy. I sensed in him immediately the driving force that would keep UNSCOP's wheels turning and be its enlivening spirit.[41]

For the Zionist movement, the intervention of the United Nations and the creation of UNSCOP represented highly significant developments, as the stakes could not be higher. As one Zionist official later recalled,

> [E]veryone knew but one thing: that the United Nations Organization, the supreme international body, was our last resort; and that our political and historical destiny would be molded by its epochal judgment.[42]

The Special Committee conducted a total of 13 public hearings, at which 37 witnesses testified representing 17 different Jewish organisations and 6 Arab states. The Special Committee held an additional 39 private meetings during the two and a half months of its work, between 15 June and 1 September 1947. The Special Committee made extensive tours of Palestine and the European displaced persons (DP) camps and also visited Lebanon, Syria, and Transjordan.[43]

### Palestinian Arab boycott

On 13 June 1947, Jamal Husseini, Vice Chairman of the Palestine Arab Higher Committee and cousin of the exiled former Grand Mufti of Jerusalem, Haj Amin al-Husseini, formally notified the Secretary General, "in a curious mixture of petulant protest and paranoia,"[44] that the Palestinian Arabs would refuse all cooperation with the Special Committee.[45] Husseini's telegram to the Secretary General repeated Palestinian Arab opposition to any possible compromise with the Zionists and invoked Palestinian Arab "rights:"

> Arab Higher Committee Palestine desire convey to United Nations that after thoroughly studying the deliberations and circumstances under which the Palestine fact-finding committee was formed and the discussions leading to terms of reference they resolved that Palestine Arabs should abstain from collaboration and desist from appearing before said committee for following main reasons – firstly United Nations refusal adopt natural course of inserting termination mandate and declaration independence in agenda special United Nations session and in terms of reference; secondly, failure detach Jewish world refugees from Palestine problem; thirdly, replacing interests Palestine inhabitants by insertion world religious interests although these are not subject of contention – furthermore Palestine Arabs natural rights are self-evident and cannot continue to be subject to investigation but deserve to be recognized on the basis of principles of United Nations charter.[46]

The ex-Mufti threatened any Palestinian who dared cooperate with UNSCOP in violation of the boycott.[47]

On 30 June 1947, the US Consul General in Jerusalem cabled the Secretary of State, noting the Special Committee had made "no headway whatever toward changing the rigid line of non-cooperation adopted by the Arab Higher Committee."[48]

Justice Sandstrom, the Chair of the Special Committee, wrote to Jamal Husseini on 8 July 1947 asking him to reconsider. Husseini responded on 10 July, again rejecting any Palestinian Arab cooperation with the Special Committee.[49]

The Special Committee members viewed the Palestinian Arab boycott as self-defeating. Garcia Granados (shown in Figure 12.2), for example, recalled how "the Arab Higher Committee's uncompromising attitude, its refusal to consider the possibility of any conciliatory course, was to prove a convincing argument for partition."[50] A Jewish Agency official later described the Palestinian Arabs' decision to boycott the Special Committee as "one of their more blatant and stupid tactical errors."[51]

Notwithstanding the Palestinian Arab boycott, the Special Committee managed to engage in a small number of informal discussions with various leading Palestinian Arabs, all of whom rejected any solution other than immediate Arab statehood and sovereignty over all of Palestine.[52]

**FIGURE 12.2** UNSCOP member Jorge Garcia Granados (Alamy images)

Given the Arab Higher Committee's boycott, the Special Committee instead invited representatives of various Arab states to testify and express their views regarding Palestine. Ultimately, the Special Committee held hearings on 22–23 July 1947 in Beirut, during which representatives of Egypt, Iraq, Lebanon, Saudi Arabia, Syria, and Yemen testified. The Special Committee also met privately with King Abdullah of Jordan in Amman on 25 July 1947.

## UNSCOP hearings, June–July 1947

The Special Committee members arrived in Palestine on 14–15 June 1947. They held their first hearings in Jerusalem on 16 June 1947, taking background testimony from witnesses representing the Mandatory Government and the Jewish Agency.

The Chief Secretary of the Palestine Government, Sir Henry Gurney, accompanied by Palestine Government official Donald MacGillivray, testified for three hours *in camera* on 16 June 1947. Gurney answered a wide variety of questions about the Palestine economy, based on statistics the Palestine Government had provided in an updated version of the same two-volume *Survey of Palestine* it had prepared for the Anglo-American Committee a year earlier.[53]

The Special Committee held its first public hearing in Jerusalem on 17 June 1947, taking background testimony regarding the Palestine economy from Moshe Shertok, head of the Political Department of the Jewish Agency, accompanied by Jewish Agency representative David Horowitz.[54] The *New York Times* reported the hearing room at the YMCA building in Jerusalem was less than half-full, comprised mostly of journalists.[55]

Following this initial hearing, the Special Committee members spent several days, from 18 June to 3 July 1947, visiting various places in Palestine, including the Christian, Jewish, and Moslem shrines of Jerusalem, plus Haifa, the Dead Sea, Hebron, Beersheba, Gaza, Ramle, Beit Dajan, Jaffa, Tel Aviv, Ramallah, Nablus, Tulkarm, Acre, Rehovot, and several Jewish agricultural settlements.[56]

The Special Committee reconvened in Jerusalem between 4 and 19 July 1947, where it conducted both public and *in camera* hearings (Figure 12.3). The Special Committee took testimony from 31 Jewish witnesses, as well as British Government and British ecclesiastical witnesses. "Some of the questions we asked were legal, and some historical," Garcia Granados recalled later.[57] A contemporaneous observer described the Jewish case as, "in the first place, a legal one, based on the Balfour Declaration and the Mandate for Palestine."[58]

**FIGURE 12.3** UNSCOP hearings, YMCA building, Jerusalem, July 1947 (Alamy images)

The Special Committee heard testimony from the Jewish Agency for Palestine, from a number of other Jewish organisations and religious bodies, and from Chaim Weizmann in his personal capacity. Nearly all the Jewish witnesses employed transformational legal framing in their testimony to the Special Committee, none more so than David Ben-Gurion.

## *Ben-Gurion testimony*

The first substantive hearing before the Special Committee took place on 4 July 1947, featuring the testimony of Jewish Agency Chairman and the future first Prime Minister of Israel, David Ben-Gurion.[59]

### *Opening statement*

Ben-Gurion (Figure 12.4), who had studied law in Istanbul decades earlier, presented the Zionist case in powerful language laden with transformational legal framing and narrative. Ben-Gurion argued the Balfour Declaration and the Mandate provided the legal basis for reconstituting Jewish statehood in Palestine. He attacked the British Government and the British administration in Palestine for actively thwarting that goal, especially with the immigration and land transfer

**FIGURE 12.4** David Ben-Gurion testifying before UNSCOP, 7 July 1947 (Alamy images)

restrictions of the 1939 White Paper. He blamed the White Paper for dooming millions of European Jews to death in Hitler's gas chambers.

Ben-Gurion continued by congratulating the Arab peoples on having achieved their nationalist aspirations throughout the Middle East after World War I. He urged the Special Committee to complete the task of recognising Zionist aspirations in Palestine as a moral and legal obligation of the international community, again invoking the Jewish justice/injustice narrative:

> The settlement of these twin problems is perhaps the supreme test of the United Nations, a test both of their freedom and ability to deal with an issue involving as it does a conflict between a small, weak people and a powerful world empire; to deal with it not as a matter of power politics and political expediency, *but as a question of justice and equity*, as far as these are attainable in human affairs, and in accordance with the merits of the case. The United Nations in our view embody the most ardent hope and the most vital needs of the peoples of the world and a need for peace, stable and lasting peace, which is possible only if based on *justice*, equality and cooperation between nations … The prophets who followed Moses – Isaiah, Hosea, Micah and others – proclaimed the gospel of *social justice* and international brotherhood and peace.[60]

Ben-Gurion described the Balfour Declaration and the Mandate as conferring *legal* rights to Palestine for the Jewish people:

> An international undertaking was given to the Jewish people some thirty years ago in the Balfour Declaration and in the Mandate for Palestine, to reconstitute our national home in our ancient homeland. This undertaking originated with the British people and the British Government. It was supported and confirmed by 52 nations and embodied in an international instrument known as the Mandate for Palestine. The Charter of the United Nations seeks to maintain "justice and respect for the obligations arising from treaties and other sources of international law." Is it too presumptuous on our part to expect that the United Nations will see that obligations to the Jewish people too are respected and faithfully carried out in the spirit and the letter?[61]

Ben-Gurion then referenced the Jewish Agency's rejection of the Morrison-Grady provincial autonomy plan and the British Government's revised version of that plan. Ben-Gurion noted the Jewish Agency's willingness to consider partition as a solution to the Palestine problem:

> [L]ast year when the so-called Morrison Plan was discussed, the Jewish Agency Executive decided that it could not accept that plan as a basis for discussion but it was ready to consider an offer for a viable Jewish State *in*

> *an adequate area* of Palestine. The same attitude was maintained last winter after the last Congress in our oral discussion with the Government in London.[62]

Ben-Gurion next attacked the legality of the 1939 White Paper's immigration restrictions and the 1940 Land Transfers Ordinance, arguing both had violated the express terms of the Mandate:

> The White Paper in destroying the Mandate has removed the moral and legal basis of the present regime in Palestine. It is an arbitrary rule based on force alone. It is contrary to the wishes of the entire population of the country, it causes untold sufferings to our people, it threatens our national existence. It is incompatible with international obligations and good faith.[63]

Ben-Gurion next compared the relative positions of the Jews and Arabs in the Middle East, noting Palestine accounted for a mere one per cent of all the land area comprising the independent Arab states. Ben-Gurion argued the Arabs would have no reason to fear a Jewish State in Palestine, given how much the Arabs had already benefitted from Jewish economic development in Palestine since the late 19th century.

Ben-Gurion, reprising Weizmann's famous formulation before the Anglo-American Committee of Inquiry one year earlier, invoked the justice/injustice narrative:

> And now I put the question to you: who is prepared and able to guarantee that what happened to us in Europe will not happen again? Can human conscience, and we believe that there is a human conscience, free itself of all responsibility for that catastrophe? There is only one safeguard: a Homeland and Statehood! A Homeland, where a Jew can return freely as of right. Statehood, where he can be master of his own destiny. These two things are possible here, and here only. The Jewish people cannot give up, cannot renounce these two fundamental rights, whatever may happen … The conscience of humanity ought to weigh this: *Where is the balance of justice, where is the greater need, where is the greater peril, where is the lesser evil and where is the lesser injustice?*[64]

Ben-Gurion concluded his opening statement with another appeal to justice, saying "[y]ou will achieve your mission successfully when you restore freedom to Palestine, *give justice to the Jewish people* and stability, progress and prosperity to the Middle East."[65]

### *Cross-examination*

Tickets to the UNSCOP hearings (Figure 12.5) were highly sought after during Ben-Gurion's testimony. By this time he had firmly established himself as the undisputed leader of the worldwide Zionists and the Palestinian Jews.

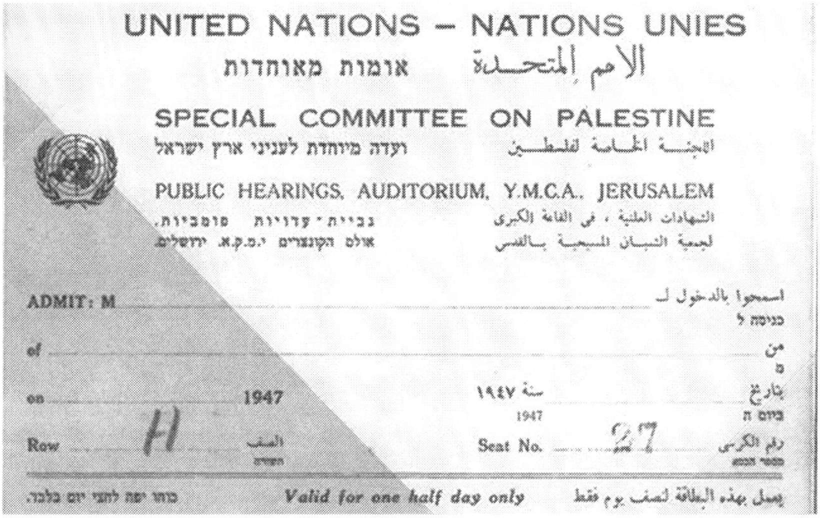


**FIGURE 12.5** Admission ticket for UNSCOP hearings, Jerusalem, July 1947 (Public Domain)

The Special Committee cross-examined Ben-Gurion on 7 and 8 July 1947, three days after his opening statement, and after several other Jewish witnesses had given their opening statements.

Ben-Gurion's cross-examination began with questions from Justice Sandstrom regarding the likelihood the United Nations would need to employ military power to enforce any decision regarding Palestine over Arab opposition. Ben-Gurion appeared evasive when asked about the potential use of military force while taking the opportunity yet again to invoke the Jewish justice narrative.

Ben-Gurion's evasiveness drew a rebuke from the Indian member of the Special Committee, Sir Abdur Rahman, a High Court Judge from Lahore, in what was shortly to become Pakistan. The tense exchanges between Ben-Gurion and Abdur Rahman resembled those which Ben-Gurion had with Justice Singleton during the Anglo-American Committee hearings 15 months earlier:

MR. BEN-GURION: I have to answer. I said that the facts are that at present force is being used against us for two purposes: for preventing us from coming here – because, without force, I want Sir Abdur Rahman to know these Jews would not have been prevented from coming back; and secondly, force is used to enforce the racial discrimination against Jews.

SIR ABDUR RAHMAM (INDIA): That is not the answer to the question. It is going absolutely beyond it. If he would only concentrate on the answer to the question put to him, it would be better, because when he says force is being used, the same force is being used against the Arabs, and the same force is being used against anybody who contravenes the law. If I contravene the law, the same force would be used against me today.

MR. BEN-GURION: I did not finish my answer.

SIR ABDUR RAHMAN (INDIA): You are going beyond it. We will not finish for two months if you go on in that way. I do not mind if we take two months or two years. Let me lead the questioning. You say you have not finished your answer?

MR. BEN-GURION: Yes. I say that the fact is, first, that force is being used against people exercising their rights. Our right is to come back. To prevent this, force is being used. *If the United Nations will give a decision in justice and equity that the Jews have a right to come back to their country, then I believe it will be their duty, if necessary, to enforce it.*[66]

Chairman Sandstrom next engaged Ben-Gurion in a legal discussion regarding the respective rights and claims of the Arabs and Jews to Palestine. Ben-Gurion first addressed the Arab legal claim, based on the original Muslim conquest of Jerusalem in the 7th century, and hundreds of years of continuous habitation of Palestine:

CHAIRMAN: Now, let us return to the Arab claim. You know well the Arab claim and the basis for it?

MR. BEN-GURION: Yes.

CHAIRMAN: It can be expressed very shortly. It is a claim based on the possession of the land for a considerable period of time and the right of self-government of the people of the land. What is your answer to this claim?

MR. BEN-GURION: My answer to that claim is the answer which was given not only by us but by human conscience almost in the whole world. The same claim was made almost twenty-five years ago. The reply was that you cannot judge this country which has a special history and special conditions which cannot be found anywhere else, and the relations of the Jews of this country cannot be judged by a rule applied to other countries not having the same unique conditions. Really, it is a unique case. You have first of all the people who were here a very, very long time ago; you know that. I can give you the Arab case. I understand the Arab case and I fully realize it. It is very simple. They state they do not care what happened, and nobody ought to care what happened fifteen hundred or two thousand years ago. We are here. We are not here from yesterday; we were here for centuries. We are the majority, and we have a right to self-determination. We will decide, just as the people in the United States or the people in Canada, whether to allow or not to allow immigrants. The fact that Jews were here some two thousand years ago is the same as the Roman legions having been in England some two thousand years ago, or when Arabs were in Spain fourteen or so many centuries ago. That is their claim. It is simple.[67]

Ben-Gurion next defended the Jewish claim to Palestine, arguing the Balfour Declaration and the League of Nations had promised Palestine to the Jewish people. Moreover, the Jewish people had never waived their right of return and their legal claim to Palestine, despite two millennia of exile:

MR. BEN-GURION: Many kinds of people come from many countries, but here you have a unique case without any parallel in history. Here is a people who for many centuries were dreaming of this country. They might have found a country anywhere else, but no, and they never gave up their claim ... The Jews are connected with this country. We [the Balfour Declaration and the Mandate] recognize their connexion. They are coming back. They have a right to come back ... Now, I return to the question: what reason have you, not you the Commission, but what reason has world conscience to reverse that decision? ... [W]e say there is no reason why you should reverse that decision, because justice and the necessity are the same, if not stronger. There is no reason whatsoever. The only reason is that those who undertook to do it failed to do it.

CHAIRMAN: You think the fact that a claim to a country has not been given up is so essential?

MR. BEN-GURION: Our claim?

CHAIRMAN: Yes.

MR. BEN-GURION: It is very. Of course, if we are invaders, then we have no right.

CHAIRMAN: And you do not think that a thousand year's possession is enough to oust the claim?

MR. BEN-GURION: Sir, I do not lay down general rules. I say on this occasion, under this historic and geographic position, no it is not, for the reasons which I gave in my address. It is not a question of the Arab race; they are fully liberated. It is not a question of the Arab individuals who are here; they are not suffering. Our claim stands; we did not give it up.[68]

Chairman Sandstrom next questioned Ben-Gurion about the provisions of the Balfour Declaration and the Mandate. Sandstrom noted neither document spoke of Jewish "statehood" in Palestine, and both documents contained language intended to protect the rights of the indigenous Palestinian Arab population:

CHAIRMAN: Let us go now to this decision that you spoke of. I suppose you mean the Mandate?

MR. BEN-GURION: The Declaration and the Mandate.

CHAIRMAN: Let us return to that act. You mean that that is an absolute promise to give the country to the Jews as a state?

MR. BEN-GURION: Sir, in human affairs you cannot speak about "absolute." I would not commit myself to the word "absolute" because it is a term whose meaning nobody understands. But, it was a definite undertaking, a definite promise based on the recognition of these unique facts to which I have referred.

CHAIRMAN: Why I use the word "absolute" there is to come to my further questions which are aiming at seeing whether you admit any reservations in the undertaking. The Mandate is based on the Balfour Declaration, and in the Balfour Declaration the word "state" is not used; the term "National Home" is used. Further, it is said "Palestine," and it has been so stressed. The phrase used is "in Palestine." You do not think there is any reservation in these terms?

MR. BEN-GURION: Yes, sir, there are two reservations: one is the reservation that the civil and religious rights of non-Jewish communities should not be prejudiced. That is one reservation. There is another reservation that the equality and political status of Jews in other countries should not be prejudiced. These are the two reservations ... What you have in mind is the first reservation concerning the Arabs. This very reservation is a clear indication as to what they meant by a National Home for the Jewish People. If, as this memorandum or the White Paper claimed, it was meant or even contemplated that the Jews remain a minority, I ask you if in a country the Jews are not a minority why must you have safeguards for the rights of a majority. It is nonsense. The whole question, after all, state or no state, is the question of whether the Jews must remain a minority or may they become a majority. This is the question, because a state follows from that ... It is true that they did not say "Palestine as a National Home;" they said "in Palestine." ... Suppose you are introducing Socialism in England, when you say Socialism in England it does not mean socialism in a part of England. But, also, it could not have meant a minority ... [69]

Chairman Sandstrom next pressed Ben-Gurion regarding the reservation of rights set forth in both the Balfour Declaration and Articles 2 and 6 of the Mandate in favour of the indigenous Palestinian Arab population. Ben-Gurion responded by arguing the rights promised to the Arabs were economic and not political. The Mandate, argued Ben-Gurion, granted political rights *solely* to the Jews:

MR. BEN-GURION: Then I say quite definitely that I would not use the word "absolute," complete conviction and knowledge that what was meant was the economic conditions and position of the population of Palestine because it is dealing with economic matters. Article 6 is dealing with two economic matters, immigration and colonization. They asked the Mandatory to facilitate immigration and to encourage close settlement of the Jews on the land on the condition – or some other phrasing, I do not remember – while ensuring that the rights and position of other sections of the population are not prejudiced. I want to say that we accept it wholeheartedly, not only because it is there but because it is right. What is meant by the economic interests of the population is that their economic position should not become worse because of Jewish immigration and settlement. This is what the Mandate meant.

CHAIRMAN: But is the immigration wholly an economic matter? Does it not also have political implications?

MR. BEN-GURION: Absolutely. But the political implication was to allow the Jews by immigration to become a Nation and have a National Home, not a minority. That was the political implication.[70]

Ben-Gurion next referred to the Peel Commission's July 1937 partition proposal, saying the Jews were willing to consider a compromise. This prompted Commissioner Lisicky of Czechoslovakia to intervene:

MR. LISICKY (CZECHOSLOVAKIA): Are you still ready to consider a compromise?
MR. BEN-GURION: I told you in my evidence that when we had the talks after our last congress with the Government in London, we told them that if a Jewish State in an adequate area of Palestine were offered, we would consider it.
MR. LISICKY (CZECHOSLOVAKIA): Does that mean partition?
MR. BEN-GURION: "To partition," according to the Oxford dictionary, means to divide a thing into two parts. Palestine is divided into three parts, and only in a small part are the Jews allowed to live. We are against that.
...
MR. LISICKY (CZECHOSLOVAKIA): Am I right in understanding that you are not opposed to the idea of partition?
MR. BEN-GURION: That means we are ready to consider it.[71]

Commissioner Lisicky asked Ben-Gurion again about partition later that day, eliciting the following response:

> I will tell you what we told the Government last year and this year. While we believe and request that our right, at least to the Western part of Palestine should be granted in full and Western Palestine be made a Jewish State, we believe it is possible. We have a right to it, but we are willing to consider an offer of a Jewish State in an area which means less than the whole of Palestine.[72]

Chairman Sandstrom then raised the Arab legal claim that Palestine belonged to them, and that no one – neither Britain nor the United Nations – had the right to act in Palestine without Arab consent. Ben-Gurion turned the argument on its head, again using transformational legal framing to characterise the issue as a matter of justice for the Jewish people:

CHAIRMAN: There is one argument in the Arab case to which I want an answer. They say, this decision of the League of Nations is all right, but nobody can dispose of our country without our consent. What do you answer to that?
MR. BEN-GURION: The answer is this is our country, including the Arabs who are in it. This country is the country of the Jewish people and of all the other inhabitants. This is our answer ... *It is a matter of justice, I am convinced.*[73]

Commissioner Lisicky took up the questioning again, pressing Ben-Gurion on the Zionist demands:

MR. LISICKY (CZECHOSLOVAKIA): You are asking the United Nations for help in accomplishing three objectives: the immediate abolition of the White Paper; the establishment of a Jewish State, and the promotion of a Jewish-Arab alliance. I am asking would it not be useful to start with the promotion of the Jewish-Arab alliance in the country and not outside, and if you think that there is no prospect of this alliance in the country, should this prospect for this Jewish-Arab alliance outside the country be greater than in the country?

MR. BEN-GURION: While there are Arabs who from the beginning were in favour of Jewish immigration, and there are still Arabs who are in favour, not a single Arab will come out publicly for Jewish immigration. I don't blame them. I don't say that the Arab is dishonest; he is under the pressure of his community ... We said we were willing to meet the Arabs and discuss proposals. Time passed and receiving no answer we asked where the people were. They said that they went back and that they refused to discuss it. What happened? In the meantime, between which these proposals were submitted to us and their refusal, a new policy was formulated by His Majesty's Government. They scrapped the policy of the Peel Commission. They scrapped the policy of having two states, which means having a Jewish State. Then the people who came to us said, "Why should we come to terms with the Jews? There is no need." So, we think as long as they will be able to prevent us they will. Their wish and policy will prevail among the Arab communities. *Since this is in our view a matter of right and wrong it should not be decided only by the Arabs, but it must be decided by a Higher Tribunal. We say you are the Tribunal.*

MR. LISICKY (CZECHOSLOVAKIA): Now, you are in the absolute. Now, do you know the definition of politics? Politics is the art of the possible.

MR. BEN-GURION: The only question is what is the possible.[74]

Commissioner Hood from Australia then asked Ben-Gurion what sort of transitional arrangement he envisioned for the governance of Palestine post-Mandate, but pre-statehood. Ben-Gurion reframed the question and invoked the Zionist claim for justice:

> What is the difference between what you call non-Mandate and transitional? Again there will have to be some Mandatory power here. I might say there would be two very important differences which will change the entire nature of the temporary supervision. One is there will be a clear assumption that what we claim is right and is approved by you. If not, and you do not approve it, the question does not arise. The question that Mr. Blom and you put to me arises only on the assumption that you admit our claim is right and should be approved by the United Nations. Then the first very important difference would be that there would be in existence a clear-cut decision by the highest tribunal in the world for a Jewish State in Palestine ... However, I do not see that it is beyond the statesmanship of the big and small nations of the United Nations to lay down definite conditions, in this special case and for a very short period providing for such an international supervision as will ensure, first the carrying out of these two decisions of the United Nations: to have a State and to have the

Jewish Agency carry out that plan. Secondly, to provide for administering the country until it is able to be a democratic independent country, and to ensure peace and justice for everybody in that country, which will be the problem of the transitional period.[75]

Ben-Gurion later clarified, in response to a question from Commissioner Garcia Granados, that if the Special Committee were to recommend partition, meaning a Jewish State were established in "a part of Palestine, we do not need any transitional period. If it is the whole of Palestine, we may need a short transitional period."[76]

Ben-Gurion repeatedly used transformational legal framing and the justice narrative throughout his cross-examination to reframe and parry questions. For example, in response to Commissioner Rand (Canada), Ben-Gurion appealed to the legal and moral authority of the United Nations:

> If there were no United Nations and, assuming for a moment that England says: "I walk out tomorrow," or that the United Nations would say: "I have nothing to do with Palestine," I think we would manage. It would be difficult. We would manage to bring in Jews, and as our work in Palestine is in its nature constructive, we would do it, under difficulties. We would try every day to come to the Arabs and say: "Let us have an agreement and settle the question by ourselves." We would be willing to listen if they would, in a spirit of cooperation, discuss a compromise. But if they said: "No," we would go on by ourselves as far as we could. But there is a United Nations; there is a will in the world ... Therefore, we come to you and say, if you admit that we are right, say so; if you admit and say that we are right, and should that right be accomplished, as you are trying to do it in every place in the world as the Court of Justice is doing – if it decides that Mr. A is right, then although Mr. B said "No," the right of Mr. A is enforced. But if you leave us alone we will do what we can alone by our own means. We will defend ourselves by all means and we will build by our own means. We will bring Jews by our own means. We will not give up.[77]

Commissioner Abdur Rahman then resumed his cross-examination, once again exhibiting hostility toward Ben-Gurion:

SIR ABDUR RAHMAN (INDIA): I would like you to be precise in your answer to the questions I will put. They will be definite questions. I have been hearing your discourse with great interest and attention, and I would like you to confine your answers to my questions. I do not want a discourse. My questions will be such that they will require short answers, and you can give me short answers. I will break the question, for your advantage, into bits. I find from your statement before the Anglo-American Committee that you did not and do not, base the Jews' right to Palestine on what has come to be known as the Balfour Declaration. Have I understood your answer correctly?

MR. BEN-GURION: I must be given the freedom to answer in the way I believe I can answer.

SIR ABDUR RAHMAN (INDIA): I think there is only one answer.

MR. BEN-GURION: If I have to answer, I have to answer in my own way. If I cannot, I will not answer.

SIR ABDUR RAHMAN (INDIA): Have I understood your position?

CHAIRMAN: I think I shall have to decide whether the answer is an answer to the question or not.

SIR ABDUR RAHMAN (INDIA): My question is a simple one. I have put to him that his statement before the Anglo-American Committee and the statement which he made here led me to think that he does not base the right of the Jews to Palestine on what has come to be known as the Balfour Declaration. Have I understood his position correctly or not.

MR. BEN-GURION: Not correctly. What I said was that the Jewish right to Palestine was prior to the Balfour Declaration. I do not think that is the same thing. Our right was existing for 3,500 years. The Balfour Declaration was merely a recognition by a Great Power of that right. The right existed before. That is what I said, and I maintain it now.[78]

Commissioner Abdur Rahman, "aggressive in manner, and loud of tone,"[79] then engaged in another testy exchange with Ben-Gurion, trying to force him to admit the term "National Home" as used in the Balfour Declaration and the Mandate did not contemplate Jewish statehood, and that Jewish legal experts such as former Palestine Attorney General Norman Bentwich had admitted as much:

SIR ABDUR RAHMAN (INDIA): Was Mr. Bentwich a Jewish international lawyer?

MR. BEN-GURION: He is still a Jew and, I think, still an international lawyer.

SIR ABDUR RAHMAN (INDIA): Did he define "National Home" in his book on the Mandatory System? Would you please read it?

MR. BEN-GURION: Do you want me to read it now? I cannot give you a judgment on what I am going to read now.

SIR ABDUR RAHMAN (INDIA): I am only drawing your attention to Mr. Bentwich's definition of a National Home.

MR. BEN-GURION: I think the best thing would be for you to read what he says.

SIR ABDUR RAHMAN (INDIA): Is it written there? I am just drawing your attention to that book. It defines National Home as a territory in which a people without receiving rights of political sovereignty has nevertheless a recognized legal position and the opportunity of developing its moral, social and intellectual side. Is that how Mr. Bentwich understands that term?

MR. BEN-GURION: I will tell you what I understand it to mean. If you ask me to say whether these words are here, you do not need to because they are here. If you want to ask me what I understand by them I will tell you. If you do not want me to, I will not.

SIR ABDUR RAHMAN (INDIA): Since you are not an international lawyer I will not trouble you.

MR. BEN-GURION: If you want to draw my attention, I want to say what is my contention.

CHAIRMAN: I would like to shorten the discussion. We are here to gain information and it is perhaps not necessary to ask the opinion of the Jewish Agency on everything that is written on this subject. We can discuss it.

SIR ABDUR RAHMAN (INDIA): No, that is not the case. The answers of Mr. Ben Gurion have been given in a certain strain and they assume that the words "National Home" mean a "National State." I am trying to draw his attention to the fact that Jewish international lawyers who have written books have meant otherwise: that is all. It is for your benefit, for my benefit, for everybody's benefit.

MR. BEN-GURION: May I again tell you what is my view, because I believe you tried to draw my attention to something which is not there, and because I believe the first part of it says when the Balfour Declaration was given it did not signify that it gave the Jews sovereignty of the country. The Jews until now had no sovereign rights in Palestine, but it gave the Jews who were not here the right to come back and develop it. That is, as far as I gather it, what you mean. Secondly, maybe Mr. Bentwich has views different from the views of others. I do not see why Mr. Bentwich is not entitled to have his own views and why his views need to bind anyone else. I think the people who formulated the Balfour Declaration knew as much about the meaning of it as Mr. Bentwich. The same thing is true for the Royal Commission. There are also lawyers among them.[80]

Later, in response to a question from Commissioner Entezam of Iran, Ben-Gurion again used the opportunity to frame the issue in legal terms:

> What we say is that here we Jews and we Jewish people have a State and have a right. No State, no political regime can be created in accordance with justice, with history, and with international law which recognizes this Jewish State and this Jewish right, which will preclude the realization of our right. And our right consists of two things: our right to immigrate into Palestine as our right … There are certain rights of self-determination, and when I say the right of the Jew to come back to his country and the right of our people to be here as equal partners in the world family, it is an overriding right which applies to Palestine, and therefore no regime – not only an Arab State, should be created, even no trusteeship, no mandate should be created – which will make that right impossible of realization. This is why we oppose it.[81]

## *Weizmann testimony*

Chaim Weizmann (Figure 12.6) testified before the Peel Commission multiple times in 1936–1937, both publicly and *in camera*. Weizmann, as described in

FIGURE 12.6 Chaim Weizmann testifying before UNSCOP (future Israeli Foreign Minister Abba Eban seated behind, to Weizmann's right), 8 July 1947 (Alamy images)

Chapter Eight, also testified before the Anglo-American Committee of Inquiry, where he invoked his famous "least injustice" transformational legal reframing. On 8 July 1947, Weizmann testified before the Special Committee, but this time only in his personal capacity, as he no longer held any official position with the Jewish Agency.

### *Weizmann opening statement*

In his opening statement, Weizmann retraced the history of the Balfour Declaration and the Zionist enterprise during the British Mandate. Weizmann noted statehood had *always* been the ultimate aim of Zionism, "eventually, in the fullness of time."[82] Weizmann also argued the British Government itself had always recognised Jewish statehood in Palestine as the logical outcome of the National Home project.

Weizmann also employed transformational legal framing during his opening statement. For example, Weizmann characterised as a "*Treaty* of Friendship" a document he and Prince Feisal signed in January 1919, in which Feisal had accepted Zionist aspirations (but not explicitly statehood) in Palestine.[83] Weizmann had previously and more tentatively referred to that same document as a "treaty" during his testimony before the Peel Commission. This time, however, Weizmann used the word "treaty" multiple times, transformationally framing the document to the Special Committee as vested with the force of international law.[84]

Weizmann then made clear his support for partition, going further than Ben-Gurion and Shertok had been willing to say in public at that point in time.[85] Weizmann argued Palestine had already been partitioned once previously, in 1923, when Britain divided Palestine into eastern (Transjordan) and western (Cisjordan) sections. Now, with only the western side of Palestine still in play, Weizmann recommended a second partition of the remainder:

> Knowing all that, we are – I think I am speaking the mind of a great many Jews, after a great deal of hardship, after a great deal of testing, after a great deal of evaluating the possibility of what we can do, for a form of partition which would satisfy the just demands of both the Jews and the Arabs. We realize that we cannot have the whole of Palestine. God made a promise; Palestine to the Jews. It is up to the Almighty to keep His promise in His own time. Our business is to do what we can in a very imperfect human way. I do not like to play on the sentiment of the distinguished Indian representative who sits here. I should say partition is *la mode*. It is not only in small Palestine; it is in big India. But at least there you have something to partition. Here we have to do it with a microscope. There you can do it with a big knife.[86]

### *Weizmann cross-examination*

Chairman Sandstrom began the cross-examination by questioning Weizmann's reliance on the agreement he signed with Prince Feisal in January 1919. Sandstrom then extracted a significant concession from Weizmann:

CHAIRMAN: Now I would like to ask you a question with regard to the agreement you made with Emir Feisal. In that document was inserted the condition that the undertaking of Emir Feisal would be void if the promises given to the Arabs were not carried out. Emir Feisal and the Arabs have contended that by later events the undertakings were not carried out. I suppose it referred then to the events which took place in Syria; was that not so?

MR. WEIZMANN: Yes, *the promises were not carried out at the time*. He was expelled from Syria, he had to go to Iraq. What I contend now is that the Arabs have obtained all the independence they had been claiming under Feisal.

CHAIRMAN: I should like to ask you the question whether Emir Feisal, after he had been driven out from Damascus, was entitled to consider the agreement made with you as void?

MR. WEIZMANN: I think he was. I think he was, and this agreement was never pressed.

CHAIRMAN: I should like to ask you a question, which is perhaps a legal question, and that is whether the agreement can be revived by further accomplishment of the condition he had put?

MR. WEIZMANN: I really believe, sir, that it can be revived under new authority, under new conditions; since then much has changed.[87]

But Weizmann was able to recover during Commissioner Abdur Rahman's cross-examination, arguing Prince Feisal never intended to claim Palestine for Arab independence:

SIR ABDUR RAHMAN (INDIA): Was Palestine included in the Feisal agreement?

MR. WEIZMANN: No, definitely not.

SIR ABDUR RAHMAN (INDIA): So, the immigration in Palestine was included but the liberty of people living in Palestine was not included?

MR. WEIZMANN: I do not quite get it. It was not included in the sense that it was not considered by Feisal as an Arab country, as a country on which he had a claim.

SIR ABDUR RAHMAN (INDIA): He had no claim at that time to any country.

MR. WEIZMANN: Oh, yes. He laid claim to Arab countries. He was ready to exclude Palestine from that claim.

SIR ABDUR RAHMAN (INDIA): But there is no mention of the exclusion of Palestine in the agreement?

MR. WEIZMANN: No, but if he allowed immigration into Palestine – that we should conduct it and we should support it and develop it, it means that he lays no claim to Palestine as an Arab country.[88]

## *Eliash testimony*

Several other leaders of the Zionist movement and the Palestinian Jewish community also testified before UNSCOP during the Jerusalem hearings. The most prominent such witness was the famous lawyer Dr Mordechai Eliash of Jerusalem. Dr Eliash had served as one of the "assessors" during the Haycraft Commission's investigation of the 1921 Jaffa Riots. He testified before the Shaw Commission in 1929 and served as the lead trial lawyer for the Jewish side before the Lofgren Commission in 1930. He also testified before the Anglo-American Committee of Inquiry in 1946.

Dr Eliash, like Ben-Gurion and Weizmann, invoked the Jewish "justice" narrative in his opening statement:

> The organised conscience of mankind has found it possible *to do justice to the Jew* individually in almost every nation. The great ideals of the French Revolution have taught the world liberty, equality, fraternity as regards individual Jews in each of these countries. Perhaps the great ideals which now animate the United Nations *will teach the organised conscience of mankind to do justice to the Jews as a people.* And then we in Palestine shall be given the status not of a religious community merely, as we are now, but of the People of Israel in the Land of Israel.[89]

## *Magnes testimony*

Judah Magnes of the Hebrew University of Jerusalem reprised the testimony he had given one year earlier to the Anglo-American Committee of Inquiry, rejecting partition and calling again for a binational, single Jewish-Arab state based on equality:

> We have no belief in Partition for many reasons—religious, historical, political, economic. Indeed we regard Partition as not only impracticable, but, should it be carried through, as a great misfortune for both Jews and Arabs. We have not wanted to encumber our documents to you by engaging in polemics with the advocates of Partition, whom we greatly respect. We have wanted to present a positive case for a united bi-national Palestine on its own merits. Should it, however, be desired, we are ready to formulate our arguments against Partition as well. We are greatly encouraged by the advocacy of the idea of a bi-national Palestine by some of the delegates at the Special Session on Palestine of the United Nations General Assembly. It had been said by the Chief Delegate of the U.S.S.R. that Partition is only to be considered if a bi-national solution should prove to be impossible. We think it is the task of statesmanship to make this possible. In any event we think consideration of Partition entirely premature until the bi-national Palestine be given a full and fair chance to prove its worth over a number of years.[90]

Garcia Granados recalled later that while Magnes' "idealistic" views seemed "reasonable, many of us questioned its practicality … I think most of us agreed that the bi-national state had most of the inconveniences of partition without its finality."[91]

## *Jewish written legal submission*

The Jewish Agency submitted an enormous amount of written material to UNSCOP as part of the Jewish case for statehood.[92] In July 1947, the Jewish Agency also submitted a legal memorandum to UNSCOP in support of its case.[93] The legal memorandum provided the most comprehensive Jewish legal argument ever submitted during the Mandate years. The legal memorandum stands as a prime example of Zionist transformational legal framing, reflecting the long-standing Zionist legal narrative.

The legal memorandum began by reminding the Special Committee that the Balfour Declaration and the Mandate contained "international pledges made to the Jewish people."[94] The legal memorandum immediately cast those pledges as *legally* binding on the international community:

> The Pledges … include the formulations in international law (1) that there is a Jewish people; (2) that its historic connection with Palestine is internationally recognized; and (3) that the grounds for reconstituting its National Home in Palestine are accepted as internationally valid.[95]

The legal memorandum argued the "international pledge to the Jewish people is more than an incident of history; it is a declared principle of the law of nations."[96] The memorandum further noted, "the *justice* of the international settlement after World War I, and ... the overwhelming equity in support of our position today."[97]

The legal memorandum next analysed the validity of Britain's claim that the Mandate had imposed dual, equal obligations on Britain to protect both Jewish and Arab rights in Palestine, and that in practice those rights had proven irreconcilable. The legal memorandum noted the Balfour Declaration had been elevated to the status of international law by virtue of its broad acceptance among the international community and its incorporation by reference into the Treaty of Sevres and the Mandate. Britain's acceptance of the Mandate locked in Britain's role as trustee, charged on behalf of the international community with carrying out "the fundamental international law" pledges to the Jewish people contained in the Balfour Declaration.[98]

The legal memorandum emphasised this point again, several pages later:

> Logic supports this view. It is not to be supposed that the framers of the Mandate considered that, the Jews having been promised facilities for the establishment of the Jewish National Home, the Arabs, on their side, must be promised facilities for obstructing its establishment.[99]

The legal memorandum then focused on the specific language of various provisions of the Mandate to determine the overall purpose and scope of the document. The legal memorandum argued that nothing in the Mandate could be read to justify *any* limit on Jewish immigration, or *any* restriction on Jewish land acquisition anywhere in Palestine:

> On the contrary, if the duties of the Administration to facilitate immigration and to encourage close settlement in the land are carried out as expressly required, a Jewish majority is likely to accrue as a direct consequence of the fulfillment of the positive obligations.[100]

The Jewish majority contemplated by the Balfour Declaration and the Mandate also, according to the legal memorandum, included Jewish *statehood* as the ultimate goal of establishing the Jewish National Home in Palestine; indeed, Jewish statehood was "taken for granted by the statesmen who framed the Balfour Declaration."[101]

The legal memorandum further argued the Mandate had survived the dissolution of the League of Nations. The legal memorandum pointed to the resolution the League Assembly adopted at its final session on 18 April 1946, as well as Article 80 of the UN Charter.[102]

The legal memorandum also contained the most comprehensive Jewish response to the long-standing Arab legal argument regarding Article 22 of the

Covenant of the League of Nations. The Arabs had argued since the early 1920s that Article 22, when read together with Article 20, contained promises of future independence *solely* to "certain communities formerly belonging to the Turkish empire," meaning the Arab inhabitants of Palestine and not the Jewish people throughout the world. Therefore, Article 20, according to the Arab legal argument, abrogated the Balfour Declaration, because Balfour's prior promises to the global Jewish people to create a National Home in Palestine were inconsistent with the League's subsequent commitments in Article 22 to the indigenous Palestinian Arab population.

The legal memorandum offered the following response to the Arab legal arguments:

> It is sometimes suggested by Arab spokesmen that immediate independence of Palestine is required under Art. 22(4) of the Covenant of the League of Nations. The answer seems clear: (1) Para. 4 speaks of "*certain* communities formerly belonging to the Turkish Empire," not of "*the* communities" of the Turkish Empire; (2) That Palestine was not intended was pointed out in the correspondence attached to the British White Paper of 1922 (letter of Colonial Office to Palestine Arab Delegation, 1 March 1922); (3) In any event, the provisions of para. 4 are permissive, not mandatory; (4) The special treatment of Palestine was in view before para. 4 was drawn, which explains why the reference was to "*certain* communities" only; (5) Art. 94 of the Treaty of Sevres specifically referred to Art. 22(4), but Art. 95, dealing with Palestine, omitted such reference; (6) The preamble to the Palestine Mandate makes no reference to para. 4, while the preamble to the Syria and Lebanon Mandate does, thus making it clear that Palestine was considered to be *sui generis*.[103]

The remainder of the Jewish legal memorandum attacked the juridical basis for the 1939 White Paper, which still represented official British policy as of 1947. The memorandum noted the White Paper and the process leading to it, including consultations with Arab states rather than the Council of the League of Nations, violated Britain's international legal obligations under the Mandate.[104]

Garcia Granados wrote later, "it seemed to me that the legal case of the Jews was decisive,"[105] and "far stronger than that of the Arabs."[106]

By the time the Special Committee had reached the end of its stay in Palestine, the "full scale-hearing of the Jewish case and the Arab boycott of its own were turning delegates towards partition, however reluctantly."[107]

Just prior to leaving Palestine, the UNSCOP secretariat met with Hussein Khalidi of the Arab Higher Committee. Khalidi said the Palestinian Arabs would consider only one solution: Arab statehood over the *entirety* of Mandatory Palestine, and the cessation of *all* further Jewish immigration.[108]

## *Testimony from Arab states*

The Special Committee travelled from Jerusalem to Beirut to hear testimony on 22–23 July 1947 from representatives of Lebanon, Egypt, Syria, Iraq, Saudi Arabia, and Yemen.[109]

The Foreign Minister of Lebanon, Hamid Frangie, opened the proceedings, invoking the long-familiar Arab transformational legal framing of the conflict. Frangie reprised the Palestinian Arab narrative regarding the legal invalidity of the Balfour Declaration and the Mandate:

> The origin of Palestine's troubles is to be found in two documents, which are null and valueless, although it is upon them that Zionist claims are based: the Balfour Declaration and the Mandate. In the first of these documents, the British Government undertook to facilitate the establishment of a Jewish National Home, thereby violating the principle of self-determination and the rules of international law. At the time when the undertaking was given, Great Britain had no legal relations with Palestine, which then formed part of the Ottoman Empire. Further, the Balfour Declaration violates the undertakings given by the British Government concerning the Arabs in the letters exchanged between Sherif Hussein and Sir Henry McMahon, recognizing Arab independence within boundaries which included Palestine. Finally, the Balfour Declaration contravened the 1918 Declaration which stated that the British Army was entering Palestine not as a conquering but as a liberating army. As for the Mandate, it contains the same redhibitory defects as the Balfour Declaration. It also violates Article 22 of the League of Nations Covenant.[110]

Frangie continued by framing the Balfour Declaration and the Mandate as violating "the sacred rights of the Arabs."[111] He urged the Special Committee "to propose such a solution as may put an end to the present unrest and *ensure the triumph of justice* and the establishment of peace."[112]

During the cross-examination portion of his testimony, Frangie addressed the issue of Jewish immigration, insisting "all Jews who entered Palestine since the Balfour Declaration are illegal immigrants."[113]

The Saudi and Iraqi representatives appeared next. They argued that creating a Jewish State in even a tiny portion of Palestine would violate the UN Charter:

CHAIRMAN: Would you consider even the Jewish State constituted under the auspices of the United Nations as established by violence?

MR. FOUAD HAMZA (SAUDI ARABIA): We have confidence that the United Nations will not make such a decision. It will exceed the terms of the Charter of the United Nations to impose such a foreign State on Arab land. It will be against the will of the population.

MR. FADEL JAMALI (IRAQ): I would like to state, Mr. Chairman, that the example of the League of Nations is before us. When the League of Nations supported a Mandate which was against its own Covenant, against the terms of its covenant and against the principles of democracy and self-determination, the decision of the League of Nations did not preclude violation in Palestine. Since the Balfour Declaration was issued a violation started, and that violation involved the Arab world. Ever since, one revolution followed another and the Arab States surrounding Palestine were involved, whether officially or semi-officially, and yet the League of Nations was in existence. This was one of the grave mistakes of the League of Nations, in having passed the terms of a Mandate which were against the very terms of the Covenant. So we do hope that the United Nations will not make the mistake of the League of Nations by going against the spirit of its own Charter ...[114]

Sir Abdur Rahman of India, who had cross-examined Weizmann regarding the agreement with Prince Feisal, took up the same issue with the Arab representatives:

SIR ABDUR RAHMAN (INDIA): Now, referring to the Feisal-Weizmann Agreement. I know the contention that King Feisal was not authorized by Arabs. I also know the contention that the condition made by him had not been given effect to and that independence was not secured. I know all that. It is not necessary for me to ask you that. What I am asking you is, since most of the countries have obtained independence would it be too much now to enforce that Agreement that was made by King Feisal and Dr. Weizmann?

EMIR ADEL ARSLAN (SYRIA): I wish to say that as I had been a counsellor to the late King Feisal I had the opportunity of speaking of this draft Agreement with him. It was presented to him by Lawrence, himself. After this draft Agreement had been read to him and translated, he added with his own hand: "Under the condition that all the Arab nations be united under one same regime." Since this was the condition that could not be realized either by Weizmann or Lawrence, of course the Agreement fell by itself. Therefore, what is called an Agreement is not an Agreement at all.

SIR ABDUR RAHMAN (INDIA): I did not ask you that question at all. What I did ask you is what objection would there be in enforcing that Agreement now that most of the Arab countries have obtained their independence? That was the point I meant.

MR. RIAD SOLH (LEBANON): It would be necessary then that Palestine also should be independent. Therefore we come back to the same point.

SIR ABDUR RAHMAN (INDIA): That takes me to the next question. Was Palestine also to be independent before the document was to take effect, or was Palestine not to be included as was stated by Dr. Weizmann in his statement?

MR. FOUAD HAMZA (SAUDI ARABIA): It is self-evident in the draft Agreement itself that all the Arab nations should be independent and unified.

MR. FADEL JAMALI (IRAQ): The fact that the Committee is meeting here to investigate the question of Palestine shows that Feisal's part of the agreement

> had not been fulfilled. And, moreover, His Majesty, the late King Feisal, in his lifetime on several occasions rejected Zionist claims on that Agreement. Moreover, that Agreement never took a final, official shape, and was never ratified by any State, any government, or any permanent body.[115]

The Arab representatives then raised the McMahon-Hussein correspondence and the familiar Arab transformational legal frame that the correspondence had imposed a *legal* obligation on Britain to confer independence on the Palestinian Arabs after World War I. This led to a long and important exchange between Commissioner Garcia Granados and the Arab representatives:

MR. GARCIA GRANADOS (GUATEMALA): I think that a very interesting point of international law has just been raised. Before putting any question to the representative of the Arab States, I would like to ascertain certain facts. Is it true that in 1918 Palestine and all Arab countries belonged to Turkey?

MR. RIAD SOLH (LEBANON): No, we did not belong to Turkey, we were part of the Ottoman Empire. There is a great difference between belonging to a State and being part of it.

MR. GARCIA GRANADOS (GUATEMALA): Legally, these territories belonged to the Ottoman Empire. We have seen in history that after war the defeated countries had to cede some parts of their territory to the victorious countries. I need not give you many examples, but Europe has been formed to a great extent in this way. Russia obtained territories from Sweden, from Turkey, from Poland, from Austria; Germany from Austria and so on. In 1918, Turkey was beaten and had to sign the Treaties of Sevres and of Lausanne. By these treaties, Turkey surrendered the territories, now known as Arab territories, to the Allies.

MR. FOUAD HAMZI (SAUDI ARABIA): They were ceded to the Allies by the Treaty of Sevres but that clause was modified in the Treaty of Lausanne; the phrases "the Allies" was substituted by the phrase "the parties concerned," i.e., the inhabitants of the country.

MR. GARCIA GRANADOS (GUATEMALA): Yes, but the Treaty of Sevres ceded these territories to the Allies who were, during this time, settling the question of the Balfour Declaration and of the Jewish National Home in Palestine, in accordance with this Treaty of Sevres, signed in 1918.

MR. FRANGIE (LEBANON): The Balfour Declaration was issued in 1917 and the Treaty of Sevres was signed in 1918.

MR. GARCIA GRANADOS (GUATEMALA): Yes, but the Allies began to put the Balfour Declaration into effect in accordance with the Treaty of Sevres. They brought that question before the League of Nations and declared that Palestine would be the Jewish National Home, again in accordance with the Treaty of Sevres. Later they signed the Treaty of Lausanne. But by that time the Jewish National Home had already been created. This involves an important point of international law, which it would be interesting to discuss.

MR. FRANGIE (LEBANON): There is one point which I should like to make clear.

CHAIRMAN: We are not going to discuss that legal question here. I recognize Mr. Frangie, who wishes to make an explanation.

MR. HAMID FRANGIE (LEBANON): I should like to recall that the Sevres Treaty was signed in 1920 and was never ratified. It therefore has no legal value. In 1920, the Balfour Declaration had already been in effect for three years. Therefore, one cannot say that it is supported in any way by the Sevres Treaty. Further, I would like to say that we never belonged to Turkey but that we were a province of the Ottoman Empire, as were the other provinces. Finally the question had to be solved. If it was solved by the Lausanne Treaty; that is to say, that certain territories were yielded to the parties concerned, to the inhabitants of the countries. This explains why the Mandate aimed at the final independence of those States concerned. Unfortunately, Palestine was a state which received a different type of Mandate.

MR. GARCIA GRANADOS (GUATEMALA): That is a question of interpretation.

MR. FOUAD HAMZA (SAUDI ARABIA): It seems to me that the honourable member from Guatemala implied disposition by right of conquest by Great Britain to this territory. I think this is irrelevant, because at the time when the country was occupied, the Arabs had already become associated with the Allies. In fact, they were called "the Allied and Associated Powers." The Arabs were considered an Associated Power of the Allies. Therefore, the disposition by right of conquest does not apply. This is a point of fact that I want to mention.

EMIR ADEL ARSLAN (SYRIA): I should like to add further proof that the Arabs signed the Armistice with the Allies. The representative of the Arab States signed on the same footing, as France and the United Kingdom signed the Treaty with the Turks. Therefore, we were really allies of the Allies. Therefore, it is impossible to say that Palestine had been conquered; there is no question of conquest there. Now as regards the Sevres Treaty, the best proof that it was never put into force is that Turkey was not partitioned, was not divided, and the Treaty was signed at a time when Istanbul was occupied by the Allied troops. It also gave rise to the Kemalist movement, and it was also because of that Treaty that Turkey deposed its Sultan. The Allies further recognized the right of the Turks to decide their own fate, and that gave rise to the Lausanne Treaty. Therefore, on this occasion, there was no question of Palestine or of the Balfour Declaration. The Lausanne Treaty recognizes the right of the Arabs to decide their own fate for themselves. Therefore, the right of the Arabs to decide their own fate has been recognized.

MR. FARID ZEINEDINE (SYRIA): It is very difficult … to speak about the right of conquest. For, in regard to any justification of the situation by reference to such right, it must be remembered, first, that there is a Charter of the United Nations, or even when there was no Charter of the United Nations, there was the Covenant of the League of Nations. These two Charters were based on something very different and quite contrary to the right of conquest. Even so, as has already been explained, that right of conquest cannot apply because it is the Arabs who were the allies of the Allies, and therefore, they have helped to effect this conquest, if it can be called that. It was a liberation,

> not a conquest. Furthermore, the Treaty of Sevres, as has already been explained, was the basis according to which the Mandates were distributed, because the Ottoman Empire, according to that Treaty, ceded its territories to the principal Allied and Associated Powers. But the Treaty of Sevres was not ratified. The Treaty of Lausanne took its place. From Article 16 of the Treaty of Lausanne it is clear that it ceded them to the interested parties. It should be noted – and this is the main consideration I should like to bring forth – that in the Treaty of Lausanne there are no principal Allied and Associated Powers. Therefore, the Mandate given under the Sevres Treaty was never confirmed or accepted by the Treaty of Lausanne which never gave any right whatsoever to the principal Allied and Associated Powers to dispose of Palestine or any other Ottoman territory. Therefore, this is one of the reasons why the Mandate juridically speaking is non-existent.[116]

The Iraqi delegate, Fadel Jamali, also invoked the Palestinian Arab legal narrative. Interestingly, just as many Palestinian witnesses had previously argued, Jamali began by claiming "Palestine is only the southern part of the whole of natural and historical Syria. Nationally the indigenous people of Palestine are one and the same people as those of Syria, and culturally and nationally united with the rest of the Arab world."[117]

Jamali then invoked the Palestinian Arab transformational legal framing of the conflict:

> The Mandate violated in general all the principles of democracy and self-determination which were contained in the Covenant of the League of Nations. In particular, it violated the very spirit and letter of Paragraph 4, Article 22 of the Covenant of the League of Nations … [which] clearly recognizes the right of the Arabs of Palestine to independence and to the choice of the Mandatory power by the inhabitants. These rights the Mandate for Palestine ignored, just as it ignored the real object of the Mandate, that of holding people as a trust with the object of helping them toward self-government and independence and not with the object of imposing an alien body whose object is to dominate the country and establish a state therein. Thus we find that the Mandate over Palestine has no moral or legal foundations for the League of Nations had no legal or moral authority to violate the letter and spirit of its own Covenant … the Arabs from the very beginning never recognized the legality or the validity of the Mandate over Palestine … it is not right or just that the Arabs of Palestine should have been deprived of their rights to self-government and self-determination.[118]

Jamali concluded by again invoking legal framing and narrative:

> What is involved in the Palestine issue is whether the principles of peace and justice can prevail or whether domination by the force of money,

> distorted propaganda, political pressure and terrorism will succeed ... An experience of thirty years proved that *flagrant injustice was done to the political rights of the Arabs of Palestine*. That injustice led to strife and unrest throughout this period. Many committees and commissions were sent and made reports, with no avail. The Arabs have become desperate and they have lost hope in committees. May this Committee at last, guided by the principles of the Charter, *make such recommendations which will finally remove the source of trouble and injustice*, bring about clarity and finality in the situation so that peace and harmony may prevail in the Land of Peace and in all the Middle East.[119]

The Saudi representative, Fouad Hamza, went even further with his use of transformational legal framing:

> *Never in the history of human conflicts have any people or country suffered an injustice so grave as the injustice and calamities suffered by the Arabs of Palestine ... We are firmly convinced of the justice of the Arab case.* Our belief is strong in the desire of the United Nations to carry out a just course in the interests of peace and security in this part of the world. Thus in resting our case upon your sense of justice we sincerely hope for the establishment of permanent peace. You will thereby have rendered service to a just cause in the interests of humanity. You will have rendered service to the Arabs who will long remain.[120]

## *Meeting with King Abdullah*

Following the Beirut testimony, the Special Committee flew to Amman for a private meeting with King Abdullah on 25 July 1947.

Ralph Bunche of the UNSCOP secretariat prepared a memorandum several days later summarising the Committee's meeting with Abdullah:

> [T]he King tended to parry all questions by taking the position that there were many proposed solutions for Palestine and many positions on the question of Palestine which might be taken. What was necessary was to adopt one solution and firmly enforce it. But, he added, in any solution the incontestable Arab rights must be protected. It would be very difficult, he pointed out, for Arabs to accept a Jewish State even in a part of Palestine.[121]

The British Embassy in Amman later reported to the Foreign Office that the Commissioners were "disappointed at the line of extreme discretion taken by King Abdullah who failed to give them any lead as to his real views."[122] Abdullah would later confide to Greek and US diplomats that he did not object to partitioning Palestine, so long as he could annex the portion allocated to the Palestinian Arabs.[123]

Abdullah and the Jewish leadership also had reached, according to some historians, an unwritten understanding that Palestine would be divided among them:

> From the summer of 1946 an unwritten agreement of principle existed between the Jewish Agency and King Abdullah, that in the event of a decision to divide Palestine into two states, Abdullah would annex the Arab area to his kingdom, and the Jews would establish their state in the territory designated for that purpose. This understanding did not stipulate mutual aid in implementing annexation or the establishment of the state, and each side undertook mutually not to prevent the other from carrying out its part of the agreement. The understanding was reaffirmed in a meeting between Golda Meyerson (Meir), the acting head of the Jewish Agency's Political Department, and King Abdullah at Naharayim on 17 November 1947 less than two weeks before the United Nations passed the resolution partitioning Palestine into two states, one Arab and one Jewish.[124]

## UNSCOP deliberations and report

### *Deliberations*

Near the end of the Special Committee's stay in Palestine, the British High Commissioner in Jerusalem, Sir Alan Cunningham, reported to Colonial Secretary Arthur Creech Jones that the Special Committee seemed favourably disposed toward recommending the partition of Palestine into separate Jewish and Arab states.[125] But when the Special Committee arrived in Geneva in early August 1947, after conducting a week-long tour of European DP camps, the outcome seemed less certain.

Indeed, the American diplomat Ralph Bunche, serving as a top staffer to UNSCOP, privately doubted the Special Committee's ability to render a sound verdict:

> As to the Committee, there is little that I can say, or rather should say in writing. It is not by any means a strong committee and that may be a very great understatement. Geneva, which we will reach on Friday, will soon reveal if there are any hidden qualities of genius in this group.[126]

The Special Committee spent the next three weeks deliberating its verdict.[127] The leading historian of UNSCOP has emphasised the fairness and objectivity of the Special Committee's deliberative process:

> The Arabs' claim that the committee was pre-directed to the solution of partition is entirely refuted. At the outset of the inquiry the forces were balanced and the Zionists and the Palestinian Arabs had an equal chance to convince the members of the committee of their arguments.[128]

According to Garcia Granados' notes, the Special Committee members focused on legal issues as much as political issues during their deliberations. By the end of their first deliberation session, according to Garcia Granados, the Special Committee members unanimously agreed the Mandate should be terminated.[129] They also unanimously agreed, "it would not be just to place all the Arabs of Palestine under Jewish rule, nor all the Jews of Palestine under Arab rule."[130] But the Special Committee could not agree whether to recommend partitioning Palestine into separate Jewish and Arab states or creating a single, binational state.[131]

Indeed, partition commanded the support of less than a majority of the delegates during the early stages of the deliberations and continued to lack majority support as late as the last week of August.[132] As one historian aptly observed, "[t]he committee, which was accused by the Arabs of bringing a pre-prepared solution with them, was unable to reach a decision four days before the end of its term."[133]

The Special Committee conducted its deliberations in systematic fashion, ruling out the most extreme options first. Accordingly, the Special Committee rejected versions of the one-state solution in which either the Jews or the Arabs (but not both) would be vested with control of the entire country.[134]

From there, the Committee rejected two variations of the one-state solution: the binational state advocated by Judah Magnes and the provincial autonomy or cantonisation plan advocated by the British. The Special Committee found the binational scheme "patently artificial and of dubious practicality." The Special Committee likewise rejected the provincial autonomy plan as "quite unworkable."[135]

That left the Special Committee with two remaining options: first, a two-state solution in which Palestine would be partitioned into separate Jewish and Arab sovereign countries, with Jerusalem internationalised and some form of economic union between the two states for a fixed period of years; or second, a "federal-state" variant of the one-state solution, in which the Jewish and Palestinian areas would enjoy more self-governance than contemplated under the original and modified provincial autonomy plans.[136]

The Special Committee could not agree which of the two remaining solutions to endorse. The Special Committee's discussion of the two issues on 6 August 1947 "broke into a melee of dissenting views, and finally ended in dramatic confusion."[137]

The Special Committee resolved the tension by creating two working groups to explore the two competing proposals. The first working group, containing the Iranian, Indian, and Yugoslav members, focused on the single state, binational proposal, eventually producing a minority proposal advocating that solution. The second working group comprised the remaining eight members of the Special Committee, who focused on developing the partition proposal. The second working group was divided into two subgroups, one focusing on drawing boundaries, and the second on the organisation of the two new states and the operational mechanics of partition.[138]

**FIGURE 12.7** Justice Ivan Rand (Public Domain)

During their deliberations, the Special Committee briefly considered the possibility of inviting the Mandatory Government in Palestine to offer further input. Justice Rand (Figure 12.7) shot down the idea in decidedly judicial language:

> The Mandatory Government *is a party in this dispute*, and any invitation issued to it for official consultation at this stage of the proceedings will impair the Committee's independence and neutrality.[139]

Although the Special Committee rejected any consultation with the Mandatory Government, it did hear from British Labour MP Richard Crossman on 14 August 1947. Crossman had played a key role on the Palestine issue as a member of the Anglo-American Committee of Inquiry one year earlier. Crossman reiterated his support for partition, noting an imposed, "organized partition" would be better than Britain leaving a vacuum in Palestine. Crossman also expressed support for a "pro-Jewish" solution as "the more just."[140]

As the deliberations proceeded in Geneva, Jewish Agency officials monitoring the situation grew concerned the Special Committee might either agree to a two-state solution, but with far less territory earmarked for the Jewish State than the Zionists needed to meet their most minimal requirements, or the Special

Committee would opt for a one-state solution, which to the Zionists meant a majority-ruled Palestinian Arab State.

As one Zionist official recalled, Jewish prospects seemed "dismal ... we were told more than once in meeting UNSCOP personnel that there wasn't a scrap of hope of achieving our full demands."[141] The Zionist official, invoking the Jewish legal framing, expressed the hope that the Special Committee would acknowledge Jewish "claims of right and justice, the suffering and agony of a harassed people ..."[142]

Zionist officials took no chances, realising UNSCOP's verdict represented their last chance for statehood in at least a portion of Palestine. One official made an emergency visit to Justice Rand immediately prior to the Special Committee's most important deliberation session, begging him not to reduce the geographic area for the prospective Jewish State to a "near sham." Justice Rand, who had expressed great sympathy and admiration for Zionism during his travels with the Special Committee the prior month in Palestine, said "I won't allow you to be placed in a territorial ghetto."[143]

Justice Rand ultimately played a key role in helping cobble together a majority of the Special Committee members to support partition. Evidently swayed by the Jewish transformational legal framing, Justice Rand employed decidedly legal argumentation to persuade other UNSCOP members to support his position:

> As for the argument that partition fulfilled pre-established legal requirements to create a Jewish National Home in Palestine, Rand believed that an Arab state in all of Palestine would be a "betrayal of the Jewish people and a violation of international agreements." The international agreements that Rand was referring to were the Balfour Declaration of 1917 and the Mandate granted in 1922, which the Zionists used effectively to facilitate the creation of a "national home for the Jews in Palestine ..."[144]

Ultimately, the Special Committee could not agree unanimously on which of the final two options to recommend to the General Assembly. A majority (seven out of eleven) of the Special Committee members (Canada, Czechoslovakia, Guatemala, the Netherlands, Peru, Sweden, and Uruguay) supported the two-state solution (partition). A minority of four countries (Iran, India, Australia, and Yugoslavia) favoured the one-state solution (federal-state plan).

The majority's partition proposal is reflected in Map 12.1.

## *UNSCOP report*

The Special Committee submitted its Report to the Secretary General on 1 September 1947, the deadline fixed in the Terms of Reference.

The full Report started with a detailed description of the Committee's activities and methodology and then moved into a discussion of the historical background of the Mandate and the current social and economic conditions in the country.

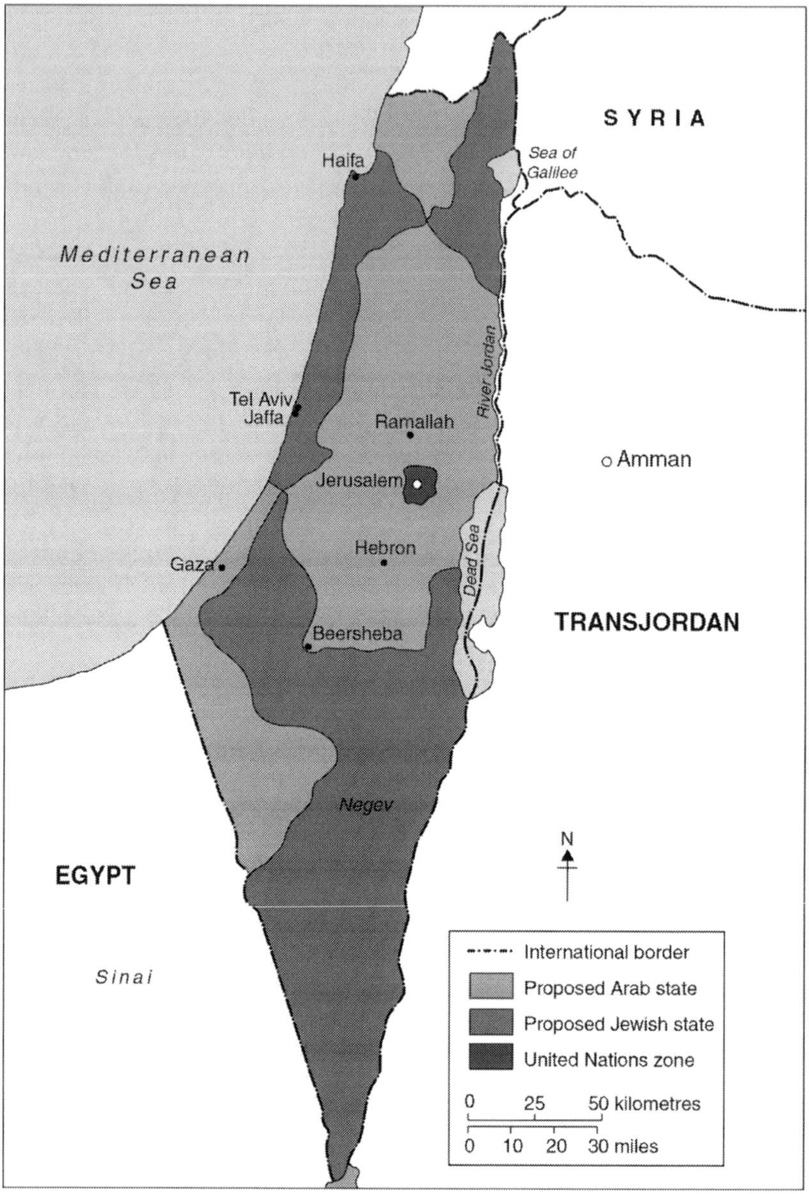


**MAP 12.1** The UNSCOP Partition Plan, September 1947 (Public Domain)

The Report began with a recitation of 11 unanimous recommendations and then described the separate recommendations of the majority and minority factions of the Special Committee.[145] The 11 unanimous recommendations included terminating the Mandate and granting independence to Palestine at the earliest possible date, following a short transition period. The unanimous recommendations also addressed the need to preserve access to the Holy Places in Palestine, protect the human rights and religious freedom of minority groups in Palestine, and preserve the economic unity of the country. The Special Committee also recommended unanimously that the international community takes steps to deal urgently with the problem of European Jewish displaced persons, including admitting 150,000 Jewish Holocaust survivors into Palestine.

The Majority Report endorsed the two-state solution. It recommended partitioning Palestine into three separate entities – a Jewish State, an Arab State, and Jerusalem under international control as a *corpus separatum*. In addition to Justice Rand, Justice Sandstrom played an instrumental role in advocating for the two-state solution and persuading the UNSCOP majority to concur.[146]

The Majority Report then engaged in a lengthy analysis justifying its recommendation of partition and the two-state solution. The analytical portion of the Majority Report seemed to borrow significantly from Jewish transformational legal framing.

The Majority Report began by assessing the competing nationalist claims of the Jews and Palestinian Arabs. The Majority Report first addressed the Jewish claim, examining whether the term "National Home for the Jewish People," as used in the Balfour Declaration and the Mandate, could be deemed as a matter of law to mean a Jewish State in all or part of Palestine:

> The notion of the National Home, which derived from the formulation of Zionist aspirations in the 1897 Basle program has provoked many discussions concerning its meaning, scope and legal character, especially since it has no known legal connotation and there are no precedents in international law for its interpretation. It was used in the Balfour Declaration and in the Mandate, both of which promised the establishment of a "Jewish National Home" without, however, defining its meaning. The conclusion seems to be inescapable that the vagueness in the wording of both instruments was intentional. The fact that the term "National Home" was employed, instead of the word "State" or "Commonwealth" would indicate that the intention was to place a restrictive construction on the National Home scheme from its very inception. This argument, however, may not be conclusive since "National Home," although not precluding the possibility of establishing a Jewish State in the future, had the advantage of not shocking public opinion outside the Jewish world, and even in many Jewish quarters, as the term "Jewish State" would have done.[147]

The Majority Report next recognised the legal force of the Balfour Declaration and the Mandate:

> Nevertheless, neither the Balfour Declaration nor the Mandate precluded the eventual creation of a Jewish State. The Mandate in its Preamble recognized, with regard to the Jewish people, the "grounds for reconstituting their

> National Home." By providing, as one of the main obligations of the mandatory Power the facilitation of Jewish immigration, it conferred upon the Jews an opportunity, through large-scale immigration, to create eventually a Jewish State with a Jewish majority. Both the Balfour Declaration and the Mandate involved international commitments to the Jewish people as a whole.[148]

The Majority Report acknowledged the provisions of both the Balfour Declaration and the Mandate regarding the civil and religious rights of the indigenous Arab population. But the Report, in language impossible to find in modern-day UN parlance, rejected any notion that the Palestinian Arabs enjoyed a superior claim to Palestine than the Jews:

> The Jewish assurance that no political injustice would be done to the Arabs by the creation of a Jewish State in Palestine, since the Arabs have never established a government there, gains some support from the fact that not since 63 B.C., when Pompey stormed Jerusalem, has Palestine been an independent State.[149]

The Majority Report then turned to an assessment of the Palestinian Arab case. Significantly, again in language one would never see from the modern-day United Nations, the Report cast doubt on the strength of Palestinian Arab nationalism:

> The Arabs consider that all of the territory of Palestine is by right Arab patrimony. Although in an Arab State they would recognize the right of Jews to continue in possession of land legally acquired by them during the Mandate, they would regard as a violation of their "natural" right any effort, such as partition, to reduce the territory of Palestine. The desire of the Arab people of Palestine to safeguard their national existence is a very natural desire. However, Palestinian nationalism, as distinct from Arab nationalism, is itself a relatively new phenomenon, which appeared only after the division of the "Arab rectangle" by the settlement of the First World War. The National Home policy and the vigorous policy of immigration pursued by the Jewish leadership has sharpened the Arab fear of danger from the intruding Jewish population.[150]

The Majority Report then addressed the Arab claim regarding the McMahon-Hussein correspondence. The Majority Report noted that Prince Feisal's statement to the Versailles Peace Conference and his written agreement with Weizmann undercut the Arab claim that Britain had promised Palestine exclusively to them:

> A Memorandum presented by Amir Feisal to the Paris Peace Conference, however, would indicate that the special position of Palestine was recognized in Arab circles. He said: "The Jews are very close to the Arabs

> in blood and there is no conflict of character between the two races. In principle we are absolutely at one. Nevertheless, the Arabs cannot risk assuming the responsibility of holding level the scales in the clash of races and religions that have, in this one province, so often involved the world in difficulties. They would wish for the effective superposition of a great trustee, so long as a representative local administration commended itself by actively promoting the material prosperity of the country." It was also Amir Feisal who, representing and acting on behalf of the Arab Kingdom of the Hejaz, signed an agreement with Dr. Weizmann, representing and acting on behalf of the Zionist Organization. In this agreement, Feisal, subject to the condition that the Arabs obtained independence as demanded in his Memorandum to the British Foreign Office of 4 January 1919, accepted the Balfour Declaration and the encouragement of Jewish immigration into Palestine.[151]

The Majority Report, in a stunning blow to Palestinian Arab nationalism, decisively rejected Palestinian Arab rights of self-determination in all of Palestine:

> With regard to the principle of self-determination, although international recognition was extended to this principle at the end of the First World War and it was adhered to with regard to the other Arab territories, at the time of the creation of the "A" Mandates, it was not applied to Palestine, obviously because of the intention to make possible the creation of the Jewish National Home there. Actually, it may well be said that the Jewish National Home and the *sui generis* Mandate for Palestine run counter to that principle.[152]

The Majority Report likewise flatly rejected the long-standing Palestinian Arab claim that the Mandate was void *ab initio* because it conflicted with Article 22 of the Covenant of the League of Nations:

> There would seem to be no grounds for questioning the validity of the Mandate for the reason advanced by the Arab States. The terms of the Mandate for Palestine, formulated by the Supreme Council of the Principal Allied Powers as a part of the settlement of the First World War, were subsequently approved and confirmed by the Council of the League of Nations.[153]

The Majority Report then offered various reasons in support of the majority recommendation of the two-state solution:

> The basic premise underlying the partition proposal is that the claims to Palestine of the Arabs and Jews, both possessing validity, are irreconcilable, and that among all of the solutions advanced, partition will provide

> the most realistic and practicable settlement, and is the most likely to afford a workable basis for meeting in part the claims and national aspirations of both parties. It is a fact that both of these peoples have their historic roots in Palestine, and that both make vital contributions to the economic and cultural life of the country. The partition solution takes these considerations fully into account. The basic conflict in Palestine is a clash of two intense nationalisms. Regardless of the historic origins of the conflict, the rights and wrongs of the promises and counter promises and the international intervention incident to the Mandate, there are now in Palestine some 650,000 Jews and some 1,200,000 Arabs who are dissimilar in their ways of living and, for the time being, separated by political interests which render difficult full and effective political cooperation among them, whether voluntary or induced by constitutional arrangements. Only by means of partition can these conflicting national aspirations find substantial expression and qualify both peoples to take their places as independent nations in the international community and in the United Nations. The partition solution provides that finality which is a most urgent need in the solution. Every other proposed solution would tend to induce the two parties to seek modification in their favour by means of persistent pressure. The grant of independence to both States, however, would remove the basis for such efforts.[154]

The Majority Report is a remarkable document, for many reasons. Largely drafted by Ralph Bunche, who personally disfavoured Jewish statehood in Palestine, it nevertheless stands as a powerful endorsement of Jewish national aspirations in Palestine. Moreover, in today's world, it would be unimaginable for any Committee of the United Nations to offer such a powerful endorsement of Zionism. Indeed, less than three decades later the General Assembly voted to condemn Zionism as a form of "racism."

## Reactions to the UNSCOP report

### *British reaction*

The British Cabinet met on Saturday morning, 20 September 1947, to consider the UNSCOP report. Foreign Minister Bevin prepared a briefing memorandum in advance of the meeting, in which he harshly criticised the UNSCOP majority report as "manifestly unjust to the Arabs."[155] Bevin predicted the Palestinian Arabs and the surrounding Arab states would never accept partition. He viewed the creation of a Jewish State in a portion of Palestine as "poor compensation for the loss of Arab goodwill and with it our prospect of establishing that firm strategic hold on the Middle East which is an indispensable part of Commonwealth defence policy."[156]

Bevin concluded by noting the situation in Palestine had become "intolerable" for Britain and that Britain's "only remaining course would be to withdraw from Palestine."[157]

The Cabinet debated Bevin's memorandum two days later and approved the recommendation to announce Britain's withdrawal from Palestine.[158]

## *Arab reaction*

Arab reaction to the majority report was "one of uncompromising and intransigent hostility … [their] threats of violence were quite opposed to the letter and spirit of the Charter of the United Nations and were obviously aimed at intimidating the delegates to the [General] Assembly."[159] Jamal Husseini, on behalf of the Palestinian Arabs, reacted to the report by threatening "blood will flow in the rivers of the Middle East."[160]

The Palestinian Arabs declared a general strike to protest the UNSCOP report, and the Supreme Muslim Council sent a formal protest to the British High Commissioner in Jerusalem.[161]

Emile Ghory, spokesperson for the Arab Higher Committee, employed transformational legal framing in his characterisation of the Report as "an *excess of injustice* to Palestine, a flagrant violation of the natural rights of the Arabs in their own country."[162]

## *Jewish reaction*

The Zionist leadership expressed satisfaction with the UNSCOP report. The official reaction came from Golda Meyerson (later Meir), the Political Director of the Jewish Agency in Jerusalem, who "paid high tribute to the efficiency and 'deep insight' of the Committee."[163] Ben-Gurion likewise was "elated" with the Majority Report.[164]

Zionist officials knew, however, they would face many obstacles in the weeks and months ahead.

## Notes

1 CAB 129/16/28, C.P. (47) 28 (Top Secret), Palestine: Reference to United Nations, Memorandum by the Secretary of State for Foreign Affairs (attaching memorandum from the legal advisers to the Foreign Office and the Colonial Office) (13 January 1947).

2 *Id.*, para. 3.

3 *Id.*, para. 4. The British Government began discussing internally as early as October 1946 whether prior approval from the United Nations would be required to partition Palestine into separate Jewish and Arab states. FO 371/52563, Letter from C.W. Baxter (Foreign Office) to John Martin (Colonial Office) (18 October 1946); *Id.*, Reply letter from John Martin (Colonial Office) to C.W. Baxter (Foreign Office) (4 November 1946); *Id.*, Draft Minute from H. Beeley (Foreign Office) to British UN delegation (13 November 1946).

4 CAB 129/16/28, C.P. (47) 28 (Top Secret), Palestine: Reference to United Nations, Memorandum by the Secretary of State for Foreign Affairs (attaching memorandum from the legal advisers to the Foreign Office and the Colonial Office) (13 January 1947). para. 4.

5 *Id.*, para. 7.

6 CAB 128/11/2, C.M. (47) 6 (Top Secret) Conclusions of Cabinet Meeting, Confidential Annex at 2–3 (15 January 1947).
7 UNSCOP A/AC.14/8, *The Political History of Palestine under British Administration Memorandum by His Britannic Majesty's Government,* at paras. 146–148 (1 July 1947); *see also* A. Kochavi, *op. cit.*, at 159–160.
8 CAB 129/16/49, C.P. (47) 49, Palestine: Joint Memorandum (Top Secret) by the Secretary of State for Foreign Affairs and the Secretary of State for the Colonies (6 February 1947) at para. 1.
9 *Id.*, paras. 2–4.
10 *Id.*, para. 5.
11 *Id.*, para. 6 (emphasis added).
12 Bevin later told Parliament the modified provincial autonomy plan "envisaged the establishment of local areas, Arab and Jewish, with a substantial degree of autonomy within a unitary State, with a central government in which both Arabs and Jews would share. These proposals provided that Jewish immigrants should be admitted over the next two years at the rate of 4,000 a month, and that thereafter the continuation of the rate of Jewish immigration should be determined, with due regard to economic absorptive capacity, by the High Commissioner in consultation with his advisory council, or, in the event of disagreement, by an arbitration tribunal appointed by the United Nations. This plan, while consistent with the principles of the Mandate, added an element which has hitherto been lacking in our administration of Palestine, namely, a practical promise of evolution towards independence by building up, during a five year period of trusteeship, political institutions rooted in the lives of the people." Hansard, HC Deb. vol. 433, cols. 986–987 (18 February 1947).
13 CAB 129/16/49, C.P. (47) 49, Palestine: Joint Memorandum (Top Secret) by the Secretary of State for Foreign Affairs and the Secretary of State for the Colonies (6 February 1947) at para. 12.
14 *Id.*, para. 12; *see also* R. Ovendale, *Britain, the United States and the End of the Palestine Mandate, 1942-1948* at 193–194 (Royal Historical Society, Boydell Press, 1989).
15 CAB 128/9/18, C.M. 18 (47), Conclusions (Secret) of a Meeting of the Cabinet (7 February 1947) at 120.
16 CAB 129/17/9, C.P. (47) 59, Palestine: Memorandum (Top Secret) by the Secretary of State for Foreign Affairs and the Secretary of State for the Colonies (13 February 1947) at para. 1.
17 *Id.*, para. 5.
18 *Id.*, para. 12.
19 CAB 128/9/22, C.M. 22 (47), Conclusions (Secret) of a Meeting of the Cabinet (14 February 1947) at 146.
20 Hansard, HC Deb. vol. 433, cols. 988–989 (18 February 1947).
21 Library Special Collections, Charles E. Young Research Library, UCLA, Ralph Bunche papers, Box 97, Folder 6, Letter from N. Feinberg to T. Lie (23 February 1947). Feinberg's letter likely represented the first time during the conflict when either the Arab or Jewish side employed transformational legal framing with the United Nations. In the modern era, the United Nations has embraced the Palestinian transformational legal framing of the conflict. *See* ch. 1, *supra*.
22 Hansard, HC Deb. vol. 433, cols. 1901–1902 (25 February 1947).
23 United Nations A/286, Letter from Alexander Cadogan to Dr Victor Chi Tsai Hoo, Assistant Secretary General (2 April 1947); *see also* United Nations A/364, Official Records of the Second Session of the General Assembly, Supplement No. 11, *United Nations Special Committee On Palestine, Report To The General Assembly*, Vol. 1 at Ch. I, para. 1 (3 September 1947) (hereafter "UNSCOP Report"); J. Robinson, *Palestine and the United Nations* at 50–53 (Public Affairs Press, 1947).
24 The leading historian of UNSCOP, the Israeli scholar Elad Ben-Dror, has demonstrated UNSCOP began its work with no preordained outcome. The Palestinian Arab boycott of UNSCOP stood in stark contrast to the effectiveness of Jewish lobbying. Both factors

played a significant role in persuading the UNSCOP majority to support the two-state solution. *See* E. Ben-Dror, *The Arab Struggle Against Partition: The International Arena of Summer 1947*, Middle Eastern Studies 43:2, 259–293 (2007).

25 United Nations A/PV.28, Twenty-Eighth Meeting (29 April 1947). For a detailed description of the First Committee's debates, *see* J. Robinson, *op. cit.*, Part Two.

26 UNSCOP Report, *op. cit.*, Ch. I, para. 12.

27 United Nations A/307, Special Committee on Palestine: Report of the First Committee (13 May 1947).

28 United Nations A/2/PV.78, Seventy-Eighth Plenary Meeting (14 May 1947).

29 United Nations A/2/PV.77, Seventy-Seventh Plenary Meeting (14 May 1947).

30 *Id.*

31 United Nations A/RES/106 (S-1) (15 May 1947); *see also* United Nations A/2/PV.79, Seventy-Ninth Plenary Meeting (15 May 1947) (roll-call vote on General Assembly Resolution 106).

32 United Nations Archives, S-0504-0004-0009-00001, *Special Committee on Palestine, Summary Record of the First Meeting (Private), Held at Lake Success, Monday, 26 May 1947* (29 May 1947).

33 UNSCOP, A/AC.13/PV.2, Verbatim Record of the Second Meeting of the Special Committee on Palestine (2 June 1947). The Canadian delegate, Ivan C. Rand, was also a lawyer and a Justice of the Canadian Supreme Court.

34 J.G. Granados, *The Birth of Israel: The Drama As I Saw It*, at 13 (Alfred A. Knopf, 1948).

35 Eight of the eleven members of the Special Committee had law degrees. Four had served as judges. United Nations Archives, S-0504-0009-0004-00003, Memorandum from M. Arakie, Assistant Secretary, Special Committee on Palestine, to Secretary General T. Lie and Assistant Secretary General V. Hoo, "Biographical Notes on Members of Special Committee on Palestine" [Undated].

36 D. Horowitz, *op. cit.*, at 162.

37 *Id.*

38 *Id.* at 165.

39 *Id.* at 63.

40 *Id.* at 7–8. Ambassador Granados incorrectly described UNSCOP as the "first" international tribunal to investigate and render judgement on issues related to Palestine. The first such tribunal was the British-appointed Lofgren Commission of 1930, comprising judges from Sweden, Switzerland, and the Netherlands serving under the auspices of the League of Nations, to conduct a trial and render judgement regarding the respective rights and claims of Muslims and Jews to the Wailing Wall. *See* S. Zipperstein, *op. cit.*, Ch. 4.

41 D. Horowitz, *op. cit.*, at 159–160.

42 *Id.* at 158.

43 United Nations PAL/91, Press Release (31 August 1947).

44 M. Jones, *op. cit.*, at 269.

45 United Nations Archives, S-0472-0086-0011-00001, Cablegram from Arab Higher Committee to UN Secretary General (13 June 1947); *see also* E. Ben-Dror, *The Success of the Zionist Strategy vis-à-vis UNSCOP*, Israel Affairs 20:1 at 23 (2014).

46 United Nations Archives, S-0472-0086-0011-00001, Cablegram from Arab Higher Committee to UN Secretary General (13 June 1947); *see also* FRUS, 501.BB Palestine/6–1147, Telegram No. 243 (Confidential) from US Consul General, Jerusalem to Secretary of State (11 June 1947) (noting some local Palestinian Arabs opposed the Arab Higher Committee's decision to boycott UNSCOP, and further reporting Jamal Husseini had alleged to local Arab leaders that UNSCOP had already decided to recommend partition in advance of any hearing); United Nations Archives, S-0504-0004-0008-00001, translation of article in Palestinian newspaper *Al Wahda* (16 June 1947) (accusing Chairman Sandstrom and UNSCOP of predisposition against the Palestinian Arabs and justifying Arab Higher Committee boycott of UNSCOP, arguing "the Palestinian case is right, just and clear … and needs no inquiry or investigation"). Ben-Dror

has since debunked the Palestinian Arab claim that UNSCOP had been predisposed in favour of partition prior to its arrival in Palestine to hear evidence. E. Ben-Dror (2007), *op. cit.*, at 268 ("with every detail revealed in this research it should become clear that at the outset of the inquiry, on the axis between the Jews and the Arabs, [UNSCOP] was a balanced entity").

47 E. Ben-Dror (2007), *op. cit.*, at 269.

48 FRUS, 501.BB Palestine/6–3047, Telegram (Secret) No. 113 from the US Consul General, Jerusalem, to the Secretary of State (30 June 1947).

49 UNSCOP, A/AC.13/42, Letter from Chairman Sandstrom to Arab Higher Committee (8 July 1947) (repeating invitation to cooperate with the Special Committee); United Nations A/AC.13/NC/52, Letter from Jamal Husseini, Arab Higher Committee to Chairman Sandstrom (10 July 1947) (rejecting Special Committee's request for cooperation); *see also* UNSCOP Report, Ch. I, paras. 32–34; E. Ben-Dror, *The Success of the Zionist Strategy vis-a-vis UNSCOP*, Israel Affairs 20:1 at 23 (2014) ("Despite all the efforts to persuade it to recant, the AHC (Arab Higher Committee) continued to shun UNSCOP to the end and managed to impose the boycott on the entire Palestinian public").

50 J.G. Granados, *op. cit.*, at 39.

51 D. Horowitz, *op. cit.*, at 160.

52 *See, e.g.*, United Nations Archives, S-0504-0009-0003-00002, *Notes on a Conversation with Mr. Khalidy, Secretary of the Arab Higher Committee*, Special Series No. 9 (7 August 1947) (reporting on conversation at a 16 July 1947 dinner party in Jerusalem between Justice Sandstrom, Victor Hoo, and Khalidy, during which Khalidy described the Arab case but reiterated the decision to boycott UNSCOP would not be reversed); E. Ben-Dror (2007), *op. cit.*, at 271–272.

53 UNSCOP, A/AC.13/SR.6, Verbatim Record of the Sixth Meeting (Private) (16 June 1947).

54 UNSCOP, A/AC.13/SR.8, Summary Record of the Eighth Meeting (Public) (17 June 1947). The Guatemalan member of the Special Committee, Jorge Garcia Granados, described his colleague from India, Sir Abdur Rahman, as acting like a "prosecutor" during cross-examination of Shertok. J.G. Granados, *op. cit.*, at 48.

55 "Zionist Rules Out Unity in Palestine," *New York Times*, 18 June 1947 at 13.

56 United Nations, Press Release PAL/91, George Symeonides, UNSCOP Press Officer, "Background Story on Palestine Report" (31 August 1947).

57 J.G. Granados, *op. cit.*, at 145.

58 J. Robinson, *op. cit.*, at 203.

59 UNSCOP, A/AC.13/PV.16, Verbatim Record of the Sixteenth Meeting (Public) (4 July 1947).

60 *Id.* (emphasis added).

61 *Id.*

62 *Id.* (emphasis added).

63 *Id.*

64 *Id.* (emphasis added).

65 *Id.* (emphasis added).

66 UNSCOP, A/AC.13/PV.19, Verbatim Record of the Nineteenth Meeting (Public) (7 July 1947) (emphasis added).

67 *Id.*

68 *Id.*

69 *Id.*

70 *Id.*

71 *Id.*

72 *Id.*

73 *Id.*

74 *Id.* (emphasis added).

75 *Id.*

76 *Id.* The Zionist leadership throughout the UNSCOP hearings was careful not to endorse partition in public but frequently did so in private, especially at a 14 July 1947 secret meeting at Shertok's home with Zionist officials and nearly all members of the Special Committee. *See* E. Ben-Dror (2014), *op. cit.*, at 27–29.

77 UNSCOP, A/AC.13/PV.19, Verbatim Record of the Nineteenth Meeting (Public) (7 July 1947).

78 *Id.*

79 FRUS, 501.BB Palestine/7–1447, Telegram No. 123 (Secret) from the US Consul General, Jerusalem, to the Secretary of State (14 July 1947). According to a contemporaneous top secret British military intelligence report, Rahman was "obviously pro-Arab" and waging a "campaign against the Jews." The Mufti, anxious to maintain the official Palestinian Arab boycott of the Special Committee, but equally eager to supply Rahman with anti-Zionist talk points, surreptitiously supplied information to Rahman via the Lebanese and Syrian Governments, an arrangement British intelligence characterised as "devious and complicated." KV 2/2091, Dispatch (Top Secret) from Lieutenant M.W.L. Kitson, S.I.M.E. (Security Intelligence Middle East) General Headquarters, Middle East Land Forces, to Director General (9 July 1947).

80 UNSCOP, A/AC.13/PV.19, Verbatim Record of the Nineteenth Meeting (Public) (7 July 1947).

81 UNSCOP, A/AC.13/PV.21, Verbatim Record of the Twenty-First Meeting (Public) (8 July 1947).

82 *Id.*

83 *Id.*

84 The Palestinian Arabs, of course, had also repeatedly framed the McMahon-Hussein correspondence as constituting a legally binding "treaty" on Britain, under which Britain had committed itself in 1915–16 to an internationally enforceable pledge of Arab independence in Palestine following the end of World War I.

85 Following his testimony, Weizmann sent a letter to Justice Sandstrom reiterating his support for partition as superior to the cantonisation and provincial autonomy proposals for Palestine. Weizmann Archives, 13-2760, Letter from Weizmann to Sandstrom (14 July 1947).

86 UNSCOP, A/AC.13/PV.21, Verbatim Record of the Twenty-First Meeting (Public) (8 July 1947).

87 *Id.* (emphasis added.) Weizmann sent two follow-up letters to Sandstrom several days later elaborating on various other aspects of his testimony, noting he preferred partition to a cantonal/federal plan, and explaining why he believed Palestine could absorb an additional 1.5 million Jewish immigrants in the near term. Weizmann Letters and Papers, *op. cit.*, Series A, Vol. XXII, Letters No. 364 and 365 from Weizmann to Sandstrom at 367–373 (both dated 14 July 1947).

88 *Id.*

89 UNSCOP, A/AC.13/PV.24, Verbatim Record of the Twenty-Fourth Meeting (Public) (9 July 1947) (emphasis added).

90 UNSCOP, A/AC.13/PV.30, Verbatim Record of the Thirtieth Meeting (Public) (14 July 1947).

91 J.G. Granados, *op. cit.*, at 143.

92 UNSCOP Report, *op. cit.*, Annex 9/IV. The Arab Higher Committee published a memorandum in April 1947 setting forth its case, but the memorandum was not submitted to UNSCOP due to the Palestinian Arab boycott of the proceedings. *See The Palestine Arab Case: A Statement by the Arab Higher Committee* (April 1947).

93 UNSCOP Report, *op. cit.*, Annex 9/IV(h), The Jewish Agency for Palestine, *Some Legal Aspects of the Jewish Case, Memorandum Submitted to the United Nations Special Committee on Palestine* (July 1947).

94 *Id.*, para. 1.

95 *Id.*

96 *Id.*, para. 12.
97 *Id.*, para. 2 (emphasis added).
98 *Id.*, para. 7.
99 *Id.*, para. 24.
100 *Id.*, para. 16.
101 *Id.*, para. 21.
102 *Id.*, para. 19.
103 *Id.*, para. 24(3), n. 40 (emphasis in original).
104 The Jewish Agency made several other written submissions to the Special Committee, as did the Mandatory Government of Palestine. The written submissions laid bare the intense hostility each party felt toward the other. *Compare* UNSCOP Report, op. cit., Annex 9/II(a), *Memorandum on the Administration of Palestine under the Mandate* (June 1947) *and* Annex 9/II(k), *Supplementary Memorandum by the Government of Palestine, including Notes on Evidence Given to the United Nations Special Committee on Palestine up to 12 July 1947* (July 1947) *with* Annex 9/IV(n), *Reply to the Government of Palestine's Memorandum on the Administration of Palestine under the Mandate* (August 1947) *and* Annex 9/IV(s), *Observations on the Supplementary Memorandum of the Government of Palestine* (August 1947).
105 J.G. Granados, *op. cit.*, at 64.
106 *Id.* at 67. Garcia Granados specifically rejected the Palestinian Arab legal argument that Article 22 of the Covenant of the League of Nations intended the Palestine Mandate be created as a sacred trust of civilisation for the sole benefit of the Palestinian Arabs, with future statehood promised solely to the Palestinian Arabs: "The final conclusion of my study was clear. A country possessing sovereign rights (Turkey) over a territory (Palestine) had ceded them unconditionally [in Article 16 of the Treaty of Lausanne, 1923] to a group of nations (the European allies). These nations, in accord with traditional international usages, were entitled to pass upon the destinies of that land, to make provision for any kind of immigration into it, and to establish the form of government they saw fit. Consequently the allies had assigned Palestine to Great Britain (the Mandatory) and had charged her to bring about a specific objective (the constitution of the Jewish National Home)." J.G. Granados, *op. cit.*, at 67.
107 D. Mandel, *H.V. Evatt and the Establishment of Israel: The Undercover Zionist* at 90 (Routledge, 2004).
108 E. Ben-Dror (2014), *op. cit.*, at 29.
109 On 18 July, several days before the Special Committee departed Palestine, Sandstrom and the Yugoslav delegate visited the Jewish refugee ship *Exodus*. British troops had forcibly boarded the ship at sea and taken it to Haifa, eventually deporting the passengers to Cyprus. Sandstrom reported to the full committee the next day that "[t]hey had witnessed the transport of passengers from the ship to the freighter which it had been understood would take them to Cyprus. The people looked very poor and tired. There had been no brutal handling of the passengers by the troops. Later they went on board the freighter and spoke to the immigrants who gave them messages for their friends in Palestine. They were mainly concerned to be given food and drink. They learnt the story of the boarding during the night by the officers of the boarding party. The officers thought that the boarding had taken place not more than two or three miles off the shore, while the ship was steering towards Haifa. The party had had to fight their way down to the wheelhouse, which had been surrounded by barbed wire. They had used something like Chinese firecrackers to frighten off the crowd. Tin boxes and other missiles had been thrown at them. They had used tear gas after tear gas had been used against them. During this fight he understood there were 2 killed and some 150 injured. Mr. Simic (Yugoslavia) confirmed the Chairman's account adding that he had seen twelve people gravely wounded lying on stretchers. Wounded soldiers had also been observed." UNSCOP, A/AC.13/SR.37, Summary Record of the Thirty-Seventh Meeting (19 July 1947).

110 UNSCOP, A/AC.13/PV.38, Verbatim Record of the Thirty-Eighth Meeting (Public) (22 July 1947).
111 *Id.*
112 *Id.* (emphasis added).
113 UNSCOP, A/AC.13/PV.39, Verbatim Record of the Thirty-Ninth Meeting (Private) (23 July 1947).
114 *Id.*
115 *Id.*
116 *Id.*
117 *Id.*
118 *Id.*
119 *Id.* (emphasis added).
120 *Id.* (emphasis added). The British Embassy in Beirut summarised the Arab representatives' statements in two cables to London. FO 371/61876, Telegram No. 550 from British Embassy, Beirut to Foreign Office (22 July 1947); FO 371/61876, Telegram No. 558 from British Embassy, Beirut to Foreign Office (24 July 1947).
121 United Nations Archives, S-0504-0009-0003-00001, Special Series No. 1, *Notes on Visit of Some Members of the Committee to Amman, Transjordan, 24 July 1947* at 4–5 (3 August 1947). Bunche also noted, in response to a question from Justice Sandstrom, that King Abdullah rejected the legal validity of the agreement Abdullah's brother Feisal had signed with Chaim Weizmann at Versailles in January 1919, in which Feisal recognised the Balfour Declaration and Zionism. Feisal, according to Abdullah, signed the agreement without prior approval from their father, Sherif Hussein of Mecca. Abdullah's admission that Feisal had signed the agreement contradicted the Palestinian Arab claim during the 1929 Shaw Commission trial that Feisal had *never* signed the agreement and was unaware of its existence.
122 FO 371/61769, Cypher Telegram No. 236 from British Embassy, Amman to Foreign Office (28 July 1947).
123 E. Wilson, *op. cit.*, at 115; *see also* M.J. Cohen, *Palestine and the Great Powers, 1945-1948* at 325 (Princeton University Press, 1982); *see also* A. Shlaim, *Collusion Across the Jordan: King Abdullah, the Zionist Movement and the Partition of Palestine* at 91–94 (Clarendon Press, 1988).
124 A. Sela, Transjordan, *Israel and the 1948 War: Myth, Historiography and Reality*, Middle Eastern Studies 28:4 at 631 (1992); *but see* E. Karsh, *The Collusion That Never Was: King Abdallah, the Jewish Agency and the Partition of Palestine*, Journal of Contemporary History 34:4, 569–585 (1999) ("there was not and could not have been a Jewish-Transjordanian collusion to divide Palestine in a way contradictory to the UN Partition Resolution …").
125 CO 537/2362, Letter from Chief Secretary of Palestine Government (Shaw) to J. Martin, Colonial Office (9 July 1947) ("There is clear indication of a majority view in favour of partition and Weizmann's evidence yesterday will have strengthened this"); *see also* R. Ovendale, *op. cit.*, at 207, citing CO 537/2272, Cunningham to Creech Jones (Private and Personal) (19 July 1947).
126 Library Special Collections, Charles E. Young Research Library, UCLA, Brian Urquhart papers, Box 5, Folder 2, Letter from Ralph Bunche to G. Benjamin Gerig, Division of Dependent Area Affairs, Department of State (23 July 1947).
127 United Nations, Press Release PAL/91, G. Symeonides, UNSCOP Press Officer, "Background Story on Palestine Report" (31 August 1947) ("A sub-committee visited displaced persons camps between 8 and 14 August 1947. During its tour the sub-committee visited Munich, Salzburg, Vienna, Berlin, Hamburg and Hanover, and met the Austrian Chancellor, the Military Governor of the United States zones of Germany and Austria, several American and British officials in charge of displaced person's affairs, as well as officials of the Preparatory Commission of the International Refugee Organization. The sub-committee visited the children's camp of Indersdorf

(near Munich) comprising 168 children between the ages of 8 and 16 years; camp of Landsberg (Bavaria) comprising about 3,000 displaced persons, infiltrees, refugees of which four-fifths were from Poland; the camp of Bad Reichenhall (near Berchtesgaden) comprising about 5,000 displaced persons, infiltrees and refugees of which four-fifths also were from Poland; Rothschild hospital (Vienna) sheltering about 4,100 refugees almost entirely from Romania; camp of Dueppel (Berlin) comprising about 3,400 displaced persons and refugees almost entirely from Poland; camp of Hohne (near Belsen) comprising about 9,000 displaced persons and 1,800 infiltrees chiefly from Poland, the rest from Hungary and Romania. 42 DP's were interrogated in detail").

128 E. Ben-Dror (2007), *op. cit.*, at 286.

129 J.G. Granados, *op. cit.*, at 236.

130 *Id.* at 237.

131 *Id.* at 238–240.

132 E. Ben-Dror (2007), *op. cit.*, at 280, 283–284.

133 *Id.* at 284.

134 UNSCOP Report, *op. cit.*, Ch.V, paras. 2–3.

135 *Id.*, paras. 4–5.

136 *Id.*, para. 6.

137 P. Mann, *Ralph Bunche: UN Peacemaker* at 197 (Coward, McCann & Geoghegan, 1975).

138 J.G. Granados, *op. cit.*, at 240–241 (emphasis added).

139 Quoted in D. Horowitz, *op. cit.*, at 187.

140 *Id.* at 207. During Crossman's visit to Geneva, Horowitz invited him to meet with Bunche. Horowitz later wrote about the meeting, describing one particularly poignant exchange: "Crossman, who regarded psychological complexes, prejudice, and hatred of Hebrews as one of the chief barriers to an equitable Palestine solution, expressed this opinion to Bunche and asked the latter jestingly if he had already managed to turn anti-Semitic as a result of being immersed in the Jewish question. Bunche returned curtly, 'That would be impossible … I've been a Negro for 42 years … I know the flavor of racial prejudice and racial persecution. A wise Negro can never be an anti-Semite.'" *Id.* at 204; *see also* M. Jones, *op. cit.*, at 275–276. Bunche noted in his contemporaneous account of the meeting with Crossman that Crossman criticised both Bevin and the Anglo-American Committee of Inquiry. Bunche quoted Crossman saying, "it was never intended that the Anglo-American Committee should make a sincere effort to find a solution." United Nations Archives, S-0504-0009-0003-00001, *Notes on Conversation with Mr. Richard Crossman, M.P., 13 August 1947.*

141 D. Horowitz, *op. cit.*, at 214.

142 *Id.*

143 *Id.* at 218–219.

144 H. Husseini, *A "Middle Power" in Action: Canada and the Partition of Palestine*, Arab Studies Quarterly 30:3 at 47 (2008).

145 One of Bunche's biographers claims he drafted the entire report, including both the majority and minority recommendations. P. Mann, *op. cit.*, at 200. The Israeli historian Elad Ben-Dror, however, noted Bunche received help with the drafting from UN officials Henri Vigier and John Reedman, who flew from New York to Geneva to assist Bunche. Ben-Dror also notes, contrary to the typical narrative regarding Bunche's pro-Zionism, that Bunche in fact "opposed the establishment of an independent Jewish state," and "made strenuous attempts to torpedo its establishment." E. Ben-Dror, *Ralph Bunche and the Establishment of Israel*, Israel Affairs, 14:3 at 520, 522 (July 2008). Another historian credits Bunche with drafting the entire report. M.N. Penkower, *op. cit.* (2019, Vol. II) at 459–460.

146 E. Ben-Dror (2014), *op. cit.*, at 32.

147 UNSCOP Report, *op. cit.*, Ch. II, para. 141.

148 *Id.*, paras. 145–146.

149 *Id.*, para. 154.

150 *Id.*, paras. 165–166.
151 *Id.*, paras. 173–174.
152 *Id.*, para. 176.
153 *Id.*, para. 179.
154 *Id.*, Ch. VI, paras. 1–5. The *New York Times* editorial board reacted negatively to the UNSCOP majority report, noting how "[s]ome of us have long had doubts as to the wisdom of erecting a political state on a basis of religious faith." *New York Times*, 1 September 1947 at 18.
155 CAB 129/21/9, C.P. (47) 259, Memorandum (Top Secret) by the Secretary of State for Foreign Affairs, para. 8 (18 September 1947).
156 *Id.*, para. 9.
157 *Id.*, para. 18.
158 CAB 128/10/27, Cabinet 76 (47), Conclusions (Secret) of a Meeting of the Cabinet at 19 (20 September 1947).
159 H.G. Evatt, *The Task of Nations* at 126–127 (Duell, Sloan and Pearce, 1949).
160 E. Ben-Dror (2007), *op. cit.*, at 285.
161 Israel State Archives, 120/39, Letter from Amin Abdul Hadi on behalf of Supreme Muslim Council to High Commissioner (3 October 1947).
162 "Zionists Ask U.N. To Pass New Plan," *New York Times*, 2 September 1947 at 1 (emphasis added).
163 "Jewish Agency Welcomes UNSCOP Report; Wants Shortest Possible Interim Period," *Jewish Daily Bulletin*, 2 September 1947 at 1; *see also* D. Horowitz, *op. cit.*, at 222–223; Z. Elipeleg, *op. cit.*, at 3–22 (Jews were "overjoyed" with partition plan).
164 T. Segev, *A State At Any Cost: The Life Of David Ben-Gurion* at 404 (Farrar, Straus and Giroux, 2019).

# 13

# AD HOC COMMITTEE HEARINGS AND VERDICT

## Ad Hoc Committee formation

After receiving the UNSCOP report, the General Assembly on 23 September 1947 established the Ad Hoc Committee on the Palestinian Question.[1] The General Assembly referred a broad range of tasks to the Ad Hoc Committee, including an in-depth examination of both the UNSCOP majority report and a competing proposal from Saudi Arabia and Iraq to terminate the Palestine Mandate and recognise the country's independence as a single, majority-Arab State.[2]

The Ad Hoc Committee held its first meeting on 25 September 1947 and elected the Australian Foreign Minister and former High Court Judge Herbert V. Evatt (Figure 13.1) as Chair, and Prince Subhasvasti Svastivat of Siam as Vice-Chair.[3]

Evatt's appointment as Chair continued the dominant role judges and lawyers had played in the Palestine Conflict, beginning with the British inquiry commissions of the 1920s and 1930s, and continuing through the London Conferences of 1939, the Anglo-American Committee of Inquiry, UNSCOP, and now the Ad Hoc Committee.

Before serving as Foreign Minister, Evatt had been the youngest person ever appointed to Australia's High Court. Evatt had overseen Australia's participation as one of the 11 members of UNSCOP during the spring and summer of 1947, and he was very familiar with the Palestine file. Evatt ordered the Australian member of the Special Committee, John Hood, to remain neutral during the Special Committee's deliberations in Geneva in August 1947. Evatt's biographer described Evatt as an "ambitious schemer" who deliberately hid Australia's hand (and his own preference for partition) during UNSCOP's work.[4]

When Evatt convened the first meeting of the Ad Hoc Committee on 27 September 1947, he immediately "sought to establish … his complete independence and the

DOI: 10.4324/9781003225263-18

**FIGURE 13.1** Herbert V. Evatt (Public Domain)

quasi-judicial nature of the proceedings."[5] He viewed the Ad Hoc Committee's role "as akin" to a court of law, requiring a judgement inevitably favouring one side over the other.[6]

On 26 September 1947, British Colonial Secretary Arthur Creech Jones appeared before the Ad Hoc Committee and announced the British Government agreed with the recommendation of the UNSCOP majority that the Mandate for Palestine "be terminated at the earliest practicable opportunity."[7] Creech Jones also informed the Ad Hoc Committee (just as Britain had hinted when it referred the Palestine matter to the United Nations months earlier) that if the UN General Assembly recommended a policy not acceptable to *both* the Arabs and Jews, Britain would be unable to enforce it.[8]

Evatt viewed Britain's insistence on an outcome acceptable to both sides as absurd, given the judicial nature of the Ad Hoc Committee's work:

> The very purpose of submitting the question to the jurisdiction of the United Nations Assembly was to ascertain what was the fair and just solution of the problem quite irrespective of whether that just solution would be accepted by both parties directly interested. As well ask a court of justice to decide a case in a way which would be agreed to by both sides![9]

The Ad Hoc Committee engaged in a "general debate" on the Palestine question from 29 September 1947 until 17 October 1947 at the temporary UN headquarters at Lake Success, New York. The Ad Hoc Committee heard from representatives of the Jewish Agency and Palestinian Arab Higher Committee, as well as from other delegates.

## Testimony before the Ad Hoc Committee

### *Husseini testimony*

Jamal Husseini, who had led the Arab boycott against UNSCOP, decided to cooperate with and testify before the Ad Hoc Committee. Indeed, Husseini made three separate appearances before the Ad Hoc Committee between September and November 1947.

#### *First appearance: 29 September 1947*

Husseini travelled to New York to address the Ad Hoc Committee on 29 September 1947, on behalf of the Palestinian Arabs and the Arab Higher Committee. Husseini's appearance, coming on the heels of the Palestinian Arab boycott of UNSCOP, was significant, marking the first official Palestinian Arab response to the UNSCOP report.

Husseini told the Ad Hoc Committee he categorically opposed partition and the two-state solution. Husseini laid the groundwork for the Palestinian Arabs' eventual refusal of the General Assembly's 29 November 1947 offer of the two-state solution. As will be discussed further in Chapters 14 and 16, that refusal had legal consequences for the Palestinian Arabs that remain highly relevant and important today.

At the beginning of his statement to the Ad Hoc Committee, Husseini immediately invoked the transformational legal framing and the justice/injustice narrative the Palestinian Arabs had been employing for the last quarter century:

> The Palestine Arab case is simple and self-evident. The Arabs of Palestine are there where Providence and history have placed them. As all other nations, they are entitled to live in freedom and peace and to develop their country in accordance with their traditions and in harmony with universal exceptions of justice and equity. The Arabs are and have always been in actual possession of Palestine and thus have one binding, lawful and sacred duty: to defend it against all aggression.[10]

Husseini then criticised the many previous investigations and fact-finding commissions that had been sent to Palestine:

> Investigation and fact-finding ... should have, by all means, been set afoot a long time ago. When enquiries are conducted for the removal of injustices, they are understandable and commendable. But when they take the

> course finding ways and means to cover and justify aggressive acts ... they become hazardous and futile ... such recommendations as were made in favor of the Arabs were ignored by the Mandate and those in favor of the Zionists were carefully enforced.[11]

The Palestinian Arabs, Husseini added, lacked confidence in any outside investigative commissions, and "[i]t is for this and other reasons that were duly communicated to the United Nations that we refused to appear before the Special Fact Finding Committee on Palestine."[12]

Nevertheless, Husseini expressed to the Ad Hoc Committee his "desire to assure you in the name of the committee that represents the Arabs of Palestine of our great veneration for your august body, and to impress upon you the fact that *we look to the United Nations for justice* and equity, and we pin our faith and find our salvation in its Charter."[13]

Husseini repeatedly employed transformational legal framing throughout his testimony. He said there were two scales of justice in Palestine, one, less favourable, for the Arabs; and the other, more favourable, for the Jews. Husseini further characterised Zionist claims to Palestine as having "no legal basis."

> The Zionist case ... is based on the association of the Jews with Palestine 2000 years ago. If that claim had any legal or moral value, the Arabs could have better and stronger claims over Spain, parts of France, Turkey, Persia, Afghanistan and even parts of India, Russia and China.[14]

Husseini also criticised the Balfour Declaration, as Great Britain had never "owned Palestine" and thus had no legal right to promise it to the Jews. The Balfour Declaration, according to Husseini, contradicted the Covenant of the League of Nations, and was "an immoral, unjust and illegal promise."[15]

Husseini also argued Britain had, prior to issuing the Balfour Declaration, made legally binding promises of Arab independence in the McMahon-Hussein correspondence, a promise "that did not exclude Palestine."[16]

Husseini then noted Article 22 of the Covenant of the League of Nations had upheld the rights and interests of the indigenous population as a "sacred trust of civilization" in the hands of the mandatory. Britain, however, had failed to ensure those rights to the Palestinian Arabs:

> Deprived of their rights, the Arabs were rendered helpless spectators to behold the funeral of their national existence passing slowly before their eyes. This policy and that atmosphere in general continue to present day.[17]

Husseini said the Palestinian Arabs rejected the UNSCOP report, and that "it could not be a basis for discussion." Husseini criticised not only the majority's partition recommendation, but also the minority's federal-state recommendations, even though the Muslim Commissioners from Iran and India had advocated those recommendations on behalf of the Palestinian Arabs. Husseini slammed both the majority and minority recommendations as "based on considerations that are, in the opinion of the Arabs of Palestine, inconsistent with and repugnant to their rights, the UN Charter, and the Covenant of the League of Nations."[18]

The Arabs of Palestine were therefore "solidly determined to oppose, with all the means at their disposal, any scheme that provides for the dissection, segregation or partition of their country or that gives to a Minority on the ground of creed, special and preferential rights or status."[19]

Husseini concluded by demanding nothing less than immediate Arab statehood over the whole of Palestine.

## *Second appearance: 18 October 1947*

Husseini made his second appearance before the Ad Hoc Committee three weeks later, on 18 October 1947. According to the summary of the meeting released to the press:

> Mr. Husseini quoted various historical works to support his contention that the Jews of Eastern Europe are descended from the Khazars and therefore without any connection with Palestine ... Mr. Husseini denied that Jewish immigration benefits the Arabs economically, and that Jewish colonization has achieved as much as some delegations claim. In any case, said Mr. Hussein, the question for the Arabs is on a much higher level, namely liberty and independence. Mr. Husseini emphasized the contribution of the Arabs to the war effort and declared that the Arabs, as the indigenous majority population of Palestine, are entitled to self-determination and to all the consequences that this principle entails.[20]

## *Third appearance: 24 November 1947*

Husseini made his third appearance before the Ad Hoc Committee on 24 November 1947, when he gave the closing statement for the Palestinian Arabs. Husseini argued vehemently against the two-state solution, once again employing transformational legal framing:

> Palestine was Arab by virtue of centuries of permanent occupation and possession and the Arabs were entitled to the right of shaping the government and forming the constitution of their own country. There was no provision in the Covenant of the League of Nations or the Charter of the United Nations that enabled the minority of the population to impose its will on the majority by constituting itself a distinct political entity and forming an independent State in Palestine. The Zionists claimed that the Balfour Declaration gave them the right, but both the Declaration and the Mandate had been drawn up without the knowledge of the indigenous

> population of Palestine. Furthermore, he added, there is nothing in either the Balfour Declaration or the Mandate that can be construed as enabling the Jewish Agency to establish a Jewish State in any part of Palestine.[21]

Husseini continued his argument with the familiar Palestinian Arab legal claims regarding Britain's obligations under Article 22 of the Covenant of the League of Nations. He sharply criticised Britain's failure to grant independence to the Palestinian Arabs, arguing Britain "was morally and legally bound to surrender the whole territory and the administration of the territory to a Palestinian government." Husseini added that the Arab Higher Committee stood ready to take over the administration of the country. Britain's refusal to transfer power to the Palestinian Arabs, therefore, was neither morally nor legally justifiable."[22]

Husseini concluded by threatening violence and bloodshed – including against Jewish citizens of Arab countries – if the United Nations were to adopt the two-state solution for Palestine:

> [I]t was idle to think that the creation of a Jewish State would not arouse a general uprising in the Arab world, and it should be remembered that there were as many Jews in the Arab world as there were in Palestine, whose positions might become very precarious, even though the Arab States did their best to protect them. If partition were forced upon Palestine, it would have little chance of permanence in the midst of a strongly aroused and genuinely apprehensive Middle East. The fight would continue, as it had in the Crusades, *until the injustice was completely removed*. By imposing partition, the United Nations would virtually precipitate Palestine into a blood bath ... One delegation defending partition had referred to the boundary line as final and a boundary line of peace. As the representative of the Arabs of Palestine, Mr. Husseini wished to place on record the serious conviction that it would be nothing but a line of fire and blood.[23]

## *Silver testimony*

Rabbi Abba Hillel Silver, representing the Jewish Agency, appeared before the Ad Hoc Committee on 2 October 1947. Rabbi Silver criticised both the majority and minority recommendations of the UNSCOP report. Regarding partition, Rabbi Silver noted Palestine had already been partitioned in 1923, when Palestine was split into Transjordan and Cisjordan. The Arabs received Transjordan, and therefore Cisjordan should have been allocated to the Jews. Dividing Cisjordan into two states meant the Arabs would end up receiving not one, but two separate countries from the original Palestine Mandate, leaving the Jews with only a small portion of Cisjordan. That outcome, Rabbi Silver argued, was unfair to the Jews.[24]

But Rabbi Silver then struck a conciliatory note:

> Dr. Silver nevertheless declared that he would be prepared to recommend to the Jewish people acceptance of the majority proposals – subject to further discussion of the constitutional and territorial provisions – because the proposals made possible the immediate re-establishment of the Jewish State, and because it would ensure immediate and continuing Jewish immigration.

## *Jamali testimony*

The Foreign Minister of Iraq, M.F. Jamali, testified before the Ad Hoc Committee on 6 October 1947. Jamali invoked transformational legal framing in his argument on behalf of the Palestinian Arabs:

> Palestine belongs to the Palestinians alone. Not only is it theirs through the right of ownership through long possession, but also by right of "prescription." No one, other than the rightful inhabitants of Palestine, has any right to Palestine ... The problem of Palestine would be very simple if treated according to the well-established rules of democracy, justice and international law.[25]

Ambassador Jorge Garcia Granados of Guatemala, who had served as a member of UNSCOP, appeared before the Ad Hoc Committee on 10 October 1947, explaining the legal basis for his government's support for the UNSCOP majority's two-state solution:

> [B]oth peoples have rights and material claims to the disputed territory – the Jews by reason of historical ties and the legality of the Mandate – and the Arabs by virtue of a numerical majority, long possession and on the principle of self-determination. But the phrase "self-determination," while a beautiful principle, had not been given application after either world war, and cannot, therefore, be taken as an axiom of international law solely and exclusively for the case of Palestine.[26]

## *Zafrullah Khan statements*

The Pakistani Ambassador to the United Nations, Sir Mohammed Zafrullah Khan, made a lengthy statement to the Committee on 8 October 1947, and a follow-up statement five days later. Khan invoked the Palestinian Arab legal framing and argued partition would be illegal and unjust. He urged the Ad Hoc Committee to refer the matter to the International Court of Justice (ICJ) for a ruling on whether the Mandate violated McMahon's October 1915 pledge of Arab independence on behalf of the British Government to the Arabs, including the Arabs of Palestine.[27]

### El-Khoury statement

On 11 October 1947, Faris el-Khoury of Syria addressed the Ad Hoc Committee, also invoking transformational legal framing and the Palestinian Arab legal narrative. El-Khoury also supported the possibility of an Arab petition to the ICJ seeking an opinion declaring illegal the "Jewish National Home" provisions of the Palestine Mandate:

> [F]rom the start, the Arabs had objected to the fact that the political aspects of the Palestine question were given precedence over the legal aspects. *The Arabs wished to contest the legality of the Mandate on Palestine*, particularly in regard to its terms concerning the establishment in Palestine of a Jewish National Home. On the legal aspect, we shall submit a proposal for its discussion and request the International Court of Justice for a legal opinion on the subject … Such a body could decide whether the terms of the Mandate regarding the introduction of hordes of immigrants by force into Palestine to form themselves a national home is or is not consistent with the provisions of the Covenant of the League of Nations, and with the fundamental rights of peoples.[28]

El Khoury continued his testimony by criticising those countries who had expressed support for the UNSCOP majority's proposed two-state solution. El Khoury again framed the argument in the context of the justice/injustice narrative:

> Is this the justice to which the [United Nations] Charter refers – to decide the fate of [the Palestinian Arab] people by expelling them from their homes and robbing them of their independence, in order to make room for foreign intruders?[29]

### Other Arab testimony

Mostafa Adl of Iran, who had served as a member of UNSCOP, spoke next to the Ad Hoc Committee to express Iran's opposition to the two-state solution, as it "did not conform to the principles which ought to guide the United Nations – namely justice, equality, and respect for the right of all peoples to self-determination without outside interference."[30]

Another Syrian representative, Dr Farid Zein Eddini, appeared before the Ad Committee on 14 October 1947, warning against a decision on Palestine which would be "unjust."[31]

On 15 October 1947, the Yemeni representative, Hassan Baghdadi, addressed the Ad Hoc Committee. He too invoked the Palestinian Arab legal framing, attacking the "injustice" of the Mandate and characterising it as contrary to the "letter and spirit" of Article 22 of the Covenant of the League of Nations.[32]

Baghdadi further argued as a matter of law that both Article 22 and the Mandate prohibited partitioning Palestine into separate states. Britain, as the League of Nations-appointed trustee of Palestine, bore a legal obligation to return the *entire* country to the indigenous Palestinian Arab population, on whose *sole* behalf Britain had acted as trustee:

> The Mandatory, having received an undivided territory, must in conformity with the principles of the "scared trust of civilization" provided for by Article 22 of the Covenant, give it back to the people whose rights were suspended by the Mandate.[33]

### *Creech Jones testimony*

On 16 October 1947, British Colonial Secretary Creech Jones appeared for a second time before the Ad Hoc Committee and repeated Britain's position that it would not enforce any UN decision that did meet the approval of both Jews and Arabs.[34]

### *Shertok testimony*

On 17 October 1947, Moshe Shertok, the future second Prime Minister of Israel, spoke forcefully on behalf of the Jewish Agency. Shertok quickly invoked the Jewish transformational legal framing. According to the Ad Hoc Committee press release summarising Shertok's presentation:

> Mr. Shertok then turned to the question of the international validity of the Palestinian settlement which resulted from World War I. Of the McMahon promises and the Hogarth measure which the Pakistan representative had cited as proofs that Palestine was not excluded from the plans for independence of the Arab countries, Mr. Shertok said that both documents were at most instruments regulating the relations between Great Britain and a certain Arab dynasty, but that *no amount of legalistic casuistry could avail to undermine the overriding authority of the Palestine Mandate*. Mr. Shertok declared that under Article 80 of the Charter, the Mandate, as long as it had not been replaced by any other instrument, was part of the law of the United Nations.[35]

Shertok buttressed his legal argument with a new variant of Jewish framing, based on language in the UN Charter:

> Mr. Shertok quoted from the opening passage of the Charter the sentence reaffirming "faith in fundamental human rights, in the dignity and worth of the human person, in the equal rights of men and women and of nations large and small." The dignity and worth of a Jew as a human person, he

said, could not fully assert itself, nor could Jewish men and women attain equal rights with others, unless the people to which they belong were placed on a footing of complete equality with other peoples ...[36]

### *Weizmann testimony*

Chaim Weizmann, the former Chair of the Jewish Agency and future first President of the State of Israel, appeared in his personal capacity before the Ad Hoc Committee on 18 October 1947, the same day as Jamal Husseini's second appearance.

Weizmann argued "there is nothing new in the idea of a Jewish State. It is no departure from the Mandate. It is the inevitable and foreseen consummation of the Mandate."[37] Weizmann also, as he had done in his testimony to the Palestine Royal Commission in 1937, referred to the document he and Prince Feisal signed at Versailles in January 1919 as a "treaty ... declaring that if the rest of Arab Asia were free, the Arabs would concede the Jewish right freely to settle and develop in Palestine which would exist side by side with the Arab State."[38]

Weizmann concluded his testimony by invoking the Jewish justice/injustice frame, placing Zionism at the forefront of the global social justice and progressive movements:

> When this Committee comes to the creation of a Jewish State, it will be fulfilling a proud historic mission. Despite its small scope, this enterprise stands high in the esteem of liberal thought. *So many considerations of justice and humanity are involved.* There is redress for a persecuted people; equality for Jewish people amongst the nations; the redemption of desert soil by cultivation; the creation of a new economy and society; the embodiment of progressive social ideas in an area that has fallen behind the best standards of modern life; the revival of one of the oldest cultures of mankind.[39]

★★★★★

David Horowitz, observing the proceedings on behalf of the Jewish Agency, described later how well the Jewish witnesses had invoked legal narrative and framing in their presentations to the Ad Hoc Committee. However, Horowitz doubted the reliance on legal framing would be enough to win the day, noting "[t]he voice of justice and logic spoke through the throats of our representatives. But in this arena of power politics and mighty vested interests, considerations of justice and logic were relegated to secondary place."[40]

## Ad Hoc Committee deliberations and verdict

On 18 October 1947, the Ad Hoc Committee began its deliberations. On 22 October, the Ad Hoc Committee approved Evatt's proposal to create three subcommittees to examine the UNSCOP majority and minority recommendations, and to attempt conciliation between the Arabs and Jews.[41]

### *The three subcommittees*

Evatt assigned the first subcommittee (Canada, Czechoslovakia, Guatemala, Poland, South Africa, Soviet Union, United States, Uruguay, and Venezuela) to draft a detailed plan implementing the UNSCOP majority's partition recommendation.

Evatt tasked the second subcommittee (Afghanistan, Colombia, Egypt, Iraq, Lebanon, Pakistan, Saudi Arabia, Syria, and Yemen) with studying and consolidating various Arab proposals for a one-state solution, meaning an independent, unitary Palestinian State governed by the Arab majority.[42] Provincial autonomy and Trusteeship had both been abandoned as potential solutions by this point.

Evatt later noted the importance of creating subcommittees to explore both sides of the question:

> There was opposition to the Arab proposal [to create the second subcommittee]. I had to intervene in the interests of just procedure. I pointed out to the committee that we were in a semi-judicial position and that it was absolutely necessary to be acquainted with the Arab proposal in detail ...[43]

Evatt gave both subcommittees a deadline of 29 October 1947 to complete their work. He later granted extensions of time to both subcommittees.[44] Both subcommittees submitted their reports to the Ad Hoc Committee on 19 November 1947.

The focus in Subcommittee I was whether or not to recommend including the Negev Desert in the area allotted for the Jewish State. Ultimately, Subcommittee I approved allocating the Negev to the Jews. Subcommittee II, on the other hand, focused an enormous amount of effort on the Palestinian Arabs' legal arguments, including legal challenges to the competency of the United Nations to determine Palestine's future.

A third subcommittee, consisting of Australia, Siam, and Iceland was appointed to attempt to conciliate the Jews and Palestinian Arabs.[45] Evatt, however, mostly ignored the third subcommittee and undertook no meaningful effort to attempt conciliation between the parties. Evatt dismissed conciliation as likely to fail, and in any event, inconsistent with the inherently judicial task of the Ad Hoc Committee to render judgement for one side against the other:

> He [Evatt] saw the task of conciliation, though theoretically crucial, as practically irrelevant and in any case altogether subsidiary to that of planning detailed proposals for the consideration and vote of the Assembly. It is here that one can detect Evatt's judicial pedigree. A court of law, particularly in the adversarial system of British countries, serves to bring a sound and informed judgment to complex problems. It permits the fullest

> presentation of competing claims. It does not seek to reconcile parties. Conciliation tends to take place, if it happens at all, out of court. Where the prospects of conciliation were practically nil, Evatt went through the motions but did not generate his characteristic rigour and persistence. These were reserved for enabling both sides to develop their respective cases unhindered.[46]

The full Ad Hoc Committee met again on 21 October 1947. The Egyptian and Pakistani delegates focused on legal issues. Mahmoud Bey Fawzi of Egypt reiterated his proposal "that the International Court of Justice be asked for an advisory opinion as to whether it lies within the competence of the General Assembly to recommend any of the two solutions proposed by the Majority or by the Minority Reports; and as to whether it lies within the rights of any Member State or group of Member States to implement any of the proposed solutions without the consent of the people of Palestine." Fawzi asked that the matter be taken up urgently.[47]

Sir Mohammed Zafrullah Khan of Pakistan asked for a subcommittee to consider the legal implications of British promises to the Arabs during World War I, the competence of the United Nations to determine the fate of Palestine, and the legality of the Mandate. Khan repeated his earlier request that all three questions be referred to the ICJ.

The Belgian representative described the Egyptian proposal for a decision by the ICJ as "of paramount importance." Evatt, however, rejected the Belgian proposal.[48] Nevertheless, Subcommittee II created three working groups, the second of which ("Working Group B") would "look into the legality of the mandate, the request for ruling by the International Court of Justice and the legal limitations of the United Nations in regard to implementation."[49]

## *Subcommittee II report: The Palestinian Arab legal case*

Subcommittee II devoted more than one-third of its report to Working Group B's analysis of the "legal issues connected with the Palestine problem."[50] The discussion completely embraced the Palestinian Arab transformational legal framing and narrative of the conflict.

Working Group B's analysis began by arguing the solution of the Palestine problem "raises various legal points as to the legality of any proposal for the future of Palestine, as well as the competence of the General Assembly to make and enforce recommendations in this regard."[51]

Working Group B then attacked the UNSCOP majority report:

> The Special Committee failed to consider and determine some issues and juridical aspects of the Palestine question ... The Special Committee considered neither the juridical validity of the Balfour Declaration, nor the meaning of the term "Jewish National Home" nor the validity and scope

> of the provisions of the Palestine Mandate relating thereto. So also the Special Committee evaded the issue of the [British] pledges made to the Arabs.[52]

Working Group B next addressed the McMahon-Hussein correspondence, as well as the Hogarth Message and other contemporaneous British-Arab communications, arguing "Palestine was included within the territories which Sherif Hussein claimed should become independent at the end of the war." Working Group B ignored McMahon's July 1937 public denial that Palestine was included in the pledges of independence to the Arabs, and that Hussein fully understood Palestine was not included.[53] Instead, Working Group B insisted the proper interpretation of McMahon's correspondence "can be satisfactorily settled only by obtaining the opinion of an authoritative and impartial tribunal such as the International Court of Justice."[54]

Working Group B also urged various questions regarding the legality of the Balfour Declaration be referred to the ICJ. Those questions included whether the Balfour Declaration was made without the knowledge or consent of the Palestinian Arabs, whether the Declaration was contrary to the principles of self-determination and democracy, and whether the Declaration was legally invalid because it conflicted with prior British pledges to the Arabs regarding Palestine.[55]

Working Group B next raised a series of legal questions regarding the Mandate. The key legal issue, according to Working Group B, was whether the phrase "National Home for the Jewish People" meant "no more than a cultural centre for a limited number of Jews, which does not affect or diminish the rights and position of the indigenous population of Palestine."

Working Group B identified a number of additional legal issues, including whether the Mandate conflicted with Article 22 of the Covenant of the League of Nations; whether the dissolution of the League after World War II meant the Mandate had become null and void as a matter of law; whether a "National Home" had already been established for the Jewish people in Palestine, meaning nothing further need be done on their behalf to fulfil the Mandate; and whether the 26 September 1947 British announcement to the Ad Hoc Committee of its intent to terminate the Mandate and withdraw from Palestine at the "earliest practicable date" deprived the United Nations of lawful authority to take any further actions in Palestine on behalf of the Jews.[56]

Working Group B addressed each of these issues in turn and suggested each issue also be referred to the ICJ.

First, Working Group B argued Article 22 of the Covenant was intended to place Palestine under temporary guardianship as a "sacred trust of civilization," but only until such time as Palestine would be ready for independence. Legally, therefore:

> [T]he only limitation upon the sovereignty of the people of Palestine was the imposition of a temporary tutelage under the Mandatory Power. It cannot be suggested that the entry of an unlimited number of Jewish

> immigrants into Palestine, or the creation of a Jewish State against the wishes of the majority of the people of the country, was in accordance with the aims and objectives of the Mandate and the principles embodied in Article 22 of the Covenant.[57]

Second, Working Group B argued the dissolution of the League of Nations meant, as a matter of law, that the Mandate itself had also ceased to exist, "and with it has disappeared the legal basis for the Mandate." Moreover, Working Group B argued, "the United Nations organization had not inherited the constitutional and political powers and functions of the League of Nations, [and] cannot be treated in any way as the successor of the League of Nations insofar as the administration of mandates is concerned."[58]

Third, Working Group B noted the British Government in the 1939 White Paper had proclaimed the process of creating the Jewish National Home in Palestine would be completed once the immigration of a total of 75,000 additional Jews over the subsequent 5-year period had occurred.[59]

Fourth, Britain's 26 September 1947 announcement of its intent to withdraw from Palestine and relinquish the Mandate as soon as practicable had removed all legal obstacles to converting *all* of Palestine into an independent Arab state.[60]

Working Group B next cited Chapter XII and Article 79 of the UN Charter, arguing that Britain (as the outgoing Mandatory) was required to negotiate a successor Trusteeship agreement for the General Assembly's approval. Unless and until that occurred, neither the General Assembly nor the Security Council had any power to "entertain, much less recommend or enforce, any solution … other than the recognition of the independence of Palestine."[61]

Working Group B then reiterated its position that the United Nations lacked jurisdiction to impose any solution on Palestine. This argument reprised the decades-long Palestinian legal narrative that neither the British, the League of Nations, nor any outside body had jurisdiction over Palestine:

> To sum up, the dissolution of the League of Nations, and the consequential removal of the legal basis for the Mandate, and the more recent declarations by the Mandatory of its intention to withdraw from Palestine, opens the way for the establishment of an independent Government in Palestine by the people of the country, without the intervention of either the United Nations or any other party … no further discussion of the Palestine problem seems to be necessary or appropriate, and this item should be struck off the agenda of the General Assembly.[62]

Working Group B therefore recommended the ICJ be asked to render an opinion regarding the jurisdiction and legal authority of the United Nations "to make any recommendations or enforce any scheme in Palestine not acceptable to the majority of the population."[63]

Working Group B then addressed the legality of the UNSCOP majority's proposed two-state solution. Working Group B first argued that Articles 5 and 28 of the Mandate, when read together with Article 22 of the Covenant of the League of Nations, required Britain to preserve the territorial and political integrity of Palestine, and to return the country in one piece to the indigenous population upon the termination of the Mandate.

The UNSCOP majority's partition plan therefore was unlawful, not only because it violated the relevant provisions of the Mandate and the Covenant, but also because it violated the UN Charter, especially Article 1 (requiring member states "to act in conformity with the principles of justice and international law") and Article 73 (requiring member states to respect "the right of self-determination of peoples").

Working Group B also attacked the UNSCOP majority's recommendation that Jerusalem be placed under international Trusteeship, arguing Jerusalem should instead be recognised as the capital of the independent Arab state of Palestine.

## *Advisory legal ruling proposal rejected*

On 22 November 1947, the Ad Hoc Committee met in an atmosphere of high drama and tension to consider the proposal from Subcommittee II to seek an advisory opinion from the ICJ on the legal issues Working Group B had raised. The proposal lost by one vote, with Evatt casting the deciding vote against it.[64]

It was no surprise that Evatt, a former High Court Judge in Australia, preferred to protect the "court" over which he presided – the Ad Hoc Committee – and therefore objected to referring the matter to the ICJ:

> In exercising his vote against a proposal for judicial review, Evatt's conduct seems uncharacteristic. In fact, he knew a decision would have been derailed by this unpromising reference to the Hague ... Evatt's instinct to avoid a reference to the Court ... had been correct: too much energy had been invested in grappling with the conundrum to make the prospect attractive to over-strained delegates. The law, as Evatt knew, was on his side: the United Nations Charter specifically empowered the Assembly to determine such matters referred by mandatory powers under Article 14. Advising the Security Council on matters of international peace and security was authorised under Article 11.[65]

Evatt's view echoed his prior rulings as a Judge of Australia's High Court regarding the legal status of mandated territories. The League of Nations had appointed Australia as the mandatory for New Guinea after World War I. In 1937, the Australian High Court considered whether the New South Wales Fugitive Offenders Act applied to a defendant alleged to have committed murder in New Guinea.

Evatt, writing for the Australian High Court, rejected the claim, noting "every recognized authority on international law accepts the view that the Mandated Territory of New Guinea is not part of the King's dominions."[66] Interestingly, Evatt supported his decision by citing a prior ruling from the UK Privy Council that "[Palestine] is not within the King's dominions."[67]

Evatt therefore dismissed the Arab push to "refer almost every aspect of the problem to the International Court of Justice" as "patently absurd ... for instance the question whether or not the Balfour Declaration is a legally binding declaration."[68] Evatt also argued the United Nations had sufficient legal authority to decide Palestine's future:

> As to the validity of the action proposed to be taken by the U.N. Assembly, I never had any doubt. The Palestine situation was obviously one likely to impair friendly relations among nations, and accordingly the Assembly was competent under Article 14 of the Charter to recommend measures for its peaceful adjustment, regardless of the origins of the situation. In addition the question also concerned the maintenance of international peace and security and accordingly the General Assembly could act under Article 11 of the Charter to call the attention of the Security Council to the position and make the appropriate recommendations to all States concerned.[69]

Moreover, it would have made no sense to interpret the UN Charter as *depriving* the United Nations of jurisdiction over former League of Nations mandated territories. The United Nations clearly possessed the power to decide whether and how to convert a League of Nations mandate into a Trusteeship or terminate a mandate entirely.[70]

## Final verdict: The two-state solution

On 24 November 1947, the Ad Hoc Committee met, in an atmosphere of "mounting tension,"[71] to debate the recommendations of Subcommittees I and II. Jamal Husseini (in his third and final appearance before the Ad Hoc Committee) gave a closing statement on behalf of the Palestinian Arabs. Moshe Shertok gave the closing statement for the Jewish Agency, arguing "[t]he fact that Jews were at home in Palestine had received official international recognition twenty-five years before and that recognition had extended to the entire area of Palestine, including Transjordan."[72] The Jewish Agency was ready, however, to consider partition and the two-state solution.

Later that same evening, the Ad Hoc Committee voted to reject Subcommittee II's recommendation to establish a unitary, independent state in Palestine.[73] The Ad Hoc Committee then voted to adopt the recommendation of Subcommittee I for partition and the two-state solution.[74]

That same evening, 24 November 1947, British Foreign Secretary Bevin had dinner in London with US Secretary of State George Marshall and others.

Marshall cabled Washington the next day, noting how Bevin had expressed bitter regret and frustration with the United Nations' handling of the Palestine issue:

> [Bevin] had directed his delegate to abstain in the voting. He summarized the British position rather elaborately stating that the unanimous political reaction in Great Britain was against the Jewish influence in Palestine … He referred to the Jewish influence from the United States making impossible his efforts to successfully solve the difficulty prior to its reference to the United Nations. He referred to Balfour's declaration for a Jewish home rather than Jewish state, stated that he had had thorough legal advice that the declaration did not commit British Government to development of Jewish state, characterized the declaration as an unfortunate error and outlined the good faith in which he insisted Great Britain had conducted its mandate obligations.[75]

The Ad Hoc Committee issued its formal report the following day, 25 November 1947.[76] The stage was set for the final, crucial debate and vote in the General Assembly four days later.

## Notes

1 The members of the Ad Hoc Committee were Dr Herbert V. Evatt (Australia), Prince Subhasvasti Svastivat (Siam), Oswald Aranba (Brazil), Guillermo Belt (Cuba), Vladimir Simic (Yugoslavia), Henrik Kauffman (Denmark), C. Setalvad (India), Hernan Santa Cruz (Chile), Thor Thors (Iceland), and M.R. Scheyven (Belgium). All 57 member states of the United Nations also had the right to participate in the deliberations of the Ad Hoc Committee.

2 United Nations, A/516, Report of the Ad Hoc Committee on the Palestinian Question (25 November 1947).

3 United Nations Archives, S-0504-0025-0001-00004, *Report of the Ad Hoc Committee on the Palestinian Question* at 1 (25 November 1947); United Nations, A/AC.14/SR.1, Summary Record of First Meeting of Ad Hoc Committee on the Palestinian Question at para. 1 (25 September 1947); D. Mandel, *H.G. Evatt and the Establishment of Israel: The Undercover Zionist* at 119 (Frank Cass, 2004).

4 D. Mandel, *op. cit.*, at 94, 118.

5 *Id.* at 125.

6 *Id.* at 118.

7 United Nations, GA/PAL/2, Ad Hoc Committee on Palestinian Question, Press Release (26 September 1947).

8 *Id.*; *see also* FRUS, 501.BB Palestine/9–2547, Memorandum (Secret) of Conversation (25 September 1947) (discussing lunch meeting in New York City between Secretary of State George Marshall, British Colonial Secretary Creech Jones, Britain's Ambassador to the United States, and a member of the British delegation to the United Nations, during which Creech Jones disclosed what he intended to tell the Ad Hoc Committee the following day regarding Britain's refusal to enforce any UN decision that did not obtain both Jewish and Arab backing).

9 H.G. Evatt, *op. cit.*, at 127–128.

10 United Nations, GA/PAL/3, Ad Hoc Committee on Palestinian Question, Summary Press Release (29 September 1947); *see also* Library Special Collections, Charles E. Young Research Library, UCLA, Ralph Bunche papers, Box 97, Folder 7, Memorandum from

C. Rolfe to V. Hoo summarising Husseini's testimony (29 September 1947). Several days later, the Pakistani Delegate, Sir Zafrullah Khan, made a four-hour speech to the Ad Hoc Committee, reprising and emphasising Husseini's legal arguments. GA/PAL/7, Ad Hoc Committee on Palestinian Question, Press Release (7 October 1947). Jewish Agency representative David Horowitz later praised Khan as a "skilled lawyer … aided by an impeccable Oxford English accent, brilliant and polished style, and keen power of logic" D. Horowitz, *op. cit.*, at 241.

11 United Nations, GA/PAL/3, Ad Hoc Committee on Palestinian Question, Summary Press Release (29 September 1947).

12 *Id.*

13 *Id.* (emphasis added).

14 *Id.*

15 *Id.* Modern-day Palestinian scholars have continued invoking the "illegality" narrative regarding the Balfour Declaration. *See, e.g.*, E. Said, *The Question of Palestine* at 15–16 (Vintage, 1979), H. Husseini, *op. cit.*, at 47.

16 *Id.*

17 *Id.*

18 *Id.*

19 *Id.*

20 United Nations, GA/PAL/21, Summary Press Release (18 October 1947).

21 United Nations, A/AC.14/SR.31, Ad Hoc Committee Debate on Reports of Subcommittee I and II (24 November 1947).

22 *Id.*

23 *Id.* (emphasis added).

24 United Nations, GA/PAL/4, Press Release (2 October 1947).

25 United Nations, GA/PAL/6, Press Release (6 October 1947).

26 United Nations, GA/PAL/11, Press Release (10 October 1947).

27 Library Special Collections, Charles E. Young Research Library, UCLA, Ralph Bunche papers, Box 97, Folder 7, Memorandum from C. Rolfe to V. Hoo summarising Ad Hoc Committee debates (8 October and 13 October 1947).

28 United Nations, GA/PAL/12, Press Release (11 October 1947) (emphasis added). El Khoury's desire to seek an advisory opinion from the International Court of Justice regarding the legality of the Mandate presaged the Palestinian Authority's successful effort to obtain an Advisory Ruling in 2004 from the International Court of Justice declaring Israel's "wall of separation" illegal.

29 *Id.*

30 *Id.*

31 United Nations, GA/PAL/15, Press Release (14 October 1947).

32 United Nations, GA/PAL/16, Press Release (15 October 1947).

33 *Id.*

34 United Nations, GA/PAL/17, Press Release (16 October 1947).

35 United Nations, GA/PAL/20, Press Release (17 October 1947).

36 *Id.*

37 Israel State Archives, 2272/18, *Text of Statement of Dr. Chaim Weizmann, Former President of the Jewish Agency, Before the Ad Hoc Committee on the Palestinian Question*, para. 6 (18 October 1947).

38 *Id.*, para. 16. Regarding Weizmann's prior use of the term "treaty" to characterise the document he signed with Feisal, *see* S. Zipperstein, *op. cit.*, at 307.

39 Israel State Archives, 2272/18, *Text of Statement of Dr. Chaim Weizmann, Former President of the Jewish Agency, Before the Ad Hoc Committee on the Palestinian Question*, para. 24 (18 October 1947) (emphasis added).

40 D. Horowitz, *op. cit.*, at 245.

41 Library Special Collections, Charles E. Young Research Library, UCLA, Ralph Bunche papers, Box 97, Folder 7, Memorandum from C. Rolfe to V. Hoo summarising Ad Hoc Committee meetings (22 October 1947).

42 United Nations, GA/PAL/22, Press Release (21 October 1947). The Ad Hoc Committee also approved the formation of a smaller subcommittee (the Chair, Vice-Chair, and Rapporteur of the Committee) to examine the potential for achieving conciliation between the Palestinian Arabs and the Jews. A later Arab legal commentator argued the creation of the two subcommittees unfairly prejudiced the Palestinian cause: "The Ad Hoc Committee chose a path which widened the cleavages between proponents of the majority and minority plans. It seems anomalous that the procedure adopted for the consideration of the report was delegated to two subcommittees of the Ad Hoc Committee, one composed of pro-partition delegates and the other of Arab delegates plus Colombia and Pakistan, which were sympathetic to the Arab cause. It was obvious that those two subcommittees were so unbalanced as to be unable to achieve anything constructive. As was later made evident, the task of reconciling their conflicting recommendations was impossible. In such circumstances, it was not surprising that no serious attention was given to the legitimate aspirations of the Palestinians." N. Elaraby, *Some Legal Implications of the 1947 Partition Resolution and the 1949 Armistice Agreements*, Law and Contemporary Problems 33:1 at 101 (1968).

43 H.G. Evatt, *op. cit.*, at 137.

44 United Nations, GA/PAL/23, Press Release (23 October 1947). The Ad Hoc Committee Chair granted a request from Subcommittee II to extend the 29 October deadline. United Nations, GA/PAL/39, Press Release (29 October 1947).

45 United Nations, GA/PAL/22, Press Release (21 October 1947).

46 D. Mandel, *op. cit.*, at 143.

47 *Id.*

48 *Id.*

49 United Nations, GA/PAL/28, Press Release (23 October 1947).

50 United Nations, A/AC.14/32 (11 November 1947).

51 *Id.,* para. 6.

52 *Id.*, para. 7.

53 *See* Ch. 3, *supra* for a discussion of McMahon's 23 July 1937 letter to the editor of the *Times.*

54 *Id.*, para. 9.

55 *Id.*, para. 10.

56 *Id.*, para. 11.

57 *Id.*, para. 12(a).

58 *Id.*, para. 15(c).

59 *Id.*, para. 12(c).

60 *Id.*, para. 12(d).

61 *Id.*, paras. 16–17.

62 *Id.*, paras. 20–21.

63 *Id.,* para. 21.

64 United Nations, A/AC.14/SR.32, Palestine Question, Ad Hoc Committee Debate on Reports of Subcommittee I and II (24 November 1947); Mandel, *op. cit.*, at 147. The United States also announced at the 22 November meeting (after Weizmann had appealed directly to Truman at an Oval Office meeting on 19 November) its support for including the Negev region in the area to be allocated to the Jews. A. Radosh and R. Radosh, *op. cit.*, at 261–265.

65 D. Mandel, *op. cit.*, at 147; *see also* B. Oppenheim and H. Lauterpacht, *International Law, a Treatise* (6th ed.) at 208 (Longman, Greens, 1940) ("Although, according to its wording, the [United Nations] Charter imposes no clear obligation upon states which were mandatories by virtue of Article 22 of the Covenant [of the League of Nations] to place the territories in question under the system of trusteeship, it is clear that an obligation to this effect closely approaching a legal duty follows from the principles of the Charter"); *see also* J. Robinson, *op. cit.*, at 56 ("[T]he United Nations has clear jurisdiction with regard to former mandated territories. This jurisdiction is outlined in detail with regard

to procedures and powers in so far as they concern the conversion of a mandate into a trusteeship agreement. The way is left open for any other solution of the problem of an existing mandate").

66 *Ffrost v. Stevenson* (1937) 58 C.L.R. 528, 581–582 (Evatt, J.); *see also* J.L. Brierly, *The Law of Nations: An Introduction to the International Law of Peace* (5th ed.) at 165–167 (Oxford University Press, 1956).

67 *Ffrost v. Stevenson* (1937) 58 C.L.R. 528, 581 (Evatt, J.).

68 H.G. Evatt, *op. cit.*, at 155.

69 *Id.* at 156.

70 J. Robinson, *op. cit.*, at 56. For a contrary view, *see* H. Kelsen, *The Law of the United Nations: A Critical Analysis of Its Fundamental Problems* at 195–197 n.7 (Stevens & Sons, 1951) (agreeing with Arab objections that the General Assembly had exceeded its "recommendation" authority by adopting the Plan of Partition for Palestine in Resolution 181(II)).

71 H.G. Evatt, *op. cit.*, at 147.

72 United Nations, A/AC.14/SR.31, Palestine Question, Ad Hoc Committee Debate on Reports of Subcommittee I and II (24 November 1947).

73 United Nations, GA/PAL/85, Press Release (24 November 1947); see also J.G. Granados, *op. cit.*, at 265–266.

74 Subcommittee I focused its efforts on delineating the boundaries of the proposed Jewish and Arab states. At one point during those deliberations, the British delegation to the United Nations reported to London that the "[d]iscussions on boundaries have throughout been conducted … in an atmosphere very favourable to the Jews, the majority of the members showing themselves deliberately blind to all facts inconsistent with Jewish claims." FO 371/61888, Cypher Telegram No. 3440 from United Kingdom Delegation to Foreign Office (18 November 1947). It is impossible to imagine any committee or agency of the United Nations harbouring a similar pro-Israeli attitude today.

75 FRUS, 867N.01/11–2547, Telegram (Top Secret) from Secretary of State to Acting Secretary of State (25 November 1947).

76 United Nations Archives, S-0504-0025-0001-00004, *Report of the Ad Hoc Committee on the Palestinian Question* (25 November 1947); United Nations, A/516 (25 November 1947).

# 14

# THE UNITED NATIONS AND THE TWO-STATE SOLUTION

## The general assembly approves resolution 181 and the two-state solution

Following a lengthy and extraordinarily tense debate featuring a variety of Arab appeals for "justice" on behalf of the Palestinians[1] and intense Jewish lobbying efforts,[2] the United Nations General Assembly on 29 November 1947 approved, by the required two-thirds majority, the two-state solution for Palestine embodied in the "Plan of Partition with Economic Union" set forth in General Assembly Resolution 181(II).[3] Thirty-three nations (including *both* the United States and the Soviet Union) voted in favour, 13 voted against, and 11 (including Great Britain) abstained.[4]

### *Legality of resolution 181(II)*

The Arab delegates relied extensively on transformational legal framing during the General Assembly debate on 26 November 1948. The Arab delegates raised a long list of legal objections to the partition resolution, including: (i) the United Nations lacked jurisdiction over Palestine; (ii) the General Assembly could only make "recommendations" and lacked the legal authority to "impose" partition; (iii) partition constituted an act of "aggression" against the Palestinian Arabs, in violation of the UN Charter; (iv) partition violated Palestinian Arab rights of self-determination and Palestinian Arab "natural" and "historic" rights to sovereignty over all of Palestine; (v) partition violated principles of democratic rule, as the Palestinian Arabs comprised two-thirds of the country's population; (vi) Zionism represented a form of colonialism and/or communism; and (vii) the Palestinian Arabs had the right under the self-defence principles of the UN Charter to resist with violence the partition plan (leading to the absurd and

DOI: 10.4324/9781003225263-19

FIGURE 14.1 United Nations General Assembly, 29 November 1947, Lake Success, New York (Public Domain)

illogical proposition that the UN Charter allows parties to respond to United Nations resolutions with armed conflict and bloodshed).

During the General Assembly debate (Figure 14.1), for example, the Saudi delegate declared, "today … is the day when either justice or tyranny will prevail … Is not what is being attempted today in Palestine a case of flagrant aggression? … I hope I am not wrong in my confidence—that there are here amongst you those whose conscience and deep sense of justice would not allow them to be instruments of tyranny or abettors of aggression."[5]

The Syrian delegate also invoked transformational legal framing, imploring the General Assembly to consider "the legal side of the question."[6] The Syrian delegate continued:

> The Arab delegations, as everyone knows, have not failed to point out to their colleagues the real danger involved in the partition plan. On several occasions, we have reminded the world that this Organization cannot trample on its own Charter, to which it owes its existence, without running the risk of dealing itself a very dangerous blow. We have voiced here the uneasiness of the Arabs in Palestine and in all the Arab countries. In their opinion this plan is contrary to the principles of justice and to their natural rights, since their right to independence is not questioned. Yesterday, however, certain delegations invoked, in support of the Jewish argument, an alleged "historic right" to Palestine. Even supposing that this

> right existed, it could not be considered equal to the historic and acquired rights of the Arabs, rights which we have moreover explained to you on more than one occasion.[7]

The UN rejected every one of the Arab legal arguments. The "Jewish State and the Arab State," wrote Garcia Granados in his own version of transformational legal framing, "had been *legally created* by the supreme authority of civilized mankind."[8] As one commentator explained later:

> The United Nations was thus the most competent international body to determine the future of the Mandate on its termination in light of the fact that (a) the rights of the parties under the Mandate required preservation under article 80, and (b) the supervisory powers of the League of Nations, which included the interpretation of sovereign rights under the terms of the Mandate, had passed to the United Nations. The General Assembly's Partition Resolution was, moreover, a product of maximum international consideration and analysis of both Arab and Jewish positions. In this light, the United Nations Resolution must, as the Jewish Agency maintained at the time, be termed *sui generis* and to have been legally binding upon the parties.[9]

Other authorities agreed at the time that the United Nations, acting through the General Assembly, had the full legal authority to adopt partition and the two-state solution for Palestine. The State Department's legal advisor, for example, noted "the mandatory power and Great Britain together were competent to make a legally effective political settlement for Palestine. By virtue of the Assembly's passage of the resolution and Great Britain's 'acceptance' of the plan, these authorities appear to have made a *legal disposition* for the future of Palestine."[10]

The Legal Adviser further noted the legitimacy of Resolution 181(II) stemmed from the international community's elevation of the Balfour Declaration to the status of an internationally binding legal instrument when it was incorporated into the Mandate for Palestine:

> [T]he disposition of Palestine by the competent Powers after World War I included a provision, having the nature of a trust, in favor of a Jewish national home in Palestine. This was to be, however, without prejudice to the civil and religious rights of existing communities in Palestine. One of the ways in which this trust might be carried out would be through the establishment of a Jewish state in Palestine. The existence of this trust together with the inherent right recognized in international law afford a legal basis for the formation of a state and government by the Jewish community in the areas of Palestine which that community occupies. Such action would also have the moral sanction of the partially implemented

> disposition of Palestine made by the mandatory and the United Nations General Assembly in the Partition Plan. Similarly, the Arab Community would be entitled to organize a state and government in the areas of Palestine which it occupies.[11]

Arab legal commentators differ whether the General Assembly resolution carried any legal weight. The most common Arab legal arguments contend Resolution 181(II) was either legally invalid or, even if it were legally valid, as a General Assembly resolution, it merely set forth a *recommendation* and carried no legal weight:

> The Assembly's powers according to Articles 10, 11, 12, and 14 of the Charter are only recommendatory and without binding force on Member States. Hence, the Arab states did not contravene their Charter obligations when they, responding to the will of the Palestine Arab majority, rejected the Partition Plan … the General Assembly could do no more than recommend a solution and … its recommendation was not accepted by an Arab majority in Palestine.[12]

Other Arab legal commentators have taken this argument even further. They insist the Mandate for Palestine was never formally terminated, primarily because Resolution 181(II) was recommendatory only and carried no legal weight. Therefore, the Mandate *remains in effect today* and constitutes the sole governing international legal instrument for Palestine. Accordingly, the unilateral Zionist declaration of statehood in May 1948 was invalid, as the Mandate says nothing about Jewish *statehood* in Palestine. Instead, when read together with Article 22 of the Covenant of the League of Nations, the Mandate's *sole* purpose was to create an *Arab* State in Palestine.[13] Thus, the only permissible outcome under international law today would be the termination of the State of Israel and the establishment of Palestinian Arab statehood over the entirety of mandatory Palestine.

In the same breath, however, some of those same commentators take the logically inconsistent position that Resolution 181(II) *does* carry the force of law, and through it, the General Assembly established the maximum legal boundaries of the Jewish State:

> The General Assembly took great care in drawing their respective boundaries … the boundaries allotted to the Jewish state constitute a categorical limitation on Israel to claim legitimacy beyond them.[14]

Other Arab commentators explicitly recognize the legality of Resolution 181(II). One, for example, has recently argued "the Partition Plan was viewed as a legally binding decision," and the United Nations had the legal authority to modify and terminate the Mandate when it adopted Resolution 181(II).[15]

## *Recommendatory only, or legally binding?*

Even if the General Assembly had the legal power to adopt the two-state solution and partition plan, some question whether the General Assembly resolution created legally binding obligations on the Palestinian Arabs and Jews. General Assembly resolutions (unlike Security Council resolutions) ordinarily are non-binding as a matter of law. Legal scholars, therefore, disagree on the extent to which Resolution 181(II) carried any legal weight.

Some legal scholars have urged Resolution 181(II) possessed a "special status" in international law, for three reasons.[16] First, in addressing the Palestine issue, the General Assembly essentially stepped into the shoes of the League of Nations and "assumed the [League's] functions relative to the supervision of mandated territories."[17] This meant, according to one scholar, that "the General Assembly's action in voting for partition may have been legally binding and not merely recommendatory, as General Assembly resolutions normally are."[18]

Second, when Britain handed the Palestine question to the United Nations in early 1947,

> [This] amounted to the return of the Mandate to a sovereign or responsible party representing the international community. General Assembly Resolution 181 possessed, therefore, a special status and was not merely a "recommendation." Accordingly, the General Assembly resolution to regulate sovereignty in the mandate territory did not involve a change in international law, but rather was an authoritative decision regarding the fate of territory under its control and thus entitled to recognition as an expression of international law.[19]

Third, all the permanent members of the Security Council (except the United Kingdom) voted in favour of Resolution 181(II), further vesting the Resolution with "special status" under international law. Significantly, the General Assembly added language to the resolution requesting that the Security Council take steps to *enforce* the resolution, including "the necessary measures as provided for in the plan for its implementation."[20] This request gave the Security Council the option to take jurisdiction over Palestine and issue legally binding resolutions regarding Palestine.[21]

Finally, and most significantly, the General Assembly requested the Security Council "determine as a threat to the peace, breach of the peace or act of aggression, in accordance with Article 39 of the Charter, *any attempt to alter by force the settlement envisaged by this resolution*." This language, of course, anticipated that the Arabs would make good on their repeated threats to resist the two-state solution and partition with violence and armed conflict. The language, therefore, provided further evidence of the General Assembly's intent not just to make mere "recommendations" for future options for Palestine, but instead to impose binding and enforceable legal obligations on Arabs and Jews alike.

The Secretary General formally transmitted Resolution 181(II) to the President of the Security Council on 2 December 1947, asking the President of the Council to "draw the Council's attention particularly" to the various requests from the General Assembly regarding enforcement of the resolution.[22] Although the Security Council never took any steps to *enforce* Resolution 181(II), that does not mean Resolution 181(II) lacked legal force *ab initio*. Moreover, it would make no sense to argue that the Security Council's reluctance to enforce Resolution 181(II) deprived the resolution of any legal force, especially since the Security Council's reluctance stemmed from the violence the Mufti had precipitated *in response to* Resolution 181(II).

Nevertheless, the legal status of Resolution 181(II) continues to provoke debate among international lawyers and scholars. Crawford (2007), for example, argues the United Nations acted lawfully in adopting Resolution 181(II):

> Three views of the validity and legal effects of GA resolution 181(II) are possible. It might have been *ultra vires*; it might have been only a recommendation, or it might have constituted a valid and effective disposition of Palestine, at least to the extent of authorizing those concerned to implement it. The view that the resolution was *ultra vires* derives from a general implication as to the dispositive powers of the General Assembly. However, even earlier practice suggested that United Nations organs can make binding dispositions of territory in appropriate circumstances, pursuant to a delegation of power from States concerned or otherwise. This view has been twice reaffirmed, in the context of the Mandate system, by the International Court in the *Status Opinion* and the *Namibia Opinion*. There is no basis for treating the resolution as *ultra vires* ... the resolution was binding by virtue of the Assembly's own authority with respect to Mandates and of the referral of the Mandatory.[23]

Crawford further argues, however, that Resolution 181(II) only amounted to a recommendation and did not legally bind the parties. Accordingly, subsequent events in Palestine caused the United Nations to abandon the partition plan and the Resolution to lapse:

> The conclusion must be that the partition plan, though valid, was intended as no more than a recommendation. This conclusion is reinforced by the history of the resolution after 29 November 1947. Both the Security Council and the United Kingdom refused to enforce the partition plan, and various alternative schemes were mooted ... By 14 May 1948 the Assembly itself had, in effect, abandoned the partition plan as a whole.

## Palestinian Arabs and Arab states reject the two-state solution

The Palestinian Arabs were "incensed" at the General Assembly vote approving partition.[24] The Arab Higher Committee insisted the United Nations lacked jurisdiction to do anything other than adopt the one-state solution for Palestine and confer immediate sovereignty on the Arabs over the entire country.

The Palestinian Arabs and their Arab brethren had previously rejected both the UNSCOP majority and minority recommendations. They threatened violence if the General Assembly were to adopt the two-state solution. Now that the General Assembly had done so, the Arabs immediately launched war.

## *Palestinian Arab opposition to partition and preparation for war*

From his base in Beirut, the ex-Mufti Haj Amin al-Husseini declared the partition resolution and offer of the two-state solution "null and void."[25] The Mufti responded to the United Nations offer of Palestinian Arab statehood as part of a two-state solution by calling a three-day general strike and provoking the immediate outbreak of civil war, with Arab attacks against Jews throughout the country.[26]

The Mufti also formed an "Arab Liberation Army" to launch civil war in Palestine and thwart the implementation of the two-state solution.[27] The Mufti's goal was to gain the upper hand militarily in Palestine, which he hoped would enable him by mid-1948 to replace the outgoing British administration with a Palestinian Arab Government in control of the entire country.[28]

The Mufti had been preparing for this moment for months. For example, according to a CIA report from November 1946, the Mufti told a Lebanese newspaper owner that if the United Nations were to partition Palestine, the "Arabs of Palestine will resort to arms and will attack the Jews."[29] British Intelligence reported in July 1947 that the Mufti was "rapidly" readying armed and violent resistance to any potential United Nations partition plan.[30] In late July 1947, MI-6 reported the Mufti's envoys warned the attendees at a meeting of the Arab Higher Committee in Haifa that the rebellion against the possible two-state solution would begin "shortly," and that any Arabs opposing the Mufti would be "finished."[31]

In early September, 1947, Emile Ghory, spokesperson of the Palestine Arab Higher Committee, condemned the Special Committee's recommendations for partition as "an excess of injustice to Palestine, a flagrant violation of the natural rights of the Arabs in their own country, and an echo of the influence of Zionism and world Jewry."[32]

Also during September 1947, the British Government sent two police officials from Palestine to Cairo on an unofficial visit to contact the Mufti to ascertain whether he was "irrevocably opposed to any form of partition." The Mufti's reply was "emphatically yes."[33]

Garcia Granados recalled that Jamal Husseini, speaking on 29 September 1947, "uncompromisingly rejected both our majority partition and our minority federation plan, and warned that the Arabs would fight both solutions."[34]

In early October, 1947, the Arab Higher Committee formally notified the United States Government that the "Arabs of Palestine refuse definitely to acquiesce in any solution entailing the partitioning of Palestine ... The Arabs of Palestine unanimously demand the termination of the mandate over Palestine, the establishment of an Arab democratic state, and the withdrawal of British Troops and Government personnel."[35]

On 12 October 1947, the Mufti told a British newspaper the Palestinian Arabs would "resist [the two-state solution] with all their means."[36] On 26 October 1947, Jamal Husseini categorically rejected partition, declaring, "[i]f partition is approved, the U.N. will add another grave resolution to the list of prejudicial and unjust resolutions hitherto taken against the Arabs."[37]

In early November 1947, MI-6 reported the Mufti was "encourage[ing] preparations for eventual clandestine and guerilla warfare" against the two-state solution.[38]

In early February 1948, less than three months following the adoption of Resolution 181, the Arab Higher Committee sent a letter to the Secretary General reiterating the Palestinian Arab rejection of the two-state solution. The letter argued Resolution 181(II) was illegal because various countries were "forced" to vote for partition against their will:

> It is an elementary rule of law and justice that any decision, agreement, or act made or done under pressure, or undue influence or duress, is null and void. The aforementioned facts prove how the partition recommendations were extorted from member states of the United Nations. The Arabs therefore consider them null and void and of no legal or moral force.[39]

The letter closed with a shocking threat to the Secretary General:

> The Arabs of Palestine made a solemn declaration before the United Nations, before God and history, that they will never submit or yield to any power going to Palestine to enforce partition. *The only way to establish partition is first to wipe them out – man, woman and child.*[40]

## *Arab states' opposition to partition and preparation for war*

The Arab states followed the Mufti's lead, proclaiming they were not legally bound by the partition resolution. The Arab League in Cairo issued a communique on 19 September 1947 declaring the Palestinian Arabs "would wage war, in which no quarter would be shown" against the two-state solution.[41] The former Australian High Court Judge and recent Chair of the Ad Hoc Committee, H.G. Evatt, characterized the Arab bellicosity in reaction to Resolution 181(II) as "defiance of the United Nations."[42]

The Arab states joined the Palestinian Arabs in rejecting partition during autumn 1947: "Day after day the Arab states representatives threatened that partition meant war, and demanded the same solution they had demanded when we began our work months earlier: all Palestine as an Arab State."[43]

On 26 October 1947, King Ibn Saud wrote to President Truman, threatening the Arabs would reject partition and choose war instead:

> The Arabs have definitely decided to oppose establishment of a Jewish state in any part of the Arab world. The dispute between the Arab and Jew will be violent and long-lasting and without doubt will lead to more shedding of blood. Even if it is supposed that the Jews will succeed in gaining support for the establishment of a small state by their oppressive and tyrannous means and their money, such a state must perish in a short time. The Arabs will isolate such a state from the world and will lay siege to it until it dies by famine. Trade and possible prosperity of the state will be prevented; its end will be the same as that of those crusader states which were forced to relinquish coveted objects in Palestine.[44]

Immediately following the General Assembly's approval of Resolution 181(II), the delegates from the Arab states issued a joint statement condemning the resolution as legally invalid and unjust to the Arabs:

> All the delegations of the Arab states to the General Assembly ... consider that the resolution adopted today by a majority of the Assembly to partition Palestine goes beyond the mandate given to the members of the United Nations by the Charter, which is the only valid source of authority they might have ... the conscience of the world will not tolerate the dire consequences which will inevitably follow if nothing is done to remedy the injustice that has been meted out to the Arabs ... we trust that through the steadfastness of our people and through our belief in God and the justice of our cause, our right will prevail.[45]

The Arabs "flatly refused to accept the verdict of the United Nations."[46] For example, in early December 1947, King Farouk told the US Ambassador to Cairo that Egypt and other Arab states would use military force to drive the Jews completely out of Palestine.[47] Ali Jinnah of Pakistan cabled President Truman directly, invoking the Palestinian Arab justice narrative:

> At this hour when the Muslim world has received a terrible shock owing to the most unfortunate decision of the United Nations Organization to enforce partition of Palestine, I would like to address to you, Mr. President, this personal appeal. The decision is *ultra vires* of the United Nations charter and basically wrong and invalid in law ... May I therefore, at this eleventh hour, appeal to you and through you to the great and powerful American nation, which has always stood for justice, to uphold the rights of the Arab race.[48]

Azzam Pasha, the Secretary General of the Arab League, who had testified before the Anglo-American Committee of Inquiry one year earlier, reacted to the General Assembly's approval of Resolution 181(II) by threatening "a war of extermination and momentous massacre."[49]

## The Security Council takes jurisdiction to enforce the two-state solution

The Security Council met on 9 December 1947 to determine whether to take jurisdiction over Resolution 181(II). After much discussion, the Security Council agreed as follows:

> The Security Council received the letter from the Secretary-General enclosing the resolution of the General Assembly concerning Palestine, and, *being seized of the question*, decided to postpone discussion.[50]

The Soviet delegate, Andrei Gromyko, insisted on the term "seized of" during the Security Council's consideration of how to treat the transmittal letter from the Secretary General:

> The Security Council should implement the resolution of the General Assembly, and it should be stated that the Security Council is seized of the Palestinian question from now on. The Security Council should not mention the resolution of the General Assembly in passing and just take note of it. The resolution of the General Assembly should be implemented.[51]

The term "seized of" indicates the Security Council's determination to take jurisdiction of an issue from the General Assembly. Article 12 of the United Nations Charter grants the Security Council such authority:

> While the Security Council is exercising in respect of any dispute or situation the functions assigned to it in the present Charter, the General Assembly shall not make any recommendation with regard to that dispute or situation unless the Security Council so requests.

As a matter of international law, therefore, the Security Council's decision not merely to "take note" of Resolution 181(II), but to assert jurisdiction over the implementation and enforcement of the Resolution elevated the resolution and its offer of the two-state solution to the Palestinian Arabs and the Jews to the status of international law.[52]

On 5 March 1948, the Security Council adopted a resolution urging the implementation of Resolution 181(II).[53] The Resolution stated, in part:

> The Security Council, [h]aving received General Assembly resolution 181(II) of 29 November 1947 on Palestine ... Resolves to call on the permanent members of the Council to consult and to inform the Security Council regarding the situation with respect to Palestine and to make, as the result of such consultations, recommendations to it regarding the guidance and instructions which the Council might usefully give to the Palestine Commission with a view to implementing the resolution of the General Assembly.[54]

The same Arab legal commentators who rejected the binding legal nature of Resolution 181(II) have also argued that once the Security Council deems a matter to fall within its "threat to peace" jurisdiction, "the Council establishe[s] for itself the exclusive right of complete supervision" of the matter.[55] By the same reasoning, therefore, even if Resolution 181(II) lacked legally binding force when the General Assembly adopted it, it subsequently rose to the level of a legally binding instrument when the Security Council became "seized of" the issue and took jurisdiction over Palestine.

## Palestine between November 1947 and May 1948

The Mufti-inspired civil war in Palestine raged throughout the months following the General Assembly's approval of the partition plan. The war continued beyond Britain's 14 May 1948 withdrawal from Palestine, well into 1949.

On 19 January 1948, the Arab Higher Committee formally notified the United Nations that it had declined an invitation to appoint representatives to the United Nations Palestine Commission. The Arab Higher Committee said it would "persist in the rejection of partition" and that it "refus[ed] to recognize the United Nations Resolution [181(II)] or anything deriving therefrom."[56] Garcia Granados characterized the Palestinian Arabs' refusal to cooperate with the Palestine Commission as "an attack on the United Nations."[57]

On 30 January 1948, Britain announced it would terminate the Palestine Mandate on 15 May 1948.[58]

Meanwhile, the Jews focused during the ongoing civil war in the late winter and spring of 1948 on securing the territory the United Nations had allocated to them for their future state. The *Haganah* offensive, known as "Plan "D," or in Hebrew "*Dalet*," was intended "to ensure its control of the area designated for the Jewish state according to the partition plan."[59]

The Arab Higher Committee, the Arab League, and the Government of Transjordan each wanted to serve as the lead voice for the Palestinian Arabs and began jockeying for position beginning in late 1947. No one, however, took any steps to lay the groundwork for Palestinian Arab self-rule in the areas of Palestine the General Assembly had allocated to the Arabs in the partition plan. Having completely renounced the two-state solution, the Palestinian Arabs focused on fomenting violence and bloodshed instead of state-building during the crucial period between November 1947 and May 1948.

Some Arab historians take a dim view of the Arab Higher Committee's performance during the winter and spring of 1948:

> In Israel it is quite common to say that the Arabs fought against the partition plan and refused to accept it. It is standard to claim that this is what the Arab leadership chose, and that that decision led to the war. These statements are correct. That decision was an error and a foolish one … There was no Palestinian leadership. The Arab Higher Committee was composed of a group of *Mukhtars*, who were the representatives of a few large families. They were never elected to office in any way, shape or form, and were not representatives of the law … The Arab Higher Committee, contrary to what is usually thought today, did not take upon itself the role of leadership with sufficient seriousness. It did not invest any effort in the study of the Palestinian economy or its planning. It never examined the territorial question or similar issues. It did not function as the leadership of a country or even like a neighborhood committee. The members of the committee were decorative leadership (*zaamah*) and not a representative one.[60]

On 18 May 1948, the Assistant Secretary-General for Security Council Affairs wrote to the Arab Higher Committee seeking information, in light of the Arab invasion of Israel, about whether and how the Palestinian Arabs were governing themselves in the portion of Palestine the United Nations had allocated to them in Resolution 181(II).

Jamal Husseini, in his new capacity as the Arab Higher Committee's representative to the United Nations, replied to the letter on 24 May 1948. Husseini said the Arab Higher Committee considered itself the governing body for *all* of pre-May 1948 Palestine, other than for military matters, which it had ceded to the invading forces of the Arab League:

> When the Mandatory started their gradual withdrawal from Palestine, some weeks ago, the Arab Higher Committee asked all Arab Government Officials to carry on in their respective posts after the Mandatory's withdrawal. They were instructed that the senior Palestinian officer in each department is to act as temporary director of his department. These senior officers will be held responsible for the proper functioning of the departments and for the registers and documents, as well as for all their belongings. Arab officials have accepted the offer and are executing their duties in a satisfactory manner, under the present circumstances.[61]

Husseini concluded his reply letter by reiterating the Palestinian Arabs had completely renounced the United Nations 29 November 1947 offer of a two-state solution:

> Arabs claim to have authority over all the area of Palestine as being the political representative of the overwhelming majority of the population. They regard Palestine a one unit. All forces that oppose majority wherever they may be are regarded as unlawful.[62]

The Mufti continued opposing the two-state solution even after the State of Israel had declared its independence and the armies of Egypt, Jordan, Syria, Lebanon, Iraq, and Saudi Arabia invaded the nascent state. Following a ceasefire declaration in July 1948, British Intelligence reported the Mufti was "indignant" and committed to waging a guerilla warfare campaign against the two-state solution.[63]

Indeed, nearly a full year after the General Assembly had offered the Palestinians statehood pursuant to the partition plan's two-state solution, the Arab Higher Committee continued arguing vehemently *against* the two-state solution. The Palestinian lawyer Henry Cattan appeared on behalf of the Arab Higher Committee at a United Nations meeting in Paris on 22 November 1948, employing and expanding the traditional Palestinian Arab framing of the justice/injustice narrative:

> It was thus the greatest injustice, the greatest treachery in the history of the world; a violation of the very principles proclaimed in the Covenant and in the Mandate. The Arabs had even been refused recourse to the International Court of Justice; and the Mediator had based his observations on the *fait accompli*, and not on the merits of the problem, or on justice. The proposed solution had had tragic consequences: it was not, in fact, a real solution at all. Politically, historically and economically, Palestine was an entity. Partition would involve not simply a division of the territory; it would be a mutilation ...[64]

Against this chaotic backdrop, King Abdullah of Jordan had implicitly accepted the reality of partition, but he rejected the notion of a Mufti-led Palestine on Jordan's western border. Abdullah, therefore, wanted to occupy and annex for Jordan the area of Palestine the United Nations had designated for the Palestinian Arab State.[65]

The bitter rivalry between King Abdullah and the Mufti continued to play out during the months following Israel's proclamation of statehood. The Arab League, suspicious of Abdullah's designs, but reluctant to fight him, offered half-hearted support for the Mufti.

## October 1948: A Palestinian Arab "Government"?

### *Background*

One aspect of the three-way struggle between the Mufti, King Abdullah, and the Arab League involved the Mufti's desire both to pre-empt Abdullah and negate the existence of the Jewish State by establishing a Palestinian Arab "Government" ruling *all* of Palestine.

The Arab Higher Committee, with the backing of the Arab League, took various symbolic steps toward establishing a "government" for Palestine. For example, as early as August 1947, the Beirut newspaper *Al Naha* reported the Mufti had rented space in an Egyptian hotel, where he intended to establish a Palestinian Arab Government in exile.[66]

In early November 1947, British Intelligence reported the Arab League intended "in due course" to establish a government in exile for Palestine under its auspices and not under the Mufti's control.[67] The British Ambassador in Beirut speculated later that the Palestinian Arabs realized their renunciation of the United Nations offer of statehood jeopardized their legal claim to sovereignty over the portion of Palestine the international community had offered to them. The British Ambassador noted the Palestinian Arabs may have believed they needed to set up a "government in exile" as a way to preserve their juridical position.[68]

In late January 1948, MI-6 reported the Mufti, against opposition from Iraq, Egypt, and Transjordan, wanted to establish a symbolic Palestinian Arab Government for all of Palestine, with the Mufti at its head.[69] Also in January 1948, Syria, Egypt, and Saudi Arabia proposed the creation of an "Administrative Apparatus" (consisting of a national council, an executive council, and a president) to assume control of Palestine upon the British departure from the country. Jamal Husseini, however, hastened to clarify that this did not mean the Palestinian Arabs were forming a functioning government.[70]

Within weeks, however, the Arab League withdrew support for the fledgling "Administrative Apparatus." The withdrawing British took no steps to hand over any responsibility for governing the country to the Arab Higher Committee.[71] Nor had the Palestinian Arabs, as of February 1948, even "attempt[ed] to work out any kind of civil administration for their part of Palestine after 15th May."[72]

On 26 April 1948, less than three weeks before the 14 May termination of the Mandate, Jamal Husseini appeared in person at Lake Success and notified the General Assembly that the Palestinian Arabs intended to establish an Arab State throughout *all* of Palestine upon the termination of the Mandate. Husseini reiterated the Palestinian Arabs' renunciation of the United Nations' offer of Arab statehood in a portion of Palestine, invoking the long-standing Palestinian Arab transformational legal framing regarding the Covenant of the League of Nations and the Mandate:

> Jamal Bey Husseini (Arab Higher Committee) stressed the injustice and inequality of what he termed the Anglo-Zionist Mandate … The Mandate had been ratified in 1922 without the people of the Holy Land being given a hearing, that is to say, in disregard of the principle of the right of peoples to self-determination … In the course of its second regular session, the General Assembly had heard the people of Palestine proclaim their

> intention to defend their national patrimony to the last man; yet two-thirds of its members, ill-advised, misled or acting under compulsion, had accepted an illegal scheme which could not be carried out and which was contrary to the rights and interests of the Arabs ... In 1917, an Anglo-Zionist conspiracy had resulted in the Balfour Declaration, which was opposed by the Arabs of Palestine and the whole of the Arab and Moslem world. That Declaration was an unprecedented negation of the principles of justice and equity and was also in contradiction with the promise made to the Arabs of Palestine ... neither the Covenant of the League of Nations, nor the Mandate, nor any other authority had authorized the division of the country after the termination of the Mandate. What the United Kingdom Government had to hand over was the whole of Palestine as one unit, and this could be done only to one Palestinian government representing all the lawful citizens of Palestine ... The Arab Higher Committee was utterly opposed to partition under any form. UNSCOP had, however, ignored this attitude of the Arabs of Palestine ... Failing agreement, the overwhelming majority of the people of Palestine would establish an independent Palestinian government in conformity with Article 22 of the Covenant and Article 28 of the Mandate, which provided for the establishment of such a government on the termination of the Mandate.[73]

Once the surrounding Arab armies invaded the newly declared State of Israel on 15 May 1948, King Abdullah moved swiftly to supplant the Mufti as the supreme authority over the Palestinian Arab population. The Palestinian Arabs had still taken *no* steps to create a functioning government for the portion of Palestine the General Assembly had offered them in Resolution 181(II). An Egyptian newspaper columnist harshly criticized the Palestinian Arab leadership in a surprisingly candid August 1948 editorial for failing to establish a government for their portion of Palestine, alongside the new Jewish State:

> The Arab-controlled part of Palestine has no government to administer its affairs. The Jews were wiser than the Arabs in this respect. They hastened to form a government as soon as the U.N. Assembly voted for partition ... Palestine, however, is still without an Arab government. It may be argued that the establishment of an Arab government in Palestine was delayed because the Jews drove several hundred thousand Palestinian Arabs out of their homes, and because the Arab governments wanted to avoid disputes among themselves over this matter. *Both excuses are silly.*[74]

## *Rise of the "All-Palestine Government"*

By July 1948, the Arab League was pushing back on Abdullah's effort to claim the Arab portions of Palestine for Jordan. The League thus revived the idea of a Palestinian Arab "civil administration" to govern the entire country. The Arab

League was motivated more by the desire to check Abdullah's ambitions than to promote Palestinian Arab nationalism:

> Furthermore, the Arab League general secretary, with the encouragement of Egypt and Syria, launched an overt political effort to foil the Bernadotte plan and deny Abdullah its innate advantages, enlisting for this purpose the Palestinian national movement. Thus, on the eve of the termination of the first truce, the Arab League decided to establish an autonomous Palestinian administration, allegedly to bear responsibility for the affairs of the local Arab population. As a further step in this direction, the Arab League, with Egyptian prodding, created the All-Palestine Government, which took Gaza as its base.[75]

In September 1948, the Arab League approved the conversion of the administrative council into a "government" for Palestine.[76] Accordingly, the Arab Higher Committee announced on 22 September 1948 that, based on the Arab League's approval, it would establish a government in Gaza to rule *all* of Palestine.[77] On 30 September 1948, a group of 75 Palestinians met in Gaza and declared the creation of the "Palestinian National Council." The "National Council" elected the ex-Mufti as "President," who, in turn, appointed his cousin Jamal Husseini as "Foreign Minister."[78]

The Palestinian Arabs proclaimed their "government" in an announcement to the international community:

> In virtue of the natural right of the people of Palestine for self-determination which principle is supported by the Charters of the League of Nations, the United Nations and others and in view of the termination of the British mandate over Palestine which had prevented the Arabs from exercising their independence, the Arabs of Palestine, who are the owners of the country and its indigenous inhabitants and who constitute the great majority of its legal population, have solemnly resolved to declare Palestine *in its entirety* and within its boundaries as established before the termination of the British mandate an independent state and constituted a government under the name of the All Palestine Government deriving its authority from a representative council based on democratic principles and aiming to safeguard the rights of minorities and foreigners, protect the holy places and guarantee freedom of worship to all communities, I wish to take this opportunity to express to Your Excellency the earnest desire of the All Palestine Government to establish relations of cordiality and cooperation with your country.[79]

Jamal Husseini told an American official in Amman several days earlier the "government" would be formed on paper only, "so that Palestine Arabs would have legal position vis-à-vis Arab League and as evidence Palestine Arabs determination continue fight against Jews."[80]

Significantly, however, the Palestinian Arabs never asserted *any* legal reservation of rights as to the portion of Palestine the United Nations had allocated to them for statehood in Resolution 181(II). Instead, the Palestinian Arabs laid claim to *all* of Palestine. In so doing, the Palestinian Arabs purported to preserve the *same* legal arguments the United Nations had *already* rejected, namely, that the United Nations had no legal authority to adopt the partition resolution, that the partition resolution itself was illegal, and that the Palestinian Arabs, therefore, were entitled to sovereignty over the *entirety* of Palestine.

In any event, the Mufti's focus was not on preserving legal claims but creating "a focal point of opposition to Abdullah and … frustrating [Abdullah's] ambition to federate the Arab regions of Palestine with Transjordan."[81] The Lebanese Foreign Minister noted the "Gaza Government was set up as opposition to Abdullah. … popular reaction is that other Arabs wish to thwart Abdullah's ambitions for federation of Arab regions with Transjordan; [and] concomitant tacit recognition of Israel."[82]

On 2 October 1948, the Mufti's "National Council" issued the "Palestine Declaration of Independence," asserting sovereignty over all of Palestine. The State Department responded swiftly, cabling every United States Ambassador in the Middle East with instructions to contact their host governments and relay the following statement of United States policy regarding the supposed "Arab Palestine Government":

> US Govt considers establishment of "Arab Palestine Govt" under present circumstances prejudicial to successful solution Palestine problem as well as to best interests Arab States and Arab inhabitants Palestine. "Govt" apparently being set up without prior consultation wishes Arab Palestinians. Also appears dominated by Mufti, an adventurer, whose reprehensible wartime activities in association with our enemies cannot be forgotten or forgiven by US. Best interests Arab States being prejudiced by published indications that Arab unity disturbed by formation of 'Govt.' Moreover by claiming speak for all Palestine "Govt" affords ready pretext to Jewish revisionists make similar claims for right … control all Palestine.[83]

As noted, the Arab League had offered tepid support to the Mufti, but as with most Middle East politics, the undercurrent of conflicting and complex rivalries created even further ambiguity. Egypt, for example, had joined the Arab League vote supporting the establishment of a Palestinian Arab Government. But the British Ambassador in Cairo cabled London on 8 October 1948, advising Egypt's vote had been given without King Farouk's consent.[84]

In any event, the All-Palestine "Government" proved to be nothing more than an illusory, paper government. It controlled no territory, employed no people, mustered no army, exercised no functions, provided no public services, collected no revenue, and vanished one month after it was established. It boasted only one actual achievement: managing to print about 14,000 "passports" (Figure 14.2),

**FIGURE 14.2** Passport issued by "All-Palestine Government" (Public Domain)

a symbol of a would-be "government" that never became a reality. As one historian noted:

> [T]he contrast between the pretensions of the All-Palestine Government and its capability quickly reduced it to the level of farce. It claimed jurisdiction over the whole of Palestine, yet it had no administration, no civil service, no money, nor real army of its own … Ostensibly the embryo for an independent Palestinian state, the new government, from the moment of its inception, was thus reduced to the unhappy role of a shuttlecock in the ongoing power struggle between Cairo and Amman.[85]

## *Collapse of the "All-Palestine Government"*

The third phase of the 1948–1949 war began in mid-October 1948 with an Israeli offensive in the south of the country. On 29 October 1948, the British Consulate in Jerusalem notified London the Gaza "Government" had collapsed less than one month after it had been created. The Consulate noted there had been "a perceptible movement towards King Abdullah" among the Palestinian Arab population.[86]

Every member of the Gaza "Government" fled, including the Mufti. Jamal Husseini even spoke of agreeing to serve under King Abdullah. As one historian concluded, the "All Palestine Government" vanished "under the weight of its own impotence."[87]

In March 1949, British Intelligence prepared an extensive report regarding the Mufti's effort to establish an "All Palestine Government" in Gaza. The report noted the so-called government existed only on paper, and only briefly. The "Government" exercised no authority, ruled no territory, and held no legal status. It aspired to rule all of Palestine, in violation of Resolution 181(II). Other than the Arab League, no international organizations, including the United Nations, recognized the "All Palestine Government." No countries, including no Arab countries, exchanged Ambassadors with it.

According to the British Intelligence report, the nominal head of the Government, Ahmed Filmy Pasha, was ready to defect to King Abdullah along with several other members of the Government, as the Mufti "keeps everything under his own control." The report also noted the Mufti had embezzled the funds received from Arab states.[88] Filmy Pasha had concluded the Gaza Government "could not carry on any longer, i.e., they have created a state without financial resources and that now is the time to face facts and call it a failure."[89]

The "All Palestine Government" continued to "exist," but solely on paper, from a new base in Cairo until the 1952 overthrow of King Farouk.

The Palestinian Arab failure to embrace the two-state solution in 1947–1948 and engage in state-building and peaceful coexistence rather than violence and bloodshed proved catastrophic for the Palestinian Arab people. That failure was the true *Nakba* for the Palestinians.

## Abdullah takes control

Many Palestinian Arabs themselves refused to recognize the validity of the Mufti's paper government, deciding instead their best hope lay in pledging loyalty to King Abdullah and submitting to Jordanian rule. Thus, on 1 October 1948, on the same day the Mufti and his team declared their new Government in Gaza, a different group of Palestinian Arabs gathered in Amman. The delegates adopted resolutions slamming the formation of the "All Palestine Government" and declaring their loyalty to King Abdullah. The delegates affirmed that Transjordan and Arab Palestine constituted a single territorial and political entity.[90]

On 18 October 1948, the anti-Mufti Palestinians met again, this time in Ramallah, and reiterated their desire to merge the Arab areas of Palestine into Jordan under King Abdullah's rule.

On 1 December 1948, the pro-Abdullah Palestinian Arabs met in Jericho to formalize their allegiance to the King and Jordan. "It was an especially large gathering," one historian has noted, "with hundreds of representatives from all sectors of the Palestinian population, attended by religious leaders, the Jordanian military governors and many reporters."[91]

The Jericho Conference marked King Abdullah's victory over the Mufti for control of the Arab portion of Palestine. Convening the day after Transjordan and Israel had agreed to a truce, the Palestinian Arabs (those not controlled by the Mufti and his henchmen) formally pledged their loyalty to the King:

> The Jericho Conference, as it came to be known, which was held with the encouragement and support of the Arab Legion, and attended by local Palestinians, recognized Abdullah as "King of Palestine" and effectively granted him power-of-attorney to resolve the 'Palestine problem' as he saw. The Jericho Conference further aggravated the king's position in the Arab world, which viewed this as yet another step towards annexation. Indeed, the king was now eager to actualize the Jericho resolutions for immediate and formal annexation of the Arab territory held by his army. Abdullah was convinced that through immediate annexation of Palestine, he could end the war with Israel and ease his resulting economic difficulties.[92]

The 1 December 1948 Jericho meeting sealed Abdullah's victory over the Mufti and the Arab League:

> The all-Palestine government did its best to overlook the fact that it was, in effect, a regime with neither territory nor subjects. It held meetings and outlined plans to form sovereign frameworks hoping to give them some content in the future ... This almost pathetic experiment was soon doomed to failure. Prominent figures in the all-Palestine government and its National Council deserted to King Abdallah's camp ... The final stage was a Palestinian congress held on 1 December 1948, in Jericho, which denounced the Gaza government and expressed its non-confidence in [the Arab Higher Committee]. The Congress granted Abdallah a mandate to solve the Palestine question as he saw fit and to unite it with Transjordan.[93]

Abdullah notified the US Government a few days later that he would accept the request from the Palestinian Arab delegates to the Jericho conference and "proclaim the annexation of Arab Palestine to Transjordan."[94]

## Legal significance of Jordan's "annexation" of the West Bank

Despite Abdullah's purported annexation of the Arab portion of Palestine in late 1948, some scholars have questioned whether the Palestinian Arabs, as a matter of law, formally ceded sovereignty over the Arab portions of Palestine to Jordan at the 1 December 1948 Jericho meeting. For example, Gerson (1973) has argued:

> Assuming *arguendo* that the decision to merge expressed at the Jericho Conference represented in fact the free choice of the West Bank inhabitants, it would still remain questionable whether that decision indicated an intent wholly and irrevocably to transfer such sovereign rights.[95]

Gerson further notes that both the Arab League and the broader international community refused to recognize Jordanian sovereignty over the West Bank between 1949 and 1967. Only two countries – Britain and Pakistan – recognized Jordanian claims to the West Bank during those years.

On 23 December 1948, the CIA reported information received from a source in Egypt (via a source in Lebanon) indicating the Mufti, as part of his ongoing struggle against Abdullah, "made an agreement with the Soviets to work toward bringing the Arabs into the Soviet orbit if they would help aid him to gain control of Palestine."[96]

*****

In June 1949, more than one year after the establishment of Israel and after the War of Independence had ended with various armistice agreements, the Arab Higher Committee reiterated the Palestinian Arab rejection of Resolution 181's two-state solution, while continuing to employ transformational legal framing and the justice/injustice narrative:

> The Jews and their unjustified admission to the United Nations have obstructed every chance of a pacific settlement of the Palestine Problem. Every day the Jews are giving grounds for censure by the Security Council, the General Assembly and world conscience and public opinion. Yet the Jews are being constantly shielded, presented as justified while in the wrong, as the innocent party while deep in their aggression. Surely there must be an end to this one-sided treatment of the Palestine Problem. The concepts of the Arabs of Palestine about justice, fair play, and ethics in International Affairs have been paralyzed by the events of the last year ... the wickedness, the fantastic demands, and aggressive intentions of Jews ... are responsible for failure ... to bring justice and peace to Palestine.[97]

In many respects, this early statement set the tone for Palestinian transformational legal framing for the next seven-plus decades.

## The State Department's trusteeship gambit

As the Mufti-inspired violence worsened in early 1948, the United States increasingly harboured second thoughts about the two-state solution. Various State Department officials who had opposed partition in 1947 began actively looking for a way to reverse course. Those officials seized on the Mufti's campaign of terror and violence in Palestine as "proof" that partition was unworkable.

Indeed, "[a]lmost from the first day, the U.S. State and Defense establishment waged a relentless campaign to undermine partition and President Truman's support for it."[98] The campaign almost succeeded.

Given their institutional preference for strong United States relations with the Arab states, and their concerns about the impact of the Truman Administration's support for partition on American political and economic interests in the Arab world, those officials (especially Undersecretary of State Robert Lovett, Near East Division Chief Loy Henderson, and Policy Planning Staff Chief George Kennan and their staffs) worked behind the scenes to sabotage the President's Palestine policy. The anti-partitionists urged an alternative to the two-state solution, in which Palestine would be placed under trusteeship rather than be divided into two sovereign states.[99]

The Policy Planning Staff (under the leadership of George Kennan) at the State Department, for example, prepared a lengthy memorandum in mid-January 1948, less than two months after the United States had voted in favour of the partition resolution, recommending the United States "take no further initiative in implementing or aiding partition." The memorandum urged the United States to consider advocating the Palestine issue be returned to the United Nations for further study, including "investigat[ing] the possibilities of any other suggested solution such as a federal state or trusteeship."[100]

The State Department drumbeat against partition intensified further in a 27 January 1948 top-secret memorandum from Samuel Kopper, a young lawyer and Arabist in the Near Eastern Affairs Division, who would later serve as Assistant to the Chairman of the Arabian American Oil Company (Aramco).[101] Kopper, advocating for trusteeship instead of partition, framed his argument in legal terms:

> The growing tendency to refer to the recommendation of the General Assembly as a decision which must be carried out must not be allowed to divert our attention from the fact that the action of the General Assembly was only a recommendation. The United Nations has above all an obligation to preserve peace by peaceful methods so long as this is possible. The United Nations should retain a degree of flexibility and be able to alter its suggested solution of a matter when such is necessary in the light of changing conditions. There are serious doubts as to whether the Arabs of Palestine are under any obligations whatsoever, legal or moral, to be bound by the General Assembly recommendation.[102]

On 18 March 1948, Chaim Weizmann met with President Truman in the Oval Office. The President initially refused to take the meeting, agreeing only after a personal appeal from his friend and former business partner, Eddie Jacobson.[103] Weizmann left the meeting feeling he had secured the President's promise of continued support for the two-state solution.[104]

But the next day, 19 March 1948, US Ambassador to the United Nations Warren Austin announced, with authorization from Secretary of State George Marshall, [105] but seemingly without Truman's knowledge or consent, that the American Government had reversed its position and now preferred trusteeship over partition for Palestine:

> [M]y Government believes that a temporary trusteeship for Palestine should be established under the Trusteeship Council of the United Nations to maintain the peace and to afford the Jews and Arabs of Palestine, who must live together, further opportunity to reach an agreement regarding the future government of that country. Such a United Nations trusteeship would, of course, be without prejudice to the character of the eventual political settlement, which we hope can be achieved without long delay. In our opinion, the Security Council should recommend the establishment of such a trusteeship to the General Assembly and to the Mandatory Power.[106]

Austin's announcement stunned Jewish leaders in Palestine and the United States and put Truman "in the most embarrassing position of his political career."[107]

That same day (19 March 1948), the State Department's Legal Adviser sent a memorandum to State Department official (and future Secretary of State) Dean Rusk, setting forth a series of conclusions regarding the legal status of Palestine. The memorandum argued the Principal Allied and Associated Powers "held and exercised the legal power to dispose of Palestine" following World War I. It noted the Mandate empowered Britain "to complete the tutelage of Palestine," to enable the people of that country to attain full independence, "which had been provisionally recognized in the Covenant of the League of Nations."

The Legal Adviser's memorandum then turned to a discussion of Resolution 181(II), noting it remained in force, unless it appeared "unworkable" due to the ongoing violence in Palestine and "inaction by the Security Council." The memorandum then noted that Britain's intention to abandon the Mandate, before completing the role the League of Nations had entrusted to it, raised questions "as to the existence of legal continuity for the governing of Palestine," including the possibility of an absence of constituted authority in Palestine."[108]

On 25 March 1948, Truman made a public statement appearing to support both a "temporary trusteeship" *and* eventual partition, creating even further confusion regarding American policy.[109]

On 9 April 1948, Weizmann wrote to Truman. Weizmann made a powerful argument for partition and against trusteeship, invoking again the Jewish legal framing:

> The clock cannot be put back to the situation which existed before November 29. I would also draw attention to the psychological effects of promising Jewish independence in November and attempting to cancel it in March … The choice for our people, Mr. President, is between Statehood and extermination. History and providence have placed this issue in your hands, and I am confident that you will decide it in the spirit of the moral law.[110]

At one point in early 1948, Truman asked his friend Oscar Ewing, an attorney who worked in the Administration, for advice regarding the Palestine situation.

Ewing volunteered to study the legal aspects of the Palestine question for the President. More than two decades later, in an oral history interview with the Truman Library, Ewing recalled his findings and his legal advice to Truman:

> The study proved fascinating. Being a lawyer, naturally I investigated the legal claims that the Arabs and Jews respectively had to the land in question. I found that under international law, when land is taken by conquest, the conqueror can dispose of it as he wishes. For instance, after the Norman conquest of England in 1066, William the Conqueror granted lands to his various lords and the titles to land in England today start with these grants. Therefore, the grant of sovereignty given by the Allies to the Jews of lands conquered from Turkey had the same validity as had similar grants of sovereignty to Jordan, Syria, Lebanon, and Saudi Arabia. The claim of the Arabs that Palestine had been their land for thousands of years was untrue. For several hundred years it had been Turkish territory and with Allenby's conquest in World War I the territory became Allied territory for the Allies to dispose of as they wished. When the title of the Allies to a part of this conquered land was transferred to the Jews, their title to it became indisputable; and I so advised the President.[111]

The President's Special Counsel, future Secretary of Defense Clark Clifford, also pushed back against the State Department's effort to reverse the Administration's position regarding partition. On 6 March 1948 Clifford wrote, "[t]his Government urged partition upon the United Nations in the first place and it is unthinkable that it should fail to back up that decision in every possible way."[112]

Two days later, Clifford wrote directly to the President, offering a staunch defence of partition as the best outcome for the United States, consistent with decades of US policy. Clifford began by slamming critics of the President's support for partition:

> There are some who criticize your actions last fall in actively supporting partition in Palestine. They argue that this embarked the United States on a new policy; that this new policy involves military commitments which we are unable to perform; and that, therefore, we should seek some other solution. This argument is completely fallacious. Your action in supporting partition is in complete conformity with the settled policy of the United States. Palestine was Turkish territory prior to World War I. It was captured by the Allies. The Balfour Declaration favoring "the establishment in Palestine of a national home for the Jewish people," was made November 2, 1917 ... The substance of the Balfour Declaration has been restated by Presidents Harding, Coolidge, Hoover, Franklin D. Roosevelt and yourself. The Balfour Declaration was approved by joint resolution of Congress June 30, 1922. It was reaffirmed in the American-British Palestine Mandate Convention of December 3, 1924 ... Your active support of partition was

> in complete harmony with the policy of the United States. Seldom has any policy of this government been so clearly and definitely established. Had you failed to support partition, you would have been departing from an established American policy and justifiably subject to criticism.[113]

Clifford concluded by urging that "[p]artition unquestionably offers the best hope of a permanent solution of the Palestine problem that may avoid war."[114]

Two weeks later, as Weizmann was preparing to attend a Passover Seder, he received an urgent message that a close friend of the President, Judge Samuel Rosenman, needed to speak to Weizmann. Rosenman reported he had just met with the President, who said, "I have Dr. Weizmann on my conscience." The President authorised Rosenman to convey the following message to Weizmann:

> [The President] went over the events of the 19th of March, explaining how he was inadequately informed about the United States brief to the U.N.O., and, it seems, somewhat blaming himself for the ensuing muddle. He explained that his object now was to get the American position in [the] U.N.O. back to what it had been before the 19th when official American policy was in support of the resolution of November, 1947. If this could be done, he said, and if a Jewish State was proclaimed, he would recognize it immediately. He made one stipulation. He would deal with only one Jewish representative, and that was Dr. Weizmann.[115]

Weizmann would later present President Truman with a Torah scroll on behalf of the new State of Israel (Figure 14.3).

## Israel declares independence; Arab Palestine in Abeyance

On 14 May 1948, hours before the departure of the British High Commissioner and the formal termination of the Mandate at midnight 14/15 May,[116] the Palestinian Jews declared their independence and established the State of Israel.[117] Truman kept his word to Weizmann and recognized the State of Israel only ten minutes later.

The Palestinian Arabs and the surrounding Arab nations responded with declarations of war, in blatant violation of Resolution 181(II), the United Nations Charter, and international law.[118]

The legal status of the portions of Palestine allocated for the Arab state remained unsettled. The ill-fated attempt to establish an Arab Government to rule *all* of Palestine changed nothing as a matter of law. By the time the first Arab-Israeli War ended with a series of armistice agreements in 1949, Jordan had emerged as the occupying power in the West Bank and East Jerusalem, and Egypt stood as the occupying power in the Gaza strip. The situation remained unchanged until the Six-Day War in June 1967, when Israel replaced both Egypt and Jordan as the occupying powers in the territories.

**FIGURE 14.3** President Truman receiving a Torah from Chaim Weizmann (Public Domain)

## Notes

1 *See, e.g.*, FO 371/61890, Telegram No. 3554 (Immediate) from United Kingdom delegation to United Nations to Foreign Office (27 November 1947) ("Feisal appealed for justice saying that if it were not granted by the United Nations the states concerned must defend it by themselves"); *see also* J. Strawson, *op. cit.*, at 108–117.

2 *See* N. Goldmann, *op. cit.*, at 244–245; R. Ovendale, *op. cit.*, at 241–245. The Jewish lobbying campaign included a successful effort to delay the vote until after the Thanksgiving Holiday, allowing the Jewish side several additional, crucial days to lobby the White House and the wavering General Assembly members to secure the necessary two-thirds support among the members of the General Assembly. A. Radosh and R. Radosh, *op. cit.*, at 268–274; *see also* M.J. Cohen (1990), *op. cit.* at 163–168.

3 United Nations General Assembly, Resolution 181(II), A/RES/181(II) (29 November 1947). The vote followed a successful French effort to obtain a one-day delay, from Friday 28 November to Saturday 29 November. *See* D. Mandel, *op. cit.*, at 153–154.

4 Prior straw votes on 22 and 26 November failed to produce the required two-thirds majority necessary to adopt the Resolution. K. Roosevelt, *op. cit.*, at 13–14.

5 United Nations, A/PV.125 at 1337 (26 November 1947).

6 *Id.* at 1338.

7 *Id.* at 1338–1339.

8 J.G. Granados, *op. cit.*, at 268 (emphasis added). The International Court of Justice, in the *Namibia* opinion, ruled the demise of the League of Nations had no legal effect on the ongoing validity of the various post–World War I Mandates: "To the question whether the continuance of a mandate was inseparably linked with the existence of

the League, the answer must be that an institution established for the fulfilment of a sacred trust cannot be presumed to lapse before the achievement of its purpose. The responsibilities of both mandatory and supervisor resulting from the mandates institution were complementary, and the disappearance of one or the other could not affect the survival of the institution." International Court of Justice, *Legal Consequences for States of the Continued Presence of South Africa in Namibia (South West Africa) Notwithstanding Security Council Resolution 276 (1970)*, ICJ Reports at para. 55 (21 June 1971). Therefore, Britain lawfully continued as mandatory for Palestine following the termination of the League's existence; Britain lawfully referred the Palestine matter to the United Nations in February 1947; and the General Assembly, therefore, lawfully adopted Resolution 181(II).

9 A. Gerson, *Trustee-Occupant: The Legal Status of Israel's Presence in the West Bank*, 14 Harv. Intl. L. J. at 35 (1973); *see also* G. Watson, *The Oslo Accords: International Law and the Israeli-Palestinian Peace Agreements* at 26 (Oxford University Press, 2000) ("Britain's abdication in favour of UN disposition of the Mandate for Palestine plainly gave the United Nations authority to act").

10 FRUS, 867N.01/5–1048, Memorandum by the Legal Adviser to the Under Secretary of State, "Recognition of New States and Governments in Palestine" (11 May 1948).

11 *Id.*

12 N. Elaraby, *op. cit.*, at 102–103.

13 *See* M. de Blois, *The Unique Character of the Mandate for Palestine*, 49 Israel Law Review at 365, 388–389 (2016).

14 *Id.* at 103.

15 V. Kattan, Blog post, *op. cit.*

16 *See, e.g.*, R. Gavison (ed.), *The Two-State Solution: The UN Partition Resolution of Mandatory Palestine* at xx-xxi (Bloomsbury, 2013).

17 A. Gerson, *Israel, The West Bank and International Law* at 47–48 (Frank Kass, 1978).

18 *Id.* at 48; *see also* G. Watson, *op. cit.*, at 22–23 (Resolution 181(II) had "some legal effect" at the time of its adoption, although it most likely lapsed as of 14 May 1948 when Israel declared its independence).

19 R. Gavison, *op. cit.*, at xxi.

20 United Nations General Assembly, Resolution 181 (II), A/RES/181(II) (29 November 1947); *see also* H. Kelsen, *op. cit.*, at 210 n.7 (General Assembly had the legal authority under Article 10 of the United Nations Charter to recommend to the Security Council that it take steps to enforce the partition resolution). Article 10 states, "The General Assembly may discuss any questions or any matters within the scope of the present Charter or relating to the powers and functions of any organs provided for in the present Charter and, except as provided in Article 12, may make recommendations to the Members of the United Nations or to the Security Council or to both on any such questions or matters." United Nations, Charter of the United Nations, Art. 10, 1945, 1 UNTS XVI; *see also* FO 371/61889, Telegram No. 3453 from British Delegation, United Nations to Foreign Office, paras. 4, 5 (19 November 1947) (reporting on Ad Hoc Committee discussions regarding the legality of the partition proposal under the United Nations Charter and noting the Ad Hoc Committee agreed the proposals were legal, and that the request to the Security Council to take the necessary measures to implement the partition plan was also intended to convey the partition proposal carried legal weight beyond serving as a mere "recommendation" by the General Assembly), *reprinted in* P. Toye and A Seay, *Israel: Boundary Disputes with Arab Neighbours, 1946–1964*, Vol. 2 at 39–40 (Archive Editions 1995).

21 The General Assembly also requested the Security Council "consider, if circumstances during the transitional period require such consideration, whether the situation in Palestine constitutes a threat to the peace. If it decides that such a threat exists, and in order to maintain international peace and security, the Security Council should supplement the authorization of the General Assembly by taking measures, under Articles 39 and 41 of

the Charter, to empower the United Nations Commission, as provided in this resolution, to exercise in Palestine the functions which are assigned to it by this resolution." United Nations General Assembly, Resolution 181(II), *op. cit.*

22 United Nations, S/614, Letter from Secretary-General to President, Security Council (2 December 1947).

23 J. Crawford, *The Creation of States in International Law* (2d ed.) at 430–432 (Oxford 2007).

24 Z. Elipeleg, *op. cit.*, at 3–22.

25 M. Tessler, *A History Of The Israeli-Palestinian Conflict* at 261 (Indiana University Press, 2009).

26 C. Sykes, *op. cit.*, at 333, 337–339; B. Morris, *The Birth of the Palestinian Refugee Problem, 1947–1949* at 29 (Cambridge University Press, 1987); E. Karsh, *Palestine Betrayed* at 100 *et seq.* (Yale University Press, 2010); M.J. Cohen (1982), *op. cit.* at 302–303; A. Radosh and R. Radosh, *op. cit.*, at 280; M. Maoz, *The UN Partition Resolution of 1947: Why Was It Not Implemented?*, Palestine-Israel Journal of Politics, Economics, and Culture, 9:4 at 18–19 (2002).

27 R. Yitzhak, *Transjordan's Occupation of Jerusalem in the 1948 War*, Israel Affairs 25:2 at 308–309 (2019).

28 J. Nevo, *op. cit.*, at 14–15 ("From his Cairo residence, the president of the AHC, al-Hajj Amin al-Husayni, promised a swift Arab offensive in order to make maximum military gains which would make the Arabs the leading power in the country to whom the British would delegate the reins of authority when they departed. Al-Hajj Amin also sought to secure his own position as the unchallenged leader of the Palestinian Arabs and to guarantee his nomination as the head of the Palestinian state, once military successes ensured its foundation"); M.N. Penkower (2019, Vol. II) *op. cit.*, at 521 (the Palestinian Arabs "launched a civil war" in response to the UN's offer of the two-state solution).

29 Central Intelligence Agency, CIA-RDP82-00457R000300140006-1, "Mufti's Declarations on Palestine Situation" (Secret) (27 January 1947) (reporting on meeting "last November" [1946] between the Mufti and Afif Tibi, the owner of the Lebanese newspaper *al-Yawm*).

30 KV2/2091, Report No. 82 (28 July 1947) (relaying information received from sources on 17 July 1947).

31 KV2/2091, *Extract from Account forwarded by S.I.S. re Palestine – Political. The Arab "National Conference" at Haifa* (29 July 1947).

32 "Zionists Ask U.N. to Pass New Plan; Arabs Inflamed," *New York Times*, 2 September 1947 at 1. Ghory further threatened that if the General Assembly were to accept the Special Committee's partition recommendation, "the Arabs will oppose it by every means at their disposal." *Id.*

33 KV2/2091, C.S. 808/2, Memorandum (Top Secret) from Officer Administering the Government of Palestine to Secretary of State for the Colonies (23 September 1947) enclosing 21 September 1947 Report (Top Secret) regarding unofficial meeting between Palestine Government police officials with Mufti in Cairo (9 October 1947).

34 J.G. Granados, *op. cit.*, at 249.

35 FRUS, 501.BB Palestine/10–1647, Letter from Emil Ghory, Arab Higher Committee, to United States Consul General, Jerusalem (3 October 1947).

36 G. Bilainkin, "The Man Who May Lead the Holy War," *Sunday Despatch* (12 October 1947).

37 "Jamal: We Must Foil Partition," *Palestine Post*, 27 October 1947 at 1.

38 KV2/2091, *Extract (Secret) from Report No. 95 re the Arabs and Palestine* (4 November 1947).

39 United Nations Archives, S-0472-0090-0018-00001, Letter from I. Nakhleh, Representative of the Arab Higher Committee, to Secretary General (6 February 1948).

40 *Id.* (Emphasis added).

41 W. Khalidi (1986), *op. cit.*, at 121, 123–124; *see also* D. Mandel, *op. cit.*, at 115.

42 H.V. Evatt, *op. cit.*, at 121.

43 *Id.* at 250.
44 FRUS, 867N.01/10–3047, Letter from King Abdul Aziz Ibn Saud to President Truman (26 October 1947).
45 "Arab Leaders Call Palestine Vote 'Invalid'; Delegates Reaffirm Challenge to U.N. Action," *New York Times*, 30 November 1947 at 54.
46 *Id.* at 270; J. Nevo, *The Arabs of Palestine 1947-48: Military and Political Activity*, Middle Eastern Studies 23:1 at 26–27 (1987) (the Arab Higher Committee declared Resolution 181 and the offer of a two-state solution "null and void" and opposed "any solution that indicated either Partition or Jewish sovereignty over any part of Palestine"); *cf.* FO 371/6836, H. Beeley Minute, 22 December 1947, *reprinted in* P. Toye and A. Seay, *op. cit.*, Vol. 2 (potential pan-Arab invasion of Palestine on behalf of the Palestinian Arabs "would amount to a direct and open defiance of the United Nations by a group of its members," exposing them to sanctions under Article 41 of the Charter).
47 FRUS, 867N.01/12–347: Telegram (Secret) from United States Ambassador, Egypt to Secretary of State (3 December 1947). By February 1948, some in the British Government had become enamored of the idea of Abdullah annexing the Arab-designated area of Palestine. One Foreign Office official minuted his desire that Abdullah might even seize a portion of the Negev to create a corridor linking Gaza to the West Bank, noting "[t]his would have immense strategic advantages for us, both in cutting the Jewish State, and therefore Communist influence, off from the Red Sea ..." FO 371/68368, B. Burrows Minute at para. (d), *reprinted in* P. Toye and A. Seay, *op. cit.*, Vol. 2 at 107.
48 FRUS, 501.BB Palestine/12–947, Telegram from Governor General Mohammad Ali Jinnah of Pakistan to President Truman (undated).
49 P. Mann, *op. cit.*, at 210.
50 United Nations, S/PV.222, Palestine Question/GA Resolution 181, "Future Government of Palestine" – Security Council meeting – Verbatim record (9 December 1947) (emphasis added).
51 *Id.*
52 *But see* United Nations, A/AC.21/13, United Nations Palestine Commission, Relations Between The United Nations Commission and the Security Council, Working Paper Prepared by the Secretariat (3 February 1948) ("The phrase 'being seized of the question' was interpreted by the President of the Security Council to mean that 'the matter remain on the agenda, available for discussion at the request of any member or members at any time'"). The Working Paper went on to note, however, that the Trieste precedent provided authority for the Security Council to exercise control of the Palestine situation: "In the case of the Free Territory of Trieste, which presents some similar aspects to the present case, the Security Council answered the question in the affirmative ... Under the Peace Treaty with Italy, various responsibilities were assigned to the Security Council with regard to the Free Territory of Trieste, and as a result, the Council of Foreign Ministers requested the Security Council to adopt the three instruments relating to the administration of the Free Territory and to accept the responsibilities devolving upon it under the same instruments. During the discussion in the Security Council, a legal objection was raised by the Australian representative whether the Security Council has the power to accept new responsibilities and further, whether it had the power to assume functions having no direct connection with the maintenance of international peace and security. At the 91st meeting of the Security Council, a statement of the Secretary-General was read regarding the legal issues raised by the representative of Australia. According to the statement, the words of Article 24 'primary responsibility for the maintenance of international peace and security' coupled with the phrase 'acts on their behalf' constitute a grant of power sufficiently wide to enable the Security Council to approve the documents in question and to assume responsibilities arising therefrom." The five-member Palestine Commission, chaired by Karel Lisicky of Czechoslovakia and also containing delegates from Bolivia, Denmark, Panama, and the Philippines, was formed to oversee the implementation of Resolu-

tion 181(II) during the transition period until the formal termination of the Mandate. The Working Paper noted the Commission reported directly to the Security Council. *Id.*, *see also* United Nations, A/AC.21/SR.1, Summary Record of the First Meeting of the Palestine Commission (9 January 1948). It is also important to note that the legal status of Jerusalem, while initially subject to the internationalization provisions of Resolution 181(II), underwent substantial change as a result of the 1948–1949 war and again after the 1967 war. The author will examine the legal status of Jerusalem in a future study.

53 United Nations Security Council, S/691 (5 March 1948).

54 *Id.* Interestingly, the State Department, as part of its effort during the first several weeks of 1948 to sabotage partition, apparently devised a convoluted plan to seek a Security Council Resolution that would have rejected the assumption of responsibility for implementing Resolution 181(II). The Security Council would then have been forced to hand the matter back to the General Assembly, "which would seek to work out a new Palestine solution." The State Department's own lawyer pushed back against this approach, noting it would be "legally incorrect and a distortion of the [United Nations] Charter." FRUS, N.A. 501.BB Palestine/3-548, Memorandum from Ernest A. Gross, Legal Adviser, U.S. Department of State, to Undersecretary of State Lovett, "Precise Position of United States on Security Council Powers with respect to Palestine."

55 N. Elaraby, *op. cit.*, at 107.

56 United Nations, A/AC.21/6, United Nations Palestine Commission, Communication from the Representative of the Arab Higher Committee for Palestine (19 January 1948); *see also* "Arabs Refuse to Cooperate," *The Times*, 20 January 1948 at 3; "Arabs Again Shun Any Partition Aid," *New York Times*, 20 January 1948 at 4. The Palestine Commission notified the Security Council, in its first monthly report to the Council, of the Arab Higher Committee's refusal to cooperate and its rejection of General Assembly Resolution 181(II). The Commission noted, "No further communication has been addressed to or received from the Arab Higher Committee by the Commission. The Commission will, at the appropriate time, set forth in a separate document its views with regard to the implementations of this refusal by the Arab Higher Committee." United Nations, A/AC.21/7, United Nations Palestine Commission, First Monthly Progress Report to the Security Council (29 January 1948).

57 J.G. Granados, *op. cit.*, at 271.

58 CAB 129/24/10, Palestine: Withdrawal of British Civil Administration, Memorandum (Secret) by the Secretary of State for the Colonies (4 February 1948).

59 A. Sela, *op. cit.* at 628. Plan *Dalet* lies beyond the scope of the present study. Suffice to say it has generated considerable controversy among scholars and polemicists alike for its role in alleged atrocities against Arab civilians in 1948 and for allegedly forcing Palestinian Arabs to flee the country in the midst of the Mufti-inspired civil war.

60 N. Magally, "The Position of the Arab Leadership vis-à-vis the Partition Plan: The Crime and its Punishment," in R. Gavison (ed.), *op. cit.*, at 38–39.

61 United Nations, S/775, Letter from Jamal Husseini, Arab Higher Committee, to Secretary-General regarding Questions Submitted by the Security Council (24 May 1948).

62 *Id.*

63 KV2/2091, Intelligence Repot No. 114 (Secret), *Palestine: The Mufti's Preparations for Guerilla War* (17 August 1948); *see also* KV2/2091, SIME/P.F. 1415/B.1, Despatch (Secret) to Director General, London, from E. Richardson, *Activities of the Mufti* (18 August 1948) (enclosing Report No. 2813, *Palestine: Political Activities of the Mufti*, 31 July 1948).

64 United Nations, A/C.1/SR.207, Continuation of the discussion on the Progress Report of the United Nations Mediator on Palestine (22 November 1948).

65 *See* KV2/2091, Intelligence Report (Secret) No. 111, *Palestine: Activities of the Mufti* (15 December 1947) (Mufti instigated a "whispering campaign through paid agents" against King Abdullah, portraying the King "as a monster waiting and planning to pounce on Palestine and occupy it when the British withdraw").

66 KV2/2091, Dispatch (Secret) SIME/P1415/Blb from S.I.M.E General Headquarters, Middle East Land Forces to Director General, London, *The Mufti* (14 August 1947). Jamal Husseini publicly denied the rumors that the Mufti intended to set up a Palestinian Arab government in exile. *Id*. By early September the Mufti himself had also indicated he had no intention of establishing a Palestinian Arab government in Egypt. KV2/2091, Intelligence Report No. 80, *Palestine. The Mufti and the Arab Resistance* at 1 (2 September 1947).

67 KV2/2091, *Extract from SIME Security Intelligence Survey* (7 November 1947).

68 FO 371/68376, Telegram (Secret) No. 688 from British Embassy, Beirut to Foreign Office (21 September 1948), *reprinted in* P. Toye and A. Seay, *Israel: Boundary Disputed with Arab Neighbours, 1946-1964,* Vol. 2 at 187–190 (Archive Editions 1995) (noting motivations for creating Palestinian Arab "government" included the desire to not only "safeguard the Arab juridical position, i.e. their claim to sovereignty over the whole of Palestine," but also identifying intra-Arab disputes between Abdullah and the Mufti, and Abdullah and the Arab League, as more important factors in the move to create a Palestinian Arab "government.").

69 KV2/2091, *Extract from M.I.6. report re Palestine – Arab Dissensions* (27 January 1948).

70 J. Nevo, *op. cit.*, at 28.

71 *Id.*; *see also* A. Shlaim, *The Rise and Fall of the All-Palestine Government in Gaza,* Journal of Palestine Studies 20:1 at 38 (1990).

72 FO 371/68368, K. Buss Minute (13 February 1948), *reprinted in* P. Toye and A. Seay, *op. cit.*, Vol. 2 at 104.

73 United Nations, A_C-1_SR-126, General Assembly, 1st Committee: 126th meeting held at Lake Success, New York at 93–97 (26 April 1948). Interestingly, British intelligence reported to the Colonial Office that same day (26 April 1948) that the Mufti had apparently decided "to accept annexation of Palestine to Transjordan and to acknowledge Abdullah as King during the latter's lifetime." KV2/2091, Despatch (Secret) No. 55 to Sir Marston Logan, Colonial Office (26 April 1948). The Mufti ended up ordering Abdullah's assassination three years later. British Intelligence learned of the Mufti's orders to assassinate King Abdullah as early as the fall of 1948 and continued receiving similar information thereafter. *See* KV2/2091, Intelligence Report No. 160, *Palestine: Terrorist Intentions by the Mufti, Directed Against King Abdullah* (4 November 1948); *see also* KV2/2091, Intelligence Report (Secret) No. 13 (11 April 1949) ("The Iraqi Legation in Cairo have informed the Egyptian Government of a plot by the Mufti to assassinate King Abdullah); *see also* KV2/2091, SIME/PF.1415/3/B.1., Despatch (Secret) from S.I.M.E. General Headquarters, Middle East Land Forces to London (2 May 1949) (enclosing Report (Secret) No. 1505, *Middle East, Political, The Ex-Mufti's Plot to Assassinate King Abdullah,* 7 April 1949); see also KV2/2091, Telegram No. 685 from British Embassy, Jerusalem to Foreign Office (24 September 1949) ("Two separate sources informed Arab Legion yesterday that two Mufti agents … were planning to assassinate King Abdullah on arrival in Beirut today"). The New York Times published the written text of Husseini's statement the following day. "Text of Arab Statement on Palestine", *New York Times*, 27 April 1948 at 3 ("The British Government is morally and legally bound to hand over the administration of Palestine only to one Palestinian Government representing the lawful citizens of Palestine. This handing over must comprise the whole of Palestine in one unit … The Arabs of Palestine are determined to proceed on the following lines, at the termination of the Mandate. Article 22 of the Covenant of the League of Nations and Article 28 of the Palestine mandate explicitly and implicitly impose that there should emerge, at that date, an independent Palestinian Government. This duty, under the Covenant of the League of Nations, was the responsibility of the mandatory. Now that the mandatory has failed to fulfill this duty, the overwhelming majority of the people of the country have decided to carry it our themselves, in expression of their inalienable right to self-determination. This action on their part is in complete

harmony with the United Nations Charter and is a principal requirement of the Covenant of the League of Nations under which the mandate was given").

74 Central Intelligence Agency, RDP83-00415R001300100016-8, A. Kader al Mazny, editorial in *Al Assas* (22 August 1948) (U.S. Embassy translation, Cairo) (emphasis added); *see also* R. Khalidi, "The Palestinians and 1948: The Underlying Causes of Failure," in E. Rogan and A. Shlaim, *The War for Palestine: Rewriting the History of 1948* at 12-36 (Cambridge Univ. Press, 2001) (noting the Palestinian Arabs were plagued by "poor political calculations … disorganization, confusion and leaderless chaos").

75 A. Sela, *op. cit.*, at 668; A. Shlaim, *op. cit.*, at 39.

76 A. Shlaim, *op. cit.*, at 29–30.

77 *Id.* at 40.

78 *Id.* at 30; *see also* A. Shlaim (1990), *op. cit.*, at 42–43 (1990).

79 FRUS, Telegram from U.S. Embassy, Cairo to Acting Secretary of State (2 October 1948) (emphasis added).

80 FRUS, 867N.01/9–2648, Telegram No. 65 from Amman (26 September 1948).

81 A. Shlaim, *op. cit.*, at 40; for a different perspective, *see* W. Salem, *Legitimization or Implementation: On the UN Partition Plan*, Palestine-Israel Journal of Politics, Economics and Culture, 9:4 at 10 (2002) (arguing the formation of the All-Palestine Government is evidence of the Palestinian Arab willingness to "deal pragmatically with the results of partition").

82 FRUS, 867N.01/10–148, Telegram No. 498 (1 October 1948).

83 FRUS, 501.BB Palestine/10–248: Circular telegram (Secret) from the Acting Secretary of State to Certain Diplomatic Offices (2 October 1948).

84 KV2/2091, Telegram No. 1405 (Secret) from British Embassy, Cairo to Foreign Office (8 October 1945).

85 A. Shlaim, *op. cit.*, at 43.

86 FO 371/68643, Telegram No. 578 (Secret) from Acting British Consul General, Jerusalem to Foreign Office (29 October 1948), *reprinted in* P. Toye and A. Seay, *op. cit.*, Vol. 2 at 203–205.

87 A. Shlaim, *op. cit.*, at 50; Z. Elipeleg, *op. cit.*

88 KV2/2091, SIME/SF.2119/B.1 (Secret) (29 March 1949) (enclosing CX Report No. 1399, Palestine, Political, *The Present Position of the Gaza Government*, 5 March 1949). The report attached copies of "passports" issued by the "All Palestine Government."

89 *Id.*

90 A. Shlaim, *op. cit.*, at 44; Z. Elipeleg, *op. cit.*

91 Z. Elipeleg, *op. cit.*

92 A. Sela, *op. cit.*, at 672; see also FO 371/68644, Letter from Mohamed Ali al Ja'bari, President of the Second Arab Palestinian Conference to British Ambassador Sir A. Kirkbride, British Embassy, Amman (4 December 1948), *reprinted in* P. Toye and A. Seay, *op. cit.*, Vol. 2 at 208-09 (enclosing document entitled "Decisions Taken by 2d Arab Palestinian Conference held at Jericho on the 1st of December, 1948," including "the Conference decides that Palestine and the Hashemite Kingdom of Transjordan should be incorporated into one Kingdom and acknowledges his Majesty King Abdulla ibn Hussein as the Constitutional King of Palestine"). This gave Abdullah the political cover he needed to move ahead with attempting to annex the West Bank, as it had been the view previously that so long as Abdullah was aiming at fighting the Jews he could count on "a large measure of support in the Arab world," but if his true aim were to take control of the Arab-designated portions of Palestine, then "his action will be interpreted as personal aggrandizement and will isolate him from his neighbours and from Arab opinion generally." FO 371/68364, H. Beeley Minute, para. 4 (6 January 1948), *reprinted in* P. Toye and A Seay, *op. cit.*, Vol. 2 at 100–101; *see also* A. Plascov, *The Palestinian Refugees in Jordan, 1948-1957* at 11-13 (Frank Cass, 1981) (noting the resolutions adopted at the December 1948 conference provided the "juridical basis" for the union of Arab Palestine with Transjordan).

93 A. Shlaim, *op. cit.,* at 31; *see also* W. Salem, *op. cit.*, at 10 (2002) (describing Palestinian Arab efforts to establish a civil authority and/or government for all of Palestine during 1947–1948 and how the Arab League and Transjordan thwarted those efforts); Central Intelligence Agency, 51966ec8993294098d50a4bf, "Haj Amin al-Husseini, Mufti of Jerusalem, Biographic Sketch No. 60" (Confidential, prepared by Department of State) at 5 (10 April 1951) ("A so-called Palestine Arab Government was set up in Gaza in September 1948 … The Gaza Arab Government existed for a time, on paper only, and then folded its tents"); M. Shemesh, *The Palestinian National Revival: In the Shadow of the Leadership Crisis, 1937–1967*, at 56 (Indiana University Press, 2018). The British Government reacted to the formation of the supposed Palestinian Government by flatly refusing to recognize "this so-called government." FRUS 867N.01/10-748, Telegram No. 4423 (7 October 1948). A British official reported during a formal visit to Gaza in June 1949 that he "heard no mention of the 'Gaza Government' which had a fleeting existence toward the end of last year." FO 371/75342, Letter (Confidential) from E. Troutbeck, British Middle East Office, Cairo, to Bevin (16 June 1949), *reprinted in* P. Toye and A. Seay, *op. cit.*, Vol. 2 at 601.

94 FO 371/68644, Telegram (Confidential) No. 5566 from British Embassy, Washington to Foreign Office (7 December 1948), *reprinted in* P. Toye and A. Seay, *op. cit.*, Vol. 2 at 210.

95 A. Gerson (1973), *op. cit.*, at 37–38.

96 Central Intelligence Agency, RDP82-00457R002100850002-7 (Secret), "Contact Between the Grand Mufti and the Soviets" at para. 1 (23 December 1948).

97 United Nations, A/AC.25/Org/20, Memorandum from Arab Higher Committee to United Nations Conciliation Commission for Palestine (UNCCP) (17 June 1949). Interestingly, one modern Palestinian Arab commentator has written that "in light of the international events that preceded the partition resolution, Arab rejection of the partition plan seemed unreasonable." R. Nasrallah, *The Road to Partition*, Palestine-Israel Journal of Politics, Economics and Culture, 9:4 at 64 (2002). In fact, the Mufti himself may have had second thoughts about partition, as he reportedly planned in late 1949 to set up yet another Palestine "government" in Gaza, but this time with the intent to "claim authority over Arab Palestine only as opposed to the earlier Gaza government which claimed authority over the whole of Palestine." FO 371/75333, Telegram No. 500 (Confidential) from British Embassy, Amman to Foreign Office (4 October 1949), *reprinted in* P. Toye and A. Seay, *op. cit.*, Vol. 2 at 472. That same day the British Ambassador in Amman, Sir Alec Kirkbride, wrote separately to Bevin reporting that Syria and Lebanon had conferred with Transjordan and all agreed that "any attempt to set up an independent Arab Palestine state at the present moment would be folly …" *Id.* at 473.

98 A. Radosh and R. Radosh, *op. cit.*, at 277.

99 Truman was well aware the State Department was actively working to undermine his Palestine policy. In his memoirs, Truman expressed frustration about this, in words presaging former President Donald Trump's more contemporary (and unproven) accusations of a "deep state" actively opposed to his policies: "The difficulty with many career officials in the government is that they regard themselves as the men who really make policy and run the government. They look upon the elected officials as just temporary occupants. Every President in our history has been faced with this problem: how to prevent career men from circumventing presidential policy. Too often career men seek to impose their own views instead of carrying out the established policy of the Administration." H.S. Truman *op. cit.*, at 165.

100 FRUS, N.A. PPs/19, Lot 64, D563, Memorandum (Secret) by Policy Planning Staff, US Department of State, "To Assess and Appraise the Position of the U.S. with respect to Palestine, Taking into Consideration the Security Interests of the U.S. in the Mediterranean and Near East Areas, and in the Light of the Recommendation of the General Assembly of the United Nations Regarding the Partition of Palestine" at paras. 27, 31 (19 January 1948), *reprinted in* M.J. Cohen, *The Rise of Israel: The American Trusteeship Proposal 1948* at 12–22 (Garland 1987). Interestingly, the Memorandum also

recommended against referring the matter to the International Court of Justice, as "the fundamental issue, i.e., whether the two communities will cooperate to make the partition plan effective, is not a proper question for the Court." *Id.* at para. 33. The following week, however, Dean Rusk, the future Secretary of State and then a high-ranking official in the Department, criticized the Policy Planning Staff's memorandum, asking "What events have occurred which create a 'new situation' with respect to the action taken by the General Assembly on Palestine? Were not the considerations discussed in the attached paper known at the time of the decision to support the plan of the UNSCOP majority? At what point or points can it be reasonably concluded that the situation in Palestine will render impossible the implementation of the General Assembly resolution?" FRUS, 867N.01/2–648, Memorandum (Top Secret) by Dean Rusk to the Under Secretary of State (26 January 1948). Within days both George Kennan and Loy Henderson responded in writing with their own criticisms of Rusk's analysis. Henderson's memorandum borrowed heavily from Kennan's, suggesting a coordinated effort by the two officials to undermine the President's prior decision to support partition. *See* FRUS, PPS Files, Lot 64 D 563, Memorandum (Top Secret) by the Director of the Policy Planning Staff to the Under Secretary of State (29 January 1948); FRUS, 867N.01/2–648, Memorandum (Top Secret) by the Director of the Office of Near Eastern and African Affairs to the Director of the Office of United Nations Affairs (6 February 1948).

101 "Samuel Kopper, FRAMCO Aide, Dies," *New York Times*, 5 June 1957 at 35.

102 FRUS, 501.BB Palestine/1–2748, Memorandum (Top Secret) by Mr. Samuel K. C. Kopper of the Office of Near Eastern and African Affairs, "The Partition of Palestine and United States Security" at 31 (27 January 1948).

103 H.S. Truman, *Memoirs, op. cit.*, at 160–161; Telegrams from Edward Jacobson to Matt Connelly (Secretary to the President) (21 February 1948 and 15 March 1948), *reprinted in* M.J. Cohen, *op. cit.*, at 89, 91; *see also* A. Radosh and R. Radosh, *op. cit.*, at 299–301 (describing Jacobson's Oval Office plea to Truman, 12 March 1945); M.N. Penkower (2019, Vol. II), *op. cit.*, at 606–607 (same); M.J. Cohen (1990), *op. cit.*, at 185–187 (Jacobson's extraordinary effort to use his friendship with Truman on behalf of Weizmann secured Jacobson's place in "Zionist mythology").

104 C. Sykes, *op. cit.*, at 347.

105 FRUS, 501.BB Palestine/3–1648, Telegram (Top Secret) from Secretary of State Marshall to U.S. Ambassador Austin (16 March 1948). Truman expressed anger to Secretary of State Marshall for the lack of any prior warning to him that Austin "was going to make his statement at that particular time." FRUS, N.A. 501BB Palestine/3-2248 (22 March 1948). Truman's aide Clark Clifford told the State Department the President "had never approved" Austin's announcement of US support for trusteeship instead of partition. FRUS, 501.BB Palestine/3–2248, Memorandum by the Director of the Executive Secretariat to the Secretary of State (22 March 1948) (reporting conversation between Clifford and Undersecretary of State Lovett on 22 March 1948).

106 United Nations Security Council, S/PV.271, *Security Council Official Records, 3rd year*, 271st meeting, Lake Success, New York at 167 (19 March 1948).

107 Charles Ross (Truman aide) diary at 3 (29 March 1948), *reprinted in* M.J. Cohen, *op. cit.*, at 193. Ross reported a furious President Truman complained the State Department "have made me out a liar and a double-crosser." Clark Clifford, the President's Special Counsel, attributed the disconnect between the White House and the State Department to confusion over whether Truman had actually approved the trusteeship proposal as a *change* in US policy, rather than as a contingency plan in the event partition were to fail. A. Radosh and S. Radosh, *op. cit.*, at 304, 310. Michael Ottolenghi takes a different view, dismissing historical concern over the apparent disconnect or dispute between the Truman White House and the State Department regarding the trusteeship proposal as "completely missing the point." According to Ottolenghi, "Truman did not consider trusteeship to be a repudiation of partition; he would have accepted a trusteeship only

if partition was found to be unworkable by the UN, against the advice of Clifford. This position was not a repudiation of US objectives in Palestine, but rather an acceptance of the State Department's tactics on how best to achieve these objectives." M. Ottolenghi, *op. cit.*, at 980.

108 FRUS, U.S. Department of State, L Files, Memorandum by the Legal Adviser to the Director of the Office of United Nations Affairs (19 March 1948).

109 Truman Library, Presidential Statement (25 March 1948), https://www.trumanlibrary.gov/library/public-papers/55/presidents-news-conference (last accessed 18 December 2020).

110 Weizmann Archives, 25-2823, Letter from Weizmann to President Truman (9 April 1948). Weizmann's 18 March 1948 meeting with Truman and his 9 April 1948 letter to the President stand alongside his secret testimony before the Peel Commission in 1937 (during which Weizmann left the door open to the two-state solution) as among the most important episodes in the history of Zionism. S. Zipperstein, *op. cit.*, at 309. If not for Weizmann, the State of Israel would never have been created.

111 Truman Library, Oscar R. Ewing Oral History Interview, transcript at 277–278 (2 May 1969).

112 FRUS, Clifford Papers, Memorandum by the President's Special Counsel (6 March 1948).

113 FRUS, Clifford Papers, Memorandum by the President's Special Counsel to President Truman (8 March 1948).

114 *Id.*

115 C. Sykes, *op. cit.*, at 360; M.J. Cohen (1982), *op. cit.*, at 379–380.

116 *Palestine: Termination of the Mandate, Statement Prepared for Public Information by the Colonial Office and the Foreign Office* at 2 (15 May 1948). Watson (2000) notes the Mandate ceased to exist as a matter of law once the British withdrew from Palestine on 14 May 1948. Watson, *op. cit.*, at 25.

117 Crawford argues the legal basis for Israel's statehood was not Resolution 181(II), but secession: "It must be concluded that Israel was effectively and lawfully established as a State by secession from Palestine in the period 1948 to 1949. Its original territory was its armistice territory, not the partition territory." J. Crawford, *op. cit.*, at 434. Yuval Shany disagrees with Crawford, noting "[t]he establishment of Israel in 1948 probably did not constitute an act of secession from Mandatory Palestine, as suggested by Crawford, but rather an implementation of the right to self-determination of the Jewish people in parts of Mandatory Palestine pursuant to the 1922 Palestine Mandate." Y. Shany, *Legal Entitlements, Changing Circumstances and Intertemporality: A Comment on the Creation of Israel and the Status of Palestine*, Isr. L. Rev. 49:3, at 391, 408 (2016). The international legal scholar Julius Stone agrees with Crawford, but for a different reason. Stone argues the Palestinian Arab rejection of Resolution 181(II) rendered the partition resolution legally null and void. Israel's statehood derived, therefore, not from the partition resolution but instead from the "assertion of independence by its people and government, on the vindication of that independence by arms against assault by other states, and on the establishment of orderly government within territory under its stable control." J. Stone, *Israel and Palestine: Assault on the Law of Nations* at 61 (John Hopkins University Press, 1981). Stone further claims that if the Palestinian Arabs had accepted Resolution 181, then both the Jews and Palestinian Arabs would have obtained sovereignty in the areas allocated to them. However, Stone argues, when the opposite occurred (Arab rejection of the partition resolution and Arab warfare against Israel), "[t]here was in fact no such agreement, no such effect in vesting and delimiting titles, and no such entities as the proposed Arab state and *corpus separatum* [internationalized Jerusalem] came into being in fact or in law." *Id.* at 62–63; *see also* Y. Shany, *op. cit.*, at 403 (Resolution 181(II) lapsed and fell into "desuetude"); *but see* A. Gerson (1973), *op. cit.*, at 35–36, arguing the Palestinian Arabs received sovereignty over the areas the UN had allocated to them by operation of law immediately upon the adoption of Resolution 181(II).

118 Y.Z. Blum, *The Missing Reversioner: Reflections on the Status of Judea and Samaria*, 3 Isr. L. Rev. 279, 287 (1968).

# 15

# ASSESSMENT

The UNSCOP and Ad Hoc Committee trials brought to a close the nearly three-decade long history of judicial and quasi-judicial investigations and inquiries during the British Mandate for Palestine.

However, unlike all the previous trials, this time the Jews emerged at least partly victorious. The international community rendered an unambiguous, resounding verdict in favour of the two-state solution, endorsing the Zionist goal of statehood in at least a portion of Palestine. The United Nations had come full circle, ending up where the Palestine Royal Commission started ten years earlier and endorsing partition. In so doing, the United Nations rejected various alternative proposals that had been advanced in the span of the previous decade, including the White Paper's one-state solution, the Anglo-American Committee's no-state solution, and the Morrison-Grady provincial autonomy plan.

Palestinian Arab nationalism, on the other hand, suffered a devastating blow. The UN General Assembly, acting as the lawful successor to the League of Nations, rejected the Palestinian arguments regarding Articles 20 and 22 of the League Covenant and dismissed Palestinian claims of sovereignty over the entirety of Palestine. Both the UNSCOP and Ad Hoc Committee majorities likewise rejected every other argument the Palestinians had been advancing since the early 1920s against Zionism.

How had Palestinian fortunes declined so rapidly since the British offer of the one-state solution only eight years earlier? The answer, contrary to the modern-day Palestinian "injustice" narrative, has nothing to do with the alleged western post-Holocaust desire to recompense the Jewish people at the expense of the Palestinian Arabs. The Anglo-American Committee proceedings and verdict in 1946 stand as compelling evidence against any claim that the Holocaust somehow proved a boon to Zionism. The Committee, although sympathetic to

DOI: 10.4324/9781003225263-20

allowing more Jewish immigration to Palestine, rejected the Zionist wartime Biltmore resolutions and Jewish statehood in Palestine, recommending instead the continuation of the Mandate and/or a successor Trusteeship. Nor is there any evidence that the eventual Soviet support for partition resulted from any post-Holocaust sympathy in the Kremlin.

The answer lies instead with the Palestinians themselves, and their failed leadership. The Mufti's rejection of the White Paper's one-state solution in May 1939 astonished and exasperated even the most pro-Arab officials in the British Government. The Mufti's wartime alliance with Hitler did not help the Palestinian cause either. And the Arab Higher Committee made an unforgivable error by following the Mufti's orders, albeit under penalty of death, to boycott UNSCOP. In so doing, the Palestinians lost a crucial opportunity to make their case before the first international tribunal to adjudicate the Arab-Jewish conflict since the 1930 Lofgren Commission regarding the rights and claims of the parties to the Wailing Wall.

Although the Palestinian Arabs ended up reversing course and participating before the Ad Hoc Committee (Jamal Husseini testified three times), by then their long-standing invocation of transformational legal framing and narrative had worn thin and stalled completely during the immediately preceding UNSCOP hearings. Transformational legal framing, at least for purposes of defeating the two-state solution, had failed to achieve the Mufti's objectives.

Viewed through the prism of the modern-day conflict, the Palestinian Arabs should have embraced the two-state solution in November 1947. But the Mufti had no intention of doing so. He had already rejected the one-state solution the British Government had offered less than a decade earlier in the May 1939 White Paper because it did not provide for an immediate halt to Jewish immigration. The Mufti's position in November 1947 remained the same as his position in May 1939 – nothing less than full and immediate Arab sovereignty over *all* of Palestine and an immediate halt to Jewish immigration would satisfy his demands. It was, therefore, not surprising that the Palestinian Arabs rejected the United Nations' two-state solution in November 1947.

If the worst Palestinian Arab mistake of the last century was their decision to reject the British offer of the one-state solution in May 1939, their second-worst mistake was to renounce the United Nations' offer of the two-state solution in November 1947 and chose decades of war and terrorism instead. Those two decisions, far more than anything else, are the root causes of Palestinian statelessness today.

*****

The United Nations' November 1947 decision to offer the two-state solution to the Jews and Arabs of Palestine represented, for the first time since the League of Nations approved the Palestine Mandate in 1922, an expression of the international community's judgement regarding the most fair and "just" outcome for two peoples claiming rights to the same land. Resolution 181(II) stood as the super-majority verdict of the international community following the final two "trials of Palestine."

The Palestinian Arab leadership could have accepted the verdict of the world community and set about the task of preparing for statehood in a portion of Palestine, to be ready for self-governance once the British departed. But the Palestinian Arabs took *no* steps in that direction, choosing instead to renounce the General Assembly's partition plan and defy the will of the United Nations for decades following 29 November 1947.

The Palestinian Arabs did not simply reject the partition plan; they launched all-out warfare against it, resulting in tens of thousands killed and wounded. Hundreds of thousands more fled, including not only Palestinian Arabs but also nearly one million Jewish citizens forced to leave the Arab countries where they had resided for centuries. The reverberations of the human tragedy wrought by the Mufti's rejection of the two-state solution continue to the present day.

However, in one of the supreme ironies of human history, the Palestinian Arab leadership today insist on receiving the *same* thing they rejected in late 1947 – statehood in a portion of Mandate-era Palestine. Equally ironic is how the Palestinian Arabs, who lost legal momentum during 1947, have successfully reprised transformational legal framing during the more recent decades of the conflict, winning a series of victories at the International Court of Justice and the International Criminal Court, among other international legal and judicial fora.

We, therefore, turn now to the final portion of this study, examining the legal implications of the Palestinian Arab refusal to accept the two-state solution in November 1947. Did the Palestinian Arabs *waive* sovereignty over the Arab portions of Palestine? Are they *estopped* from changing their minds and attempting to reclaim sovereignty today? Or did the portion of Palestine allocated to the Arabs somehow mature into "statehood" sometime between 1949 and the present day? If so, *precisely when and how did the Palestinian Arabs achieve statehood in the West Bank and Gaza Strip?*

The final chapter of this study, therefore, analyses both the legal consequences of the Palestinian Arab renunciation of statehood when the United Nations offered it in 1947 and the Palestinian revival of transformational legal framing for the last several decades in an effort to gain the very statehood they previously rejected.

# PART V

# Legal consequences

# 16

# LEGAL IMPLICATIONS OF THE PALESTINIAN ARAB REJECTION OF THE UNITED NATIONS 1947 OFFER OF STATEHOOD

## Historical background

### *The Mandate system*

The League of Nations officially approved the Mandate for Palestine in July 1922. Turkey formally renounced its claims to Palestine when it ratified the Treaty of Lausanne in August 1923, paving the way for the Mandate to take effect in September 1923.

The League of Nations appointed Britain as Mandatory, but sovereignty did not pass to Britain. Sovereignty instead remained in abeyance or suspension, pending the future termination of the Mandate.[1] The Mandate established as a matter of international law the legal and political status of the Jewish people and the Palestinian Jews, but *not* the Palestinian Arabs.[2] However, the Mandate made no provision for Palestine's future sovereignty.

The post-World War I Mandate system represented a new creation of international law. The League of Nations rejected the acquisition of sovereignty through conquest. More advanced nations would serve as "mandatories" over the former Ottoman and German territories conquered during the war, including Palestine, providing tutelage until such time as those territories could inherit sovereignty and stand on their own as independent nations.

Article 22 of the Covenant of the League of Nations codified the Mandate system:

> To those colonies and territories which as a consequence of the late war have ceased to be under the sovereignty of the States which formerly governed them and which are inhabited by peoples not yet able to stand by themselves under the strenuous conditions of the modern world, there should be applied the principle that the well-being and development of

DOI: 10.4324/9781003225263-22

> such peoples form a sacred trust of civilisation and that securities for the performance of this trust should be embodied in this Covenant. The best method of giving practical effect to this principle is that the tutelage of such peoples should be entrusted to advanced nations who by reason of their resources, their experience or their geographical position can best undertake this responsibility, and who are willing to accept it, and that this tutelage should be exercised by them as Mandatories on behalf of the League.[3]

Within a short time the Council of the League of Nations had authorised the appointment of mandatories for Syria, Lebanon, Iraq, Palestine, and various other places scattered around the world. The new system eventually gave rise to questions about the status of sovereignty over the Mandated territories, especially Palestine.

## *Sovereignty in Abeyance*

Most commentators agree that sovereignty over Palestine was suspended or held in abeyance during the entire period of the Mandate. The early commentator Wright (1923), for example, addressed the issue of sovereignty over League of Nations Mandated areas. Wright noted that Article 22 of the League Covenant did not confer sovereignty to anyone over the Mandated areas:

> It is not certain that complete sovereignty rests anywhere. Although abhorrent to absolutist political theorists and to modern international law, unquestionable instances have existed which can only be described as divided or suspended sovereignty, though it is also true that they have usually proved temporary or transitional … if the makers of the Treaty of Versailles, in drafting Article XXII of the League of Nations Covenant, and if the Principal Allied and Associated Powers in assigning the ceded territory as mandates under the terms of that article expressed or implied no intention of giving sovereignty to any one, none was legally given.[4]

Therefore, Wright argued, under international law sovereignty over the Mandated areas resided in no particular nation, but instead should be viewed as *suspended*, pending the final disposition of the Mandated areas:

> It would seem that in law the mandated territories are not under the sovereignty of the mandatory … Thus the League, as the embodiment of civilization, has an equal claim with the mandatory to be considered the trustee. If we appeal to the Roman law of *mandatum*, it is clear that the *mandatarius* has no title in the property but is merely an agent … In practice also the mandatory's powers fall short of sovereignty, as is indicated by the insistence of the council, on recommendation of the Permanent Mandates Commission, that the inhabitants of mandated territories are not nationals of the mandatory,

> that mandatories must preserve fiscal autonomy in the mandated area and utilize all revenues for the benefit of the mandate, and that the administration of mandates may not be transferred by the assigned mandatory ... If a mandated territory is not under the sovereignty of the mandatory, the mandated community or the League, what is its status? One writer thinks it "highly probable that from the viewpoint of international law ... the Allied Powers, by creating the mandatory system, have placed the sovereignty of all mandated areas in suspense during the operation of the respective mandates."[5]

Nearly 30 years later, Judge McNair sounded a similar theme in his Separate Opinion in the International Court of Justice (ICJ) *Advisory Opinion on the International Status of South West Africa*:

> Upon sovereignty a very few words will suffice. The Mandates System ... is a new institution – a new relationship between a territory and its inhabitants on the one hand and the government which represents them internationally on the other – a new species of international government, which does not fit into the old conception of sovereignty and which is alien to it. The doctrine of sovereignty has no application to this new System. Sovereignty over a Mandated Territory is in abeyance; if and when the inhabitants of the territory obtain recognition as an independent State, as has already happened in the case of some Mandates, sovereignty will revive and vest in the new State.[6]

## *Termination of the Palestine Mandate*

The League of Nations met for the last time on 18 April 1946 to dissolve itself in favour of the newly created United Nations.[7] The League adopted a Resolution, supported by Great Britain among others, noting the declared intention of the Mandatory Powers to continue administering their existing mandates "until other arrangements have been agreed upon between the United Nations and the respective Mandatory Powers."[8] The Mandate for Palestine continued in full force and effect pursuant to Article 80 of the UN Charter.[9]

Thus, when Britain referred the Palestine matter to the United Nations in early 1947, the League of Nations Mandate was still in effect, and Palestine remained legally under British Mandatory control. Britain asked the United Nations to make recommendations for Palestine's future, but said it would not enforce any such recommendations against the will of either the Palestinian Jewish or Arab communities.

The United Nations, in Resolution 181(II), recommended the Mandate for Palestine be terminated no later than 1 August 1948. The British Government subsequently announced it would accelerate the timing to 15 May 1948.[10] The original plan envisioned the transfer of administrative control over Palestine to a newly appointed United Nations "Palestine Commission."[11] But the Mufti-inspired civil war rendered conditions on the ground impossible for the Palestine Commission to carry out its mission. The Palestine Commission thus was unable to assume any governmental functions from the departing British.[12]

The Mandate ceased to exist as a matter of law when Britain departed Palestine on 14 May 1948. Sovereignty continued in abeyance for the next several hours, until the Jews declared their independence "in Palestine," based on the legal authority of Resolution 181(II), but without specifying precise boundaries. The ambiguity in the Israeli declaration maintained the same "in Palestine" formulation as the Balfour Declaration and the Preamble to the Mandate, both of which spoke of establishing/reconstituting the Jewish National Home "*in Palestine*."

By importing the ambiguous "in Palestine" language into the Israeli Declaration of Independence, the drafters left open the possibility they were creating the new Jewish State solely in the specific *portion* of Palestine the United Nations had allocated for that purpose. However, the ambiguity also left open the possibility that Israel could claim sovereignty over some or all of the *remaining* portion of Palestine, where the Arabs had been offered but rejected statehood, thereby leaving a vacuum to be filled.

In any event, the armies of five Arab nations invaded the nascent State of Israel hours after it had proclaimed its independence. By the time the fighting mostly ended and the Israel-Jordan armistice agreement was signed at Rhodes on 3 April 1949, Israel had expanded its territory into a small portion of the areas allocated for the Palestinian State. Jordan occupied and purported to annex the remainder of the Arab-designated territory, comprising the area commonly referred to as the West Bank. Jordan also laid claim to East Jerusalem and the Holy Sites.

But King Abdullah's purported annexation of the West Bank likewise failed to gain sovereignty for Jordan over Arab Palestine. As Blum (1968) noted:

> [T]he Kingdom of Jordan never acquired the status of a legitimate sovereign over Judea and Samaria and enjoyed at the most the rights of a belligerent occupant there … It would seem to follow that, in a case like the present where the ousted State never was the legitimate sovereign, those rules of belligerent occupation directed to safeguarding that sovereign's reversionary rights have no application.[13]

Accordingly, only two countries – Britain and Pakistan – formally recognised Jordanian sovereignty over the West Bank between April 1949 and June 1967, when Israel replaced Jordan as the occupying power in the West Bank and East Jerusalem.

Therefore, as of the end of the 1948–1949 Arab-Israeli War, one portion of Mandate Palestine had become the sovereign, lawful territory of the new State of Israel. Sovereignty over the remaining, Arab-designated portion of Palestine remained in abeyance and has continued in abeyance ever since.[14]

As the International Law Quarterly noted in an unsigned April 1948 article, one month prior to the termination of the Mandate:

> With the League of Nations dissolved, and the United Nations not its successor in law, with the Permanent Mandates Commission dissolved and the Trusteeship Council not its successor in law, lawyers have ample opportunity to indulge in the pastime of "hunting the sovereignty" from the treble aspect of where it is now, where it will be during the transitional period (i.e., following May 15, when Great Britain relinquishes the mandate) and where it will be ultimately. The question is further complicated by the fact that alongside the mandatory Power, the mandate contemplated the existence of the "Administration of Palestine." The two were in fact mainly indistinguishable but in law were divergent, the Administration of Palestine being of course the embryonic government which would take over control on the relinquishment of the mandate by the mandatory Power ... But no country with traditions of government such as ours can fail to have regard to the legal details of such a transfer of authority as the termination of the Palestine mandate involves. It was in reply to questions touching on the legal considerations outlined above ... that the Attorney-General made the position of H.M. Government clear. There was no general rule of international law, he suggested, to prevent termination of the mandate by the United Kingdom, and insofar as on a narrower view the original mandate might be regarded as a kind of contractual undertaking, the impossibility of performing the object of that undertaking, as originally contemplated, frustrated the agreement (*ad impossibilia nemo tenetur*).[15]

When the Mandate ended on 14 May 1948, the post-World War I international control of Palestine through the League of Nations and later the United Nations also ended, thereby depriving the United Nations of legal authority thereafter to reallocate or determine sovereignty over *any* portion of post-Mandate Palestine. Therefore, subsequent United Nations actions and resolutions granting "observer status" to "Palestine," and according "Palestine" the status of a "state" for purposes of participating in various United Nations agencies and committees do not satisfy international legal requirements for conferring Palestinian Arab statehood and sovereignty over the West Bank.

## Legal ramifications of the Palestinian rejection of Resolution 181(II)

The Palestinian Arab decision to renounce the 29 November 1947 offer of statehood from the United Nations undoubtedly carried legal consequences for Palestinian nationalism. Few, if any, scholars, however, have focused on the significance of *that* day for purposes of determining Palestine's eligibility under international law to claim statehood *today*.

The Arab rejection of the United Nations 29 November 1947 offer of statehood raises two important legal questions that, until now, have received scant attention: first, what was the legal effect of the Arab rejection of the United Nations November 1947 offer of statehood? Second, if the Palestinians *waived* their right to statehood when the UN offered it to them in 1947, did they nonetheless *obtain* statehood at a later date, and if so, when?

## *Renunciation, waiver, and estoppel*

The Palestinian Arabs did not just reject the United Nations 29 November 1947 offer of statehood; they deliberately and expressly *renounced* the UN's offer. The Palestinian Arabs punctuated their renunciation by launching a violent and bloody war against the two-state solution. And the Palestinian Arabs *continued* renouncing the two-state solution for nearly 50 years after rejecting the UN's 29 November 1947 offer.

As a matter of international law, therefore, a strong argument can be made that the Palestinian Arab renunciation of Resolution 181(II) triggered the legal consequence of *waiving* sovereignty and statehood in the West Bank and Gaza Strip as of 29 November 1947. The Palestinian Arabs reiterated and reaffirmed that waiver for decades after 1947, including in the original Palestine National Charter, otherwise known as the Palestine Liberation Organization (PLO) Charter of 1964. Arguably, therefore, the Palestinian *waiver* had the legal effect of *estopping* the Palestinian Arabs from changing their minds and claiming statehood after more than a half century of renunciation.

The Palestinian Arabs, who so vociferously and violently rejected Resolution 181(II) from November 1947 until they recognised Israel's right to exist in the 1993 Oslo Accords, therefore lack the *legal right* to claim statehood today.[16]

This argument, of course, does not preclude a *political* settlement of the conflict under which the Palestinians could receive statehood in the West Bank and Gaza Strip. But it *does* preclude the Palestinians from *legal entitlement* to statehood.

Under international law, "[t]itle to territory – or a claim to it – may be abandoned. The consequence of abandonment is that the territory either becomes *res nullius* or falls under another state's sovereignty."[17] The related concept of "renunciation" in international law refers to the "unequivocal" or "deliberate" abandonment of rights.[18] The Palestinian Arab rejection of the 1947 United Nations offer of statehood clearly constituted a deliberate and unequivocal renunciation of Palestinian sovereignty over the Arab-designated portions of Palestine.

The Permanent Court of Arbitration discussed the meaning of estoppel in international law in a recent dispute between the United Kingdom and Mauritius:

> Estoppel is a general principle of law that serves to ensure, in the words of Lord McNair, "that international jurisprudence has a place for some recognition of the principle that a State cannot blow hot and cold – *allegans contraria non audiendus est*." The principle stems from the general requirement

> that States act in their mutual relations in good faith and is designed to protect the legitimate expectations of a State that acts in reliance upon the representations of another. The principle as it exists in international law was well summarized by Judge Spender in the *Temple of Preah Vihear*: the principle [of estoppel] operates to prevent a State contesting before the Court a situation contrary to a clear and unequivocal representation previously made by … either expressly or impliedly, on which representation the other State was, in the circumstances, entitled to rely and in fact did rely, and as a result the other State has been prejudiced or the State making it has secured some benefit or advantage for itself.[19]

The Court also noted the requirement for the party asserting estoppel to establish detrimental reliance on the estopped party's conduct:

> Further to this jurisprudence, estoppel may be invoked where (a) a State has made clear and consistent representations, by word, conduct, or silence; (b) such representations were made through an agent authorized to speak for the State with respect to the matter in question; (c) the State invoking estoppel was induced by such representations to act to its detriment, to suffer a prejudice, or to convey a benefit upon the representing State; and (d) such reliance was legitimate, as the representation was one on which that State was entitled to rely.[20]

The Palestinian Arabs, of course, would argue that no one detrimentally relied on the Palestinian Arab rejection of Resolution 181(II), and thus, the Palestinians were never estopped from asserting claims of sovereignty over the West Bank at a later date. However, both the Israelis and Jordanians could argue they indeed relied to their detriment on the Palestinian rejection of the two-state solution and the internationalization of Jerusalem. The Israelis did so by having to fight for control of the areas of Palestine the United Nations had allocated for the Jewish State, and by having to fight for control of West Jerusalem in 1948. The Jordanians did so by accepting the Palestinian Arab request at the December 1948 Jericho Conference to expend the money and manpower to assume control of the West Bank and East Jerusalem in 1948.

In any event, the Palestinians not only renounced the United Nations offer of statehood on 29 November 1947, but reemphasised their renunciation by starting a war. Those acts, as a matter of law, arguably constituted the deliberate *abandonment* of statehood in the Arab portion of Palestine.

In so doing, the Palestinian Arabs waived and abandoned their claim of sovereignty over those areas of Palestine. As one commentator has noted:

> [T]he UN partition plan had designated specified territory within Palestine for an Arab state, but the Arabs rejected that plan – and, concomitantly, control over such territories. That rejection strongly suggests that Arab

Palestinians rejected the UN grant of sovereignty over those portions of land designated for the Arab state. Yet, whatever one concludes in that regard, one thing is clear – following that rejection, the Palestinian Arabs have never had the opportunity to exercise full sovereign control over any Palestinian territory.[21]

## *Reverse renunciation*

The Palestinians in more recent years have tried to walk back that rejection, reversing themselves and now arguing vehemently that not only are they legally entitled to sovereignty over the West Bank and East Jerusalem, but that "Palestine" has also evolved into statehood. Palestinian legal commentators, however, differ regarding precisely *when* Palestine acquired statehood. Some rely on international recognition during the past 30 years, while others claim Palestine acquired statehood a century ago, at the issuance of the Mandate in 1922.[22]

Some Palestinian commentators even rely unabashedly on Resolution 181(II) – the *same* Resolution the Palestinians renounced in November 1947 – as providing the legal basis for Palestinian sovereignty over the West Bank today:

> It is no wonder, then, that by 1947 when the newly established UN GA weighed the fate of the territory and its people that partition along ethnic lines was favoured by many. In spite of the Partition Plan's lack of implementation as a result of the breakout of hostilities in 1948 and the concomitant Israeli declaration of statehood, this blueprint is seized on by Palestinians today as its promise of 44 per cent of the territory is far more generous that what has now become the default two-state boundary: those territories first occupied by Jordan (the West Bank) and Egypt (Gaza) in 1948/1949 and then taken over by Israel in 1967 until the present day.[23]

The Palestinian "reverse renunciation" has prompted an outcry from certain legal scholars.

Stone (1981), for example, closely examined these and other questions in his study of the interplay between international law and the Israeli-Palestinian conflict.[24] Stone recounted how the Palestinian position regarding Resolution 181(II) had flip-flopped over the decades, originally renouncing the Resolution and violating its terms when they thought they could drive the Jews out of Palestine by force, and decades later embracing the same Resolution as the legal basis for their claims of statehood in the West Bank and Gaza.

Stone concludes the Palestinian Arab rejection of Resolution 181(II) and resort to war frustrated the implementation of Resolution 181(II) and, thus, rendered it legally null. Consequently, the Palestinian Arabs *renounced* their claim to the Arab portions of Palestine and, therefore, have no ongoing legal basis for claiming statehood:

> [The rejection of partition and the armed aggression by the Arab states constituted an anticipatory repudiation and frustration of the resolution and plan [of partition], the protracted use of force by these states against the latter effectively preventing them from coming into legal effect.[25]

Stone identified additional legal and equitable reasons for his conclusion that the Palestinian Arabs had renounced their claims to the Arab portions of Palestine. Stone further argued the Palestinian Arabs, by virtue of their rejection of the United Nations offer of statehood in November 1947, were legally *estopped* from changing their minds and claiming statehood thereafter:

> Such claimants do not come with "clean hands" to seek equity; their hands indeed are mired by their lawlessly violent bid to destroy the very resolution and plan from which they now seek equity. They may also be thought by their representations concerning these documents, to have led others to act to their own detriment, and thus to be debarred by their own conduct from espousing, in pursuit of present expediencies, positions they formerly so strongly denounced.[26]

Stone reiterated his argument, grounded in international principles of equity, that the Palestinian Arabs had *forfeited* their rights under Resolution 181(II):

> Their position resembles that of a party to a transaction who has unlawfully repudiated the transaction, and comes to court years later claiming that selected provisions of it should be meticulously enforced against the wronged party. It also resembles that of a party who has by unlawful violence wilfully destroyed the subject-matter that is the "fundamental basis" on which consent rested, and now clamors to have the original terms enforced against the other party ... the Partition Resolution and Plan, since they were prevented by Arab rejection and armed aggression from entering into legal operation, could not thereafter carry any legal effects ... [27]

Gerson (1973), however, takes a different view. He argues the Palestinian Arabs, by rejecting partition and demanding statehood over the *entirety* of Palestine, did not necessarily renounce sovereignty over the *portion* of Palestine allocated to them in Resolution 181(II):

> [S]overeignty in the West Bank vested in the Palestinian Arabs in 1947. Their rejection of the Partition Plan represented a denial of its limitation rather than a renunciation *in toto*. Subsequent loss of title could be accomplished only in a manner similar to the traditional modes applicable to sovereign states – cession, prescription, or *debellatio*. In the context of a people possessing sovereign rights, the latter two modes can be said to have occurred when no attempt at the exercise of sovereignty is made when an opportunity to do so exists.[28]

Strawson (2010), however, agrees with the argument that by choosing to wage war against Resolution 181(II), the Palestinians waived sovereignty over the portion of Palestine allocated to them. "It was ironic," Strawson notes, "that just at the moment the United Nations recognized the Arab people of Palestine's right to self-determination, *their representatives were to reject it*."[29]

Karsh (2014) summarised the Palestinian Arabs' repeated rejections of opportunities for statehood throughout the 20th and early 21st centuries:

> For nearly a century, Palestinian leaders have missed no opportunity to impede the development of Palestinian civil society and the attainment of Palestinian statehood. Had Hajj Amin Husseini chosen to lead his constituents to peace and reconciliation with their Jewish neighbors, the Palestinians would have had their independent state over a substantial part of mandate Palestine by 1948, if not a decade earlier, and would have been spared the traumatic experience of dispersal and exile. Had Arafat set the PLO from the start on the path to peace and reconciliation instead of turning it into one of the most murderous and corrupt terrorist organizations in modern times, a Palestinian state could have been established in the late 1960s or the early 1970s; in 1979, as a corollary to the Egyptian-Israeli peace treaty; by May 1999, as part of the Oslo process; or at the very latest, with the Camp David summit of July 2000. Had Abbas abandoned his predecessors' rejectionist path, a Palestinian state could have been established after the Annapolis summit of November 2007, or during President Obama's first term after Benjamin Netanyahu broke with the longstanding Likud precept by publicly accepting in June 2009 the two-state solution and agreeing to the establishment of a Palestinian state.[30]

## Palestinian claims of statehood

Despite rejecting the two-state solution in November 1947 and for decades afterward, in more recent years the Palestinians have reversed course, employing transformational legal framing to argue Palestine is already a "state," entitled to all the legal rights and privileges of statehood under international law. The linchpin of Palestinian transformational legal framing for the past 30 years has focused on achieving international *recognition* of Palestine's "statehood":

> Palestine's admission into the UN would, in Abbas' view, transform the Israeli-Palestinian conflict into a matter of one UN member state violating the sovereign rights of another. That could give the Palestinians access to various international forums and mechanisms, such as the UN's human rights bodies, the International Court of Justice, and even the International Criminal Court, and offer them new avenues to seek redress.[31]

The disagreement regarding the "statehood of Palestine" involves highly complex and arcane aspects of international law. The traditional four criteria for determining statehood under international law derive from Article 1 of the 1933 *Montevideo Convention on the Rights and Duties of States*: (1) permanent population, (2) defined territory, (3) government, and (4) capacity to enter into relations with another State (some argue this fourth requirement is included in the third).[32] Brownlie (1973) described the determination of statehood under international law as "elusive."[33]

## Pre-1967

Prior to June 1967, the Palestinian Arabs *never* met the *Montevideo* criteria. They *rejected* statehood over *all* of Palestine when the British Government offered it to them in the May 1939 White Paper. They *renounced* statehood over a *portion* of Palestine when the United Nations offered it to them in November 1947.

Moreover, during the period between December 1947 and June 1967, the Palestinians did *nothing* to revoke their renunciation of Resolution 181(II) and the two-state solution. They did *nothing* to attempt to create a state in the Jordanian-occupied West Bank and East Jerusalem or in the Egyptian-occupied Gaza Strip. Indeed, the period between 1947 and 1967 saw a "shift away from international recognition of Palestinian Arab Nationhood."[34]

In 1964, Ahmed Shukheiry, who had testified before the Anglo-American Committee of Inquiry 18 years earlier, founded the PLO. The PLO's founding document, the "Palestinian National Charter," reaffirmed the Palestinian Arabs' renunciation of Resolution 181(II) and called for the destruction of the State of Israel.[35]

Moreover, the original PLO Charter said *nothing* about establishing a Palestinian State in the West Bank and Gaza Strip. In fact, the Charter expressly recognised *Jordanian* sovereignty over the West Bank and expressly *disclaimed* Palestinian Arab sovereignty over both the West Bank and the Gaza Strip, proclaiming, "This Organization does not exercise *any* regional sovereignty over the West Bank in the Hashemite Kingdom of Jordan, [or] the Gaza Strip."[36]

Legally, therefore, the PLO Charter should be viewed as a reaffirmation of the Palestinian Arab *waiver* of sovereignty over the West Bank and Gaza Strip.

## Post-1967

Following the June 1967 Six-Day War, the Palestinians continued calling for the destruction of Israel, in violation of the two-state solution the General Assembly had adopted in Resolution 181(II). By the late 1980s, however, the Palestinians began to implement a strategy to achieve "statehood" by self-acclamation as a legal weapon against Israel.

The self-acclamation strategy began on 30 November 1988 with the Palestine National Council's adoption of a "Declaration of Independence," proclaiming their "statehood."[37] The United Nations General Assembly, completely siding with the Palestinian cause since the late 1960s, recognised the

Declaration and replaced the designation "Palestine Liberation Organization" with "Palestine."[38]

Ever since then, the Palestinians and their supporters have launched an all-out effort to demonstrate Palestine truly qualifies under international law as a "state." A large part of the effort has involved legal arguments aimed at undermining the *Montevideo* criteria as the appropriate test for statehood. Palestinian advocates urge replacing *Montevideo* with a far more elastic "functional equivalent" test, aimed at making it as easy as possible for Palestine to be deemed a "state."[39]

In December 2012, the UN General Assembly gave the Palestinian effort a huge boost, adopting Resolution 67/19 and elevating the Palestinian territories to the Vatican-like status of "non-member observer state."[40] More than 100 countries currently recognise the "State of Palestine." Nevertheless, Israel and various other countries deny that Palestine has ever achieved statehood under international law.

## *Legal analysis of Palestinian claims of "Statehood"*

Much legal briefing and academic writing been devoted to the debate regarding Palestine's claim of "statehood."

### *Palestinian legal arguments*

For the past several decades, Palestinian lawyers and their supporters have argued that "Palestine" – either in its entirety or at least the West Bank and Gaza Strip – achieved statehood at some undefined point between 1919 and the present day.

Quigley (2010), for example, argues unconvincingly that Palestine achieved at least "provisional statehood" as early as mid-1919, pursuant to Article 22 of the Covenant of the League of Nations.[41]

Other Palestinian advocates offer a broad range of conflicting and muddled theories to pinpoint the precise moment Palestine achieved some form of "statehood." These advocates argue statehood arose when the Mandate for Palestine was issued; or when the Mufti established the short-lived, Gaza-based All-Palestine "government" in October 1948; or when the United Nations Security Council adopted Resolutions 242 and 338 after the June 1967 and October 1973 Arab-Israeli wars; or when Jordan renounced its claims to the West Bank in 1988; or when the PLO unilaterally declared Palestinian "statehood" in 1988; or when the Israelis agreed to limited Palestinian autonomy in certain areas of the West Bank in the 1994 Oslo Accords; or when the United Nations General Assembly granted Palestine non-member "observer state" status in 2012; or when the majority of United Nations member states subsequently "recognized" Palestine.

Palestinian advocates also offer a broad variety of arguments in support of their legal argument that Palestine is *already* a State, including statehood based on the "constitutive/recognition" theory and/or the "declaratory" theory, as well as a newly proposed "functional" approach to recognising statehood for particularised purposes.[42]

Adem (2019), for example, argues Palestine has achieved "abstract statehood" by virtue of its broad, although not unanimous, international recognition.[43] Other scholars argue the General Assembly's grant of "non-member observer State" status in Resolution 67/19 (29 November 2012) somehow equated to a grant of "statehood."[44] Still others contend many countries and international organisations have accorded various forms of *de facto* recognition to "Palestine," thereby amounting to collective recognition of Palestinian statehood.

Some scholars even argue that Palestinian "statehood" preceded World War I, and that neither the Covenant of the League of Nations nor the Mandate *deprived* the Palestinian Arabs of their putative statehood, at least as to the portions of Palestine (the West Bank, Gaza, and East Jerusalem) they continue claiming today.[45]

One Palestinian legal observer has latched onto a particularly weak basis for arguing Palestine achieved statehood long ago, proffering the Mufti's "All-Palestine Government" of October 1948 as evidence of Palestinian statehood:

> Although the APG did not last a long time, it was sufficiently "sovereign" to have proclaimed independence, drafted a constitution, issued passports, and established diplomatic relations with the Arab League and with other Arab states.[46]

However, as discussed in Chapter 14, the Mufti's short-lived and farcical effort to establish an "All-Palestine," Gaza-based "government" amounted to nothing more than a meaningless paper exercise, satisfying none of the *Montevideo* criteria.

*****

In 1968, in the wake of the Six-Day War and the Israeli occupation of the West Bank and Gaza Strip, the Egyptian diplomat and lawyer Nabil Elaraby argued the United Nations "consistently disregarded" the law when it approved the November 1947 partition resolution:[47]

> The legitimate aspirations and the high hopes of the whole Arab nation were consequently shattered when they saw with deep sorrow that the United Nations, the supposed conscience of mankind, had reached biased conclusions that brought grievous damage to the cause of justice and international morality. In fact, through the twenty-year [1947-1967] debate on Palestine in the United Nations, the international organization deviated time and again from the path which justice, law and ethics would dictate. The law of the Charter was sacrificed for the convenience of political expediency.

Elaraby further argued, as had Auni Bey Abdul Hadi decades earlier, that Article 22 of the Covenant of the League of Nations imposed a legal obligation on the international community to create an independent Arab state of Palestine after a temporary period of tutelage under a Mandatory. This legal obligation, as well as the provisions of the United Nations Charter, rendered the Balfour Declaration "subordinate" and "inferior" as a matter of law. Therefore, once the Mandate ended and the inhabitants of Palestine were ready to assume control of the country, only the "lawful" inhabitants of Palestine would have standing to choose their government via plebiscite.[48]

Elaraby's argument, however, ignored the legal implications of the Palestinian renunciation of the General Assembly's November 1947 offer of statehood.

## *Israeli legal arguments*

The Israeli side and its supporters, on the other hand, argue that Palestine, to this day, has *never* achieved statehood. They argue *no one* has held sovereignty in the West Bank since the Turks renounced their claims to Palestine in the 1923 Treaty of Lausanne. They also argue Israel acquired sovereignty over the area it controlled for the Jewish State, likely under the principle of secession, when it unilaterally declared independence on 14 May 1948. Israel's sovereignty became internationally recognised both under the 1949 armistice agreements and upon Israel's admission to the United Nations in May 1949.

Some advocates of the Israeli cause have suggested Israel also acquired sovereignty over the *entirety* of Mandate Palestine under the doctrine of *uti possidetis juris* upon the termination of the Mandate on 14 May 1948.[49] Others argue the 1949 armistice agreements froze sovereignty in the West Bank and Gaza, meaning both Gaza and the West Bank as early as 15 May 1948 (and certainly by April 1949) became *terra nullius*, with sovereignty suspended or in abeyance.[50] Jordan therefore did not acquire sovereignty when it purported to annex the West Bank and occupied it between 1949 and 1967. Nor did Egypt assert sovereignty over Gaza between 1949 and 1967.[51]

Instead, Israel's supporters argue, Jordan ruled the West Bank as a "belligerent occupant" from 1949 to 1967. Since 1967, Israel has merely stepped into Jordan's shoes as a successor "belligerent occupant" of the West Bank, and into Egypt's shoes for the Gaza Strip (until Israel withdrew from Gaza in 2005).[52]

Finally, proponents of the Israeli case argue "Palestine" is not a "state" because it cannot satisfy the requirements of the longstanding four-prong *Montevideo* test for statehood.

## *Other views regarding Palestinian "Statehood"*

Crawford (2006) has argued Palestine failed to achieve statehood after its unilateral declaration of statehood in 1988 and again after entering into the Oslo Accords with Israel:

> [I]t seems clear that this possibility [statehood] does not yet apply in the case of Palestine. In agreements welcomed by the General Assembly, the PLO has expressly accepted that an important agenda of issues remains to be resolved through permanent status negotiations. For its part, the General Assembly has stated that it has "a permanent responsibility towards the question of Palestine until the question is resolved in all its aspects in a satisfactory manner in accordance with international legitimacy." Both parties have agreed that unilateral action must not be taken in the meantime to change the status quo; this is equally the position reached by the International Court in the Wall Advisory Opinion. But the point is to change the status quo in favour of a comprehensive settlement accepted by all parties concerned—a situation that seems as remote as ever.[53]

The United States Court of Appeals for the First Circuit, in a landmark 2005 decision rejecting the PLO's argument that it was a "state" and therefore entitled to the protection of sovereign immunity against a tort suit in the United States, noted:

> [I]t is hard to pin down exactly when or how the defendants assert that Palestine achieved statehood. At various points in their briefs, they hint at three possibilities: (i) the period from the beginning of the mandate through the 1967 Arab-Israeli war; (ii) the period from the end of that war up until the creation of the Palestinian Authority (1994); and (iii) the period from 1994 forward ... the defendants have not carried their burden of showing that Palestine satisfied the requirements for statehood under the applicable principles of international law at *any* point in time.[54]

### International Court of Justice and International Criminal Court

The Palestinian Arab effort to transform the conflict from the political to the legal realm has been especially focused for the past two decades on persuading the ICJ and the International Criminal Court (ICC) to treat the Israeli-Palestinian conflict as a *legal* matter requiring *judicial* intervention and the imposition of legal/equitable remedies.

The Palestinians used their enormous influence at the United Nations General Assembly at the turn of the 21st century to persuade the ICJ to take jurisdiction over the dispute involving the Israeli security barrier or "wall of separation." The ICJ ultimately issued an Advisory Opinion in July 2004 finding the barrier illegal.[55]

The recent Palestinian effort at the ICC presents a far more serious attempt to weaponise the law against Israel. The Palestinians have pushed the ICC to accept jurisdiction and permit its prosecutor to bring potential indictments against Israeli officials for alleged "war crimes" in the West Bank, Gaza, and Jerusalem.[56]

The main hurdle to achieving this objective has been the threshold jurisdictional requirement that Palestine prove it is a "State" within the meaning of Article 12(3) of the Rome Statute, the ICC's governing document.[57] If Palestine were deemed to be a "state," then it would be eligible under the Rome Statute to delegate its criminal jurisdiction to the ICC. The stakes, therefore, for both the Palestinians and Israelis are enormous.

In January 2009, the Palestinians made their first effort to invoke the ICC's jurisdiction, filing an *ad hoc* declaration asking the ICC Prosecutor to investigate Israeli actions during Operation "Cast Lead," the late 2008 to early 2009 military conflict in Gaza between Israel and Hamas.[58] The ICC Prosecutor determined Palestine had not proven its statehood and declined to take further action.

On 15 May 2018, the Palestinian Authority, calling itself the "State of Palestine," submitted a referral to the ICC, purporting to delegate its "sovereign" criminal jurisdiction to the ICC.

The Palestinian Authority, in a brief filed in March 2020 with the ICC, claimed "statehood" over the *same* portion of Mandate Palestine the Palestinians had rejected when the United Nations offered it to them in November 1947:

> Palestine joined the Rome Statute as a State within its internationally recognized borders, as defined by the 1949 Armistice Line. That is the territory which Palestine claims as its own, which is recognized as such by the international community, and over which Palestine gave jurisdictional competence to the Court upon accession.[59]

In a highly controversial February 2021 decision, a pretrial panel of the ICC ruled in a 2-1 majority opinion that, regardless of its status under general international law, Palestine's accession to the Rome Statute followed "the correct and ordinary procedure." The pretrial panel acknowledged that Palestine lacked recognised international borders and many other attributes of statehood.

Nevertheless, the panel majority ruled the ICC lacked authority to second-guess the accession procedure. Therefore, the panel ruled, in a virtuoso demonstration of legal bootstrapping and judicial contortion, that "Palestine" could be deemed a "state" by virtue of its accession to the Rome Statute, even though Palestine might *not* otherwise qualify as a "state" under general principles of international law.[60]

The ICC panel's ruling was deeply flawed as a matter of law. The court overlooked the basic fact that Palestine *never* should have qualified for accession to the Rome Statute in the first instance, as it was not a "state" when it deposited its accession request with the Secretary General. The panel relied on the improper accession as the basis for its bizarre ruling, which essentially boiled down to the illogical proposition that even though Palestine is *not* a "state" under international law, it *is* a state for purposes of the Rome Statute.

## Assessment

Throughout the British Mandate years, the Palestinian Arabs engaged in transformational legal framing, casting the *political* dispute between competing Jewish and Arab nationalist movements in Palestine as a *legal* battle, in which the Palestinian Arabs were fighting for *justice* as the *victims* of Jewish colonisation, immigration, and land purchases. The Palestinian Arabs and their supporters throughout the Arab world invoked transformational legal framing in their testimony and arguments at the London Conferences in 1939, before the Anglo-American Committee of Inquiry in 1946, to UNSCOP and the Ad Hoc Committee in 1947, and even after the adoption of United Nations Resolution 181(II) in late November 1947.

Indeed, the Palestinian Arabs and their supporters continue utilising such framing to the present day, with far greater success than during their failed effort in 1947 to block the two-state solution. Advocates and scholars for the Palestinian cause have churned out an enormous amount of material invoking the justice/injustice/victimisation transformational legal frame.[61]

Throughout the Mandate years and afterward, the Palestinian Arabs also used violence alongside transformational legal framing, often justifying terrorism through the lens of legal narrative. For example, the Palestinian Arabs argued before the Shaw Commission in 1929 that the August 1929 Arab massacre of Jews in Hebron resulted from British and Zionist *injustices* perpetrated against the local Arab population. The Palestinian Arabs continue to the present day invoking transformational legal framing to justify violence as a lawful form of "self-defense" against Israeli "injustices."

The Palestinian Arab century-long effort to characterise the *political* conflict between Palestinian nationalism and Zionism as a *legal* conflict has succeeded in many ways, even though it has completely failed to achieve Palestinian Arab statehood. The Palestinian Arabs have cloaked themselves in the twin mantles of *justice* and *victimhood*, attracting enormous support from the vast majority of the world community. The United Nations has enthusiastically embraced the Palestinian transformational legal framing, focusing more attention in the last four decades on the Israel-Palestine dispute than *all* other global issues combined.

Ironically, however, treating the Israel-Palestine political conflict as a legal dispute also threatens Palestinian success, because the Palestinian *legal* case on the merits suffers from a fatal weakness. When the Palestinian Arabs knowingly and voluntarily renounced the General Assembly's 29 November 1947 offer of statehood and launched all-out war, they effectively *waived* their legal right to sovereignty over the portion of Palestine the United Nations had allocated to them, thereby condemning their own people to perpetual statelessness. That *waiver*, under international law, *estopped* the Palestinian Arabs from changing their minds decades later and insisting on the *same* General Assembly offer of statehood they previously rejected.

Between 1949 and 1967, Jordan occupied and purported to annex the West Bank. During those years, the Palestinian Arabs did *nothing* to seek statehood over the area the United Nations had allocated to them in Resolution 181(II). The Palestinian Arab leadership during those years failed to pursue independence for their own people living in the Arab portion of Palestine under Jordanian rule. Nor did they take *any* steps to repatriate their brethren languishing in refugee camps in neighbouring Arab states.

Instead, the Palestinian Arabs continued renouncing the two-state solution between 1949 and 1967 and thereafter for an additional two-plus decades. The Palestinian Arabs consistently maintained the Mufti's all-or-nothing approach, insisting on obtaining sovereignty over the *entirety* of Mandate Palestine and renouncing the two-state solution.

The Palestinian Arab decades-long rejection of the two-state solution undermines their modern-day legal argument that they are legally *entitled* to that very same solution. If anyone caused a *legal* wrong to the Palestinians, it was their *own leadership* for renouncing and waiving separate offers of statehood from Britain in the May 1939 White Paper and from the United Nations in the November 1947 partition plan.

Moreover, the decades-long Palestinian Arab renunciation of the two-state solution undermines their modern-day legal argument that "Palestine" somehow achieved statehood at some point during the last century. The West Bank has remained under various forms of continuous military occupation from 1949 until today. No legal event sufficient to confer Palestinian statehood in the West Bank *ever* occurred between November 1947 and the present day.

The Palestinian renunciation of sovereignty in November 1947 maintained the post-World War I vacuum in sovereignty over the West Bank and Gaza Strip during the Jordanian and Egyptian occupations of those areas between 1949 and 1967. Sovereignty continued in abeyance after Israel replaced Jordan and Egypt as the occupants in June 1967. Jordan's subsequent renunciation of its claims to the West Bank and East Jerusalem in 1988 had no legal effect, as Jordan never possessed sovereignty over those areas, and thus could not lawfully transfer sovereignty to anyone else.[62]

The most that can be said regarding sovereignty over the areas Israel has occupied since 1967 is that *neither* the Palestinian Arabs *nor* Israel can establish, as a purely legal matter, a perfected claim to sovereignty over what most observers still regard as occupied *terra nullius*. As between the Palestinian Arabs, who renounced the United Nations offer of statehood in November 1947, and the Israelis, who captured the West Bank and Gaza Strip in a lawful, defensive war in June 1967, the Israeli claim to sovereignty may be stronger than the Palestinian claim, but it is not a perfected claim.

This *legal* outcome, however, does not preclude the Palestinians from arguing, as a *political* matter, their entitlement to statehood in the West Bank and Gaza. But such statehood may arise only from a negotiated *political* settlement with Israel, not as the result of any Palestinian *legal* claim to the *same* area they rejected in November 1947. Palestinian statehood in the West Bank and Gaza Strip can and should be resolved through diplomatic negotiation, *not* adversarial litigation.

## Notes

1 *See* J. Stoyanovsky, *op. cit.*, at 261–262 (sovereignty over mandated territories "is not vested in the mandatory Powers … This is equally the case in Palestine"); *see also* A. Gerson, *op. cit.*, at 24–27 (sovereignty of mandated territories deemed in "suspension" or "abeyance").
2 J. Strawson, *op. cit.*, at 46–49.
3 Covenant of the League of Nations, Art. 22 (1920).
4 Q. Wright, *Sovereignty of the Mandates*, 17:4 Am. J. Int'l L. 694 (1923).
5 *Id.* at 695, 697–698.
6 *International Status of South-West Africa*, Advisory Opinion, 010-19500711-ADV-01-01, I.C.J. Reports at 150 (11 July 1950). Britain acted in derogation of these principles when it offered sovereignty without League of Nations approval to the Palestinian Arabs in the 1939 White Paper.
7 League of Nations Archives, R4090/6A/43880/761, Letter from S. Lester, Secretary-General of the League of Nations, to Lord Hailey (2 May 1946).
8 FO 371/52563, Letter from J. Martin, Colonial Office to C.W. Baxter, Foreign Office (4 November 1946).
9 United Nations, Charter of the United Nations, 1945, 1 UNTS XVI, Article 80, para. 1 ("Except as may be agreed upon in individual trusteeship agreements, made under Articles 77, 79, and 81, placing each territory under the trusteeship system, and until such agreements have been concluded, nothing in this Chapter shall be construed in or of itself to alter in any manner the rights whatsoever of any states or any peoples or the terms of existing international instruments to which Members of the United Nations may respectively be parties"); *see also id.*, Article 77, para. 1(a) ("The trusteeship system shall apply to such territories in the following categories as may be placed thereunder by means of trusteeship agreements: a. territories now held under mandate"); CO537/2362, Letter (Top Secret) from T. Smith, Colonial Office to H. Beeley, Foreign Office, enclosing notes of 18 July 1947 meeting of Colonial Office Legal Advisers (7 August 1947) (noting both Colonial Office and Foreign Office legal advisers agreed that "with the demise of the League, we could in theory disregard the Mandate, but we had informed the United Nations that we would continue to administer Palestine under the terms of the Mandate until other arrangements were made … [t]he Charter does not say that Mandates must now be placed under trusteeship … [i]t may be argued therefore that for the time being at least H.M.G. can continue to govern Palestine by virtue of the Mandate … ").
10 *Id.*
11 United Nations, A/AC.21/W.2, Working Paper, General Assembly, United Nations Palestine Commission (9 January 1948).
12 "Text of the British Statement on Palestine, Chronicling History and Policy of the Mandate," *New York Times*, 14 May 1948 at 4 ("When this advance party had visited Palestine and seen for themselves the conditions prevailing there, the Commission reported to the Security Council that they would be unable to carry out their task without the assistance of armed forces, which the Security Council declined to provide. It then became obvious that the Commission would not themselves be able to arrange for the transfer of the functions exercised by the Central Government and steps were accordingly taken to devolve upon local authorities those functions which could appropriately be assumed by them").

13 Y. Blum, *op. cit.*, at 292, 293. Blum further argued, "The legal standing of Israel in the territories in question is thus that of a State which is lawfully in control of territory in respect of which no other States can show a better title. Or, if it is preferred to state the matter in terms of belligerent occupation, then the legal standing of Israel in the territories in question is at the very least that of a belligerent occupant of territory in respect of which Jordan is not entitled to the reversionary rights of a legitimate sovereign." *Id.* at 294.

14 M. Shaw, *The League of Nations Mandate System and the Palestine Mandate: What Did and Does It Say About International Law and What Did and Does It Say About Palestine*, 49 Isr. L. Rev. 287, 304 (2016); *but see* N. Erakat, *op. cit.*, at 80–81 ("Palestinians had successfully inscribed their right to self-determination in the White Paper of 1939, in the UN Partition Plan (1947), and in the UN draft Trusteeship Agreement (1948). Thus, when the British Mandate for Palestine expired in May 1948, sovereignty vested in the people of Palestine"). Bell and Kontorovich, however, argue Israel inherited the boundaries of the entirety of Mandate Palestine as of the moment the Mandate ended on 15 May 1948. They rely on the doctrine of *Uti Possidetis Juris*, arguing the boundaries of Mandate Palestine automatically became the boundaries of the new State of Israel at the moment of the state's creation on 15 May 1948, given that no one else had claimed sovereignty over the areas of Palestine the United Nations had allocated to the Arabs. A. Bell and E. Kontorovich, *Palestine, Uti Possidetis Juris, and the Borders of Israel*, 58 Arizona Law Rev. 633–692, 688 (2016). Bell and Kontorovich's argument, however, ignores that Israel itself did not assert sovereignty over the Arab areas at the time; indeed, it had *accepted* the two-state solution embodied in Resolution 181(II). Other evidence indicates the Zionist leadership may have been ready to accept *Jordanian* sovereignty over those areas, at least prior to King Abdullah's decision to join the war against the Jewish State.

15 *Termination of the British Mandate for Palestine*, 2 Int'l L. Q. 58 (April 1948).

16 Indeed, it was not until the signing of the Oslo Accords that the PLO formally accepted the existence of Israel and refocused its aspirations for sovereignty on the West Bank and Gaza. Even then, however, the Palestinians agreed that most of the West Bank (Area C) would remain under Israeli control.

17 K. Parlett, "State Conduct in Territorial Disputes Beyond *Effectivites*: Recognition, Acquiescence, Renunciation and Estoppel," in M. Kohen and M. Hebie, *Research Handbook on Territorial Disputes in International Law* at 183 (Edward Elgar, 2018).

18 L. Oppenheim and H. Lauterpacht, *International Law: A Treatise*, Vol. I (7th Ed.) at 875 (Longmans, Green, 1948); *see also Case of Certain Norwegian Loans*, Judgment of 6 July 1957, I.C.J. Reports 1957, 9, 26 (express abandonment of known rights constitutes waiver under international law); *Armed Activities on the Territory of the Congo (Democratic Republic of the Congo v. Uganda)*, Judgment, I.C.J. Reports 2005, 168, para. 293 ("waivers or renunciations of claims or rights must either be express or unequivocally implied from the conduct of the State alleged to have waived or renounced its right … [s]imilarly, the International Law Commission … points out that '[a]lthough it may be possible to infer a waiver from the conduct of the States concerned or from a unilateral statement, the conduct or statement must be unequivocal'").

19 *In The Matter Of The Chagos Marine Protected Area Arbitration* (Mauritius v. U.K, Case No. 2011-03) Award, Permanent Court of International Arbitration, para. 435 (18 March 2015).

20 *Id.* paras. 436–438.

21 R.W. Ash, *Is Palestine a State: A Response to Professor John Quigley's Article, the Palestine Declaration to the International Criminal Court*, 36 Rutgers L. Rec. 198 (2009).

22 *See, e.g.*, V. Kattan, *From Co-Existence to Conquest: International Law and the Origins of the Arab-Israeli Conflict, 1891-1949* at 133–140 (Pluto Press, 2009).

23 M.L. Burgis-Kasthala, *op. cit.*, at 681.

24 J. Stone, *Israel and Palestine: Assault on the Law of Nations* at 64 (Johns Hopkins University Press, 1981).

25 *Id.* at 65.
26 *Id.*
27 *Id.*; *see also* D. Benoliel and R. Perry, *Israel, Palestine and the ICC*, 32:1 Mich. J. Int'l L. 73–127 (2010) (arguing neither the West Bank nor Gaza are "states" under international law).
28 A. Gerson (1973), *op. cit.*, at 35–36.
29 J. Strawson, *op. cit.*, at 102 (emphasis added).
30 E. Karsh, *Palestinian Leaders Don't Want an Independent State*, 21:3 Middle East Q. 11 (2014).
31 K. Elgindy, *Palestine Goes to the UN: Understanding the New Statehood Strategy*, 90:5 Foreign Aff. 107 (2011); *see also* N. Erakat, *op. cit.*, at 221–222 (explaining ulterior legal motives for Palestinian efforts to achieve "statehood").
32 Montevideo Convention, Art. I (1933). The United States standard for determining statehood is set forth in the Restatement (Third) of Foreign Relations, deeming a state to be "an entity that has a defined territory and a permanent population, under the control of its own government, and that engages in, or has the capacity to engage in, formal relations with other such entities." *Restatement (Third) of Foreign Relations* § 201 (1987). More recent scholarship has questioned the ongoing validity of the four *Montevideo* criteria as determinants of statehood. *See, e.g.*, J. Crawford, *The Creation of States in International Law* (2d ed.) at 47 (Oxford Univ. Press, 2006); T. Grant, *Defining Statehood: The Montevideo Convention and its Discontents*, 37:2 Colum. J. Transnat'l L. 403–445 (1999).
33 I. Brownlie, *Principles of Public International Law* at 91 (2d ed.) (Oxford Univ. Press, 1973).
34 O. Dajani, *Stalled Between The Seasons: The International Legal Status Of Palestine During The Interim Period*, 26 Denv. J. Intl'l L. & Pol'y 40 (1997).
35 Palestinian National Charter, Preamble and Art. 2 (28 May 1964).
36 *Id.*, Art. 24 (emphasis added).
37 United Nations General Assembly, A/43/827, Palestine Declaration of Independence (18 November 1988).
38 United Nations General Assembly, Resolution 43/177, UN Doc. A/RES/43/177 (15 December 1988); *see also* S. Adem, *Palestine and the International Criminal Court* at 62 (Springer, 2019). Adem concedes, however, that "it is difficult to reach a definite conclusion on the statehood of Palestine on a mere reliance on the declaration of independence and the engagement of Palestine with international law and organisations." *Id.* at 64; V. Tsilonis, *op. cit., at* 56 ("the term 'State' has for each international organisation and court a 'variable geometry,' that is, a constantly changing definition; a fact which undoubtedly proves that the term 'State' does not have such a strictly defined meaning from a legal perspective as one would initially think").
39 *See generally* E. Kontorovich, *Israel/Palestine – The ICC's Uncharted Territory*, 11 J. Int'l Crim. Just. 979 (2013).
40 United Nations, UNGA A/RES/67/19 "Status of Palestine in the United Nations" (4 December 2012).
41 J. Quigley, *The Statehood of Palestine: International Law In the Middle East Conflict* (Cambridge Univ. Press, 2010).
42 The "declaratory" theory holds that statehood may be recognized based on another State's willingness to engage in diplomatic relations with the emerging State. The "constitutive" theory requires formal recognition from other States. Proponents of the "functional" theory argue the ICC should be free, under the *Kompetenz-Kompetenz* principle, to treat Palestine as a "state" for purposes of applying the Rome Statute. *See* S. Adem, *op. cit.*, at 55–76; J. Crawford (2006), *op. cit.*,at 17–25; I. Brownlie, *op. cit.*, at 91–93; L. Oppenheim and H. Lauterpacht, *International Law: A Treatise*, Vol. I (7th Ed.) at 120–134 (Longmans, Green, 1948).
43 S. Adem, *op. cit.*, at 68.
44 United Nations, General Assembly Resolution 67/19, (A/67/L.28 and Add.1), *Status of Palestine in the United Nations* (29 November 2012).

45 *See, e.g.*, J. Quigley, *op. cit.*; F. Boyle, *The Creation of the State of Palestine*, 1 Eur. J. Int'l L. 301 (1990); *but see* J. Crawford, *The Creation of the State of Palestine: Too Much Too Soon*, 1 Eur. J. Int'l L. 307, 313 (1990) (criticizing Boyle's argument for Palestinian statehood as "weak and unconvincing. Indeed it is weaker and more unconvincing than it need have been, having regard to some of the post-1945 developments, and in particular to the case of Guinea Bissau. But if that case is to be justified on the premise '*nasciturus pro jam natus habetur*,' the fact remains that a real State of Palestine is by no means yet assured. For a Palestinian State to be properly described as '*nasciturus*,' what is needed is statesmanship on all sides, and respect for the rights of the peoples and states of the region. The manipulation of legal categories is unlikely to advance matters").

46 V. Kattan, "A Critical Assessment of the Government of Israel's Memorandum to the ICC – Part I," Blog (30 January 2020), https://victorkattan.com/work/1077-2/ (last accessed 4 January 2021). As discussed in detail in Chapter 14, *supra*, the Palestinian "government" in Gaza was nothing more than a paper creation, exercising no governmental authority at all. The fact that it managed to print a few thousand passports is meaningless.

47 *Id.*

48 *Id.* at 98–99.

49 A. Bell and E. Kontorovich, *op. cit.*, at 633–692, 688.

50 The Jordan-Israel armistice agreement contained language expressly preserving both parties' rights and claims to the West Bank and East Jerusalem: "No provision of this Agreement shall in any way prejudice the rights, claims and positions of either Party hereto in the ultimate peaceful settlement of the Palestine question." United Nations Security Council, S/1302/REV.1 1/, cablegram from the United Nations Acting Mediator to the Secretary-General transmitting the text of the General Armistice Agreement between the Hashemite Jordan Kingdom and Israel, Art. II.2 (3 April 1949). The British Government also took the legal position that the Arab renunciation of Resolution 181(II) would result in the Arab areas of Palestine becoming a "'no man's land' on and after May 15." 867N.01/5–248, L. Henderson, Memorandum (Top Secret), "British-American Cooperation with Regard to Palestine," at 3–4 (2 May 1948).

51 A. Sharon, *Why is Israel's Presence in the Territories Still Called "Occupation"?*, 23:3/4 Jew. Pol. Stud. Rev. 46 (2011) (Egypt claimed sovereignty over Sinai Peninsula but not Gaza).

52 Regarding Gaza's status, the Israeli Supreme Court ruled in 2008 that Israel's unilateral withdrawal from Gaza in 2005 ended Israel's status as a "belligerent occupant," but did not end Gaza's status as *terra nullius*. *Ahmad et al. v. Prime Minister*, Israel Supreme Court (sitting as the High Court of Justice), HCJ 9132/07 (30 January 2008) at 8, para. 12 ("The State argued before us that it acts according to the rules of international law and respects its humanitarian obligations under the laws of warfare. According to counsel for the State, these are limited obligations, derived from the state of warfare in existence between the State of Israel and the Hamas organization that controls the Gaza Strip, and from the need to prevent harm to the civilian population caught in the area of the hostilities. In this context, we note that since September 2005, Israel no longer has effective control over what takes place within the territory of the Gaza Strip. The military government that previously existed in that territory was abolished by means of a decision of the government, and Israeli soldiers are not present in that area on a permanent basis and do not direct what occurs there. In these circumstances, under the international law of occupation, the State of Israel has no general obligation to care for the welfare of the residents of the Strip").

53 J. Crawford (2006), *op. cit.*, at 448.

54 *Ungar v. Palestine Liberation Organization*, 402 F.3d 274, 289, 292 (1st Cir. 2005) (emphasis added).

55 *Legal Consequences of the Construction of a Wall in the Occupied Palestinian Territory*, Advisory Opinion, I.C J. Reports 136 (2004). For an interesting discussion of the Court's decision from an Israeli perspective, *see* R. Sabel, *The Status of the Territories: The International Court of Justice Decision on The Separation Barrier and the Green Line*, 38 Isr. L. Rev. 316–378 (2005).

56 International Criminal Court, *Situation in Palestine*, PAL-180515-Ref, *State of Palestine, Referral by the State of Palestine Pursuant to Articles 13(a) and 14 of the Rome Statute* (15 May 2018). Israel has raised a variety of jurisdictional objections to the referral, including that Palestine is not a "state" and therefore lacks legal standing to delegate jurisdiction to the ICC; but even if it were deemed to be a "state," pursuant to the Oslo Accords it has waived jurisdiction "either in law or in fact over Area C, Jerusalem and Israeli nationals – and thus cannot validly delegate such jurisdiction to the Court." International Criminal Court, *Situation in Palestine*, PAL-180515-Ref, *State of Israel, Office of the Attorney General, The International Criminal Court's Lack of Jurisdiction over the So-Called "Situation In Palestine"* (20 December 2019). The Israeli submission to the ICC also preserved Israel's own claims to the West Bank, the Gaza Strip, and East Jerusalem, arguing sovereignty over those areas has been in "abeyance" since the termination of the Palestine Mandate on 14 May 1948. *Id.* paras. 29–30.

57 Article 12 is entitled "Preconditions to the Exercise of Jurisdiction." Article 12(3) provides as follows: "If the acceptance of a State which is not a Party to this Statute is required under paragraph 2, that State may, by declaration lodged with the Registrar, accept the exercise of jurisdiction by the Court with respect to the crime in question. The accepting State shall cooperate with the Court without any delay or exception in accordance with Part 9." Legal commentators have disagreed as to whether Palestine qualifies as a "state" within the plain meaning of Article 12(3). Some have argued it does not, based on traditional norms of international law such as the *Montevideo* criteria for statehood. Others have urged a more liberal, "functional" reading of Article 12(3), urging Palestine be deemed a state "for purposes of" effectuating the purpose of Article 12(3). *See, e.g.*, H. Lee, *Defining State for the Purpose of the International Criminal Court: The Problem Ahead After the Palestine Decision*, 77 U. Pitt. L. Rev. 345, 384 (2016) ("The term 'state' in the [Rome Statute] should be defined broadly to include self-proclaimed entities that exercise *de facto* governmental function, regardless of whether the entity received any formal recognition"); W. Worster, *The Exercise of Jurisdiction by the International Criminal Court Over Palestine*, 26:5 Am. Univ. Int'l L. Rev. 1208 (2011) ("Although the text of the Rome Statute appears to limit membership to 'states,' the practice of international organizations is that the term 'state' may be used liberally to include quasi-states with some degree of statehood, notwithstanding the clear language of the text. There is no requirement of international law that the term be interpreted restrictively … Thus, there is no barrier under international law to Palestinian accession to the Rome Statute or acceptance of the ICC's jurisdiction"); A. Zimmermann, *Palestine and the International Criminal Court Quo Vadis: Reach and Limits of Declarations under Article 12(3)*, 11:2 J. Int'l Crim. Just. 303–330 (2013) (arguing Palestine satisfies the requirements of Article 12(3) as of the 2012 UN resolution upgrading Palestine's status to "non-member observer state"); J. Quigley, *Palestine is a State: A Horse with Black and White Stripes is a Zebra*, 32:4 Mich. J. Int'l L. 749 (2011) (arguing Palestine is a state, consistent with Quigley's previous writings); *but see* R. Barnidge, *Palestinian Engagement With The International Criminal Court: From Preliminary Examination To Investigation?*, 7:2 J. Middle East Afr. 122 (2016) ("When the Palestinians engage with international institutions such as the ICC as a state in the absence of a final settlement that enshrines Palestinian statehood, there is a strong argument to be made that they are acting contrary to international law, since this *prima facie* would seem to prejudice the final (negotiated) status of the territories"); R.W. Ash, *Is Palestine a State: A Response to Professor John Quigley's Article, the Palestine Declaration to the International Criminal Court*, 36 Rutgers L. Rec. 200 (2009) ("[I]t is difficult to fathom how anyone could argue that there is a state of Palestine currently in existence. Even the Palestinian leaders themselves, through both their frequent statements and their voluntary participation in a process whose goal is to establish a Palestinian 'State,' testify that what they hope to achieve in the future is the creation of a viable Palestinian state. If creation of a viable Palestinian state is the goal Palestinian leaders continue to pursue, that is proof positive that no such 'State' currently exists"); J. Vidmar, *Palestine and the Conceptual Problem of Implicit Statehood*, 12 Chinese J. Int'l L. 19, 40–41 (2013) ("Setting

Palestine next to States and giving it the competencies to do certain things that States tend to do does not automatically and implicitly make it a State … Palestine, in many respects, has the capacity to act like a State internationally, yet such a capacity does not create Palestinian statehood"); E. Kontorovich, *Israel/Palestine – The ICC's Uncharted Territory*, 11 J. Int'l Crim. Just. 979 (2013) (noting potential ICC recognition of Palestinian "statehood" would lead to many similarly questionable claims around the world).

58 S. Adem, *op. cit.*, at 50–55.

59 ICC-01/18-82 16-03-2020 12/32 NM PT, International Criminal Court, Pre-Trial Chamber, *The State of Palestine's observations in relation to the request for a ruling on the Court's territorial jurisdiction in Palestine*, para. 28 (16 March 2020). Interestingly, in the *Kosovo* case, the ICJ recognized the validity under general international law and the applicable Security Council Resolution of Kosovo's declaration of independence, but also emphasized the Court was *not* deciding one way or the other whether that declaration meant Kosovo had attained statehood as a matter of law. *Accordance with International Law of the Unilateral Declaration of Independence in Respect of Kosovo*, Advisory Opinion, I.C.J. Reports 2010, 403 at para. 51.

60 International Criminal Court, No. ICC-01/18, *Situation In The State Of Palestine* at paras. 106–107 (5 February 2021) ("Therefore, the reference to '[t]he State on the territory of which the conduct in question occurred' in article 12(2)(a) of the Statute cannot be taken to mean a State fulfilling the criteria for statehood under general international law … the Rome Statute insulates the Court from making such a determination, relying instead on the accession procedure and the determination made by the United Nations General Assembly. The Court is not constitutionally competent to determine matters of statehood that would bind the international community. In addition, such a determination is not required for the specific purposes of the present proceedings or the general exercise of the Court's mandate.") The Court, in a 2–1 majority ruling, further noted, "in accordance with the ordinary meaning given to its terms in their context and in the light of the object and purpose of the Statute, the reference to '[t]he State on the territory of which the conduct in question occurred' in article 12(2)(a) of the Statute must be interpreted as a reference to a State Party to the Statute." *Id.* para. 109. Judge Kovacs issued a lengthy, partial dissent from the majority opinion, noting "I agree neither with the conclusion, nor with the Majority's reasoning and analysis in reaching such a conclusion" regarding the issue of Palestine's "statehood" for purposes of the Rome Statute. *Judge Péter Kovács' Partly Dissenting Opinion*, para. 2.

61 *See, e.g.*, W. Boustany, *The Palestine Mandate, Invalid and Impracticable: A Contribution of Arguments and Documents Towards the Solution of the Palestine Problem* (American Press, 1936); N. Erakat, *Justice For Some: Law and the Question of Palestine* (Stanford Univ. Press, 2019); J. Quigley, *Palestine and Israel, A Challenge to Justice* (Duke University Press, 1990); J. Quigley, *The Case for Palestine: An International Law Perspective* (Duke University Press, 1990); V. Kattan, *From Coexistence to Conquest: International Law and the Origins of the Arab-Israeli Conflict, 1891-1949* (Pluto Press, 2009); S. Akram et al., *International Law and the Israeli-Palestinian Conflict: A Rights-Based Approach to Middle East Peace* (Routledge, 2011); M. Muzzawi, *Palestine and the Law: Guidelines for the Resolution of the Arab-Israel Conflict* (Ithaca Press, 1997); H. Cattan, *Palestine and International Law: The Legal Aspects of the Arab-Israeli Conflict* (2d Ed.) (Longman, 1973); H. Cattan, *Palestine, the Arabs and Israel: The Search for Justice* (Longman, 1969); W. Mallison and S. Mallison, *The Palestine Problem in International Law and World Order* (Longman, 1986); E. Said, *The Question of Palestine* (Random House, 1980).

62 For a contrary view, *see* United Nations A/CN.4/557, V. Rodríguez Cedeño, Special Rapporteur, *Unilateral Acts of States (Eighth Report)* at para. 53 (2005) ("The question arises whether the King of Jordan was competent to act at the international level and to formulate the waiver on behalf of Jordan. It is significant that the Constitution of Jordan prohibits any act related to the transfer of territory, so that it would appear that the King exceeded his authority. However, that did not prevent the waiver from producing legal effects, and in fact a transfer of the territory of the West Bank to the State of Palestine actually took place").

# CONCLUSION

The Arab-Israeli conflict has featured a battle of competing narratives for the last century, especially competing legal narratives. Both sides have employed transformational legal framing since the inception of the conflict to portray themselves as *victims* fighting for *justice*.

Throughout the Mandate years, the British Government also used legal framing to justify substantive law and legal procedure as the preferred frame for discharging their responsibilities as Mandatory, and for managing the conflict between Arabs and Jews. This dynamic reached a climax in the key decade between 1939 and 1948. Four separate quasi-legal proceedings, in relatively quick succession, produced three dramatically different outcomes: the *one-state* solution in 1939, the *no-state* solution in 1946, and finally the *two-state* solution in 1947.

Despite the differing results, the Palestinian Arabs repeatedly invoked the injustice narrative to renounce statehood and justify violence and bloodshed. Today, however, the Palestinians have come full circle, repeatedly invoking the injustice narrative to demand the very same outcome they rejected throughout the 1930s and 1940s – statehood in a portion of the former Mandatory Palestine.

This complete reversal of position has attracted wide support around the world for the Palestinian legal narrative, especially at the United Nations and other international bodies. The International Criminal Court (ICC) represents the most recent example of an international organisation embracing Palestinian legal framing. The Court gave an enormous boost to Palestinian aspirations with its controversial and bizarre February 2021 ruling that although Palestine does *not* qualify as a "state" under principles of general international law, it *does* qualify as a "state" for ICC purposes by virtue of its accession to the Rome Statute (something that never should have been allowed in the first instance). In a supreme twist of irony, the ICC *itself* employed transformational legal framing to reach far beyond its jurisdictional limits and characterise a nonjusticiable political issue as one cloaked in legal garb.

The Palestinian success at the ICC follows a long line of similar successes during the various legal proceedings under British rule in Palestine. Both the Palin (1920) and Haycraft (1921) Commissions issued reports sympathising with Palestinian Arab fears of Zionism. The Shaw Commission verdict (1930) led directly to new British policies curtailing Jewish immigration and land acquisition in Palestine, initially proposed in the Hope Simpson report and White Paper of 1930, and culminating eventually in the White Paper of May 1939.

Tragically, however, the Palestinians never leveraged those legal successes to help their own people by ending the conflict, preferring instead, as they continue doing today, to promote conflict *perpetuation* through legal framing and "lawfare" rather than conflict *resolution* through diplomacy.

The Palestinian preference for continuing rather than resolving the conflict was most starkly on display during the London Conferences in February and March 1939. The Palestinians and their Arab allies refused to sit in the same room with the Jews, forcing Prime Minister Chamberlain to conduct separate opening ceremonies and Colonial Secretary Malcolm MacDonald to engage in the original version of shuttle diplomacy. Although the British Government had already decided before the conferences began to reward the Palestinian Arabs with a new policy withdrawing support for Zionism, the conferences nevertheless represent the greatest missed opportunity for the Palestinians in the entire history of the conflict.

The legal wrangling at the London Conferences provided Whitehall political cover for the White Paper's radical departure from Britain's obligations to the Jewish people under the Mandate. The extensive re-examination during the conferences of the McMahon-Hussein correspondence, cast as a *legal* exercise featuring both the Lord Chancellor and the former Chief Justice of the Palestine Supreme Court, served Britain's *political* objective of appeasing Arab sentiment on the eve of war with Germany.

The conferences broke down without agreement, leading the British unilaterally to follow the plan they had formulated in advance of the conferences to issue the May 1939 White Paper. In one swift motion, the British Government all but ended Jewish immigration and land acquisition while offering to set Palestine on a path to a majority-ruled Arab State in ten years. Yet the Palestinians inexplicably *rejected* the offer, preferring instead to continue invoking the justice/injustice/victimhood narrative for the next 80-plus years. The Palestinian failure to embrace their sweeping victory in London, the fruit of a successful two-decade battle to delegitimise Zionism, represents the greatest failure of Palestinian leadership in the history of the conflict.

Following World War II, the plight of Jewish Holocaust survivors, the rising importance of oil, and the emerging rivalry between the Soviet Union and the West changed the strategic calculus in the Middle East irrevocably. Never again would the Palestinian Arabs be offered sovereignty over the entirety of pre-1948 Palestine. Yet once again their effective use of transformational legal framing during the 1946 hearings before the Anglo-American Committee of Inquiry helped avoid a resurrection of the Peel Commission's 1937 two-state solution.

Although Justice Singleton and Judge Hutcheson grew to despise each other, they and their colleagues agreed unanimously on the *no-state solution*, ruling that neither Arab nor Jew should dominate each other in Palestine. The Anglo-American Committee preferred instead for Palestine to remain a ward of the international community under some form of Trusteeship. The United States resurrected the Trusteeship idea briefly in March 1948, four months after the UN General Assembly had approved Resolution 181 and the two-state solution.

In the end, however, the United Nations delivered the final verdict for Palestine after three decades of legal battles under British rule. Both the Special Committee and the Ad Hoc Committee decided on partition – the two-state solution – as the best outcome for Palestine. The final verdict at the General Assembly on 29 November 1947 followed an intense Jewish lobbying campaign in the face of British opposition and American ambivalence.

Far more significant was the off-again, on-again engagement of the Palestinian Arabs with the United Nations in 1947. Boycotting UNSCOP turned out to be an egregious and self-defeating blunder. The belated decision to participate in the Ad Hoc Committee process came as too little, too late, for the Palestinian Arabs. The United Nations decided on the two-state solution, the *same* solution the Palestinians demand today. Yet in late 1947, the Palestinians not only rejected the two-state solution and renounced sovereignty over the portion of Palestine offered to them but also launched all-out war to prevent it.

The Palestinian Arabs, who had originally rejected the two-state solution when the Peel Commission recommended it in July 1937, maintained their rejection of the two-state solution for decades thereafter, finally agreeing to recognise Israel's existence in the Oslo Accords of 1993.

The Palestinians and the United Nations have never acknowledged the legal consequences of the Palestinian rejection/renunciation of Resolution 181(II) and the two-state solution. It is of vital legal significance that the Palestinians *themselves* knowingly and wilfully rejected the two-state solution in 1947 and *continued* rejecting it until 1993. The Palestinians, as a matter of law, waived and renounced the United Nations' offer of statehood in November 1947, punctuated their waiver and renunciation by launching a violent and bloody war, and continued their waiver and renunciation for decades afterward.

Legally, therefore, despite the Palestinian Arab long-standing effort to cast the inherently *political* conflict between themselves and the Israelis as a *legal* dispute, the Palestinian legal case on the merits is weak at best. The Palestinian Arabs, who themselves insisted there was no such entity as "Palestine" well into the 1940s,[1] did *not* obtain statehood from the League of Nations either pursuant to Article 22 of the League Covenant or under any provision of the Mandate for

Palestine. While the Mandate was still in effect, the Palestinians rejected *both* the British Government's offer of sovereignty in the May 1939 White Paper *and* the United Nations' offer of sovereignty less than a decade later.

Nor did the Palestinian Arabs obtain statehood when they briefly set up the Gaza-based "All Palestine" paper Government in October 1948. Nor did they obtain statehood between 1949 and 1967, when Jordan occupied the West Bank. Indeed, the Palestine Liberation Organisation included language in its founding Charter (1964) expressly *waiving* sovereignty over the West Bank and Gaza. Nor did the Palestinians acquire sovereignty after June 1967, when Israel replaced Jordan as the occupying power. The *only* claim to sovereignty the Palestinians made between 1922 and 1993 was over the *entirety* of Palestine, in derogation of the Mandate, Resolution 181(II) and international law.

Moreover, rejecting the two-state solution of 1947 and insisting on sovereignty over *all* of Palestine failed to preserve Palestinian Arab legal claims to the smaller *portion* of Palestine the United Nations had offered to them. The original Palestinian Charter of 1964 expressly reaffirmed their waiver of sovereignty over the West Bank and Gaza. The Palestinians deliberately opted for an all-or-nothing approach and ended up with nothing. The Palestinians thus lack *any* legal or equitable basis, after decades of renouncing the 1947 two-state solution through warfare and terrorism, to demand the originally offered and rejected two-state solution.

From a purely legal perspective, the Jewish people, whom the Romans violently ousted from their ancient homeland 2,000 years ago but who never gave up the dream of return, obtained international legal recognition in the Mandate for the "*reconstitution*" of their National Home in Palestine.

The local Arabs, on the other hand, who for decades insisted they were "southern Syrians" and not "Palestinians," and who rejected *every* offer of sovereignty – from the Peel Commission's offer in 1937 to Prime Minister Ehud Olmert's offer in 2006 – have a shaky legal claim to statehood, despite their success in transformationally framing the conflict as one grounded in victimhood and injustice.

Palestinian Arab "victimisation," therefore, rests entirely on the shoulders of the decisions their own leaders made for the last century, from the Mufti to Arafat to Abbas.

International law thus provides *no* support for Palestinian Arab legal claims of sovereignty over the West Bank, Gaza, and Jerusalem. Both the Covenant and the Mandate suspended sovereignty, and sovereignty over the Arab portion of Palestine has remained in abeyance ever since. As between the Palestinians, who renounced and waived sovereignty over the West Bank and Gaza in November 1947, and the Israelis, who have neither claimed nor waived sovereignty over the West Bank to the present day, the Israelis have a slightly better although not a perfected claim of *legal* title to the area.

Yet Palestinian transformational legal frame entrepreneurs have brilliantly exploited the world community's disregard of the historical facts and the associated legal consequences, successfully positioning Palestinian nationalism and the Palestinian people at the centre of the global social justice movement as the *victims* of ongoing "injustices" perpetrated against them.

The Israeli-Palestinian conflict, inherently political and not legal in nature, must be resolved through *political*, not judicial means. If the Palestinian Arabs deserve statehood in the West Bank and Gaza, despite rejecting it at every prior opportunity, it is *not* because they have any *legal* right to it, but instead because the two-state solution continues to represent perhaps the most viable long-term *political* outcome for the conflict. But the Palestinian insistence on invoking transformational legal framing and the "victimhood" narrative have become so overwhelmingly identified with Palestinian nationalism that little or no room remains for the hard work and serious diplomacy required for the future task of state-building.

★★★★★

Can any lessons be gleaned from the last century of Arab-Jewish legal battles and transformational legal framing? The answer seems clear: *the conflict ultimately must be addressed and resolved through diplomacy, not litigation.* Politics and diplomacy require far more skill, creativity, and nuanced thinking than lawfare. The sooner both sides realise this, the better for everyone, most especially their own people.

## Note

1 *See* S. Zipperstein, *op. cit.* at 4, 63–64.

# BIBLIOGRAPHY

## Books and articles


Abbas, M. (2017). *Lord Balfour's Burden*. Cairo Review of Global Affairs 27, 1–7.

Abdul Hadi, A. (1932). *The Balfour Declaration*. Annals of the American Academy of Political and Social Science 164:1, 12–21.

Adem, S. (2019). *Palestine and the International Criminal Court*. Berlin: Springer.

Adler, C. (1930). *Memorandum on the Western Wall Prepared for the Special Commission of the League of Nations on the Wailing Wall on Behalf of the Jewish Agency for Palestine*. Philadelphia, PA: Jewish Agency.

Agne, R. (2007). *Reframing Practices in Moral Conflict: Interaction Problems in the Negotiation Standoff at Waco*. Discourse and Society 18:5, 549–578.

Akram, S., *et al.* (eds.) (2011). *International Law and the Israeli-Palestinian Conflict: A Rights-Based Approach to Middle East Peace*. Abingdon: Routledge.

Alimi, E. (2007). *Israeli Politics and the First Palestinian Intifada: Political Opportunities, Framing Processes and Contentious Politics*. London; New York, NY: Routledge.

Allen, L.A. (2017). *Determining Emotions and the Burden of Proof in Investigative Commissions in Palestine*. Comparative Studies in Society and History 59:2, 385–414.

Allena, P. and Keller, A. (2006). *What Is a Just Peace?* Oxford: Oxford University Press.

Al-Omar, A.K. (ed.) (1999). *The Memoirs of Al-Haj Mohammed Amin Al-Husseini*. Damascus: Al-Ahly Press.

Amar-Dahl, T. (2017). *Zionist Israel and the Question of Palestine: Jewish Statehood and the History of the Middle East Conflict*. Berlin: De Gruyter.

Andrews, F. (1931). *The Holy Land under Mandate*. Westport, CT: Hyperion.

Anheier, H., *et al.* (1998). *Movement Cycles and the Nazi Party: Activities of the Munich NSDAP, 1925-1930*. American Behavioral Scientist 41:9, 1262–1281.

Antonius, G. (1939). *The Arab Awakening: The Story of the Arab National Movement*. Forest Grove, OR: Allegro.

Ash, R.W. (2009). *Is Palestine a State: A Response to Professor John Quigley's Article, the Palestine Declaration to the International Criminal Court*. The Rutgers Law Record 36, 186–200.

Bakan, A. and Abu-Laban, Y. (2009). *Palestinian Resistance and International Solidarity: The BDS Campaign*. Race & Class 51:1, 29–54.

Barghouti, O. (2014). *Opting for Justice: The Critical Role of Anti-Colonial Israelis in the Boycott, Divestment, and Sanctions Movement*. Settler Colonial Studies 4:4, 407–412.

Barghouti, O. (2015). *Upholding International Law, Asserting Palestinian Rights*. The Palestine Yearbook of International Law, Birzeit University Institute of Law 2013-2014: 15-40. Leiden: Brill Nijhoff.

Barnidge, R. (2016). *Palestinian Engagement with the International Criminal Court: From Preliminary Examination To Investigation?* The Journal of the Middle East and Africa 7:2, 109–123.

Bartal, S. (2017). *The Peel Commission Report of 1937 and the Origins of the Partition Concept*. Jerusalem: Jerusalem Center for Public Affairs.

Baumgart-Ochse, C. (2017). *Claiming Justice for Israel/Palestine: The Boycott, Divestment, Sanctions (BDS) Campaign and Christian Organizations*. Globalizations 14:7, 1172–1187.

Becker, A. (1988). *The United Nations and Israel: From Recognition to Reprehension*. Lexington, MA: Lexington Books.

Beckerman, C. (2020). *Unexpected State, British Politics and the Creation of Israel*. Bloomington, IN: Indiana University Press.

Bell, A. and Kontorovich, E. (2106). *Palestine, Uti Possidetis Juris, and the Borders of Israel*. Arizona Law Review 58, 633–692.

Ben-Arieh, Y. (2020). *The Making of Eretz Israel in the Modern Era: A Historical-Geographical Study (1799–1949)*. Berlin: De Gruyter and Jerusalem: Magnes.

Ben-Bassat, Y. (2013). *Petitioning the Sultan: Protests and Justice in Late Ottoman Palestine 1865–1908*. London; New York, NY: I.B. Tauris.

Ben-Dror, E. (2007). *The Arab Struggle against Partition: The International Arena of Summer 1947*. Middle Eastern Studies 43:2, 259–293.

Ben-Dror, E. (2008). *Ralph Bunche and the Establishment of Israel*. Israel Affairs 14:3, 519–537.

Ben-Dror, E. (2014). *The Success of the Zionist Strategy Vis-a-Vis UNSCOP*. Israel Affairs 20:1, 19–39.

Ben-Gurion, D. (1971). *Letters to Paula*. Pittsburgh, PA: University of Pittsburgh Press.

Ben-Gurion, D. (1973). *My Talks with Arab Leaders*. New York, NY: The Third Press.

Benford, R. and Snow, D. (2000). *Framing Processes and Social Movements: An Overview and Assessment*. Annual Review of Sociology 26, 611–639.

Benoliel, D. and Perry, R. (2010). *Israel, Palestine and the ICC*. Michigan Journal of International Law 32:1, 73–127.

Bentwich, N. (1929). *Judicial Interpretation of the Mandate for Palestine*. Zeitschrift für Ausländisches Öffentliches Recht und Völkerrecht 1:1, 212–222.

Bentwich, N. (1932). *England in Palestine*. London: Kegan Paul.

Bentwich, N. and Bentwich, H. (1965). *Mandate Memories 1918-1948*. New York, NY: Schocken.

Benvenisti, E. (2017). *An Article that Changed the Course of History*. Israel Law Review 50:3, 269–298.

Bethell, N. (1979). *The Palestine Triangle: The Struggle for the Holy's Land, 1935-1948*. New York, NY: G.P. Putnam's Sons.

Bishara, A. (2003). *House and Homeland: Examining Sentiments about and Claims to Jerusalem and Its Houses*. Social Text 21:2, 141–162.

Blizzard, E. (2017). *Peace Journalism in Palestine's BDS Campaign*. Peace Review: A Journal of Social Justice 29:4, 467–474.

Blum, Y.Z. (1968). *The Missing Reversioner: Reflections on the Status of Judea and Samaria*. Israel Law Review 3:2, 279–301.

Blum, Y.Z. (2018). *The Status of Judea and Samaria Revisited: A Response to Eyal Benvenisti*. Israel Law Review 51:2, 165–168.

Blum, S. (2019). *Between the Lion Cub of Judea and the British Lion: Cause Lawyers, British Rule and National Struggle in Mandatory Palestine*. Comparative Legal History 7:1, 2–36.

Bosco, D. (2016). *Palestine in the Hague: Justice, Geopolitics, and the International Criminal Court*. Global Governance 22, 155–171.

Boustany, W.F. (1936). *The Palestine Mandate Invalid and Impracticable: A Contribution of Arguments and Documents towards the Solution of the Palestine Problem*. Beirut: American Press.

Boyle, F. (1990). *The Creation of the State of Palestine*. European Journal of International Law 1:1, 301–306.

Brierly, J.L. (1963). *The Law of Nations: An Introduction to the International Law of Peace* (6th ed.). Oxford; New York, NY: Oxford University Press.

Brownlie, I. (1973). *Principles of Public International Law* (2nd ed.). Oxford: Oxford University Press.

Bullock, A. (1983). *Ernest Bevin: Foreign Secretary 1945-1951*. London: Heinemann.

Burgis-Kasthala, M.L. (2014). *Overstating Palestine's UN Membership Bid? An Ethnographic Study on the Narratives of Statehood*. European Journal of International Law 25:3, 677–701.

Cammarata, M. (2010). *La Palestina Del Mandato Nell'Editoria Italiana, 1918–1939*. Trieste: Edizioni Universita di Trieste.

Capek, S. (1993). *The "Environmental Justice" Frame: A Conceptual Discussion and an Application*. Social Problems 40:1, 5–24.

Caplan, N. (1978). *Palestine Jewry and the Arab Question, 1917–1925*. London: Frank Cass.

Caplan, N. (1983). *Futile Diplomacy: Early Arab-Zionist Negotiation Attempts, 1913–1931*. London: Frank Cass.

Carroll, W. and Ratner, R. (1996). *Master Frames and Counter-Hegemony: Political Sensibilities in Contemporary Social Movements*. Canadian Review of Sociology and Anthropology 33:4, 407–435.

Cattan, H. (1969). *Palestine, the Arabs and Israel: The Search for Justice*. London; New York, NY: Longmans.

Cattan, H. (1973). *Palestine and International Law: The Legal Aspects of the Arab-Israeli Conflict* (2nd ed.). London; New York, NY: Longmans.

Cohen, M.J. (1973). *Appeasement in the Middle East: The British White Paper on Palestine*. The Historical Journal 16:3, 571–596.

Cohen, M.J. (1976). *The British White Paper on Palestine, May 1939. Part II: The Testing of a Policy, 1942–1945*. The Historical Journal 19:3, 727–757.

Cohen, M.J. (1978). *Palestine: Retreat from the Mandate, the Making of British Policy, 1936–45*. New York, NY: Holmes and Meier.

Cohen, M.J. (1979). *The Genesis of the Anglo-American Committee on Palestine, November 1945: A Case Study in the Assertion of American Hegemony*. The Historical Journal 22:1, 185–207.

Cohen, M.J. (1982). *Palestine and the Great Powers, 1945–1948*. Princeton, NJ: Princeton University Press.

Cohen, M.J. (ed.) (1987a). *The Rise of Israel*. New York, NY; London: Garland.

Cohen, M.J. (1987b). *The Origins and Evolution of the Arab-Zionist Conflict*. Berkeley, CA; Los Angeles, CA; London: University of California Press.

Cohen, N. (1988). *The Year after the Riots: American Responses to the Palestine Crisis of 1929–30*. Detroit: Wayne State University Press.

Cohen, M.J. (1990). *Truman and Israel*. Berkeley, CA: University of California Press.

Cohen, H. (2008). *Army of Shadows: Palestinians and Collaboration with Zionism, 1917–1948*. Berkeley, CA; Los Angeles, CA; London: University of California Press.

Cohen, M.J. (2014). *Britain's Moment in Palestine: Retrospect and Perspectives, 1917–48*. Abingdon; New York, NY: Routledge.

Cohen, H. (2015). *Year Zero of the Arab Israeli Conflict: 1929*. Detroit: Wayne State University Press.

Cohen, M. and Freilich, C. (2018). *War by Other Means: The Delegitimisation Campaign against Israel*. Israel Affairs 24:1, 1–25.

Cover, R. (1983). *Nomos and Narrative*. Harvard Law Review 97:1, 4–69.

Crawford, J. (1990). *The Creation of the State of Palestine: Too Much Too Soon*. European Journal of International Law 1:1, 307–313.

Crawford, J. (2006). *The Creation of States in International Law* (2nd ed.). Oxford: Oxford University Press.

Crossman, R. (1946). *Palestine Mission*. London: Hamish Hamilton.

Crum, B. (1947). *Behind the Silken Curtain: A Personal Account of Anglo-American Diplomacy in Palestine and the Middle East*. New York, NY: Simon & Schuster.

Cust, L.G.A. (1927). *Jerusalem, the Status Quo, Its Origin and History Till the Present Time*. Oxford: Bodleian Libraries. Jerusalem: High Commission. Chancellor Papers, MSS. Brit. Emp. S.284, Box 24/2.

Dajani, O. (1997). *Stalled between the Seasons: The International Legal Status of Palestine During the Interim Period*. Denver Journal of International Law and Policy 26, 27–92.

De Blois, M. (2016). *The Unique Character of the Mandate for Palestine*. Israel Law Review 49:3, 365–389.

De Bruycker, I. (2017). *Framing and Advocacy: A Research Agenda for Interest Group Studies*. Journal of European Public Policy 24:5, 775–787.

Derrida, J. (1992). *Acts of Literature*. New York, NY; London: Routledge.

Derrida, J. (1994). *Specters of Marx: The State of the Debt, the Work of Mourning and the New International*. New York, NY; London: Routledge.

Dershowitz, A. (2011). *Countering Challenges to Israel's Legitimacy*. Jerusalem: Jerusalem Center for Public Affairs.

Destani, B. (ed.) (2004). *The Zionist Movement and the Foundation of Israel, 1839–1972*. Cambridge: Archive Editions.

Dinnerstein, L. (1980). *America, Britain, and Palestine: The Anglo-American Committee of Inquiry and the Displaced Persons, 1945–46*. Diplomatic History 4:3, 283–301.

Dresner, C. and Litvinoff, B. (eds.) (1978). *The Letters and Papers of Chaim Weizmann*. New Brunswick: Transaction.

Dugard, J. (2013). *Palestine and the International Criminal Court: Institutional Failure or Bias*. Journal of International Criminal Justice 11, 563–570.

Eddy, W.A. (1954). *FDR Meets Ibn Saud*. New York, NY: American Friends of the Middle East, Inc..

Eddy, W.A. (1963). *King Ibn Sa'ūd: Our Faith and Your Iron*. Middle East Journal 17:3, 257–263.

Elaraby, N. (1968). *Some Legal Implications of the 1947 Partition Resolution and the 1949 Armistice Agreements*. Law and Contemporary Problems 33:1, 97–109.

Elaraby, N. (2017). *Palestine and the Law of Nations*. Cairo Review of Global Affairs 27, 47–57.

Elgindy, K. (2011). *Palestine Goes to the UN: Understanding the New Statehood Strategy*. Foreign Affairs, 90:5, 102–113.

Elipeleg, Z. (1989). *Why Was "Independent Palestine" Never Created?* Jerusalem Quarterly 50, 3–22.

Elipeleg, Z. (2009). *Through the Eyes of the Mufti: The Essays of Haj Amin Al Husseini Translated and Annotated*. London: Valentine Mitchell.

Elmendorf, D. (1912). *A Camera Crusade through the Holy Land*. New York, NY: C. Scribner's & Sons.

Entman, R.M. (1993). *Framing: Toward Clarification of a Fractured Paradigm*. Journal of Communication 43:4, 51–58.

Epstein, L. (2016). *The Dream of Zion: The Story of the First Zionist Congress*. Lanham, MD: Rowman & Littlefield.

Erakat, N. (2019). *Justice for Some: Law and the Question of Palestine*. Stanford, CA: Stanford University Press.

ESCO Foundation for Palestine. (1947). *Palestine, a Study of Jewish, Arab and British Policies*. New Haven, CT: Yale University Press.

Evatt, H.G. (1949). *The Task of Nations*. New York, NY: Duell, Sloan and Pearce.

Feinberg, N. (1970). *The Arab-Israel Conflict in International Law: A Critical Analysis of the Colloquium of Arab Jurists in Algiers*. Jerusalem, Magnes Press.

Frankfurter, F. (1931). *The Palestine Situation Restated*. Foreign Affairs 9:3, 409–434.

Friedman, I. (1970). *The McMahon-Hussein Correspondence and the Question of Palestine*. Journal of Contemporary History 5:2, 83–122.

Friedman, I. (1973a). *The Question of Palestine, 1914–1918: British-Arab-Jewish Relations*. New York, NY: Schocken.

Friedman, I. (1973b). *The Response to the Balfour Declaration*. Jewish Social Studies 35:2, 105–124.

Friedman, I. (1999). *Palestine, A Twice Promised Land? The British, the Arabs and Zionism 1915–1920*. New Brunswick: Transaction.

Fromkin, D. (1989). *A Peace to End All Peace: The Fall of the Empire and the Creation of the Modern Middle East*. New York, NY: Henry Holt.

Galnoor, I. (1991). *Territorial Partition of Palestine: The 1937 Decision*. Political Geography Quarterly 10:4, 382–404.

Galnoor, I. (2009). *The Zionist Debates on Partition (1919–1947)*. Israel Studies 14:2, 74–87.

Gamson, W., *et al.* (1982). *Encounters with Unjust Authority*. Homewood, IL: Dorsey Press.

Gamson, W. (1992). *Talking Politics*. Cambridge: Cambridge University Press.

Garcia Granados, J. (1948). *The Birth of Israel: The Drama as I Saw It*. New York, NY: Alfred A. Knopf.

Gardiner, R. (2015). *Treaty Interpretation* (2nd ed.). Oxford; New York, NY: Oxford University Press.

Gavison, R. (ed.) (2103). *The Two-State Solution: The UN Partition Resolution of Mandatory Palestine*. New York, NY; London: Bloomsbury Academic Press.

Gendzier, I. (2011). *U.S. Policy in Israel/Palestine, 1948: The Forgotten History*. Middle East Policy, 18:1, 42–53.

Gerber, H. (2008). *Remembering and Imagining Palestine: Identity and Nationalism from the Crusades to the Present*. Basingstoke: Palgrave Macmillan.

Gerson, A. (1973). *Trustee-Occupant: The Legal Status of Israel's Presence in the West Bank*. Harvard International Law Journal 14, 1–49.

Gerson, A. (1978). *Israel, the West Bank and International Law*. London: Frank Kass.

Ghandour, Z. (2010). *A Discourse on Domination in Mandate Palestine: Imperialism, Property and Insurgency*. Abingdon: Routledge.

Gilbert, M. (2012). *The Routledge Atlas of the Arab-Israeli Conflict* (10th ed.). Abingdon; New York, NY: Routledge.

Gillan, K. (2008). *Understanding Meaning in Movements: A Hermeneutic Approach to Frames and Ideologies*. Social Movement Studies 7:3, 247–263.

Glick, E. (1959). *Latin America and the Palestine Partition Resolution*. Journal of Inter-American Studies 1:2, 211–222.

Goda, N., *et al.* (2015). *To the Gates of Jerusalem: The Diaries and Papers of James G. McDonald, 1945-1947*. Bloomington, IN: Indiana University Press.

Goffman, E. (1974). *Frame Analysis: An Essay on the Organization of Experience*. New York, NY: Harper Colophon.

Golani, M. (2013). *Palestine between Politics and Terror*. Waltham, MA: Brandeis University Press.

Goldmann, N. (1969). *The Autobiography of Nahum Goldmann: Sixty Years of Jewish Life.* New York, NY: Holt, Rinehart and Winston.

Grant, T. (1999). *Defining Statehood: The Montevideo Convention and Its Discontents.* Columbia Journal of Transnational Law 37:2, 403–45.

Grantham, D. (2019). *Argentina, the Arab World, and the Partition of Palestine, 1946–1947.* Journal of Global South Studies 36:1, 88–115.

Graves, P. (1923). *Palestine, the Land of Three Faiths.* London: J. Cape.

Gribetz, L. (1930). *The Case for the Jews: An Interpretation of Their Rights under the Balfour Declaration and the Mandate for Palestine.* New York, NY: Bloch.

Grief, H. (2008). *The Legal Foundation and Borders of Israel under International Law.* Jerusalem: Mazo.

Haiduc-Dalen, N. (2013). *Arab Christians in British Mandate Palestine: Communalism and Nationalism, 1917–1948.* Edinburgh: Edinburgh University Press.

Haim, Y. (1978). *Zionist Attitudes toward Partition, 1937–1938.* Jewish Social Studies 40:3, 303–320.

Handmaker, J. (2015). *Taking Academic Freedom Seriously: Exploring the Legal and Moral Underpinnings of BDS.* Leiden: Brill Nijhoff. The Palestine Yearbook of International Law, Birzeit University Institute of Law 2013-2014: 101–14.

Haron, M.J. (1982). *Palestine and the Anglo-American Connection.* Modern Judaism 2:2, 199–211.

Harpaz, G. (2015). *When Does a Court Systematically Deviate from Its Own Principles? The Adjudication by the Israel Supreme Court of House Demolitions in the Occupied Palestinian Territories.* Leiden Journal of International Law 28:1, 31–47.

Hatoum, N.A. (2017). *Framing Visual Politics: Photography of the Wall in Palestine.* Visual Anthropology Review, 33:1, 18–27.

Hattis, S. (1970). *The Bi-National Idea in Palestine during Mandatory Times.* Haifa: Shikmona.

Heidborn, A. (1908). *Manuel De Droit Public Et Administratif De l'Empire Ottoman.* Vienna: C.W. Stern.

Heller, J. (1982). *The Anglo-American Commission of Inquiry on Palestine (1945-1946): The Zionist Reaction Reconsidered.* In E. Kedourie and S. Haim (eds.). Zionism and Arabism in Palestine and Israel. Abingdon: Frank Cass and Co. Ltd.

Herf, J. (2014). *Haj Amin Al-Husseini, the Nazis and the Holocaust: The Origins, Nature and Aftereffects of Collaboration.* Jewish Political Studies Review 26:3/4, 13–37.

Hershco, T. (2006). *Le Grand Mufti De Jérusalem En France: Histoire d'Une Evasion.* Controverses 1, 244–273.

Hershco, T. (2008). *France and the Partition Plan: 1947–1948.* Israel Affairs 14:3, 486–498.

Hollis, R. (2016). *Palestine and the Palestinians in British Political Elite Discourse: From 'The Palestine Problem' to 'The Two-State Solution'.* International Relations 30:1, 3–28.

Horowitz, D. (1953). *State in the Making.* New York, NY: Alfred A. Knopf.

Hughes, M. (2010). *From Law and Order to Pacification: Britain's Suppression of the Arab Revolt in Palestine, 1936–39.* Journal of Palestine Studies 39:2, 6–22.

Huneidi, S. (1998). *Was Balfour Reversible, the Colonial Office and Palestine, 1921-23.* Journal of Palestine Studies 27:2, 23–41.

Huneidi, S. (2001). *A Broken Trust: Herbert Samuel, Zionism and the Palestinians.* New York, NY: I.B. Tauris.

Hurevitz, J.C. (1976). *The Struggle for Palestine.* New York, NY: Schocken Books.

Husseini, H. (2008). *A "Middle Power" in Action: Canada and the Partition of Palestine.* Arab Studies Quarterly 30:3, 41–55.

Hutcheson, J.C. (1929). *The Judgment Intuitive: The Function of the Hunch in Judicial Decision.* Cornell Law Review 14:3, 274–288.

Jager, E. (2018). *The Balfour Declaration: Sixty Seven Words, One Hundred Years of Conflict*. Jerusalem: Geffen.

Jeffries, J.M.N. (1938). *Palestine: The Reality*. London: Longmans, Green.

Jones, A.P. (1979). *Britain and Palestine, 1914-1948: Archival Sources for the History of the British Mandate*. Oxford: Oxford University Press for the British Academy.

Jones, M. (1986). *Failure in Palestine: British and United States Policy after the Second World War*. London: Bloomsbury.

Ju'Beh, N. (2001). *Jewish Settlement in the Old City of Jerusalem after 1967*. Palestine-Israel Journal of Politics, Economics, and Culture VIII 1, 48–54.

Junk, W.M. and Rasmussen, A. (2019). *Framing by the Flock: Collective Issue Definition and Advocacy Success*. Comparative Political Studies 52:4, 483–513.

Karlinsky, M. (1990). *Premeditation in the Palestine Disturbances of August 1929?* Middle East Studies 26:1, 18–34.

Karlinsky, M. (1993). *Law, Order and Riots in Mandatory Palestine, 1928–35*. Basingstoke: Macmillan; New York, NY: St. Martin's Press.

Karsh, E. (1999). *The Collusion That Never Was: King Abdallah, the Jewish Agency and the Partition of Palestine*. Journal of Contemporary History 34:4, 569–585.

Karsh, E. (2008). *Zionism and the Palestinians*. Israel Affairs 14:3, 355–373.

Karsh, E. (2010). *Palestine Betrayed*. New Haven, CT: Yale University Press.

Karsh, E. (2014). *Palestinian Leaders Don't Want an Independent State*. Middle East Quarterly 21:3, 1–11.

Kattan, V. (2009). *From Coexistence to Conquest: International Law and the Origins of the Arab-Israeli Conflict 1891–1949*. New York, NY: Pluto.

Kattan, V. (2014). *The Implications of Joining the ICC after Operation Protective Edge*. Journal of Palestine Studies, 44:1, 61–73.

Kedourie, E. (1976). *In the Anglo-Arab Labyrinth: The McMahon-Husayn Correspondence and Its Interpretations 1914–1939*. London; Portland: Frank Cass.

Kedourie, E. and Haim, S. (eds.) (1982). *Zionism and Arabism in Palestine and Israel*. Abingdon: Frank Cass.

Kelsen, H. (1951). *The Law of the United Nations: A Critical Analysis of Its Fundamental Problems*. London: Stevens & Sons.

Khader, N. (2014). *Interview with Noura Erakat: Framing the Palestinian Narrative*. Journal of Palestine Studies 44:1, 106–117.

Khalidi, R. (2006). *The Iron Cage: The Story of the Palestinian Struggle for Statehood*. Boston: Beacon Press.

Khalidi, W. (2005). *On Albert Hourani, the Arab Office, and the Anglo-American Committee of 1946*. Journal of Palestine Studies 35:1, 60–79.

Kisch, F.H. (1938). *Palestine Diary*. New York, NY: AMS Press. Reprint from London: Victor Gollancz.

Kittrie, O. (2016). *Lawfare: Law as a Weapon of War*. New York, NY: Oxford University Press.

Klein, C. (2005). *Zionism Revisited*. Israel Affairs 11:1, 238–253.

Klieman, A. (ed.) (1987). *The Rise of Israel: A Documentary Record from the Nineteenth Century to* 1948. New York, NY: Garland.

Kochavi, A. (1998). *The Struggle against Jewish Immigration to Palestine*. Middle Eastern Studies, 34:3, 146–167.

Kohen, M. and Hebie, M. (2018). *Research Handbook on Territorial Disputes in International Law*. Cheltenham: Edward Elgar.

Kontorovich, E. (2013). *Israel/Palestine – The ICC's Uncharted Territory*. Journal of International Criminal Justice 11:5, 979–999.

Kontorovich, E. (2014). *When Gravity Fails: Israeli Settlements and Admissibility at the ICC.* Israel Law Review 47:3, 379–399.

Kramer, G. (2008). *A History of Palestine: From the Ottoman Conquest to the Founding of the State of Israel.* Princeton, NJ; Oxford: Princeton University Press.

Kretzmer, D. (2012). *The Law of Belligerent Occupation in the Supreme Court of Israel.* International Review of the Red Cross 94:885, 207–236.

Lahav, P. (1997). *Judgment in Jerusalem: Chief Justice Simon Agranat and the Zionist Century.* Berkeley, CA; London: University of California Press.

Lapidoth, R. and Hirsch, M. (eds.) (1992). *The Arab-Israeli Conflict and Its Resolution: Selected Documents.* Dordrecht; Boston, MA; London: Martinus Nijhoff Publishers.

Laurens, H. (2002). *La Question Du Palestine.* Paris: Fayard.

Leachman, G. (2013). *Legal Framing.* Studies in Law, Politics and Society 61, 25–59.

Lee, H. (2016). *Defining State for the Purpose of the International Criminal Court: The Problem Ahead after the Palestine Decision.* University of Pittsburgh Law Review 77:3, 345–384.

Lemire, V. (2011). *The Awakening of Palestinian Hydropolitical Consciousness: The Artas Jerusalem Water Conflict of 1925.* Jerusalem Quarterly 48, 31–53.

Lesch, A.M. (1979). *Arab Politics in Palestine, 1917–1939: The Frustration of a Nationalist Movement.* Ithaca, NY: Cornell University Press.

Likhovski, A. (2006). *Law and Identity in Mandate Palestine.* Chapel Hill, NC: University of North Carolina Press.

Litvinoff, B. and Rose, N. (eds.) (1980). *The Letters and Papers of Chaim Weizmann, Series A, Letters.* Piscataway, NJ: Transaction; Jerusalem: Israel Universities Press.

Loeffler, J. (2018). *Rooted Cosmopolitans: Jews and Human Rights in the Twentieth Century.* New Haven, CT: Yale University Press.

Loevy, K. (2016). *Reinventing a Region (1915-22): Visions of the Middle East in Legal and Diplomatic Texts Leading to the Palestine Mandate.* Israel Law Review 49:3, 309–337.

Long, C.W.R. (2018). *The Palestinians and British Perfidy: The Tragic Aftermath of the Balfour Declaration of 1917.* Brighton; Portland; Toronto: Sussex.

Louis, W. and Stookey, R. (eds.) (1986). *The End of the Palestine Mandate.* Austin, TX: University of Texas Press.

Lundsten, M.E. (1978). *Wall Politics: Zionist and Palestinian Strategies in Jerusalem, 1928.* Journal of Palestine Studies 8:1, 3–27.

Lustick, I. (2000). *Yerushalayim and Al-Quds: Political Catechism and Political Realities.* Journal of Palestine Studies 30:1, 5–21

Mallison, W. and Mallison, S. (1974). *The Role of International Law in Achieving Justice and Peace in Palestine-Israel.* Journal of Palestine Studies 3:3, 77–87.

Mallison, S. and Mallison, W.T. (1984). *The Juridical Basis for Palestinian Self-Determination. The Palestine Yearbook of International Law.* Nicosia: al-Shaybani Society of International Law Ltd.

Mallison, W. and Mallison, S. (1986). *The Palestine Problem: International Law and World Order.* Harlow: Longman.

Mandel, D. (2004). *H.G. Evatt and the Establishment of Israel: The Undercover Zionist.* London: Frank Cass.

Mann, P. (1975). *Ralph Bunche: UN Peacemaker.* New York, NY: Coward, McCann & Geoghegan.

Maoz, M. (2002). *The UN Partition Resolution of 1947: Why Was It Not Implemented?* Palestine-Israel Journal of Politics, Economics, and Culture 9:4, 15–30.

Marlowe, J. (1959). *The Seat of Pilate: An Account of the Palestine Mandate.* London: Cresset Press.

Marshall, A.M. (2003). *Injustice Frames, Legality, and the Everyday Construction of Sexual Harassment.* Law & Social Inquiry 28:3, 659–689.

Mattar, P. (1983). *The Role of the Mufti of Jerusalem in the Political Struggle over the Western Wall, 1928-29.* Middle East Studies 19:1, 104–118.

Mattar, P. (1992). *The Mufti of Jerusalem: Haj Amin Al Husseini and the Palestinian National Movement.* New York, NY: Columbia University Press.

Matthew, W. (2014). *The Palestine Deception, 1915–1923: The McMahon-Hussein Correspondence, the Balfour Declaration, and the Jewish National Home.* Washington, DC: Institute for Palestine Studies.

Matthews, W. (2003). *Pan-Islam or Arab Nationalism? The Meaning of the 1931 Jerusalem Islamic Congress Reconsidered.* International Journal of Middle East Studies 35:1, 1–22.

Mazzawi, M. (1997). *Palestine and the Law: Guidelines for the Resolution of the Arab-Israeli Conflict.* Reading: Garnet.

McKee, E. (2018). *Environmental Framing and Its Limits: Campaigns in Palestine and Israel.* International Journal of Middle East Studies 50:3, 449–470.

McMahon, S. (2014). *The Boycott, Divestment, Sanctions Campaign: Contradictions and Challenges.* Race & Class 55:4, 65–81.

McTague, J. (1978). *The British Military Administration in Palestine 1917-1920.* Journal of Palestine Studies 7:3, 55–76.

Meir, G. (1975). *My Life.* London: Cox and Wyman Ltd.

Miller, R. (2010). *Britain, Palestine and Empire: The Mandate Years.* Farnham: Ashgate.

Montell, J. (2016). *Learning from What Works: Strategic Analysis of the Achievements of the Israel-Palestine Human Rights Community.* Human Rights Quarterly 38:4, 928–968.

Moore, J.N. (1974). *The Arab-Israeli Conflict.* Princeton, NJ: Princeton University Press.

Morris, B. (1987). *The Birth of the Palestinian Refugee Problem, 1947-1949.* Cambridge: Cambridge University Press.

Muller, P. and Slominski, P. (2019). *Legal Framing and the EU's External Relations: How NGOs Shaped the Negotiations for an Israel-Europol Cooperation Agreement.* Journal of European Public Policy 26:6, 906–926.

Muslih, M. (1988). *The Origins of Palestinian Nationalism.* New York, NY: Columbia University Press.

Nachmani, A. (1987). *Great Power Discord in Palestine: The Anglo-American Committee of Inquiry into the Problems of European Jewry and Palestine, 1945-1946.* London; New York, NY: Routledge.

Nasrallah, R. (2002). *The Road to Partition. Palestine-Israel Journal of Politics, Economics & Culture* 9:4, 58–66.

Nevo, J. (1987). *The Arabs of Palestine, 1947-48: Military and Political Activity.* Middle Eastern Studies 23:1, 3–38.

Ofer, P. (1985). *The Commission on the Palestine Disturbances of August 1929: Appointment, Terms of Reference, Procedure and Report.* Middle Eastern Studies 21:3, 349–361.

Omer, A. (2009). *'It's Nothing Personal:' The Globalisation of Justice, the Transferability of Protest, and the Case of the Palestine Solidarity Movement.* Studies in Ethnicity and Nationalism 9:3, 497–518.

Oppenheim, B. and Lauterpacht, H. (eds.) (1955). *International Law: A Treatise* (8th ed.). London: Longmans, Green.

Orzeck, R. (2015). *The Jewish Agency's Case before the UNSCOP: Image and Discourse.* Jerusalem Quarterly 63/64, 7–23.

Ottolenghi, M. (2004). *Harry Truman's Recognition of Israel.* The Historical Journal, 47:4, 963–988.

Ovendale, R. (1989). *Britain, the United States, and the End of the Palestine Mandate: 1942–1948.* Woodbridge; Wolfeboro, NH: Royal Historical Society; Boydell Press.

Ovendale, R. (2004). *The Origins of the Arab-Israeli Wars* (4th ed.). Harlow; New York, NY: Pearson Longman.

Palestine Information Center. (2017). *Al-Buraq Wall: Targeted Historical Identity.*

Pappe, I. (2004). *A History of Modern Palestine: One Land, Two Peoples.* Cambridge: Cambridge University Press.

Pappe, I. (2015). *The Framing of the Question of Palestine by the Early Palestinian Press: Zionist Settler-Colonialism and the Newspaper Filastin, 1912–1922.* Journal of Holy Land and Palestine Studies 14:1, 59–81.

Pedersen, S. (2010). *Getting Out of Iraq in 1932: The League of Nations and the Road to Normative Statehood.* The American Historical Review 115:4, 975–1000.

Pedriana, N. (2006). *From Protective to Equal Treatment: Legal Framing Processes and Transformation of the Women's Movement in the 1960s.* The American Journal of Sociology 111:6, 1718–1761.

Penkower, M.N. (2016). *The Earl Harrison Report: Its Genesis and Its Significance.* The American Jewish Archives Journal 68:1, 1–75.

Penkower, M.N. (2019). *Palestine to Israel, Mandate to State, 1945-1948, Volume I: Rebellion Launched.* New York, NY: Touro University Press.

Peteet, J. (2016). *Language Matters: Talking About Palestine.* Journal of Palestine Studies 45:2, 24–40.

Phillips, W. (1953). *Ventures in Diplomacy.* Boston, MA: Beacon Press.

Plascov, A. (1981). *The Palestinian Refugees in Jordan, 1948-1957.* London: Frank Cass.

Podet, A.H. (1986). *The Success and Failure of the Anglo-American Committee of Inquiry, 1945–1946: Last Chance in Palestine.* Lewiston, ME: Edwin Mellen Press.

Porath, Y. (1974). *The Emergence of the Palestinian-Arab National Movement, 1918–1929.* London; Portland: Frank Cass.

Porath, Y. (1977). *The Palestinian Arab National Movement: From Riots to Rebellion, 1929–1939.* London: Routledge.

Priestland, J. (ed.) (2002). *Records of Jerusalem 1917-1971.* Cambridge: Cambridge University Press, Archive Editions.

Quigley, J. (1990). *Palestine and Israel, a Challenge to Justice.* Durham; London: Duke University Press.

Quigley, J. (2005). *The Case for Palestine: An International Law Perspective.* Durham: Duke University Press.

Quigley, J. (2009). *Palestine Statehood: A Rejoinder to Professor Robert Weston Ash.* The Rutgers Law Record 36, 257–263.

Quigley, J. (2010). *The Statehood of Palestine: International Law in the Middle East Conflict.* Cambridge: Cambridge University Press.

Quigley, J. (2011). *Palestine Is a State: A Horse with Black and White Stripes Is a Zebra.* Michigan Journal of International Law 32:4, 749–764.

Radosh, R. and Radosh, R. (2009). *A Safe Haven, Harry S. Truman and the Founding of Israel* New York, NY: Harper Collins.

Regan, B. (2017). *The Balfour Declaration: Empire, the Mandate and Resistance in Palestine.* London; New York, NY: Verso.

Reichman, S., *et al.* (1997). *The Absorptive Capacity of Palestine, 1882-1948.* Middle Eastern Studies 33:2, 33–361.

Reiter, Y. (2017). *Contested Holy Places in Israel-Palestine: Sharing and Conflict Resolution.* Abingdon; New York, NY: Routledge.

Rettig, E. and Avraham, E. (2016). *The Role of Intergovernmental Organizations in the "Battle Over Framing:" The Case of the Israeli–West Bank Separation Barrier.* International Journal of Press/Politics 21:1, 111–133.

Reynold, N. (2014). *Britain's Unfulfilled Mandate for Palestine.* Lanham, MD: Lexington Books.

Rhett, M. (2016). *The Global History of the Balfour Declaration: Declared Nation.* New York, NY; London: Routledge.

Riedel, B. (2019). *Kings and Presidents: Saudi Arabia and the United States since FDR.* Washington, DC: Brookings.

Rizk, E. (1968). *The Palestine Question, Seminar of Arab Jurists on Palestine, Algiers, 22–27 July, 1967.* Beirut: Institute for Palestine Studies.

Roberts, N. (2017). *Islam under the Palestine Mandate: Colonialism and the Supreme Muslim Council.* London; New York, NY: I.B. Tauris.

Robinson, J. (1947). *Palestine and the United Nations.* Washington, DC: Public Affairs Press.

Rogan, E. (2015). *The Fall of the Ottomans: The Great War in the Middle East.* New York, NY: Basic Books.

Roosevelt, K. (1948). *The Partition of Palestine: A Lesson in Pressure Politics.* The Middle East Journal 2:1, 1–16.

Rose, N. (1973). *The Gentile Zionists: A Study in Anglo-American Diplomacy, 1929–1939.* London: Frank Cass.

Rose, N. (1986). *Chaim Weizmann: A Biography.* New York, NY: Viking Penguin.

Royal Institute of International Affairs. (1946). *Great Britain and Palestine, 1915–1945.* Welwyn Garden City: Broadwater Press.

Sabel, R. (2005). *The Status of the Territories: The International Court of Justice Decision on the Separation Barrier and the Green Line.* Israel Law Review 38, 316–378.

Said, E. (1979a). *The Question of Palestine.* New York, NY: Random House.

Said, E. (1979b). *Zionism from the Standpoint of Its Victims.* Social Text 1, 7–58.

Said, E. (1994). *The Politics of Dispossession: The Struggle for Palestinian Self-Determination, 1969–1994.* New York, NY: Pantheon Books.

Said, E. (2006). *A Method for Thinking About Just Peace.* In P. Allan and A. Keller (eds.). *What is a Just Peace?* Oxford: Oxford University Press.

Salem, W. (2002). *Legitimization or Implementation: On the UN Partition Plan.* Palestine-Israel Journal of Politics, Economics and Culture 9:4, 7–14.

Samuel, M. (1929). *What Happened in Palestine: The Events of August 1929, Their Background and Their Significance.* Boston, MA: Stratford.

Samuel, H. (1930). *Beneath the Whitewash, a Critical Analysis of the Report of the Commission on the Palestine Disturbances of August, 1929.* London: Leonard and Virginia Woolf at the Hogarth Press.

Samuel, M.T. (2014). *Punitive House Demolitions in the West Bank: The Hague Regulations, Geneva Convention IV, and a Jus Cogens Bypass.* Berkeley Journal of Middle Eastern and Islamic Law 6:1, 1–24.

Sanger, C. (1995). *Malcolm MacDonald: Bringing an End to Empire.* Montreal: McGill-Queen's University Press.

Scham, P., *et al.* (2002). *Roundtable Discussion: Narratives of 1948.* Palestine – Israel Journal of Politics, Economics, and Culture 9:4, 22–38.

Schlosberg, D. (2013). *Theorising Environmental Justice: The Expanding Sphere of a Discourse.* Environmental Politics 22:1, 37–55.

Schneer, J. (2010). *The Balfour Declaration: The Origins of the Arab-Israeli Conflict.* London; Berlin; New York, NY: Bloomsbury.

Schorr, D. (2014). *Water Law in British-Ruled Palestine.* Water History 6, 247–263.

Schwebel, S. (1979). *The Effect of Resolutions of the U.N. General Assembly on Customary International Law*. Proceedings of the Annual Meeting (American Society of International Law) 73, 301–309.

Segev, T. (1999). *One Palestine, Complete: Jews and Arabs under the British Mandate*. New York, NY: Henry Holt & Co.

Segev, T. (2005). *1967: Israel, the War, and the Year That Transformed the Middle East*. New York, NY: Henry Holt & Co.

Segev, T. (2019). *A State at Any Cost: The Life of David Ben-Gurion*. New York, NY: Farrar, Straus and Giroux.

Sela, A. (1992). *Transjordan, Israel and the 1948 War: Myth, Historiography and Reality*. Middle Eastern Studies 28:4, 632–688.

Seller, M. (1968). *Isaac Leeser's Views on the Restoration of a Jewish Palestine*. American Jewish Historical Quarterly 58:1, 118–135.

Shamir, R. (1990). *"Landmark Cases" and the Reproduction of Legitimacy: The Case of Israel's High Court of Justice*. Law and Society Review 24:3, 781–806.

Shany, Y. (2016). *Legal Entitlements, Changing Circumstances and Intertemporality: A Comment on the Creation of Israel and the Status of Palestine*. Israel Law Review 49:3, 391–408.

Sharon, A. (2011). *Why Is Israel's Presence in the Territories Still Called "Occupation"?* Jewish Political Studies Review 23:3/4, 40–64.

Shaw, M. (2016). *The League of Nations Mandate System and the Palestine Mandate: What Did and Does It Say About International Law and What Did and Does It Say About Palestine*. Israel Law Review 49:3, 287–308.

Shemesh, M. (2018). *The Palestinian National Revival: In the Shadow of the Leadership Crisis, 1937–1967*. Bloomington, IN: Indiana University Press.

Shepherd, N. (2000). *Ploughing Sand: British Rule in Palestine, 1917-1948*. New Brunswick: Rutgers University Press.

Sherman, A.J. (1997). *Mandate Days: British Lives in Palestine, 1918-1948*. London: Thames and Hudson.

Shindler, C. (2009). *Opposing Partition: The Zionist Predicaments after the Shoah*. Israel Studies 14:2, 88–104.

Shlaim, A. (1988). *Collusion across the Jordan: King Abdullah, the Zionist Movement and the Partition of Palestine*. New York, NY: Columbia University Press.

Shlaim, A. (1990). *The Rise and Fall of the All-Palestine Government in Gaza*. Journal of Palestine Studies 20:1, 37–53.

Shorrock, W. (1976a). *French Suspicion of British Policy in Syria, 1900-1914*. Journal of European Studies 6:3, 190–208.

Shorrock, W. (1976b). *French Imperialism in the Middle East: The Failure of Policy in Syria and Lebanon, 1900-1914*. Madison, WI; London: University of Wisconsin Press.

Sicker, M. (2000). *Pangs of the Messiah, the Troubled Birth of the Jewish State*. Westport, CT: Praeger.

Sidebotham, H. (1937). *Great Britain and Palestine*. London: MacMillan & Co.

Silverburg, R. (ed.) (2001). *Palestine and International Law: Essays on Politics and Economics*. London: McFarland & Co.

Singleton, J. (1933). *Conduct at the Bar and Some Problems of Advocacy*. London: Sweet & Maxwell.

Sobel, R. (2011). *The Campaign to Delegitimize Israel with the False Charge of Apartheid*. Jewish Political Studies Review 23, 18–31.

Sosebee, S. (1991). *Seeds of a Massacre: Israeli Violations at Haram Al-Sharif*. American-Arab Affairs 36, 104–116.

Sperber, J. (2015). *BDS, Israel, and the World System*. Journal of Palestine Studies 45:1, 8–23.

Stein, L. (1930a). *The Palestine White Paper of 1930*. London: Jewish Agency for Palestine.

Stein, L. (1930b). *Memorandum on the "Report of the Commission on the Palestine Disturbances of 1929"*. London: The Jewish Agency for Palestine.

Stone, J. (1981). *Israel and Palestine: Assault on the Law of Nations*. Baltimore, MD; London: The Johns Hopkins University Press.

Storrs, R. (1937). *The Memoirs of Sir Ronald Storrs*. New York, NY: G.P. Putnam's Sons.

Stoyanovsky, J. (1928). *The Mandate for Palestine: A Contribution to the Theory and Practice of International Mandates*. London: Longmans, Green.

Strawson, J. (2010). *Partitioning Palestine: Legal Fundamentalism in the Palestinian-Israeli Conflict*. London: Pluto Press.

Susser, A. (2018). *The Historical Linkage: Israel's Legitimacy and the Idea of Partition*. Israel Studies 23:3, 216–227.

Swart, W.J. (1995). *The League of Nations and the Irish Question: Master Frames, Cycles of Protest, and "Master Frame Alignment"*. The Sociological Quarterly 36:3, 465–481.

Sykes, C. (1965). *Crossroads to Israel: 1917–1948*. Bloomington, IN: Indiana University Press.

Terry, P. (2018). *Britain in Palestine (1917–1948) – Occupation, the Palestine Mandate, and International Law*. University of Bologna Law Review 2:2, 187–251.

Tessler, M. (2009). *A History of the Israeli-Palestinian Conflict*. Bloomington, IN: Indiana University Press.

Teveth, S. (1985). *Ben-Gurion and the Palestinian Arabs: From Peace to War*. Oxford; New York, NY: Oxford University Press.

Teveth, S. (1987). *Ben-Gurion: The Burning Ground, 1886–1948*. Boston, MA: Houghton, Mifflin.

Townshend, C. (2002). *Going to the Wall: The Failure of British Rule in Palestine, 1928–31*. Journal of Imperial and Commonwealth History 30:2, 25–52.

Toye, P. (ed.) (1989). *Palestine Boundaries 1833-1947*. Cambridge: Cambridge University Press, Archive Editions.

Toye, P. and Seay, A. (eds.) (1995). *Israel: Boundary Disputes with Arab Neighbours 1946–1964*. Cambridge: Cambridge University Press, Archive Editions.

Toynbee, A. (1970). *The McMahon-Hussein Correspondence: Comments and a Reply*. Journal of Contemporary History 5:4, 185–201.

Trachtman, J. (2016). *Integrating Lawfare and Warfare*. Boston College International and Comparative Law Review 39:2, 267–282.

Troen, I. (1989). *Calculating the "Economic Absorptive Capacity" of Palestine: A Study of the Political Uses of Scientific Research*. Contemporary Jewry 10:2, 19–38.

Truman, H. (1956). *Memoirs, Volume Two: Years of Trial and Hope*. New York, NY: Doubleday.

Tsilonas, V. (2019). *The Jurisdiction of the International Criminal Court*. Berlin: Springer.

Urquhart, B. (1993). *Ralph Bunche: An American Life*. New York, NY: W.W. Norton.

Vareilles, G. (2010). *Les Frontieres De La Palestine, 1914–1947*. Paris: L'Harmattan.

Vidmar, J. (2013). *Palestine and the Conceptual Problem of Implicit Statehood*. Chinese Journal of International Law 12, 19–41.

Voltolini, B. (2016). *Non-State Actors and Framing Processes in EU Foreign Policy: The Case of EU–Israel Relations*. Journal of European Public Policy 23:10, 1502–1519.

Wasserstein, B. (1978). *The British in Palestine: The Mandatory Government and the Arab-Jewish Conflict, 1917-1929*. London: Royal Historical Society.

Watson, G. (2000). *The Oslo Accords: International Law and the Israeli-Palestinian Peace Agreements*. Oxford: Oxford University Press.

Watson, G. (2018). *The Balfour Declaration in International Law*. Journal of Levantine Studies 8:1, 101–120.

Weizmann, C. (1942). *Palestine's Role in the Solution of the Jewish Problem*. Foreign Affairs 20:2, 324–338.

Weizmann, C. (1949). *Trial and Error: The Autobiography of Chaim Weizmann*. New York, NY: Harper & Bros.
Werner, W. (2010). *Historical and Semiotic Origins of "Lawfare": The Curious Career of Lawfare*. Case Western Reserve Journal of International Law 43:1/2, 61–72.
Wheatley, N. (2015). *Mandatory Interpretation: Legal Hermeneutics and the New International Order in Arab and Jewish Petitions to the League of Nations*. Past and Present 227:1, 205–248.
Whitman, C. (2013). *Palestine's Statehood and Ability to Litigate in the International Court of Justice*. California Western International Law Journal 44, 73–112.
Williams, F. (1952). *Ernest Bevin: Portrait of a Great Englishman*. London: Hutchinson.
Wilson, E. (1973). *The Palestine Papers, 1943-1947*. Journal of Palestine Studies 2:4, 33–54.
Wilson, E. (1979). *Decision on Palestine: How the U.S. Came to Recognize the State of Israel*. Stanford, CA: Hoover Institution Press.
Worster, W. (2011). *The Exercise of Jurisdiction by the International Criminal Court over Palestine*. American University International Law Review 26:5, 1153–1209.
Wright, Q. (1923). *Sovereignty of the Mandates*. The American Journal of International Law 17:4, 691–703.
Yazbak, M. (2000). *From Poverty to Revolt: Economic Factors in the Outbreak of the 1936 Rebellion in Palestine*. Middle Eastern Studies 36:3, 93–113.
Yitzhak, R. (2019). *Transjordan's Occupation of Jerusalem in the 1948 War*. Israel Affairs 25:2, 307–317.
Yusuf, M. (2002). *The Partition of Palestine (1947) – An Arab Perspective*. Palestine – Israel Journal of Politics, Economics, and Culture 9:4, 39–49.
Zelden, C. (1998). *The Judge Intuitive: The Life and Judicial Philosophy of Joseph C. Hutcheson*. South Texas Law Review 39, 905–1071.
Zimmermann, A. (2013). *Palestine and the International Criminal Court Quo Vadis: Reach and Limits of Declarations under Article 12(3)*. Journal of International Criminal Justice 11:2, 303–330.
Zipperstein, S. (2020). *Law and the Arab-Israeli Conflict: The Trials of Palestine*. London; New York, NY: Routledge.

★★★★

New Zionist Organization. (1937). *Evidence Submitted to the Palestine Royal Commission*. London: New Zionist Press.
Note. (2017). *Recent Resolution: International Law – Israel's Settlement Activities – United Nations Security Council Asserts Illegality – S.C. Res. 2334 (Dec. 23, 2016)*. Harvard Law Review 130:8, 2267–2276.
Pamphlet. (1968). *The Rights and Claims of Moslems and Jews in Connection with the Wailing Wall at Jerusalem*. Beirut: Institute for Palestine Studies.
Proceedings. (2016). *The Mandate for Palestine: Past and Present: Proceedings of an International Workshop Held at the Hebrew University Faculty of Law, 11 February 2016*. Israel Law Review 49:3, 409–435.
*Termination of the British Mandate for Palestine*. (1948). International Law Quarterly, Vol. 2 at 58.
*The McMahon-Hussein Correspondence of 1915-16*, 16 Bulletin of International News no. 5 at 6–13 (11 March 1939).

## US government documents

### *Foreign relations of the United States (FRUS)*

867N.01/4-545, Letter from President Franklin Roosevelt to King Abdul Aziz Faisal (5 April 1945).
867N.01/8-3145, President Truman to Prime Minister Attlee (31 August 1945).

867N.01/9-1745, Memorandum (Top Secret) from Prime Minister Attlee to President Truman (16 September 1945).
867N.01-145, Memorandum from Loy Henderson, Director, Division of Near Eastern Affairs to Dean Acheson, Acting Secretary of State (1 October 1945).
867N.01/10-245, Memorandum (Top Secret) from Dean Acheson, Acting Secretary of State, to President Truman (2 October 1945).
867N.01/11-2545, Telegram from Byrnes to Halifax (27 November 1945); FO 371/45387, Telegram No. 12555 (Secret and Personal) from Bevin to Halifax (7 December 1945).
867N.01/11-1945, Memorandum of Conversation between Byrnes and Halifax (19 November 1945).
867N.01/11-2045, Letter from Halifax to Byrnes (20 November 1945).
867N.01/11-2445, Letter from Halifax to Byrnes (24 November 1945).
867N.01/11-2545, Letter from Byrnes to Halifax (25 November 1945).
867N.01/12-1045, Telegram from Byrnes to Halifax (10 December 1945).
867N.01/6-1046, Telegram (Secret) from Secretary of State to U.S. Ambassador W. Averill Harriman, London (10 June 1946).
867N.01/6-1446, Telegram (Secret) from Truman to Attlee (14 June 1946).
867N.01/7-1546, Telegram from U.S. Embassy, London to State Department (12 July 1946).
867N.01/7-1946, Telegram No. 6851 (Top Secret) from U.S. Embassy, London (Grady) to Secretary of State (19 July 1946).
867N.01/7-1946, Telegram No. 5541 (Top Secret) from Byrnes to Grady (22 July 1946).
867N.01/72446, Telegram (Top Secret) No. 6970 from U.S. Embassy, London (Grady) to State Department (24 July 1946).
867N.01/7-2546, Telegram No. 6975 (Confidential) from Grady to Byrnes (25 July 1946).
867N.01/7-2646, Telegram No. 7030 (Top Secret) from Grady to Byrnes (26 July 1946).
867N.01/7-2646, Record of Teletype Conference between Washington and London (Secret) (26 July 1946).
867N.01/7-2746, Telegram No. 7082 from Grady to Byrnes (27 July 1946).
867N.01/7-3046, D. Acheson, Memorandum of Conversation, by the Acting Secretary of State (30 July 1946).
867N.01/7-3146, Telegram No. 3744 (Top Secret) from Harriman to State Department (31 July 1946).
740.00119 Council/7-3146, Telegram No. 3743 (Top Secret) from Byrnes to Truman (31 July 1946).
867N.01/8-1246, Telegram No. 5973 (Top Secret) from Acting Secretary of State to U.S. Ambassador Harriman (12 August 1946).
867N.01/8-1246, Telegram (Top Secret) from Truman to Attlee (12 August 1946).
867N.01/8-1546, Telegram No. 7552 (Top Secret) from U.S. Embassy, London to State Department (15 August 1946).
867N.01/8-1946, Telegram (Top Secret) from Attlee to Truman, para. 4 (19 August 1946).
740.00119 Council/8-2146, Telegram (Top Secret) from Harriman to Acting Secretary of States (21 August 1946).
867N.01/9-1746, Telegram No. 8214 (Secret) from U.S. Embassy, London to State Department (17 September 1946).
867N.01/9-2346, Telegram No. 8349 (Secret) from U.S. Embassy, London to State Department (23 September 1946).
867N.01/10-246, Telegram No. 8572 (Urgent) from U.S. Embassy, London to State Department (2 October 1946).
867N.01/10-346, Telegram from Truman to Attlee (3 October 1946).
867N.01/10-1546, Letter from Abdul Aziz Ibn Saud to President Truman (15 October 1946).
501.BB Palestine/6-1147, Telegram No. 243 (Confidential) from United States Consul General, Jerusalem to Secretary of State (11 June 1947).

501.BB Palestine/6-3047, Telegram (Secret) No. 113 from the United States Consul General, Jerusalem, to the Secretary of State (30 June 1947).
501.BB Palestine/7-1447, Telegram No. 123 (Secret) from the United States Consul General, Jerusalem, to the Secretary of State (14 July 1947).
501.BB Palestine/9-2547, Memorandum (Secret) of Conversation (25 September 1947).
867N.01/11-2547, Telegram (Top Secret) from Secretary of State to Acting Secretary of State (25 November 1947).
867N.01/5-1048, Memorandum by the Legal Adviser to the Undersecretary of State, "Recognition of New States and Governments in Palestine" (11 May 1948).
501.BB Palestine/10-1647, Letter from Emil Ghory, Arab Higher Committee, to United States Consul General, Jerusalem (3 October 1947).
867N.01/10-3047, Letter from King Abdul Aziz Ibn Saud to President Truman (26 October 1947).
867N.01/12-347, Telegram (Secret) from United States Ambassador, Egypt to Secretary of State (3 December 1947).
501.BB Palestine/12-947, Telegram from Governor General Mohammad Ali Jinnah of Pakistan to President Truman (Undated).
501.BB Palestine/3-548, Memorandum from Ernest A. Gross, Legal Adviser, U.S. Department of State, to Undersecretary of State Lovett, "Precise Position of United States on Security Council Powers with respect to Palestine" (5 March 1948).
867N.01/9-2648, Telegram No. 65 from Amman (26 September 1948).
867N.01/10-148, Telegram No. 498 (1 October 1948).
501.BB Palestine/10-248, Circular Telegram (Secret) from the Acting Secretary of State to Certain Diplomatic Offices (2 October 1948).
867N.01/10-748, Telegram No. 4423 (7 October 1948).
PPs/19, Lot 64, D563, Memorandum (Secret) by Policy Planning Staff, U.S. Department of State, "To Assess and Appraise the Position of the U.S. with Respect to Palestine, Taking into Consideration the Security Interests of the U.S. in the Mediterranean and Near East Areas, and in the Light of the Recommendation of the General Assembly of the United Nations regarding the Partition of Palestine" (19 January 1948).
867N.01/2-648, Memorandum (Top Secret) by Dean Rusk to the under Secretary of State (26 January 1948).
PPS Files, Lot 64 D 563, Memorandum (Top Secret) by the Director of the Policy Planning Staff to the under Secretary of State (29 January 1948).
867N.01/2-648, Memorandum (Top Secret) by the Director of the Office of Near Eastern and African Affairs to the Director of the Office of United Nations Affairs (6 February 1948).
501.BB Palestine/1-2748, Memorandum (Top Secret) by Mr. Samuel K. C. Kopper of the Office of Near Eastern and African Affairs, "The Partition of Palestine and United States Security" (27 January 1948).
501.BB Palestine/3-1648, Telegram (Top Secret) from Secretary of State Marshall to U.S. Ambassador Austin (16 March 1948).
501BB Palestine/3-2248 (22 March 1948).
501.BB Palestine/3-2248, Memorandum by the Director of the Executive Secretariat to the Secretary of State (22 March 1948).
U.S. Department of State, L Files, Memorandum by the Legal Adviser to the Director of the Office of United Nations Affairs (19 March 1948).
Clifford Papers, Memorandum by the President's Special Counsel (6 March 1948).
Clifford Papers, Memorandum by the President's Special Counsel to President Truman (8 March 1948).

### Central intelligence agency documents

RDP82-00457R000300140006-1, "Mufti's Declarations on Palestine Situation" (Secret) (27 January 1947).
RDP83-00415R001300100016-8, A. Kader al Mazny, editorial in Al Assas (22 August 1948).
51966ec8993294098d50a4bf, "Haj Amin al-Husseini, Mufti of Jerusalem, Biographic Sketch No. 60" (10 April 1951).
RDP82-00457R002100850002-7, "Contact between the Grand Mufti and the Soviets" (Secret), para. 1 (23 December 1948).

## British government documents

### Reports of the Palin, Haycraft, Shaw, Lofgren and Peel commissions

Palin Commission. *Secret (Unpublished) Report of the Court of Inquiry Convened by order of H.E. the High Commissioner and Commander-in-Chief,* Foreign Office file FO 371/5121 (1920).
Haycraft Commission. *Palestine Disturbances in May 1921, Report of the Commission of Inquiry with Correspondence Relating Thereto,* Command Paper 1540 (1921).
Shaw Commission. *Report of the Commission on the Palestine Disturbances of August, 1929,* Command Paper 3530 (1930).
Lofgren Commission. *Report of the Commission Appointed by His Majesty's Government in the United Kingdom of Great Britain and Northern Ireland, with the Approval of the Council of the League of Nations, to Determine the Rights and Claims of Moslems and Jews in Connection with the Western or Wailing Wall at Jerusalem,* 58-9096 (December 1930).
Peel Commission. *Palestine Royal Commission Report,* Command Paper 5479 (July 1937).

### Transcripts (public and secret) of the Shaw, Lofgren and Peel commission hearings

Shaw Commission:
*Palestine Commission on the Disturbances of August, 1929, Evidence Heard by the Commission in Open Sittings and a Selection from the Exhibits Put in During those Sittings,* Colonial Paper 48 (1930).
*Palestine Commission of Enquiry on Disturbances of August, 1929, In Camera Evidence to the Commission,* National Library of Wales, Sir Rhys Hopkin Morris Papers, Series 2–21, Files 2–5.
Lofgren Commission:
*Wailing Wall Commission, Minutes of the Session at Jerusalem (1930),* King's College London, Foyle Special Collections Library, Foreign and Commonwealth Office Historical Collection FOL. DS126 INT'.
Peel Commission:
Palestine Royal Commission, *Minutes of Evidence Heard at Public Sessions,* Colonial Paper 134 (1937).
Palestine Royal Commission, *Minutes of Evidence Heard at Secret Sessions,* Foreign Office File FO 492/19 (1937).

### Command papers

*Mandate for Palestine, Together with a Note by the League of Nations Secretary General Relating to its Application to the Territory Known as Transjordan, under the Provisions of Article 25,* Command Paper 1785 (1922).

*Palestine: Correspondence with the Palestine Arab Delegation and the Zionist Organisation*, Command Paper 1700 (1922).
*The Western or Wailing Wall at Jerusalem*, Command Paper 3229 (1928).
*Palestine: Report on Immigration, Land Settlement and Development*, Command Paper 3686 (1930).
*Palestine: Statement of Policy by His Majesty's Government in the United Kingdom*, Command Paper 3692 (1930).
*Palestine: Statement of Policy*, Command Paper 5513 (1937).
*Policy in Palestine*, Command Paper 5634 (1938).
*Palestine Partition Commission Report*, Command Paper 5854 (1938).
*Palestine: Statement by His Majesty's Government in the United Kingdom*, Command Paper 5893 (1938).
*Correspondence between Sir Henry McMahon, His Majesty's High Commissioner at Cairo and the Sherif Hussein of Mecca, July 1915-March 1916*, Command Paper 5957 (1939).
*Report of a Committee Set up to Consider Certain Correspondence Between Sir Henry McMahon and the Sharif of Mecca in 1915 and 1916*, Command Paper 5974 (1939).
*Statements Made on Behalf of His Majesty's Government during the Year 1918 in Regard to the Future Status of Certain Part of the Ottoman Empire*, Command Paper 5964 (1939).
*Palestine: Statement of Policy*, Command Paper 6019 (1939).
*Palestine Land Transfers Regulations*, Command Paper 6180 (1940).
*Report of the Anglo-American Committee of Enquiry regarding the Problems of European Jewry and Palestine*, Command Paper 6308 (1946).

## Cabinet papers and minutes

Cabinet Paper (Secret) 149 (37), *Desire of Royal Commission on Palestine to Quote Extracts from the McMahon-Hussein Correspondence in their Report* (27 May 1937).
Cabinet Paper (Secret) 23(37), *Extract from Conclusions of a Meeting Held on Wednesday* (2nd June 1937).
Cabinet Paper (Secret) CAB 24/275/10, C.P. 46 (38), *Memorandum by the Secretary of State for the Colonies, Control of Immigration into Palestine* (24 February 1938).
Cabinet Paper (Secret) CAB 24/278/25, C.P. 190 (38), *Memorandum by the Secretary of State for the Colonies* (21 August 1938).
Cabinet Paper (Secret) CAB 24/280/5, C.P. 250 (38), *Memorandum by the Secretary of State for the Colonies, Final Draft of the Statement of Policy* (5 November 1938).
Cabinet Paper (Secret) CAB 23/96/12, *Minutes of a Meeting of the Cabinet* (21 December 1938).
Cabinet Paper (Secret), CAB 24/282/4, C.P. 4 (39), *Memorandum by the Secretary of State for the Colonies* (18 January 1939).
Cabinet Paper (Secret) CAB 24/282/19, *Memorandum by Lord Halifax, Secretary of State for Foreign Affairs, Palestine: Legal Arguments Likely to be Advanced by Arab Representatives* (23 January 1939).
Cabinet Paper (Secret) CAB 24/283/2, C.P. 29 (39), *Cabinet Committee on Palestine Report* (30 January 1939).
CAB 23/97/3, *Minutes (Secret) of Cabinet Meeting* (1 February 1939).
CAB 24/284/3, *Minutes (Secret) of Meeting of Cabinet Committee on Palestine* (23 February 1939).
CAB 23/97/9, *Minutes (Secret) of Cabinet Meeting* (2 March 1939).
C.P. 9 (39), *Extract (Secret) from Conclusions of a Meeting of the Cabinet* (2 March 1939).
CAB 23/97/10, *Minutes (Secret) of Cabinet Meeting* (8 March 1939).
C.P. 10 (39), *Extract (Secret) from Conclusions of a Meeting of the Cabinet* (8 March 1939).
CAB 24/285/1, *Memorandum by the Secretary of State for the Colonies* (13 April 1939).
CAB 23/99/3, *Minutes (Secret) of Cabinet Meeting* (26 April 1939).
CAB 23/99/4, *Minutes (Secret) of Cabinet Meeting* (1 May 1939).

CAB 23/99/7, *Minutes (Secret) of a Meeting of the Cabinet* (17 May 1939).
CAB 23/100/6, *Minutes (Secret) of Cabinet Meeting* (19 July 1939).
C.P. 38(20), *Minutes (Secret) of Meeting of the Cabinet Committee on Palestine, Draft Commentary on the Observations of the Permanent Mandates Commission* (22 July 1939).
CAB 24/288/24, C.P. 174 (39), *Memorandum (Secret) by the Secretary of State for Foreign Affairs, Forthcoming Discussions at Geneva regarding the Palestine White Paper* (2 August 1939).
CAB 95/14, P.(M) (45)13, *Palestine Cabinet Committee, Note by the Secretaries* (3 September 1945).
CAB 129/2/6, C.P. (45) 156, *Cabinet Palestine Committee, Report (Top Secret) by the Lord President of the Council* (8 September 1945).
CAB 129/2/46, C.P. (45) 196, *Palestine: Memorandum (Top Secret) by the Secretary of State for the Colonies* (28 September 1945).
CAB 128/1/21, C.M. (45) 38, *Conclusions (Secret) of a Meeting of the Cabinet* (4 October 1945).
CAB 95/14, *Cabinet Palestine Committee, Proposed Anglo-American Commission of Enquiry, Note (Top Secret) by the Secretary of State for Foreign Affairs and the Secretary of State for the Colonies* (9 October 1945).
CAB 129/3/16, C.P. (45) 216, *Palestine: Report (Top Secret) by the Lord President of the Council* (10 October 1945).
CAB 128/1/23, C.M. (45) 40, *Conclusions of Cabinet Meeting* (11 October 1945).
CAB 128/2/5, C.M. 52 (45), *Conclusion of a Meeting of the Cabinet* (13 November 1945).
CAB 128/5/37, C.M. 37 (46), *Conclusions (Secret) of a Meeting of the Cabinet* (24 April 1946).
CAB 129/9/23, C.P. (46) 173, *Palestine: Report of Committee of Officials* (27 April 1946).
CAB 128/5/39, C.M. 39 (46), *Conclusions (Secret) of a Meeting of the Cabinet* (1 May 1946).
CAB 128/5/45, C.M. (46) 45, *Conclusions (Secret) of a Meeting of the Cabinet* (13 May 1946).
CAB 128/5/50, C.M. (46) 50, *Conclusions (Secret) of a Meeting of the Cabinet* (20 May 1946).
CAB 129/111/8, C.P. (46) 258 (Secret), *Report of the Anglo-American Committee of Enquiry regarding the Problems of European Jewry and Palestine, Memorandum by the Secretary of State for the Colonies* (8 July 1946).
CAB 129/11/19, C.P. 46 (259) (Top Secret), *Long-Term Policy in Palestine: Memorandum by the Secretary of State for the Colonies* (8 July 1946).
CAB 128/6/5, C.M. 67 (46), *Conclusions (Secret) of a Meeting of the Cabinet* (11 July 1946).
CAB 129/10/20, C.P. (46) 220 (Secret), *Arab Reactions in Palestine to the Report of the Anglo-American Committee of Inquiry* (6 June 1946).
CAB 128/6/10, C.M. (46) 72, *Conclusions (Secret) of a Meeting of the Cabinet* (23 July 1946).
CAB 129/11/45, C.P. (46) 295 (Top Secret), *Palestine: Statement of Policy* (24 July 1946).
CAB 128/6/11, C.M. 73 (46), *Conclusions (Secret) of a Meeting of the Cabinet* (25 July 1946).
CAB 129/12/8, C.P. (46) 308 (30 July 1946).
CAB 129/16/28, C.P. (47) 28 (Top Secret), *Palestine: Reference to United Nations, Memorandum by the Secretary of State for Foreign Affairs* (13 January 1947).
CAB 128/11/2, C.M. (47) 6, (Top Secret), *Conclusions of Cabinet Meeting, Confidential Annex* (15 January 1947).
CAB 129/16/49, C.P. (47) 49, *Palestine: Joint Memorandum (Top Secret) by the Secretary of State for Foreign Affairs and the Secretary of State for the Colonies* (6 February 1947).
CAB 128/9/18, C.M. 18 (47), *Conclusions (Secret) of a Meeting of the Cabinet* (7 February 1947).
CAB 129/17/9, C.P. (47) 59, *Palestine: Memorandum (Top Secret) by the Secretary of State for Foreign Affairs and the Secretary of State for the Colonies* (13 February 1947).
CAB 128/9/22, C.M. 22 (47), *Conclusions (Secret) of a Meeting of the Cabinet* (14 February 1947).
CAB 129/21/9, C.P. (47) 259, *Memorandum (Top Secret) by the Secretary of State for Foreign Affairs* (18 September 1947).

CAB 128/10/27, Cabinet 76 (47), *Conclusions (Secret) of a Meeting of the Cabinet* (20 September 1947).
CAB 129/24/10, *Palestine: Withdrawal of British Civil Administration, Memorandum (Secret) by the Secretary of State for the Colonies* (4 February 1948).
PREM 8/627:
*Memorandum to the Prime Minister from the President* (24 July 1945).
Telegram No. 10268 (Cypher) from Foreign Office to British Embassy, Washington, DC (13 October 1945).
Telegram (Top Secret) from British Embassy, Washington, DC to Foreign Office (14 October 1945).
Telegram No. 6964 (Top Secret) from Lord Halifax to Bevin (19 October 1945).
Telegram No. 7013 (Top Secret) from British Embassy, Washington, DC to Foreign Office (22 October 1945).
Telegram No. 7026 (Top Secret) from Halifax to Bevin (23 October 1945).
Telegram No. 7036 (Top Secret) from Halifax to Bevin (24 October 1945).
Telegram No. 7037 (Top Secret) from British Embassy, Washington, DC to Foreign Office (24 October 1945).
Telegram No. 10750 (Top Secret) from Foreign Office to British Embassy, Washington, DC (25 October 1945).
Telegram No. 7113 (Top Secret) from British Embassy, Washington, DC to Foreign Office (25 October 1945).
Telegram No. 10754 (Top Secret) from Bevin to Halifax (26 October 1945).
Telegram No. 7157 (Top Secret) from Halifax to Bevin (27 October 1945).
Telegram No. 7159 (Top Secret) from Halifax to Bevin (27 October 1945).
Telegram No. 7192 (Top Secret) British Embassy, Washington, DC to Foreign Office (28 October 1945).
Telegram No. 7206 (Top Secret) from Halifax to Bevin (29 October 1945).
Telegram No. 7264 (Top Secret) from British Embassy, Washington, DC to Foreign Office (31 October 1945).
Telegram No. 7422 (Top Secret) from British Embassy, Washington, DC to Foreign Office (6 November 1945).
Telegram No. 11227 (Top Secret) from Foreign Office to British Embassy, Washington, DC (7 November 1945).
Telegram No. 7445 (Top Secret) from Lord Halifax, British Ambassador to the United States to Foreign Office (7 November 1945).
Telegram No. 11264 (Top Secret), from Foreign Office to British Embassy, Washington, DC (8 November 1945).
Telegram No. 7509 (Top Secret), from British Embassy, Washington, DC to Foreign Office (9 November 1945).
Telegram No. 11317 (Top Secret) from Foreign Office to British Embassy, Washington, DC (9 November 1945).

## *Parliamentary debates*

Hansard, HL Deb. 27 March 1923 vol. 53.
Hansard, HC Deb. 2 November 1928, vol. 222.
Hansard, HC Deb. 26 November 1928, vol. 223.
Hansard, HC Deb. 13 February 1931, vol. 248.
Hansard, HC Deb. 19 June 1936, vol. 313.
Hansard, HC Deb. 29 July 1936, vol. 315.

Hansard, HL Deb. 20 July 1937 vol. 106.
Hansard, HC Deb. 21 July 1937, vol. 326.
Hansard, HC Deb. 4 March 1938, vol. 333.
Hansard, HL Deb. 23 May 1939, vol. 113.
Hansard, HC Deb. 23 May 1939, vol. 347.
Hansard, HC Deb. 7 June 1939, vol. 348.
Hansard, HC Deb. 13 November 1945, vol. 415.
Hansard, HC Deb. 31 July 1946, vol. 426.
Hansard, HC Deb. 18 February 1947, vol. 433.
Hansard, HC Deb. 25 February 1947, vol. 433.

## Foreign office documents

FO 371/6237:
Foreign Office, *Relations between His Majesty's Government and the Arabs* (January 1921).
FO 371/6247:
Foreign Office, Arab Bureau (Secret), *Summary of Historical Documents from the Outbreak of War between Great Britain and Turkey, 1914, to the Outbreak of the Revolt of the Sherif of Mecca in June 1916* (January 1921).
FO 371/7797:
Foreign Office, *Draft Reply to Parliamentary Inquiry of 11 July 1922.*
FO 371/10820:
Childs, W.J., *Decisions regarding Publication of the McMahon-Hussein Correspondence* (1930).
FO 371/14495:
Childs, W.J., Memorandum (Confidential) No. 13778, *Memorandum on the Exclusion of Palestine from the Area assigned for Arab Independence by McMahon-Hussein Correspondence of 1915–16* (24 October 1930).
FO 371/20810:
Arab Higher Committee to High Commissioner of Palestine (23 July 1937).
Telegram No. 427 from Lampson to Foreign Office (27 July 1937).
Cypher Telegram from High Commissioner to Secretary of State (29 July 1937).
Rendell Minute Discussing Meeting at Colonial Office (31 July 1937).
Unsigned Minute, 23 Sept. 1937 to Rendell, Enclosing Copy of McMahon's Despatch No. 131 of 26 Oct. 1915; Rendell Minute (11 October 1937).
FO 371/23219:
MacKenzie Memorandum (draft, 19 December 1938).
Baggallay to Downie (19 January 1939).
FO 371/23222:
McMahon-Hussein Correspondence: Notes for Mr. Trott (23 January 1939).
Baggallay Minute (30 January 1939).
Baggallay Memorandum, *The Juridical Basis of the Arab Claim to Palestine: Views of the Lord Chancellor* (30 January 1939).
Conferences on Palestine, 1939, United Kingdom Delegation, *Note of Informal Discussion with Palestinian Arab Delegation* (31 January 1939).
Trott, A.C., *McMahon-Hussein Correspondence: Results of the Examination of the Arabic Texts of Certain Obscure Passages* (31 January 1939).
FO 371/23223:
Conferences on Palestine, United Kingdom Delegation, (Secret) *Note of Informal Discussion with Members of the Jewish Agency Executive* (1 February 1939).

*Note of Mr. MacDonald's Discussion with Dr. Weizmann* (4 February 1939).
Conferences on Palestine, United Kingdom Delegation, Programme for Opening Meetings (4 February 1939).
Baggallay Minute, *Formal Opening of Palestine Conferences at St. James's Palace, London* (6 February 1939).
Conferences on Palestine, United Kingdom-Jewish Agency Delegation, *Notes of the First Meeting Held at St. James's Palace, London* (7 February 1939).
Conferences on Palestine, United Kingdom-Jewish Agency Delegation, *Draft Notes of the Second Meeting Held at St. James's Palace, London* (8 February 1939).
Conferences on Palestine, United Kingdom-Jewish Agency Delegation, *Draft of Secretary's Notes of the Third Meeting Held at St. James's Palace, London* (10 February 1939).
Conferences on Palestine, United Kingdom-Jewish Agency Delegation, *Draft Notes of the Second Meeting Held at St. James's Palace, London* (12 February 1939).
FO 371/23225:
Conferences on Palestine, 1939, *Informal Discussions with Arab and Jewish Delegates* (23 February 1939).
Baxter Minute (19 May 1939).
FO 371/23226:
Conferences on Palestine, Colonial Office, *Note (Confidential) on Jewish Agency's Memorandum of 20th February* (28 February 1939).
Conferences on Palestine, (Secret) *Note of Informal Conversation with Representatives of the Jewish Agency Delegation* (25 February 1939).
Cablegram from Louis D. Brandeis to Prime Minister Neville Chamberlain (26 February 1939).
Conferences on Palestine, United Kingdom-Jewish Agency Delegation, *Draft of Secretary's Notes of the Ninth Meeting Held at St. James's Palace, London* (27 February 1939).
FO 371/23228:
Conferences on Palestine, 1939, *Informal Discussions with Arab and Jewish Delegates* (7 March 1939).
FO 371/23229:
Hogarth Note to High Commissioner, Cairo (Extract) (15 January 1918).
Conferences on Palestine, *Note (Secret) of Prime Minister's Conversation with Dr. Weizmann, Mr. Ben-Gurion and Rabbi Wise* (2 March 1939).
Letter from Baggallay to MacDonald (9 March 1939).
Baggallay Minute (10 March 1939).
Conferences on Palestine, *Note (Secret) of Informal Discussion with Delegates of Egypt, Iraq and Saudi Arabia* (10 March 1939).
Conferences on Palestine, *Informal Discussions with Jewish Delegates, Secretary's Notes of the Third Meeting Held at St. James's Palace, London* (11 March 1939).
Baxter and Butler Minutes (11 March 1939).
Conferences on Palestine, *Informal Discussions with Jewish Delegates, Secretary's Notes of the Fourth Meeting Held at the Colonial Office, London* (12 March 1939).
Cabinet Committee on Palestine, *Draft Conclusions (Secret) of the Eighth Meeting of the Committee* (13 March 1939).
FO 371/23230:
Conferences on Palestine, *Note of Conversation between Mr. MacDonald and Dr. Weizmann* (14 March 1939).
Conferences on Palestine, United Kingdom-Jewish Agency Delegation, *Draft of Secretary's Notes of the Tenth Meeting Held at St. James's Palace, London* (15 March 1939).
Cypher Telegram No. 169 (Secret) from the Secretary of State for the Colonies to the High Commissioner for Palestine (16 March 1939).

Cypher Telegram from the High Commissioner for Palestine to the Secretary of State for the Colonies (17 March 1939).

FO 371/23232:

C.W. Baxter Minute (5 April 1939).

Cabinet Committee on Palestine, *Draft Conclusions of the Ninth Meeting of the Committee (Secret)* at 2 (6 April 1939).

FO 371/23235:

C.P. 28(39), *Extract from Cabinet Conclusions* (17 May 1939).

FO 371/23248:

*Question de la convocation, en 1939, d'une session extraordinaire de la Commission permanente des Mandats consacree a la Palestine, Note preliminaire* (9 January 1939).

*Various Minutes Discussing Procedure for Obtaining Amendment of the Mandate* (10, 12, 13 and 17 January 1939).

Cabinet Committee on Palestine, *Memorandum (Secret) by the Secretary of State for the Colonies, Draft Commentary on the Observations of the Permanent Mandates Commission* (July 1939).

FO 371/45378:

Palestine Policy: Foreign Office Appreciation of International Repercussions (July 1945).

FO 371/45379:

Minutes of Meeting Held at the Foreign Office (6 September 1945).

FO 371/45400:

Telegram No. 6593 (Secret) from Lord Halifax to Prime Minister Attlee and Foreign Secretary Bevin (3 October 1945).

FO 371/45385:

Letter from Bevin to Rees (16 November 1945).

Letter from Leggett to Bevin (19 November 1945).

Letter from Bevin to Leggett (22 November 1945).

Letter from Bevin to Crossman (22 November 1945).

FO 371/45386:

Letter from U.S. Ambassador John G. Winant to Bevin (19 November 1945).

Letter from Sir George Henry Gater, Colonial Office to Sir Alexander Cadogan, Foreign Office (22 November 1945).

Letter from Sir A. Napier to Sir A. Cadogan (23 November 1945).

Telegram No. 11802 (Secret) from Foreign Office to British Embassy, Washington, DC (24 November 1945).

Telegram No. 7896 from British Embassy, Washington, DC to Foreign Office (26 November 1945).

FO 371/45387:

Letter from Foreign Secretary Bevin to Justice Singleton (25 November 1945).

Telegram No. 12019 (Cypher) from Foreign Office to British Embassy, Washington, DC (30 November 1945).

Telegram No. 8032 (Secret) from British Embassy, Washington, DC to Foreign Office (30 November 1945).

Telegram No. 8168 (Secret) from British Embassy, Washington, DC to Foreign Office (6 December 1945).

Telegram No. 12555 (Secret and Personal) from Bevin to Halifax (7 December 1945).

J.G. Donnelly Minute (7 December 1945).

FO 371/45388:

Telegram No. 8287 from British Embassy, Washington, DC to Foreign Office (11 December 1945).

FO 371/52503:

US Department of State Confidential Future Release No. 936 (13 December 1945).
Cypher Telegram No. 125 from British Embassy, Washington, DC to Foreign Office (6 January 1946).
FO 371/52504:
Telegram No. 1818 from High Commissioner, Jerusalem to Secretary of State for the Colonies (22 December 1945).
Cypher Telegram No. 247 from British Embassy, Washington to Colonial Office in Response to Palestine High Commissioner's Telegram No. 1818 (10 January 1946).
Cypher Telegram No. 279 from British Embassy, Washington, DC to Foreign Office (11 January 1946).
FO 371/52505:
Letter to C.W. Baxter, Foreign Office from H.G. Vincent (British Secretary to the Anglo-American Committee of Inquiry (9 January 1946).
FO 371/52507:
Letter to Foreign Secretary Bevin from Manningham-Buller (22 January 1946).
Letter from British Embassy, Washington, DC to Foreign Office (22 January 1946).
Telegram No. 201 (Secret) from Secretary of State for the Colonies to High Commissioner of Palestine (2 February 1946).
FO 371/52508:
Letter from Justice Singleton to Foreign Secretary Bevin (1 February 1946).
Telegram No. 175 (Cypher) from Foreign Office to British Embassy, Cairo (2 February 1946).
Letter from Foreign Secretary Bevin to Justice Singleton (6 February 1946).
Telegram No. 145 from Foreign Office to British Embassy (7 February 1946).
FO 371/52513:
H.T. Morgan Minute (Top Secret) regarding Lord Morrison's Report to Bevin
FO 371/52514:
Letter from H. Beeley to C.W. Baxter, Foreign Office (25 March 1946).
FO 371/52520:
Prime Minister's Statement in the House of Commons on the Report of the Anglo-American Committee of Enquiry (1 May 1946).
FO 371/52521:
Letter from British Embassy, Washington, DC to Foreign Office (1 May 1946).
FO 371/52522:
Royal Egyptian Embassy, London. *Aide Memoir* (6 May 1946).
FO 371/52524:
Letter from Crossman to McNeil (22 April 1946).
Note of a Meeting Held at No. 10 Downing Street, on 14 May 1946 (17 May 1946).
FO 371/52525:
Telegram No. 4799 (Top Secret and Personal) from Foreign Office to Lord Halifax, British Embassy, Washington, DC (17 May 1946).
FO 371/52526:
Telegram No. 4799 from Foreign Office to British Embassy, Washington, DC (17 May 1946).
Telegram No. 5151 (Top Secret) from Foreign Office to British Embassy, Washington, DC (26 May 1946).
FO 371/52529:
Telegram (Cypher) No. 543 from British Embassy, Beirut to Foreign Office (16 June 1946).
FO 371/52532:
*Correspondence with the States Members of the Arab League, with the Jewish Agency for Palestine, and with the Palestine Arab Higher Committee, Concerning the Report of the Anglo-American Committee of Enquiry regarding the Problems of European Jewry and Palestine* (19 June 1946).

FO 371/52539:
President Truman's Statements on the Admission of 100,000 Jewish Immigrants to Palestine (15 July 1948).
FO 371/52546:
Telegram No. 4862 (Cypher) from Lord Inverchapel to Foreign Office (31 July 1946).
FO 371/52556:
Telegram No. 59 (Secret) from British Embassy, Amman to Foreign Office (27 August 1946).
FO 371/52558:
Letter from C. Cane to J. Balfour (Very Confidential) (7 September 1946).
FO 371/52563:
Letter from C.W. Baxter (Foreign Office) to John Martin (Colonial Office) (18 October 1946).
Letter from John Martin (Colonial Office) to C.W. Baxter (Foreign Office) (4 November 1946).
Draft Minute from H. Beeley (Foreign Office) to British United Nations Delegation (13 November 1946).
FO 371/52565:
Cover Note to Bevin Enclosing Memorandum (Secret) Entitled "Palestine," Prepared by Foreign Office for US Secretary of State Byrnes (23 November 1946).
FO 371/61888:
Cypher Telegram No. 3440 from United Kingdom Delegation to Foreign Office (18 November 1947).
FO 371/61890:
Telegram No. 3554 (Immediate) from United Kingdom Delegation to United Nations to Foreign Office (27 November 1947).
FO 371/68376:
Telegram (Secret) No. 688 from British Embassy, Beirut to Foreign Office (21 September 1948).
FO 371/75342:
Letter (Confidential) from E. Troutbeck, British Middle East Office, Cairo, to Bevin (16 June 1949).
FO 816/83:
Letter to Palestine High Commissioner Sir Alan Cunningham from Emir Abdullah (3 May 1946).

## *Colonial office documents*

CO 537/1754:
John M. Martin Minute (2 January 1946).
CO 537/1759:
Telegram No. 2918 (Secret) from British Embassy, Washington, DC to Foreign Office (7 May 1946).
CO 537/2362:
Letter from Chief Secretary of Palestine Government (Shaw) to J. Martin, Colonial Office (9 July 1947).
CO 733/179/7:
*Memorandum on Discussions with the Parties with a View to Voluntary Settlement of the Wailing (Western) Wall Dispute* (10 October 1930).
Draft memoranda to be endorsed and exchanged between the parties dated 10 September 1930; Jewish and Muslim letters rejecting draft memoranda (dated 12 and 14 September 1930, respectively).

CO 733/195/6:
*Memorandum by Acting Attorney General regarding Draft Palestine (Western or Wailing Wall) Order-in-Council* (21 April 1931).
CO 733/343/10:
Abdul Hadi to Wauchope (18 December 1936).
CO 733/344/11:
Memorandum from Emir Abdullah (March 1937).
CO 733/344/22:
Abdul Hadi to Secretary, Palestine Royal Commission (20 January 1937).
CO 733/346/8:
*Report of the Commission Appointed by His Excellency the High Commissioner for Palestine by Notification No. 1561*, Published in the Palestine Gazette (16 November 1933).
CO 733/346/9:
Coupland, Note for Discussion of Partition (7 December 1936).
Coupland, Note regarding "Clean Cut" (23 May 1937).
Hammond, Note regarding "Clean Cut" (21 May 1937).
CO 733/353/2:
Wauchope to Parkinson Enclosing Two Memoranda, Each Dated 25 July 1937, from Emir Abdullah (31 July 1937).
Ormsby-Gore to McMahon (23 July 1937).
CO 733/364/1:
Downie Minute (19 January 1938).
Downie Minute (7 February 1938).
Downie Minute (4 March 1938).
Downie Minute (22 June 1938).
CO 733/390/5:
Letter from Lord Hankey to MacDonald (30 June 1939).
CO 733/392/8:
Harris to Downie (15 March 1939).
CO 733/401/15:
Letter from MacMichael to Sir Cosmo Parkinson, Permanent Undersecretary of State for Colonial Affairs (14 July 1939).
CO 733/406/11:
C.P. 6 (39), *Conclusions (Secret) of a Meeting of the Cabinet* (8 February 1939).
Letter from Malcolm MacDonald to Sir Alexander Hardinge (10 February 1939).
Cabinet 7(39), *Extract (Secret) from Conclusions of a Meeting of the Cabinet* (15 February 1939).
C.P. 10 (39), *Extract (Secret) from Conclusions of a Meeting of the Cabinet* (8 March 1939).
C.P. 9 (39), *Extract (Secret) from Conclusions of a Meeting of the Cabinet* (2 March 1939).
Cypher Telegram No. 121 from Foreign Office to R.C. Lindsey (15 March 1939).
Telegram No. 176 from Secretary of State for the Colonies to High Commissioner for Palestine (17 March 1939).
Telegram No. 199 from Lampson to Foreign Office (18 March 1939).
C.P. 11 (39), *Extract (Secret) from Conclusions of a Meeting of the Cabinet* (15 March 1939).
Code Telegram from Foreign Office to British Ambassadors to Egypt, Iraq and Saudi Arabia (19 March 1939).
Code Telegram from Foreign Office to British Ambassadors in Egypt, Iraq and Saudi Arabia (20 March 1939).
C.P. 14 (39), *Extract (Secret) from Conclusions of a Meeting of the Cabinet* (22 March 1939).
CO 733/407/6:

Telegram from United Zionist Organization of Poland and Agudas Israel of Poland to Prime Minister (17 March 1939).
CO 733/408/15:
Letter from Kingsley Heath to Sir Harold MacMichael, High Commissioner for Palestine (14 July 1939).
CO 733/409/13:
Downie to Baggallay (1 February 1939).
Bushe Minute (6 February 1939).
CO 733/410/5:
Code Telegram No. 129 from Foreign Office to Sir Ronald Lindsay, British Ambassador to the United States (20 March 1939).
CO 733/410/9:
Note from Sir Grattan Bushe, Legal Advisor, Colonial Office (19 January 1939).
Malcolm MacDonald Handwritten Draft of White Paper (Undated).
Letters to Colonial Office on Behalf of the Lord Chancellor with Suggested Edits to the Draft White Paper, and Requesting Opportunity to Review a Revised Draft (21 March and 31 March 1939).
Cabinet 21(39), *Extract (Secret) from Conclusions of a Meeting* (19 April 1939); Cabinet 24(39), *Extract (Secret) from Conclusions of a Meeting* (26 April 1939).
Cabinet 25(39), *Extract (Secret) from Conclusions of a Meeting* (1 May 1939); Cabinet 26(39), *Extract (Secret) from Conclusions of a Meeting* (3 May 1939).
Downie, H.F., *Palestine: Points for Geneva* (10 June 1939).
CO 733/410/17:
Letter from MacDonald to Attorney General Donald Somervell (15 May 1939).
Letter from Sir Grattan Bushe to Attorney General Enclosing Memorandum Entitled *Palestine Statement of Policy: The Legal Aspect* (16 May 1939).
Letter from Attorney General D.B. Somervell to MacDonald Enclosing Memorandum Entitled *Palestine* (18 May 1939).
CO 733/410/18:
Weizmann to MacMichael (31 May 1939).
Weizmann to MacMichael (4 June 1939).
Jewish Agency for Palestine, *Memorandum on the Legal Aspects of the Statement of British Policy in Palestine (Cmd. 6019)* (5 June 1939).
*Notes on Jewish Agency Memorandum of the Legal Aspects of the White Paper* (9 June 1939).
CO 733/411/16:
Letter from Selig Brodetsky on Behalf of the Jewish Agency to Malcolm MacDonald (28 March 1939).
Bennett, J.S., Colonial Office, Note on Jewish Criticisms of the Report of the "McMahon-Hussein Committee" (3 April 1939).
CO 733/415/17:
Conferences on Palestine, 1939: Notes on General Arrangements.
CO 733/418/13:
Palestine Land Transfer Regulations: Notes on League of Nations Aspect (4 March 1940).
Note from Downie to Bushe and MacDonald Confirming Legal Advice Received from Bushe (18 May 1939).
Sir W. Malkin's Memo on Legal Aspects (4 March 1940).
R. Makins, *Palestine Land Transfers Regulations: Notes on Legal Aspects* (3 March 1940).
*Palestine Land Transfers Regulations: Notes on League of Nations Aspect* (4 March 1940).

## British intelligence documents

KV 2/2091:

Dispatch (Top Secret) from Lieutenant M.W.L. Kitson, S.I.M.E. (Security Intelligence Middle East) General Headquarters, Middle East Land Forces, to Director General (9 July 1947).

Report No. 82 (28 July 1947) (Relaying Information Received from Sources on 17 July 1947).

Extract from Account Forwarded by S.I.S. re Palestine – Political. The Arab "National Conference" at Haifa (29 July 1947).

C.S. 808/2, Memorandum (Top Secret) from Officer Administering the Government of Palestine to Secretary of State for the Colonies (23 September 1947).

Extract (Secret) from Report No. 95 re the Arabs and Palestine (4 November 1947).

Intelligence Repot No. 114 (Secret), Palestine: The Mufti's Preparations for Guerilla War (17 August 1948).

SIME/P.F.1415/B.1, Despatch (Secret) to Director General, London, from E. Richardson, Activities of the Mufti (18 August 1948).

Intelligence Report (Secret) No. 111, Palestine: Activities of the Mufti (15 December 1947).

Dispatch (Secret) SIME/P1415/Blb from S.I.M.E General Headquarters, Middle East Land Forces to Director General, London, The Mufti (14 August 1947).

Extract from SIME Security Intelligence Survey (7 November 1947).

Extract from M.I.6. Report re Palestine – Arab Dissensions (27 January 1948).

Despatch (Secret) No. 55 to Sir Marston Logan, Colonial Office (26 April 1948).

Intelligence Report No. 160, Palestine: Terrorist Intentions by the Mufti, Directed Against King Abdullah (4 November 1948).

Intelligence Report (Secret) No. 13 (11 April 1949).

SIME/PF.1415/3/B.1., Despatch (Secret) from S.I.M.E. General Headquarters, Middle East Land Forces to London (2 May 1949).

Telegram No. 685 from British Embassy, Jerusalem to Foreign Office (24 September 1949).

Telegram No. 1405 (Secret) from British Embassy, Cairo to Foreign Office (8 October 1945).

SIME/SF.2119/B.1 (Secret) (29 March 1949).

## League of nations documents

League of Nations. (1919). The Covenant of the League of Nations. Montreal: A.T. Chapman.

League of Nations, Permanent Mandates Commission, C. 405.M.144.1926 vi (C.P.M./9th Sess./P.V.), *Minutes of the Ninth Session Held at Geneva* (8–25 June 1926).

League of Nations Information Section, League of Nations Secretariat (1927). The Mandate System. Geneva: League of Nations.

League of Nations, Permanent Mandates Commission, *Minutes of the Fourteenth Session Held at Geneva* (26 October–13 November 1928).

League of Nations, Permanent Mandates Commission, *Minutes of the Fifteenth Session Held at Geneva*, C.P.M. 837 (1–19 July 1929).

League of Nations Archives, R2286, 6A/23373/224, *On the Palestine White Paper of 1930*, Memorandum by Auni Bey Abdul Hadi on behalf of the Arab Executive Committee (December 1930).

League of Nations, Permanent Mandates Commission, *Seventeenth (Extraordinary) Session of the Commission (Geneva, 3–21 June 1930)*, Official No. C.355.M.147.1930.VI, C.P.M. 1042(1) and 1043(1).

League of Nations, Permanent Mandates Commission, *Seventeenth (Extraordinary) Session of the Commission (Geneva, 3–21 June 1930), Comments by the Mandatory Power* (Letter Dated 2 August 1930), Official No. C.355.M.147.1930.VI.

League of Nations, Permanent Mandates Commission, *Seventeenth (Extraordinary) Session of the Commission (Geneva, 3–21 June 1930), Report to the Council of the League of Nations on the Work of the Session*, Official No. C.355.M.147.1930.VI.

League of Nations, Permanent Mandates Commission, *Minutes of the Eighteenth Session Held at Geneva* (First Meeting, 18 June 1930).

League of Nations, Permanent Mandates Commission, C.355, M.147.1930.VI, *Seventeenth Session, Report to the Council of the League of Nations on the Work of the Session* (4 August 1930).

League of Nations, Permanent Mandates Commission, *Minutes of the Thirty-Second (Extraordinary) Session*, C.330.M.222, 1937,VI (30 July–18 August 1937).

League of Nations Archive, R4078/6A/37120/668, *Resolution of the Inter-Parliamentary Congress, Cairo* (October 1938).

League of Nations Archive, R4078/6A/668/37120, Letter from Abdur Rahman Siddiqi, All-India Muslim League, to Secretary General, League of Nations Enclosing *Statement of Indian Muslim Views on Palestine* (9 February 1939).

League of Nations, Permanent Mandates Commission, *Minutes of the Thirty-Sixth Session, Held at Geneva from June 8 to June 29, 1939*, Official No. C.170.M.100.1939.VI.

League of Nations Archive, Geneva, R4076/6A/30296/668, *Reply of the Arab Higher Committee for Palestine to the White Paper Issued by the British Government on May 17, 1939* (30 May 1939).

League of Nations Archive, R4079/6A/38689/668, Folio 78, *Variante su dernier paragraphs de la conclusion* (28 June 1939).

League of Nations Archives, R4079/6A/38140/668, Letter from Lacy Baggallay, Foreign Office, to Secretary General, League of Nations, Enclosing Document Entitled *Comments of His Majesty's Government in the United Kingdom* (5 August 1939).

## Other international documents

Treaty of Versailles (1919), www.foundingdocs.gov.au/resources/transcripts/cth10_doc_1919.pdf, accessed 25 August 2019.

Covenant of the League of Nations, http://iilj.org/wp-content/uploads/2016/08/The-Covenant-of-the-League-of-Nations.pdf, accessed 25 August 2019.

San Remo Resolution (1920), https://ecf.org.il/media_items/299, accessed 26 August 2019.

Treaty of Sevres, http://sam.baskent.edu.tr/belge/Sevres_ENG.pdf, accessed 25 August 2019.

Treaty of Peace with Turkey, Signed at Lausanne (1923), http://sam.baskent.edu.tr/belge/Lausanne_ENG.pdf, accessed 25 August 2019.

Charter of the United Nations (1945), 1 UNTS XVI, https://treaties.un.org/doc/publication/ctc/uncharter.pdf, accessed 25 August 2019.

United Nations General Assembly, Resolution 181(II), A/RES/181(II) (29 November 1947).

United Nations General Assembly, Resolution 3379, A/Res/3379 (10 November 1975), *revoked*, A/Res/46/86 (16 December 1991).

United Nations Security Council, Resolution 2334, S/Res/2334 (23 December 2016).

Vienna Convention on the Law of Treaties, United Nations Treaty Series, vol. 1155, 1–18232 (23 May 1969).

Palestine National Charter (28 May 1964), *amended*, 1996.

International Criminal Court (ICC) Statute 17 July 1998, in force on 1 July 2002, United Nations, Treaty Series, vol. 2187, No. 38544.

European Union, *Final Interpretative Notice on Indication of Origin of Goods from the Territories Occupied by Israel since June 1967*, C (2015) 7834 (11 November 2015).

## Judicial decisions

*Lehrer v. Postmaster General*, High Court No. 88, Supreme Court of Palestine Sitting as the High Court of Justice (1928).
*District Governor, Jerusalem-Jaffa District v. Suleiman Murra*, (1926) A.C. 321.
*Ffrost v. Stevenson* (1937) 58 C.L.R. 528 (High Court of Australia).
International Court of Justice, *International Status of South-West Africa*, Advisory Opinion, 010-19500711-ADV-01-01, I.C.J. Reports 1950.
International Court of Justice, *Legal Consequences for States of the Continued Presence of South Africa in Namibia (South West Africa) Notwithstanding Security Council Resolution 276* (1970), I.C.J. Reports (21 June 1971).
*Public Committee against Torture v. Government of Israel*, HCJ 5100/94 (1999).
*Legal Consequences of the Construction of a Wall in the Occupied Palestinian Territory*, Advisory Opinion, I.C.J. Reports 2004, International Court of Justice (2004).
*Ahmad et al. v. Prime Minister*, Israel Supreme Court (Sitting as the High Court of Justice), HCJ 9132/07 (30 January 2008).
*Case of Certain Norwegian Loans*, Judgment of 6 July 1957, I.C.J. Reports (1957).
*Armed Activities on the Territory of the Congo (Democratic Republic of the Congo v. Uganda)*, Judgment, I.C.J. Reports (2005).
*In the Matter of the Chagos Marine Protected Area Arbitration* (Mauritius v. U.K., Case No. 2011-03) Award, Permanent Court of International Arbitration (18 March 2015).
*Ungar v. Palestine Liberation Organization*, 402 F.3d 274, 289, 292 (1st Cir. 2005).
International Criminal Court, No. ICC-01/18, *Situation in the State of Palestine* (5 February 2021).

## News articles

"Zionist Congress in Basel," *New York Times*, 31 August 1897 at 7.
"The Palestine Conference," *The Times*, 23 January 1939 at 13.
"Einstein Condemns Rule in Palestine," *New York Times*, 12 January 1946 at 7.
"Government Studying the Palestine Report," *The Times*, 2 May 1946 at 4.
Crossman, R., "War in Palestine?" *The New Statesman and Nation*, 11 May 1946.
"Anglo-U.S. Talks on Palestine," *The Times*, 23 July 1946 at 4.
"Divided Palestine is Urged by Anglo-U.S. Cabinet Body, Delaying Entry of 100,000," *New York Times*, 26 July 1946 at 1.
"Zionist Rules Out Unity in Palestine," *New York Times*, 18 June 1947 at 13.
"Jewish Agency Welcomes UNSCOP Report; Wants Shortest Possible Interim Period," *Jewish Daily Bulletin*, 2 September 1947 at 1.
"Zionists Ask U.N. to Pass New Plan; Arabs Inflamed," *New York Times*, 2 September 1947 at 1.
"Jamal: We Must Foil Partition," *Palestine Post*, 27 October 1947 at 1.
Bilainkin, G., "The Man Who May Lead the Holy War," *Sunday Despatch*, 12 October 1947.
"Arab Leaders Call Palestine Vote 'Invalid'; Delegates Reaffirm Challenge to U.N. Action," *New York Times*, 30 November 1947 at 54.
"Arabs Refuse to Cooperate," *The Times*, 20 January 1948 at 3.
"Arabs Again Shun Any Partition Aid," *New York Times*, 20 January 1948 at 4.

"Text of the British Statement on Palestine, Chronicling History and Policy of the Mandate," *New York Times*, 14 May 1948 at 4.
"Truman Appoints Mission to Israel," *New York Times*, 23 June 1948 at 24.
"Samuel Kopper, FRAMCO Aide, Dies," *New York Times*, 5 June 1957 at 35.
Palestinian News and Information Agency (WAFA), Palestinians Prepare to Mark One Hundred Years of Balfour Declaration, 24 October 2016.
Munayyer, Y., Reframing the Six-Day War, *The New Yorker*, 9 June 2017.
"Palestinian Authority Plans to Sue UK over Balfour Declaration," *Arab News*, 4 November 2017.
"Palestine Submits ICC Referral to Open Probe into 'Israel Crimes,'" *Al Jazeera*, 22 May 2018.
"Fatah: Israel Worse than Nazis, Wants to 'Crush' the Arab World," *Arutz Sheva*, 27 May 2018.
Palestinian News and Information Agency Press Release, "Ashrawi: With the Expansion of Its Illegal Settlement Enterprise, Israel Seeks Not Only to Defy but to Defeat the Whole World," 23 August 2018.
"Gaza Officials Submit Proof of Israeli Crimes to International Criminal Court," *Daily Sabah*, 2 August 2018.
"Does Anyone Take the B.D.S. Movement Seriously?," *New York Times*, 29 July 2019.
Zipperstein, S., "Uncovered, Polish Jews' pre-Holocaust Plea to Chamberlain: Let Us into Palestine," *Times of Israel*, 21 January 2020.

## Archival sources

American Jewish Archives, Cincinnati, Ohio (Podet Papers).
British National Archives, Kew, London.
Central Zionist Archives, Jerusalem.
Israel State Archives, Jerusalem (Digitized, Online Collection).
James Grover McDonald Collection, Rare Book & Manuscript Library, Columbia University in the City of New York.
King's College London, Foyle Special Collections Library, Foreign and Commonwealth Office Historical Collection.
League of Nations Archives, Geneva (Digitized, Online Collection).
Middle East Centre Archive, St. Antony's College, Oxford (Antonius Papers, Crossman Papers, Lord Killearn Papers, Cunningham Papers, Photograph Collections).
Oxford University, Bodleian Libraries (Chancellor Papers).
Truman Library, Missouri (Digitized, Online Collection).
United Nations Archives, New York (Digitized, Online Collection).
UCLA Young Research Library Special Collections (Bunche and Urquhart Papers).
University of Texas, Tarlton Law Library Special Collections (Hutcheson Papers).
University of Warwick, Modern Records Centre (Crossman Papers).
National Library of Wales Archives, Aberystwyth (Hopkin Morris Papers).
Weizmann Archives, Weizmann Institute, Rehovot.

# INDEX